KEN SCHULTZ'S
Fishing Encyclopedia

Worldwide Angling Guide

VOLUME 6

KEN SCHULTZ'S
Fishing Encyclopedia

Worldwide Angling Guide

Ken Schultz

IDG Books Worldwide, Inc.
An International Data Group Company
Foster City, CA • Chicago, IL • Indianapolis, IN • New York, NY • Southlake, TX

IDG Books Worldwide, Inc.
An International Data Group Company
919 E. Hillsdale Boulevard
Suite 400
Foster City, CA 94404

Copyright © 2000 by Ken Schultz

All rights reserved. No part of this book shall be reproduced, stored in a retrieval system, or transmitted by any means, electronic, mechanical, photocopying, recording, or otherwise, without written permission from the publisher. No patent liability is assumed with respect to the use of the information contained herein. Although every precaution has been taken in the preparation of this book, the publisher and author assume no responsibility for errors or omissions. Neither is any liability assumed for damages resulting from the use of the information contained herein.

Webster's New World is a registered trademark of Macmillan General Reference USA, Inc., a wholly owned subsidiary of IDG Books Worldwide, Inc.

The IDG Books Worldwide logo is a registered trademark under exclusive license to IDG Books Worldwide, Inc., from International Data Group, Inc.

For general information on books from IDG Books Worldwide's in the U.S., please call our Consumer Customer Service department at 800-762-2974. For reseller information, including discounts and premium sales, please call our Reseller Customer Service department at 800-434-3422.

For information on a multimedia version of this book, available from Tricom Intrtactive, Inc., please go to this Web site: intellipedia.com

To contact the author, please visit: www.kenshultz.com

Library of Congress Cataloging-in-Publication Data

This edition of *Ken Schultz's Fishing Encyclopedia*, which is published in 7 volumes, contains the entire contents of the work as previously published in a single volume: *Ken Schultz's Fishing Encyclopedia*, ISBN 9780028620572

This is Volume 6 of 7

Schultz, Ken, 1950–
Ken Shultz's fishing encyclopedia: worldwide angling guide/ Ken Schultz. — 1st ed.
p. cm.
ISBN 0-02-862057-7
Volume 6: ISBN 9781684427734 (hardcover) | ISBN 9781684427741 (paperback)

1. Fishing—Encyclopedias. 2. Fishes—Encyclopedias. I. Title.
SH411.S38 2000
799.1'03—dc21 99-033719
CIP

Manufactured in the United States of America

First Edition

Trademarks

All terms mentioned in this book that are known to be trademarks or service marks have been appropriately capitalized. IDG Books cannot attest to the accuracy of this information. Use of a term in this book should not be regarded as affecting the validity of any trademark or service mark.

Table of Contents

Introduction
vii

Acknowledgments
ix

Photo Credits
xix

FISHING ENCYCLOPEDIA ENTRIES
S
1

Appendix: Conversion Charts for Weights and Measures
295

Introduction

*"Ah, the gallant fisher's life! It is the best of any;
'Tis full of pleasure, void of strife, And 'tis beloved by many."*
—IZAAK WALTON

"All men are equal before fish."
—HERBERT HOOVER

WHILE PRODUCING THIS FISHING ENCYCLOPEDIA I SPOKE TO MANY HUNDREDS OF informed anglers. Nearly all of them thought the compilation of all things piscatorial was too overwhelming to contemplate because the angling universe is so enormous and diverse.

Certainly a modern fishing encyclopedia—if it truly provides a full field of knowledge—runs counter to the short and specialized tenets of today's journalism. Yet it is precisely because there is so much to the sport of fishing, plus an increasing profusion of specialized equipment and confusing terminology, that it was necessary to bring order and perspective to all of this in one definitive book.

Ken Schultz's Fishing Encyclopedia & Worldwide Angling Guide has been a long time in the making. I started thinking about it in 1991. Since work began in earnest in 1995, the project became even more expansive than expected, and indeed there were times when it was nearly overwhelming. As a result, the book grew much bigger than originally planned, becoming 50 percent larger than any fishing encyclopedia that has heretofore been published.

As a result, however, this encyclopedia contains the equivalent of thirty standard-length books, meaning that there is ample space to devote to the species, equipment, techniques, locations, and ancillary matters that encompass the angling universe. Consider that nearly one-third of the encyclopedia is comprised of the most comprehensive information on worldwide angling opportunities ever assembled. There is absolutely no place to find these details together; indeed, some elements of the *Worldwide Angling Guide* cannot be found anywhere else at all.

Likewise, the coverage of angling methods and equipment has never been addressed more comprehensively between the covers of any other book. In fact, *Ken Schultz's Fishing Encyclopedia* contains the most modern, illuminating, and extensive dis-courses on the basic elements of fishing tackle—baitcasting, big-game, conventional, flycasting, spinning, and spincasting—ever found in one place. Each of these entries undoubtedly contain more than all but the most scrupulous person will want to know.

Great lengths were also taken, however, to make sure that the less obvious subjects in the angling universe were included and reviewed in comprehensive fashion. For example, nowhere else is there a more extensive review of the principles, methods, and pros and cons of catch-and-release—perhaps the most important angling conservation development of the twentieth century.

Topics like fisheries management, angling-related travel, choosing guides and charter boats, and the care and preparation of fish for consumption, which are among many unglamorous subjects taken for granted elsewhere, receive complete explanation and review here. Likewise the otherwise oft-ignored subjects of ethics and etiquette—increasingly important issues as human pressures increase—are included.

Although there's an enormous amount of information in this book, every topic was approached with the intent to take nothing for granted and to present information in straightforward language. Angling is not like nuclear physics, and if it was half as complicated as some people try to make it, no one would enjoy it or have success. The extensive insertion of cross references is thus intended to direct you through a continuing stream of appropriate topics, so you can take any subject as far as you want to go. Some cross references appear within entry text next to topics that are more thoroughly reviewed elsewhere; many cross references appear at the end of entry text, either to direct you to the appropriate subject entry or to note related topics.

We've tried to make things easy to find and to place subjects where you're most likely to look for them, even if you're unsure of the proper terms or spelling. As an example, you'll find rainbow trout under the "T" entries (trout, rainbow) rather than under the "R" entries. Also, at the back of the book is a weights and measures conversion chart; this will be convenient for many readers since there's a liberal mix of metric and U.S. customary weights and measures throughout this book, just as there is at boat docks, fish camps, and tackle shops throughout the world.

Because the text is encyclopedic in format, however, it does not provide a full sense of the joy or spirit of sportfishing—the pleasure that makes it "beloved by many," as Izaak Walton said. Perhaps the accompanying photos help convey this. Photos and line art, incidentally, were planned and selected to reflect the broad, eclectic places and situations that so many anglers experience, as well as to reflect the great diversity of its participants. Angling is a very democratic recreation; as the quotation from President Hoover implies, the fish don't care who hooks them.

It is a special delight to publish this encyclopedia at the close of the twentieth century—a period with the most phenomenal sportfishing growth in the history of mankind—and at the advent of a new millennium. Knowing that the decades ahead will require proper stewardship of aquatic resources—something that anglers in particular have always demonstrated personal and financial support for—this text has been written and edited with sensitivity to conservation issues while also being realistic about the role that humans play as the highest predators and the diverse motivations they bring to angling.

In a sense, the sport of fishing is like a book with as many footnotes as main text. It is full of variables, especially individual skills, weather issues, peculiarities among species, habitat differences, and so forth. You may notice that the words "usually" and "generally" occur often in portions of the text. This isn't meant to be vague; it's because there are often no hard-and-fast rules in catching fish, no matter what you may have heard to the contrary. There are norms, but straying from norms is common for one reason or another, as any angler who has been humbled at a "hot" site at the "best" time of the season can attest.

While there is a wealth of reliable information here, a caveat is in order with regard to the contents of the *Worldwide Angling Guide*. Many of the countries profiled have not in the past provided, or do not currently provide, or may not in the future provide stable travel environments, especially to tourists of certain nationalities. Jungle fishing opportunities are especially among those that may present danger. Angola, Colombia, and Zambia come immediately to mind in this regard. Civil unrest can likewise make travel in certain places dangerous; recent troubles in Kenya, Indonesia, Russia, Uganda, and the Balkans serve as examples. The adventurous angler needs to use good judgment.

Things change the environmental order and aquatic resources, too. Yugoslavia hadn't been wrecked by bombs when that entry was written; Nicaragua and Honduras were leveled by Hurricane Georges right after those entries were written. Environmental changes sometimes radically alter the presence or availability of certain gamefish species, and in the more remote pockets of the world only native people and intrepid explorers are likely to know it.

On a final note, it is tempting to say, as marketers and publicists are wont to do, that this book contains everything an angler will ever need to know about fish and fishing. But new developments in fishing tackle will surely come along, changes in some habitats or in fish populations will alter the techniques and equipment used, and certainly natural changes will take place in some of the world's best angling spots. However, a lot of the fundamentals—the underlying principles of fish behavior, the function of basic equipment, and angling methodology—will be constant, making most of the information in this book relevant to the discerning angler even in years to come.

I expect to add to this body of knowledge in time, so if you think there's something that should have been included, if you have knowledge about fishing in a country that wasn't covered, or if you can suggest an improvement to any aspect of this book, please visit my website—www.kenschultz.com— and post a message about it.

Now, turn to any page and become absorbed.
—Ken Schultz

"If I fished only to capture fish, my fishing trips would have ended long ago."

—ZANE GREY

Acknowledgments

Producing a book of this magnitude required the involvement of a tremendous number of people and a great array of talents. This encyclopedia would not have gone beyond a mere suggestion, however, had it not been for the endorsement and encouragement of Natalie Chapman, a former publisher at Macmillan General Reference, now IDG Books Consumer Reference, whose confidence and vision made this book possible, and who gave me free rein to produce it as necessary. I'm also indebted to publisher Marie Butler-Knight, who took this project over in mid-stream, marshaled all the resources, and fervently shepherded the book to completion. Sincere appreciation is also extended to Renee Wilmeth and Kristi Hart, who directed the publisher's nitty-gritty editorial and production work with outstanding dedication and professionalism, plus a reassuring enthusiasm; to Pamela Benner, who paid excellent attention to details in the copyediting process and made good suggestions; and to many other directly involved personnel, particularly Beth Jordan, Faunette Johnston, and Jeanine Bucek.

This book could also not have been completed without the special assistance of my wife, Sandy, and my daughters, Alyson, Megan, and Kristen. They each helped in a variety of ways, especially by being patient. Sandy's assistance with a host of matters was very beneficial, and Kristen was particularly vital, pitching in for a second time during a desperate period with important research and writing assistance.

In order to make this encyclopedia truly comprehensive and of worldwide significance it was imperative to involve a host of contributors with expertise in technical fisheries matters, regional angling opportunities, and specialized sportfishing topics. I'm grateful for their participation and excellent contributions, the bulk of which made up the *Worldwide Angling Guide*. In particular, appreciation is extended to the incomparable Ed Migdalski, who provided technical scientific fisheries advice and vetted all of the fish art.

I'm also indebted to the late, and incomparable in his own right, A. J. McClane. His fishing encyclopedia of 1965 and 1974, though now outdated, was not only a phenomenal reference work, but a monumental achievement in an era before personal computers, electronic mail, fax machines, scanners, laser printers, and the various modern technology that made putting this book together far easier than it was in his time. Unlike me, he was unable to write and edit on a laptop computer in cars, planes, airports, hotel rooms, and other places, or receive electronically transmitted text. More significantly, McClane set a very high bar for what a real fishing encyclopedia ought to be, and provided a template for such a book for the twenty-first century. Without his accomplishment, it would have been much more difficult to plan and publish this book. (Aside to historians: four contributors to this project—Ed Migdalski, George Reiger, Jack Samson, and Bill Scifres—were also contributors to McClane's encyclopedia.)

Just as McClane, the contributors to this book, and the people at IDG Books Worldwide are the best in their fields, so is *Field & Stream* the largest and best fishing and hunting magazine in the world, and I've been privileged to be part of this publication continuously since 1973. I appreciate the confidence and opportunities provided me over that time by its editors. Those opportunities laid the groundwork for this encyclopedia. I'm especially grateful to Editor Slaton White and Managing Editor Mike Toth for allowing me leeway over the last several years that I've been working on this project.

Information, suggestions, encouragement, technical advice, reference paraphernalia, reviews and critiques, and assorted material assistance were received from so many individuals and organizations that some will likely be overlooked in these acknowledgments, for which I apologize.

I'm very grateful to the following individuals:

Blaine Anderson
John Anthon
Dick Ballard
Ron Ballanti
LaVerne Barnes
Cameron Baty
Susan Baumgartner
Gene Bay
Dick Bengraff
Virginia Benoit
Walt Boname
Toby Bradshaw
Eric Burnley

Cyril Calendini
Bill Chapman, Jr.
Jim Chapralis
Larry Columbo
David Cosby
Gary Dollahon
Lou Duarte
Todd DuPuis
Jack Erskine
Mike Fine
Paul Fuller
Riccardo Galigani
Ken Gangler

Guy Geffroy
Lois Gerber
Alessandro Giangio
Barry Gibson
Gary Giudice
Fred Golofaro
Jerry Gomber
George Gowen
Garry Gurke
Judy Hammond
Bill Hilts, Jr.
Bruce Holt
Dr. James Imai
Jimmy Kano
Nick Karas
Glenda Kelley
Gary King
Jason Klein
Bob Lang
Steen Larsen
Mike Leech
Bill Liston
Chun Liu
George Loechl
Paulo Loes
Frank Longino
Jim Matthews
John Mazurkewicz
Tom Melton
Paul Merzig
Ed Mesunas
Bill Miller
Gail Morchower

András Nagy
Andy Newman
Stuart Newman
Donald J. Orth
Tom Pagliaroli
Sheldon Pasternack
Dennis Phillips
Stanko Popovic
Norville Prosser
Jim Reist
Al Ristori
Milt Rosko
Gail Ross
Sharon Rushton
Pat Salimeno
Marty Salovin
Glenn Sapir
Christine Moore Serrao
Vin Sparano
Ron Speed, Sr.
Roy Stiner
Mick Thill
Roger Tucker
Jerry Valentine
Mike Walker
Ben Wechsler
Mark Weintz
Fenner Weller
Jim White
Anthony M. Williams
Dick Wood
Peter Yaskowski

I'm also grateful to the following companies and organizations (and specific people where noted in parenthesis):

American Sportfishing Association (Mike Hayden)
American Wire (Michael Shields)
Arkie Lures
The Atlantic Salmon Federation
Bay de Noc Lure Co.
Bead Tackle (Peter Renkert)
Bear Advertising (Dick Bear, Mark Malkin)
Big Jon (Jerry Livingstone)
Bullet Weights (Douglas Crumrine)
Bushnell Sports Optics (Barbara Mellman)
Cabela's Inc. (Tony Dolle)
Classic Fishing Products (Mike Richards)
C-Map USA (Pam Oldham)
Computrol, Inc.
Cossack Bait Products (Garry Shaw)
Cuba Specialty Mfg. Co. (Craig Osterhus, Dana Pickup)
Daiwa Corp.
Earie Dearie Lure Co. (Helen Galbincea)
EZE Lap Diamond (Donna Long)
Fin-Nor (Niels Stenhoj)
Flambeau Products Corp. (Jason Sauey)
Florida Keys and Key West Visitors Bureau
Flow-Rite of Tennessee (Don Zielinski)
Furuno
Future Fisherman Foundation
Garmin International (Steve Featherstone)
G. Loomis (Gary Loomis, Steve Rajeff)
Gudebrod
International Game Fish Association (Jim Brown)
Hudson River Foundation
Interphase Technologies
K-C Tackle (Raymond Packer)
L. L. Bean (Mary Rose MacKinnon)
L&S Bait Co. (Eric Bachnik)
Lowrance Electronics (Darrell Lowrance, Steve Schneider)
Luhr Jensen & Sons (Phil Jensen, Barry Ternahan)
Magellan Systems Corp. (Don Meyer)
Mann's Bait Co.
Marado Inc.
Old Town Canoe (Jim Kaiser)
O. Mustad & Sons USA (John DeVries)
National Freshwater Fishing Hall of Fame
Nomadic Expeditions (Denise Gogarty)
Normark Corp. (Ron Weber, Craig Weber)
The Orvis Company
Outdoor Technologies
Owner America Corp. (Kat Shitanishi)
Penn Fishing Tackle
Pradco (Joe Hughes, Bruce Stanton)
Scientific Anglers
Shakespeare Fishing Tackle (Mark Davis)
Sheldon's Inc.
Shimano American Corp.
Si-Tex Marine Electronics
Storm Lures (Sharon Andrews, John Storm)
Sufix USA, Inc.
Techsonics Industries
Len Thompson Lures (Richard Pallister)
Top Brass Tackle (Eric Cosby)
Tru-Turn Hooks (Wes Campbell)
Wisconsin Pharmacal
H. D. Wood Advertising
Worden's Lures
The Worth Co.
Wright & McGill Co. (George Large)
Yakima Bait Co. (Rob Phillips)
Zebco Corp. (Jenni Foster)

Gratitude is also due the following government agencies and government-funded programs (and the people noted in parenthesis), which provided research and reference materials, and, in some cases, other forms of assistance:

Alabama Cooperative Extension Service (Richard Wallace)
Alabama Department of Conservation and Natural Resources (Stan Cook)
Alabama Sea Grant Extension Program
Alaska Department of Fish and Game (Jon Lyman)
Alaska Sea Grant College Program (Kurt Byers)
Alberta Department of Environmental Protection

Acknowledgments

Arizona Game and Fish Department
Arkansas Cooperative Extension Program, Univ. of Arkansas (Nathan Stone)
Arkansas Game and Fish Commission (Keith Sutton)
Auburn University Marine Extension (Richard Wallace, William Hosking, Stephen Szedlmayer)
Brazil Embratur
British Columbia Ministry of Environment, Fisheries Branch
California Department of Fish and Game (A. Petrovich)
Canada Department of Fisheries and Oceans
Canadian Consul General
Cayman Islands Department of Tourism
Colorado Department of Natural Resources
Connecticut Department of Environmental Protection
Delaware Division of Fish and Wildlife
Florida Department of Environmental Protection, Marine Research Institute and Division of Marine Resources (Jim Lewis)
Florida Game and Freshwater Fish Commission, Division of Fisheries (Henry Cabbage)
Georgia Department of Natural Resources (Chris Martin)
Great Lakes Fishery Commission
Guam Department of Agriculture (Gerry Davis)
Hawaii Department of Land and Natural Resources, Division of Aquatic Resources
Idaho Department of Fish and Game (Jack Trueblood)
Illinois Department of Natural Resources
Indiana Department of Natural Resources (Jon Marshall)
International Center for Living Aquatic Resources Management/Food and Agriculture Organization of the United Nations
Iowa Department of Natural Resources (Steve Suman)
Kansas Department of Wildlife and Parks (Mike Miller)
Kentucky Department of Fish and Wildlife Resources (J. Beth Garland)
Louisiana Department of Wildlife and Fisheries
Louisiana Sea Grant College Program
Maine Department of Inland Fisheries and Wildlife (V. Paul Reynolds)
Manitoba Department of Natural Resources, Fisheries Branch (Carl Wall)
Maryland Department of Natural Resources (Eugene Deems, Jr.)
Maryland Sea Grant College Program (Jack Greer)
Massachusetts Division of Fisheries and Wildlife
Michigan Department of Natural Resources, Fisheries Division
Michigan Sea Grant College Program (Martha Walter)
Minnesota Department of Natural Resources (Tom Dickson)
Mississippi Department of Wildlife, Fisheries and Parks (Jim Walker)
Missouri Department of Conservation (John McPherson)
Montana Division of Fish, Wildlife, and Parks
Nevada Department of Conservation and Natural Resources
New Brunswick Department of Economic Development and Tourism
New Brunswick Department of Natural Resources, Fish and Wildlife Branch (Peter Cronin)
Newfoundland Department of Natural Resources
New Hampshire Fish and Game Department (Patricia Fleurie)
New Jersey Division of Fish, Game and Wildlife (Dave Chanda)
New Mexico Department of Game and Fish (Ruth Anderson)
New York Department of Environmental Conservation (Robert Brandt)
New York Sea Grant Program (David MacNeill, Mark Malchoff)
NOAA/Gray's Reef National Marine Sanctuary (Beth Kostka)
NOAA/National Marine Fisheries Service
NOAA/National Weather Service
North Carolina Division of Boating and Inland Fisheries (Fred Harris)
North Carolina Sea Grant
North Dakota Game and Fish Department (Terry Steinwand)
Nova Scotia Department of Fisheries (Murray Hill)
Nova Scotia Department of Lands and Forests (Barry Sabean)
Ohio Department of Natural Resources
Ohio Sea Grant College Program
Oklahoma Department of Wildlife Conservation (Nels Rodefeld)
Ontario Ministry of Economic Development, Trade & Tourism (Tom Boyd)
Ontario Ministry of Natural Resources
Oregon Department of Fish and Wildlife (Randy Henry)
Oregon Sea Grant (Pat Kight)
Parátur, State of Pará, Brazil
Pennsylvania Fish and Boat Commission
Portuguese National Tourist Office (Maria João Ramires)
Prince Edward Island Department of Environmental Resources
Quebec Department of Recreation, Fish and Game
Rhode Island Division of Fish and Game
Rhode Island Sea Grant
Saskatchewan Department of Environment, Fish and Wildlife (Bruce Howard)

Acknowledgments

South Carolina Department of Natural Resources (Greg Lucas)
South Carolina Sea Grant Consortium (John Tibbetts)
South Dakota Department of Game, Fish and Parks
Spain Ministry of Commerce and Tourism
Tennessee Wildlife Resources Agency (Dave Woodward)
Texas Parks and Wildlife (Steve Lightfoot)
Tourism British Columbia
Tourism New Brunswick
Tourism Newfoundland and Labrador
Tourism Nova Scotia (Randy Brooks)
Tourism Prince Edward Island (Carol Horne)
Tourism Quebec (Siegfried Gagnon)
Tourism Saskatchewan (Gerard Makuch, Nadine Howard)
Travel Alberta (Peter Gregus)
Travel Manitoba (Dennis Maksymetz, Colette Fontaine, Gord Richardson)
University of Connecticut Sea Grant Marine Advisory Program (Nancy Balcom)
University of Delaware Sea Grant College Program
University of Florida Cooperative Extension Service
University of New Hampshire and University of Maine Sea Grant College Program
U.S. Fish and Wildlife Service
Utah Department of Natural Resources (Gerry Schlappe)
Vermont Department of Fish and Wildlife (John Hall)
Virginia Department of Game and Inland Fisheries (Mitchell Norman)
Washington Department of Fish and Wildlife (Nina Carter, James Chandler)
Washington Sea Grant Program (Kris Freeman)
West Virginia Division of Natural Resources (Hoy Murphy)
Wisconsin Department of Natural Resources (David Kunelius)
Woods Hole Oceanographic Institute (Tracey Crago)
Wyoming Game and Fish Department
Yukon Territory Department of Renewable Resources (Susan Thompson)

Finally, I'm also grateful to four student interns, whose early work compiling and organizing research materials was of much help—Kristen Schultz of Oberlin College, Alyson Schultz of Boston University, Mathew Kane of Hamilton College, and John Kuhner of Princeton University—and to Megan Schultz of Ithaca College, for Web site development and advice.

—Ken Schultz

About the Author, Artists, and Contributors

PRINCIPAL AUTHOR AND EDITOR

Ken Schultz has been a staff fishing writer and editor for *Field & Stream* since 1973. His feature articles and columns for that publication appear monthly, and he contributes to the magazine's nationally syndicated weekly radio show and to its Web site. Schultz is a frequent author of the outdoors column of the *New York Times*, and he previously was a syndicated newspaper columnist for Gannett. He has authored a dozen books on sportfishing and angling travel topics, has been a featured guest on CNBC, ESPN, and The Nashville Network, and appears regularly in assorted fishing segments for the Outdoor Life Network. A widely traveled angler, Schultz is a former holder of seven line-class world records and was inducted into the Fishing Hall of Fame in 1998. He lives in Forestburgh, New York.

THE ARTISTS

Steve T. Goione is a rising star in the world of fishing and boating art, working in mixed mediums to present his lifelong passion for angling in a dynamic and realistic style. Although he drew the distinctive pen-and-ink illustrations for this book as well as the dust-jacket cover, Goione is primarily a creator of fine art. From his studio in Toms River, New Jersey, he produces commissioned fishing scenes for private collections and limited-edition prints, and he has created original artwork for Sea World in Florida. Goione has also made a mark among boat builders and owners for commissioned renderings of big-game sportfishing craft, and he recently created original artwork for the latest products of Hatteras Yachts. A frequent guest artist on the big-game fishing tournament circuit, Goione appears at exclusive contests each year from Nantucket to Venezuela, and his work is regularly featured at fund-raising events for prominent conservation organizations.

David Kiphuth, whose renderings of fish appear in this book, has had a varied career in the field of art, having been a professional illustrator since 1969. His work has included portraiture, architectural renderings, maps, and book illustration. Kiphuth has created archaeological and scientific book and exhibit renderings for the Yale Peabody Museum, the Yale Department of Anthropology, and Yale University Press. He formerly maintained a studio and gallery in Branford, Connecticut, where he created and sold wildlife and nature art and animal portraits. Since 1989, he has been the staff illustrator for the *Gazette Newspapers* in Schenectady, New York. He lives in Saratoga Springs, New York.

THE CONTRIBUTORS

Brett Albanese of Virginia is a Ph.D candidate at the Department of Fisheries and Wildlife Sciences at Virginia Polytechnic Institute; he formerly worked at the Mississippi Museum of Natural Sciences.

Ken Allen of Maine is Associate Editor of *Maine Sportsman* and a prolific writer, photographer, newspaper columnist, book author, and guide.

Michael Babcock of Montana is Outdoors Editor of the *Great Falls Tribune*.

Ken Bailey of Alberta is Manager of Field Operations in central Alberta for Ducks Unlimited Canada; he is a prolific writer and President of the Outdoor Writers Association of Canada.

Dick Ballard of Missouri is President of Dick Ballard's Fishing Adventures and a foremost authority on Amazonian angling; he's sent anglers fishing around the world for 18 years, and established the first travel service for Bass Pro Shops.

Scott Bannerot of Pennsylvania and Florida has a Ph.D. in fisheries science and has worked in marine biological research and consulting; he is a photojournalist and a charter boat captain.

John A. Barnes of Bermuda is the Director of Agriculture and Fisheries for Bermuda; he authors a weekly fishing column in the Bermuda *Mid Ocean News*, and is an IGFA representative.

Rob Barraclough of Indonesia and England works in the oil industry and is a charter boat captain and freelance writer.

Carlos M. Barrantes of Costa Rica established the first two sportfishing camps in Costa Rica; he is an IGFA representative and was the first President of the Costa Rican Fishing Federation.

Cody Beers of Wyoming works for the Wyoming Game and Fish Department as Associate Editor of *Wyoming Wildlife* magazine and Editor of *Wyoming Wildlife News and Wild Times*; he is also a freelance writer and photographer.

Bob Berry of California is one of the world's top fish carvers and sculptors, and swept all divisions of the 1986 world championship of fish carving; he is a foremost competition judge, a former professional taxidermist, and author of the book *Fish Carving*.

Mike Bleech of Pennsylvania is a writer and photographer whose work has appeared in most major U.S. fishing and hunting magazines.

Larry Blomquist of Louisiana is Publisher of *Breakthrough*, the world's largest taxidermy trade magazine, and one of the top competition judges in North America; he is a retired award-winning taxidermist, and former President of the National Taxidermists Association.

Fred Bonner of North Carolina is Editor of *Carolina Adventure* magazine; he is also a syndicated newspaper columnist, fisheries biologist, and an IGFA representative.

Judith Bowman of New York has been a foremost sporting books dealer for over twenty years; she produces two sporting book catalogs a year, with special emphasis on fishing.

John Brownlee of Florida is Senior Editor of *Salt Water Sportsman* and a former charter boat captain; he has served on the South Atlantic Fishery Management Council, is former Chairman of the Florida Conservation Association, and is an IGFA representative.

Eric B. Burnley of Virginia is the author of *Surf Fishing the Atlantic Coast* and a radio show host; he is a charter boat captain and Regional Editor of both *Salt Water Sportsman* and *The Fisherman* magazines.

Erwin Bursik of South Africa is Publisher of *Ski-Boat* and *Flyfishing* magazines of Durban, a member of the executive board of the South African Deep Sea Angling Association, and an IGFA representative.

Mac Campbell of Great Britain works for *Angling Plus*, a match fishing magazine, and has previously worked for *Sea Angler*, *Trout Fisherman*, and *Angling Times*.

Jim Casada of South Carolina is the author of many books, including *Modern Fly Fishing*; he is Senior Editor of *Sporting Classics* magazine, and outdoor columnist for the Rock Hill *Herald* and Greensboro *News and Record*.

Göran Cederberg of Sweden has been Editor of several international fact-packed large-format angling books, including *The Complete Book of Sportfishing*; he contributes regularly to north-European publications and has been chief editor of a Swedish sportfishing magazine.

Matthew D. Chan of Virginia is a Ph.D candidate at the Department of Fisheries and Wildlife Sciences at Virginia Polytechnic Institute; he formerly worked as a fisheries biologist for the U. S. Army Corps of Engineers.

Dawn Charging of North Dakota is Outdoors Director for the North Dakota State Tourism Department; she is also a writer and photographer whose family owns a successful fishing resort on Lake Sakakawea.

Homer Circle of Florida has been Angling Editor of *Sports Afield* magazine for 34 years; the dean of American outdoor writers, he is the recipient of numerous media and achievement awards, a former member of the Arkansas Game & Fish Commission, and a renowned television and video host.

Barry Ord Clarke of Norway is a professional photographer and writer and the author of several books on fly fishing and fly tying; he contributes regularly to most European fishing magazines, and is fishing consultant to Norway's largest private sporting estate.

Soc Clay of Kentucky is an accomplished and prolific fishing writer and photographer whose work has appeared in every major outdoor periodical in North America.

Angelo Cuanang of California is a Pacific Regional Editor for *Salt Water Sportsman* and a freelance writer and photographer.

Paula J. Del Giudice of Nevada is Outdoor Columnist for the *Las Vegas Sun*; a freelance writer, photographer, and book author; and former President of the Nevada Wildlife Federation.

Arthur De Mello of Uganda is a representative for the IGFA in Uganda.

Hansjörg Dietiker of Switzerland is Editor of the Swiss Anglers Magazine *Petri-Heil*, and an IGFA representative.

Philippe Dolivet of France is the Chief Editor of the French fly fishing magazine *Plaisirs de la Pêche* and a professional photographer; he is a fly fishing instructor and competitor, an ichthyologist, and an IGFA representative.

Gary Edwards of Wyoming is a longtime fishing guide and a television show host; he is the former Editor and Publisher of *Salmon Fever* magazine, and a former fly rod world record holder.

D'arcy Egan of Ohio has been a sportswriter for *The Cleveland Plain Dealer* for over 20 years; he authored the book, *Guide to Ohio Fishing*, and is host of the American Outdoorsman Radio Network.

Bill Ensor of New Brunswick works for the Fish & Wildlife Branch of the New Brunswick Department of Natural Resources; he was formerly marketing manager of fishing and hunting for the New Brunswick Department of Tourism, and is a longtime fishing guide.

Jack Erskine of Australia is a foremost big-game tackle designer and technical innovator who has helped design many of the modern rods, reels, and drag systems in use today.

Stan Fagerstrom of Oregon is one of the world's best known trick and accuracy casters, and has been featured at sport shows worldwide for half a century; he is also a book, magazine, and newspaper writer.

Jan Fogt of Florida is Editor of *The Bahamas Sportfishing Guide* and was the founding editor of

Bahamas Blue Water Magazine; she is a contributing editor for *Sport Fishing* and *Marlin* magazines, and is also a book author.

Frank Fry of the Yukon Territory has worked with the Yukon Territory's Department of Natural Resources on various fishing projects.

Mike Garzillo of New Hampshire has been a newspaper columnist for 24 years; he is a regular contributor to various publications and a former regional editor for *Outdoor Life*.

Alessandro Giangio of Italy writes for Italy's premier fishing magazine, *Pesca in Mare*, and has been published worldwide; he has authored five books, is owner and master instructor of the Fishbuster Trolling School and Sportfishing Travel, and has a charter boat in Huatulco, Mexico.

Jerry Gibbs of Vermont is Fishing Editor of *Outdoor Life*, where his career as a staff writer has spanned three decades and made him one of North America's most respected angling authors; he has written several books and has been inducted into the Fishing Hall of Fame.

Barry Gibson of Massachusetts is Editor of *Salt Water Sportsman* and a longtime Maine charter boat captain; he is a former member of the New England Fishery Management Council, and former advisor to the International Commission for the Conservation of Atlantic Tunas.

Jerry Gomber of New Jersey has over twenty-five years of experience in design, development, and marketing of fishing rods and reels; during that period he has been responsible for several successful product innovations.

George Gruenefeld of Quebec and Saskatchewan is Editor of *Canadian Outdoor Publications*; he has written for many magazines in Canada and the U.S., is a book author, and was formerly Outdoors Editor for the *Montreal Gazette*.

Chris Hanks of the Northwest Territories is an anthropologist, freelance writer, and author of the book *Fly Fishing in the Northwest Territories*.

Steve Harper of Kansas is the Outdoors Editor of the *Wichita Eagle* and author of the book *Kansas Day Trips*; in 1995 he was named Conservation Communicator of the Year by the Kansas Wildlife Federation.

Dan Heiner of Alaska is an advertising agency executive and former editor and writer for *Alaska Outdoors* magazine; he is the author of four books on Alaska fishing, including *Fly Fishing Alaska's Wild Rivers*.

Bob Hodge of Tennessee is the Outdoors Editor of the *Knoxville News-Sentinel*; he was named the state's Best Outdoor Writer for 1996-97 by the Tennessee Sportswriters Association.

Grant Hopkins of Ontario is the outdoor columnist for the *Ottawa Citizen*, a frequent contributor to *Ontario Out of Doors*, and retired from the Royal Canadian Air Force.

John Husar of Illinois is the longtime outdoors columnist and general sportswriter of the *Chicago Tribune* and co-host of a Chicago radio show; he has worked for newspapers in Kansas, Texas, and New Mexico, and has covered the last nine Olympics.

Jim Imai of California has a Ph.D in physics and is Professor of Physics at California State University, Dominguez Hills; he is a Consulting Physicist for the Daiwa Corporation, and a leading authority on the design and performance of fishing reels and rods.

James Kano of Ontario is the Marketing Director of Japan Communications in Toronto and Outdoor Coordinator for the Press and Tourism division of the Ontario government; his articles have appeared online and in newspapers, guide books, and magazines.

Nick Karas of New York is the retired outdoor columnist for (New York) *Newsday* and a charter boat captain and ichthyologist; he has written for many national magazines and authored a dozen books, including *The Striped Bass* and *Brook Trout*.

Lee Kernen of Wisconsin is the retired Director of Fisheries for the State of Wisconsin; he is also a writer, fishing guide, and fisheries consultant.

Ronnie Kovach of California is a radio and television show host, educator, magazine writer, guide, and author of five books, including *Bass Fishing in California*, *Trout Fishing in California*, and *Saltwater Fishing in California*.

Steen Larsen of Denmark is one of Europe's leading sportfishing writers and photographers; he is a book author and lecturer, and contributes widely to many European angling publications.

Dick Lewers of Australia is Technical Editor of *Encyclopaedia of Australian Fishing*, author of seven books on angling, a former IGFA representative, 35-year columnist for *Modern Fishing Magazine*, and past President of the Australian National Sportfishing Association.

Bill Loftus of Idaho is the Outdoors Editor of the *Lewiston Morning Tribune* and the author of two guidebooks to Idaho.

Maurice Loustau-LaLanne of Seychelles is the Principal Secretary in the Ministry of Tourism and Transport for the Seychelles, and an IGFA representative.

Carl. F. Luckey of Alabama is a writer specializing in antiques and collectibles; he has authored ten books, including his best-selling, 618-page work, *Old Fishing Lures and Tackle*.

Joe Macaluso of Louisiana is an award-winning outdoors sportswriter/editor for the *Baton Rouge Advocate*; his weekly fishing reports have appeared in Louisiana newspapers since 1976.

Rosanne Macfarlane of Prince Edward Island recently received her Masters degree in Biology at

Acadia University; she works for the Department of Fisheries and Environment.

Dennis Maksymetz of Manitoba is Manager of Tourism Marketing for the Industry, Trade and Tourism division of the Manitoba government.

Don Mann of Florida is a longtime contributor to *Florida Sportsman*, a record-holding big-game angler, and book author; his articles and photographs have appeared in many publications.

Al Marlowe of Colorado has written numerous articles for outdoor magazines; he authored a trail guide for the Flat Tops Wilderness area and a fly fishing guide for the Colorado River.

Peter B. Mathiesen of Missouri is Executive Editor and Producer of the *Field & Stream Radio Hour*; he is also a magazine writer, photographer, and video and television show producer.

John McCoy of West Virginia is Outdoors Editor for the *Charleston Daily Mail*, Regional Editor for *Field & Stream*, and a frequent contributor to regional and national magazines.

Tom Meade of Rhode Island writes about the outdoors for the *Providence Journal-Bulletin*; he is the author of *Essential Fly Fishing*, and writes for various magazines.

Ed Migdalski of Connecticut is the retired Director of Yale University's Outdoor Education and Club Sports Programs, retired Ichthyologist for the Yale Peabody Museum, and holder of the current world record for the largest strictly freshwater fish (pirarucú) ever caught on rod and reel.

Kent Mitchell of Georgia has covered outdoor sports for the *Atlanta Journal-Constitution* for three decades; he has received the Communicator of the Year Award from the Georgia Wildlife Federation, and has authored three books on martial arts.

Bill Monroe of Oregon has covered the outdoors for his state's largest daily newspaper, *The Oregonian*, for 18 years.

Gary W. Moore of Vermont is a freelance writer and photographer; he is former Commissioner of the Vermont Fish and Wildlife Department and former Chairman of the Vermont Water Resources Board.

Sam Mossman of New Zealand is Special Projects Editor for *New Zealand Fishing News* magazine; he is the author of three books and hundreds of magazine articles, and has held five world and numerous New Zealand fishing records.

Perry Munro of Nova Scotia is a writer and artist who contributes to *The Atlantic Salmon Journal* and various other magazines; he is also an outfitter, master guide, operator of Maple Mountain Lodge, and a Director of Trout Unlimited Canada.

Iain Nicolson of Angola is an IGFA representative and has a Ph.D. in molecular genetics; he and his family pioneered fishing for blue marlin in Angola and collectively established six world fishing records.

Chris Niskanen of Minnesota is the Outdoors Editor of the *St. Paul Pioneer Press*.

Donald J. Orth of Virginia is a Professor of Fisheries Science in the Department of Fisheries & Wildlife Sciences at Virginia Polytechnic Institute.

Tom Pagliaroli of New Jersey is an advertising agency executive, freelance writer, and photographer whose work has appeared in various regional and national publications.

Ali Pasiner of Turkey is an attorney, the author of two fishing books, and a consultant to the Turkish version of the *Encyclopaedia Britannica*; he is also a writer, editor, and representative of the IGFA.

C. Boyd Pfeiffer of Maryland is a longtime journalist and photographer, a regular columnist for many angling magazines, and the author of numerous books on fishing topics, the latest of which is *Fly Fishing Salt Water Basics*.

Larry Porter of Nebraska has been on the sports staff of the *Omaha World-Herald* for over three decades and their outdoors writer since 1990; he has been named Nebraska Sportswriter of the Year three times, and is a former professional tournament angler.

Steve Price of Texas is a longtime Senior Writer for *Bassmaster* magazine and contributor to a wide variety of national sporting magazines; he is an accomplished photographer and author of several books.

Gareth Purnell of England is Editor of Britain's leading angling magazine, *Improve Your Coarse Fishing*, and former News Editor of *Angling Times*; he has fished annually in the World Freshwater Angling Championships since 1993.

George Reiger of Virginia is Conservation Editor of *Field & Stream* and *Salt Water Sportsman* magazines and the most widely respected conservation writer in North America; he has been a staff writer for *Field & Stream* since 1972, is the author of seven books on angling and marine ecology, and the recipient of numerous honors and awards.

Tim Renken of Missouri has been the outdoors writer for the *St. Louis Post-Dispatch* since 1963; he previously worked for the Nebraska Game Commission.

Len Rich of Newfoundland is the author of two books and many outdoor magazine articles; he operates Awesome Lake Lodge in Labrador, is a former Hunting and Fishing Development Officer for Newfoundland and Labrador, and is a past representative of the Atlantic Salmon Federation.

Tom Richardson of Massachusetts is Managing Editor of *Salt Water Sportsman* magazine, as well as a freelance writer and photographer.

Al Ristori of New Jersey is Saltwater Fishing Editor of the *Newark Star-Ledger*, Regional Editor of *Salt Water Sportsman*, Conservation Editor of *The Fisherman* magazine, and the author of several books; he is also a charter boat captain and has served on the Mid-Atlantic Fishery Management Council.

Jim Rizzuto of Hawaii is Hawaii Editor for *Salt Water Sportsman* and *Western Outdoors*, a longtime columnist for *West Hawaii Today* and *Hawaii Fishing News*, and the author of the books *Modern Hawaiian Gamefishing* and *Fishing Hawaii Style*.

Nels Rodefeld of Oklahoma is an avid angler and hunter who frequently covers Oklahoma's hunting and fishing scene.

Milt Rosko of New Jersey is a writer for *Big Game Fishing Journal* and various other publications and a longtime authority on saltwater sportfishing; he is a photographer, book author, magazine feature writer, and lecturer.

Terry Rudnick of Washington has been writing articles on Northwest fishing subjects for more than 25 years; he is the author of the book *Washington Fishing, the Complete Guide*, and co-author of *How to Catch Trophy Halibut*.

Bob Sampson, Jr. of Connecticut is a writer, photographer, science teacher, and fisheries biologist; his work has appeared in numerous national and regional magazines.

Jack Samson of New Mexico is the retired Editor-in-Chief of *Field & Stream* and a former Associated Press columnist; he is Saltwater Editor of *Fly Rod & Reel* magazine, author of twenty books, and the first angler to catch both Atlantic and Pacific sailfish and all five species of marlin on a fly.

Ray Sasser of Texas is the Outdoor Editor of *The Dallas Morning News* and a freelance contributor to various magazines; he has been writing about outdoor sports for over 25 years.

Carl Werner Schmidt-Luchs of Germany is a contributor to *Blinker*, the largest angling magazine in Europe; he is a photographer, writer, and author of a dozen angling books.

Kristen Schultz of Massachusetts is a writer who recently graduated from Oberlin College; she works for an engineering consulting firm.

Bill Scifres of Indiana has been the Outdoor Editor of the *Indianapolis Star* since 1953; he is a book author, freelance writer, and photographer.

Eric Sharp of Michigan is Outdoor Editor of *The Detroit News*, and was formerly Outdoor Editor of *The Miami Herald*.

Luis Sier of Argentina is a newspaper columnist, a former magazine publisher, and an outfitter who operates several Argentinian fishing camps.

Jeff Simpson of South Dakota is an information officer for the State of South Dakota, a book author and freelance magazine writer, and former project developer for Cowles Creative Publishing.

DeWayne Smith of Arizona is an information officer for the Maricopa County Parks and Recreation Department; he covered the outdoors for over 30 years for *The Phoenix Gazette*.

Ryan Smith of Virginia is a research assistant with the Department of Fisheries and Wildlife Sciences at Virginia Polytechnic Institute.

Michael Snook of Saskatchewan is a freelance writer, conservationist, outdoor educator, and television producer.

Frank Sousa of Massachusetts is a writer for the *Springfield Sunday Republican* and the *Union News*, Editor/Publisher of *Northeast Woods and Waters*, and a freelance writer and photographer.

Vin T. Sparano of New Jersey is Senior Field Editor and retired Editor-in-Chief of *Outdoor Life*, for whom he worked for over three decades; he is a former syndicated columnist for *Gannett Newspapers*, and the author/editor of fourteen books, including *The Complete Outdoors Encyclopedia*.

Vladimir Stakic of Yugoslavia is Deputy Editor-in-Chief of the Yugoslavian angling magazines *Ribolovacka Revija* and *Ribolovacke Novine*, a freelance writer, and the author of three books of short stories.

Bob Stearns of Florida has been the staff boating/saltwater fishing writer of *Field & Stream* for 20 years and is the Electronics Editor of *Salt Water Sportsman*; the author of two books, he is a renowned fly fishing and light tackle expert, and has held two fly rod world records for sailfish.

Larry Stone of Iowa has been a writer and photographer for over three decades, and writes about the outdoors for the *Des Moines Register*.

Keith Sutton of Arkansas is Editor of *Arkansas Wildlife magazine*, a conservation publication of the Arkansas Game & Fish Commission, and a prolific freelance writer and photographer.

Ferenc Szalay of Hungary is Editor-in-Chief of *Magyar Horgász*, Hungary's premier fishing magazine; he is also President of the Hungarian National Committee for Match Fishing and Executive Board member of the Federation Internationale de la Pêche Sportive en Eau Douce.

Allan Tarvid of Texas is a contributing editor for *Sport Fishing* magazine and has authored hundreds of articles on electronics for sporting and commercial fishing and emergency service use; he has been a fishing guide and search and rescue diver.

Rikk Taylor of British Columbia is Editor and Publisher of *British Columbia Sport Fishing* magazine.

Mick Thill of Illinois and England is one of the world's top professional match fishing anglers and the first and only person to medal in the open water and ice fishing World Freshwater Fishing Championships; he is also a prominent float designer, and coach of the U. S. World Championship fishing teams.

Albert A. W. Threadingham of Fiji is an IGFA representative for the Fiji Islands and Governor of the Hawaiian International Billfish Association and the Pacific Ocean Research Foundation; he is a former world-record fish holder.

Raj Tilak of Maryland and India is co-author of the book *Game Fishes of India and Angling*, and author of more than 200 research publications; he is experienced in fisheries and wildlife management, with extensive knowledge of gamefishes and their ecology in India.

Anssi Uitti of Finland works for the Finnish outdoor magazine *Metsästys ja Kalastus*, and his articles have appeared in *Urheilukalastus* (Sportfishing) and *Perhokalastus* (Flyfishing) magazines.

Luis Umpierre of Puerto Rico is a physician, Editor of *Notipesca* (Fishing News), President of the Puerto Rico Sportfishing Association, and advisory member of the Caribbean Fishery Management Council.

Rudy Van Duijnhoven of Holland is a freelance photographer and author; his work appears monthly in *BEET-Sportvissers* magazine, and he is European Correspondent for Fly Fishing in *Salt Waters* magazine.

Carlo Vernocchi of Italy and Zanzibar introduced modern big-game fishing to the Zanzibar archipelago of Tanzania in 1992; he is an IGFA representative and charter boat captain.

Victor Villavicencio of Manila is a representative for the IGFA in the Philippines.

Tsutomu Wakabayashi of Japan is the General Manager of the Japan Game Fish Association; he has written for several Japanese fishing magazines, and is an IGFA representative.

Steve Waters of Florida is the outdoors writer for the *Fort Lauderdale Sun-Sentinel* and occasionally writes for national magazines; he was formerly a newspaper writer and video executive in New York.

Tom Wharton of Utah has been Outdoor Editor of the *Salt Lake Tribune* since 1976; he has co-authored five books, and is past President of the Outdoor Writers Association of America.

Jesse E. Williams of New Mexico is the retired Chief of Public Affairs for the New Mexico Department of Game and Fish, and a former Colorado wildlife manager and environmental education supervisor.

Juergen Willms of the Yukon Territory has worked with the Yukon Territory's Department of Natural Resources on various fishing projects.

Jorge Xifra of Paraguay operates El Pescador, a sportfishing outfitting service; he is a writer, television show host, IGFA representative, and holder of four world fishing records.

Photo Credits

All photographs by Ken Schultz except for the following:

Erwin Bursik 135, 140	Bruce Holt 14, 243	Al Ristori 76, 293
Cabela's 297, 304	Nick Karas 44	Shakespeare 161, 200
Daiwa 187, 189, 201	Steen Larsen 286	Zebco 155, 157, 158, 174, 191, 196
Fin-Nor 193	Marado 184, 190, 200	

SABIKI RIG
See: Multihook Rig.

SAFETY

Sportfishing is generally not a dangerous activity and seldom results in accidents. However, any activity that takes place on or around water; involves the operation of motorized vessels; causes people to come into contact with sharp objects like hooks, knives, and fish teeth; results in interaction with wild animals; and may be pursued in inclement weather can justly raise some safety concerns. Accidents may be rare, but they do happen.

Wading swift waters; walking on slippery jetties; floating in an inflatable tube; landing large, strong, and toothy fish; fishing on ice; and similar matters all require obvious precautions. Safety matters pertaining to these and other specific activities have been addressed within the respective entries. Although anglers can find themselves in an unsafe situation in many not-so-obvious ways—encountering a grizzly bear while walking the banks of a wilderness stream, for example—the greatest safety issues are related to boating, weather, and exposure to the elements.

Water Safety

The greatest concern for anyone who spends time around water is the possibility of drowning. The four major causes of drowning, in order, are: not wearing a personal flotation device; abuse of alcohol; lack of sufficient swimming skills; and hypothermia (chilling of the body because of exposure to cold). Two-thirds of the people who drown never had any intention of being in the water; this includes most people who fish, since they either wade, fish from the bank or shore, or fish from a boat, but don't intend, or expect, to get into an unsafe situation.

Personal flotation devices *(see)*, also known as PFDs, are reviewed in detail elsewhere. The most important basic points to know are that anyone who cannot swim should be wearing a PFD when on or near the water; that rough weather and water conditions and some tricky boating situations require that a PFD be worn out of prudence; and that a PFD must be worn to be helpful, because it is almost always too difficult to put on once a person is in the water and in trouble.

People who spend time around water not only should develop a healthy respect for it, but should become comfortable with it. Learning to swim, at least to be able to float and tread water, means that if you do take an unexpected plunge in the water, you know enough to somewhat help yourself. Small children, of course, need constant supervision around water.

Alcohol (and drugs) and water are a lethal mixture. More than half of the people who drown annually have consumed alcohol prior to their accident, so it is obvious that no one who is on or in the water should consume alcohol.

Being in cold water is much more of a concern than being in warm water, even if you know how to swim and are wearing a PFD. This can lead to hypothermia, which is reviewed elsewhere *(see: first aid)*.

Boating

Safety issues for boating anglers arise when towing, launching, fueling, and operating a boat, and have been mostly addressed under a separate entry *(see: boat)*. It is especially important not to overload a boat (too much weight or too many people), to make sure that a proper-fitting PFD is available for every passenger, and to have the required safety equipment (warning device, navigational lights, fire extinguisher, etc.) aboard.

Other than reckless boat handling, the chief causes of boating safety concerns for anglers are dams, dangerous currents, navigational hazards, anchoring, and winds or storms. Most of these concerns can be minimized by prudent boat operation

Fishing during a snowstorm and in very cold water, these anglers are smart to have life jackets on, but they'd be safer sitting than standing.

and good boat-handling skills, but it's important to learn to recognize situations that can present a problem and to not underestimate them. The force of current *(see)* and the effects of strong converging currents, for example, are commonly not respected enough. The dangers inherent in improper anchoring *(see: anchor)* are significant, especially in heavy winds or strong current, and many boaters run into problems by anchoring poorly or in unsafe places or circumstances.

River tailraces *(see)*, for example, can be extremely dangerous because of the velocity and turbulence of discharged water, changing water levels, and unpredictable current patterns. In these places, anglers should not tie their boat to the dam or anchor at it; downstream anchoring should be done with a quick-release device, and the engine should always be kept running in fast water. It's important to be alert for rising water and to keep a safe distance from other boats as well.

In large bodies of water and in big rivers, prudent navigation requires not just evaluating what lies ahead on the open water, but what may lie below. The water isn't like a highway, where everything is visible. Reefs, sandbars, rockpiles, and other objects are commonly present in many water bodies, and not necessarily marked; boaters must be sure of their path of travel, or proceed cautiously otherwise. The sudden striking of objects has unexpectedly and quickly sunk fishing boats, pitching occupants into the water. An otherwise delightful day can become a crisis, an emergency, or a survival situation in an instant.

Fishing and boating at night, which is common in summer for freshwater and saltwater anglers, brings added concerns for navigation and boat handling, and a greater concern for caution. This obviously applies to those who are moving under power, and not as obviously to those who are not; people in a boat that is anchored in a channel need to use lights to indicate their presence to others, or risk unintentionally being in harm's way.

Strong winds are often a natural element that causes a problem for boaters. Sometimes, coping with the wind is not terribly prudent, and the sensible thing to do is head for port. This is especially so if the winds appear to be building; don't wait for the worst conditions to arrive.

The first concern when fishing in heavy wind—especially when the water is cold, the waves are high, the boat is small or tipsy or flat-hulled, or there is a far distance to go—should be safety. You must put on and fasten a proper-fitting PFD that will keep your fully clothed body afloat and your head upright.

When the wind and weather are rough, you have to consider whether you, and the boat you expect to use, are up to fishing. On the personal comfort level, taking a pounding by running through heavy waves is hard on the back and neck, particularly for older anglers. And though the fish may be biting like crazy, that is small comfort to a companion who gets seasick *(see: seasickness)*.

But the boat is another story. You have to realistically assess what your boat can handle, going forth only if you're are completely sure and prepared, or turning back when good sense demands it. Of course, going out to fish under severe wind is much different than being on the water and angling when conditions change from calm to frothy. Too many anglers push their luck each year, not noticing shifts in wind speed or direction, or thinking they can run themselves out of trouble. Sometimes they pay for it. Most people are guilty of not looking enough to the horizon for squalls and thunderstorms. That is one reason why on large bodies of water the wise angler has a VHF radio or handheld weather radio to stay informed of weather patterns, changes, and potential problems when in a locale where these devices function.

If the wind has picked up enough to put whitecaps on the water or, worse, a trail of foam, beware. It's already late, especially on large shallow lakes, which are among the most dangerous bodies of water because big waves build up quickly there. So are lakes with many reefs and shoals. Small boaters get caught in troughs, or get pushed up into shallows or shoals or boulders and bang up the outboard's lower unit or the boat hull, maybe even causing capsizing (especially watch out in a canoe). Recognize the dangers that lie ahead and be smart enough to avoid them so that you remain safe.

In addition, you need to be sure that nothing impedes your boat's progress when you're faced with strong winds and their accompanying waves. A crippled boat is very tough to handle properly in the worst conditions. You shouldn't be out there with a motor that isn't working well, for example. And make sure that any ropes—anchor rope or otherwise—aren't laying out where rough-water bouncing could cause them to be swept overboard. If so, the rope will be in the boat's propeller in an instant, probably seizing up the motor, and you'll be in a lot of trouble.

Thunderstorms

Although all types of storms pose danger to anglers, a thunderstorm is the one significant weather event that is most likely to be encountered by people who fish. Lightning is the leading cause of weather-related deaths and a high cause of weather-related injuries. Approximately one in four lightning strikes on humans happens to people involved in recreation; many such strikes are on or near water. Over the last half century in the United States, lightning was responsible for many more deaths than tornadoes and for many more than hurricanes and floods combined.

Whenever the slightest chance of a thunderstorm exists, the first safety precaution is to check the latest weather forecast and keep an eye on the sky. Recognize the signs of an impending storm: towering thunderheads, darkening skies, lightning, and increasing wind. Tune in an NOAA weather radio, the weather band of a VHF radio, or an AM/FM radio if you can, for the latest weather information.

When a thunderstorm threatens, getting inside a home, large building, or all-metal automobile (not a convertible or the bed of a truck) is the best course of action. This is usually not possible for anglers unless they act well in advance of a storm. Many people put themselves in unnecessary danger by waiting too long to take action when a thunderstorm approaches.

Anglers who are wading or who are along the bank or shore need to get out of and away from the water. Anglers in boats should quickly get to a safe place on land whenever possible; if not possible, they may be able to get out of the storm's path by moving, but only if they act well ahead of its arrival. You cannot outrun a thunderstorm that is imminent. If the storm is still very distant, you can try to outrun it. To do so, you need to know what direction the storm is moving in. Thus, running is effective only on large bodies of water and when storms do not cover wide expanses.

If you are caught outside on land, do not stand underneath an isolated tree, a telephone pole, or isolated objects, or near power lines or metal fences. Avoid projecting above the surrounding landscape. In a forest, seek shelter in a low area under a thick growth of small trees. In open areas, go to a low place, such as a ravine or valley. If you're in a group in the open, spread out, keeping people 5 to 10 yards apart. Stay away from metal vehicles and objects, and do not carry or raise any objects. Remove any metal objects from your hair or head, and remove metal-cleated boots.

Lightning may strike up to 10 miles from the center of the storm, so precautions should be taken even though the parent cloud is not directly overhead. If you are caught in the open, far from shelter, and if you feel your hair stand on end, lightning may be about to strike you. Drop to your knees and bend forward, putting your hands on your knees. Do not lie flat on the ground.

If you are stuck in a boat and the same thing happens, or your fishing rod begins to buzz or the line rises out of the water, lightning is about to strike. Immediately crouch down, lean forward, and put your hands on your knees, making sure not to touch anything else in the boat.

The reason behind these positions—and why you don't lie flat—is that when lightning strikes, it seeks the quickest way through the object it strikes. The more things that you touch or have contact with, the more lightning will travel through the body in an effort to seek a way out.

Many lightning strikes occur without the warning of thunder, so precautions are necessary even when there is no thunder. When there is both thunder and lightning, you can tell how many miles the lightning is from your position by counting the seconds between the sound of the thunder and the sight of the lightning, then dividing that by five. Scientists say that if you can hear thunder, then you are in range of being struck.

Thus, to avoid becoming a statistic, anglers should watch the sky for signs of an impending storm, get off the water early and especially if they hear thunder, and pick the proper places for refuge on land.

See: Boat; Navigation; Survival; Waves; Weather.

SAILFISH *Istiophorus platypterus.*

Other names—spindlebeak, bayonetfish; French: *voilier, espadon vela;* Hawaiian: *a'u lepe;* Italian: *pesce vela, pesce ventaglio;* Japanese: *bashôkajiki;* Portuguese: *veleiro, algulhão;* Spanish: *pez vela, aguja voladora, aguja de faralá, aguja de abanico.*

With its characteristic large dorsal fin and superlative aerial ability, the sailfish is arguably the most striking member of the Istiophoridae family of billfish. Although present taxonomy suggests that the Atlantic and Pacific sailfish are the same species, some experts are not yet convinced. It has long been believed that Indo-Pacific specimens of sailfish attain a much greater size than their Atlantic counterparts (and this is reflected in record catches), but a recent study of size data from the Japanese longline fishery provided evidence that eastern Atlantic specimens (identified by some ichthyolo-

An Atlantic sailfish provides a thrill near American Shoal in the Florida Keys.

Sailfish

Sailfish

gists as *I. albicans*) can attain much larger sizes than previously recorded.

The speedy sailfish is among the most exciting light-tackle big-game fish to catch. Light conventional gear, as well as spinning, baitcasting, and fly outfits, are all suitable for pursuing sailfish. The smaller specimens found in the Atlantic are especially good fun and are relatively easy for even inexperienced anglers to enjoy. Sailfish are rarely kept by western Atlantic anglers (and many are tagged when released) but are commonly kept in other places, especially off Mexico and Central America. They do have commercial significance in many parts of their range and are heavily exploited.

Identification. The sailfish is dark blue on top, brown blue laterally, and silvery white on the belly; the upper jaw is elongated in the form of a spear. This species' outstanding feature is the long, high first dorsal fin, which has 37 to 49 total elements; it is slate or cobalt blue with many black spots. The second dorsal fin is very small, with six to eight rays. The single, prominent lateral line is curved over the pectoral fin and otherwise straight along the median line of the flanks. The bill is longer than that of the spearfish *(see)*, usually a little more than twice the length of the elongated lower jaw. The vent is just forward of the first anal fin. The sides often have pale, bluish gray vertical bars or rows or spots.

Although sailfish look like similar-size white marlin *(see: marlin, white)* and blue marlin *(see: marlin, blue)*, they are readily distinguished by their large sail-like dorsal fin.

Size/Age. Sportfishing records for sailfish have long been maintained by the International Game Fish Association (IGFA) according to their Atlantic and Indo-Pacific distribution; the all-tackle world record for Atlantic fish is a 141-pounder caught off Angola in 1994; its counterpart in the Pacific is a 221-pounder caught off Ecuador in 1947. Fish from 20 to 50 or 60 pounds are commonly caught off the eastern U.S., and fish from 50 to 100 pounds are common in many places in the Pacific. They can exceed 10 feet in length.

Distribution/Habitat. Sailfish occur worldwide in tropical and temperate waters of the Atlantic, Indian, and Pacific Oceans. They are pelagic and migratory in warm offshore waters, although they may migrate into warm nearshore areas in parts of their range. In the eastern Pacific, sailfish range from Baja California, Mexico, to Peru, and in the western Atlantic from Massachusetts to Brazil. They are most common in warm waters along the edges of the Gulf Stream.

Life history/Behavior. Like other pelagic species that spawn in the open sea, sailfish produce large numbers of eggs, perhaps 4 to 5 million. These are fertilized in the open water, where they float with plankton until hatching. Sailfish grow rapidly and reportedly can attain 4 to 5 feet in length in their first year. They reportedly swim at speeds approaching 68 mph, making them the swiftest short-distance gamefish. Sailfish may form schools or small groups of from 3 to 30 individuals and sometimes travel in loose aggregations spread over a wide area. They appear to feed mostly in midwater along the edges of reefs or current eddies.

Food and feeding habits. Sailfish eat squid, octopus, mackerel, tuna, jacks, herring, ballyhoo, needlefish, flyingfish, mullet, and other small fish. They feed on the surface or at mid-depths.

Angling. Fishing methods for this species are similar to those for other billfish, although lighter tackle is more appropriate. Fishing methods include trolling with strip baits, whole mullet or ballyhoo, plastic offshore trolling lures, and trolling feathers or spoons. Another option is live-bait fishing with or without kites, using jacks, mullet, and other small natural baits. Sailfish are usually caught in depths exceeding 6 fathoms but are occasionally caught in lesser depths and even from ocean piers where currents and baitfish bring this species near shore. Generally, however, they are pursued in clear, blue offshore water and are located on or near the surface.

The spectacular jumping of the sailfish makes it a superb light-tackle quarry, as this leaping and a generally small size prevent it from having long-term stamina. Spinning and baitcasting rods with 12- through 30-pound line are standard, and fly gear is very effective with bait-and-switch *(see)* tactics.
See: Big-Game Fishing; Billfish; Billfish on Fly Tackle; Offshore Fishing.

SALINITY

The total amount of inorganic minerals or salts dissolved in a kilogram of seawater. Rain, snowfall, and the inflow of rivers dilute seawater and lower salinity; evaporation and freezing increase salinity. Other factors that may affect salinity at a given time and place include wind, wave motion, and ocean currents. These elements cause vertical and horizontal mixing.

The average salinity of seawater is 35 parts per thousand (35 pounds of salt per 1,000 pounds of seawater), which is 220 times saltier than fresh lake water. Concentrations as high as 40 parts per thousand have been observed in the Red Sea and the Persian Gulf. Salinities are much less than average in coastal waters, in the polar seas, and near the mouths of large rivers.

The salinity of seawater may affect the availability of species, because some gamefish are much more tolerant of low salinity or variable salinity.
See: Brackish Water.

SALMON, AMAGO *Oncorhynchus rhodurus*.
Other names—Japanese: *amago, biwamasu.*

This small member of the Salmonidae family is one of two species of Pacific salmon *(see: salmon, Pacific)* that occur only in Asia and the western Pacific. It is closely related to masu salmon *(O. masou; see: salmon, masu)*, and there are diverging ichthyological opinions about whether the two are the same; they are currently considered separate species. Compounding the matter is the existence of anadromous and freshwater versions of both species. Technically, the word "amago" refers to the anadromous or stream-dwelling version, *O. rhodurus macrostomus;* the nonanadromous and permanently freshwater-dwelling version is *O. rhodurus rhodurus,* which in Japan is known as *biwamasu.* Thus, "amago" refers to the seagoing salmon and "biwamasu" to the freshwater dweller, although the word "amago" is often used interchangeably to refer to both.

Both amago and biwamasu are small, the former being half the size of the latter on average, and generally less than 10 inches long. Their distribution in Japan is extremely limited, ranging from the Tokyo Bay area southwesterly along the Pacific coast of Honshu Island to the northern tip of Kyushu Island, including Shikoku Island. Most amago salmon remain in rivers for their full life span, but some are anadromous, and most of the latter remain in bays and inlets rather than wandering through the open ocean. Those that migrate to the ocean spend only six months there. Spawning in coastal rivers occurs in spring. Amago were reportedly introduced unsuccessfully in Germany.

SALMON, ATLANTIC *Salmo salar.*
Other names for sea-run fish—grilse, grilt, fiddler, Kennebec salmon; Danish and Norwegian: *laks;* Dutch: *zalm;* Finnish: *lohi;* French: *saumon Atlantique, saumon d'eau douce;* German: *lachs, las, salm;* Italian: *salmo, salmone;* Japanese: *sake masu-rui;* Portuguese: *salmao;* Russian: *losos;* Spanish: *salmón del Atlantico;* Swedish: *lax.*

Names for post-spawn adult fish—black salmon, slink, kelt.

Names for salmon living entirely in freshwater—landlocked salmon, ouananiche, grayling, lake Atlantic salmon, Sebago salmon; French: *ouananiche.*

Atlantic salmon are possibly the most important single species of fish in a historical and an economic sense, having been esteemed since the days of the Romans and being mentioned even in the Magna Carta, not to mention the high price that fishing on a beat of prime Atlantic salmon river fetches. The only salmon in the Salmonidae family that occurs in the Atlantic Ocean and its tributaries, the Atlantic salmon has been coveted for its excellent flesh since recorded history. Likewise, anglers since before Izaak Walton's time have known it for its acrobatics when caught, which gave rise to its name *salar,* derived from the Latin word *salio,* meaning leaper.

Confusion sometimes arises because the Atlantic salmon is classified as a member of the *Salmo* genus, which consists of various trout species, rather than the *Oncorhynchus* genus, which includes all seven Pacific salmon species. Despite the confusion, this system is unlikely to change. The name "salmon" arose in Europe and originally referred to the Atlantic salmon. New World settlers carried the name with them from the Old World and applied it not only to the Atlantic salmon in eastern North America, which was identical to the species in Europe, but also to the similar-bodied fish of western North America.

Although it has been proposed that the name Atlantic salmon be changed to end confusion concerning its taxonomical relationship to trout, this name is deeply rooted in history and has been published in the literature worldwide. The fish is broadly regulated under the name Atlantic salmon as well, and it is reasoned that a name change might cause greater confusion and be an injustice to the species with which the name "salmon" originated.

Ironically, the Atlantic salmon is like some members of the Pacific salmon group in that it has both anadromous and freshwater forms. The former migrate from freshwater streams to the ocean

Atlantic Salmon

and then return to those streams to spawn, whereas the latter remain in freshwater all their lives. Called landlocked salmon or ouananiche in North America, the freshwater form is the same species as the anadromous Atlantic salmon and shares identical characteristics, except that the freshwater fish is smaller. Landlocked salmon occurred naturally in some large lakes that were cut off from saltwater many thousands of years ago. In modern times, stocking has spread the landlocked form to many other waters. Landlocked Atlantics are also fine gamefish and excellent food fish.

Atlantic salmon have suffered greatly throughout large portions of their range due to dams, other habitat alteration, pollution, and overfishing, especially by commercial interests. Some stocks of sea-run and landlocked Atlantic salmon have become extinct, and many are endangered or threatened. As a consequence of industrial and agricultural development, for example, most of the runs native to New England have been extirpated.

Concern for Atlantic salmon accelerated after the mid-1960s. Until that time, little was known about the life of the Atlantic salmon in the sea. Then, a common feeding ground for Atlantic salmon was discovered off Greenland and exploited by commercial fishermen. Another feeding ground was later located off Norway. The ensuing commercial pressure and the return of these fish to birth rivers they found impassable or unsuited to spawning accelerated the decline.

Atlantics have been reared in hatcheries for decades to provide smolts for river stocking programs, and although this has been of limited success, it has not proven an antidote to greater problems and has also resulted in stocks with different, and often lesser, genetic adaptability to specific rivers. Atlantic salmon are also commercially farmed in large ocean pens. This is a rapidly growing industry in some locations, one that supplies many salmon to market. Some concern does exist, however, regarding escapees and their possible interaction with natural stocks.

As a gamefish, the Atlantic salmon is showy when it leaps out of the water, capable of making strong runs up and down (usually the latter) swift-flowing rivers when hooked, and often a challenge to entice. Landlocked fish are known for long runs and superior fighting ability, and they are widely sought by anglers in lakes and rivers. The reddish orange flesh of both, but especially of the sea-run fish, is excellent to eat and is highly valued when fresh or either hot- or cold-smoked.

Identification. Compared to the size of its body, a mature Atlantic salmon has a small head. Its body is long and slim, and in adults the caudal or tail fin is nearly square. Individuals that return to spawn prematurely (called grilse) are mostly males and have a slightly forked tail. While in the sea, the Atlantic salmon is dark blue on the top of its head and back; its sides are a shiny silver, and the belly is white. The fins are dark, and there are numerous black marks in the shape of an X or Y on its head and along its body above the lateral line.

When the fish enters freshwater to spawn, it gradually loses its metallic shine and becomes dull brown or yellowish. Many, particularly males, are splotched with red or have large black patches on the body, and may look a lot like the brown trout *(Salmo trutta)*, their closest relative. Often brown trout may have circles, or halos, around some of their spots, and the spotting may be heavier than in the Atlantic salmon, extending onto the lower half of the sides and the fins, including the adipose fin. The spots do not normally take the form of Xs or Ys. At spawning time the males are further distinguished by their greatly elongated hooked jaws that meet only at the tips; the fins become thicker, and a heavy coat of slime covers the body. Post-spawn fish appear very dark, leading to the name "black salmon."

In a general sense, the body shape of an Atlantic salmon is similar to that of a trout and is distinguished from salmon and trout of the genus *Oncorhynchus* by coloration, size, and location of occurrence, among other characteristics.

Landlocked Atlantics look the same as their anadromous counterparts, although spawning fish may be darker.

Size/Age. The Atlantic salmon can live for eight years and is the second largest of all salmon. It is capable of attaining weights to 80 pounds, although no such sizes have been recorded in decades. Unofficial historical reports talk of specimens weighing as much as 100 pounds. The largest known sport-caught fish is the all-tackle world record, a specimen weighing 79 pounds, 2 ounces when taken from Norway's Tana River in 1928. Most specimens today weigh 20 pounds or less, and fish exceeding 30 pounds are rare, even in the better waters. Historically, the biggest fish came from Europe. In North America, the largest known Atlantic salmon was a 55-pounder caught in the Grand Cascapedia River, Quebec.

Landlocked Atlantic salmon do not grow to such ultimate sizes, although they are capable of growing to between 30 and 40 pounds. A 22-pound, 11-ounce specimen from Lobstick Lake in Labrador is often cited as the largest sport-caught landlocked salmon, but these fish historically grew to 45 pounds in New York's Lake Ontario, and modern introductions in that lake and in Lake Michigan have produced numerous fish in excess of 30 pounds. A $35^{1}/_{2}$-pound specimen was once taken from Sebago Lake in Maine. Lake Vanern in Sweden, and some Russian lakes, have reportedly grown landlocks to 40 pounds. In most places, the average size is under 10 pounds and closer to 5 pounds.

Distribution. The anadromous Atlantic salmon is native to the North Atlantic Ocean and coastal rivers in North America and Europe. Its endemic range in the western Atlantic was from Long Island Sound and the Housatonic River in Connecticut north to Ungava Bay, Quebec, including the Gulf of St. Lawrence and the Labrador Sea; in the central North Atlantic, its range included southwestern Greenland and most of Iceland; in the eastern Atlantic, it ranged from the Dour River in Portugal north to the Kara River in Russia, including the British Isles, the North and Baltic Seas, the Norwegian Sea, and the Barents and White Seas.

In North America, landlocked Atlantic salmon were endemic to many lakes in eastern Canada and Maine, as well as to Lakes Champlain and Ontario; in Europe they existed in Norway, Sweden, and northwestern Russia.

Although anadromous Atlantic salmon still inhabit much of their original range, some stocks are no longer of the original genetic strain, which was wiped out. They therefore consist of introduced or augmented anadromous fish. Anadromous Atlantic salmon have been extirpated from most of their more southerly range on both sides of the Atlantic, a victim of industrial growth, dams, pollution, and other factors. In North America, numerous self-supporting runs of anadromous Atlantics exist in Canada, especially Quebec, but also in Newfoundland, New Brunswick, and Nova Scotia, although the size of these stocks is severely depleted. Self-supporting runs of Atlantic salmon in the United States are found only in Maine. Restoration efforts have been attempted in various rivers and presently continue in the Connecticut, Pawcatuck, Merrimack, and Penobscot Rivers of New England, which is a far cry from the 28 New England rivers that once contained this species.

Although some original landlocked populations have also been extirpated, landlocked Atlantic salmon have been introduced to many waters where they did not originally exist, and reintroduced to waters where they once existed. Landlocked Atlantics have been widely introduced to the Great Lakes, where the larger specimens exist today, and are widely dispersed in eastern Quebec, Newfoundland, and Labrador.

Habitat. Anadromous Atlantic salmon spend most of their lives in the ocean, ascending coastal rivers to spawn. They are found in freshwater only during their spawning runs, after engaging in extensive and complex migrations throughout their range by relying on their acute sense of homing for navigation. In coastal rivers, they primarily inhabit deep runs and pools, and seldom favor fast water or riffles.

Although some landlocked salmon may exist in rivers all year, the great majority spend most of their lives in the open water of lakes, ascending tributaries to spawn. In rivers, they inhabit deep runs and pools. In lakes they stay in cooler, deeper levels, where baitfish are abundant.

Life history/Behavior. Spawning usually occurs in gravel bottoms at the head of riffles or the tail of a pool, and in the evening or at night. The female looks for places where the water seeps down into clean gravel. The female digs a nest, or redd, 6 to 14 inches deep in the gravel by turning on her side, flipping her tail upward, and pulling the gravel up until a hole is excavated. After the female and male spawn in the redd, the 5- to 7-millimeter eggs are buried with gravel by the female. The whole process is repeated several times until the female has shed all of her eggs. Females produce an average of 700 eggs per pound of body weight. After spawning, the adults, which are then called kelts, usually drop downstream to rest in a pool.

Unlike Pacific salmon *(see: salmon, Pacific)*, the adults do not die after spawning. Exhausted and thin, they often return to sea immediately before winter or remain in the stream until spring. Some will survive to spawn a second time, but few survive to spawn three or more times.

Salmon eggs develop slowly (roughly 110 days) over the winter while water flowing through the nest keeps the eggs clean and oxygenated. In most rivers, the eggs survive well and are protected from freezing or silt. The eggs hatch in the spring, usually April, and the young salmon, called alevins, remain buried in the gravel for up to 5 weeks while they absorb their large yolk sac. Many young fish are lost at this stage. Over the winter, silt and sand often move into the nest and can trap the young fish. If they survive this stage, the young salmon that emerge are about 1 inch long in May or June. During this freshwater stage, before they migrate to sea, they are known as parr. Salmon parr are territorial, feed during the day, and live in shallow riffle areas 10 to 26 inches deep that have gravel, rubble, rock, or boulder bottoms.

After roughly three years (but within two to eight years) in freshwater, salmon parr become smolts and prepare for life in saltwater. In the spring, these parr become slimmer and turn silvery. During the spring runoff, as water temperatures rise, smolts form schools and migrate downstream at night. It is during this downstream migration that smolts "learn," or become imprinted with, the characteristics of their particular river, which will play a role in their eventual return.

Atlantic salmon will stay at sea (or in a lake) for one or more years and are known to travel long distances. Many salmon from Canada's Maritime rivers travel as far as the western coast of Greenland, where the waters are rich in food. Grilse, or salmon that spend only one year at sea before returning to freshwater, are smaller, weighing from 3 to 6 pounds; most are males. Salmon that return after two winters usually weigh from 6 to 15 pounds. Salmon that remain in the sea for two years or longer before making their first spawning run become the largest, heaviest individuals. Rivers with runs of fish that spend more than two years in the ocean, therefore, are known for larger salmon. Some Atlantics may make a spawning run only once or twice during their lifetime of roughly eight years; others will spawn three or four times, returning in consecutive years to the same spawning grounds, and these are usually the largest fish of all.

Atlantic salmon that are ready to spawn begin moving upriver from late spring through fall. The exact timing varies according to the particular river and the distance the fish travel upstream, but these spawning runs are surprisingly consistent and occur at the same time each year for each river. Salmon populations are often spoken of as "early run" or "late run," and these are relative, overall designations. In some places, the spawning areas are actually close to the sea, not far above the high-tide level. In other streams, the spawners may travel long distances, as much as 312 miles upstream; they are known for their ability to leap small waterfalls and other obstacles. During this journey, the salmon does not eat. Landlocked salmon living in lakes move up into tributary streams to spawn in a similar manner, although they usually don't do so until late summer.

The early spawners appear in streams in spring and are usually the largest fish. These individuals have the firmest flesh and are most sought after. They are followed soon by the grilse and then by more mature fish, the runs slacking off during the hot summer months but increasing again in early autumn. Early-run fish do not move upstream rapidly; their gonads are not yet well enough developed for the actual spawning act. Sometimes the late arrivals catch up with them, and they reach their destination at the same time. Spawning occurs from October through December.

Large river systems may have several runs, which reflects different races heading to their own tributaries. In a few rivers, especially in northerly regions, some Atlantics enter rivers in late summer, fall, or early winter, a year before they spawn.

Food. In rivers, salmon parr feed mainly on the immature and adult stages of aquatic insects. In the ocean, salmon grow rapidly, feeding on crustaceans and other fish such as smelt, alewives, herring, capelin, mackerel, and cod. Landlocked salmon in lakes eat pelagic freshwater fish, primarily smelt and alewives. Neither feeds during its upstream spawning migration, which leads to endless curiosity and speculation as to why it strikes a lure or fly during this time.

Angling (for Atlantic and landlocked salmon). Much has been written about salmon fishing and the intricacies thereof, and even a volume such as this cannot do justice to the full scope of fishing techniques and strategies for both the sea-run and freshwater fish in their respective environments, so the following information is intended as an overview.

It is during their limited spawning run that seagoing Atlantics are pursued by anglers in rivers; there is no ocean sportfishing for this species in North America, although Scandinavian anglers practice ocean fishing for this species in the Baltic Sea. The average sea-winter fish weighs less than 15 pounds, and one weighing more than that is considered large in most rivers. Nevertheless, smaller fish fight extraordinarily well, and the possibility of landing older 20- to 30-pound fish exists in some rivers.

Atlantic and landlocked salmon hug the river bottom, resting in pools and deep-water sections. They are not usually caught in the fast-water reaches, although they will frequent the head and tail of pools, and slick-water runs. A common tactic is to start fishing above the head of a pool or run, methodically working down through a stretch, casting down and across and letting the fly swing at the end of each cast. Most fish are caught when the fly makes its swing or hangs momentarily in the current at the end of the swing.

Fly fishing is the angling method by law or tradition in most of North America for seagoing Atlantic salmon. These fish usually hold shallower than other salmon, making sight fishing—casting to a specific fish that has been seen rather than casting blindly for unobserved fish as is usually done when angling for coho or chinook salmon—a favored method. Some waters have restrictions on weighted hooks or flies to minimize accidental or deliberate foul hooking of fish.

Wet flies in various colorful patterns and sizes are popular for Atlantic salmon fishing, and the larger flies are generally reserved for fast, high rivers. Dry flies work at times, too, which is an anomaly considering the nonfeeding disposition of these fish; the dries used, however, such as Bombers, are large flies typically tied with tightly packed deer hair.

Atlantics may take on the first, fiftieth, or one-hundredth cast, acting out of reflex or annoyance, and they may be put down easily or be relatively undisturbed by the angler's presence and activities. Unlike other salmon in rivers, Atlantics and landlocks are prone to jump high and often, in addition to making long, demanding runs. Long rods and reels with plenty of backing are required. Standard fly tackle consists of an 8- or 9-weight rod equipped with a floating fly line and a reel with 200 yards of 20- or 30-pound-test backing. Leader length should match rod length, or be slightly shorter. A sinking fly line or sink-tip fly line is not used. A 9-foot rod with 9-weight line is a standard outfit in North America. This setup accommodates the bulk of some salmon flies; however, longer rods, including two-handed versions, are popular in many European rivers.

Long casts in the 70- to 100-foot-plus range are the norm on many Atlantic salmon rivers, although they aren't always a necessity. Getting a good drift on the fly, mending it where necessary, and at times even riffling it across the surface gently, are important aspects of presentation. The evening and early-morning hours are good times, and overcast days bode well for daylong fishing, although there is no guarantee on such matters. When pools are fished by a number of anglers, it is customary to take turns; anglers slowly work their way downstream from the head of the pool, with one angler beginning at the top of the pool as the previous angler approaches the end of it.

The principal method of pursuing landlocked salmon in lakes is trolling. Most activity occurs in the spring, after ice out and until these fish move deep. Although some salmon are caught when the ice is breaking up and water temperatures are in the 39° to 42°F range, better action doesn't begin until the water hits the mid 40s. Landlocks are caught from the surface to 20 feet deep at this time and are found near shore over relatively shallow bottom or in open areas over deep water.

As the surface temperature increases, landlocks are more likely to be found near tributaries if they attract large spawning runs of smelt, or inshore where schools of smelt or spawning alewives may be located. Water temperatures then are in the low to mid-50s. This activity takes place in May and throughout June, but by mid- to late June in a normal year the surface water is warming, and landlocks will move to deeper water and locate in the thermocline, roughly staying in 52° to 57°F water and roaming as widely as the size of the lake and water temperature zones will allow. They are usually hardest to locate and catch at this time.

The traditional and still widely practiced method of landlocked salmon trolling employs a fly rod and a streamer fly. The rod is between 8 and 9 feet long and equipped with a large-capacity fly reel loaded with 100 yards of backing, a level sinking line, and a long leader. The leader is between 20 and 30 feet in length and usually 6 to 10 pounds in strength. A streamer fly is tied to the end, and

A landlocked Atlantic salmon is released on a river in Labrador.

sometimes a split shot or two is added to the leader. The rod is often held in the angler's hand and kept parallel to the water, and it is jerked backward frequently to give the fly a darting motion.

Another traditional method is to use a fly rod or conventional rod with a levelwind reel and leadcore line, fishing a spoon or fly at the business end. The favored rods are long, and anglers pulsate them as they do fly rods. Downrigger and sideplaner fishing have increased on the landlocked salmon scene, especially where spoons and plugs are preferred. These are fished in conventional manners.

Lure selection should follow the baitfish patterns in a given lake. Smelt are the foremost, and preferred, landlocked salmon food. Alewives are a major forage in some locales. Elsewhere, cisco, shiners, and yellow perch make up part of their lake diet. Smelt are usually the bread-and-butter prey, and most landlocked salmon lures are meant to imitate smelt. These lures include minnow-imitating plugs in straight and jointed versions from 4 to 6 inches in length, long thin spoons, and single or tandem streamer flies.

The best fishing, especially in spring, is often in the first few hours of the day, but a late-afternoon or evening flurry is common. Midday, particularly under bluebird conditions, is dubious. A relatively fast trolling speed is employed for landlocks, and whereas lines are usually set from 75 to 200 feet behind the boat on flatlines, and from 40 to 80 feet back on deep downriggers, some spring fish are literally caught in the prop wash.

SALMON, AUSTRALIAN
See: Kahawai.

SALMON, CHINOOK *Oncorhynchus tshawytscha.* **Other names**—king salmon, spring salmon, tyee, quinnat, tule, blackmouth, Sacramento River salmon, Columbia River salmon; French: *saumon chinook, saumon royal*; Japanese: *masunosuke*.

The chinook salmon is one of the most important sportfish and commercial fish in the world, especially, and historically, to the Pacific coast of North America, where this and other salmonids have long had great cultural and food significance. It is the largest member of the Salmonidae family, and both the largest and least-abundant member of the Pacific salmon genus *Oncorhynchus*. By nature an anadromous species, it can adapt to an entirely freshwater existence and has done so with such remarkable success in the Great Lakes of North America that it has formed the backbone of an enormous and extremely valuable sportfishery there, becoming one of the greatest fisheries transplant/management/revitalization projects of all time.

Pacific stocks of chinook, as well as other Pacific salmonids, however, have suffered greatly throughout large portions of their range due to dams, other habitat alteration, pollution, and excessive commercial fishing. Some chinook runs in the Pacific Northwest are threatened or endangered.

As a gamefish, the chinook is not flashy; it rarely leaps out of the water, unlike coho salmon *(see: salmon, coho)* and Atlantic salmon *(see: salmon, Atlantic)*, but it is bulldog strong and has great staying power. Fresh river migrants are more than a handful for many anglers, and large fish in all environs are not only tenacious but also greatly prized. The sea-run chinook is the only Pacific salmon in which the meat can be regularly either red or white. Although white meat is rare, red meat commands a higher price in any Pacific salmon species. It is sold fresh, fresh-frozen, canned, or smoked, and has an excellent taste in all forms.

Identification. The body of the chinook salmon is elongate and somewhat compressed. The head is conical. For most of its life, the chinook's color is bluish to dark gray above, becoming silvery on the sides and belly. There are black spots on the back, upper sides, top of the head, and all the fins, including both the top and bottom half of the tail fin. Coloration changes during upstream migration; spawning chinook salmon range from red to copper to olive brown to almost black, depending on location and degree of maturation, and they undergo a radical metamorphosis. Males are more deeply colored than the females and are distinguished by their "ridgeback" condition and by their hooked nose or upper jaw, known as a kype. The young have 6 to 12 long, wide, well-developed parr marks, which are bisected by the lateral line, and no spots on the dorsal fin.

One distinguishing feature of the chinook is its black mouth and gums. The very similar looking coho salmon has a black mouth but white gums, except in the Great Lakes population, in which the gums may be gray or black.

Size. This species is the largest of all Pacific salmon; individual fish commonly exceed 30 pounds in Alaska and British Columbia and 20 pounds elsewhere. A 126-pound chinook salmon taken in a fish trap near Petersburg, Alaska, in 1949 is the largest known specimen. The all-tackle world sportfishing record is a 97-pound, 4-ounce fish caught in Alaska's Kenai River in 1986. Chinook transplanted to the Great Lakes commonly weigh from 15 to 30 pounds, and the largest specimens recorded weigh under 50 pounds.

Distribution. The chinook salmon is endemic to the Pacific Ocean and to the Bering Sea, the Okhotsk Sea, the Sea of Japan, and most of the rivers that flow into these waters. On the Asian coast, they occur naturally from Hokkaido in northern Japan to the Anadyr River in the former USSR, and generally from San Luis Obispo County in Southern California to the Chukchi Sea area of Alaska; the greatest concentrations are along the

Chinook Salmon (sea-run phase)

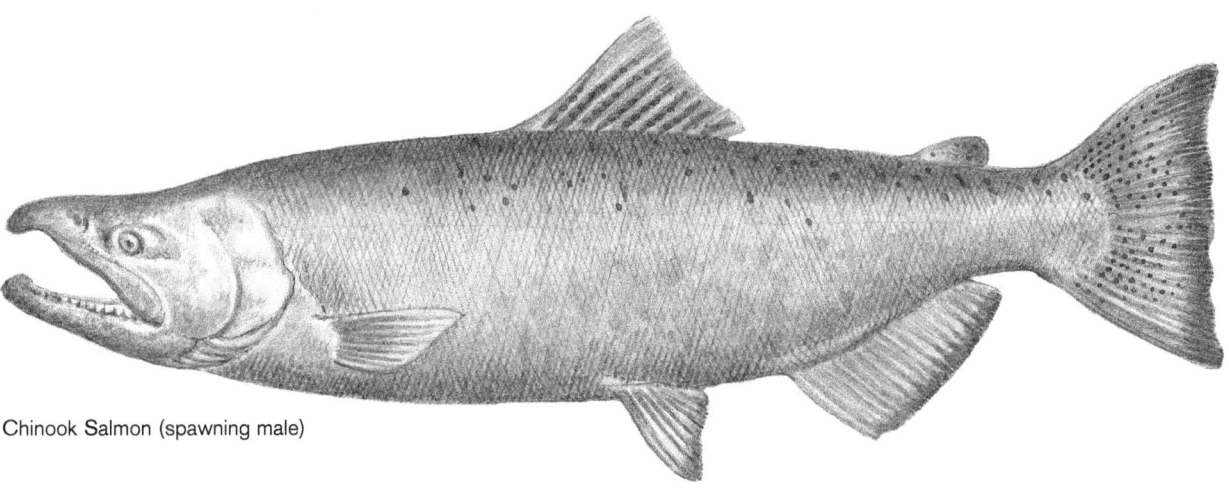

Chinook Salmon (spawning male)

British Columbia coast and Alaska. In Alaska, where the chinook is the state fish, it is abundant from the southeastern panhandle to the Yukon River. Major populations return to the Yukon, Kuskokwim, Nushagak, Susitna, Kenai, Copper, Alsek, Taku, and Stikine Rivers. Important runs also occur in many smaller streams. The chinook is rare in the Arctic Ocean. Most sea-run chinook are encountered by anglers along the coasts and in spawning rivers. Scientists estimate that there are in excess of a thousand spawning populations of chinook salmon on the North American coast. An uncertain but much lower number inhabits the Asian Coast.

Since as early as 1872, the chinook salmon has been introduced into other waters around the world, including the Great Lakes and Atlantic and Gulf states in the United States, some areas of Central and South America, Europe, and the South Pacific. These transplanted populations apparently failed due to an inability to maintain self-perpetuating spawning levels, with the exceptions of South Island in New Zealand, and to some degree in the Great Lakes of the U.S. (which experience minimal natural reproduction, although large populations are sustained by intensive stocking). Anadromous chinook have returned to sea ranching operations in southern Chile as well. Transplanted and strictly freshwater-dwelling chinook are widely distributed throughout the Great Lakes and their tributaries in Canada and the U.S., with greatest concentrations in Lakes Michigan and Ontario; these fish also exist in some large inland lakes in the U.S., and in other countries.

Life history/Behavior. Like all species of Pacific salmon, chinook are anadromous. They hatch in freshwater rivers, spend part of their life in the ocean, and then spawn in freshwater. Those chinook that have been transplanted to strictly freshwater environments (as in the Great Lakes) hatch in tributary rivers and streams, spend part of their life in the open water of the lake, and then return to tributaries to spawn. In both cases, all chinook die after spawning.

Sea-run chinook salmon may become sexually mature from their second through seventh year; as a result, fish in any spawning run may vary greatly in size. For example, a mature three-year-old in Alaska will probably weigh less than 4 pounds, whereas a mature seven-year-old may exceed 50 pounds. Females tend to be older than males at maturity. In many spawning runs, males outnumber females in all but the six- and seven-year age groups. These life spans and maturities may vary with different coastal runs of chinook as well as with freshwater transplants; in the latter case, they usually live no more than four to five years and are much larger at two and three years. Small chinook that mature after spending only one winter in the ocean or lake are commonly referred to as "jacks" and are usually males.

The period of migration into spawning rivers and streams varies greatly. Alaskan streams normally receive a single run of chinook salmon from May through July. Streams throughout the Great Lakes primarily receive chinook from late August into October, but there are some spring runs.

Chinook salmon often make extensive freshwater spawning migrations to reach their home streams on some of the larger coastal river systems. Yukon River spawners bound for the extreme headwaters in Yukon Territory, Canada, will travel more than 2,000 river miles during a 60-day period. In the Great Lakes, however, some migrating salmon are restricted to only a few miles of river (and do not spawn successfully in that stretch).

Chinook salmon do not feed during their freshwater spawning migration, so their condition deteriorates gradually during the spawning run. During that time, they use stored body materials for energy and for the development of reproductive products. Each female deposits from 3,000 to 14,000 eggs (usually in the lower range) in several gravel nests, or redds, which she excavates in relatively deep, moving water. They usually hatch in late winter or early spring, depending on time of spawning and water temperature. The newly hatched fish, called alevins, live in the gravel for several weeks until they gradually absorb the food in the attached yolk sac. These juveniles, called fry, wiggle up through the gravel by early spring. Most juvenile chinook salmon remain in their natal water until the following spring, when they migrate to the ocean in their second year of life. These seaward migrants are called smolts.

Scientific understanding of the distribution of chinook in the ocean is still sketchy. It has been speculated that most North American chinook do not wander more than 1,000 kilometers from their natal river, and that fish from western Alaska streams roam farther than others from North America. Large numbers are found relatively close to their respective shores, and also in distant offshore waters, and their depth preferences vary.

In the Great Lakes, chinook migrate many miles from their natal water, apparently in relation to the abundance of forage and appropriate water temperature. Thus, as surface levels warm, the colder water preferred by both salmon and their forage is found deeper (or shallow but farther offshore, depending on wind and other factors). The fish wander considerable distances, and their location varies regularly.

Food and feeding habits. Juvenile chinook in freshwater feed on plankton, then later eat insects. In the ocean, they eat a variety of organisms, including herring, pilchards, sand lance, squid, and crustaceans. Salmon grow rapidly in the ocean and often double their weight during a single summer season. Likewise, chinook that live entirely in freshwater feed on plankton and insects as juveniles, and pelagic freshwater baitfish in the lakes. Alewives and smelt are the primary food items, and, in fact, chinook and other salmonids were introduced to the Great Lakes and other inland waters especially to help control massive populations of baitfish, which they consume voraciously. Thus, they quickly develop large, stocky bodies.

Angling (for chinook and coho). Because coho and chinook salmon inhabit a variety of environments, anglers practice multiple fishing methods to pursue them. Overall, angling for these fish is far more prevalent in freshwater—either in rivers when the spawning run occurs or in the open water of the Great Lakes—than in saltwater. Identifying habitat, structure, and so forth, as one might do for many other fish, is less critical when targeting Pacific salmon than when enticing nonfeeding river fish to strike through careful presentation, or locating the right depth and temperature of open water in which salmon schools will be located. Essentially, then, open-water and river fishing techniques are the primary angling methods.

The coastal fishery for sea-run salmon in Pacific waters primarily occurs in nearshore, tidewater, and estuary environs. The favored angling methods are trolling with spinners and cut herring, trolling with flies (mostly for coho), mooching (see), some jigging, and some live-bait fishing. The most opportune time to pursue these fish is when they have returned from their sea wandering and are gathering in the vicinity of coastal rivers, waiting for rains to send new water out the rivers and signal the beginning of the "run." Salmon in the midst of their life cycle—not ready to spawn and not migrating to natal waters—are rarely sought far at sea, especially by small-boat anglers. The great travel distances are inconvenient, and because of the deep-wandering nature of salmon, finding them is akin to locating a needle in a haystack. Confronted by these obstacles, coastal anglers wait for sea-run fish to come close to shore during their migration toward coastal rivers.

When pursuing chinook in the ocean, anglers principally troll dead baits or artificial lures. Occasionally, they offer live baits or use metal jigs while stillfishing or drifting. Chinook salmon normally stay well beneath the ocean's surface, making a heavy weight or downrigger necessary to maintain a trolled bait at the desired depth. Chinook favor depths between 40 and 250 or more feet, depending on location, temperature, currents, and other factors. Channels, passes, and straits that funnel current are popular sites, particularly along current seams and where a back eddy exists. In northern areas, steep rocky shores—near the mainland or islands—that are well washed by current and tidal movement are prime spots; here, anglers offer a cut herring, fished very close to the bottom. Fishing in low light, especially at sunset and at dusk, is often more productive than during bright midday light, especially for chinook. Surface trolling with light tackle for coho salmon is possible when the fish are congregated on or near shoals where food is abundant. Streamer flies are the main offering, trolled fairly fast over bull kelp beds so that the fly skips over the water.

Coho and chinook in the Great Lakes are widely pursued throughout the season in open water. They are inshore early in the season and ultimately seek out a water temperature of between 48° and 55°F, which occurs at the thermocline. The thermocline is usually deeper as summer progresses; its depth changes, however, due to shifting winds. Coho tend to remain closer to shore than do chinook, although the depth and location of each species is a highly variable factor. Both gather in schools and traverse great distances as they seek out desirable water conditions and alewives or smelt forage.

Because freshwater salmon migrate extensively and exist at varied levels in open water, particularly below 30 feet and as much as 70 to 120 feet deep in the summer, anglers must typically search and fish deep in open water where there are few, or no, shoals or islands. Thus, freshwater tactics differ considerably from the tactics practiced in coastal fishing for sea-run salmon. Various trolling techniques are the primary focus, and among them downrigger fishing is most popular. Some drift fishing and limited jigging are also done.

Although open-water salmon fishing is essentially a boating proposition, the land-bound angler can score on open-water salmon in the spring and fall, and occasionally in the winter. Spring is the best all-around time for salmon in the Great Lakes. When the fish are in close to shore seeking out the most comfortable water temperature (influenced by wind direction and the introduction of warm tributary waters), they are just as accessible and vulnerable to shore-based anglers as they are to boaters. The only edge boaters have at this time is mobility, as they can cover a large expanse of water. Shore fishing close to the tributaries is generally best, as this is where the warmer water is. At this time, breakwaters, piers, beaches, and other access points become jammed with casters equipped with long rods. As the fish move out, shore fishing becomes markedly less productive. It increases in productivity again in late summer and early fall, when many salmon return to migrate upriver.

Chinook and coho salmon anglers seldom practice live-bait fishing in freshwater, principally due to the wandering nature of the quarry and the prodigious amount of available natural forage, including alewives, smelt, herring, and anchovies. Under these circumstances, a hooked offering often goes unrecognized. In Pacific waters, cut herring is extremely effective and has been used much more in recent years inland. Particularly effective baits, salmon eggs are used for drift fishing in coastal rivers and Great Lakes tributaries; they are usually fished in gobs or egg sacks and are sometimes combined with crayfish meat or tails, frequently with just a pencil or ball lead rig, or with a float.

Tributary fishing is the predominant Great Lakes method of catching chinook and coho salmon in late summer and fall. Fish that have just entered rivers or have been in them only a short while may still exhibit a feeding urge, striking a lure or fly as a conditioned, reflexive act. But the longer they are in the river, the less this is so. The same is true in coastal rivers where sea-run fish are migrating, although these fish have a much longer distance to run and their behavioral timing is more spread out. None of these fish actually feed, however, so imitating a natural food source in appearance or action is unnecessary. Getting the attention of a fish that will aggressively swipe at your offering is the whole game.

Often it can be difficult to get river fish to strike any offering, and it is usually vital to make the presentation right in front of the salmon. A precise presentation, therefore, is of foremost importance; the trick is to position the bait or lure on the bottom and directly ahead of the fish.

Long rods, medium-heavy lines, and small offerings are the main outfits for coho and chinook fishing in small to medium streams. Eggs, spinners, spoons, and wobbling plugs all have devotees. Fly fishing is more popular in western waters than in the Great Lakes, primarily because the rivers in the former are bigger and longer than those in the latter, affording a greater expanse of fishing oppor-

A chinook salmon from the coastal waters of Rivers Inlet, British Columbia.

tunities and somewhat less crowding. Shallower sections, however, provide the best opportunity for anglers using fly tackle and light spinning or baitcasting tackle. Bright flies and fast-sinking fly lines (usually the high-density full-sink versions) get the nod.

Salmon hug the bottom, resting in pools and deep-water sections. They gather in the tail of a run, ahead of swifter water, and in holes and runs along deep-water banks. They are not usually caught in the fast-water reaches. Lures must be cast slightly upstream and quartered, drifting with the current to the end of the swing. Whatever the offering, it must bounce or swim along the bottom, and the right-size sinker is critically important: too little, and the offering never reaches the bottom and is totally ineffective; too much, and it drags in the current, acting unnaturally or hanging up repeatedly.

Much river salmon fishing is done by bank or wading anglers, but in large rivers, angling from boats for coho and chinook is not only practical but also effective. Nonfly anglers usually use wobbling plugs in the river more than they do other hardware, or they use salmon eggs or spawn sacks. Forward trolling is not a popular tactic, not least because of boat and angler traffic. Anchoring or controlled drifting via backtrolling (see) are the primary boat fishing methods. Those who anchor do so in or above selected pools, setting their lines out 50 to 75 feet behind the boat and allowing the plugs to work constantly in current, perhaps bouncing them back slowly and then retrieving to repeat the procedure.

In rivers, tackle ranges from 14- to 30-pound-test line, the latter used in narrow rivers and where heavy weights and big fish are encountered. Levelwind reels are preferred, and long (8- to 9-foot) rods are employed. Fly rods suitable for 9- and 10-weight lines with plenty of reel backing are necessary. In open-water trolling, 8- to 9-foot downrigger rods get the most play; for this method, levelwind reels are most popular, and line strength ranges from 12 to 20 pounds, although lighter line can be used.

See: Salmon, Pacific.

SALMON, CHUM *Oncorhynchus keta*.

Other names—calico salmon, dog salmon, fall salmon, autumn salmon, chum, keta; French: *saumon keta*; Japanese: *sake, shake*.

The late spawning run of the chum salmon severely affects its popularity as a sportfish. In general, it is caught by anglers fishing for other Pacific salmon. In arctic, northwestern, and interior Alaska, this member of the Salmonidae family is an important year-round source of fresh and dried fish for subsistence and personal use, although elsewhere its flesh is not favored for human consumption. Overall, it is not as popular or as desirable as other Pacific salmon. The frequently used name dog salmon reportedly originates with its prevalent use as dog food among aboriginals.

The flesh is creamy white or pinkish to yellowish and the lowest of all salmon in fat content; it is sold fresh, frozen, dried/salted, smoked, and canned. After entering freshwater, chum salmon are most often prepared as a smoked product. The chum was formerly commercially cultured in Russia and used as dog food in Canada. The development of markets for fresh and frozen chum in Japan and northern Europe has increased the demand for these products.

Identification. In the ocean, the slender, somewhat compressed, chum salmon is metallic greenish blue on the back, silvery on the sides, and has a fine black speckling on the upper sides and back but no distinct black spots. Spawning males turn dark olive or grayish; blood-red coloring and vertical bars of green and purple reach up the sides, giving the fish its "calico" appearance. It develops the typical hooked snout of Pacific salmon, and the tips of the anal and pelvic fins are often white. The breeding male develops distinctly large front teeth, another explanation for the name dog salmon. The color of spawning females is essentially the same as that of males but is less vivid, with a dark horizontal band along the lateral line. Young fish are exceptionally slender and have 6 to 14 narrow, short parr marks along the sides, located mostly above the lateral line.

The chum salmon is difficult to distinguish from the sockeye (see: salmon, sockeye) and the coho salmon (see: salmon, coho), which are of similar size, without examining gills or caudal fin scale patterns; the chum salmon has fewer but larger gill rakers than do other salmon. The sockeye salmon also lacks the white marks on the fins, and the chum salmon is generally larger than the sockeye.

Size/Age. The chum salmon varies in size from 4 to more than 30 pounds, but the average weight is 10 to 15 pounds. Females are usually smaller than males. These fish can reach 40 inches in length. The all-tackle world record is a 35-pounder from British Columbia. Chum salmon can live as long as seven years.

Distribution. Chum salmon are the most widely distributed of the Pacific salmon, native to the Pacific and Arctic Oceans, the Bering Sea, the Sea of Japan, and the Okhotsk Sea. They range south to about the Sacramento River in California and to the island of Kyushu in the Sea of Japan. In the north, they range east in the Arctic Ocean to the Mackenzie River in Canada and west to the Lena River in Siberia. In the Mackenzie, they travel all the way to the mouth of the Hay River and to the rapids below Forth Smith on the Slave River, entering both Great Bear and Great Slave Lakes and traveling through the Northwest Territories to the edge of Alberta.

Life history/Behavior. The chum salmon is an anadromous fish; with the exception of a few landlocked populations, chum salmon inhabit both ocean environments and coastal streams. Spawning takes place from ages 2 to 7, most commonly at age 4 and at a weight of 5 to 10 pounds. Like

A chum salmon from King Salmon, Alaska.

Chum Salmon (spawning phase)

pink salmon (see: salmon, pink), chum salmon are sometimes called "autumn salmon" or "fall salmon" because they are among the last salmon in the season to take their spawning run, entering river mouths after mid-June but reaching spawning grounds as late as November or December. Occasionally there is one run of chum salmon in summer and another in fall in the same river; the summer-spawn fish are smaller and less likely to swim far upstream. In general, they are not strong leapers, swimming upstream only as far as the first significant barrier, although some fish in the Yukon River have been known to travel more than 2,000 miles to spawn in the Yukon Territory. Chum salmon often spawn in the same places as pink salmon, such as small streams and intertidal zones and in small side channels. As many as 4,000, but an average of 2,400 to 3,100, eggs are deposited in nests, or redds, dug by females in gravel riffles. The female guards the redd for a few days, then both sexes die.

Chum salmon enter streams in an advanced state of sexual maturity and thus do not stay in freshwater as long as chinook, coho, and sockeye salmon, remaining for perhaps two to three weeks. Their fry do not move out to sea as quickly as do pink salmon fry in the spring. They move to saltwater estuaries in schools, remaining close to shore for a few months and waiting until fall to move into the ocean. Chum salmon are known to hybridize naturally with pink salmon.

Food. Juvenile chum salmon in freshwater feed on plankton, then later eat insects. In the ocean, they eat a variety of organisms, including herring, pilchards, sand lance, squid, and crustaceans. Adults cease feeding in freshwater.

Angling. Chum salmon are not a focused target of anglers. They are an incidental catch on occasion, both in coastal nearshore saltwaters and in tributaries.

See: Salmon, Pacific.

SALMON, COHO Oncorhynchus kisutch.
Other names—silver salmon, silversides, hookbill, hooknose, sea trout, blueback; French: *saumon coho;* Japanese: *gin-zake.*

A member of the Salmonidae family, the coho salmon is an extremely adaptable fish that occurs in nearly all of the same waters as does the larger chinook salmon (see: salmon, chinook), but it is a more spectacular fighter and the most acrobatic of the Pacific salmon. It is one of North America's most important sport- and commercial fish, especially to the Pacific coast of North America, where this and other salmonids have long had great cultural and food significance.

By nature an anadromous species, the coho can adapt to an entirely freshwater existence and has done so with remarkable success in the Great Lakes of North America. Like the chinook, it has declined through large portions of its endemic range due to dams, other habitat alteration, pollution, and excessive commercial fishing. Some runs in the Pacific Northwest are threatened or endangered.

Although they are smaller on average than chinook salmon, and in many places less abundant, coho are popular sportfish wherever they are found. Their Pacific coastal range parallels the chinook's. As with the chinook, coho populations in the Great Lakes are supported almost entirely by hatchery production. Both species are intensively sought by boat anglers in coastal estuaries and bays and in the Great Lakes proper, and by boat, bank, and wading anglers in rivers.

As a gamefish, the coho is a much more suitable light-tackle quarry than the chinook, although it is caught with most of the same tackle and methods. Unlike the chinook, it is a streaky, near-surface, and aerial battler, rather than a deep and dogged fighter, although it, too, has great stamina. The coho's flesh is red and of excellent quality. It is a significant commercial catch for food markets, and is processed fresh, fresh-frozen, canned, or smoked.

Identification. The body of the coho salmon is elongate and somewhat compressed, and the head is conical. For most of its life (in saltwater or lake as well as newly arrived in a spawning river), this species is a dark metallic blue or blue green above,

Coho Salmon (sea-run phase)

becoming silvery on the sides and belly. There are small black spots on the back and on the upper lobe of the caudal fin. They can be distinguished from chinook salmon *(see: salmon, chinook)* by their lack of black spots on the lower lobe of the tail, and the white or gray gums at the base of the teeth; chinook have small black spots on both caudal lobes of the tail, and they have black gums.

Spawning adults of both sexes have dark backs and heads, and maroon to reddish sides. The males turn dusky green above and on their head, bright red on their sides, and blackish below. The females turn a pinkish red on their sides. The males develop a prominent doubled-hooked snout, called a kype, with large teeth, which make closing the mouth impossible.

Juvenile coho salmon have 8 to 12 well-developed parr marks evenly distributed above and below the lateral line; the parr marks are narrower than the interspaces. The adipose fin is uniformly pigmented. The anal fin has a long leading edge usually tipped with white, and all fins are frequently tinted with orange.

Size. Coho do not attain the size of their larger chinook brethren and in most places are caught around the 4- to 8-pound mark. The all-tackle world record is a Great Lakes fish of 33 pounds, 4 ounces, caught in the Salmon River, New York, in 1989. Fish to 31 pounds have been caught in Alaska, where the average catch is 8 to 12 pounds and 24 to 30 inches long. All coho are exciting to catch, as they are strong and acrobatic, but coho exceeding 15 pounds are a real handful for most anglers.

Distribution. The coho salmon is endemic to the northern Pacific Ocean and the rivers flowing into it, from northern Japan to the Anadyr River, Russia, and from Point Hope, Alaska, on the Chukchi Sea south to Monterey Bay, California. It has been infrequently reported at sea as far south as Baja California, Mexico. Most sea-run chinook are encountered along the coasts and in spawning rivers.

The coho has been transplanted into the Great Lakes and into freshwater lakes in Alaska and along the U.S. Pacific coast, as well as into the states of Maine, Maryland, and Louisiana; the province of Alberta, Canada; and in Argentina and Chile. Natural successful spawning has not noticeably occurred in these transplanted populations, with the possible exception of the Great Lakes in Michigan; the Great Lakes contain substantial populations of coho, which are sustained through extensive stocking.

Life history/Behavior. Like all species of Pacific salmon, coho are anadromous. They hatch in freshwater rivers, spend part of their life in the ocean, and then spawn in freshwater. Those coho that have been transplanted to strictly freshwater environments (as in the Great Lakes) hatch in tributary rivers and streams, spend part of their life in the open water of the lake, and then return to tributaries to spawn. All coho die after spawning.

Adult male sea-run coho salmon generally enter streams when they are either two or three years old, but adult females do not return to spawn until age 3. All coho salmon, whether male or female, spend their first year in the stream or river in which they hatch.

Generally speaking, the larger the female, the greater the number of eggs produced. Females spawn from 1,500 to 4,500 eggs, but the average production is 2,500 eggs. This number also varies with specific runs.

The timing of runs into tributaries varies as well. Coho salmon in Alaska, for example, enter spawning streams from July through November, usually during periods of high runoff. In California, the runs occur from September through March, and the bulk of spawning occurs from November through January. Streams throughout the Great Lakes primarily receive coho from late August into October. Run timing has evolved to reflect the requirements of specific stocks. In some streams with barrier falls, adults arrive in July when the water is low and the falls are passable. In large rivers, adults must arrive early, as they need several weeks or months to reach headwater spawning grounds. Run timing is also regulated by the water temperature at spawning grounds: Where temperatures are

Coho Salmon (spawning male)

low and eggs develop slowly, spawners have evolved early run timing to compensate; conversely, where temperatures are warm, adults are late spawners.

Coho salmon do not feed during their freshwater spawning migration, so their condition deteriorates gradually during the spawning run as they use stored body materials for energy and for the development of reproductive products. Adults hold in pools until they ripen, then move onto spawning grounds; spawning generally occurs at night. The female digs a nest, or redd, and deposits her eggs, which are fertilized by the male. The eggs develop during the winter and hatch in early spring, and the embryos remain in the gravel utilizing the egg yolk until they emerge. The emergent fry occupy shallow stream margins and, as they grow, establish territories, which they defend from other salmonids. They live in ponds, lakes, and pools in streams and rivers, usually among cover in quiet areas free of current, from which they dart out to seize drifting insects.

During the fall, juvenile coho may travel miles before locating off-channel habitat, where they pass the winter free of floods. Some sea-run fish leave the river in the spring and rear in brackish estuarine ponds, then migrate back into freshwater in the fall. Coho spend one to three winters in streams and may spend up to five winters in lakes before migrating to the sea as smolts. Time at sea varies. Some males (called jacks) mature and return after only 6 months at sea, at a length of roughly 12 inches, whereas most fish stay 18 months before returning as full-size adults.

Little is known of the ocean migrations of coho salmon. Evidently there are more coho salmon in the eastern Pacific and along the coast of North America than in the western Pacific. High-seas tagging shows that maturing southeast Alaska coho move northward throughout the spring and appear to concentrate in the central Gulf of Alaska in June. They later disperse toward shore and migrate along the shoreline until they reach their stream of origin. Although most coho do not seem to migrate extensively, tagged individuals have been recovered up to 1,200 miles from the tagging site.

In the Great Lakes, coho migrate many miles from their natal water as abundance of forage and appropriate water temperature dictate. Thus, as surface levels warm, the colder water preferred by both salmon and their forage is deeper (or shallow but farther offshore, depending on wind and other factors). The fish wander considerable distances, and their location varies regularly.

Food and feeding habits. Juvenile coho in freshwater feed on plankton, then later eat insects. In the ocean, coho salmon grow rapidly, feeding on a variety of organisms, including herring, pilchards, sand lance, squid, and crustaceans. Likewise, coho that live entirely in freshwater feed on plankton and insects as juveniles, and on pelagic freshwater baitfish in the lakes. Alewives and smelt are the primary food items, and, in fact, coho and other salmonids were introduced to the Great Lakes and other inland waters especially to help control massive populations of baitfish, which they consume voraciously and thus quickly grow large, stocky bodies. Like all Pacific salmon, the coho does not feed once it enters freshwater on its spawning run.

Angling. Because the coho's habits are similar to those of the chinook salmon, angling methods and locations are similar as well. Coho are at times an incidental catch when chinook are the focus; most likely, however, fishing efforts target either or both species. The timing of availability may be different, especially in coastal rivers and in nearshore coastal waters. In addition, coho salmon are likely to remain shallower in open water than are chinook. Sometimes coho hold on or close to the surface, which is not a likelihood for chinook. Fishing methods are detailed under the entry for chinook salmon.
See: Salmon, Pacific.

SALMONFLIES
See: Stoneflies.

SALMONID
A term for any member of the Salmonidae family; this includes the various trout, salmon, charr,

A coastal coho salmon from Campbell River, British Columbia.

whitefish, and grayling. It is frequently, but erroneously, expressed as salmonoid.

SALMON, LANDLOCKED

A term for strictly freshwater-dwelling salmon, which spend the greater portion of their life in a lake and return to their natal river or stream to spawn. Any species of salmon with such behavior and without access to saltwater is "landlocked"; this includes freshwater sockeye salmon, which are called kokanee, as well as coho and chinook salmon. In the northeastern United States and Canada, however, the term "landlocked salmon" specifically refers to freshwater-dwelling Atlantic salmon (see: salmon, Atlantic).

SALMON, MASU *Oncorhynchus masou*.
Other names—cherry salmon, cherry trout; Japanese: *honmasu, sakuramasu, yamame, yamabe*.

This member of the Salmonidae family is one of two species of Pacific salmon (see: salmon, Pacific) that occur only in Asia and the western Pacific. It is generally called cherry salmon in English, because the meaning of its most common Japanese name, *sakuramasu*, is "cherry trout." This appellation alludes to the masu's presence on the spawning grounds at cherry blossom time, which occurs from March through May in Japan.

Although ichthyological opinion varies as to whether this species and amago salmon (*O. rhodurus*; see: salmon, amago) are the same, these species are currently classified as separate but closely related. Moreover, there are anadromous and freshwater versions of both species. Technically the word "masu" refers to the anadromous fish, *O. masou masou*, which in Japan is known as *sakuramasu*; the nonanadromous and permanently freshwater-dwelling version is *O. masou ishikawae*, which in Japan is known as *yamame*. Thus, "masu" refers to the seagoing salmon, and "yamame" to the freshwater dweller. The masu is subject to commercial fishing in the ocean and is reared in hatcheries in Japan.

Size. Masu salmon on spawning grounds in Russian rivers may range up to 8.5 kilograms, but the average fish weighs between 2 and 3 kilograms. They are generally smaller in Japanese rivers. On average, yamame are roughly half the size of masu.

Distribution. The masu salmon occurs in more southerly waters than do any of the other Pacific salmon. It is found in the Sea of Japan and the Sea of Okhotsk, and migrates up rivers on all sides of the Japanese islands of Hokkaido and Honshu and on some of Russia's Kuril Islands and Sakhalin Island; along the Asian mainland in rivers from southeastern Korea to Russia's Amur River; as well as in rivers of the western Kamchatka Peninsula. It is not found in the Bering Sea and was unsuccessfully introduced in Canada. The yamame has the same range but is also present on Japan's Kyushu Island and some southernmost Korean rivers fronting the western Korea Strait, as well as on Taiwan.

Habitat. Masu live in the Japan and Okhotsk Seas while maturing and migrate up large and small coastal rivers for spawning. Their migration range in the Pacific is extremely limited compared with that of other Pacific salmon. Yamame are present in coastal rivers.

Life history/Behavior. Spawning takes place from March through early July; the exact time varies among the rivers but begins earlier in the southern part of the spawning range. Masu and yamame salmon have been observed spawning together. Male yamame salmon mature at age 1 and females at age 2—a year earlier than their masu counterparts, some of which do not mature until age 4. Yamame do not migrate downstream in spring after one winter in freshwater, as masu do. Adult masu do not feed while in freshwater, and yamame do not feed when undergoing the reproductive process. Both die after spawning, although in some hatchery rearing experiments, some yamame males have successfully spawned two or more times.

SALMON, PACIFIC

The term "Pacific salmon" describes certain members of the genus *Oncorhynchus* that occur naturally in the North Pacific Ocean and its drainages in Asia and North America. They are members of the Salmonidae family of fish, which includes trout,

Masu Salmon

salmon, charr, whitefish, and grayling, all of which are endemic to the temperate and cool regions of the Northern Hemisphere but have been introduced widely outside their native range, including the Southern Hemisphere.

In the Salmonidae family there are either 11 or 7 "salmon" of Pacific origin, and 1 of Atlantic origin. The latter is *Salmo salar*, simply known as Atlantic salmon *(see: salmon, Atlantic)*. In order of general prominence and value to anglers, the 7 most widely recognized Pacific salmon include chinook *(Oncorhynchus tshawytscha)*, coho *(O. kisutch)*, pink *(O. gorbuscha)*, sockeye *(O. nerka)*, chum *(O. keta)*, masu *(O. masou)*, and amago *(O. rhodurusi)*. Masu and amago salmon occur naturally only in Asia, and the others occur naturally in both Asia and North America.

Some scientists count 11 species because 4 additional species that were historically called "trout" and were, at least among nonscientists, not considered "salmon" have been classified taxonomically as belonging to the *Oncorhynchus* genus. Not even a taxonomist can explain the reasons for this very well, but these newcomers include two prominent "trout" species that were formerly in the *Salmo* genus—steelhead/rainbow trout *(O. mykiss)* and cutthroat trout *(O. clarki)*—as well as the lesser-known golden trout *(O. aguabonita)* and the Apache trout *(O. apache)*. The placement of these four "trout" in this Pacific salmon genus would seem to make them members of the Pacific salmon family.

Biologically, salmon and their relatives are primitive fish, with fossil remains dating to more than 100 million years ago. Evidence indicates that many of the more advanced or specialized families of modern-day bony fish have ancestral stocks closely resembling these primitive fish.

The most clearly evident primitive feature of the group is the lack of spines in the fins. Most of the soft rays in the fins are branched. The pelvic fins are situated far back on the body—in the "hip" region, where the legs of amphibians articulate with the body *(see: anatomy)*. This location contrasts with the placement of the pelvic fins in many other species, including largemouth bass, for example, which are so far forward they are almost directly beneath the pectoral fins. Other indications of their primitive nature are an adipose fin and a primitive air bladder.

Most members of the Salmonidae family are in some way associated with cold, often rushing waters and high oxygen demands. Some, including all of the salmon, are also tied to the sea, spending a good portion of their lives there. All members of the family spawn in freshwater, and most require cold running water. Members of some sea-running species, including most salmon, have become accidentally or deliberately landlocked, living and reproducing successfully entirely in freshwater without ever taking a journey to saltwater.

Pacific salmon spawn in gravel beds in rivers and streams, and sometimes along the lakeshore. Their progeny have a relatively short freshwater existence and migrate out to the sea. When mature, Pacific salmon usually return to the waters of their birth to reproduce, after which all but some amago and some nonanadromous masu males die.

Contrary to earlier beliefs, many salmon from North American rivers roam far at sea in the North Pacific Ocean and the Bering Sea. The oceanic distribution of the salmon is dependent on the species and point of origin. Sockeye and chinook salmon from northwest Alaska, for example, may migrate across the Bering Sea to areas close to Kamchatka, Russia, and south of the Aleutian Islands into the North Pacific Ocean; the sockeye also migrate eastward to the Gulf of Alaska. Salmon such as the pink, chum, and coho from central and Southeast Alaska, British Columbia, and Washington State migrate out into the northeastern Pacific Ocean and the Gulf of Alaska. Some salmon migrate several thousand miles from the time they leave the rivers as juveniles until they return as adults. A chinook salmon tagged in the central Aleutian Islands and recovered a year later in the Salmon River, in Idaho, had traveled roughly 3,500 miles.

The homing instinct of salmon is one of nature's greatest wonders, and something that is still not fully understood by scientists. Some degree of straying from natal waters does occur, but all Pacific salmon species are likely to develop reproductively isolated populations, which are known as stocks, and these stocks are individually vulnerable to highly efficient harvesting and to adverse conditions affecting the waters where they spawn.

Collectively and individually, the Pacific salmon species are of great historical, cultural, food, and sport significance to people of the coastal regions of the North Pacific Rim. The market for chinook, coho, pink, and sockeye salmon, because of their excellent table qualities and high value in canning, has long been strong, and the subsistence catch has been important for centuries. Although a long tradition of recreational fishing for these species exists, only since the 1950s has it gained momentum. Today, it is of great economic value, especially for tourism in Alaska and British Columbia.

Virtually all angling attention focuses on chinook and coho salmon, especially in North America. Today, for example, although five species of Pacific salmon occur along the Pacific coast, more than 99 percent of all salmon caught in the ocean off California are either chinook or coho. Most sportfishing for Pacific salmon occurs in rivers and streams when these species are undergoing their spawning migrations, and a fair amount occurs in saltwater, predominantly in bays, estuaries, and inshore waters near the coast. In these waters, anglers target fish that are migrating to their natal tributaries, or those that are gathered nearby awaiting the run. Sportfishing for this species is almost entirely centered around fish that are pre-

Most Pacific salmon, such as this chinook from the Taku River, British Columbia, are caught during their upstream spawning migration.

paring to spawn, as this is when they are most accessible. (An exception to this is the chinook and coho salmon that have been introduced into the Great Lakes of North America; these fish live their entire lives in freshwater and are pursued extensively in lakes, where they feed heavily.)

Although some commercial and subsistence fishing for Pacific salmon occurs once they have entered or are in the process of entering spawning rivers, the bulk of the harvest is in nearshore and offshore waters through gillnetting and trawling. The U.S., Canada, Japan, Russia, and North and South Korea are the major harvesters, essentially in that order. Alaskan vessels harvest the highest percentage of the North American catch.

The troubles plaguing Pacific salmon stocks have been well publicized throughout the 1990s and have resulted in harvest treaties between some of the aforementioned countries, harvest quotas, and assorted management plans; these have not stemmed the decline of some Pacific salmon stocks (especially in California, Oregon, Washington, and certain portions of British Columbia), although they are supposed to address overharvesting.

Some salmon stocks are at historically low levels. Catch reductions have been imposed on all recreational anglers and on commercial fishermen. Anglers are a small part of the overfishing problem, however. In British Columbia, where salmon sportfishing is a big business, anglers account for 4 percent of the total annual salmon harvest.

Excessive commercial fishing is just one of the problems affecting Pacific salmon. Dams, logging, pollution, water use, overfishing, habitat destruction, hatchery impacts, mismanagement, and other human-induced factors are among the factors. No single factor is responsible for the full extent of the decline, and no single action will restore the fish. Because salmon cross so many state and national jurisdictional boundaries, there is insufficient focus and accountability to ensure effective management of the overall system, as well as a lack of coordinated overall fisheries management.

Some observers feel that the entire Pacific salmon fishery could suffer the same fate as the Atlantic striped bass did in the late 1970s: perilously low stocks, curtailment of sport and commercial fishing, a ban on sale. But Pacific salmon differ greatly from Atlantic striped bass, which have rebounded strongly and are a single species dependent on relative few major rivers and estuaries. There are five eastern Pacific species of salmon. They eat different food, return to a wide range of home waters (more than 1,000 for chinook alone), and migrate according to different cycles.

See: Salmon, Amago; Salmon, Chinook; Salmon, Chum; Salmon, Coho; Salmon, Masu; Salmon, Pink; Salmon, Sockeye.

SALMON, PINK *Oncorhynchus gorbuscha.*
Other names—humpback salmon, humpy, fall salmon, pink, humpback; French: *saumon rose;* Japanese: *karafutomasu, sepparimasu.*

An important commercial catch, the pink salmon is the smallest North American member of the Pacific salmon group of the Salmonidae family. In many Alaskan coastal fishing communities, particularly south of Kotzebue Sound, it is considered a "bread and butter" fish because of its commercial significance to fisheries and thus to local economies. It has some sportfishing value in Alaskan rivers, less so than coho or chinook salmon, but little elsewhere. The flesh is pinkish, rather than red or white, and it is mostly sold canned but also utilized fresh, smoked, and frozen. It is valued for caviar, especially in Japan. The flesh is of most value when the fish is still an open-water inhabitant, as it deteriorates rapidly once the fish enters rivers.

Identification. The pink salmon is known as the "humpback" or "humpy" because of its distorted, extremely humpbacked appearance, which is caused by the very pronounced, laterally flattened hump that develops on the backs of adult males before spawning. This hump appears between the head and the dorsal fin and develops by the time the male enters the spawning stream, as does a hooked upper jaw, or kype.

At sea, the pink salmon is silvery in color, with a bright metallic blue above; there are many black, elongated, oval spots on the entire tail fin, and large spots on the back and the adipose fin. When the pink salmon moves to spawning streams, the bright appearance of the male changes to pale red or "pink" on the sides, with brown to olive green blotches; females become olive green above with dusky bars or patches, and pale below. Young pink salmon are entirely silvery and lack the parr marks, or dark vertical bars, that the young of other salmon species have. All pink salmon have small, deeply embedded scales.

Size/Age. The average pink salmon weighs 3 to 6 pounds and is 20 to 25 inches long, although these fish can grow to 15 pounds and 30 inches. The all-tackle world record is a 13-pound, 1-ounce Great Lakes fish taken from Ontario, Canada. It lives for only two years.

Distribution. Pink salmon are native to Pacific and arctic coastal waters from the Sacramento River in Northern California northeast to the Mackenzie River in the Northwest Territories, Canada, and from the Lena River in Siberia to eastern Korea. They occur throughout the Aleutian Islands, the Bering and Okhotsk Seas, the Sea of Japan, and the island of Hokkaido, Japan, as well in the rivers that flow into these waters.

Pink salmon have been introduced to Newfoundland and to the western coast of Lake Superior, and currently maintain populations in these locations; there have been sporadic reports of pink salmon in Labrador, Nova Scotia, and Quebec since their introduction into Newfoundland. Introduced accidentally into Lake Superior, pink salmon are now spawning in tributaries of Lake Huron and are possibly the only isolated freshwater population to ever survive.

Habitat. These anadromous fish spend 18 months at sea and then undertake a spawning migration to the river or stream of their birth, although they sometimes use other streams. They tend to migrate as far as 40 miles inland of coastal waters, occasionally moving as far as 70 miles inland.

Life history/Behavior. Pink salmon are often referred to as "autumn salmon" or "fall salmon" because of their late spawning runs; these occur from July through mid-October in Alaska. Females dig a series of nests, or redds, depositing hundreds to thousands of eggs, which hatch from late December through February. Young become free-swimming in the early spring soon after hatching, often returning to sea in the company of young chum and sockeye salmon. Adults die soon after spawning. Pink salmon can hybridize with chum salmon.

Almost all pink salmon mature in two years, which means that odd-year and even-year populations are separate and essentially unrelated. In particular streams and overall areas, the odd- or even-year cycle is dominant, whereas elsewhere

Pink Salmon (sea-run phase)

Pink Salmon (spawning male)

odd- and even-year pink salmon are equally abundant. Sometimes cycle dominance will transfer, so that the previously abundant cycle becomes weak, and vice versa.

Food and feeding habits. While in freshwater on spawning runs, sea-run pink salmon may eat insects, although they often do not feed at all. At sea, they feed primarily on plankton, as well as on crustaceans, small fish, and squid. They do not feed during the spawning run.

Angling. In open waters, pink salmon are caught by anglers trolling for other Pacific salmon, although generally smaller lures and flies are necessary to attract this species. They become a deliberate open-water target when either coho (see: salmon, coho) or chinook (see: salmon, chinook) are unavailable. They may be fairly abundant off river mouths for several weeks prior to spawning. In rivers, they are readily caught on small spinners, small spoons, and flies, and on the spinning and fly tackle used for trout.

See: Salmon, Pacific.

SALMON PLUG
Term for a cutplug (see).

SALMON, SOCKEYE *Oncorhynchus nerka.*
Other names—sockeye, red salmon, blueback salmon, big redfish; French: *saumon nerka;* Japanese: *beni-zake, himemasu.* The landlocked form is called kokanee salmon, Kennerly's salmon, kokanee, landlocked sockeye, kickininee, little redfish, silver trout; French: *kokani.*

A member of the Salmonidae family, the sockeye is like some other members of the Pacific salmon group in having both anadromous and freshwater forms. The former migrate from freshwater streams to the ocean and then return to those streams to spawn, whereas the latter remain in freshwater all their lives. Called kokanee, the freshwater form was once thought to be the subspecies *O. kennerlyi* but is now accepted as the same species with characteristics identical to that of the anadromous sockeye, although it is a smaller fish. It occurred naturally in some waters in the drainages of the Pacific and has been spread through stocking to many other waters. Kokanee can be fine gamefish and excellent food fish; sockeye salmon are predominantly prized more for their food value than for sport, however, as the upstream migrants are not aggressive at taking baits or lures.

The name of sockeye salmon is a corruption of the coastal Indian word *suk-kegh,* which meant medium salmon. Sockeye leave the ocean to spawn in freshwater, as do other Pacific salmon, but they enter only those rivers having lakes at their headwaters. These fish were so abundant historically, especially in North America, that they left indelible imprints on the culture and geography of states and provinces. Many place names were derived from these salmon, and the spawning red sockeye were both an important food source and an element of religion for native tribes. In some places they remain an important mainstay of many subsistence users. The erection of dams and alteration of habitat, however, as well as commercial overfishing and other factors, have caused an overall decline in sockeye stocks and the loss of some specific runs. Sockeye populations in the Pacific Northwest outside of Alaska are especially troubled.

The flesh of the sockeye is deep red and high in oil content, making it the most commercially valuable of all the Pacific salmon. The meat is especially delicious when smoked, excellent for canning due to the rich orange red color, and also marketed fresh, dried/salted, and frozen. Canned sockeye salmon is marketed primarily in the United Kingdom and the United States; most frozen sockeye salmon is purchased by Japan. Sockeye salmon roe is also valuable, and is salted and marketed to Japan.

Identification. The sockeye is the slimmest and most streamlined of Pacific salmon, particularly immature and pre-spawning fish, which are elongate and somewhat laterally compressed. They are

Sockeye Salmon (sea-run phase)

metallic green blue on the back and top of the head, iridescent silver on the sides, and white or silvery on the belly. Some fine black speckling may occur on the back, but large spots are absent. Juveniles in freshwater have the same general coloration as immature sockeye salmon in the ocean but are less iridescent; they also have dark, oval parr marks on their sides. These parr marks are short, less than the diameter of the eye, and rarely extend below the lateral line.

Breeding males develop a humped back and elongated, hooked jaws filled with sharp, enlarged teeth. Both sexes turn brilliant to dark red on the back and sides, pale to olive green on the head and upper jaw, and white on the lower jaw. The totally red body distinguishes the sockeye from the otherwise similar chum salmon, and the lack of large, distinct spots distinguishes it from the remaining three Pacific salmon of North America. The number and shape of gill rakers on the first gill arch further distinguish the sockeye from the chum salmon; sockeye salmon have 28 to 40 long, slender, rough or serrated closely set rakers on the first arch, whereas chum salmon have 19 to 26 short, stout, smooth rakers.

Kokanee are smaller but otherwise identical to sea-run sockeye in coloration; they undergo the same changes as sockeye when spawning.

Size. Adult sockeye usually weigh between 4 and 8 pounds. The all-tackle world record is an Alaskan fish that weighed 15 pounds, 3 ounces. Kokanee are much smaller; in many places they do not grow much over 14 inches or 1 pound, especially where the plankton food resource is low or where many other species compete for it; the all-tackle world record is a British Columbia fish that weighed 9 pounds, 6 ounces.

Distribution. The sockeye salmon is native to the northern Pacific Ocean and its tributaries from northern Hokkaido, Japan, to the Anadyr River, Russia, and from the Sacramento River, California, to Point Hope, Alaska. Kokanee exist in Japan, Russia, Alaska, at least three western provinces in Canada, seven western U.S. states, and three eastern states.

Habitat. Sockeye salmon are anadromous, living in the sea and entering freshwater to spawn. They mainly enter rivers and streams that have lakes at their source. Young fish may inhabit lakes for as many as four years before returning to the ocean. Kokanee occur almost exclusively in freshwater lakes, migrating to tributaries in the fall to spawn (or to outlet areas or shoreline gravel in waters without suitable spawning streams).

Life history/Behavior. Sockeye salmon return to their natal stream to spawn after spending one to four years in the ocean. Mature sockeye salmon

Sockeye Salmon (spawning male)

Kokanee Salmon

that spend only one year in the ocean are called jacks and, almost without exception, are males. They enter freshwater systems from the ocean during the summer months or fall, some having traveled thousands of miles. Most populations show little variation in their arrival time on the spawning grounds from year to year; kokanee spawn from August through February, sockeye from July through December.

Once near their natal system, these fish use olfactory cues to guide them home. Freshwater systems with lakes produce the greatest number of sockeye salmon, as fish run upstream to just below a lake outlet, some spawning in the lake itself or in inlet streams. The female selects the spawning site, digs a nest, or redd, with her tail, and deposits eggs in the downstream portion of the redd. One or more males swims beside her and fertilizes the eggs as they are released. After each spawning act, the female covers the eggs by dislodging gravel at the upstream end of the redd with her tail while males drive off intruders. Depending on size, a female produces from 2,000 to 4,500 eggs. Like all Pacific salmon, sockeye die within a few weeks after spawning.

Eggs hatch during the winter, and the young alevins remain in the gravel, living off the material stored in their yolk sacs until early spring. At this time they emerge from the gravel as fry and move into rearing areas. In systems with lakes, juveniles usually spend one to three years in freshwater before migrating to the ocean in the spring as smolts weighing only a few ounces. In systems without lakes, however, many juveniles migrate to the ocean soon after emerging from the gravel.

Although most sockeye salmon production results from the spawning of wild populations, some runs have been developed or enhanced through human effort.

Food and feeding habits. Anadromous salmon rarely feed after entering freshwater, although young fish will feed mainly on plankton and insects. In the ocean, sockeye salmon continue to feed on plankton, plus crustacean larvae, larval and small adult fish, and occasionally on squid. Kokanee feed mainly on plankton but also on insects and bottom organisms.

Angling. The largely plankton-eating sockeye was often judged difficult to catch in the past, which may in part have been due to anglers using the same approach for the sockeye as for the larger and more aggressive chinook and coho salmon. Sockeye are strong, however, and leap out of the water, and they have become the object of more angling effort. Small hooks baited with eggs or a piece of worm, small flies, and small spoons or spinners will catch them in rivers; because they don't feed on their river spawning run, however, deep presentations that place the offering directly in front of the fish are necessary to provoke a reflexive strike.

The same items work for river kokanee, and in lakes the best approach is deep trolling, using tactics not unlike those for other trout and salmon species, although with offerings that are on the small side. Some fly fishing opportunities exist when the fish are shallow in early-season cold water, and ice fishing is generally productive, using small ice jigs and small natural baits.

Open-water fishing for kokanee is similar to fishing for lake trout or other salmon in open water: the angler must find cool (usually deep) waters and fish them consistently at the correct depth. These tactics require lead-core lines, downriggers, and weighted flatlines with attractors when the fish are deep, and unweighted flatlines and floating fly lines when the fish are shallow after ice out.

Once the surface water has warmed, kokanee move into deeper, cooler (roughly 50°F) water. They cluster in a small deep band or, in lakes with entirely warm water, on or near the bottom where there are springs or in old channels where it is as cool as possible. Very small spoons, spinners, and occasionally plugs are used, often tipped with a piece of natural bait. Small cowbell attractors are especially popular with many deep trollers, and a rubber snubber may be used to help prevent ripping the hook from the kokanee's tender mouth. Sometimes a piece of nightcrawler or other bait is fished without a lure, directly behind the attractor.
See: Salmon, Pacific; Trolling.

SALMON TAILER
A nooselike device that cinches over the caudal peduncle of a salmon for landing.
See: Landing Fish; Tailer.

SALMON, THREADFIN
See: Threadfin, King.

SALTER
A sea-run brook trout (see). This fish is not truly anadromous but may go to saltwater for short periods to feed or for temperature reasons.

SALT FRONT
The upper limit of saline intrusion in a tidal river. Saltwater is more dense than freshwater and pushes

upriver as a wedge beneath the freshwater to a certain point, which is then known as the salt front.

SALT MARSH
See: Marsh.

SALTWATER/SEAWATER
Commonly used terms for water with many dissolved salts in or from the ocean, as well as in connected seas, bays, sounds, estuaries, marshes, and the lower portion of tidal rivers.
See: Brackish Water; Freshwater.

SALTWATER TAPER
A specially designed type of weight-forward fly line for casting large flies.
See: Flycasting Tackle.

SAMOA
Previously known as Western Samoa, the independent Pacific state of Samoa consists of nine volcanic islands, four of which are inhabited. It is situated in the heart of the South Pacific Ocean, west of American Samoa and northeast of Tonga.

The population is 170,000, three-quarters of which lives on the island of Upolu, where the capital city of Apia and the international airport are both located. Most of the rest of Samoa's population lives on the largest island in the group, Savai'i.

Upolu and Savai'i constitute most of Samoa's landmass. They are high, rugged, volcanic islands, still covered in many areas by lush rain forest. Both islands are roughly 75 kilometers long. The capital of Apia is clean and progressive by Pacific island standards. Although violent crime is minimal, theft is a problem in urban areas.

Indigenous Samoans are of Polynesian descent and make up more than 90 percent of the population, the bulk of whom maintain a traditional village way of life. For example, the traditional waist-to-knees body tattoo of Samoan men is still popular and is still achieved with bone tools in the old way. An extremely painful ritual, the tattoo is a sign of a warrior who has suffered and shown courage.

Samoa became independent in 1962. The official languages are Samoan and English. Samoans are an affable people, and most of them do speak English. Good-quality hotels, as well as resort, motel, and guest house accommodations, are available. One famous landmark is the former home of Robert Louis Stevenson, who spent his last years in Samoa. Stevenson, who was buried on the summit of Mount Vaea overlooking Apia, still casts a long shadow in Samoa, where he is known as "Tusitala," the teller of tales.

Temperatures average between 25° and 30°C, and December through April is the wet season. Samoa is subject to trade winds from the southeast quarter throughout much of the year. Because Upolu and Savai'i Islands lie in a northwest-southeast direction and have high mountainous interiors, they tend to split the winds like a sharp rock in a stream. Consequently, there is little in the way of a lee shore for anglers fishing in windy conditions.

Sportfishing is still in its infancy in Samoa, and the Western concept of fishing for recreation remains somewhat alien to the locals, who have always considered fishing as a way of putting food on the table. The first tagging and release of a billfish here was recorded in only 1995; the fish, a black marlin, was recaptured 17 days later in American Samoa, 75 nautical miles away.

In 1994, Samoan anglers became affiliated with the International Game Fish Association (IGFA) under the banner of the Tautai-O-Samoa Association. In 1996 they ran their first international gamefishing tournament, which has shown strong growth, drawing boats from American Samoa and New Zealand.

One full-time charter boat works out of Apia, and New Zealand boats occasionally spend their winter off-season (June through September) working here. These boats offer good-quality sportfishing gear. Other, less formal, charters can sometimes be organized with local boatowners; in these instances, anglers are advised to bring their own equipment.

Sea temperatures are usually around 28° to 32°C, and a wide range of tropical sportfish are available throughout the year. Blue marlin are the predominant billfish, gathering here in good numbers. Rod-and-reel captures to 300 kilograms have been recorded, and longliners have brought in fish weighing more than 1,000 pounds.

Black marlin are also present, although the waters seem to be a bit too warm for striped marlin in any numbers. Pacific sailfish are also regular captures, and shortbill spearfish have been taken. Other offshore gamefish include yellowfin tuna averaging around 40 kilograms, and plentiful skipjacks, tuna, wahoo, and dolphin (called *masimasi* here).

About 5 nautical miles off Apia, the inshore shallow water drops from 60 to 80 meters down to 3,000 meters, and this spot is where gamefishing normally starts, including visits to several fish aggregation buoys installed by the Samoan government. Trolling with lures is the favored technique.

In the mid- to late 1990s, the domestic longline commercial fishing effort increased, based from Apia. This fishery was aimed mainly at tuna for the domestic market and had evidently not made significant inroads into the local fish populations at that time.

Trolling small lures along the reef edge can provide fine sportfishing for species such as rainbow runner, bluefin trevally, barracuda, kawakawa, giant trevally, and dogtooth tuna. Anglers catch many of these species by casting lures, including surface poppers.

Fishing from the shore with both cut baits and small metal or soft-plastic lures produces a wide range of small emperors, snapper, trevally, and grouper. Some lagoon areas reportedly produce bonefish, but this has not been confirmed.

SAMSON FISH *Seriola hippos.*

Other names—sea kingfish, sambo, samsonfish.

Often confused with the yellowtail kingfish and the amberjack to which it is closely related, the samson fish is a power-packed sportfish and a member of the Carangidae (jacks) family. It has a formidable reputation among anglers and is renowned for its astonishing strength and unrelenting efforts to escape when hooked. There is a small commercial fishery for them, especially in Western Australia, where they are caught together with yellowtail kingfish on handlines and drop lines. The flesh tends to be coarse in older specimens but reasonable in smaller fish, especially if the fish is bled immediately when captured.

Identification. Samson fish have elongate, moderately compressed bodies that are bluish green above, fading to a golden yellow on the sides and white on the belly. There is usually a golden stripe along the midline. Young specimens have three or four brown vertical stripes along the body. The head, by comparison with the slender head of the yellowtail kingfish, is blunt and more rounded, although this is less pronounced as the fish ages. The first dorsal fin is usually dark blue, and the other fins are greenish gray. The second dorsal fin is elevated in front.

The teeth and tail of the samson fish are distinguishing characteristics. Its teeth are reddish (the kingfish's teeth are white), and the forked tail, which has a keel at the base, is never yellow (the kingfish's is yellow). They are also more trevally-like in appearance, although they lack sickle-shaped pectorals.

Size. Samson fish are known to grow to 55 kilograms and a length of 1.8 meters. An Australian record stands at 35 kilograms. Specimens exceeding 30 kilograms are rare.

Distribution. Samson fish are endemic to New Zealand and Australian waters. In Australia, they are distributed along two regions of the southern coastline: from the Brisbane area (Moreton Bay) in southern Queensland to Montague Island off the coast of New South Wales, and from Marion Bay in South Australia around the coast to Shark Bay in Western Australia. The specimens in Western Australian waters are usually bigger than their counterparts from the east.

Habitat. This species prefers deep water, both inshore and offshore, and is found around reefs, bomboras, and coastal headlands. Their habitat closely parallels that of the yellowtail kingfish; unlike kingfish, however, which tend to school in large numbers, older samson fish travel in pairs. Smaller fish move around in small schools.

Life history/Behavior. Very little is known about the history and behavior of the samson fish. No details of spawning activity are available.

Food. Samson fish feed on small fish, squid, and crustaceans.

Angling. Most samson fish are taken incidentally by anglers pursuing yellowtail kingfish, although Western Australian anglers fishing off Rottnest Island just west of Perth, and the Abrolhos Islands to the north, will target this species with success. Occasionally they are taken by shore-based anglers fishing from rocky headlands along the coast, but mostly they're caught over rocky reefs from anchored or drifting boats.

The tackle of shore-based anglers fishing from rock platforms and cliffs usually consists of a 3.6- to 3.8-meter rod and a sturdy reel spooled with 10- to 15-kilogram line. Both spinning and baitfishing are practiced. Where a rock platform formation allows safe fishing, shorter roller-tipped rods to 2.4 meters and medium game rods are popular. Long-handled gaffs to 6 meters are essential, as are sliding gaffs (fed down a line), when cliff fishing.

Boat anglers prefer light- to medium-weight tackle comprising fully rollered or roller-tipped rods wedded to conventional reels holding at least 400 meters of line. Hook sizes vary from 5/0 to 9/0. Stout handlines to 50 kilograms are also occasionally used. Baits include whole live fish or dead yellowtail (scad), mullet, and garfish; strips of mullet and bonito; small squid and octopus; and king prawns.

Samson fish will respond to trolled dead fish, or lures such as plastic squid, metal jigs, spoons, offshore trolling lures, and feathered lures, and they will show interest in lures dropped to the bottom and retrieved in a series of upward sweeps. Chumming with a mix of fish scraps, chopped squid, pilchards, and tuna oil, all tossed with sand and bran to help it sink to the bottom quickly, will attract this fish within angling distance and hold them in the area.

SANDDAB, LONGFIN *Citharichthys xanthostigma.*

Other names—sanddab, soft flounder, Catalina sanddab; Spanish: *lenguado alón.*

A member of the Bothidae family of left-eyed flatfish *(see),* the longfin sanddab is a small but common bottom fishing catch by anglers, particularly in Southern California.

Identification. The body of the longfin

sanddab is oblong and compressed. The head is deep, the eyes are large and located on the left side, and the mouth is large. The color is uniformly dark with rust orange or white speckles, and the pectoral fin is black on the eyed side. The blind side is white.

This species can be distinguished from the Pacific sanddab *(see: sanddab, Pacific)* by the length of the pectoral fin on the eyed side, which is always shorter than the head on the Pacific sanddab and longer than the head on the longfin. Sanddabs are always left-eyed and can be distinguished from all other left-eyed flatfish by having a lateral line that is nearly straight along its entire length.

Size. These fish are common to 10 inches in length but are reported to reach a maximum length of $15^3/_4$ inches.

Distribution. Longfin sanddabs occur in the eastern Pacific from Costa Rica to Monterey, California, including the Gulf of California. They are rare north of Santa Barbara.

Habitat. These flatfish are usually dwell on sand or mud bottoms from 8 to 660 feet deep.

Spawning behavior. Females are larger than males and normally mature when three years old and roughly $7^1/_2$ inches long. They produce numerous eggs, and each fish probably spawns more than once a season. The peak of the spawning season is July through September.

Food. The diet of longfin sanddabs is wide ranging and includes small fish, squid, octopus, shrimp, crabs, and worms.

Angling. Where these and other sanddabs are abundant, it is difficult to keep them off the hook. Anglers use bait on small hooks, often two or more on one bottom setup. A food-gathering variation from the typical rig incorporates several dozen small hooks dangled on an iron ring or hoop. This rig is lowered on a stout line to a position just off the bottom and allowed to remain a sufficient period to fill all the hooks. Normally this does not require as much time as is needed to rebait the rig after removing the catch. Small pieces of squid or octopus are best because they are tough and stay on the hook best, but fish works equally well as a bait.

See: Drift Fishing; Flatfish; Inshore Fishing.

SANDDAB, PACIFIC *Citharichthys sordidus.*
Other names—mottled sanddab, sole, sanddab, soft flounder, megrim; Spanish: *lenguado.*

A member of the Bothidae family of left-eyed flatfish *(see)*, the Pacific sanddab is an excellent food fish that has both commercial significance and a popular sportfishing following. This species is often listed on the seafood menu of California restaurants, and is viewed by some as a delicacy.

Identification. The body of the Pacific sanddab is oblong and compressed. The head is deep, and the eyes are large and on the left side. The color is light brown mottled with yellow and orange on the eyed side, and white on the blind side.

Longfin Sanddab

The Pacific sanddab can be distinguished from the longfin sanddab *(see: sanddab, longfin)* by the length of the pectoral fin on the eyed side. It is always shorter than the head of the Pacific sanddab and longer than the head of the longfin. Sanddabs are always left-eyed and can be distinguished from other left-eyed flatfish by their lateral line, which is nearly straight for its entire length.

Size. These fish may reach 16 inches and 2 pounds but are common to just 10 inches in size and under a half-pound.

Distribution. Pacific sanddabs occur in the eastern Pacific from the Sea of Japan, Aleutian Islands, and Bering Sea to Cabo San Lucas, Baja California, Mexico. They are common in shallow coastal water from British Columbia to California.

Habitat. These flatfish are found on sand bottoms in water that ranges from 30 to 1,800 feet deep, but they are most abundant at depths of 120 to 300 feet.

Spawning behavior. Females are larger than males and normally mature at age 3, at roughly 8 inches in length. They produce numerous eggs, and each fish probably spawns more than once in a season. The peak of the spawning season is July through September.

Food. The diet of Pacific sanddabs is wide

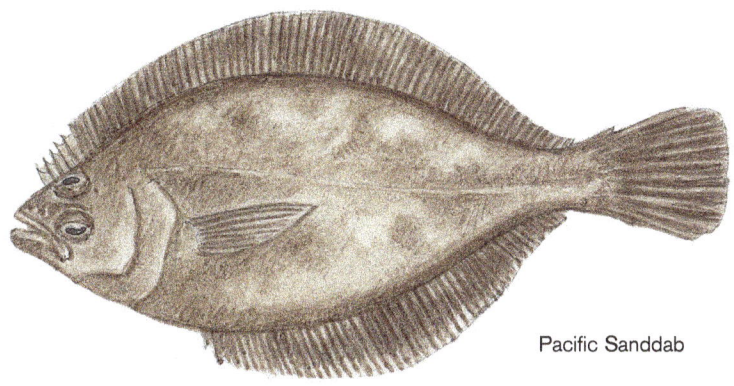
Pacific Sanddab

ranging and includes small fish, squid, octopus, shrimp, crabs, and worms.

Angling. Sportfishing activities are similar to those for the longfin sanddab.
See: Drift Fishing; Flatfish; Inshore Fishing.

SAND EEL
Common term for sand lance *(see)*.

SAND LANCE
American Sand Lance *Ammodytes americanus.*

Northern Sand Lance *Ammodytes dubius.*

Pacific Sand Lance *Ammodytes hexapterus.*

Other names—Sand launce, sand eel, launce-fish, sandlance; French: *lançon*.

Resembling small eels, sand lance are burrowing fish that are important as food for many gamefish. They are excellent to eat when prepared in the style of whitebait.

Identification. Sand lance are small, slim, elongated, and round-bodied fish with no teeth, usually no pelvic fins, no fin spines, and a forked tail. Although they have a long soft dorsal fin, they do not have a first dorsal fin. The body has sloping fleshy folds, and there is a distinct fleshy ridge along the lower side; the straight lateral line is close to the base of the dorsal fin.

Fin-ray and vertebral counts distinguish the American sand lance from the northern sand lance; the American sand lance has 51 to 62 dorsal fin rays, 23 to 33 anal fin rays, and 61 to 73 vertebrae, whereas the northern sand lance has 56 to 68 dorsal fin rays, 27 to 35 anal fin rays, and 65 to 78 vertebrae. Sand lance can be distinguished from young eels by their separate rather than continuous dorsal and anal fins, and by the rounded caudal fin of the eel.

Size. Sand lance grow to a length of about 6 inches.

Distribution. Sand lance occur in temperate and colder parts of the Atlantic and Pacific Oceans and in the Indian Ocean. On the western Atlantic coast, sand lance range from north Quebec to North Carolina. Northern sand lance are believed to inhabit deeper waters, whereas American sand lance inhabit inshore areas. Pacific sand lance range from the Sea of Japan to arctic Alaska, the Bering Sea, and to Balboa Island in Southern California. The arctic and Pacific sand lance may be separate species, distinct from Atlantic populations.

American Sand Lance

Habitat. Schools of American sand lance are often abundant in shallow water along sandy shores and are found in salinities of 26 to 32 percent. For protection, the fish quickly burrow into the sand, snout first, to a depth of about 6 inches. Quantities of sand lance are often dug up in the intertidal zone by people seeking clams.

Angling. There is no angling value to sand lance; they are important as a food for many gamefish, including arctic charr, coho salmon, mackerel, and striped bass, and their appearance and burrowing activity invite angling imitation both with lures and technique.

SAND SPIKE
A rod-holding tube, pointed at one end for insertion into the sand, used by surf anglers to secure a rod.
See: Surf Fishing.

SÃO TOMÉ AND PRÍNCIPE
The independent and democratic Republic of São Tomé and Príncipe comprises islands of the same name, as well as several small islets anchored in the Atlantic Ocean in the Gulf of Guinea. São Tomé and Príncipe is 320 kilometers off the west coast of Africa and 230 kilometers from Gabon. It is recognized as an exciting and different location for tourists and offshore fishing enthusiasts.

Part of an archipelago, the islands are volcanic in origin, leaving a jumbled mass of rocky peaks, tropical rain forests, and striking waterfalls. The southern portion of São Tomé Island crosses the equator, yet the weather is unexpectedly sublime.

Sportfishing in São Tomé and Príncipe is limited exclusively to the exclusive Bom-Bom Island Resort on the northern end of Príncipe. One of the most elegant and full-featured resorts in Africa, it caters to diving and ecotours in addition to sportfishing.

The waters off Bom-Bom (also known as Bombom) host an enormous range of gamefish, particularly sailfish, blue marlin, kingfish, yellowfin tuna, dorado, snapper, barracuda, and bonito. Many world records have been established locally, especially for Atlantic sailfish. The best fishing times appear to be between July and December; January through March are largely unproductive. Blue marlin are plentiful in August, and sailfish run in packs in October and November.

The resort has a fleet of well-equipped charter boats with English-speaking skippers and mates from South Africa (Portuguese is the official language), and both offshore and inshore fishing are offered. Anglers access São Tomé and Príncipe from Lisbon, via Abidjan (Ivory Coast), and arrive on the island of São Tomé, where they overnight at the Marlin Beach Hotel before flying to Bom-Bom the following morning.

SARATOGA *Scleropages leichardti.*
Other names—spotted barramundi, 'toga, Dawson River salmon, southern saratoga, spotted bonytongue.

Not to be confused with the barramundi, to which it is unrelated, the saratoga is one of eight species of the family Osteoglossidae, two of which live in Australia. Its counterpart is the gulf sara-toga (or northern spotted barramundi; *Scleropages jardinii*). Both species appear, naturally, to be confined to the freshwater streams of the Northern Territory, Gulf of Carpentaria, and Cape York in Australia, and the latter also appears in Indonesia. Spectacular fighters when in open water away from weedbeds and underwater obstructions, they are highly respected by recreational anglers who practice catch-and-release. Being very bony and lacking in flavor, saratoga do not make good table fare.

Identification. The saratoga is a long-bodied fish with a straight forehead profile, a scaleless head, and a large, upturned mouth with two chin barbels, large body scales, and a small, convex caudal fin. Both the dorsal and anal fins are posteriorly placed and dark brown in color and a bluish tinge along the edge. The lighter-colored pectorals are pointed, and the pelvic fin is small. Body coloration changes from dark brown on the back to silvery below, and there are one or two large orange or red spots on most of the scales. The gulf saratoga, which is of similar body design, has a convex forehead profile, and spotted dorsal, caudal, and anal fins.

Size. The saratoga grows to a length of 900 millimeters and a weight exceeding 4 kilograms. A record for this species stands at 4.2 kilograms. The gulf saratoga has been recorded to 17.2 kilograms and more than 900 millimeters in length.

Distribution. The range of the saratoga extends from the Adelaide River in the Northern Territory to the Jardine River in Cape York, and into southern Queensland, where it has been stocked in some impoundments and river systems.

Habitat. Although found in numerous freshwater streams, the saratoga prefers stillwater conditions such as those encountered in billabongs *(see),* backwaters, and lagoons. In these waterways, they prefer areas of lily pads, weedbeds, and overhanging banks and pandanus trees.

Life history/Behavior. The fecundity of the saratoga is low, up to 200 eggs, and spawning usually occurs during spring (September through November) and at night. The eggs are carried in the female's mouth, and although the larvae leave her mouth from time to time, they return until the egg sac is used up. As the upturned mouth indicates, this fish is a surface feeder, and adult fish patrol close to the surface as they seek out insects and other food. They are known to jump from the water to take dragonflies or other insects.

Food and feeding habits. The saratoga's diet is a varied one, consisting of insects, small fish, frogs, crayfish, shrimp, lizards, mice, and whatever else they happen upon as they cruise just below the surface.

Angling. Lure casters will find the saratoga an exciting fish to catch, especially on lines of up to 4- to 5-kilograms breaking strength. Subsurface plugs, surface poppers, spinners, and streamer flies are effective. Sight fishing to surface-feeding saratoga, or tossing lures under overhanging pandanus trees or along the edges of lily pads, are favored methods.

The flycaster who tosses a streamer about a meter in front of a patrolling fish can expect a split-second attack when the fly settles on the water. The resulting fight will be both spectacular and hard, provided the fish can be prevented from gaining sanctuary among subsurface structures or weedbeds.

Natural-bait anglers frequently use floats rather than probing the bottom, where it is unlikely fish will be searching for food. If the bait, which can be pieces of fish, frogs, shrimp, and the like, is suspended about 50 to 60 centimeters under the float, it will lie in the path of any patrolling saratoga. Hook size can be as large as 4/0. A wire or heavy mono leader is not necessary unless the fish is being sought in waters where barramundi are likely to exist.

SARDINE, PACIFIC *Sardinops caeruleus.*
Other names—pilchard, California pilchard, California sardine, sardina; Spanish: *pilchard California, sardina de California, sardina Monterrey.*

Unlike the young of herring *(see),* which are often marketed as sardines, the Pacific sardine is a true sardine. Once one of the most important commercial fish along the Pacific coast, the Pacific sardine population has been depleted by pollution and overfishing. The bulk of commercial fish is canned or processed to make fish meal, fertilizer, or oil, but Pacific sardines are not marketed fresh.

Identification. The Pacific sardine has an elongated body, a compressed head, and a small mouth with no teeth. It is silvery with dark blue on the back, shades of purple and violet along the sides, and black spots along both the sides and the back. It can be distinguished from the typical herring by the absence of a sharp ridge of scales (which is found down the midline of the belly of herring), and by vertical ridges on its gill covers.

Distribution. In the eastern Pacific, Pacific sardines occur from southeastern Alaska to Cabo San Lucas, and throughout the Gulf of California, Mexico.

Life history/Behavior. In summer, Pacific sardines migrate northward from California to British Columbia and return in autumn or winter. They form large schools of various-size fish. Their eggs are pelagic, and unlike the eggs of herring, they float.

Sardine, Pacific

Pacific Sardine

Individuals generally mature in their second year.

Food. The Pacific sardine feeds mainly by filtering zooplankton and phytoplankton.

SARGO *Anisotremus davidsonii*.

Other names—China croaker, blue bass, black croaker, grunt, xantic sargo; Spanish: *burro piedrero*.

The sargo is the largest of the Pacific grunts and is commonly caught incidentally by anglers fishing for other species, primarily during the summer.

Identification. The body of the adult sargo is a compressed oval shape, and the back is elevated. The head has a steep, straight upper profile and a small mouth. The sargo's coloring is a metallic silver, with a grayish tinge on the back. It is silvery below, and there is a distinguishing dark vertical bar running across the body from the dorsal fin to the base of the pectoral fin. Occasionally, sargo are entirely bright yellow, orange, or pure white.

Young sargo, up to 4 inches, have several dark horizontal stripes. The vertical bar begins to appear when they are 2 to 3 inches long.

Size. These fish can reach a maximum length of 22 inches.

Distribution. Sargo occur in the eastern central Pacific from Magdalena Bay in Baja California, Mexico, to Santa Cruz, California.

Habitat. Sargo are found inshore and in bays over rocky and rock-sand bottoms, often near kelp beds, and around pilings or submerged structures. Although they can dwell in up to 130 feet of water, they are most common in water between 8 and 25 feet deep.

Life history/Behavior. Sargo swim close to the bottom in loose schools. The fish spawn in late spring and early summer. Spawning first occurs when the fish are about 7 inches long and two years old.

Food and feeding habits. Sargo are bottom feeders that primarily forage on small shrimp, crabs, clams, and snails.

Angling. *See:* Grunts.

SASKATCHEWAN

Driving through Saskatchewan on the Trans-Canada Highway, a traveler might form the impression that this province is an arid one dominated by wheat fields and dusty rolling hills with cattle ranches. This major-highway vantage point, however, doesn't reveal that this prairie province is home to more than 94,000 lakes and countless rivers and streams. In fact, fully one-eighth of Saskatchewan's one-quarter million square miles is covered with freshwater, resulting in a rich and varied sportfishery.

Indeed, Saskatchewan has several important river systems that drain large areas and provide significant habitat for many popular sportfish. Prominent native species include lake trout, grayling, walleye, sauger, northern pike, perch, whitefish, burbot, goldeye, and lake sturgeon. Throughout Saskatchewan, however, introduced species have also enriched the opportunities. Brown, rainbow, brook, cutthroat, and tiger trout, as well as splake, have been stocked in ponds, lakes, and streams throughout the province for most of the past 50 years, and a strong trout fishery is the result. One southern lake even offers a successful largemouth bass fishery.

Saskatchewan boasts an exceptional road-accessible fishing, especially in the far northern reaches of the province. Several paved and gravel highways and roads reach remote wilderness fishing lakes that would otherwise require long and expensive flights. And these same roads take the adventurous angler to jumping-off points where floatplanes provide still greater wilderness exploration.

More than 200 outfitters are scattered throughout the central and northernmost areas of the province, providing services that range from rustic to downright luxurious. In addition, outpost camps exist on hundreds of remote lakes where few have wet a line.

Although Saskatchewan's far north offers numerous trophy fisheries, especially for northern pike and lake trout, the southern region also has outstanding opportunities to catch trophy specimens. In the valleys of the North and South Saskatchewan Rivers, walleye (called pickerel here by many anglers) over 10 pounds are caught with remarkable frequency, and northern pike in the 10- to 20-pound range are fairly numerous. Although they are increasingly rare, large lake sturgeon are available, and big carp are a definite possibility. And some of the largest members of all species are caught in winter through the ice.

Sargo

Southern Region

Trout streams. Most of the southwest corner of Saskatchewan is characterized by rolling hills, remnants of short grass prairie, and one of the driest climates in western Canada. But tucked into small valleys and the folds of the Cypress Hills are among the best and most unheralded small trout streams in the Canadian west. Cypress Hills is named for a tree that doesn't actually grow in the area; the one that does is the lodgepole pine, and it suggests an alpine region far from the prairies. The hills rise to an altitude of more than 4,000 feet, on a par with Banff in the Rocky Mountains. Brown, brook, and rainbow trout inhabit streams and ponds throughout the area. Some of these streams have been managed since the 1920s, whereas others have been enhanced more recently.

One of the more notable trout waters is Battle Creek, which flows from Alberta through Fort Walsh National Historic Park and the west block of Cypress Hills Interprovincial Park, eventually joining Montana's Milk River. It is accessible by a dry-weather road, Highway 27, southwest of the town of Maple Creek. Some parts of Battle Creek can be reached only on foot. Cool water flows through alternating cobble riffles and deep pools. Parts of the creek are heavily overgrown and are best fished with small fly rods or light spinning tackle. Rainbow trout in the 1- to 2-pound range are common between the Alberta-Saskatchewan border and the southern boundary of Fort Walsh National Historic Park.

Another good site is Boiler Creek, which runs through the center of Cypress Hills Park. Surrounded by lodgepole pine in its upper reaches and open meadows below, the creek holds a series of beaver ponds that have good angling for pan-size brook trout. Anglers can reach it on foot or on a dry-weather vehicle trail. The creek is stocked annually with brookies.

Flourishing populations of brown, brook, and rainbow trout exist in Belanger Creek, which flows out of the Cypress Hills into Frenchman River to the south. Large brown trout are found in the slower waters of the southern reaches of the creek, and large rainbows dominate in the central section. Brook trout are most abundant in the upper reaches, which have lower water temperatures and fast riffles. The creek is accessible by road at several points along Highway 21 south of the town of Maple Creek.

Bear Creek runs down the north slope of the Cypress Hills south of the town of Piapot. Initially stocked in the 1920s with brown trout, it is now managed for brookies, which have been naturally reproducing for years. The population is occasionally supplemented by stocking, but fishing is generally rated from fair to excellent. Some sections of the creek are overgrown, but there are open sections and beaver ponds.

Bone Creek rises near the eastern edge of the Cypress Hills and flows eastward into Swift Current Creek. It has been managed as a brown trout fishery since the 1930s and is known as the area's best trout stream. Browns up to 10 pounds have been taken along its 27-mile length from reaches such as Klintonel, Tompkins, Garden Head, and Carmichael Bridges. Brown trout are still stocked annually to supplement natural reproduction in the creek. Big browns have been caught on dry and wet flies, and on spinning tackle.

Anglers land brown trout in Conglomerate Creek as well, which flows south out of the Cypress Hills to join Frenchman River. Browns are stocked here each year to augment natural reproduction. A number of reaches are readily fished by anglers, as there is plenty of open pasture land along the length of the creek. Access and parking are available at several points just off the Highway 614 grid road north of the town of Eastend. Calf Creek, a tributary to Conglomerate, has brook trout; the upper section runs swiftly over cobbles and farther down is a series of beaver dams that hold fish in good numbers.

Nearby Caton Creek runs south out of the Cypress Hills. Its cold upper reaches are home to pan-size brook trout. Fly fishing opportunities are very limited because of heavy cover along the stream bank, but fishing with light spinning tackle can be excellent, especially in some of the beaver ponds along the creek's length.

Swift Current Creek, an important watershed, flows north and east into the river arm of Lake Diefenbaker. As it passes through Pine Cree Regional Park, 33 miles south of the town of Tompkins, it is accessible to anglers seeking pan-size brook trout.

Running through a steep valley south of the Cypress Hills, Sucker Creek provides excellent fishing for pan-size brookies. South of the town of Maple Creek on Highway 21, Sucker Creek is best fished with light spinning tackle, as dense cover grows along the stream's banks.

Flowing across the southwest corner of Saskatchewan is the Frenchman River, the area's main watershed, which has brook, brown, and rainbow trout, as well as walleye and northern pike. Accessible at many points, the Frenchman can be fished from shore or boat.

South Saskatchewan River. The waters that flow through the South Saskatchewan River rise in the Alberta foothills of the Rockies, then wander across southern prairies and the Badlands to meet with the North Saskatchewan River. The South Saskatchewan is home to trophy walleye, as well as sauger, pike, perch, rainbow trout, burbot, lake sturgeon, whitefish, goldeye, and carp.

In its western reaches toward the border with Alberta, the South Saskatchewan produces small numbers of the increasingly rare and pressured lake sturgeon, which are protected from overfishing by catch-and-release regulations, severe limits, or closed seasons, depending on the location. Both the South and North Saskatchewan Rivers hold lake sturgeon.

At Saskatchewan Landing Provincial Park, a half-hour north of the town of Swift Current, the river begins to widen into a classic impoundment called Lake Diefenbaker.

Lake Diefenbaker. One of the finest big-water fisheries in western Canada, T-shaped Lake Diefenbaker is 84 miles long from the southwest end at the park to the junction with the top of the T at the town of Elbow. From here it is 15 miles in either direction to the two dams. Although it is no more than a few hours' drive north of the border with the United States, and is accessible from all directions by paved highways, Lake Diefenbaker holds northern pike in excess of 20 pounds, walleye into the midteens, jumbo perch, and big rainbow trout. A rainbow trout over 20 pounds was caught by a shore angler in 1997, in the fast water below Gardiner Dam.

Big walleye are the most sought-after species in the lake. They're caught by anglers jigging off hundreds of lake points, trolling the edges of dropoffs and weedbeds with live-bait rigs, or trolling crankbaits for active fish feeding on minnows. Prime times for trophy walleye are spring and fall. In spring, look in shallower bays off the main lake where water temperatures have made the fish more active. In fall, large fish are linger off points, and in riprap near both dams.

Rainbow trout, some of which are escapees from commercial fish-farming operations, have done well in Diefenbaker Lake, and 5- to 10-pounders are not uncommon. They are caught by anglers casting from shore, trolling in boats, and fishing through the ice.

This large lake is underfished, in part because it is big and subject to high prairie winds from time to time. Big winds make for big waves and dangerous conditions for small craft. Close to almost every launch access on the lake, however, are areas that are protected from wind and that hold fish throughout the summer season.

This lake has notable opportunities for shore-bound anglers. When the region was flooded, many small side valleys, called coulees, filled with water. In springtime these sites are havens for large walleye that succumb to anglers casting jigs, crankbaits, or in-line spinners, and to those still-fishing with bait rigs from shore. Each year, large rainbow trout are caught on spinning or fly gear cast from the rocky face of the Qu'Appelle Dam at the southeast end of the reservoir. In fall, good-size rainbows are caught by shore anglers within sight of the Riverhurst Ferry, on the western arm of the lake.

Beyond Gardiner Dam at the northeast corner of Lake Diefenbaker, the South Saskatchewan continues to flow north through farmland and past Saskatoon, ultimately joining the North Saskatchewan River east of Prince Albert. The river produces excellent fishing along its length. Anglers working the banks in Saskatoon have caught walleye over 10 pounds during autumn.

Qu'Appelle River system. The Qu'Appelle River originates at the rock rubble dam at the southeast corner of Lake Diefenbaker. The Qu'Appelle drainage, which influences most of southeastern Saskatchewan, is a series of natural lakes and impoundments linked by the river as it flows eastward to meet the Assiniboine, which flows eastward into Manitoba.

Buffalo Pound, a very shallow impoundment, is the first significant lake to the east of Diefenbaker. It produces good numbers of perch, walleye, and pike in both summer and winter.

Downstream and about 60 miles northeast of the capital city of Regina lie Pasqua, Echo, Mission, and Katepwa Lakes. All four natural lakes hold good populations of walleye, perch, pike, and whitefish, as well as suckers, burbot, and some very large carp weighing in at 30-plus pounds.

Available launch facilities, provincial parks, major paved highways, and nearby services in the town of Ft. Qu'Appelle, make these four lakes amongst the most popular summer fishing holes in southern Saskatchewan. They are very fertile, and produce excellent numbers of pan-size perch, walleye in the 1- to 4-pound range, and pike over 10 pounds. Trophy walleye in excess of 10 pounds are taken from these lakes each year. Among the largest walleye are those taken during late-season ice fishing in March, off the mouths of the channels connecting these lakes.

Still farther east, Round and Crooked Lakes hold good populations of pike, walleye, perch, and whitefish. All of the Qu'Appelle drainage lakes sprout small towns of ice fishing shacks during the winter season.

Souris River drainage. One of the more unusual fishing opportunities in Saskatchewan is Boundary Dam Reservoir, a few miles south of the town of Estevan and virtually on the Saskatchewan–North Dakota border. This lake is home to a successfully reproducing population of introduced largemouth bass that are doing extremely well, protected by a reduced limit. Three- to 4-pounders are not uncommon, and trophies up to 7 pounds have been taken in the weedbeds and along the riprap of this reservoir.

The water from the reservoir is used to cool a coal-fired power-generating plant, and the warm water returning into the lake keeps its average temperatures well above normal year-round. Open-water fishing is possible near the warmwater discharge well after the rest of the province's lakes are frozen solid.

Two of Saskatchewan's newest reservoirs, created by the Rafferty and Alameda Dams on the nearby Souris River, are proving fertile and productive for walleye.

Last Mountain Lake. Locally known as Long

Lake, this narrow body of water runs nearly 70 miles from its southern edge at the Valeport Marsh to the shallow, rocky spawning waters at its northern end.

A one-hour drive from the capital city of Regina, it is accessible at numerous points along its length. Both shorelines host numerous resort communities with excellent launch facilities that are open to the public. Despite its southern location and ease of access, this is a world-class trophy lake for the patient angler.

Large walleye, many over 10 pounds, are caught in this lake every year. In spring, big fish concentrate at opposite ends of the lake near spawning areas. As summer progresses and water temperatures warm, large schools of walleye migrate toward the central portion of the lake, where they can be caught off main lake points, bars, and sunken rockpiles. The biggest fish are usually caught in fall, or just after freeze-up through the ice.

Last Mountain Lake also holds good populations of northern pike; fish over 10 pounds are common in spring and fall. Excellent carp, some over 30 pounds, are taken each year by anglers traveling here from as far away as Great Britain. Good populations of jumbo perch, some well over a pound, are here, too. Larger pike inhabit shallower bays off the main lake in spring and are taken by anglers casting plugs, spoons, and large streamer flies. In fall, large pike will strike spoons or plugs trolled along the outer edge of shoreline weedbeds and dropoffs.

Lake of the Prairies. Lake of the Prairies is formed by a dam on the Assiniboine River, which rises in eastern Saskatchewan and flows through Manitoba. One-third of the lake lies in Saskatchewan.

It is home to an excellent population of walleye, pike, perch, and large carp. Visiting anglers should note that Manitoba angling rules apply to this body of water regardless of where it is fished.

North Saskatchewan River. The North Saskatchewan River winds its way across central Saskatchewan, creating a majestic river valley and rich habitat for the production of large fish. Big walleye, pike, perch, suckers, carp, sauger, lake sturgeon, and goldeye are here. In many places the river is shallow, braiding its way through sandbars that shift with water at varying levels and changing currents. It is fishable from shore or from a boat.

Anglers fishing from shore in the city of Prince Albert have caught walleye well over 10 pounds, some on a simple leadhead jig adorned with bright plastic tail. Jigs tipped with frozen or salted minnows (live minnows are not legal for fishing in Saskatchewan) are often used for walleye, and are more effective the farther north in the province one travels.

Saskatchewan River. Formed from the merger of the North and South Saskatchewan Rivers just east of Prince Albert, the Saskatchewan River flows easterly toward Manitoba through a series of impoundments that produce some of the best walleye fishing in North America.

The first of these is the newest, Codette Lake, formed when Francois-Finlay Dam was built. This relatively new reservoir is a good place to fish for pike and walleye, and many of the latter are in the 3- to 5-pound range. Jigs and live-bait rigs are the tools of choice, but take lots of extras for working the plentiful flooded timber here.

Just downstream of Codette Lake is a section of the Saskatchewan River that runs past the town of Nipawin and into Tobin Lake. This stretch is one of North America's top producers of trophy walleye. The provincial record was broken every year for four consecutive years in the mid-1990s, and the largest lunker weighed in at more than 18 pounds.

Both drifting downcurrent with jigs, and trolling crankbaits along the breakline between shoreline flats and the deep river channel, produce trophy fish, but the primary tactic here is drifting with a long-snelled (10 feet or more) bottom-bouncing bait rig with small hooks and a live leech.

Although the river has been subjected to intense angling pressure, and catches of 4- to 8-pound fish have declined, the patient angler can still find success. Fish over 10 pounds are caught almost daily throughout September and October. Anglers fishing the river will also catch good numbers of sauger, goldeye, suckers, and the occasional lake sturgeon. The river produces best for walleye in spring and fall, and fishing in Tobin Lake is good throughout the warmer summer months. Tobin also produces pike from 15 to well over 20 pounds in the open-water angling season. Tobin is one of the most heavily fished waters in the province, and special regulations have been placed on it to protect the midrange walleye and pike.

Below the E. B. Campbell Dam, which forms Lake Tobin, and downriver to Cumberland Delta and Cumberland Lake, a number of fishing lodges and camps host anglers looking for walleye, large pike, sauger, sturgeon, whitefish, and goldeye in a wilderness setting. Cumberland Lake links the Saskatchewan River, which continues eastward into Manitoba, to the Churchill River to the north, through the Sturgeon-Weir River; this was a crucial hub in the historic "Voyageur Highway" canoe route that brought fur traders all the way from Montreal to the Northwest Territories. Much of this part of Saskatchewan is still isolated wilderness, not much changed from the days of the *voyageurs*.

Central Region
Prince Albert National Park. Prince Albert National Park is one of two national parks in Saskatchewan. Within its boundaries are Crean, Waskesiu, and Kingsmere Lakes. Crean and Kingsmere hold lake trout, pike, walleye, and whitefish. Waskesiu has no viable lake trout population. Anglers wishing to fish in national parks

> In 1915, 400 million pounds of salmon were harvested in Alaska, an amount that would then have filled 10,000 freight cars whose total length would have exceeded 100 miles. According to surveys, each year anglers in Minnesota keep about 3 1/2 million walleye totaling 4 million pounds.

should note that separate regulations and licenses apply within these parks.

Hanson Lake Road. Known both as Highway 106 and Hanson Lake Road, this route runs north through Narrow Hills Provincial Park and then east to the Manitoba border, providing access to exceptional fishing. It leads anglers along prime trout waters in the Narrow Hills Park area, including such stocked streams as McDougal Creek, Mossy River, Steep Creek, and White Gull Creek. For anglers willing to drive on gravel roads a little farther off the beaten track, this highway affords access to lakes like Piprell, Little Bear, East Trout, and Big Sandy.

Piprell is a trophy rainbow trout fishery and has produced a 19.2-pound specimen. Other species of trout are stocked in nearby lakes. East Trout and Little Bear Lakes hold lake trout, northern pike, whitefish, and perch. Big Sandy holds walleye, pike, and whitefish.

A short drive to the southwest are the Whiteswan Lakes, which contain good populations of lake trout and pike, and Candle Lake, which is an excellent walleye, pike, and whitefish site in both open-water and ice fishing seasons.

Farther east are larger lakes like Big Sandy, Hanson, Deschambault, Jan, Amisk, and Mirond.

One of the largest lakes in the area, Deschambault has a big, southern sandy basin that is particularly good for pike. The two northern arms of the lake are rocky and better habitat for walleye. Fish creek mouths in spring until the water starts warming up, then move out to the deeper edges of points. Jan holds an excellent population of pan-size walleye.

All of the lakes along the Hanson Lake Road are "drive-to" wilderness lakes serviced by outfitters and lodges set in the rugged scenery of the Canadian Shield. They hold a variety of species, from walleye and perch to northern pike and whitefish, and—in those lakes farther north of the road—lake trout.

Meadow Lake area. The region north of the town of North Battleford in west-central Saskatchewan is dotted with dozens of lakes and a number of parks, and has very little human population. Most of the lakes here, like Chitek, Ministikwan, Makwa, and Delaronde, are home to good populations of perch, northern pike, walleye, and whitefish. Turtle Lake holds large trophy pike and is the home of the "turtle lake monster," a creature occasionally sighted by anglers and boaters and thought to be a very large sturgeon.

Flotten Lake, in the northeast corner of Meadow Lake Provincial Park, is a northern walleye lake with rocky islands, reefs, and points. This lake has such classic walleye structure as rocky shoals and steep dropoffs, and serves up lots of 2- to 6-pound fish. Farther north, Dore and Canoe Lakes are remote wilderness waters that can be driven to on paved and gravel highways. They hold good numbers of walleye, pike, and whitefish.

Limited services are available at nearby First Nations communities, and provincial campgrounds exist in the area. Lac La Plonge, deeper and colder than other area lakes, has lake trout in addition to other typical species.

Lac La Ronge and vicinity. In the center of Saskatchewan amidst hundreds of fishing lakes, Lac La Ronge is a seven-hour drive north from the province's capital city of Regina. This huge northern Canadian Shield lake has two distinct characters: The northern half is dotted with hundreds of islands, and the shoreline is cut with long, fiord-like bays; the southern half is a large open basin, exposed to strong winds that sometimes whip its waters into 9- and 10-foot waves.

Lac La Ronge has literally hundreds of good fishing spots for walleye, northern pike, and lake trout. Although lakers have been severely pressured in recent years and stocks are lower than they once were, recent reductions in both commercial and sportfishing limits have helped to strengthen lake trout numbers. Prime time for walleye and pike is between mid-June and the last week of August. Lake trout are in shallow water in early to mid-June for a short period, and again during spawning in the fall, between mid-September and mid-October, depending on weather and water temperatures. During the warmer days of midsummer, lake trout are deep and are found off midlake reefs or deep-water points, perhaps as far as 100 feet down.

The lake is well serviced by outfitters, guide services, and lodges, especially those based in the town of La Ronge, and on the eastern shoreline in the Hunter's Bay area.

La Ronge is not only a significant fishing lake in its own right, but it is also the hub for hundreds of fishing destinations farther north. In summer, constant floatplane traffic buzzes over the town as anglers head for fly-in destinations lying within an hour or two of their departure point.

For the drive-in angler, however, there are dozens more road-accessible lakes and rivers to the north. Just an hour from the town of La Ronge, on gravel Highway 102, is Saskatchewan's largest northern river, the Churchill. Along the way, anglers will drive past several excellent fisheries. Nemeiben Lake, just north and east of La Ronge, is a high-quality walleye, lake trout, and pike fishery, serviced by resorts and campgrounds.

As the road winds northward, it passes many small pothole lakes holding rainbow and speckled trout, as well as McKay Lake, which is a small lake trout fishery. Anglers who like to canoe and get off the beaten path should seek out lakes like Mekewap, to find rainbow trout that are not heavily fished and will rise to dry flies readily throughout July and August. Getting there is half the fun. From Highway 102, paddle across Lynx Lake and portage across to Duck Lake. Travel up Duck Lake and cross over into Sulphide Lake, then portage into Mekewap.

The world's longest bony fish is the oarfish, which has a red fin, blue gills, a horselike face, and a snakelike body that can attain a length of 50 feet; it has accounted for many sea serpent sightings.

North of the Churchill River, 102 continues far into the northern bush. It travels past wilderness lakes such as Waddy, Brabant, and McLennan, which are noted pike and lake trout fisheries. It also connects to Highway 905, a gravel road that runs north past Reindeer Lake to Wollaston Lake and remote northern Saskatchewan.

There is no lack of opportunity throughout the area along 102, as well as farther east and west. West of La Ronge, in fact, is Besnard Lake—a large, rocky walleye and pike lake that provides especially good fishing in the peak season between June and August. Reached via Highway 2 north from Prince Albert Park to Highways 165 and 910, this lake has recovered in recent years from depressed walleye numbers and now produces steady action.

Churchill River drainage. In the northwestern section of the central region, the waters of Turnor, Frobisher, and Peter Pond Lakes flow into Churchill Lake and then into the Churchill River, one of Canada's most historic river systems. The Churchill River flows southeast through Lac Isle-à-la-Crosse, runs northward to the village of Patuanak, and then turns eastward and winds across Saskatchewan into northern Manitoba and eventually to Hudson Bay.

This river was at the heart of the old Voyageur Highway. The Saskatchewan portion of the Churchill was the essential link between southern and northern watersheds. Today the Churchill has been nominated as one of Canada's Heritage Rivers, in recognition of its cultural, historical, social, and environmental significance.

In Saskatchewan, the Churchill forms the boundary between the true Canadian Shield country to the north and the forest lands to the south. This is a territory of rocks and clear water, spruce and birch. It is also an area in which opportunities for great fishing abound. The Churchill is a series of lakes connected by short passages of fast water, rapids, or waterfalls. It is home to abundant wildlife and waters containing walleye, northern pike, whitefish, and lake trout. The Churchill River is also a world-class canoeing destination, and few trippers paddle it without adding meals of fresh fish to their packed-in food.

The Churchill drainage is home to literally dozens of fishing camps and lodges, located all along its length. Although it is a true wilderness river, in many areas virtually unchanged since the days of the fur traders, it is accessible by numerous roads.

Highway 155 is a paved two-lane highway that runs to the village of Buffalo Narrows on Churchill Lake at the river's headwaters. Gravel road No. 918 runs north to the village of Patuanak. Gravel road No. 914 runs north to Pinehouse Lake in the middle section of the river. Gravel Highway 102 runs north from La Ronge to Otter Rapids and Otter Lake, a favorite departure point for anglers and canoeists. It is the site of several lodges, the village of Missinipe (which is the Cree name for the Churchill, meaning "big river"), and a floatplane base for north-bound adventurers. Just before it enters Manitoba, the Churchill meets gravel road No. 135 at the village of Sandy Bay, just downstream from the Island Falls Dam. This is the only dam on the Churchill in Saskatchewan. Up to this point, its flow is unimpeded along its entire length.

Some anglers tow their own boats along these roads and launch them on the Churchill, where provincial parks have provided access, or at outfitters, where they may be charged a modest docking fee. The Churchill River is drive-in wilderness fishing at its peak. Lakes all along the Churchill that aren't accessible by road are readily reached by floatplane from La Ronge or Otter Lake.

Northern Region
Smaller lakes. Gravel Highway 905 gives anglers access to some of the northernmost drive-in fishing in Canada. Lakes like Davin, Pardoe, and Wathaman lie adjacent to this route and provide excellent angling for lake trout, northern pike, and walleye. The Geikie River crosses the highway as it flows into the south end of Wollaston Lake, and here, in ice-cold fast water below rapids and falls, anglers find arctic grayling holding behind rocks and in eddies.

The highway travels remote northeastern Saskatchewan all the way past the west side of Wollaston Lake to Points North Landing. From here, floatplanes take anglers into the most remote northern fly-in lakes in northern Saskatchewan (many of these lakes are also accessed directly from points south, such as Regina or Saskatoon or Winnipeg, via wheeled charter planes that land on private airstrips).

Although a few of the big waters in this region can be accessed by driving to their southern extremity, these and other near-north wilderness lakes are mainly or entirely accessed by air. Fly-in-only sites include Cree, Foster, Hatchet, Waterbury, Close, Deception, Paul, Hepburn, and Unknown Lakes. These locations are typically supported by one or more full-service lodges. They hold excellent populations of lake trout, northern pike, and whitefish. Some, like Cree and Hatchet, are well known and have produced trophy pike and lakers for many years. The more southerly lakes, or those with areas of shallower water and sand, may hold walleye as well, although seldom huge specimens. The farther north a lake is situated, the more likely it is to hold arctic grayling. Grayling are typically found where there is moving water; a stream flowing into or out of a lake is a good place to look for them.

From the Churchill River drainage northward, there are scores of small, isolated lakes that have only an outpost camp or are accessed only for day trips. Many lodges established on big lakes will fly anglers in to these places. Some such lakes are virtually virgin waters, seeing at most only a few dozen anglers a year.

Reindeer, Wollaston, and Athabasca Lakes. In the same northern reaches of Saskatchewan are the three largest lakes in the province. Two, Wollaston and Reindeer, are accessible by road, although many anglers prefer to avoid the lengthy wilderness drives and fly in. The third, Athabaska, is accessible only by air.

These lakes are big water. Reindeer, the most southerly of the three and partly stretching into Manitoba, stretches more than 120 miles from end to end. It is littered with thousands of islands and is especially known for an abundant northern pike population, as well as for producing many specimens over 20 pounds. The lake harbors large numbers of medium-size lake trout and loads of walleye. Several full-service fishing lodges accommodate anglers.

Wollaston Lake is farther north than and roughly half the size of Reindeer, yet it has more than 800 square miles of water, making it the third largest lake in the province. All of that water holds good-size lake trout as well as a tremendous population of northern pike and plenty of walleye in shallow, sandy areas. The walleye are average in size, but the pike here grow big, and Wollaston is known for pike over 20 pounds. Some specimens are in the 25-pound class and range up to as large as 35 pounds. Wollaston is also serviced by a number of lodges, and some of these have plenty of fly-out opportunities. The season on these two northern lakes is from early June to early September.

Of the three great northern fishing lakes, Athabaska is by far the largest. It lies between the 59th and 60th parallels, just south of the Northwest Territories border. It runs 180 miles east to west, extending from Ft. Chippewyan in Alberta to Fond du Lac at its eastern end. One of Canada's largest lakes, Athabaska covers more than 1.3 million acres and is part of the Mackenzie River drainage that flows to the Arctic Ocean.

Athabaska is home to huge lakers and monster pike. Lake trout over 50 pounds have been caught on rod and reel, and a reported 102-pounder was landed here in a commercial net in the 1960s; 20-pound pike are common. The lake also has walleye and arctic grayling. Despite these attributes, Athabaska has light fishing pressure and is serviced by very few outfitters. Remoteness has something to do with that, as do the lake's enormity and open expanses. Athabaska can be a dangerous lake in high winds. The best fishing occurs between mid-June and late August.

The far north. Still farther north are several wilderness lakes situated virtually or actually on the border with the Northwest Territories. Accessible only by air, these include Ena, Tazin, Scott, and Selwyn Lakes. With minimal fishing pressure, these remote lakes are trophy waters for northern pike and lakers. Catch-and-release policies are the rule. Two lodges operate on Tazin, and one each on the others. Opportunities exist to fly to remote sites for day trips or to more isolated outpost lakes. Grayling thrive at some sites. Although they are typically in the $1^1/_2$-pound range, specimens weighing more than 3 pounds inhabit some waters.

Lake trout over 20 pounds are probable, and lakers ranging from 30 to 50 pounds are possible; pike are numerous to 15 pounds, and specimens from 20 to 25 pounds or more are caught fairly often. Anglers often catch 5- to 12-pound fish of either species all day long. The period following ice out is favored for shallow action, but good deep-water anglers can score on lakers throughout the summer. The big fish are caught late in the season when they come to spawn on reefs. Because late August and early September can bring rugged weather, these periods are often bypassed; but hard-core trout anglers score very well then. It's a very limited season, of course, generally running from the second week of June through the first week of September.

Scott Lake, which sprawls over the 60th parallel into the Northwest Territories, is somewhat typical of these far-north lakes. Scott is a big, interesting lake, 40 miles long and 40 miles wide at its greatest points. Just 100 miles below the arctic tree line, the lake bears some tundra influence in the north, yet in the south it is distinctly reminiscent of southern Ontario, with craggy cliffs, jackpine shorelines, and plenty of birch trees. It has five long arms, an extraordinary number of bays, and all the islands, nooks, crannies, and shoreline you can possibly imagine.

Pike fishing starts with ice out in early June and continues throughout the summer. Many visitors will catch a 20-pounder if they work at it, and some do far better. Pike up to 38 pounds having been landed here. Lake trout are plentiful, too, including trophy specimens in the 20- to 40-pound class. These fish tend to cluster in deep-water areas throughout the summer. Anglers catch many of the biggest lakers from mid-July through August, when the fish are

Pike anglers navigate the back bays of Scott Lake.

deep and hard to access, favoring more sophisticated angling methods than those used in most far-north camps. For both pike and lake trout, the camp policy is catch-and-release only, with barbless hooks.

Several top-quality fly-out experiences are available from Scott Lake. There is an outpost camp at Premier Lake, a distant water connected to Scott where a 30-pound pike and 40-pound laker have been caught, and there's an outpost camp on Wignes Lake. Outstanding day-trip fishing for grayling is available on the Dubawnt River, and also at Lefty Falls.

Lefty Falls, officially known as Hunt Falls and the tallest waterfall in central Canada, is packed with grayling. This falls is among the province's most impressive natural wonders and a site often used for advertising the wilderness charm of Saskatchewan. It is theoretically accessible by boat: You would have to run 60 miles of the Griese River from Scott and Wignes Lakes, negotiate its rapids, and make a grueling portage around the falls. Otherwise, you fly in by floatplane and trek through thick and mosquito-laden bush to reach the splendorous falls.

A premier Saskatchewan lake trout haven, Ena Lake is a 15-mile-long glacial-carved body of water that straddles the 60th parallel northeast of Tazin Lake. It has never known commercial fishing (a factor that impacts resources in northern lakes) and has been visited by relatively few anglers since a lodge opened there in 1990.

A well-sheltered scenic wilderness lake that sports many bays and islands, Ena is blessed with numerous deep troughs that keep the water cool all season. The best angling for lake trout occurs in June, following ice out, and in September, when the fish are spawning on reefs. Many 25- to 30-pound trout thrive here, and lakers have been caught to 53 pounds. Ena Lake also provides good fishing for northern pike. They, too, are frequently caught in trophy proportions, from 18 to 26 pounds, and all are released alive. Bays and islands provide suitable cover, and in summer, pike are favored over deep lakers. This is a catch-and-release, barbless-hook-only fishery.

SAUGER *Stizostedion canadense.*
Other names—sand pickerel, sand pike, blue pickerel, pike, gray pike, blue pike, river pike, pike-perch, spotfin pike, jack, jack fish, jack salmon; French: *doré noir*.

A member of the perch family, the sauger is a smaller, slimmer relative of the walleye, which it closely resembles. It is an important commercial species in some places, especially in Canada, and a gamefish that is often overlooked in some parts of its range. Most of the commercial Canadian catch is taken in Manitoba, where fishing with gillnets and pound nets occurs in summer, autumn, and winter. Sauger are marketed almost entirely as fresh and frozen fillets, and much of the catch is exported to the United States. Their flesh is slightly softer, sweeter, and finer in texture than that of the walleye, but this difference is generally indistinguishable to most people, and commercially they are sold as one and the same fish.

Identification. The sauger's body is slender and almost cylindrical, and the head is long and cone shaped. The back and sides are a dull brown or olive gray flecked with yellow and shading to white over the belly. There are three or four dark saddle-shaped blotches on the back and sides. It is easily distinguished from the smooth-cheeked walleye by the presence of rough scales on its cheeks and two or three rows of distinct black spots on the membranes of its spiny dorsal fin, by the absence of a large blotch on the anterior portion of its spinous dorsal fin, and by the absence of a white tip on its tail. The eyes are large and glossy, and the teeth are large and sharp.

Size/Age. Sauger are commonly caught at sizes ranging from 10 to 16 inches and up to 1 1/2 pounds. Specimens exceeding 22 inches and 5 pounds are rare. The maximum size is about 9 pounds, and the all-tackle world record is an 8-pound, 12-ounce fish caught in North Dakota in 1971. The life span is 10 to 12 years.

Distribution. This species has a general distribution in mid-central North America from Quebec to Tennessee and Arkansas, and northwesterly through Montana to about central Alberta. Between Alberta and Quebec it occurs in southern Saskatchewan, Manitoba, and Ontario and throughout the Great Lakes to James Bay. It does not occur east of the Appalachians or much south of Tennessee except in a few drainages where it has been introduced, principally from the Carolinas around through the lower coastal states to as far south as Texas on the lower Gulf of Mexico.

Habitat. Habitat preferences of the sauger tend to large, turbid, shallow lakes and large, silty, slow-flowing rivers. It is more tolerant of muddy water and swifter current than are walleye, and it prefers water temperatures between 62° and 72°F. It is often found in tailwaters below dams, and along rocky riprap. Eddies near turbulent water are often staging and feeding areas. Gravel bars and points are prominent holding locations in lakes.

Life history/Behavior. Male sauger mature at age 2, females at ages 3 or 4. They spawn

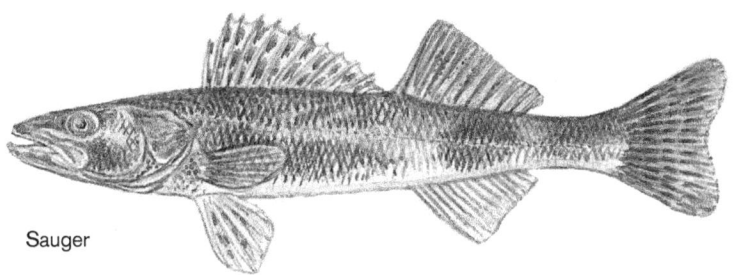
Sauger

when the water temperature is between 41° and 46°F. Adults enter backwaters or tributaries or congregate in tailwaters and search for gravel or rock substrate where they can deposit their eggs. In large river systems, the upstream spawning run can cover 100 to 200 miles, although it will be just a short distance from reservoirs into tributaries. In waters where they occur with walleye, they will usually spawn immediately after walleye. Sauger can naturally interbreed with walleye, producing a fish called a saugeye (see). Sauger grow more slowly than do walleye, however, and are primarily a river fish that locate near the bottom on a variety of bottom types. Like walleye, they are a schooling species.

Food and feeding habits. Sauger feed on such small fish as shad, sunfish, and minnows, as well as on crayfish, leeches, and insects. Most feeding occurs over rocky gravel bottoms or along sparsely weeded sandy bottoms.

Angling. Sauger can provide year-round fishing, although they are often deliberately targeted only in specific seasons in certain locales (through the ice in the north, or in winter and spring in the south) and are otherwise caught incidentally. Although locations and fishing methods for sauger are similar to those for walleye (see), these fish tend to live deeper and are also more aggressive when located, usually striking solidly. They also are even more bottom-oriented. Scaled-down presentations, including lighter and smaller lures, are more appropriate. Blade baits, tail-spinners, in-line spinners, and jigs tipped with minnows are good artificials, and deep-running small-bodied plugs are also effective when deep-trolled. Live minnows are preferred baits, and bait rigs fished deep are also productive.

SAUGEYE

The saugeye is a hybrid fish resulting from the interbreeding of walleye and sauger. It occurs naturally, although infrequently, where the two species mix together. Most populations are produced in hatcheries and are usually stocked in locations where neither parent species has been able to maintain a population. In some literature, it is identified as *Stizostedion vitreum x S. canadense*, which refers to a cross between a female walleye and a male sauger. The meat of saugeye is similar to that of its parents, making it excellent table fare.

Identification. The body of the saugeye is more similar to that of a walleye than to that of a sauger, although the dorsal fin is sometimes spotted (it is on the sauger and is not on the walleye). It also has saddlelike markings on the back and sides, as the sauger does; and the caudal fin has a white border on its lower lobe, as the walleye does. Saugeye also have a dark blotch on the membranes of the spiny dorsal fin. The body may have a yellowish cast.

Saugeye

Size/Age. This fish grows rapidly and has the potential to reach the intermediate sizes, although not the overall size, that walleye typically attain. The all-tackle world record is a 12-pound, 6-ounce fish from Ohio. Typical saugeye are about 15 inches in length, and normally range from 10 to 24 inches.

Distribution. The saugeye has been introduced to waters in the United States from western Ohio, Kentucky, and Tennessee to the eastern Dakotas and southward to Oklahoma.

Habitat. Like their sauger parent, saugeye are more tolerant of muddy or turbid water than are walleye, and seem better suited to impoundments that receive a high rate of water exchange (which increases turbidity). The introduction of saugeye to new waters, however, is still in its early stages.

Spawning behavior. Unlike some hybrid species, saugeye are not sterile and do have the ability to produce offspring with either parent stock. Spawning occurs in tributaries or in tailwater areas when the temperature is between 40° and 50°F.

Food. Small fish are the primary food for saugeye. Shad are especially favored in many lakes and rivers.

Angling. Winter tailwater fishing for saugeye is especially popular in some areas, as these fish are aggressive and one of the few gamefish that are concentrated and active then. Many of the same areas that would be fished for walleye (see) are appropriate for saugeye, although saugeye are likely to hold deeper. Midsummer fishing on lakes or impoundments can be tough, as the fish are more scattered, although they are highly structure oriented. Jigs tipped with minnows or worms, live-bait rigs, and medium-size crankbaits (which are trolled) are all good saugeye catchers.

SAURIES

Abundant offshore fish, sauries are members of the four-species Scomberesocidae family. They have only moderately elongated jaws that are beaknon, and are easily distinguished from needlefish (see) and halfbeaks (see: halfbeaks and balao) by the five to seven finlets behind the dorsal and anal fins, as in mackerel. Sauries as a group have small scales, a relatively small mouth opening, small teeth, and no swim bladder. These relatively abundant fish are heavily preyed upon by tuna, marlin, bluefish, and other predators.

Pacific Saury

The Atlantic saury (*Scomberesox saurus*) travels in schools containing thousands of fish. They are commonly attacked by a variety of predators that sometimes drive the schools into shallow nearshore waters. Often a whole school will rise simultaneously from the sea and skitter across the surface (for this reason commercial fishermen refer to them as "skippers"). They are sometimes caught commercially when abundant, but they are not fished for regularly.

The Atlantic saury occurs in the eastern Atlantic from Iceland and Norway along the British Isles to the Baltic Sea and throughout the Mediterranean, Adriatic, and Aegean Seas to Morocco. In the western Atlantic, they occur from the Gulf of St. Lawrence south to North Carolina and Bermuda. Atlantic saury are also known as, in French: *balaou;* Italian: *costardella;* Norwegian: *makrelle-jedde;* Portuguese: *agulhao;* Turkish: *zurna.*

The Pacific saury (*Cololabis saira*) is similar and has a significant commercial interest as well. Also known as mackerel pike and skipper (and *sanma* in Japanese), it also occurs in large schools, generally offshore near the surface, and, like the Atlantic saury, feeds on small crustaceans and the eggs and larvae of fish. The Pacific saury occurs from Japan eastward to the Gulf of Alaska and south to Mexico.

Both species may reach a length of about 14 inches but are usually shorter.

SAWFISH
See: Rays and Skates.

SCALE
A scale for weighing fish is one of the most popular accessories that anglers have, although it may be one of the least discussed and least used, since it is generally reserved for weighing fish that are of significant size.

Handheld scales are of the spring variety, and they have exterior incremental markings to show weight or depict weight on a digital readout. They are notoriously variable and, with few exceptions, are best for getting a "ballpark" estimate of the weight of a fish. Some, however, are surprisingly accurate—enough to be used for record purposes. If absolute weight is a concern to the angler for any reason, it's a good idea to verify the ability of a given scale by checking it against a known weight (take it to the grocery store, put a bag of potatoes/apples/grapefruit on their certified scale, then weigh it with your own scale), so you'll know if it's off the mark and by how much. A fish that might be a world record must be weighed on a certified scale, however, and not in a rollicking boat, so you need to observe certain protocol for such special fish.

Fish to be released shouldn't be indiscriminately weighed. Weighing can be harmful, as can taking the fish out of the water for the extra handling and time necessary to weigh it. If you must weigh a fish to be released, it's best to keep the fish in a cradle *(see)* and weigh the whole thing with the fish properly supported horizontally, then weigh the cradle separately and deduct that from the total. An alternative is to get a girth and length measurement and use a formula for estimating weight. This and other aspects of weighing and handling fish are covered in greater detail in other entries.
See: Catch-and-Release; Landing Fish; Measuring Fish; Records.

S-CAST
An in-air technique for presenting a fly or mending a fly line.
See: Mending.

SCENTS
An aromatic substance applied to or made part of artificial lures. These substances may be applied to hard or soft lures in the form of a paste, gel, or similar element, or in the form of a liquid that is sprayed or used as a dip; they are also incorporated into soft lures in the manufacturing process, or in some cases are added to a pouch or other receptacle that is part of a lure or attached to it. Most usage with lures occurs with items that are capable of absorbing and retaining the scent for a period of time. Scents are more popular in freshwater than in saltwater. They are viewed with suspicion by many anglers, yet used religiously by some, particularly catfish and bass anglers in freshwater.

The major question regarding scents is whether they attract fish and/or mask offensive odors, thereby increasing hooking success. This is difficult to prove in actual angling conditions due to the number of variables that influence fish behavior and angling effort.

It is well known that some fish have much more developed smell and taste senses than others. Any fish with barbels or whiskers is an example. However, many predatory fish rely primarily on their vision, some rely heavily on their hearing, and some use both; these fish rely little, if at all, on their sense of taste and smell.

Many scents are generally targeted at all fish, and others are targeted for particular species. Advertising claims notwithstanding, whether any fish are attracted to scents, to what extent they may be attracted, and under what conditions (how close it is to the fish, the effect in current versus stillwater, and other factors) is difficult to prove. In freshwater, catfish are well known to prefer baits that emit odors; scents are used regularly in fishing for these bottom-scrounging creatures. Beyond this, however, the major predators are not known to heavily rely on scent in natural environs. Most scents are aimed at bass, but these fish principally use their vision and lateral line for detecting prey when feeding. In saltwater, a high use of bait, and in some cases chum *(see)*, for certain species, plus an abundance of clear water to aid visual feeding, diminishes angler interest in scent products.

Equally uncertain is whether fishing scents mask odors that might be offensive to fish, such as human scent or chemicals (as in sunscreen or insect repellent). This, too, is a claim of scent manufacturers and one that is hard to prove or disprove. Some frequently cited instances of lures that were dipped into gasoline and lubricant and yet fished successfully have been used to refute the merits of this aspect of scents.

It is fairly clear that using scents or scented products is not repelling to fish. Therefore, if it is a confidence booster for anglers and helps them to fish more effectively, it may have some value. But there are many instances in both freshwater and saltwater fishing (using most flies, fishing with surface lures, and casting spinners) where there is little if any merit to these products.

See: Anatomy; Bait; Chumming; Processed Bait.

SCHEDULED WATER
A term used in some Canadian provinces for waters that (usually) contain significant runs of Atlantic salmon and that are subject to regulations restricting angling to the use of flies and fly fishing. Other species may be present besides salmon, but only fly fishing is permitted regardless of the species targeted. Both lakes and rivers may be scheduled, although rivers, and often their tributaries, are the primary scheduled waters and may be scheduled only during that portion of the season when salmon are historically present, leading to open and closed seasons.

SCHISTOSOMIASIS
See: First Aid.

SCHOOL
A closely spaced collection of fish that swim in association with each other. Fish in a school are often of the same species and of similar size, but species may intermingle and vary in size. Some species are noted for their tendency to school, while other species are more solitary.
See: Schooling.

SCHOOLIES
Small fish that run together, often used to refer to saltwater fish that are sub-legal size or less than a foot long, especially bluefish and striped bass.
See: Schooling.

SCHOOLING
(1) The behavioral grouping of fish, usually of the same or related species, which move together as a unit and exhibit a specific geometrical relationship. Similar to herding, schooling may be a natural means of reducing predation and ensuring survival of some individuals. Many species of fish school throughout their lives, and young fish, as well as prey species, are especially likely to school. Fish of different species seldom intermingle, although related species (such as white bass and striped bass, for example) may do so.

Schooling of fish has very little to do with their education. It does have much to do with their ability to survive and reproduce in sufficient numbers. Schools are composed of many fish of the same species moving in more or less harmonious patterns throughout the oceans. A very prevalent behavior, schooling is exhibited by almost 80 percent of all fish species during some phase of their life cycle. Many of the world's commercial fishing industries rely on this behavior pattern to produce their catch, especially for species like cod, tuna, mackerel, and menhaden.

Fish school for a number of reasons. For some, schooling helps reduce water friction. When traveling in schools, fish that swim in fairly precise, staggered patterns create a to-and-fro motion with their tails that produces tiny currents called vortices, which are swirling motions similar to little whirlpools. Each individual, in theory, can use the tiny whirlpool of its neighbor to assist in reducing the water's friction on its own body.

Another advantage is the safety factor against predators. A potential predator hunting for a meal might become confused by the closely spaced school, which can give the impression of one vast and frightening fish. Additionally, schooling fish benefit from the concept of safety in numbers. A predator cannot consume an unlimited quantity of prey; the sheer number of fish in a school allows species to hide behind each other, thus confusing a predator by the alteration of shapes and colors presented as the school swims along. Of course, those on the outside edges of the school are more likely to be eaten than those in the center. Predatory fish also benefit from schooling because it gives them the ability to travel in large numbers in search of food and to corral prey.

Schooling fish respond quickly to changes in the direction and speed of their neighbors, and can do so while still retaining a close swimming pattern. They can move from one configuration to another and then regroup almost as one unit.

When young, most fish species do not exhibit the schooling pattern. As they mature, they begin to swim in pairs and then in larger and larger clusters until they attain the classic parallel pattern. Thus, schooling appears to be a formed behavior pattern genetically imprinted. Researchers believe that as the sense organs of the young fish mature, their schooling behavior strengthens. The first sense used is that of sight, which begins to function immediately after birth to allow for feeding. Fish eyes cannot focus directly forward because they are located on the sides of the head. This placement does, however, permit the eyes to be especially sensitive to lateral movement—a very helpful attribute in schooling. The fish can see what other members of the school are doing in relation to themselves and respond accordingly.

Of special interest in the phenomenon of schooling is the lateral line system on the sides of a fish. This is a series of sensory cells usually running the length of both sides of the fish's body; it performs an important function in receiving low-frequency vibrations. These two lateral lines are highly sensitive to movements and the displacement of water as a fish swims close to its neighbor. They aid in keeping all the fish in a neat, orderly pattern. Some fish do not have lateral lines, nor do they have the sensitive cells; thus, they rely on their eyesight. Research suggests that if fish are blinded and their lateral lines cut, schooling does not take place; but if the lateral lines are left in place on blind fish, they are still able to school. The lateral lines are especially important to fish living in murky waters where sight is not particularly useful.

See: Anatomy.

(2) The phenomenon of gamefish actively feeding upon prey species and vulnerable to angling effort. Some species of gamefish, especially those that are pelagic or roam open water, like tuna and salmon, forage as a school and prey upon schools of baitfish. Some species do not ordinarily school but will do so in a loose sense when there is ample feeding opportunity; largemouth bass, for example, which are a cover-oriented fish, may school in reservoirs when large numbers of shad are available in shallow water. When gamefish are grouped and actively feeding upon large numbers of prey, they are said to be schooling, which refers both to their own association as well as to their (sometimes frenzied) foraging behavior. They may be particularly vulnerable to angling at that time, and the activity may generate a high level of action and angler enthusiasm, although it is usually a phenomenon of short duration.

Angling for Schooling Fish

The phenomenon of schooling is commonly associated with freewheeling activity. However, it does not occur everywhere and with all species. Some of the more popular fish that school in saltwater include dolphin, bluefish, striped bass, and tuna. Tuna are caught by trolling and baitfishing and very rarely by casting; they are such fast movers that they are seldom appropriate for the school-fishing tactics that are characteristic of most other species.

In some places people actually depend on schooling fish behavior for the bulk of their deliberate angling activities. In many freshwater locales in the fall, striped bass, hybrid stripers, and white bass chase and consume pods of baitfish (usually threadfin or gizzard shad) and roam over a wide area as they keep up with the bait and maraud them. Often this phenomenon is best observed in early and late daylight hours. With white bass, it happens on points and along rocky shores as well as in open water, but with stripers it may happen anywhere. The key to finding it is observation.

Striper anglers usually motor to places where schooling fish are frequently observed or were seen the morning or evening before. They shut the outboard motor off, and watch and wait. When a sudden splashing occurs in the distance, and/or a flock of seagulls is seen hovering expectantly and diving to the water, that is a giveaway and also the signal to shift into breakneck gear.

The tactic is to race to the site of the commotion, glide to the outer edge of it, cut the motor, and cast into the melee. Sometimes nearly any lure will do; sometimes it must be close in size and shape to the baitfish being pummeled. Two or three anglers may get into fish this way; if the school moves on, you try to move with it, being careful not to put the fish down (which often happens anyway, because of the fish you catch or the intrusion of your boat or that of others) and trying not to lose their direction.

The same thing happens with bluefish in saltwater, except that when bluefish and bait are really

Striped bass are the quest of these Oklahoma anglers; boats in the background are moving to keep up with the fast-traveling school of fish.

thick, the blues are reasonably undisturbed by boats, and fish-catching can be fast and furious for a longer period of time.

Likewise, bird activity in inshore or offshore waters can be an indication of feeding by schools of some species or several species, from mackerel to albacore to dolphin, and here the open waters may be conducive to trolling around the edges of the melee to pick off fish, as well as getting into position to cast lures or pitch out live bait. Many offshore anglers will use the high vantage point of towers to spot dolphin schools near floating weedlines, and will pitch some unhooked live bait to them to start a flurry of feeding, then cast some hooked bait among the fray. It is also possible to use chum to get the fish into casting position with light spinning tackle or a fly rod, since the school will keep feeding toward the boat.

Some species of freshwater fish are known as "schooling" fish because they tend to be found in groups. Walleye, yellow perch, and crappie are popular species that are usually clustered, and it is common knowledge that in nearly any place that you catch one of these fish, there are surely others. Panfish anglers well know that they can locate a school of fish, especially crappie, and catch them by the score with jigs or live bait as long as they are fishing at the proper depth. Crappie will school heavily in deep locales in summer and fall, and stay in one particular area. They require a presentation with some finesse, rather than the slam-bang action that is associated with the frenzied behavior of other species. But at least with these fish, once you have found a concentration, you don't have to work to keep locating them.

More species of freshwater fish may cluster than what people think. And in places with little or no fishing pressure, this is more likely to be observed; the difference being that fish in highly pressured waters are wary and more likely to be spooked by any activity, whereas those in virgin or lightly pressured waters are more tolerant.

Northern pike and chain pickerel are great examples of fish that can be deceptively abundant, although not actually schooled per se. In northern Canadian waters, schools of 2- to 5-pound lake trout cruise shallow rocky shorelines on summer evenings to feed on bugs, and they are caught by stealthy anglers using flies and small jigs on light tackle, who cast to wandering pods of fish. If you're patient, you can sit and wait for these trout to come by; if not, you can intercept them by boat, shutting the motor off before getting to the fish, then casting to their midst as they cruise by. These fish are in no way behaving like surface-busting striped bass would, yet they are cruising en masse and they are aggressive. In these shallow, clear waters, you can actually stalk the school, and several fish will charge your lure.

Walleye, charr, and lake trout may be found in heavy concentrations in those northern locales where there is a large inlet to a lake at various times of the season, and the fish seem to be secure because of the depth and heavy current present. Such a place can provide fast fishing for a while, but it may need to be rested when the action slows, perhaps for 30 to 60 minutes before you return and get into more fish. This seems to be more likely for charr and lakers than for walleye, but it also seems to be because the fish come in to feed and then leave, rather than taking up permanent local residence. In any event, finding these types of situations—where there's an abundance of active schooling fish—can result in terrific action.

Largemouth bass, which are very oriented to cover for hiding and feeding purposes, do gather in loosely defined schools, as previously mentioned, when there is ample open-water bait. The bait are primarily surface or near-surface feeding fish, usually detected by observation. Their appearance may be short-lived and may be fairly obvious to those close enough to be able to observe this behavior. Bass that appear to be schooling generally herd baitfish, primarily shad but sometimes alewives, against some type of underwater structure, like a reef, hump, or weed edge. Keeping up with these fish is often difficult, and they are usually spooked easily by boats that get too close.

This is a liberal definition of schools and schooling behavior, however, since largemouth and smallmouth bass are generally not a schooling type of fish once they have passed the juvenile stage. Many anglers refer to bass schools when discussing an abundance of these fish in one particular location, but this is not a school nor is it true schooling behavior, just a lot of fish of the same species co-existing, usually in an area with plenty of cover and forage opportunity.

SCOOTER

A shallow water low-freeboard style of flats boat *(see)* used in the Gulf Coast, primarily for anglers seeking redfish and seatrout in calm inshore waters.

SCOPE

The term for rode (anchor line) length in relation to water depth and anchoring point on a boat.
See: Anchor.

SCORPIONFISH, CALIFORNIA *Scorpaena guttata.*

Other names—spotted scorpionfish, scorpion, rattlesnake, bullhead, scorpene, sculpin; Spanish: *rascacio californiano.*

The California scorpionfish is an excellent food fish and the most venomous member of the scorpionfish family. It has venom glands that are attached to the dorsal, pelvic, and anal fin spines, and if these spines penetrate the skin, an intense and excruciating pain in the area of the wound occurs almost immediately. If there are multiple punctures, the wound can induce shock, respiratory distress, or abnormal heart action, and sometimes leads to hospitalization of the victim. The California scorpionfish is often called sculpin but is not a member of the sculpin family.

Identification. The California scorpionfish has a stocky and slightly compressed body as well as a large head, mouth, and pectoral fins. Colored red to brown with dark patches and spots on the body and fins, this fish is capable of dramatic color changes to blend with its background. It has large pectoral fins, 12 poisonous dorsal spines, and poisonous anal and ventral fin spines.

Size/Age. The California scorpionfish can grow to 17 inches and live 15 years.

Distribution. In the eastern Pacific, this species occurs from Santa Cruz, California, to Punta Abreojos, Baja California, including a cloistered population in the northern Gulf of California and at Guadalupe Island in Mexico.

Habitat. California scorpionfish usually live in caves, crevices, and rocky areas of bays along the shore, from just below the surface to 600-foot depths. Resting quietly during the day among rocky reefs and kelp beds, they emerge at night and are often seen by night divers in the open near kelp and eelgrass beds. Some are occasionally found over sand or mud bottoms.

Life history/Behavior. California scorpion-fish start spawning at age 3 or 4. Spawning activity occurs from April through August, most likely at night. The eggs are implanted in a single layer on the gelatinous walls of hollow, pear-shaped "balloons" of 5 to 10 inches in length; these are released on the bottom and rise to the surface, and the eggs hatch within the next five days.

Food. The California scorpionfish feeds on crabs, squid, octopus, fish, and shrimp.

Angling. California scorpionfish readily take a hook that has been baited with a piece of squid or fish and lowered to the bottom in a rocky area they are known to inhabit. Tough baits like squid are useful because they are difficult to steal and save rebaiting time. On occasion, a considerable amount of chumming with ground fish will attract California scorpionfish to the surface. Hooked California scorpionfish are not noted for their fighting qualities.

California Scorpionfish

SCOTLAND

For general information about fishing in Scotland as a country within the United Kingdom, *see: England.*

Gamefishing

Trout. Scotland offers excellent wild brown trout fishing on its abundant rivers, lochs, and tarns, and on the lochs in the Shetland, Hebrides, and Orkney Islands. The season for brown trout varies considerably from river to river, running from spring to autumn, and the visiting angler should check this beforehand if possible. Stocking is carried out in comparatively few of these waters, and catching a 3-pounder is often a considerable feat.

Preferred flies for these small wild brownies include such old favorites as Black Gnat, Black and Peacock Spider, Teal Blue and Silver, Peter Ross, Black Pennell, Zulu, Kate McLaren, Kingfisher Butcher, Alexandra, Whickham's Fancy, Soldier Palmer, and various sedge patterns.

This angling comes at a reasonable price. If you wish to stick strictly to wild browns, you can fish at a low cost; indeed the fees for getting to some of these out-of-the-way places will be far greater than the direct angling costs. Boat hire is often extremely cheap as well, although boaters should beware of being caught out in the big lochs in rough weather, which can blow up suddenly. On waters that support a run of salmon and sea trout, the charge for fishing will be greater than that for angling solely for brown trout.

In addition to browns, Scotland offers some rainbow trout as well. Stocking rainbows in Loch Leven in the early 1990s was a controversial move because of the natural brown trout population. But the rainbows have settled in well and have put on a surprising amount of weight.

The Scottish Tourist Board can direct you to the main inland trout fishing areas, but British angling publications will give you much more detailed help, as the beats on rivers change hands frequently. They may also be able to put you in touch with a local expert.

There is also a thriving and steadily increasing business in commercial, small, stillwater (in a broad sense, anything that is not a river, stream, or tributary) trout fisheries, primarily in the south of Scotland. These waters hold mainly rainbows. Some are open most of the year, closing only in winter. As the climate is colder here, the trout tend to be fitter than in some commercial stillwater trout fisheries in England, but they tend not to be stocked as large at most sites, although some specialize in bigger fish.

Salmon and sea trout. Scotland is famous for its salmon fishing, and anglers travel from all over the world to partake of the sport and the tradition, but above all to fish in beautiful locations that range from deep majestic lowland rivers to faster runs through magnificent glens, with mountains all around. Scotland offers salmon fishing for anglers from all walks of life, including royalty. Anglers can rent private beats and association waters on a daily or weekly basis. The prices range widely and are dictated by exclusivity and previous years' yields. It is possible, however, to catch good numbers of salmon from the cheapest of beats, given perfect conditions, especially when there is plenty of water to encourage Atlantic salmon to run upriver.

It is illegal to fish for migratory fish (salmon and sea trout) in Scotland on a Sunday; hence, many weekly accommodation/fishing packages run from Sunday to Sunday.

Until the mid-1990s it was common for nearly all sport-caught salmon on Scottish rivers to be kept by anglers, but this has changed somewhat—on a voluntary basis on some rivers and by legislation on others. Many waters now restrict the number of salmon that can be kept. These restrictions vary, and in some cases a strict one-fish limit followed by catch-and-release is practiced, to conserve future salmon stocks. Such practices are essential on Scottish rivers, as some have lost their spring salmon runs altogether, and the main run on many rivers is now from June onward. Diminishing stocks of sand eels—a major element of the diet of salmon and sea trout in the sea—and netting in the high seas and estuaries have had an enormous, negative impact on stocks.

As a basic guideline, salmon rivers in the west of Scotland can be classed as spate rivers. They are shorter than those in the east and are heavily reliant for their flow on rainfall coming down from the mountains, which produces quick changes in water levels. Increases in flows quickly bring fish into the river, but the run stops rapidly if levels decrease rapidly. These rivers include the Doon, Nith, Anann, Ayr, Cree, and Bladnoch. On the east side are the more famous rivers, including the Tweed, Spey, Tay, Aberdeenshire Dee, Helmsdale, Beauly, Deveron, Don, and the North and South Esk.

Many of these rivers have runs of both salmon and sea trout. The Spey, for example, has a fine run of sea trout of good average size, but they are rarely sought by anglers obsessed with catching the mighty salmon. Large sea trout (6-plus pounds) are taken on the Spey by salmon anglers using double-handed rods and salmon flies.

The Spey, of course, is arguably Scotland's premier salmon river and—along with the Tweed, Tay, and Dee—among the rivers most noted for large fish and large populations. The Spey courses northerly about 48 miles, from its origins in the Highlands southeast of Loch Ness to the sea. It is a fast flowage with plenty of breadth and wide, shallow runs. Casting a long line across large pools is a trademark of salmon fishing here, but heavily wooded banks have led to so-called Spey rods and casting methods. This gear enables anglers to overcome the intrinsic difficulties of big water and little casting room.

The Scottish Tourist Board relies heavily on visiting salmon anglers, so they will be helpful to those looking for waters to fish.

If you are tempted by the wild salmon fishing in Scotland, you should be armed with the right equipment. On some of the smaller spate rivers, it is possible, and sometimes a benefit, to use a single-handed 10-foot rod suited to an 8- or 9-weight line. If you're fishing a river in spate, or one of the longer and more well-known rivers, however, you'll need a rod of around 15 feet with a 10- or 11-weight fly line. Take various densities of line to cope with circumstances.

Flies vary depending on water conditions, but in general low water is fished with a fly of size 6 down to a size 14, and in high water a size 6 up to a brass Tube or Waddington that is almost 3 inches long. Favorite patterns include variations of Willie Gunn, Stoat's Tail, Hairy Mary, Munro Killer, and the ever-popular Ally's Shrimp. Tie these on single, double, and treble hooks, and on brass tubes and Waddingtons, and you shouldn't go far wrong. Local experts may have a few secrets in their fly box; it might be worthwhile to befriend them.

A pair of chest waders is essential in most cases, and on some of the bigger, more treacherous rivers, a wading staff is advisable.

Coarse Fishing

The only coarse fishing commonly associated with Scotland is for the beautifully marked pike present in many of the country's lochs. Several are renowned for producing pike over 30 pounds, and

River Spey anglers display their salmon catch.

anglers go there in the hope that they can produce a fish to match the legendary Endrick pike. The Endrick legend surrounds the skull of a pike that was found at the mouth of the River Endrick and Loch Lomond, which experts have calculated could have weighed more than 70 pounds.

The Scottish record specimen of 47 pounds, 11 ounces came from Lomond, which is just outside Alexandria, and many experts believe giants over 50 pounds favor the Endrick (south) bank of the 26-mile-long loch. The River Endrick itself produces excellent coarse fishing, offering large catches of roach and dace; giant bream are taken at night. On the loch itself, there is excellent roach fishing at Balmaha, where you can also hire boats.

Many other lochs are capable of producing pike that weigh 20 or more pounds, including Loch Ken in Dumfries and Galloway County, which is also a superb roach water; the underrated Loch Awe in Strathclyde, which is also home to giant wild brown trout; and Kilbirnie Loch, where it's also easy to find plenty of roach. Excellent bream and carp fishing are available at Castle Loch at Lochmaben in Dumfries and Galloway County. This venue boasts the Scottish bream record and also holds plenty of carp. Lochrutton Loch, which is full of bream and roach, is another venue that offers a large mixed catch in summer.

Of the rivers, the old River Forth at Stirling is good for roach, and the River Clyde from Motherwell down to Glasgow harbors roach, dace, and bream. The River Tay at Perth has built a superb reputation for big roach to over 2 pounds and is known for large catches. Another jewel is the Forth and Clyde Canal. This venue is rarely fished, and "swims" (immediate fishing areas) need to be created, but it offers fantastic tench fishing, and large catches are possible throughout the summer around Kirkintilloch and Cumbernauld.

No national license is required to fish in Scotland, and there is no officially closed coarse fishing season on still waters, rivers, or canals. You might have to respect local bylaws, however, which restrict fishing at certain spawning times. Although some fishing is free—and what isn't is all pretty cheap—you will often have to buy day tickets to fish. These are best purchased in advance and are generally available from local shops, hotels, and farmers. Unlike salmon and sea trout fishing, coarse fishing is permitted on Sundays.

Sea Fishing

Nearly 4,000 miles of coastline surrounds Scotland, and like its neighbor England, Scotland's species vary according to whether one is fishing in the North Sea, in the Atlantic Ocean, or fronting the Irish Sea.

The southeast corner of Scotland around the Solway Firth fronts the Irish sea and holds among the best marine fish populations in the United Kingdom. Available everywhere, dogfish are considered a local pest but have saved many anglers from a blank day. Also expect flounder from the many estuaries, and pollack, wrasses, small conger (known in the UK as "strap" conger), possibly thornback ray, and dabs from most other marks. Boat fishing around Luce Bay can be fantastic, especially for tope in summer. The main ports are Whithorn, Luce Bay, Drummore, and Stranraer.

Up the coast is the Firth of Clyde, where incredible catches of cod to 30-plus pounds were taken from the shore in the 1960s. Now it is but a shadow of its former self, although there are plenty of keen anglers, and flounders tend to be the main quarry.

Farther north anglers will find good fishing around the coast from hundreds of estuaries and sea lochs, although local advice is essential. Just getting to some of these out-of-the-way venues can be difficult. But the scenery is breathtaking. On this rocky coast, wrasses, pollack, and conger are among the targeted fish.

The Isle of Mull is famous for common skate, which run to 150-plus pounds; the main season is in July and August, and advance booking is essential. Look in the sea fishing magazines for advertisements from the few charter boats offering fishing for common skate. All common skate are returned, usually tagged. Oban is another port where boats target common skate. Up to 2.5 kilograms of lead may be required to hold bottom in the fast tides found off this coast, so be prepared for heavy-tackle angling.

The Hebrides offer excellent shore fishing, and visitors may be able to assemble a boat trip in conjunction with local anglers. Well-organized clubs exist on the islands. Halibut are caught occasionally and are perhaps the most prized marine sportfish in the UK. Some haddock are caught hereabout in winter.

Moving to the northeast mainland, Scrabster is a good charter port, and codling (small cod) are the main winter species. Local specialists occasionally land huge catches of porbeagle sharks, primarily in November. Shore fishing all around the northern and eastern coasts tends to be for codling and flounder; wrasses and red codling are prevalent in summer. Again, local knowledge is essential, and visitors should contact the local fishing club.

The marine waters of the southern part of Scotland are naturally more heavily fished than those in the north, because they're closer to Glasgow and Edinburgh. The southeast corner of Scotland, from Aberdeen south to Edinburgh, offers very good year-round sport, including excellent winter fishing for flounder in the estuaries and for codling from the rocks. The winter codling sport is superb, although weather conditions can curtail boating activities. Anglers also take haddock in winter. The main charter ports are Peterhead, Stonehaven, Johnshaven, Arbroath, Anstruther, North Berwick, Burnmouth, and Eyemouth. Many small-boat owners, and several clubs, ply the area south of Edinburgh, targeting plaice and codling.

The Orkney and Shetland Islands tend to be ignored by UK sea anglers because of the traveling required, but visitors will find plenty of fish, and some local clubs are willing to help.
See: Wales.

SCROD
Fish market terminology for a small cod or haddock with the head on.
See: Cod, Atlantic; Haddock.

SCUD
Scuds are small freshwater crustaceans of the order Amphipoda that are a favorite food of trout and other fish. They are side swimmers, moving rapidly on their sides, and are usually associated with aquatic vegetation. Unlike most crustaceans, the scud has no upper shell; it breathes by means of gills, a fact that sets it apart from insects.

Scuds have a shrimplike appearance but lack the large hard covering over the head and upper body. The body is white to clear with many segments, and is flattened laterally, being higher than it is wide. Scuds have two pairs of antennae and seven pairs of tiny legs.

SCULPIN
The Cottidae family of sculpin is made up of more than 300 species, most of which are marine but many of which also occur in freshwaters throughout the Northern Hemisphere. They are important as food for larger fish and as predators of the eggs and young of gamefish. Bottom-dwelling fish of cold waters, sculpin live in shelf waters and in rocky tidalpools. A few species of larger sculpin inhabit depths of up to 4,200 feet in saltwater.

Sculpin are characterized by wide bodies that taper to slender, compressed tails. They may be unscaled or have spiny prickles or platelike scales,

Cabezon

Staghorn Sculpin

although the development of these vary within species depending on habitat and are not necessarily useful in identification. All sculpins have a bony support beneath the eye, which connects bones with the front of the gill cover. The dorsal fin is deeply indented between the spiny and soft-rayed portions, and the pectoral fins are large and fannon. The color and pattern vary, although they are mainly mottled with various shades and are protectively camouflaged by their mottled pattern; freshwater sculpin are among the most difficult North American fish to identify because of their indistinct mottling. Freshwater sculpin are tiny, ranging from 2 to 7 inches, whereas saltwater sculpin are slightly larger; most species of sculpin are less than 1 foot long. Sculpin are primarily carnivorous, clinging to the bottom and pouncing on small invertebrates, crustaceans, and mollusks for food.

Of the marine species, the cabezon, or great marbled sculpin *(Scorpaenichthys marmoratus)*, is the largest and best known, weighing up to 30 pounds. It is good table fare and is a coveted catch in California waters, taken on cut baits or with jigs. The staghorn sculpin *(Leptocottus armatus)* inhabits the same waters as does the cabezon and is sometimes caught accidentally by anglers and used for bait. The grunt sculpin *(Rhamphocottus richardsonii)* is so called because of the noises it makes when removed from the water. It is featured in aquariums.

Of the freshwater species, the banded sculpin *(Cottus carolinae)* and the mottled sculpin *(C. bairdi)* often inhabit the cold rapids of streams. The prickly sculpin *(C. asper)* is so called because of the many prickles on its body, and it can reach a foot in length. The deep-water sculpin *(Myoxocephalus thompsoni)* of the Great Lakes is threatened.

Scud (greatly enlarged)

SCUP *Stenotomus chrysops*.
Other names—porgy.

A member of the Sparidae family of porgies, which includes about 112 species, the scup is most commonly known as "porgy" and is a common angling catch along the eastern United States. It is a fine food fish that has had significant commercial interest. Primarily caught through trawling, it was overexploited and at low population levels throughout the 1990s.

Identification. Somewhat nondescript, the scup is rather dusky colored, being brownish and almost silvery, with fins that are mottled brown. It has a deep body, about the same depth all the way to the caudal peduncle, where it narrows abruptly. The fins are spiny. The caudal fin is lunate (crescent-shaped). The front teeth are incisor-form, and there are two rows of molars in the upper jaw.

Size/Age. Scup attain a maximum length of about 16 inches. The all-tackle world record is a 4-pound, 9-ounce Massachusetts fish. Ages up to 20 years have been reported.

Distribution. Scup are found in the western Atlantic from Nova Scotia to Florida but are rare south of North Carolina, occurring primarily in the Mid-Atlantic Bight from Cape Cod to Cape Hatteras. An introduction to Bermuda was unsuccessful.

Habitat/Behavior. A schooling species, scup are common in summer in inshore waters from Massachusetts to Virginia; in winter, they frequent offshore waters between Hudson Canyon and Cape Hatteras at depths ranging from 70 to 180 meters. Sexual maturity is essentially complete by age 3, when the fish $8^{1}/_{4}$ inches long; spawning occurs during summer months.

Food and feeding habits. The diet of scup consists of crabs, shrimp, worms, sand dollars, snails, and young squid. Although they sometimes eat small fish, scup usually browse and nibble over hard bottoms.

Angling. Sportfishing for scup mostly occurs when these fish are in inshore environs. They are a common catch of anglers on small boats and party boats, especially those fishing with bait on bottom. Because of their schooling tendencies, they can be a nuisance when larger fish are sought, usually causing boaters to change locations. Specific fishing for scup may entail the use of a chum pot to attract them. Two-hook bottom rigs (and occasionally small jigs) baited with shrimp, worms, clam pieces, or squid are effective.

See: Inshore Fishing; Porgies.

Scup

SEA ANCHOR

A sea anchor is a large megaphone- or parachute-shaped bag that is used in fishing applications to slow down a drifting or trolling boat. Sea anchors, also known as drogues, have long been used by sailboaters and cruisers, can be found in very large sizes, and have varying uses for controlling a boat's action in heavy seas; smaller sea anchors have been adopted by big-water, big-boat trollers who need to reduce speed, either in flat, calm conditions or in a stiff tailwind, and by anglers who are drifting while casting or bottom bouncing but need some way to decrease or neutralize the speed of their drift in order to fish effectively.

The need for using a sea anchor arises when a boat is moving so fast that a lure or bait cannot be presented properly, or spends almost no time in the strike zone. It is also important on windy days when you have to fish a particular place where the fish are very finicky about presentation, or are tightly grouped. An alternative to using sea anchors is to set out one or two bottom anchors so that the boat does not move, but often this does not fill the bill for the circumstances.

Sea anchors usually are made of ripstop nylon and open up like a huge funnel or rounded bag when pulled through the water. Their wide-mouth opening can be restricted to lessen drag according to conditions, so that a lesser amount of water passes through the narrow end.

Many anglers attach sea anchors to the gunwales amidship, especially for drifting in open water and in situations where two or three anglers are casting downwind across an area (often a flat). Guides who

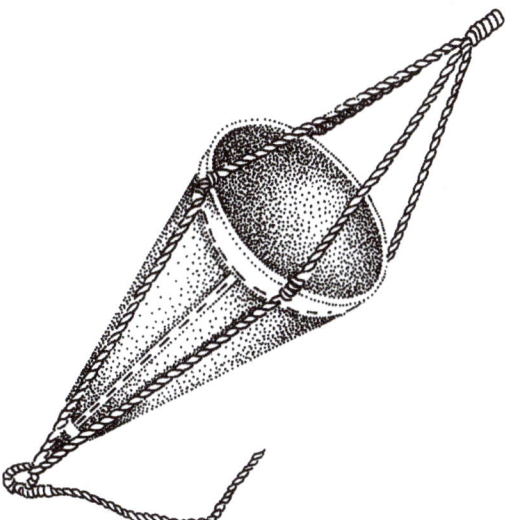
A sea anchor works by catching water in its wide end and funneling it through a narrow end, which slows momentum.

use flat-bottomed boats and who ordinarily pole may, on windy days, employ a sea anchor amidship on the windward side of the boat, and use their pushpole to help maintain position parallel and within casting distance of a shoreline, weedline, or grassbed. This is commonly used in redfishing on grassy windblown flats.

Similarly, a walleye angler might use a sea anchor in conjunction with an electric motor or small outboard motor to maintain position while drifting along a flat or around a point. The sea anchor slows the boat, and the motor does the maneuvering without the boat being blown around as it might otherwise if just relying on motor power.

Sea anchors are often tied amidship, but may be tied to the bow if conditions warrant. For forward trolling, a sea anchor can be tied to the bow, with just enough rope to reach midship; tie a tail rope to the funnel end so that when you need to retrieve the bag, you can pull on the tail to collapse it. For slow backtrolling *(see)* with the wind you can tie a sea anchor to the bow so that it extends in front of the boat facing the bow, and then, if necessary, supplement control with a transom-mounted electric motor or outboard motor. If you backtroll into a wind, the bow-tied sea anchor helps reduce splashing by keeping the bow angle lower. With boats that are easily pushed around by the bow in a wind (high-riding aluminum boats, for example), a bow-tied sea anchor negates the sideways wind push and makes the bow a pivotal point for very effective boat control.

Sometimes one anchor will slow a boat adequately, but when trolled, it may cause the boat to veer to the side. Port and starboard sea anchors, both fixed to the bow, may be necessary, perhaps decreasing the size of the opening on each to get the proper speed. Some anglers use two sea anchors when drifting, one positioned close to the bow, the other close to the stern. Others keep two sea anchors of different size on hand, a small one for use on nearly calm days and a large one for wind.

Sea anchors need to be tied to sturdy cleats or to bow eye bolts. Sometimes it has to be off the bow eye bolt and not a gunwale cleat for best results. These devices exert a lot of pull, especially in the larger sizes, so they must be tied to the sturdiest points. Be leery of tying them to a handrail or guardrail or around rod holders. And be prepared to bring one in quickly if necessary should some problem arise; a line tied to the tail and to the boat will make it easy to collapse the bag. Lastly, try to position them so as not to interfere with your fishing.

See: Drifting.

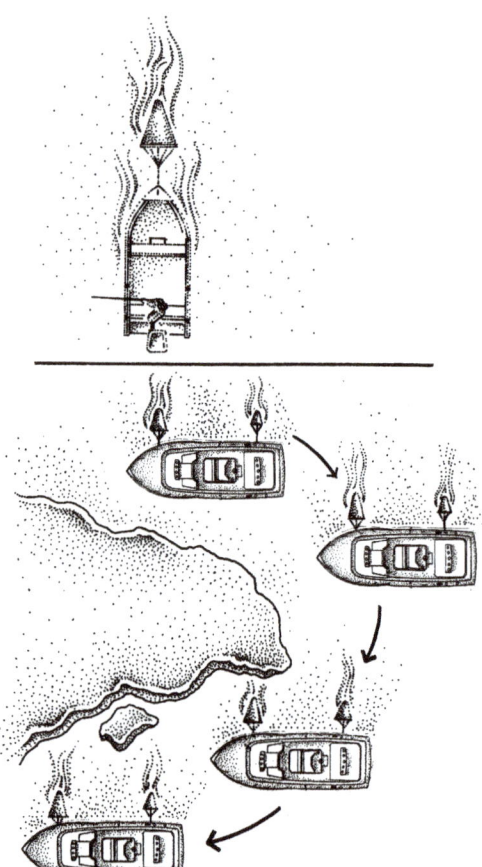

When trolling downwind in open water, you can slow boat movement by heading backward and dragging a sea anchor off the bow (top). For two people to effectively drift and slowly fish around an object, such as a point (bottom), hang two sea anchors off the starboard side of the boat, and use an electric motor to position the boat around the point.

SEA BASS

(1) Members of the Serranidae family of fish, which includes over 400 species of widely varying physiques, habitats, and natures. Many are important gamefish and food fish. They include such diverse and large-growing species as striped bass *(see: bass, striped)*, jewfish *(see)*, giant sea bass *(see: sea bass, giant)*, barramundi *(see)*, and Nile perch *(see: perch, Nile)*, as well as kelp bass *(see: bass, kelp)*, black sea bass *(see: sea bass, black)*, white perch *(see: perch, white)*, and many different grouper *(see)*.

(2) A spelling variation of "seabass," which are actually members of other fish families *(see: seabass, blackfin; seabass, Japanese; seabass, white)*.

SEA BASS, BLACK *Centropristis striata.*
Other names—blackfish, sea bass, black bass, black will, black seabass, rockbass, common sea bass, humpback (large males), pin bass (small specimens); Spanish: *serrano estriado*.

Black sea bass are members of the Serranidae family and popular sportfish in the western Atlantic along the coast of North America. Their firm, white flesh makes excellent eating, especially if they are iced after capture and properly cared for, as their flesh deteriorates rapidly when warm. Anglers must handle this fish with caution, as the dorsal fin has stiff, sharp spines that can puncture human skin. These stand straight up when the black sea bass is alive, but even when the fish is dead and the spines lie flat on the back, they can be dangerous.

Identification. The black sea bass has a relatively stout body that is three times as long (excluding the tail) as it is deep. It also has a high back, a flat-topped head, a slightly pointed snout, and a sharp spine near the apex of each gill cover. Both dorsal fins are joined into one continuous dorsal fin, and the tail is rounded; the elongated top ray of the tail that sticks out past the rest of the tail, particularly pronounced in larger specimens, is the most distinguishing feature of this fish. Because of the high back, which creates a noticeable rise just behind their heads, some large male black sea bass are called "humpbacks."

Like many rock-bottom dwellers, the body color of the black sea bass is variable, ranging from black to gray or brownish gray. The dorsal fins are marked by several slanting, white spots arranged into lengthwise lines or a more random pattern; the spots in rows make the dorsal fins appear to be striped a light color. There also appear to be thin stripes on the sides, with wide vertical bands overlapping the stripes on some fish, and a large dark spot on the last dorsal spine. The upper and lower edges of the tail are white, as are the outer edges of the dorsal and anal fins. Smaller fish may lack the white edge on the tail and anal fins.

Males differ from this coloration, having a completely bluish black body, except for some white areas on the head and the edges of fins. Their tail lobes are prolonged, although on smaller fish they may be very short.

Size. Big sea bass range from 3 to 8 pounds, and the average fish weighs between 1 and 3 pounds; the all-tackle world record is a 9-pound, 8-ounce fish. They can grow to 2 feet long, averaging 6 to 18 inches. They are known to live for 10 years, but in rare cases they may live longer. Females rarely live beyond 8 years of age, whereas males may live up to 15 years.

Distribution. Found in the western North Atlantic Ocean along the United States, the black sea bass ranges as far north as Maine and south to northern Florida, as well as into the Gulf of Mexico. It is most common between Cape Cod, Massachusetts, and Cape Hatteras, North Carolina. It also occurs in southern Florida during cold winters.

Black sea bass consist of two stocks, one north and the other south of Cape Hatteras, North Carolina. The northern group winters along the 55-fathom depth contour off Virginia and Maryland, then migrates north and west into the major coastal bays.

Habitat. The black sea bass is a bottom-dwelling species found around wrecks, reefs, piers, jetties, and breakwaters, and over beds of shells, coral, and rock. Small fish are found in shallow and quiet waters near the shore, such as in bays, whereas most larger fish prefer offshore reefs, in water ranging from roughly 10 feet deep to several hundred feet deep. Black sea bass prefer relatively cool waters, living offshore in winter and moving inshore in spring.

Life history. Black sea bass are hermaphrodites; most begin their lives as females and later become males. Large fish are males, and females reach reproductive ability in their second year. Transformation from female to male gener-

Black Sea Bass

ally occurs between ages 2 and 5. Their protracted spawning season extends from February through May in the southern range and from June through October in their northern range. Spawning begins in March off North Carolina and occurs progressively later farther north.

Food and feeding habits. Clams, shrimp, worms, crabs, and small fish constitute the diet of the omnivorous black sea bass, and most anglers offer them some form of bait. Many bass that are caught in deep water and quickly brought to the surface will regurgitate all or part of their stomach contents, which may attract more fish.

Angling. When hooked on light tackle, the black sea bass fights hard all the way to the surface. The action is fast and vigorous, and in spite of its generally small size, this species is very much a gamefish. The best angling is in depths of 6 to 20 fathoms from May through June and from November through December, especially around ledges and rocky heads, although these fish are landed year-round. Some are caught by anglers on docks, piers, or the shore, but most are taken by anglers bottom fishing with baits or by anglers jigging with 2- to 4-ounce metal jigs from anchored or drifting boats. Fishing over wrecks often produces large specimens. Finding the structure that produces the large fish is the real trick, as the better places are usually a well-guarded secret, especially among the party boats. Preferred baits includes fish pieces, shrimp, squid, and assorted crabs, worms, and clams, especially skimmer clams.

Black sea bass have a fairly good-sized mouth and can take a relatively large offering. Where bigger sea bass are likely, a large piece of clam or squid or a small whole fish might be used for bait, although smaller baits are used inshore. It is practical to use a two-hook rig, leaving the lower hook on the bottom and the upper one 2 to 3 feet off the bottom. Sea bass can be nibblers and bait stealers, so it pays to keep an eye on your bait.

Appropriate sinkers vary with the conditions. Bank sinkers are popular, ranging from perhaps 3 ounces in shallower water to 8 ounces in deep water where current is swift. Medium-action boat rods and 15-pound line are the tackle used to catch these spirited fighters. They are predominantly caught in the spring and summer.

SEABASS, BLACKFIN *Lateolabrax latus*.
Other names—Japanese: *hira-suzuki*.

Similar in shape to the striped bass, the blackfin seabass is highly regarded as both a food fish and a gamefish.

Identification. The blackfin seabass has a large mouth, a lower jaw that projects beyond the upper jaw, and a slightly forked tail. It has an elongate, compressed, silvery body, that is deeper, more stocky, and more silvery than that of the Japanese

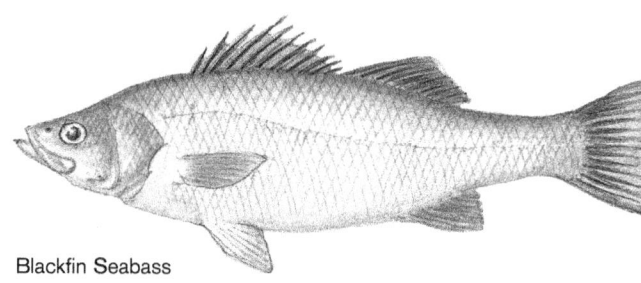

Blackfin Seabass

seabass (see: seabass, Japanese). Other elements that distinguish the two are the row of scales on the lower jaw of the blackfin seabass; the blackfin seabass also has 12 dorsal fin spines, 15 to 16 soft rays, and 3 anal fin spines with 9 to 10 soft rays; the Japanese seabass has 12 to 15 dorsal fin spines, 12 to 14 soft rays, and 3 anal fin spines with 7 to 9 soft rays. The eyes of the blackfin seabass seem slightly larger than those of the Japanese seabass, possibly due to its deeper body. Unlike the Japanese seabass, the blackfin seabass rarely has any spots.

Size. The blackfin seabass grows to 40 inches and 23 pounds. The all-tackle world record is an 18-pound, 4-ounce fish taken off of Wakayama, Japan, in 1990.

Distribution. This species occurs in the northeastern Pacific Ocean from the Shizuoka and Chiba Prefecture in central Japan to the Nagasaki Prefecture and the East China Sea.

Habitat. Blackfin seabass inhabit shallow rocky areas. They are often caught in the vicinity of shallow rocks and reefs, and large individuals are sometimes caught in the brackish waters of river mouths.

Angling. In the southern waters of Japan, the blackfin seabass is caught more often than its close relative, the Japanese seabass (*L. japonicus*). Anglers land this fish by surf casting with flashy, minnow-shaped artificial lures or metal jigs; by using small live baits; and by fly fishing with streamers.

SEA BASS, GIANT *Stereolepis gigas*.
Other names—California black sea bass, California jewfish, giant bass, black, black sea bass; French: *bar gigantesque*; Japanese: *kokuchi-ishinagi, ishinagi-zoku*; Spanish: *lubina gigante*.

The giant sea bass, a member of the Serranidae family, is not only a formidable fish in size, it is also renowned for its lengthy life span. Mostly an eastern Pacific gamefish, specimens exceeding 500 pounds have been caught.

Identification. The body of the giant sea bass is elongate and has dorsal spines that fit into a groove on the back. Greenish brown or black, the giant sea bass has black or transparent fins, with the exception of the ventral fins, which appear lighter because of a white membrane between the black spines. There is usually a white patch on the throat and underneath the tail, and the membranes between the rays are also light. Young fish are mottled with prominent dark spots and a few pale-yellow blotches on a mostly brick-red body; these markings are periodically seen on fish up to and exceeding 25 pounds.

The first dorsal fin is separated from the second by a single notch; the first is extremely low and has 11 spines, whereas the second is higher and has 10 soft rays. The presence of more spines on the first dorsal fin than soft rays on the second distinguishes the giant sea bass from similar related species such as the jewfish *(Epinephelus itajara; see: jewfish)*, with which it has been confused in the past.

Size/Age. The giant sea bass reaches maturity by the age of 11 or 12 and weighs roughly 50 pounds, although it has been known to weigh more than 600 pounds and measure more than 7 feet in length. The all-tackle world record is 563 pounds, 8 ounces; the most common catch is in the 100- to 200-pound range, and much smaller fish are seldom caught. Large specimens are usually found in water deeper than 100 feet. Some of the largest giant sea bass are believed to be 75 years or older; a 434-pound fish was estimated by ichthyologists at between 72 and 75 years of age. The ovaries of a 320-pound female fish were estimated to contain 60 million eggs.

Distribution. Giant sea bass occur in tropical and subtropical inshore waters of the northeast Pacific off the California and Mexico coasts, specifically from the Gulf of California southward to Humboldt Bay and Guadalupe Island. They have also been found off the Asiatic Pacific coast. In California waters these fish have been in short supply but were rebounding in the 1990s due to a moratorium on keeping them.

Habitat. Inhabiting inshore waters, giant sea bass are bottom-dwelling fish, preferring hard, rocky bottoms around kelp beds. The young occur in depths of about 6 to 15 fathoms, whereas larger specimens usually inhabit depths of 15 to 25 fathoms.

Food and feeding habits. The giant sea bass diet includes crustaceans and a wide variety of fish. Anchovies and croaker are a prominent food source off California, mackerel, sheepshead, whitefish, sand bass, and several types of crabs are also favored. Although these bulky fish appear to be slow and cumbersome, they are reputedly capable of outswimming and catching a bonito in a short chase.

Angling. Fishing methods include live- or dead-bait fishing from an anchored or drifting boat with cut baits and such large natural baits as mullet and mackerel. Fishing is best in the 10- to 25-fathom range in summer, over rocky bottoms and around kelp beds.

Giant sea bass do not instinctively run for cover when they are caught, and they have no teeth to cut the line, so catching them is primarily a matter of having the tackle to match the fish and being able to outlast the fish. Encountering larger specimens, which often happens while using lighter tackle for calico bass or halibut, requires staying on top of

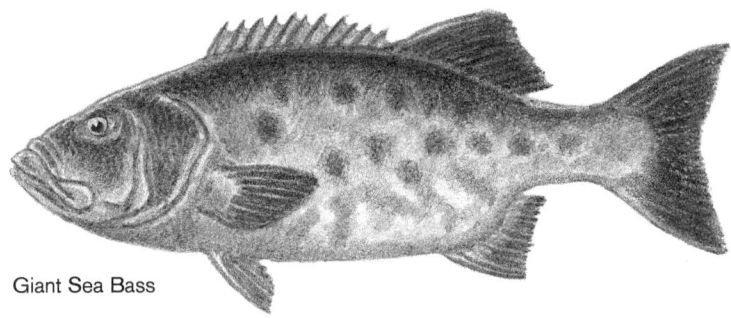
Giant Sea Bass

the fish to minimize the chance of the line running into an obstruction, and applying enough constant pumping pressure to pull the fish away from the bottom. Real giant specimens are seldom landed by anglers, and deeply caught species will need to have their swim bladder deflated *(see: releasing fish)* before being returned to the bottom.

SEABASS, JAPANESE *Lateolabrax japonicus.*
Other names—sea perch; Japanese: *suzuki.*

Apparently more wide ranging than its very close "cousin" the blackfin seabass *(see: seabass, blackfin)*, the Japanese seabass is a less frequent catch in southern Japan waters but is a highly rated gamefish and valued as table fare, making it also the object of commercial fishermen.

Identification. The Japanese seabass has an elongate and compressed body, resembling the weakfish or spotted seatrout in shape. It has a large mouth, a lower jaw that projects beyond the upper jaw, and a slightly forked tail. Its body is less deep and stocky than that of the blackfin seabass. Other elements that distinguish the two species are the fin spines and rays. The Japanese seabass has 12 to 15 dorsal fin spines, 12 to 14 soft rays, and 3 anal fin spines with 7 to 9 soft rays; the blackfin seabass has 12 dorsal fin spines, 15 to 16 soft rays, and 3 anal fin spines with 9 to 10 soft rays. Young Japanese seabass have small black spots on the back and dorsal fin, which usually disappear as the fish grows, although some adults retain small spots and others may have large spots. The eyes of the Japanese seabass seem slightly higher on its head than those on the blackfin seabass, possibly because its body is not as deep. The Japanese seabass is also darker on its

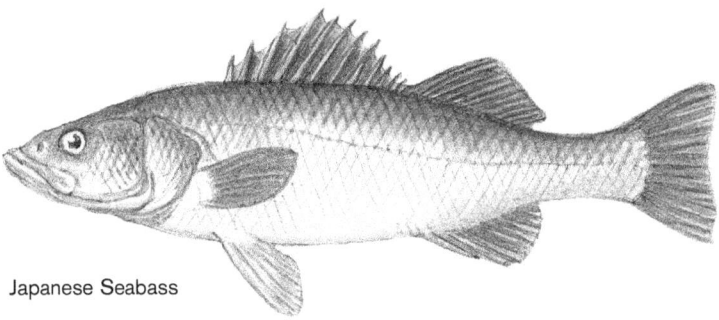
Japanese Seabass

back than the more silvery blackfin seabass.

Size. The Japanese seabass grows to 40 inches and 23 pounds. The all-tackle world record is a 19-pound, 2-ounce fish taken off of Shizuoka, Japan, in 1988.

Distribution. This species occurs in the northeastern Pacific Ocean from Japan south to Taiwan and the East and South China Seas.

Habitat. Japanese seabass inhabit river mouths, shallow inshore bays, surf, moving water of inshore rocky reefs, and deeper waters. The young may ascend rivers in summer.

Spawning behavior. Japanese seabass spawn from November through January on deep rocky reefs, then move shallow to feed.

Food. The diet of adult Japanese seabass consists of anchovies, sardines, and other small fish, plus crustaceans and shrimp.

Angling. Anglers land Japanese seabass by baitfishing with small fish or crustaceans; slow trolling; jigging; and casting with minnow-type plugs, flashy jigs, or spoons at any level from the surface to the bottom. The best fishing is said to be at night and at dawn near the surface. The largest fish are caught in fall and winter.

SEABASS, WHITE *Atractoscion nobilis* (also *Cynoscion nobilis*).
Other names—Catalina salmon, white corvina, corvina blanca, white weakfish, weakfish, king croaker; French: *acoupa blanc;* Spanish: *corvinata bronzeada*.

A member of the Sciaenidae family, the white seabass belongs to the grouping of weakfish or corvina and is not a true bass or sea bass. The name "weakfish" refers to the tender, easily torn mouth tissue characteristic of these fish, and not their fighting ability. "Seabass" is a misnomer for the *Atractoscion* species, not related to bass.

The white seabass is a fish that has been much sought after commercially and by anglers. Its flesh is white and tender and highly valued, but it spoils quickly without proper care. White seabass stocks have struggled due to overfishing by commercial gillnets, which are now illegal in California for this species. Attempts have been made to assist white seabass stocks through hatchery means and by raising newly hatched fish in enclosed marine grow-out facilities until they are large enough to be released; the results have been encouraging.

Identification. The body of the white seabass is elongate and somewhat compressed. There is a characteristic raised ridge along the middle of the belly between the vent and the base of the pelvic fins. The head is pointed and slightly flattened. The mouth is large, with a row of small teeth in the roof and a projecting lower jaw. The first dorsal fin has nine spines and the second two spines and 20 soft rays. The anal fin has two spines and 10 soft rays. There are no barbels on the chin. Its coloring is bluish to gray above, with dark speckling, and becomes silver below. Juveniles have several dark vertical bars; with a sleek profile, young fish are often mistaken for sea trout, which can be a problem where size restrictions are in effect.

The white seabass can be distinguished from its Atlantic relatives, the weakfish *(see)* and the spotted seatrout *(see: seatrout, spotted),* by its lack of canine teeth. It is most closely related to the California corbina *(see: corbina, California),* but it is the only California croaker to exceed 20 pounds. It is most easily separated from other croaker by the presence of a ridge running the length of the belly.

Size/Age. The average weight of a 28-inch fish is $7^1/_2$ pounds. The all-tackle record is 83 pounds, 3 ounces, which was established in 1953 at San Felipe, Mexico. White seabass generally live for five years. In Southern California they are commonly caught in late fall and early winter, and weigh between 5 and 15 pounds. Larger fish, including some up to 60 or more pounds, are landed from midwinter through May. A 30-pounder is a good catch.

Distribution. White seabass inhabit the eastern Pacific, mainly between San Francisco, California, and Baja California, Mexico, and in the northern Gulf of California. They are found as far north as southern Alaska and as far south as Chile.

Habitat. Preferring deep, rocky environments, white seabass are usually hold near kelp beds in depths of 12 to 25 fathoms. They are sometimes found in shallow surf or deeper waters. Juveniles inhabit shallow nearshore areas, bays, and estuaries.

Life history. Spawning occurs in spring and summer. White seabass are schooling fish and are present in California waters all year long. They are especially popular in the spring, and also in the winter when they converge on spawning squid.

Food and feeding habits. White seabass feed on anchovies, pilchards, herring, and other fish, as well as on crustaceans and squid.

Angling. White seabass are fished primarily with live baits in relatively shallow water, but they will also take a fast-trolled spoon, an artificial squid, or a bone jig. Live natural baits appear to be the best offering, but large anchovies and medium-size sardines are also good. At times, large white seabass will strike only large, live Pacific mackerel.

Live and dead squid are the primary natural baits in the winter off Southern California, when the squid are abundant and spawning. Fished on

White Seabass

a jig or a baited hook with a sliding egg sinker, the squid is freespooled to the bottom, often being pecked by other fish on the way, then worked a few feet off the bottom by repeated lifting and dropping movements. Tackle with 25- to 30-pound line is used on party boats and where there is a lot of kelp; 10- to 15-pound gear can be used on smaller boats.

SEABREAM
See: Bream, Sea.

SEA GRANT
Sea Grant, formally known as the National Sea Grant College Program, is a network of 29 university-based programs in coastal and Great Lakes States involving more than 300 institutions nationwide in research, education, and transfer of technology regarding coastal, marine, and Great Lakes issues. Through a cost-sharing relationship with universities, Sea Grant plays a vital national role in estuarine research, science-based fisheries management, marine education, coastal engineering, resource policy analysis, pollution remediation, seafood safety, and marine engineering. Focal points of Sea Grant leadership are research expertise in aquaculture and marine biotechnology, and research in areas promising new products, job creation, economic growth, and improved international competitiveness.

The National Sea Grant College Program has succeeded despite little public fanfare or significant taxpayer dollars. Few citizens, and few recreational anglers, have heard of Sea Grant, but the 100 million Americans living within 100 miles of a coastal waterway—the Great Lakes, the Atlantic and Pacific Oceans, and the Gulf of Mexico—have likely benefited from its works and, at the very least, educational programs.

Sea Grant provides critical, objective information leading to the intelligent use, conservation, and management of coastal and marine resources through problem- and issue-oriented basic research. Its scientific research is peer-reviewed with a unique value-added component that also enables Sea Grant to educate and transfer technology to citizens. By addressing its research into areas that will make a difference in large sectors of society, such as coastal communities, Sea Grant is a model for inventive and flexible approaches to problem solving.

The real-world problem-solving applications of Sea Grant research have built bridges between academic scientists and the needs of citizens, and have produced, among many things, improved hurricane-resistance construction designs, new medical products produced from crab shell wastes, desalination of sea water for irrigation and drinking water, oil spill cleanup procedures, and a better understanding of the science of fisheries resources to ensure that they will be available for the future.

The Program
Congress established the National Sea Grant College Program in 1966 to hasten the development, use, and conservation of the nation's marine and Great Lakes resources. The legislation called for a network of Sea Grant colleges that would conduct education, training, and research in all fields of marine study, and directed that grants and contracts would go to "suitable public and private institutions of higher education, institutes, laboratories, and public or private agencies which are engaged in, or concerned with, activities in the various fields related to the development of marine resources."

The Secretary of Commerce has designated 29 Sea Grant college programs in coastal and Great Lakes states and Puerto Rico. These programs are the heart of a nationwide network of over 300 participating institutions and over 3,000 scientists, engineers, educators, students, and outreach specialists. This network has provided a powerful national capability in marine resource research and public outreach.

Some notable examples of Sea Grant achievement include leading the development of hybrid striped bass aquaculture, which has grown from a university demonstration project to a valuable fish-farming industry; developing new strains of salmon that grow three times faster than wild stocks; conducting research on nutrient runoffs from agriculture into bays that has led four states to adopt management practices resulting in improved water quality; improving marine safety and lifesaving practices, from survival training for the fishing industry to major advances in the revival of coldwater drowning victims; and supporting the training of thousands of students in oceanography and marine biology. It also organized the first systematic effort in the United States to discover and develop new drugs from marine organisms; this biotechnology effort resulted in the discovery of more than 1,000 compounds—including at least 50 with significant potential for treating inflammatory diseases like arthritis and asthma—and the awarding of numerous patents.

Although many Sea Grant programs are oriented toward general resource and commercial issues, some are focused on issues of direct concern to consumers and to recreational anglers. The 29 Sea Grant programs have extensive educational materials, especially relating to environmental matters, seafood, and recreation, that are available to the public; and some of their work has been incorporated into various sections of this encyclopedia.

Addressing Resource Issues of Public Concern
Sea Grant plays a unique and important role in advancing the nation's interest in marine resources. Together with the Office of Naval Research (ONR) and the National Science Foundation (NSF), Sea

Grant provides the only sustained federal contact and funding source for universities with marine research capabilities. Moreover, Sea Grant provides the major source of research support for marine-related subjects that fall outside biological, physical, and chemical oceanography, and marine geology and geophysics. These include, for example, coastal and ocean engineering, fisheries science, and marine-related social sciences and law. Where NSF and ONR have remained steadfast in their support of basic oceanographic research, Sea Grant has supported scientific research to address marine and coastal resource issues of more immediate public concern. To ensure that programs respond to local as well as national concerns, the law requires that one-third of the program funds come from state or local governments, industry, or other sources. This has provided outstanding leverage to limited federal funds.

Sea Grant is also the only National Oceanic and Atmospheric Administration (NOAA) marine program with sustained, legislatively mandated responsibility for linking NOAA with university researchers and educators. The Marine Advisory Service (MAS) provides a key link between NOAA programs and residents in coastal and Great Lakes states and in Puerto Rico. Many Sea Grant–supported research projects are pursued in collaboration with NOAA specialists associated with the Office of Coastal Resources Management, the Coastal Ocean Program, the National Marine Fisheries Service, and the National Weather Service; and these projects contribute to a wide range of NOAA responsibilities, including fisheries and coastal management, aquaculture development, coastal water quality, habitat protection and restoration, marine sanctuaries and estuarine reserves management, and protection of life and property from natural hazards. Sea Grant is strengthened to the extent that it draws on the extensive technological and scientific resources available in NOAA. These include its forecasting and remote sensing capabilities; sophisticated environmental and resource information databases; and access to NOAA ships, laboratories, and computing capabilities.

Planning for the Future

The strategic planning framework for Sea Grant assumes the persistence of various trends. One of the most important of these is continued population growth along coastal areas; 127 million people are expected to live in coastal areas by 2010, and this population growth will place increased demands on the coastal environment and its resources as well as engender conflicts over use and access. The cumulative effect is to disrupt the natural processes of coastal ecosystems and to threaten the ecological, aesthetic, and economic values that attract people to the coast. Contaminated waters, saltwater intrusions, erosion, habitat and wetlands losses, fishery declines, and shellfish bed closures are indicative of these pressures and are not likely to diminish.

Public support for environmental protection is widespread but is moderated by a belief that it is possible to use natural resources while, at the same time, minimizing environmental destruction and preserving resources for future generations. These attitudes foster expectations for a balanced approach toward resource use and conservation and for expanded public access to coastal resources. At the same time, technological innovations continue to shape events, although the development and use of these technologies, and understanding their social, economic, and political implications, will continue to be a challenge.

Despite general public support, political support for ocean and coastal programs is severely limited by fiscal and political conditions. Prospects are limited for major capital investments and for increased funding of ocean programs, so collaborative approaches become necessary. Although the variety of issues facing Sea Grant far exceeds available resources, Sea Grant's intent is to respond to those conditions likely to persist and to identify areas where it can have greatest impact.

SEAGRASS

An aquatic plant of the marine environment, primarily of the intertidal zone. Seagrasses are a major component of coastal regions and may grow to depths of 20 feet, but they are mostly associated with the shallows of flats and estuaries. Seagrasses provide life for a wide variety of organisms and help to stabilize the substrate. Some prominent sportfish use seagrasses as a nursery, and others frequent seagrasses during certain tidal stages to feed.

Environments that contain seagrass are vulnerable to habitat destruction, which may happen via anchors being dragged through the grass and motorboats run through the shallows. Damaged seagrass does not grow back readily.
See: Aquatic Plants.

SEAMOUNT

A mountain rising 1,000 meters or more from the sea floor with limited extent across the summit. Seamounts are usually fairly isolated but may exist in groups or chains; they are seldom very steep on the sides, being more elliptical in shape. The vicinity of seamounts may provide fishing opportunity, particularly for big-game species; the presence of currents and the upwelling of water in the vicinity of this structure may enhance feeding opportunities and cause predator fish to frequent that area.

SEA ROBIN

Sea robins are mostly tropical and subtropical

fish of the Triglidae family, characterized by split pectoral fins that consist of stiff separate rays on the lower half and broad, soft, winglike rays on the upper half. The upper rays are not as large as in the similar-looking flying gurnard *(see: gurnard, flying)* but are used for the same purpose—swimming; the lower rays are used to find food by sifting through debris and turning over rocks. Sea robins also use their pelvic and pectoral fins to "walk" across the bottom as they search for fish, shrimp, squid, clams, and crabs to satisfy their insatiable appetites. They are often brightly colored, are capable of making loud noises by vibrating muscles attached to the air bladder, and inhabit moderately deep waters. At least 19 species occur in the Atlantic and a few in the Pacific off the coasts of the United States and Canada; other species exist off the coasts of Europe, Africa, and in the western Pacific south of Japan. These fish spawn throughout the summer, their eggs float on the surface, and the young grow quickly during the first year.

One of the more well-known fish of this group is the northern sea robin *(Prionotus carolinus)*, which occurs from Nova Scotia to northern South America but is uncommon north of Massachusetts. It averages 12 inches in length and may reach a length of 18 inches. A black, mottled fish with an olive brown or gray background, the northern sea robin has a large head that is covered with bony plates and spines and has a distinct black chin. It is a bottom-dweller, moving close to shore during the summer and to deeper water in winter. Other Atlantic species are the striped sea robin *(P. evolans)*, which is distinguished by a few dark bands on its sides, and the leopard sea robin *(P. scitulus)*, an almost foot-long species with dark blotches, common in the Gulf of Mexico and the southern Atlantic.

Sea robins are a delicacy in some areas and are occasionally caught by anglers in particular seasons and localities, although they are more often thought of as bait stealers and oddities.

Northern Sea Robin

SEA-RUN

Another term for anadromous *(see)*, referring to fish that move from the sea to freshwater to spawn.

SEASICKNESS

Seasickness is a form of motion disorder due to sensory confusion. It results from a sensory mismatch in the brain in which the vestibular system of the inner ear sends messages about body position and movement that contradict information relayed by the eyes. Inside the cabin of a rocking boat, for example, the inner ear detects changes in body position as it bobs with the movement of the boat. But since the cabin moves with the passenger, the eyes register a relatively stable scene. The brain is confused by the information it receives, and this causes dizziness, blurred vision, nausea, and other symptoms. It happens to many people and can afflict anyone as a normal consequence of putting the body into unnatural motion.

Seasickness usually does not occur in freshwater except on the largest bodies of water, and then chiefly when waves cause a lot of boat rocking. For this reason, many people who have boating experience in freshwater do not realize that they are susceptible to this disorder until they venture out into the more rollicking surface of the sea (perhaps that is why it is not called "water sickness"). In any case, many people experience seasickness for the first time, more or less as a surprise, when the symptoms start occurring while they are out on a boat in saltwater—and when it is too late to take any drugs to ward off the problem. If you get sick, don't expect the boat to turn around and return to the dock. Deal with it as best you can, because you will get better.

Adapting. One school of thought in the treatment of seasickness is similar to the adage about treating the common cold: An untreated cold will last about seven days, and a treated cold will go away in about a week.

Over time, most people adapt to the motion that makes them sick. Once the brain determines that the confused sensory signals are the "norm," it shuts down the nausea, cold sweats, drowsiness, and other symptoms. Unfortunately, this does not happen quickly enough for many people. For some, it is possible to ease symptoms naturally, especially if they act fast at the onset of symptoms.

The more you move around, the sooner you become accustomed to the motion of the boat. Be sure you have a broad view of the horizon, and try to anticipate the vessel's motions. Do not lie down, even though it may allow you to feel better temporarily. Don't do anything that requires a close visual focus. It may help to join the captain near the helm, so you can focus attention on the boat's course; this corresponds to the fact that automobile drivers almost never get car sick.

Treatment. Prescription and over-the-counter drugs are the most common treatments for seasickness, but the wide variety available indicates that there is still no ideal solution, and they must be taken in advance of a boat trip. For the most part, these treat symptoms, not causes. On an extended voyage, they can help keep symptoms under control while you adapt to your new surroundings or get your "sea legs."

How a specific drug will affect anyone is unpredictable. What works for one person may not work for another. The only way to know for sure is to try it after consulting with a physician.

If you know that you're prone to seasickness, you might first try a nonprescription drug like Marezine, Dramamine, or Bonine. Marezine may be more desirable because it does not cause drowsiness, but this side effect varies among users of all of these drugs. If nonprescription drugs aren't effective, a doctor can prescribe prescription medication. Transderm-Scop is a prescription drug that works well for many people. It comes in the form of a small patch worn behind the ear, and it dispenses medication into the bloodstream over time.

Most drugs for seasickness must be taken 1 to 2 hours before the boat leaves the dock, so plan ahead. Like all drugs, seasickness preventives can have side effects. If you have a history of drug effects, consult your family doctor and, if possible, try the drug on land before you use it at sea.

Ginger root has recently received some attention as a seasickness preventive. Capsules of powdered ginger root have been reported to curb motion sickness better, in some cases, than over-the-counter anti-nausea drugs. Powdered ginger, available in health food stores, is effective because it works in the digestive tract where the problem is, rather than on the brain as drug remedies do.

The use of acupressure point treatment for seasickness has also become popular recently. This technique can be used after the onset of symptoms, which can be a real advantage over preventive drugs. Fabric wristbands are commercially available that operate by exerting carefully controlled pressure on an acupuncture point on both wrists (called the neikuan point). Some users have had good results, but many people are skeptical. As with almost all seasickness remedies, if it works for you, use it.

Diet. Some people believe that eating can lessen motion sickness symptoms. Your diet before going aboard and during a voyage can play a role. Eating lightly and wisely so that your digestive tract is relaxed is a good idea, because a light or calm stomach is not as easily disturbed as a stuffed one. Enjoy the food you like to eat, in moderation. There really is no scientific evidence that consuming specific foods prevents or causes seasickness. For some people, eating after they have gotten the queasy or dizzy symptoms of sickness, or even watching others eat, can induce nausea. Most importantly, do not consume alcoholic beverages; alcohol affects inner ear function and can make a seasick person feel worse.

Additional measures. Although seasickness is not a life-threatening condition, some of the symptoms (i.e., dizziness, drowsiness, loss of balance) have the potential to cause personal injury onboard a rolling, tossing vessel. If you do become seasick on a boat, tell the captain. You will probably be directed to the area of the vessel with the least motion and away from fumes.

If you feel as if you might vomit, get to the rail or head (toilet) before you do. The rail is a better spot, because the smells that accompany vomiting are reduced by boat movement and wind, and are less likely to cause others to feel nauseated. If you must lie down on a bunk (not recommended unless you have serious symptoms), make sure you leave a bucket or container handy. Most captains treat their seasick passengers with kindness, unless they lose their lunch in the wrong place. Lying down, however, stimulates the inner ear and will probably make you queasy all over again.

If you do vomit, you'll probably feel better afterward. This may be temporary or it may be the onset of recovery. To improve your chances of rebounding, once your stomach has quieted, move around and get your body in tune with the motion of the boat. Try to adapt. There's a good chance that you may still be able to enjoy the outing.

SEASON

(1) Fisheries agencies regulate fishing by recreational and commercial fishermen for certain fish or groups of fish, setting opening and closing dates and thus creating open and closed seasons. Seasons differ by species, locality, type of water, and other considerations.

See: Regulations.

(2) In a broader, fishing-parlance sense, season refers to the time when migratory species of fish are present, as in: Shad are in season in the Northeast during May.

SEA TROUT

A term for the anadromous or sea-run brown trout; this is not to be confused with purely saltwater seatrout.

See: Seatrout, Sand; Seatrout, Silver; Seatrout, Spotted; Trout, Brown.

SEATROUT, SAND *Cynoscion arenarius*.

Other names—white trout, sand weakfish, white weakfish.

A member of the Sciaenidae family (drum and croaker), the sand seatrout is a small and frequently caught fish. Found primarily in the Gulf of Mexico, it supports a minor commercial and sportfishing industry. It is closely related to the weakfish *(see)* of the Atlantic coast.

Identification. Its coloring is pale yellow on the back and silver to white below, without any real defined spots. Young sand seatrout have cloudy backs, sometimes forming crossbands. The inside of the mouth is yellow. There are 10 to 12 soft rays in the anal fin. It does not have any chin barbels and can be distinguished from the silver seatrout *(see: seatrout, silver)* by the presence of 10 anal rays, the silver seatrout having only 8 or 9.

Size. The average fish is 10 to 12 inches in length and rarely weighs more than a pound. The all-tackle record is a 2-pound, 3-ounce fish caught in Texas.

Distribution. The sand seatrout occurs mainly in the Gulf of Mexico from the west coast of Florida through Texas and into Mexico and as far south as the Gulf of Campeche. It also exists on the extreme southeastern Atlantic portion of Florida.

Habitat. The sand seatrout is predominantly an inshore fish found in bays and inlets. The young inhabit shallow bays, particularly in less saline areas. Adult fish move offshore in winter.

Spawning behavior. There is a prolonged spawning season inshore from spring through summer. Fish mature during their first or second year.

Food and feeding habits. The main food source is shrimp and small fish.

Angling. See: Seatrout, Spotted.

SEATROUT, SILVER *Cynoscion nothus.*
Other names—silver trout, silver weakfish.

A member of the Sciaenidae family (drum and croaker), the silver seatrout is smaller than other

Sand Seatrout

seatrout and generally similar in body shape. It is often misidentified with the spotted seatrout *(see: seatrout, spotted).*

Identification. Its coloring is pale straw or walnut on the back and silver to white below, without any real defined spots, although faint diagonal lines may be present on the upper body. There are 8 to 9 rays in the anal fin, which distinguish it from the sand seatrout *(see: seatrout, sand),* which has 10 rays. Silver seatrout have large eyes and a short snout, no chin barbel, and one to two prominent canine teeth usually present at the tip of the upper jaw. The lower half of the tail is longer than the upper half.

Size. Silver seatrout seldom weigh more than a half pound and are usually less than 10 inches long.

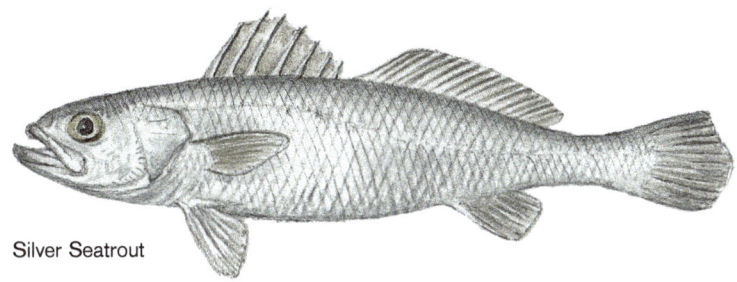
Silver Seatrout

Distribution. The silver seatrout occurs mainly throughout the Gulf of Mexico and is also in the Atlantic from southern Florida to Maryland.

Habitat. Predominantly an offshore fish, the silver seatrout is usually found over sandy and sandy mud bottoms. It migrates in bays in winter months.

Spawning behavior. There is a prolonged spawning season offshore during spring, summer, and fall.

Food and feeding habits. The main food sources are shrimp, small crustaceans, and small fish.

Angling. Owing to their size and the availability of other species, silver seatrout are seldom the deliberate target of anglers but may enter the inshore catch in winter, especially over sandy bottoms near beaches and inlets.

SEATROUT, SPOTTED *Cynoscion nebulosus.*
Other names—trout, speckled trout, speck, spotted weakfish, spotted squeteague, gator trout, salmon trout, winter trout, black trout; Spanish: *corvinata pintada.*

The spotted seatrout is a member of the Sciaenidae family of drum and croaker. It belongs to the genus *Cynoscion* (weakfish and seatrout), which is named for their tender mouths from which hooks tear easily. Considered a exceptionally valuable commercial fish, and an even more valuable sportfish to anglers, it is intensely pursued throughout its range, especially in the Gulf of Mexico. Most Gulf and Atlantic coast states have experienced a decline in spotted seatrout populations due to overfishing and exploitation, and fishing is strictly controlled; in some areas the cessation of gillnetting is leading to stock recoveries and providing optimism for the future.

The spotted seatrout is also known as an excellent table fish. Its flesh is fine and delicately flavored, but it spoils quickly and should be cleaned or stored on ice when possible after being caught. It usually appears on the menus of Southern restaurants as "trout" and can be substituted in recipes for seabass or redfish.

Identification. The spotted seatrout has an elongated body with a slightly more regular and even tail fin, with a black margin, than that of sand or silver seatrout *(see: seatrout, sand; seatrout, silver).* Its coloring is dark gray or green on the back, with

Seatrout, Spotted

Spotted Seatrout

sky-blue tinges shading to silvery and white below; the dorsal fins are gray green, and many round black spots speckle the back, tail, and dorsal fins. The lower jaw protrudes beyond the upper, which has one or two prominent canine teeth. The first dorsal fin has one spine and 24 to 27 soft rays, and the anal fin has two spines and 10 to 11 soft rays. There are eight or nine short, stubby gill rakers on the lower limb of the first gill arch. There are no barbels, and the interior of the mouth is orange. Very young fish have a broad, dark lateral band. The presence of spots on the fins can distinguish the spotted seatrout from other seatrout.

Size/Age. Mature spotted seatrout commonly range from 12 to 24 inches and average 4 pounds, although they can reach 48 inches and weigh as much as 16 pounds. The all-tackle record is 17 pounds, 7 ounces, caught at Fort Pierce, Florida, in 1995. They can live up to 10 years; three-year-old fish in Alabama are generally 12 to 13 inches long, and four-year-old fish are 14 to 15 inches long. Anglers commonly catch spotted seatrout weighing between 1 and 3 pounds; fish exceeding 7 pounds are considered large, and 10-pounders are definitely trophies.

Distribution. Spotted seatrout occur along Atlantic and Gulf of Mexico coasts. They are most abundant along the coasts of Georgia, Florida, Alabama, Mississippi, eastern Louisiana, and Texas but range as far westward as Tampico, Mexico. In late spring, they can range as far north as Long Island, New York, but are more prominent in the mid-Atlantic in the Carolinas, Virginia, and Maryland.

Habitat. An inshore bottom-dwelling species, the spotted seatrout is inhabits shallow bays, estuaries, bayous, canals, and Gulf Coast beaches. They prefer nearshore sandy and grassy bottoms, and may even frequent salt marshes and tidal pools with high salinity. They also live around oil rigs, usually within 10 miles of shore. Ideal water temperatures are between 58° and 81°F. Cold water is lethal to spotted seatrout, and although some move into slow-moving or still, deep waters in cold weather, the majority remain and may be killed by the low temperatures.

Life history/Behavior. It is believed that water temperature and salinity levels are more important to spawning than a specific location, because newly hatched spotted seatrout will not survive low salinity and low temperature conditions. Optimum spawning conditions for spotted seatrout exist when salinity is 20 to 34 parts per thousand and temperatures reach 70° to 90°F. Spawning occurs at night in coastal bays, sounds, and lagoons, near passes, and around barrier islands from March through November. Females may lay up to 10 million eggs. The eggs hatch within 20 hours and are transported to estuaries by winds and currents.

Spotted seatrout are schooling fish and are not considered migratory, as they rarely move more than 30 miles, although they do move into deeper waters or deep holes to avoid cold temperatures. Juveniles spend two to four years in shallow grassy areas and then tend to move into the nearshore passes and along beaches.

Food and feeding habits. Spotted seatrout are predatory, feeding primarily on shrimp and small fish. When shrimp are scarce, they often consume mullet, menhaden, and silversides. The larger specimens feed more heavily on fish. Juveniles feed on grass shrimp and copepods.

Angling. In Florida and on the Gulf Coast, especially in Louisiana and Texas, spotted seatrout are caught throughout the year, although the most productive time is during summer and early fall for overall numbers of fish, and in mid- to late fall and early spring for big fish.

Lures and live baits are both effective. Live shrimp and minnows are the most common live baits, but cut mullet, soft-shelled crabs, worms, and squid are among other effective natural baits. Popular lures include soft worms, bucktail jigs, grubs and jigs with assorted soft tails, surface and shallow-swimming plugs, spoons, and streamer flies. Light tackle is very appropriate for these fish, and many anglers use light baitcasting or light to medium-light spinning tackle. A lesser number employ flycasting gear.

In the gulf, especially throughout Texas, sight fishing for trout and redfish *(see: drum, red)* is extremely popular. Anglers use shallow-water craft to negotiate the abundant grassflats—many of which are just inches deep—where they visually locate and then cast to the fish with baits, lures, or flies. In other areas, fishing by wading or casting from boats is common, usually for unseen fish that are moving through an area or are located in feeding or resting places, such as grassbeds and shellfish beds or in deep holes or channels, where blind casting or even trolling can be effective.

Spotted seatrout are caught on a variety of offerings because they feed throughout the water column. Anchoring and casting lures or stillfishing with bait, drifting under the occasional control of an electric motor or pushpole and casting, and trolling slowly through holes and channels are all practiced in appropriate places and conditions. Among lures, however, jigs with soft tails—either curly, grub-shaped, or shrimp-shaped—are especially favored, and these are usually worked slowly via casting.

On occasion, these fish will actively feed on or close to the surface, and at such times surface plugs and popping bugs for fly rods will catch them. More productive, however, is fishing below the surface with shallow-swimming plugs that imitate small baitfish like finger mullet, or fishing along the bottom with slow-moving jigs. An extremely popular technique, particularly throughout the Gulf of Mexico, employs a popper and natural shrimp; the angler works the surface popper to attract the attention of a trout to the shrimp.

Bigger seatrout are not typically found with concentrations of smaller ones, and it is necessary to work deeper areas and, in general, to use larger baits and lures for bigger fish. The period before and after spawning is a good time for large spotted seatrout, and this is also when the coldest water is just coming or going. The coldest period of midwinter is generally not productive for spotted seatrout, as the fish are nearly dormant.

Large spotted seatrout are not as widely distributed as smaller ones. In the Gulf of Mexico, the largest trout are taken in spring, and again in winter. In the spring, fish move into shallow beach and bay habitats en masse for their first spawn of the season. For the rest of the summer and early fall, the larger fish tend to stay in cooler Gulf waters and only periodically enter the beach and bay habitats for subsequent spawns. Most of the large fish winter offshore, and a few winter in interior marshes, where they are especially sluggish.

Large trout have different food habits than do smaller ones. Smaller trout eat large amounts of shrimp and other crustaceans. As they become larger, their diet shifts more to fish, the larger the better. Studies in Texas and Mississippi have shown that really big spotted seatrout prefer to feed on mullet. They found that, invariably,

A spotted seatrout from Calcasieu Lake, Louisiana.

a large trout will find the largest mullet it can handle and try to swallow it. Often the mullet is half to two-thirds as large as the trout. Thus, the key to catching large spotted seatrout is to find those places where they are located at the respective season and to use big lures or baits.

SEAWEED
Algae that grows in the sea or on rocks; kelp *(see)* is a form of seaweed. This is distinguished from seagrass *(see)*.

SECCHI DISK
A circular black-and-white disk lowered into the water to determine transparency.
See: Water Clarity.

SEINE
(1) A small fine-mesh net used for collecting bait or other aquatic organisms, primarily used by one or two people in streams or shallow waters. A two-person seine usually has a float line (upper) and lead line (bottom) designed to be pulled through the water for the purpose of catching bait, particularly minnows, although a form of seine can be made of fine-mesh net stretched over a frame and used by one person. Such devices are normally used to catch baitfish for personal use, and their size and place of use may be regulated. In some

locations, seines may be used, under permit, to collect bait for sale.

(2) A large commercial fishing net designed to hang vertically in the water, with one end held at or near the surface with floats and the other end held at or near the bottom with weights. The sides are drawn together to encircle fish. The net and contents are drawn onto a boat or shore. A purse seine operates on a similar principle, although it is used by two boats and spread out to encircle schools of fish; it is interwoven and can be drawn together for collecting the entire contents. The size of the mesh is supposed to correlate to the target species. Purse seines have been attributed with the bycatch of porpoises, and there have been efforts to develop means of escape for nontarget mammals and fish.

See: Commercial Fisherman.

SENEGAL

Senegal is situated between the equator and the Tropic of Cancer, on the western coast of the African continent. Its coastal region is on the west facing the Atlantic Ocean. Mali lies to the east, Mauritania to the north, and Guinea and the Guinea Bissau to the south. In the middle of the country is Gambia, a small nation encircled by Senegal, which extends inland along the Gambia River and fronts the Atlantic Ocean.

Jutting into the eastern Atlantic, especially at the Cape Verde Peninsula, Senegal has a variety of notable offshore and inshore fishing opportunities, with sailfish being the premier attraction. Senegalese waters host more than 30 gamefish species, most of which are caught year-round by anglers trolling artificial lures or small natural baits just off the rocky peninsula of Cape Verde.

Much of Senegal is a flat, bush-covered plain, whereas the rest of the country encompasses gold beaches and mangrove swamps in the extreme south. The main rivers are the Sénégal, which forms the northern boundary, and the Saloum, Gambia, and Casamance; these are subject to seasonal fluctuations but are navigable in the lower reaches. Senegal experiences a wet season from June through October (wetter in the tropical south and drier in the more arid north), and a dry season from November through May. The best time for offshore fishing is during the rainy season, whereas inshore fishing is possible year-round.

Since the 1960s, this country has had a strong reputation among light-tackle billfish enthusiasts as a top Atlantic sailfish destination. The first sailfish—*espadon voilier* in the local French idiom—captured with rod and reel in the waters off Dakar, the capital city, dates to 1965 and led to the creation of the Gorée Sportfishing Centre in 1966 and the Big Game Fishing Club of Dakar in 1967. Senegalese sportfishermen soon improved their craft, realizing that they had access to a solid fishery for medium-size sailfish. Light-tackle angling became popular by 1970, and in 1973 a 96-pound sailfish caught on 12-pound line established Senegal's first International Game Fish Association (IGFA) line-class world record. In 1978, local anglers developed the Sport Fishing Centre of Dakar, and this group now organizes most Senegal's international tournaments. Further line-class records were established in the late 1980s and helped influence a new trend among local sportfishing operators, who have since standardized the use of light tackle aboard their charter boats.

Centre de Peche Sportive (also known as Air Afrique Sportfishing Centre), which is owned and managed in Dakar by Air Afrique, represents the pride of West Africa's sportfishing operators with its fleet of well-outfitted 28-foot Bertrams. This is where anglers wait to meet their charter boats, just a few minutes from the Savana Hotel. Only a few other serious sportfishing organizations exist in Senegal, including two dozen private boats at Africa Safari in Dakar, and the Club Espadon in nearby Saly.

Sailfish are scattered everywhere along the Senegal coast, but the locals usually target three precise zones where the fish feed most actively. One is between 4 and 25 miles northwest of the northernmost point of the Cape Verde Peninsula; this zone is the area's best bet for blue marlin and swordfish. The second zone is 8 to 25 miles southeast of Cape Manuel, the southernmost point of the peninsula, where sportfishing boats troll for sailfish and roaming blue marlin, zigzagging along the continental shelf. The third one, located 8 to 35 miles southwest of Dakar, is considered a "sailfish alley" because these fish are present almost year-round here.

Senegal's sailfish season starts at the end of May and runs until the end of October, peaking in July, August, and September. The average sailfish weighs around 65 pounds, but beginning at the end of August larger sailfish—up to 90 pounds and more—move into the area.

Yellowfin and bigeye tuna migrate through the area in two distinct movements. From April through July, schoolies averaging 30 pounds run offshore; from October through December, fish up to 200 pounds pass by roughly 30 miles off the coast. Along with the bigger tuna, anglers often have a chance to catch wahoo, sailfish, and, many times, blue marlin. Wahoo are present virtually all year, peaking from May through August, but they usually stay far off the coast, so the catches of this species are not plentiful. Local anglers report occasional encounters with bluefin tuna in December and January, but the bluefin also seem to prefer offshore waters from 30 to 200 miles from the coast.

Another great predator frequenting the waters off Dakar is the elusive broadbill swordfish. Night drifting becomes possible during the quiet nights of June and July, and again in December.

If there's any downside to the area's prolific sailfishing, it is that the large schools of sailfish tend to deter anglers from seriously exploring the blue marlin potential. Even those clients who do put in a few hours of trolling offshore often give in to the temptation to change gears and put out light tackle for sailfish, simply because the tactic produces reliable action.

Blue marlin generally follow two migration routes off the coast of Senegal. In May, June, and July, medium-size blue marlin swim southward down the coast; in October and November, the bigger fish seem to swim back up the coast. During this second northward migration, the marlin feed on yellowfin tuna, a species that prefers clear, blue waters. If the currents do not push blue water into the nearby continental shelf, blue marlin may stay as far as 50 miles off the coast.

Although most of the angling attention, especially from distant travelers, is focused on offshore action, plenty of inshore species thrive in Senegalese waters. Surf casting all along the wide beaches of St. Louis, Mbour, Cambérène, Sangomar, and Cape Skirring give the angler the best possibilities to catch big barracuda, meagre, jacks, sharks, snapper, drum, grouper, rays, and sea bass. These species are also caught in the estuaries of Casamance and Sine Saloum, but tarpon are present, too, especially along the mangroves and in the murky waters of the various rivers (which also host hippos and crocodiles).

The best spots for inshore fishing are located near three lodges: the Hotel Savana au Cap Skirring, the Centre de Peche de la Petite Cote au Mbour, and the Village Hotel Keur Saloum au Toubakouta.

SENNETS

Sennets are members of the Sphyraenidae family of barracuda, although they are smaller and less wide ranging than barracuda. Northern sennet (*Sphyraena borealis*) grow to a maximum of 18 inches; they occur in the western Atlantic from Massachusetts to southern Florida and the Gulf of Mexico. Southern sennet (*S. picudilla*) are similar, occurring in Bermuda, Florida, and the Bahamas south to Uruguay; also known as *picuda china*, they have more commercial relevance than the northern sennet and are found near the surface, sometimes in large schools.

These fish are seldom far from the coast, often preferring to be near rocky bottoms. They are good table fare and not known to be poisonous (as barracuda may be). They provide good sport for light-tackle anglers and have been known to take small spoons, plugs, and flies.

Northern Sennet

SETBACK

The distance that a lure or bait is placed behind the boat, or behind an object such as a sideplaner.
See: Downrigger Fishing; Planer Boards.

SET HOOK

A single hook and line attached to some object rather than to a hand-operated mechanical reel. The hook is usually baited and may or may not be attended. A set hook is prohibited in some places; where legal, its use and location may be regulated. A set hook may also be called a setline (*see*), jug hook (*see*), or limbline (*see*). This is not a sportfishing instrument.

SETH GREEN RIG

One of the oldest deep-trolling, multi-lure presentation methods, developed by renowned New York fish culturist Seth Green in the late nineteenth century. A few anglers still use this rig, or a variation, principally as an adjunct to other methods of deep trolling, and generally when they're desperate.

The Seth Green rig features five to eight lures, usually spoons or flies, on individual leaders that snap to the main fishing line and stay at a fixed position because they are attached to swivels set 10 to 20 feet apart. A heavy lead weight is used to get the rig down. To fish it, you lower the weight and line into the water until the first barrel swivel is reached, then you take a leader and snap it to the barrel swivel; the line is lowered in the water until you reach the next swivel, and attach another leader. Continue in this fashion until all lures are out.

This setup requires a heavy rod and reel and some adroit manipulation to retrieve—when you reel in, you must stop to remove each of the snapped on leaders. Leader length varies; old-timers used 15- to 30-foot leaders, but if you're fishing deep, you can use shorter ones. This setup has also been called a "thermal rig" and is primarily used in midsummer trout and salmon fishing for covering a deep column of water. It was adapted from commercial fishing applications. Anglers should check local fishing regulations to be sure that it is legal to use this many lures or hook points on one fishing line.

SETLINE

A line that is anchored at one point and is not

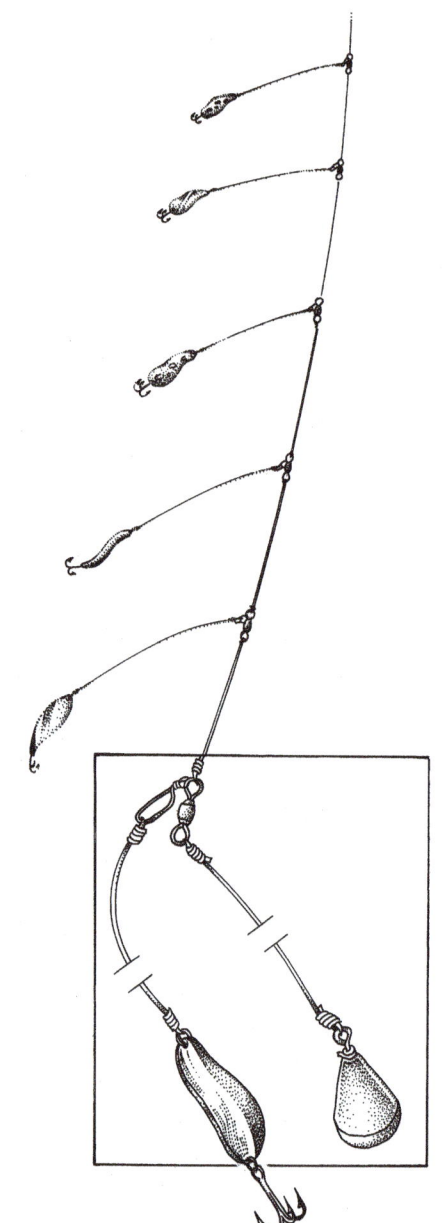

The cumbersome Seth Green Rig features multiple trolling lures attached to barrel swivels that are spaced out along the main line.

connected to a hand-operated mechanical reel. The line is attached to a hook or hooks that are baited to catch fish. A setline may also be called a limbline or logline. Setlines are illegal in some places; where legal, they usually must be tagged or marked with the owner's identifying information. Regulations also govern the length, number of hooks, spacing of hooks, and other issues. Usually a setline is not under the direct view and control of the person placing the line. From the standpoint of fishing regulations, such a line would be unattended. Although using a setline may be called fishing, and such usage may be covered under established regulations, a setline is not a sportfishing instrument, and setline fishing is not sportfishing.

SETTING THE HOOK
See: Hooksetting.

SEYCHELLES
An archipelago of 115 granite and coral islands northeast of Madagascar in the Indian Ocean, Seychelles is 4° south of the equator and 1,000 nautical miles from the east coast of Africa. Tourism is the economic mainstay of this 472-square-kilometer republic, and in the latter twentieth century the region has been a popular destination for European tourists, including anglers who have discovered outstanding and diverse big-game fishing and an abundance of bonefish.

Seychelles consists of 83 largely uninhabited coral islands, and 32 granite islands in the northerly Mahé group. The predominant islands in this group include Mahé—which is the largest and contains 90 percent of the country's population of 75,000—as well as Praslin, Silhouette, and LaDigue. Two other islands, Denis and Bird, are especially popular with big-game anglers, as they lie close to deep water.

Recreational fishing in the open sea here is a recent sport; its development coincided with the advent of tourism in 1972. Prior to this, the Seychellois fished with hook and line for daily subsistence requirements, and used fish traps inside the reefs. Spearfishing was banned with the arrival of the first tourists in 1972. Commercial fishing has become well developed, however, and is an important economic activity, the primary targets of which are yellowfin and skipjack tuna, as well as swordfish.

The tourism policy of the Seychelles champions sustainability and aims at a limited number of visitors. These restrictions allow for high-standard facilities that maximize economic benefit and minimize environmental degradation. More than 47 percent of the territory is classified as marine or national parks.

Today, most of the upmarket resort hotels on Mahé, Praslin, and La Digue, and on the islands of Desroches, Bird, and Denis, offer big-game fishing to clients. From the latter, the trip to the blue-water dropoff is just a few hundred yards; there, upwellings produce nutrient-rich conditions and excellent fishing. A typical half-day trip sees the regular tag and release of sailfish, dorado, wahoo, bonito, tuna, rainbow runners, and barracuda. Blue and black marlin are also present, and in 1996 three black marlin over 500 pounds were tagged and released. Tuna are abundant and available all year, and Seychelles has established a number of world records for dogtooth and yellowfin tuna. Great potential exists for light-tackle and fly fishing, possibly for record specimens of some species.

Being close to the equator, Seychelles experiences two annual monsoon periods. The southeast monsoon occurs from April through September, is usually associated with dry and windy conditions, and is noted for producing sailfish, marlin, and tuna. The northwest monsoon occurs from October through March, is wet but calmer, and brings a more plentiful supply of both pelagic and demersal fishes.

Desroches Island, which is part of the Amirantes Group of Seychelles islands, has recently become a hotspot for bonefish and is the bonefish capital of this country. This island group spans for 90 miles southwest of Mahé. Exploration in the late 1990s identified areas of great potential in the vicinity of Desroches, and numerous fish in the 10-pound class are reportedly present. Bird Island is also known to have bonefishing opportunity.

Seychelles are prominent grounds for Hawks Bill and Green turtles; both are protected by law, and conservation efforts are achieving encouraging results. With all of its coral reefs, the Seychelles are also popular diving sites. Travel to Seychelles is accomplished via London, Kenya, and South Africa.

S-GLASS

The common term for low-alkali, high-aluminum and -magnesium fiberglass, a very high tensile modulus fiberglass used in fishing rod construction.
See: Rod, Fishing.

SHAD, ALABAMA *Alosa alabamae*.
Other names—Gulf shad, Ohio shad.

This member of the Clupeidae family of herring *(see)* and shad is an anadromous species virtually ignored by anglers. It does have some commercial significance, however.

Identification. A silvery fish like its other relatives, the Alabama shad has a large terminal mouth with upper and lower jaws of almost equal length. Its tongue has a single median row of small teeth, there is no lateral line, the posterior of the dorsal fin lacks an elongated slender filament, and there are 18 or fewer anal rays. In general, it is nearly identical to the larger-growing American shad *(see: shad, American)*, but adult fish have 42 to 48 gill rakers on the lower limb of the first gill arch.

Size. The Alabama shad can grow to just over 20 inches but is usually under 15 inches long.

Distribution. This species occurs in the northern Gulf of Mexico from the Mississippi Delta and Louisiana eastward to Choctawhatchee River in Florida; it also occurs in rivers from Iowa to Arkansas and across West Virginia.

Habitat/Life history. The Alabama shad is a schooling species that spends most of its life in the ocean; when mature, it returns from early spring through summer to rivers and streams to spawn, inhabiting open water of medium to large rivers. Young shad descend rivers in autumn.

Food/Angling. The feeding habits of this species at sea are unknown but are presumably similar to those of hickory and American shad. The Alabama shad is anadromous and only a potential angling target during upriver spawning migrations, during which time it does not feed. This smallish shad is a largely incidental catch and a rare deliberate angling target.
See: Shad, Hickory.

SHAD, AMERICAN *Alosa sapidissima*.
Other names—poor man's salmon, common shad, Atlantic shad, Connecticut River shad, North River shad, Potomac shad, Susquehanna shad, white shad, Delaware shad, alose; French: *alose savoureuse*.

Frequently referred to simply as "shad," this species is an anadromous member of the Clupeidae family of herring *(see)* and shad and is highly regarded as a gamefish due to its strong fighting and jumping characteristics. American shad spawning runs provide a popular but seasonal sportfishery on both coasts of the United States, although these fish receive scant attention in Canada. The white, flaky flesh of this shad is full of bones but makes good table fare if prepared with patience and care; the scientific name *sapidissima* means "most delicious," an appropriate appellation for a fish that supports a considerable commercial fishery and whose roe is considered a delicacy and commands a premium price.

Other North American shad to which they are closely or distantly related include the smaller hickory shad (*A. mediocris*; see: shad, hickory), a western Atlantic species whose range overlaps with the American shad; and the Alabama shad (*A. alabamae*; see: shad, Alabama) of the Gulf Coast. Several herringlike species called shad occur in the eastern Atlantic; these include the twaite, Killarney, or Mediterranean shad (*A. fallax*); and the allis shad (*A. alosa*). These smaller species occur in western Europe and the Mediterranean, and also ascend coastal streams in spring to spawn.

The American shad has a history of intensive exploitation for its flesh and roe, and landings in the past century have steadily declined due to this and other factors. Overfishing, dams, and pollution have been the chief causes of severe declines in the abundance of American shad. Some of these factors have been mitigated but others, most recently excessive commercial ocean exploitation, have caused continued concern. Along the eastern U.S., a coastwide management plan has been created to assist cooperation and restoration efforts among states, which includes habitat improvement, fish passageways, and stocking programs. Although there has been some improvement in shad popula-

American Shad

tions in some rivers, the number of American shad continues to decline.

Identification. The laterally compressed, fairly deep body of the American shad is silvery white with some green to dark blue along the back, frequently with a metallic shine. The coloring darkens slightly when the fish enters freshwater to spawn. There is a large black spot directly behind the top of the gill cover, followed by several spots that become smaller and less distinct toward the tail; sometimes there are up to three rows of these dark spots, one under the other. The American shad has large, easily shed scales, as well as modified scales called scutes, which form a distinct ridge or cutting edge along the belly. It has a single dorsal fin in the middle of the back, the tail is deeply forked, and there are soft fin rays and long anal fins. It has weak teeth or no teeth at all.

Bearing a close resemblance to the hickory shad, the American shad is distinguished by the way its lower jaw fits easily into a deep, V-shaped notch under the upper jaw, whereas the lower jaw of the hickory shad protrudes noticeably beyond the upper jaw.

Size/Age. The normal size of American shad are 2 to 5 pounds, but specimens weighing up to 8 pounds are not uncommon when fish are abundant. They reach a maximum of $2^1/_2$ feet and possibly $13^1/_2$ pounds. The all-tackle world record is an 11-pound, 4-ounce fish taken from Massachusetts waters in 1994. Although American shad can live to age 13, few live past age 7. Females (called roe fish or hens) grow more quickly and generally larger than males (called bucks).

Distribution. The endemic range of this species is east of the Appalachians along the Atlantic coast of North America from Sand Hill River, Labrador, to the St. John's River, Florida; practically every significant coastal river along the western Atlantic seaboard has supported a distinct spawning population at one time or another. Important sportfisheries currently exist in the Connecticut and Delaware Rivers. The Hudson River has historically had major runs, but sportfishing for shad in this deep, wide river is negligible, although it has in the past been commercially significant. The Susquehanna has been undergoing restoration of its runs. In 1871, American shad were introduced into the Sacramento River in California and today are found up and down the Pacific coast, ranging from Bahia de Todos Santos in upper Baja California, Mexico, to Cook Inlet, Alaska, and the Kamchatka Peninsula. Most sportfishing occurs in the U.S. portion of this range, and a major run occurs in the Columbia River.

Habitat. American shad spend most of their lives in the ocean, ascending coastal rivers to spawn. They are found in freshwater only during their spawning runs and cannot tolerate cold waters below 41°F. Predominant in more northerly climates, American shad engage in extensive and complex migrations throughout their range, relying on their acute sense of homing for navigation. In coastal rivers, they primarily inhabit deep runs and pools.

Life history/Behavior. Most fish spawn for the first time when they weigh 3 to 5 pounds. Males reach sexual maturity at age 3 to 4, females at age 4 to 5. Some life history patterns of American shad depend on the river of origin; for instance, in Southern rivers the average spawning age is 4 and fish generally spawn only once, laying 300,000 to 400,000 eggs; however, the average spawning age for more northerly fish is 5, and these fish generally spawn several times in a lifetime, laying a smaller number of eggs per spawning, usually ranging from 125,000 to 250,000.

Shad "runs" are extremely dramatic, as thousands of fish ascend rivers within the space of a few weeks, sometimes traveling long distances up the rivers where they were hatched. When water temperatures range from 41° to 73°F, the fish swim upriver and as far inland as 300 miles. Peak migrations occur when the water temperature is in the 50s. These migrations usually take place in April in southern rivers and through July in northern regions, even beginning as early as mid-November in Florida.

Most spawning activity takes place in deep areas with moderate to strong currents, particularly during the night, when water temperatures are in the mid-60s. A single female is accompanied by several males, swimming close to the surface and splashing and rolling as anywhere from 50,000 to 600,000 eggs are laid. The nonadhesive eggs drift with the current, gradually sinking and then hatching from 3 to 12 days later. Larvae are found in rivers during the summer, feeding on insects and plankton and entering the sea by autumn, where they remain until maturity. Post-spawning adults attempt to return to the sea after spawning; many die immediately after spawning, whereas others have been known to live long enough to spawn as many as seven times.

Food and feeding habits. American shad primarily feed on plankton, swimming with their mouths open and gill covers extended while straining the water; they also eat small crustaceans, insects, fish eggs, algae, and small fish. They cease feeding during upstream spawning migration but resume during their relatively quick downstream post-spawning migration.

Angling. Shad provide drag-screeching runs, broadside-to-the current fight, and frequent aerial maneuvers. They are as spunky a river fish as there is to be found and are especially exciting when caught early in their upstream migration (they are spent after spawning and are therefore less challenging). But they are also of limited availability seasonally. The shad spawning run lasts only six to eight weeks in the spring. These fish often move through a river in stages or waves. They are affected by water conditions and are often not present in the same locales on a day-to-day basis.

Shad are not much for midday activity. Anglers often experience the best shad fishing in the evening, and early morning is considered prime time. The first two or three hours of the day may be the best because shad migrate upriver at night and there is a new wave of migrants in the morning, and perhaps also because of the low level of light. Shad will move during the day, however, particularly in cloudy or rainy weather. They may migrate from pool to pool or even move around in a large, slow-flowing section of water during the day, being vis-ible on or just below the surface as they cruise en masse. Anglers frequently see this activity when the fish are on the spawning grounds and appear to be daisy-chaining, much like tarpon.

Shad typically remain in river channels, preferring deep water to the swift, riffling, shallow sections. The primary place to fish for them is in the pools. The water is slower, calmer, and deeper here than in the rest of the river, and shad primarily rest in such spots before continuing upriver. You may find a large school of fish occupying a particular pool on a given day, or you may find few or none. Sometimes, when success tapers off in a given spot, you merely need to move slightly up, down, or across the river to find action again.

Light spinning tackle is standard for shad. A 6- to 7-foot light-action rod and a spinning reel equipped with 4- to 8-pound line are best. The reel should have a smooth drag, as large shad will take varied amounts of line during the fight. Terminal gear largely consists of shad darts; a dart is a lead-bodied bucktail jig with a tapered form and slanted nose. Darts are the perennially favored shad catcher, although some anglers have success with flies, small spinners, and tiny spoons, the latter being fished less often on a bead-chain-style sinker and more commonly behind a downrigger weight.

It is usually necessary to maneuver these offerings down to the bottom, a task that is influenced by the depth of water, strength of current, weight of lure, and size of line. Shad do not feed during their spawning runs but apparently strike out of reflexive action; thus, they don't seem to go out of their way to chase a lure. The offering has to be placed in front of a fish's nose to be effective. For this reason, it's common to get hung up and to lose many lures in the pursuit of shad.

Shore anglers, waders, and those casting from anchored boats should cast across and upstream, allowing their lure to sink to the bottom, then, with the line tight, let the lure swing downstream with the current until it reaches the end of its sweep. Boat anglers either troll into the current or anchor and stillfish their lures by letting them hang in the current. In either case, approximately

An American shad is landed on the Annapolis River, Nova Scotia.

75 feet of line is let out behind the boat, using a heavy enough lure (or weighting it with split shot on the line about 18 to 24 inches ahead of the lure) to present the offering just off the bottom.

Darts range in size from tiny to $1/2$ ounce. Heavy versions are used in early spring, when the river is high, swift, and roily; at this time, a lot of weight is needed to keep the lure down. But heavy darts are large and may not attract fish even when they do stay down, so anglers often resort to smaller darts and add split shot; the extra weight keeps the dart down, and the smaller dart is more favorable to the shad. The mostly widely used darts weigh between $1/8$ to $1/4$ ounce.

A red-headed, white-bodied dart (with white or yellow bucktail) is the time-honored favorite color and is effective. But darts come in a host of colors and combinations, and it pays to have a selection of sizes and colors available. Black head/green body, green head/chartreuse body, red head/chartreuse body, and red head/yellow body are among the most successful combinations. It's a good idea to switch colors frequently, however, especially when you know there are fish in the locale you're working but they haven't responded to your initial offering.

Especially effective for trolling are tiny spoons with No. 6 hooks. A good shine is important, and the lure must have perfect balance to run properly, as action is critical. The spoon, which should twirl fast, is fished in a manner similar to that for darts, although it is not necessary to put out as much line; 50 feet or thereabouts will do if the river section is from 8 to 12 feet deep. With spoons, use a swiveling bead-chain sinker ($1/4$ ounce is standard) about 18 inches up the line. With a downrigger, it isn't necessary to use weight, but the downrigger release must be set just right.

Fly fishing for shad is popular on both coasts, especially when the water is not in spate condition. Rods should be suited for an 8-weight line (although you can do with less) and be in the 8- to 9-foot range. Sinking, fast-sinking, and sink-tip fly lines are employed according to river depth and current flow. A short leader is adequate. Flies are mostly short-shanked streamers, sometimes brightly colored and often weighted with bead eyes. Using bead eyes and lead strips on the body is illegal in some places (especially New Brunswick) where weighted flies are prohibited (mainly for salmon fishing, to avoid deliberate snagging of fish). Check regulations carefully. It is usually necessary to get the fly down to the bottom, so an across, swing, and hang presentation is best. Most fish strike as the fly makes its downcurrent turn or when it is stripped back in retrieval. Some fly-caught shad are taken close to the surface, however, usually when milling in slow pools. Then, a short stripping retrieve is employed.

SHAD, GIZZARD *Dorosoma cepedianum.*
Other names—shad, eastern gizzard, hickory shad, mud shad, nanny shad, skipjack, winter shad.

Although the gizzard shad is important forage for large fish, its rapid growth rate causes it to exceed a consumable size for most predators early on in its life. It is often labeled as a nuisance fish by anglers and biologists, due to large die-offs, which happen because the species is especially susceptible to drastic changes in temperature and low concentrations of oxygen. A member of the Clupeidae family of herring *(see)* and shad, the gizzard shad is used to some extent as fertilizer and livestock feed.

Identification. The gizzard shad is one of two freshwater members of the herring family that has a distinctively long, slender last ray on its dorsal fin. The body is silver blue on the back and silver white underneath, with either blue-and-green or gold reflections on the head and flanks; occasionally there are six to eight horizontal dark stripes on the back, starting behind a large purple blue or black shoulder spot (which is faint or absent in large adults). The gizzard shad also has dusky fins, a blunt snout, a subterminal mouth, and a deep notch at the center of the upper jaw. It lacks scales on the nape. There are 52 to 70 lateral scales, 10 to 13 dorsal rays, and 25 to 36 anal rays.

Size/Age. Growing a maximum of $20^{1}/_{2}$ inches and averaging about 10 inches in length, this species commonly reaches more than a pound in weight. Although it is rarely pursued for sport by anglers, the all-tackle world record is a 4-pound, 6-ounce Indiana fish. Most gizzard shad die before they reach age 7, although the species is known to reach 10 years of age.

Distribution. Found in most parts of the St. Lawrence–Great Lakes, Mississippi, Atlantic, and Gulf drainages, this fish ranges from Quebec to central North Dakota and throughout New Mexico, as well as south to central Florida and Mexico; it has been introduced outside this native range.

Habitat. Gizzard shad mainly occur in the deep open water of medium to large rivers, reservoirs, lakes, and backwaters; adults are also found in brackish or saline water of estuaries or bays, as they prefer calmer open waters.

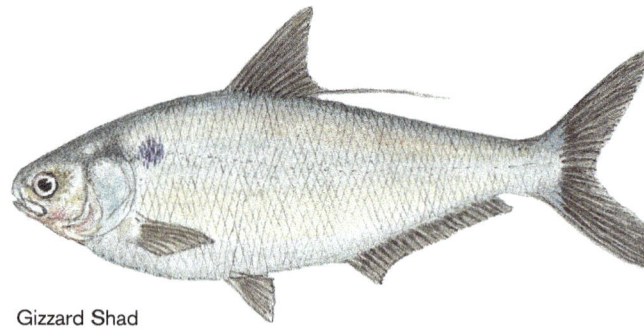

Gizzard Shad

Life history. Gizzard shad occur in schools and are first able to spawn when two to three years old or 7 to 13 inches long. They breed near the surface in freshwater from March through August, when water temperatures range from 50° to 70°F. The adhesive eggs sink to the bottom, varying in number from about 3,000 to more than 380,000. Gizzard shad prefer warm waters and cannot tolerate extreme cold conditions, which may cause a fishkill of significant numbers. They roam open waters in search of plankton, which occurs at various levels according to the season and conditions.

Food and feeding habits. Gizzard shad are filter feeders that strain microscopic organisms from the water or pick through mud and organic matter on the bottom; in some environments they appear more oriented to bottom feeding.

Angling. There is no concerted angling interest in gizzard shad, although larger specimens are sometimes caught incidentally, or when concentrated in certain areas (for example, the tailrace below a dam). Smaller specimens are caught on ultralight line and small hooks, taken in cast nets, or snagged, for bait purposes.

See: Shad, Threadfin.

SHAD, HICKORY *Alosa mediocris*.

Other names—shad herring, hickory jack, freshwater taylor, fall herring, bonejack.

A member of the Clupeidae family of herring *(see)* and shad, the hickory shad is of significant recreational interest, being a friskier although smaller cousin of the American shad *(see: shad, American)*. It is also of commercial value, particularly its roe.

Identification. Gray green on the back and fading to silver on the side, the hickory shad has clear fins with the exception of the dusky dorsal and caudal fins, which are occasionally black edged. It has a strongly oblique mouth, a lower jaw that projects noticeably beyond its upper jaw, and a cheek that is longer than or about equal to its depth. There is a blue black spot near the upper edge of the gill cover, followed by a clump of indistinct dusky spots that extend below the dorsal fin. There are also teeth on the lower jaw, and 18 to 23 rakers on the lower limb of the first gill arch.

Size. The hickory shad can reach almost 2 feet in length, and averages 1 to 3 pounds in weight. It can weigh as much as 6 pounds.

Distribution. Found only along the Atlantic coast of North America, the hickory shad ranges from Kenduskeag River, Maine, to the St. John's River, Florida. It is most common in the Southeast and in the Mid-Atlantic regions. This species overlaps with American shad and ascends some of the same rivers when spawning.

Habitat. The hickory shad is a schooling species that spends most of its life in the ocean; when mature, it returns in early spring through summer to rivers and streams to spawn, inhabiting open water of medium to large rivers. Young shad descend rivers in autumn.

Hickory Shad

Life history/Behavior. Hickory shad mature when they are two years old and about 12 inches long. Adults ascend coastal rivers during the spring. Preferred water temperatures range from 55° to 69°F, but the lower end of that range seems to trigger the spawning urge. Females lay up to 300,000 eggs. Young fish remain in rivers, estuaries, and backwaters, migrating to the sea by fall or early winter.

Food and feeding habits. At sea, hickory shad feed on small fish, as well as on squid, small crabs, other crustaceans, and fish eggs. In an irony that is common to most anadromous species, they are not pursued or caught by anglers in places where they do feed, but are pursued and caught when migrating upriver in natal waters when they do not feed.

Angling. Angling for hickory shad is akin to that for American shad.

SHADOW LINE

The sharp edge between water that is illuminated and that which is not, as created by overhead light. The shadow line is a nighttime phenomenon that exists wherever overhead lights fall on the water; it occurs on bridges, piers, bulkheads, seawalls, all types of docks, and wherever a structure is in or on the edge of the water. Usually the water close to the structure is dark while the water beyond the shadow line is brightly lit. A shadow line may also be created by moonlight in places where there is no artificial light.

Because gamefish often position themselves close to one edge of the shadow line to forage, a shadow line can be an important place to fish. Whether the fish are in the dark water facing the illuminated water, or in the illuminated water facing the dark water, may depend on the circumstances, especially if there is current.

See: Pier Fishing.

SHAD, THREADFIN *Dorosoma petenense*.

Other names—shad, threadfin.

A well-known forage fish and member of the Clupeidae family of herring *(see)* and shad, the threadfin shad rarely grows larger than 5 inches long, remaining small enough to be one of the most important open-water forage species for important freshwater gamefish, especially bass and stripers.

Identification. The threadfin shad is silvery with a deeply compressed body and is most easily recognized by the elongated, thin last ray on its dorsal fin. It has a small, dark shoulder spot, and its upper jaw does not project past the lower jaw. It is similar in appearance to other herring, including the similar-size but more northerly ranging alewives *(see)* and the larger gizzard shad *(see: shad, gizzard)*, with which it shares overlapping ranges and many of the same waters. It is distinguished from gizzard shad of similar size by its more pointed snout, terminal mouth, black dots on its chin and bottom of the mouth, and yellow fins. It has 40 to 48 lateral scales, 11 to 14 dorsal rays, and 17 to 27 anal rays.

Size. This species is commonly found at $2^{1}/_{2}$ to 4 inches long and can attain a maximum length of 9 inches. Many threadfins do not live longer than 2 years, although they can live as long as 4 or more years.

Distribution. Threadfin shad occur throughout the Mississippi River basin, from the Ohio River of Kentucky and southern Indiana southwest to Oklahoma and south to Texas and Florida, as well as in other Gulf of Mexico drainages and Atlantic drainages in Florida. They are also present in rivers around in Guatemala and Honduras. They have been introduced as a forage species in Hawaii and the western United States, and to other areas in the mainland U.S.

Habitat. Occasionally found in the brackish waters of estuaries and bays, threadfin shad are mainly a freshwater fish occurring in large rivers, reservoirs, lakes, and backwaters, where they principally inhabit open-water environs.

Life history/Behavior. Threadfin shad spawn in the spring and autumn near or over plants or other objects. They are prolific but short-lived and are highly susceptible to winter kill from extreme cold temperatures, which helps keep their numbers in check.

Food and feeding habits. Threadfins are filter feeders that primarily consume plankton and organic detritus in open water; they occasionally feed on fish larvae and on the organic material found on or over sandy or silty bottoms. In reservoirs and large lakes, these fish are constantly on the move, searching for and feeding on minute plankton, the location and level of which will vary seasonally and according to various factors.

Angling. There is no angling effort for threadfin shad, although they may be captured with cast nets for use as live baits. Like all herring, they are difficult to keep alive and must be contained in a circular, rather than rectangular, livewell that is highly aerated at the proper temperature.

SHARKING
A popular term for shark fishing.
See: Sharks.

SHARKS
Sharks evolved as predatory fish some 400 million years ago in the Devonian period, long before vertebrates began to walk on land. Ever since, they have been among the most successful predators in the sea. A rich record of fossilized shark teeth, ranging from $1/_{8}$ inch to more than 6 inches long, indicates that many species of sharks have come and gone over the ages. Fossil records show that at least one species of carnivorous shark, *Carcharodon megalodon*, which lived 4.5 million years ago, reached some 40 feet in length.

Today there are at least 370 species of sharks worldwide, and new ones are still being discovered. They range in size from 6 or 7 inches long (the dwarf dogfish, *Etmopterus perryi*) to the world's largest fish at 40 or more feet long (the whale shark, *Rhincodon typus*). Eighty percent of all sharks are less than 5 feet long when fully grown.

Sharks obviously are a diverse and adaptable group of fish. They inhabit almost every marine ecosystem, and a few species are found in freshwater. Although almost all sharks are carnivorous predators, a few—the whale, basking, and megamouth sharks—filter plankton from the water. Sharks are often thought of as solitary, but some species commonly occur in schools. Many sharks, particularly those found in temperate waters, are migratory, heading toward the equator in the winter to take advantage of food sources available in different locations at various times of the year.

Characteristics
Like all fish, sharks are vertebrates, but ichthyologists place them in a separate class from most fish because the shark's skeleton is made of cartilage instead of bone. Within this class, the Chondrichthyes, are two subclasses. One is the Holocephali, or chimaeras, strange-looking fish seldom seen outside aquariums or research facilities. The other subclass, the Elasmobranchi, includes

Threadfin Shad

sharks, skates, and rays *(see: rays and skates)*.

In addition to their unique skeletal structure, sharks have five to seven gill slits on each side, allowing each gill to vent separately into the surrounding water. Bony fish, in contrast, have one gill opening on each side of their bodies that is covered by a bony plate called the operculum.

Sharks also lack the gas-filled swim bladders of most bony fish. Instead, sharks have evolved a different means of maintaining buoyancy: They have extremely large livers (it constitutes up to 25 percent of their body weight) that contain oils that are lighter than water. These oils, coupled with the cartilaginous skeleton, make sharks almost neutrally buoyant.

Swimming ability. Not all sharks must swim constantly to force water over their gills for respiration. Some, like the nurse shark, the angel shark, and even some of the larger requiem sharks (the group that includes tiger sharks), can actively pump water over their gills and will occasionally rest motionless on the bottom, particularly in the rare places where the water is supersaturated with oxygen. And many bottom-dwelling sharks pump water over their gills most of the time. Sharks must literally swim or sink, however, because their bodies are slightly denser than water. Like airplanes, they require forward motion to stay afloat. Water is 800 times more dense than air, so swimming takes a lot of energy. Sharks have a number of physical adaptations that make them exceptionally efficient swimmers.

As mentioned, most sharks achieve near-neutral buoyancy through the oil stored in their livers. A shark's skeleton also contributes to its buoyancy and swimming efficiency, as cartilage is less dense and more flexible than bone. (Out of the water, how-ever, the skeleton isn't strong enough to support the shark's body adequately, and the shark will soon die, crushed under its own weight.) The only place heavy bone is found on the shark's body is in its teeth and scales. The scales—called placoid scales—have small bony projections that hook backward. These projections, called dermal denticles, work along with the shark's streamlined shape to facilitate the flow of water over the shark's body, reducing drag and enabling the shark to swim faster.

Not all sharks are fast; some are sluggish and stay close to the bottom. One of the fastest swimmers, however, is the mako shark, which is thought to reach speeds of more than 40 mph for short bursts and is capable of spectacular leaps into the air. The power behind this amazing ability is the tail. The sculling motion of the tail both steers and propels the shark forward. All sharks have heterocercal tails, which means that the spinal column extends into the top lobe of the tail. In most sharks, the top lobe is larger than the bottom lobe, giving the tail an asymmetrical shape. The fastest swimmers have nearly symmetrical tails.

A blue shark cruises through a chum line off Montauk, New York; a hooked bait drifts under the red balloon.

A shark's fins help create lift and stabilize the shark as it turns or dives. Because shark fins are relatively fixed and lack the pliability of fins from bony fish, sharks have more limited maneuverability than many bony fish. Some people have suggested that this is like comparing the capabilities of a fixed-wing jet, which can turn and roll but must be moving forward, to those of a helicopter, which can hover, rise straight up, or even move backward.

Sensory ability. As a shark swims, it constantly samples the water for odors and sounds. The nostrils of a shark play no role in breathing and are used only for smell. Sharks have been called "swimming noses" because they can detect odors at a few parts per million. Sharks can smell blood at the 1 part-per-million level or less and are drawn to bleeding prey.

Sound also plays a role in locating food. Low-frequency vibrations (40 Hz or less), such as the sounds made by something splashing in the water, attract sharks. A small duct connects the shark's internal ears to the outside. Hearing is further enhanced by the lateral-line system that extends along the head and sides of the body and is sensitive to vibrations, currents, and pressure changes.

Both odor and sound are important for locating possible food sources, but actual feeding is dependent on vision and the detection of electrical fields. The visual system of sharks is well developed and functions well in high and low light. A special structure in the eye called the tapetum lucidum increases their sensitivity in low light. Other animals with good night vision, such as cats, also have a tapetum. It is responsible for eyeshine, seen when light shines on a cat's eyes at night. Sharks also have eyeshine, and it varies from blue green to gold in color.

At close range, the shark's electroreception system comes into play. Receptors located in pores on the shark's snout and lower jaw can detect tiny electrical fields created by the prey's muscular movement. This sensory system may also help the shark navigate relative to the planet's magnetic field.

Feeding and digestion. When a shark has procured its prey, it swallows the food whole or in chunks. Once the shark is satiated, it may not eat again for several weeks. As the food is digested, it passes through the intestine, which has a spiral valve structure unique to sharks. The spiral valve increases the interior surface area of the intestine for more efficient absorption of nutrients.

Sharks are opportunistic feeders and will often eat whatever is available. Even extraordinary indigestible items have been among the flotsam that has turned up in their stomachs. Sharks reportedly have some ability to regurgitate unwanted food items.

Teeth. Shark teeth come in as many shapes and sizes as sharks do; in fact, they are useful in identifying individual species. They can also say something about the shark's diet. Some sharks are specialized predators; their teeth are adapted for efficient capture of their preferred prey.

The upper and lower teeth of a mako shark.

Others eat whatever is available, and their teeth are amply suited for many types of food. The great white uses its triangular, serrated, bladelike teeth for grabbing and biting off chunks of large fish and marine mammals. At the other end of the spectrum, the smooth dogfish uses its flat teeth for crushing the shells of mollusks and crustaceans. Others, like the mako or sand tiger, have narrow, pointed teeth for impaling and holding onto prey small enough to swallow whole.

Shark teeth are simply embedded in the shark's gums, not its jaws; they fall out easily but are also easily replaced. Sharks generally have several rows of teeth, one or more of which may be functional at a time. As the teeth are broken, pulled out, or worn down, they are replaced from the row behind in conveyer-belt fashion. It is estimated that some species may shed as many as 30,000 teeth in a lifetime. Each replacement tooth is larger than the one it replaces, allowing the shark's teeth to keep up with its growing body. This also allows scientists to estimate the size of a shark based solely on a tooth.

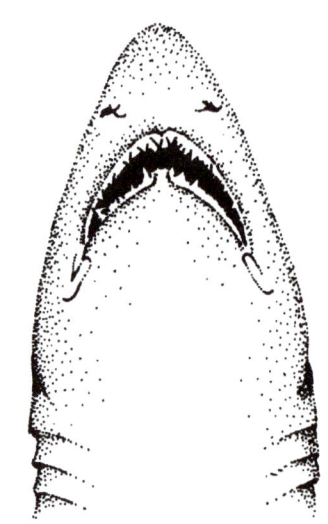

The underside of the head of a sand tiger shark.

The shark's jaw is rather loosely attached to the rest of its skull, which enables it to open its mouth very wide. A shark bite involves several distinct movements, usually taking place in a second or two. First, the shark raises its snout and lowers its bottom jaw. This not only gets the snout out of the way, it exposes the many electrosensory receptors located on the underside of the snout, which help the shark home in on the prey. This is crucial, as many sharks can't see during a strike. These species protect their eyes either with a special eyelid called a nictitating membrane or by rolling their eyes back into their heads. Next, the upper jaw protrudes forward, exposing the teeth, and the lower jaw moves upward and forward toward it. Finally, the shark lowers its head, and the upper jaw returns once more to its normal position.

Skin. Sharks don't have scales like other fish. Instead, they have placoid scales, or denticles. The denticles are tiny, bony projections implanted in the shark's skin. They come in many shapes and sizes but usually completely cover the shark's skin like a coat of armor. Their main functions are protection for the shark and reducing drag as the shark's body slices through the water. The word "denticle" means small tooth, and the teeth in the shark's mouth are actually just modified placoid scales. The teeth and the skin denticles are very similar in structure and not all that different from human teeth. A center pulp of nerve cells and blood vessels is surrounded by dentine, and the tooth has a thin, hard outer layer of enamel.

Denticles give the shark's hide a rough texture like sandpaper. In fact, shark attack victims often receive scrapes from contact with a shark. Shark skin has been dried and used as an abrasive, called shagreen, for sanding wood. This use is now rare because there are cheaper substitutes. Shark hides are used to make a strong leather, however, once the denticles have been chemically removed.

Reproduction. Sharks have a number of reproductive strategies. Some enclose fertilized eggs in tough, leathery egg cases that are released into the water for subsequent development and birth. Some female sharks retain the eggs within their bodies and hatch the young internally, so they are born alive and fully formed. Others have a sophisticated placental arrangement similar to that of mammals.

Regardless of the strategy, sharks devote most of their reproductive energy to producing a few large, well-developed young with a good chance of surviving to maturity. Shark gestation, growth, and sexual development all take a relatively long time. Many sharks take 10 to 20 years to mature sexually, and they produce as few as one pup at a time. Tagged sharks have been recaptured more than 30 years after the initial tagging. A number of species are estimated to live for 40 or 50 years.

Longevity, slow development, and low reproductive rates mean that shark populations depleted from overfishing or other causes require more time to recover.

Issues

Sharks are not only important ecologically, but they also serve humans in many ways other than sportfishing. Because they are poorly understood and the subject of fear among many people, they are also controversial and have been subject to overexploitation in recent decades.

Uses. Worldwide, sharks are a significant source of food for humans. One hundred million sharks (600,000 tons) are consumed annually. In many cultures, they are a preferred fish. In North America, sharks were considered unappetizing until the 1980s, when the demand for shark flesh rose steeply. One reason for shark meat's bad reputation may have been that proper preparation of the meat was not commonly understood. Shark blood contains high amounts of urea, which helps sharks regulate the amount of water in their bodies as they travel to areas of varying salt concentrations. If given the chance, bacteria break urea down into ammonia, which gives the meat an unpleasant odor and flavor. Freshly caught sharks should be bled and iced down immediately after capture to prevent this problem.

Sharks can command premium prices at fish markets around the world. In Hong Kong, people were buying 7 million pounds of shark fins annually in the late 1990s. To meet the demand, some commercial fishing fleets pursued sharks exclusively for their fins, cutting the fins off live sharks and returning them to the ocean to die a lingering death.

Virtually all parts of a shark have commercial value; even the entrails are used to make fish meal. Shark hide is stronger than cow hide and many times more expensive, as demonstrated by the cost of belts, shoes, and wallets made from shark skin. Indigenous people have used shark teeth to tip arrows, harpoons, and other weapons. Today, shark jaws and teeth are sold as curios or jewelry.

One of the most valuable but least-known uses of sharks is in medicine. Various parts of sharks are, and have been, used for research purposes, in antibiotics, as organic supplements to enhance human body parts (especially cartilage), and in cosmetics, as well as for other aims.

Shark attacks. A few places, such as Australia and South Africa, are infamous for shark attacks, but attacks on humans anywhere are extremely rare. Most shark attacks occur in tropical or subtropical waters, the exception being cooler waters inhabited by the great white shark. The great white is greatly feared thanks to media hype, but it is actually the tiger shark that is responsible for most attacks on humans. Many scientists now believe that most attacks by sharks are not related to predation, but rather to territoriality, or provocation.

In the entire United States, two to three dozen attacks occur on average each year. The vast majority occur in California, Florida, and/or Hawaii; fatalities are rare, and higher numbers of attack incidents seem to coincide with storms and greater

This is all that's left of an angler's bluefin tuna after being attacked by a shark.

water disturbance. The fear of shark attack is, for the most part, unwarranted. The chances of being killed by a bee sting, lightning, or a poisonous snake are much greater than those of being the victim of a shark attack. Yet, even with shark numbers declining and shark control programs being enacted in some places, lingering concerns about public safety and the possible impacts of shark attacks on tourism have led to debate concerning the desirability and practicality of shark management/control programs in certain locales.

Conservation. Sharks are remarkably suited to their role as efficient predators and are critical to the natural balance of the oceans. But human beings have been even more efficient predators of sharks, and shark populations are now in trouble throughout the world. There is widespread concern over increased commercial fishing (and also recreational fishing) and the consequences this has for the populations of some shark species in several of the world's oceans.

Unfortunately, there is a general lack of public awareness about shark conservation needs, especially in light of their low productivity. This is compounded by the historically low value of shark products, by a general lack of management efforts in many countries and a lack of international management mechanisms actively addressing the capture of sharks, by difficulties in identifying sharks at the species level, and by the lack of information about their migratory routes, seasonality, and rates of movement between different regions. A general lack of knowledge about critical habitat areas for sharks and sharklike species is also problematic. Insufficient funding for both research and management of sharks and sharklike fish compounds the problem as well.

Sportfishing

History. With a few exceptions, sportfishing for sharks has a very recent history. Classic books detailing the early days of big-game fishing don't even discuss sharks, except to mention them in a negative context, such as when they attacked hooked tuna or billfish. Prior to the 1960s, only a few areas throughout the world boasted specialists who caught sharks for sport, and in some cases they did so from shore.

Captain William Young from California was one of the early sharking pioneers at the turn of the century, and he popularized adventure with sharks in his writings about killing 100,000 of them from Hawaii to Australia and the Red Sea.

Australia became a hotbed of sharking before the sport became popular in most other areas due to a relative abundance of the great white. Alf Dean was the most famous of the early recreational sharkers, capturing six white sharks weighing more than a ton, including the 2,664-pounder at Ceduna on April 21, 1959, which the International Game Fish Association (IGFA) still recognizes as the all-tackle and 130-pound line-class world record. Dean also holds the 80-pound line-class record with a 2,344-pounder caught in November 1960. Yet those whites were small fry compared to one he lost after a $5^{1}/_{2}$-hour battle; that fish was estimated at 30 feet and 4,000 pounds. Fossil shark teeth indicate that even such modern monsters are much smaller than the really great whites that once ruled the oceans.

The once consistent white shark fishery in South Australia and the east coast of that country also produced a 2,240-pounder for Bob Dyer, who holds the 20-, 30-, and 50-pound line-class records with whites of 1,068, 1,053, and 1,876 pounds. Dyer's wife, Dolly, caught a women's record 1,052-pounder, which stood until Janet Forster boated a 1,164-pound white at The Pages in March of 1994. Ms. Dyer still holds every white shark women's record from the 20- to the 80-pound line classes, however, with fish under 1,000 pounds caught from 1954 to 1957 off Cape Moreton, Queensland.

It's unlikely that these records will be broken, at least not soon, as white sharks are becoming ever scarcer and have received protection from exploitation throughout most of the world. Furthermore, those early anglers both chummed and baited with mammals, a practice since banned by the IGFA, although the old records continue to be recognized.

South Africans were also great shark anglers. S. Schoeman, in his classic book *Strike,* cites a 986.98-kilogram shark landed from the rocks at Hermanus in 1928 by Bill Selkirk with rod and reel and 18-cord line—"certainly the biggest fish ever caught by man on rod and line from the rocks." Reg Harrison of Durban is also credited with a blue pointer (white) of 752.7 kilograms in July, 1953.

New Zealand anglers appreciated the mako long before it became popular in other areas, and Zane Grey wrote about his experiences fishing for them there. Threshers have also long been popular as a gamefish with anglers in that country.

It was Captain Frank Mundus who first popularized sharking in North America, and then Jack Casey who changed the nature of that sport from a "man against beast" killing affair to the largely tag-and-release fishery pursued today.

Mundus developed sportfishing for sharks at Montauk, New York, after World War II and brought public attention to his "monster fishing" by displaying jaws and selling shark teeth while booking charters for his boat *Cricket* from a booth at the New York Sportsmens Show during the 1950s. Mundus was as offbeat as the fish he pursued, sporting port and starboard painted toenails, harpooning porpoises and pilot whales for chum, and berating his customers' skills—all of which brought him a steady supply of business. It was Mundus who provided the inspiration for Peter Benchley's captain in *Jaws,* the book and movie that led to a huge increase in recreational sharking throughout the U.S.

Even before *Jaws,* sharking had already caught on along the south shore of Long Island by the 1960s. The first Bay Shore Tuna Club Shark Tournament resulted in such a massive catch of blue sharks that boats had to wait hours for weigh-ins, and disposal became a significant problem. All sharks were then still regarded as man-eaters to be eliminated from the ocean, but that concept changed within a decade due to the pioneering work of Jack Casey, which started when he was a fisheries scientist at the U.S. Fish and Wildlife Service Marine Fisheries Lab at Sandy Hook, New Jersey.

Casey started studying sharks and one summer took roughly 40 juvenile white sharks from longlines placed not far off Sandy Hook's beaches. He had to keep that information quiet, however, for fear of starting a panic along the Jersey Shore. He also fished with another sharking pioneer at Montauk, John Walton, an antiques dealer in New York. Not only did they catch and release many sharks, but Casey and his father also caught a great white exceeding 1,000 pounds.

When the National Marine Fisheries Service (NMFS) was formed in the early 1970s, Casey was shifted to the NMFS Lab at Narragansett, Rhode Island, where he established the shark tagging program that continues to this day. Unique among tagging *(see)* programs at that time, it relied on the volunteer efforts of anglers to place the volume of tags that would paint a picture of the migratory patterns and growth rates of sharks. Anglers responded to Casey's efforts; within a decade, sharking had turned from a killing sport to one in which the vast majority of the catch was released. It soon became almost a disgrace to bring in a blue shark (which aren't highly regarded as food), except for large specimens in tournaments.

That attitude has been further reinforced by declining shark populations in the face of commercial fishing pressures. Many tournaments have eliminated blue sharks altogether, and some don't allow tiger sharks at all. Most U.S. Mid-Atlantic contests are now strictly for the most esteemed of sharks, the mako—although threshers may also be included.

The popularity of sharking spread from Long Island to New Jersey during the 1970s, and some of the largest shark tournaments were held there for two decades before a significant drop in the resource reduced interest somewhat. *Jaws* inspired country-wide interested in sharking, and even many Florida skippers who previously hated sharks found they could improve their business with charters for the fish that created so much interest among the general public.

Another significant recreational shark fishery developed off Virginia, and there is now at least some interest all the way up the Atlantic coast to Maine. The Sarasota area along Florida's Gulf Coast had an active sportfishery for sharks even

A small bonnethead shark caught on a flat near Big Pine Key, Florida.

before *Jaws,* and the California fishery has built up steadily. West Coast fly anglers have realized that they have a unique opportunity to pursue quantities of small blue sharks, which will eat flies just about as readily as anything else. Makos are also a target off California due to a sharp decrease in the thresher population from commercial fishing pressure.

The willingness of the Chinese to pay high prices for fins to be used in shark fin soup put a big dent in North American shark populations during the 1990s, except for blues, which aren't desired for that use. At one point, some commercial fishermen were cutting the fins off sharks and throwing back the live bodies; ultimately, NMFS prohibited this practice.

Because most sharks are slow growing, take a long time to mature, and then produce few young, they can be very easily overfished—after which it can take decades to restore the fishery. Shark populations have crashed in every area, no matter how remote, where commercial shark fisheries have been established—and usually within a few years after the fishery was established. This fact was well known even during the first half of the twentieth century, but the same practices were allowed when the Chinese market for fins developed; species such as the sandbar (brown) and dusky may remain scarce for many years.

NMFS belatedly protected the extremely vulnerable sand tiger, which sports jutting teeth like a mako but is actually a lazy ground shark (making them a favorite species for aquariums) and lives in shallow waters. Also placed on the protected list were the white and basking sharks.

What used to be a wide-open sportfishery along the Atlantic coast and in the Gulf of Mexico with no restrictions has become a tightly controlled situation with a limit of two fish per boat as recently as 1998 for all except the small coastal species—and a prohibition on the sale of these fish by anglers and even most captains.

Techniques/Tackle. One of the attractions of fishing for the poor man's big-game fish is that almost any tackle will do the job under most circumstances. The vast majority of sharks are caught in open waters, where even large specimens can be handled on relatively light tackle if the angler exercises patience. Light big-game tackle, such as 20- and 30-pound-class outfits, are perfect for most sharks caught offshore. Anglers specifically seeking makos usually opt for 50-pound gear, and 80-pound tackle can be used during tournaments or when tigers, whites, and the largest of makos are sought. Modern standup rods, belts, and harnesses can entirely eliminate the need to sit in a chair to fight even the largest of sharks.

Blue sharks are usually pushovers on heavy gear but can be lots of fun on light tackle. This is especially true when they can be chummed to boatside, making it possible to select individuals of suitable size for spinning, baitcasting, or flycasting tackle. That same light tackle is standard for sharks caught on Florida Keys flats, where there is no deep water available. The sporty blacktip, which also jumps, is a favorite of flats anglers who cast lures and flies to them. Blacktips have poor eyesight, so lures must be placed close to these sharks and drawn right in front of their mouths. Lemon sharks also hit lures on the flats, but the largest sharks that wander into that area are primarily tempted with baits.

Terminal tackle for sharks is important. Their teeth make wire leaders a must; 15 feet of No. 12 to 15 single-strand wire is the usual choice for large sharks, so even if they spin in the leader they may not reach the main line. Kinking is also a problem due to a shark's tendency to spin in the leader, but braided wire presents another problem in that very large sharks can chew through it. Some skippers create leaders using very heavy monofilament attached to a large swivel, to which they add several feet of wire at the terminal end.

Sharks of one species or another may be encountered almost anywhere, from rivers and bays out to midocean. Indeed, shore and small-boat anglers catch some of the largest sharks, particularly in warm waters, where some species even enter areas barely deep enough to cover their bodies. Sharks on the Florida Keys or Bahamas flats can be as spooky as bonefish, although it's hard to imagine what they might fear.

The vast majority of sharking occurs in ocean areas, but sharks are scattered over wide areas. Unlike other fish, which tend to swarm over wrecks or dropoffs, most migratory sharks aren't tied to a particular area. Anglers usually select structure (such as a dropoff) at a likely depth to start their drift, but a means of attracting sharks to the boat is important.

By far the most common and productive method of accomplishing that is chumming *(see)*. Any oily fish can be ground up for chum, which may be mixed with water and ladled over the side to create a steady slick, or frozen in a bucket that is turned over in a net or a crate with holes so it can automatically create a slick as it gradually thaws.

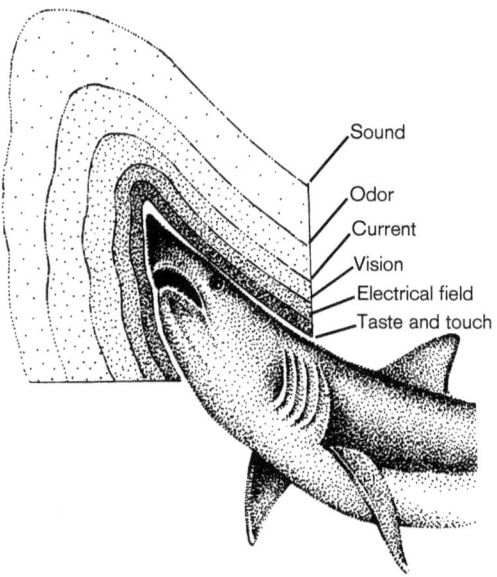

The extraordinary sensory abilities of sharks allow them to detect sounds generated miles away and to detect odor, current, and pressure at a distance of hundreds of yards. They can also see 30 to 60 or more feet away, detect electrical fields that are within inches, and utilize both taste and contact by touching.

The most common fish used for shark chum along the east coast of the U.S. is the menhaden (bunker or pogy), although mackerel and bluefish also work well.

Because sharks have an extremely fine sense of smell, they can zero in on that slick from great distances. This enables boaters to make long drifts that provide an ever-greater attraction as the slick gets longer during the day. Any sharks intersecting that aroma should follow it to its source and find the baits, which are usually distributed from just below the surface down to at least half the water depth. Floats or balloons are used to hold baits at the desired depths, and sinkers are normally required to hold the baits down.

Almost any kind of hooked bait will work at times, with the same fish used for chum being ideal. Natural baits can be fished whole or as fillets. Mackerel are most commonly used along the northeastern U.S., but fresh bluefish are even better, especially when caught on the spot as is common during the prime spring season. Any member of the tuna family is probably the best shark bait of all, as sharks can't seem to resist the smell of tuna blood.

Live baits are typically productive; small bottom fish such as silver and red hake are good choices. Live bluefish are also effective, but those caught while sharking tend to be large, and sharks often play with them and don't get hooked.

Because the vast majority of sharks are now released by anglers, it's best to use just one hook

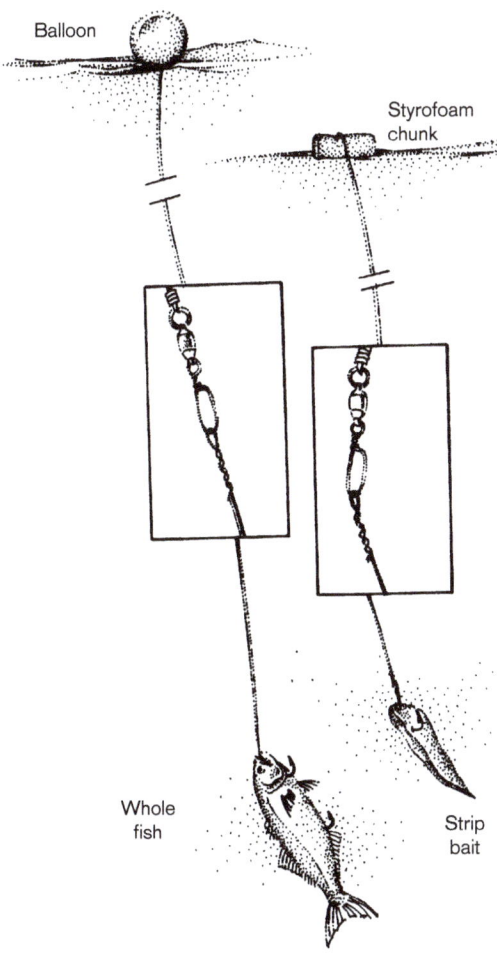

Shark fishing rigs for use offshore and when chumming include a heavy-leader rig with whole bait (left) and a light-leader rig with strip bait (right).

and to strike after allowing only a short run on freespool in order not too hook the prey deeply. Fillets are preferable to whole baits in that regard, as hooking is easier and quicker.

Some sharks, especially makos and threshers, can be trolled, although unadorned lures don't work well. California anglers add a baitfish to a heavy lure, however, which can be slow-trolled below the surface. These connect with makos regularly.

A few large sharks, such as tigers and duskys, tend to fight straight down and are no fun to

Whole and strip baits are combined on a shark hook attached to a wire leader.

catch on light tackle. Most sharks will return to the surface even if they do take a dive during the fight. This tendency permits the use of relatively light tackle and makes sharks an ideal target for standup fishing. They'll usually tow a small boat after sufficient pressure is applied, and larger boats can follow them if necessary, although the vast majority of sharks can be caught from a dead boat.

Landing care. Needless to say, sharks must be handled very carefully at boatside. Not only are the teeth a threat, but in the case of an active shark like the mako, there's always a chance that the fish could jump into the boat. A live shark in a cockpit can be a disaster for anyone trapped there and certainly for equipment and the boat itself. Tiring sharks out before bringing them alongside is the best way to avoid such scenarios.

Whereas ordinary gaffs are fine for tuna, flying gaffs are the usual choice by sharkers because those fish tend to spin when gaffed rather than run straight ahead. Secure the tail with tail ropes as soon as possible after gaffing. Some anglers use a gaffless method that involves a coated wire tail rope with a clip, which is looped around the line and slipped over the shark's body before being cinched at the tail.

Most sharkers carry firearms or a bang stick with which to dispatch sharks that are to be boated. The alternative is to hang the shark upside down, which usually kills the fish within an hour or so. As mentioned earlier, once the fish is out of the water,

Sharks

The business end of a great white shark.

its skeleton isn't strong enough to support its body adequately; the shark soon dies, crushed under its own weight. This lack of rigidity is also the reason why it can be very hard to boat if you're trying to pull it over the side or stern—the weight shifts away from you regardless which end you pull on. It's important to stay away from shark teeth, but pulling from the tail creates a great deal of friction due to the sandpaperlike skin and fins, which catch on everything. It's easy to drag a shark forward because the skin is smooth in that direction. Gin poles are ideal for raising sharks and keeping them away from people.

Shark teeth are a threat at all times. Even "dead" sharks may have active nerves that can cause the jaws to clamp down. More people have probably been cut by dead sharks than by live ones for this reason. Simple carelessness on the boat or at the dock is all it takes. Makos are particularly dangerous, as their sharp teeth protrude and can cut like razors.

Sharks to be kept for food should be bled, and smaller specimens can be completely gutted and packed in ice for prime eating. Makos are an exception to the rule, but, as noted previously, most sharks have urea in their blood and will develop an ammonia smell and tainted taste in their flesh if not bled when caught.

A tagging stick and a supply of tags is of more use these days than the gaff because the vast majority of sharks are released. Free tags are available at no charge to legitimate taggers in the Atlantic from NMFS Cooperative Shark Tagging Program, 28 Tarzwell Drive, Narragansett, RI 02882. For the Pacific, from Cabo San Lucas to Monteray Bay, those tags come from California Pelagic Shark Tagging Program, California Department of Fish and Game, Marine Resources Division, Southern Operations, 330 Golden Shore, Suite 50, Long Beach, CA 90802.

Species of Note

Atlantic angel shark *(Squatina dumeril)*. Also called sand devil, the Atlantic angel shark is frequently mistaken for a ray because of its flattened, triangular body.

This fish is unlike a ray, however, as its gill slits are lateral and create a deep indentation

Atlantic Angel Shark

Basking Shark

be-tween its head and pectoral fin. The Atlantic angel is brownish to bluish gray on the back and whitish on the belly, and it has a mid-dorsal row of denticles. The large mouth is terminal, and the teeth have a broad base with a long, pointed central cusp. The pectoral fins are not attached to the body at the rear, and Atlantic angels swim without making much use of them. Growing to 5 feet long, Atlantic angels will bite when captured and can inflict vicious wounds. In the western Atlantic, they range from southern New England to the Gulf of Mexico, also occurring around Jamaica, Nicaragua, and Venezuela; they are rarer off southern Florida and in the Gulf of Mexico. They are common during the summer along the Mid-Atlantic states.

Basking shark *(Cetorhinus maximus)*. The second largest shark in existence today, growing to 45 feet, the basking shark is a member of the mackerel shark family and is basically harmless to humans.

A dark-gray or slate-gray fish fading to a paler shade on its belly, the basking shark gets its name from its habit of swimming slowly at the surface. As a plankton feeder, it will not take bait, being too large for sportfishing anyway. Long gill slits span the sides and nearly meet below, with long, closely set gill rakers that it uses to strain zooplankton; the rakers are shed during the winter, and the basking shark fasts on the bottom while it grows new ones. Pelagic in cool, temperate waters nearly worldwide, its three-year gestation period is the longest of any shark's. Once extensively fished commercially and valued for its liver for oil, the basking shark may be a potential source of anticarcinoma drugs and is used in Chinese medicine.

Blacktip shark *(Carcharhinus limbatus)*. Sometimes called blacktip whaler, common blacktip shark, or small blacktipped shark, this shark reaches just over 8 feet in length; the all-tackle world record is a 270-pound, 9-ounce fish taken off Kenya in 1995.

It is dark bluish gray on the back and whitish below, with a distinctive silver white stripe on its flank; young fish are generally paler. As the name implies, it is black-tipped on the inside of the pectoral fin, as well as on the dorsal, anal, and lower lobe of the caudal fins in young fish. This shading may be faint, especially on the first dorsal fin, and it fades with growth. The blacktip shark has a long, almost V-shaped snout and serrated, nearly symmetrical teeth. It often forms large surface schools and is an active hunter in midwater, responsible for very few attacks on humans but dangerous when provoked.

A wide-ranging species, the blacktip extends along the western Atlantic from Massachusetts to Brazil, and in the east from Senegal to Zaire,

Blacktip Shark

Blue Shark

Madeira, the Canaries, and the Mediterranean. In the Indo–West Pacific, they occur from South Africa, Madagascar, and the Red Sea to Australia, as well as from China to Australia and also around Hawaii, Tahiti, and the Marquesas. In the eastern Pacific, it occurs from southern Baja California to Peru and the Galápagos Islands.

Blue shark *(Prionace glauca)*. This shark is also called bluedog, great blue shark, and blue whaler, the last because of its habit of trailing whaling ships and feeding off whale carcasses and ship garbage.

A member of the requiem shark family, the blue shark is very slender and streamlined, with a long and pointed snout that is much longer than the width of its mouth. Appropriately, it is a deep, brilliant blue or a dark cobalt to indigo blue above, fading gradually to white below. With up to three rows of functional teeth in each jaw, the larger teeth in the upper jaw are "saber shaped," or broadly convex on one side and concave on the other; the teeth are serrated along the edges, and those in the lower jaw are narrower.

Circumglobal in temperate and tropical waters, blue sharks hardly rate as fighters in comparison to makos and threshers, but they are much more abundant and provide fine sport on appropriate tackle in cooler temperate waters off the northeastern United States, England, and California, where there are large sportfisheries for them. They usually swim slowly, and yet they can be one of the swiftest sharks. The largest fish exceed 400 pounds and are fairly strong fighters when taken from cool waters. Viviparous, blue sharks bear live young in large litters, up to 54 at one time (135 have been recorded); they mature at a length of 7 or 8 feet but can reach upward of 13 feet. The all-tackle world record is a 454-pound fish taken off Massachusetts in 1996. Blue sharks are potentially dangerous to humans because they are related to unprovoked attacks on both humans and boats, especially during accidents and disasters at sea when injured people are in the water.

Bonnethead shark *(Sphyrna tiburo)*. Occasionally referred to simply as bonnet, the bonnethead shark is the smallest member of the hammerhead sharks, the family characterized by having eyes located at the far ends of extended lateral lobes.

The bonnethead is particularly distinctive in appearance because it has a smooth, broadly widened head, frequently described as "spade shaped," which has more curve to it than do the heads of any other hammerheads. Also, the front of the head is lacking a median groove, which is present in other hammerheads. Gray to grayish brown in color, the bonnethead shark seldom exceeds

Bonnethead Shark

Bull Shark

3 feet in length, maturing at about that length to bear 6 to 12 live young at one time.

Bonnetheads, particularly young fish, are often found over flats, where they can be taken on flies and ultralight tackle. The all-tackle world record is a 23-pound, 11-ounce fish taken off Georgia in 1994. These fish occur in the western Atlantic from North Carolina (occasionally Rhode Island) to southern Brazil, as well as around Cuba and the Bahamas, and in the eastern Pacific from Southern California to Ecuador.

Bull shark *(Carcharhinus leucas)*. A large member of the requiem shark family, the bull shark is also called freshwater whaler and river whaler because it is most common inshore around river mouths and can adapt to life in freshwater.

This is the species that is landlocked in Lake Nicaragua in Nicaragua and has gained fame as a man-eater because it has been repeatedly implicated in attacks on humans. Also known as the Zambezi shark in southern African waters, the bull shark is one of the three most dangerous sharks in that area, along with great white and tiger sharks, due to its relative abundance in inshore habitats where people are more likely to be attacked.

The bull shark gets its name from its bull-like head and is known for its heavy body and short snout, the latter of which appears very broad and rounded from below. Gray to dull brown above and growing pale below, the bull shark has a large first dorsal fin that begins above the midpectoral fin, and the upper lobe of the tail is much larger than the lower.

The bull shark can be sluggish and unwilling to strike a fly or crankbait, but it will hit natural baits readily; unlike other sharks that rise to the surface, the bull shark often stays deep and fights hard. Like the hammerhead, it will frequently attack hooked tarpon. Usually growing to a length of 6 to 9 feet, the bull shark can reach 12 feet and more 500 pounds. The all-tackle world record is a 490-pounder taken off Alabama in 1986. Bull sharks are widespread; they inhabit the western Atlantic from Massachusetts to southern Brazil, and the eastern Atlantic from Morocco and Senegal to Angola. In the Indo–West Pacific, they occur from South Africa to India and Vietnam to Australia, and in the eastern Pacific from southern Baja California, Mexico, to Ecuador and possibly Peru.

Hammerhead sharks *(Sphyrna species)*. Hammerhead sharks occur worldwide; the most prominent species include the great hammerhead

Hammerhead Shark

Lemon Shark

(S. mokarran), the smooth hammerhead *(S. zygaena)*, the scalloped hammerhead *(S. lewini)*, and the bonnethead shark *(see previous heading)*.

Hammerheads are easy for even a novice to identify, with eyes located at the ends of two thin lobes and the overall structure resembling a hammer. One possible reason why the head takes on a hammer shape may be that the shape is ideal for turning and locating odors, making the best use of the electroreceptors present in all sharks, which in turn makes detecting food an easier chore.

The largest species is the great hammerhead, which can reach a length of 20 feet and a weight of 1,000 pounds. This shark prefers warm waters and is rarely found outside tropical areas. The most widely distributed hammerhead is most likely the smooth hammerhead, which grows to 14 feet. The front edge of its head is rounded and unnotched at the center, or smooth, and it inhabits shallow, calm coastal waters of bays and harbors. The scalloped hammerhead is a gray brown to olive shark that generally grows 5 to 7 feet, usually smaller than the smooth hammerhead but sometimes reaching 15 feet. The front edge of its head is rounded and notched, or scalloped. Both smooth and scalloped hammerheads occasionally school in large numbers. Some lesser-known hammerheads include *S. couardi*, a large West African shark that bears a resemblance to the scalloped hammerhead, and *S. blochii*, whose strange appearance is due to head lobes, which often measure 50 percent of the body length and are swept back like the wings of an airplane.

Stingrays are thought to be the favored food of many hammerheads, and all species are viviparous and prolific, giving birth to many live young at a time. These sharks are exceptionally strong and can make fast, long surface and midwater runs when hooked, fighting hard and thrashing about with a great deal of excitement.

Lemon shark *(Negaprion brevirostris)*. A requiem family shark, the lemon shark grows to 11 feet at maximum, although it is usually between 5 and 8 feet long.

A potentially dangerous shark, it may rest on the bottom in coastal waters in groups of 4 to 6 and become aggressive when in the vicinity of spearfishing. It is commonly yellow brown, although it can also be muddy dark brown or dark gray with olive sides and a paler belly. It has a blunt and broad snout that appears rounded from below. The second dorsal fin is almost equal in size to the large first dorsal fin, and the upper lobe of the tail is much larger than the lower.

Lemon sharks are good inshore, light-tackle sportfish that inhabit western Atlantic waters from New Jersey to Brazil, including the Gulf of Mexico, the Bahamas, and the Caribbean, and eastern Atlantic waters from Senegal and the Ivory Coast possibly down the African continent; in the eastern Pacific they extend from southern Baja California, Mexico, and the Gulf of California to Ecuador.

Leopard shark *(Triakis semifasciata)*. Sometimes called cat shark, the leopard shark is a striking fish, so named for its leopardlike black spots, which run in crossbars across its back and sides over a lighter gray background.

Leopard Shark

Porbeagle Shark

It has an elongate body and a short snout that is bluntly rounded. Attaining lengths of up to 7 feet, the leopard shark inhabits inshore sand flats and rocky areas, often in schools with smoothhound sharks. As a smaller, less-aggressive species of shark, it is not considered dangerous. Female bear live young in moderate numbers, between 4 and 29 at each birth. Found in the eastern Pacific from Oregon to the Gulf of California, the leopard shark is good light-tackle game and very good table fare. It is often sought by commercial fishermen.

Porbeagle shark *(Lamna nasus).* The porbeagle shark is recognized by many different names, among them beaumaris shark, blue dog, bonito shark, herring shark, mackerel shark, porbeagle, and salmon shark.

It is a member of the mackerel shark family, as are the great white and the mako sharks, and bears a resemblance to both species. The porbeagle has a robust, cobalt blue body with a perfectly conical snout that ends in a point. It is easily identified by its teeth, which are smooth and have little cusps on each side of the base. It often has a distinctive white area at the base portion of the first dorsal fin; this fin is farther forward than it is on mako or white sharks. There is a large, particularly prominent flattened keel on both sides of the caudal peduncle, and beneath that but farther back on the tail is a small secondary keel, which mako and white sharks also lack. Its anal fin is directly aligned with the second dorsal fin.

The flesh of the porbeagle is of good quality and texture and is said to taste something like swordfish. Excellent sportfish, porbeagles occur in colder waters than makos or whites, which may explain why they are not implicated in attacks on humans. A widespread species, they exist in the western Atlantic from Newfoundland to New Jersey, although they rarely venture south of New England, and probably range from southern Brazil through Argentina. In the eastern Atlantic, porbeagles range from Iceland and the western Barents Sea to South Africa, being present as well in the Mediterranean; in the South Pacific, they inhabit waters around Australia, New Zealand, and Chile. They are also known in the Antarctic and in the South Indian Ocean.

Sandbar shark *(Carcharhinus plumbeus).* The

Sandbar Shark

Sand Tiger Shark

sandbar shark is an inshore fish and a good light-tackle fighter, growing usually to between 5 and 7 feet long. A relatively heavy-bodied fish, it is dark bluish gray to brownish gray and has a pale or white belly.

There is a distinct ridge on the back between the first and second dorsal fins, and the first fin is large and pointed, starting over the middle of the pectoral fin. Its snout is shorter than the width of its mouth, appearing rounded from below.

Sandbar and dusky *(Carcharhinus obscurus)* sharks are coastal migrants that have taken a particularly hard hit from longlining for both their fins and flesh. Sandbars are usually called browns by anglers along the east coast of the U.S., where they commonly migrate into large bays to spawn. Although basically ground sharks, they are extremely strong fighters. The dusky is almost indistinguishable from the sandbar but grows to more than 700 pounds; the brown never exceeds much more than 200 pounds. The most common gray shark along the coast of the Middle Atlantic states, sandbars extend in the western Atlantic from southern Massachusetts to southern Brazil, and in the east from Portugal to Zaire, including the Mediterranean. In the western Indian Ocean, they occur in the Red Sea, the Gulf of Oman, eastern Africa, Madagascar, Mauritius, and the Seychelles. In the Pacific, they occur in the west from Japan to Australia and in the east around the Hawaiian, Galápagos, and Revillagigedo Islands.

Sand tiger shark *(Carcharias taurus)*. Previously called *Odontaspis taurus*, the sand tiger shark is the most common shark sighted along Atlantic beaches. It grows to about 9 feet and is grayish brown or tan with dark brown spots along the sides that grow more numerous toward the tail; although it bears a resemblance to the tiger shark, it has a larger second dorsal fin, a longer snout, and strongly projecting teeth.

Usually caught accidentally by surf casters fishing for other fish, sand tigers are sluggish and offer little resistance when hooked. In the western Atlantic, they occur from the Gulf of Maine to Argentina, and in the east from the Mediterranean to Cameroon. In the western Indian Ocean, sand tigers extend from the Red Sea to South Africa, Pakistan, and possibly India; in the western Pacific, they extend from Japan to Australia, possibly including waters around Vietnam and Indonesia.

Sharpnose sharks *(Rhizoprionodon species)*. There are six sharpnose sharks in the *Rhizoprionodon* genus of the requiem shark family, all sharing a similar external appearance that is characterized by a long flattened snout. The best-known member of the family is the Atlantic sharpnose, which is a very popular small species as an inshore food and a small gamefish in the Gulf of Mexico.

It grows to between 2 and 4 feet in length and has the characteristic long and flattened snout, as well as a slender, brown to olive gray body with a pale belly. The dorsal and caudal fins may be edged in black, especially in the young, and often there are small, scattered whitish spots on the sides. The Atlantic sharpnose is further distinguished by well-developed furrows in the lips at the corners of the mouth, and by the second dorsal fin,

Atlantic Sharpnose Shark

Shortfin Mako Shark

which begins over the middle of the anal fin. This sharpnose ranges as far north as New Brunswick but is rarely found north of North Carolina. The Caribbean sharpnose (*R. porosus*) may actually be a subspecies of the Atlantic sharpnose but is found in mostly Caribbean waters. The Brazilian sharpnose (*R. lalandii*) is confined to Brazilian waters.

The Australian sharpnose (*R. taylori*) and gray sharpnose (*R. oligolinx*) sharks are nearly identical in appearance but are easy to distinguish because of their different ranges, the former being a western Pacific species and the latter inhabiting Indo–West Pacific waters. The Pacific sharpnose is fairly common in the Gulf of California and a frequent catch of the shark fisheries there, extending as far south as Peru.

Shortfin mako shark (*Isurus oxyrinchus*). Also called blue pointer, bonito shark, dog shark, and short-nosed mackerel shark, the shortfin mako is by far the most popular of angling sharks, exceeding 1,000 pounds in weight and 13 feet in length.

It is widely distributed throughout the oceans, ranging in the western Atlantic from the Gulf of Maine to southern Brazil, in the eastern Atlantic from Norway to South Africa, and in the Indo–West Pacific from South Africa to Australia, Russia to New Zealand, south of the Aleutian Islands to Hawaii, and Southern California to Chile. Although most abundant in temperate waters (64° to 70°F is considered ideal), some large makos adapt to temperatures in the upper 50s, and smaller makos often prefer waters in the 70s. A similar species, the longfin mako (*I. paucus*), is encountered mainly at night by anglers fishing great depths well offshore.

The shortfin mako has a streamlined, well-proportioned body that is most striking for a vivid blue gray or cobalt blue coloring on its back, which changes to a lighter blue on the sides and a snowy white on the belly; this brilliant coloring fades after death to a grayish brown. Other characteristic features are a conical, sharply pointed snout, a large flattened keel on either side of the caudal peduncle, and a lunate (crescent-shaped) tail with lobes of nearly equal size. The large, first dorsal fin begins just behind the base of the pectoral fins. The shortfin mako can be easily distinguished from all other sharks by its teeth, which are slender and curved and lack cusps or serrations.

Makos have all the characteristics of gamefish in that they fight hard, have good endurance, and are fast, active, strong swimmers that jump. Indeed, their jumps are possibly the most spectacular of all, as they may suddenly appear 20 feet in the air while the line is still pointing at another angle. At the top of their leap, makos typically turn over and reenter the water where they exited. Some makos never jump, and those that do rarely jump more than two or three times. They are also potentially dangerous, known to bite or otherwise attack boats by leaping into them, causing severe injuries and damage.

Unfortunately for makos, they are also very good food fish—a quality that has endeared them to longliners and led to a sharp decline in abundance. Mako steaks command a good price under their own name, but they used to be a cheap substitute for swordfish steaks, which they resemble in both texture and taste. Ironically, makos love to eat swordfish, which they attack by chopping their tails off while the swordfish are dozing on the surface.

Because female makos weigh more than 600 pounds before becoming mature, and only a few pregnant specimens have ever been recorded, it's something of a miracle that there are any makos left in the oceans at all. The warm-blooded mako is ovoviviparous, which means the eggs hatch inside the mother and the young are born alive; while in the uterus, the unborn young often resort to cannibalism until just one remains for birth. The all-tackle world record is a 1,115-pound fish taken off Mauritius in 1988.

Thresher sharks (*Alopias species*). Known by a variety of names, among them fox shark, longtail thresher, pelagic thresher, sea fox, sviveltail, thintail thresher, and thrasher shark, a thresher shark is characterized by its well-muscled tail, the upper lobe of which is usually as long as the rest of the body.

These sharks use their tails to herd baitfish into a mass by slapping or thrashing the water, then stunning or injuring fish before swallowing them. There are four species, including the pelagic thresher (*A. pelagicus*) and the Pacific bigeye thresher

Thresher Shark

(A. profundis), which occur in the northwestern Pa-cific, and the Atlantic bigeye thresher shark *(A. superciliosus)*, which occurs in the Atlantic. The longtail thresher *(A. vulpinus)* is cosmopolitan in temperate and tropical waters. All threshers are fundamentally pelagic but will occasionally move in close to shore.

Grayish to dark charcoal in color, thresher sharks turn abruptly white on the belly and may be mottled on the lower half of the body. Threshers are further identified by the absence of a keel on the caudal peduncle; by their small, pointed and broad-based teeth; and by their comparatively smooth skin. Longtail and pelagic threshers have moderate-size eyes, and the first dorsal fin is set almost directly in the middle of the back and far ahead of the beginning of the pelvic fins. The Atlantic and Pacific bigeye threshers have much larger eyes, and the rear margin of the dorsal fin is located at least as far back as the origin of the pelvic fins.

Threshers are excellent food fish, comparable to mako and swordfish, and they are outstanding fighters (the longtail has been known to leap out of the water). They are often hooked in the tail because of their habit of using their tail to herd potential prey. Thresher sharks were more popular than makos off California until recently and are a relatively rare catch along the U.S. Atlantic coast, although specimens in the 300- to 600-pound class are the most common size encountered from New Jersey to Massachusetts. The largest threshers have come from New Zealand, where they've been boated in excess of 800 pounds; in general they are said to reach 20 feet and 1,000 pounds, but are usually much smaller. The all-tackle world record for *A. vulpinus* is a 767-pound, 3-ounce fish taken off New Zealand in 1983.

Tiger shark *(Galeocerdo cuvier)*. One of the largest of the requiem sharks, the tiger shark grows to 24 feet. It is infamous as one of the most dangerous sharks.

Although some sharks will attack and kill humans without necessarily eating them, the tiger shark is especially fearsome because it is well-known as a man-eater, often devouring the remains of its victims. The tiger shark frequents shallow waters where people swim and is circum-global in tropical and temperate waters. One study has shown that the tiger shark can travel more than 30 miles within a 24-hour period, and that, although tiger sharks do revisit the same coastal areas, the time elapsed between visits can vary from a few days to many months.

Dark bluish gray to brownish gray above and whitish below, the tiger shark is so called because of its prominent dark brown blotches and bars, or "tiger stripes and leopard spots"; these are especially evident in juveniles and small adults but fade with age. This fish has an extremely blunt snout that appears broadly rounded from below, and a mid-dorsal ridge is present. The tiger shark is also distinguished by its broad and coarsely serrated teeth,

Tiger Shark

which have deep notches and are the same in both jaws. The first two of five gill slits are located above the pectoral fin, and there is a long, prominent keel on either side of the caudal peduncle, as well as a long upper lobe on the tail.

The tiger shark is an important species for anglers only because it is commonly in the 300- to 800-pound class when encountered, and can grow much larger. The long-standing all-tackle record of 1,780 pounds was caught from a pier at Cherry Grove, South Carolina, in 1964. Tigers are famed for eating virtually anything, including metal objects, and are generally poor fighters.

Tope *(Galeorhinus galeus)*. One of the smallest members of the requiem shark family, the tope is an active and highly sought species within its extensive range.

Tope

It is also known throughout that range by various names, including flake, greyboy, greyshark, hundshai, school shark, snapper shark, soupfin shark, and vitamin shark.

The tope has a slender body; a prominent, long, pointed snout; long pectoral fins; and a large and strong tail fin with a large lower lobe. It is a bottom-roaming inhabitant of inshore environs that commonly weighs from 20 to 40 pounds but may grow as large as 75 pounds and exceed 5 feet in length. It is reported to live as long as 55 years. Despite its size, it is favorably regarded by anglers for its vigorous fight.

Tope occur in all oceans. In the western Atlantic, they are found in southern Brazil and Argentina; in the eastern Atlantic, they range from Iceland to South Africa, including the Mediterranean Sea. In the western Indian Ocean, tope are found in South Africa; in the western Pacific, they are found in Australia and New Zealand; in the eastern Pacific, they range from British Columbia to southern Baja California, Mexico, including the Gulf of California, and also Peru and Chile.

White shark *(Carcharodon carcharias)*. The white shark goes by a few different names, such as white pointer, white death, man-eater, and great white shark, the last two of which hint at both the deadly habits and threatening size of this mackerel shark.

Although a relatively uncommon deep-water fish, the white shark occasionally enters shallow waters and will attack, without provocation, humans and small boats alike; because it often lingers near islands and offshore colonies of seals and sea lions, which are some of its preferred foods, it is thought that some attacks on humans occur because the white shark mistakes divers or surfers in wet suits for seals. It is undoubtedly the most dangerous shark due to a combination of size, strength, ability, and disposition to attack, and because of the many recorded attacks that have taken place in the twentieth century.

Growing to 26 feet but usually less than 16 feet in length, the white shark has a stout, heavy body that may be a dull slate blue, grayish brown, or almost black above, turning dirty white below. There are black edges on the pectoral fins, and often there is a black oval blotch on the body just above or behind the fins. The large head ends in a point at the conical snout, which accounts for the name "white pointer." There is a large, distinct, flattened keel on either side of the caudal peduncle and a greatly reduced second dorsal fin. A distinguishing feature of the white shark is its teeth, which are large and triangular with sharp, serrated cutting edges.

Sportfishing for whites has virtually come to an end as a result of conservation efforts aimed at preserving the greatest of the predators, which were never especially abundant in any case. Most whites are found in temperate or even cool waters

White Shark

worldwide, and close to a source of the marine mammals they prefer to eat after growing to large sizes. Actually, there are two much larger sharks, the basking shark of the North Atlantic and the whale shark of the tropics, but these are harmless plankton feeders.

Though Alf Dean's white shark record—2,664 pounds off South Australia in 1959—continues to be recognized by the IGFA, a much larger 17-foot specimen of 3,427 pounds was caught on August 6, 1986, on legitimate tackle by Donnie Braddick out of Montauk, New York. Captain Frank Mundus had found a dead whale floating offshore, a sure attraction for the huge whites and tigers that seem to appear out of nowhere for such a feast. Although sharks feeding on blubber have no interest in fish, Mundus (who had harpooned several great whites over the years) managed to slip a string of baitfish into a white's mouth to get the hookup. After much controversy, the IGFA decided not to accept the catch because the dead whale was, in effect, the forbidden mammal chum.

SHARPENER
See: Hook Sharpening.

SHEEFISH
A common term in North America for inconnu (see).

SHEEPHEAD, CALIFORNIA *Semicossyphus pulcher.*
Other names—sheepie, goat, billygoat (large), red fish, humpy, fathead; Spanish: *vieja de California.*

A member of the Labridae family of wrasses (see), the California sheephead is a strong bottom-dwelling fish that is a favorite of spearfishing divers. It has some commercial value, although declining numbers caused it to be supplanted commercially by rockfish. Its flesh is white, firm, and mild, and it is preferred in chowder and in salads.

Identification. The body of the California sheephead is elongate, robust, and compressed. This species is a hermaphrodite: It begins life as a female and becomes a male later in life. Females mature at about 8 inches in length and four to five years of age. Most females transform to males at a length of about 12 inches, or seven to eight years of age. This sex change is accompanied by a marked change in appearance. Younger fish (females) are a uniform pinkish red with a white lower jaw. As they age and become males, the head and rear third of the body turn black, the midsection of the body remains red, and the lower jaw remains white. In all stages of their development, sheephead have unusually large doglike teeth.

Size/Age. The largest sheephead recorded on rod and reel was 36 inches long and weighed $35\frac{1}{2}$ pounds, although the average fish weighs less than 15 pounds. At least two fish of 40 pounds were speared in the past. A 29-pound, 32-inch-long fish was 53 years old.

Distribution. California sheephead occur from Cabo San Lucas, Baja California, Mexico, to Monterey Bay, California. An isolated population exists in the Gulf of California, but these fish are uncommon north of Point Conception, California

Habitat. This species is generally taken in rocky kelp areas near shore, in water from 20 to 100 feet deep, although they do occur as deep as 180 feet.

Spawning behavior. Spawning takes place in early spring and summer.

Food and feeding habits. Crabs, mussels, various-size snails, squid, sea urchins, sand dollars, and sea cucumbers are typical food items. The large caninelike teeth are used to pry food from rocks. A special plate in the throat crushes shells into small pieces for easy digestion. Occasionally, large adults have been observed out of the water in the intertidal zone, hanging onto mussels after a wave has receded.

Angling. California sheephead take a variety of live and cut baits, such as anchovies or squid, fished on the bottom. Whole live mackerel fished on the bottom are often good for large specimens. These fish provide a long, determined struggle and must be kept away from kelp and rock ledges to avoid having the line cut.

SHEEPSHEAD
(1) The most commonly used term for freshwater drum.
See: Drum, Freshwater.

California Sheephead

(2) *Archosargus probatocephalus.*
Other names—convict fish, sheepshead seabream; Portuguese: *sargo;* Spanish: *sargo chopa.*

This is the most popular member of the Sparidae family of porgies with saltwater anglers in the United States, and a large one that is commonly caught around barnacle-encrusted structures along shorelines. The sheepshead is an excellent food fish and is of commercial value.

Identification. The basic color of the sheepshead is black, including the fins, but the sides and caudal peduncle are striped alternately with broad

Sheepshead

bands of silver and black. The stripes are most prominent in young fish. The mouth is small to medium in size, and the teeth are broad and flat for crushing the shells of crustaceans and mollusks.

Size. Sheepshead average about a pound in weight but may attain a weight of 25 pounds and measure as much as 3 feet in length.

Distribution. This species occurs from Nova Scotia to Florida and the northern Gulf of Mexico and south to Brazil, excluding the Bahamas and West Indies.

Habitat. Sheepshead are found in bays and estuaries and along the shoreline and commonly enter brackish water in coastal rivers.

Food and feeding habits. Sheepshead consume mollusks and crustaceans. Often traveling in schools, they are browsing feeders that forage around the pilings of wharves and docks and may be located around jetties, over rocky bottoms, and in other places where they can find oysters and mussels.

Angling. These game-fighting bottom feeders are primarily caught on bait and bottom or float rigs, usually with light or medium tackle as necessary for the depths fished and weights used. Assorted crabs, clams, mussels, shrimp, or cut baits are the primary natural baits, sometimes used with sliding sinker rigs, although small jigs may also catch fish. Because these fish are wary, chumming is popular. Although most fishing occurs around objects and structures near shore, the possibilities for stalking fewer and warier fish also exist in some backwater marsh areas. In winter, deeper artificial reefs (in 35 to 60 feet of water) in Southern waters may be the best place to find these fish, as they congregate here where the water temperature is relatively stable.

Sheepshead bite lightly, sometimes remaining undetected and stealing baits. They can be tough and frustrating fish to hook. Furthermore, the hook must be set firmly because of the fish's hard mouth.

See: **Inshore Fishing; Porgies.**

SHEET BEND
See: **Knots, Boating.**

SHELLFISH
A popular general term for crustaceans and mollusks, but not including finfish. Shellfish may be used as bait when angling, but they are not targeted by anglers, or deliberately sought with sporting equipment.

SHELL LURE
A lure made with pearl shell inserts, devised by Polynesians for tuna fishing.

SHINER
Shiners are members of the minnow, or Cyprinidae, family of freshwater fish. A number of minnows are called "shiners" because their shimmering silvery sides flash as the little fish turn in the water. There are well over a hundred species in North America. All are relatively slender fish, and their fins are relatively large compared to the size of their body. They are prominent forage species for predator fish, are used frequently as baits, and are often imitated with lures and flies.

Typical of the group is the common shiner (*Luxilus cornutus*), which is olive green above and silvery on its sides and belly. At spawning time in spring, the male's body takes on a pinkish tinge, and the tail and fins become bright orange or red, particularly at the base. Hard bumps, or tubercles, develop on the top of the head and on the fins. Males are larger than females, sometimes attaining a length of 8 inches, although they are usually sold for bait when they are half this size or smaller. The common shiner is widely distributed, inhabiting small streams from southern Canada southward over much of the northern United States east of the Rockies.

Another widely distributed minnow of this group is the emerald shiner (*Notropis atherinoides*), which often travels in tremendously large schools. It is smaller than the common shiner, rarely exceeding 3 inches in length, and has a proportionately shorter snout. The striped shiner (*Luxilus chrysocephalus*) is also common and widespread, and is similar in size to the common shiner.

Some of the more attractive and hardy shiners are kept in aquariums. Among these is the sailfin shiner (*Pteronotropis hypselopterus*), which has exceptionally high fins. The males' fins are streaked handsomely with red during the spawning season.

The golden shiner (*Notemigonus crysoleucas*) rates as one of the best bait minnows and is commonly reared specifically for this market. Unlike most members of the minnow family, the golden shiner has a scaleless keel on the midline of its belly. The lateral line bows sharply downward, and the mouth angles upward. When young, these minnows are silvery; as adults, they become a bright metallic or brassy gold. The average size varies with the environment, but in some large lakes the golden shiner attains a length of 10 inches or more; in Florida, large shiners are commonly used as live baits for largemouth bass. Found throughout eastern Canada and in the U.S. east of the Rockies, the golden shiner is adaptable to a wide range of water conditions and temperatures, from cool and swift-flowing, which it cohabits with trout, to warm and weedy sluggish streams and ponds.

See: Minnow; Shiner, Common; Shiner, Emerald; Shiner, Golden; Shiner, Striped.

SHINER, COMMON *Luxilus cornutus*.

Other names—shiner.

The common shiner is an abundant minnow of the Cyprinidae family that is commonly used as a baitfish. It has been known to hybridize with striped shiners *(see: shiner, striped)*.

Identification. The common shiner is silvery with a deep compressed body, a dusky dorsal stripe, large eyes, diamond-shaped scales that flake off easily, and nine anal rays. It has no barbels, and no dark lateral stripe, but there is a dark stripe along the middle of the generally olive-colored back. During the spawning season, males develop blue backs and red or pink bodies, with pinkish fins, and display large tubercles on the head, pectoral fins, and anterior parts of the body.

Size. Common shiners are usually 3 to 4 inches long but can grow to 8 inches.

Distribution. This species occurs throughout the Mississippi River, Hudson Bay, Great Lakes, and Atlantic basins from Nova Scotia to Saskatchewan south to Missouri and Virginia.

Habitat. Common shiners are most prevalent in small to moderate-size streams, preferring areas that are clear and without fast-moving water. They will tolerate a small amount of silt, but not muddy water.

Spawning behavior. Common shiners spawn in late spring in water temperatures ranging from 60° to 65°F. They are diverse spawners, preferring to use the nests of other minnows such as chub and fallfish, but they also spawn over gravel or in excavated depressions in gravel or sand. Groups of males gather at the spawning sight and vie for position at the upstream end of the nesting area. Spawning occurs when the male wraps his body around a female and drives her toward the nest. Because they often spawn in nests constructed by other minnow species, hybridization is common.

Food. Common shiners feed mainly on insects and insect larvae, but their diet may also include plant material, fish eggs, and small fish.

Angling. Common shiners have no angling value, but they are one of many shiners that are important forage for larger predators and are often used as baitfish by anglers.

See: Minnow; Shiner.

SHINER, EMERALD *Notropis atherinoides*.

Other names—buckeye, shiner, lake shiner, lake emerald shiner, common emerald shiner; French: *mémé émeraude*.

The emerald shiner is one of many shiners that are members of the minnow, or Cyprinidae, family. These fish are important forage for predator species and are frequently used as bait by anglers. Unlike most minnows, however, the emerald shiner is a pelagic big-water species and is abundant in large rivers and in lakes within its range.

Identification. The emerald shiner is a slender, elongated fish with a pale and silvery slab-sided body; it is faintly iridescent green on the top, fading to silver or white on the belly. Juveniles appear semitransparent. Other characteristics include a faint lateral band, a short and fairly pointed snout, large eyes, and usually 11 anal fin rays. It has no barbels. During the spawning season, males develop very small tubercles on the fins but have no breeding colors.

Size/Age. Emerald shiners are commonly 3 to 4 inches long, and seldom grow to more than 5 inches long. They typically living for only three years.

Distribution. This species has a wide range, from the St. Lawrence and Hudson River basins west to the Mackenzie River drainage of the Northwest Territories and south throughout the Great Lakes and Mississippi River drainages to the Gulf Coast from Texas to Alabama. It is probably the most abundant fish in the Mississippi River and other large rivers, and is also prominent in the Great Lakes as well as other large lakes.

Habitat. Emerald shiners travel in large schools in midwater and near-surface areas. They roam in large lakes and are common in the pools of big riv-

Common Shiner

Emerald Shiner

ers. They are known to move vertically toward the surface at night, and to deeper water in daylight.

Spawning behavior. Spawning occurs when water temperatures reach about 75°F and may be continued over an extended period, lasting from late spring through midsummer in some places. Unlike many other shiners, this species spawns in midwater in groups. It is also prone to cyclical abundance.

Food. A pelagic species, emerald shiners feed on plankton, zooplankton, blue-green algae, diatoms, and insect larvae.

Angling. Emerald shiners have no angling value, but they are one of many shiners that are important forage for larger predators, and are often used as bait by anglers.

See: Minnow; Shiner.

SHINER, GOLDEN *Notemigonus crysoleucas.*
Other names—roach, shad roach, shiner, pond shiner.

The golden shiner is a prominent and widespread minnow of the Cyprinidae family. These fish are important forage species for predators and are widely used in various sizes as baits by anglers.

Identification. The golden shiner has a deep, compressed body that is generally golden yellow or brass colored in turbid water, varying to more silvery in clear water. The fins are yellow green but become reddish in large spawning adults. The mouth is small and upturned with a slightly pointed snout, and there is a distinctive fleshy scaleless keel along the belly from the pelvic to anal fin. This keel distinguishes the golden shiner from other similar species, especially the European rudd (*see: rudd*), which is an introduced species in the native North American range of the golden shiner. The dusky lateral line of the golden shiner noticeably dips down in the middle of the body, and the caudal fin is moderately forked. The color of the fins is more pronounced during breeding season; breeding males develop fine tubercles on the dorsal surface of the head and body. The golden shiner has 7 to 9 dorsal rays, and 8 to 19 anal rays.

Size/Age. Golden shiners can grow to $10^1/_2$ to 12 inches in length, although the average size varies with the environment. Many northerly waters are likely to produce smaller fish on average, and 3 to 5 inches is the norm in many places. These fish reportedly live for up to 10 years.

Distribution. This species is widely distributed east of the Rockies in the central and eastern United States, ranging from Quebec to Saskatchewan in the north, and to Florida, Texas, and Mexico in the south. It has been introduced elsewhere, including Arizona, California, and Washington.

Habitat. Slow-water fish, golden shiners are prevalent in lakes, ponds, and backwaters, and in the slower parts of streams and small to medium rivers. They are common in weedy, clean, quiet, and shallow waters.

Golden Shiner

Spawning behavior. Golden shiners reach sexual maturity in their second year when they are usually $2^1/_2$ to $3^1/_2$ inches long, and spawn over an extended period, commencing in spring when water temperatures exceed 68°F. They do not prepare a nest as many other shiners and minnows do; rather, they scatter adhesive eggs over algae and other aquatic vegetation and do not exhibit parental care. Large females reportedly lay more than 200,000 eggs in a spawning season.

Food. The food of golden shiners consists of plankton, algae, insects, and small fish; they feed in midwater and at or near the surface.

Angling. The primary interest of anglers in golden shiners is as baits, and the species is widely cultured in ponds, as well as in large tanks, for distribution to bait shops. In some places, most notably large Florida waters, commercial bait netters (and some energetic and devoted anglers) use chum or groundbait to attract and concentrate large (7- to 10-inch) golden shiners, which are caught by throwing cast nets over the shallow baited area. These are purchased in bait shops at a premium price and used for live-bait fishing for big largemouth bass, or for striped bass. Elsewhere, smaller sizes are preferred for the majority of species.

Golden shiners can be caught on hook and line, although relatively few anglers deliberately do so, as there is little merit to them from a consumptive standpoint. They are caught incidentally, however, by anglers using small hooks and natural baits, as well as flies or tiny jigs, in shallow vegetated areas. European methods of coarse fishing, which employs fine hooks and baits and prebaiting tactics, would likely be effective, although with many other species options there is little incentive for North American anglers to pursue golden shiners as sport.

See: Minnow; Shiner.

SHINER, STRIPED *Luxilus chrysocephalus.*
Other names—shiner.

The striped shiner is a common and widespread minnow of the Cyprinidae family that is familiar to anglers who use it as bait or observe it spawning over the gravel nests built by other minnows. Two subspecies are recognized: *Luxilus chrysocephalus chrysocephalus* and *L. c. isolepis*.

Striped Shiner

Identification. The striped shiner is a silvery, laterally compressed minnow with large eyes and a terminal mouth. As in other species of *Luxilus*, the exposed portion of its scales near the anterior lateral line is much more deep than it is wide. Anterior portions of scales are darkly pigmented, giving a crescent shaped appearance to the sides of striped shiners. Its common name stems from several parallel stripes that run along each side of the upper body and converge posterior to the dorsal fin. The convergence of these lines appears as large Vs when viewed from above.

The two subspecies can be separated by the appearance of the lateral stripes; *L. c. chrysocephalus* has wavy stripes, whereas *L. c. isolepis* has straight stripes. Other characteristics of striped shiners are 8 to 10 anal fin rays, a complete lateral line with 36 to 42 scales, and a pharyngeal tooth count formula of 2-4-4-2. Nuptial males possess striking coloration, developing a rosy pink color on their head, body, and the margins of all fins. Tubercles occur on the head, snout, lower jaw, and pectoral fins of nuptial males.

Size/Age. Adults can exceed 8 inches in length, but most are less than 5 inches long; they can live up to six years.

Distribution. The subspecies *L. c. chrysocephalus* extends throughout drainages of the lower Mississippi River and Gulf Coast; *L. c. isolepis* occurs in drainages of the Great Lakes and Mississippi River basins north of the Red River in Arkansas.

Habitat. Striped shiners occur in water bodies ranging from small streams to small rivers but are most abundant in small to medium streams. Their preferred habitats are pools, runs, and backwaters of flowing streams. They are more common in free-flowing streams with clear or slightly turbid water.

Spawning behavior. Striped shiners reach sexual maturity in their second year. Adult males are larger than females. Spawning occurs from late spring to early summer in water temperatures ranging from 16° to 27°C. Striped shiners are classified as pit spawners. Males excavate small pits on the top of chub nests or directly on the stream bottom and aggressively defend these pits while attempting to secure females for spawning. Spawning occurs when the male wraps his body around a female and drives her toward the pit. Females probably release less than 50 eggs during a single spawning event. Because of their tendency to spawn over chub nests, striped shiners often hybridize with chub and with other minnows that use nests.

Food. Striped shiners feed mainly on insects, but their diet may also include detritus, algae, fish eggs, crayfish, and small fish.

Angling. Although striped shiners have no angling value, they are one of many shiners that are important forage for larger predators, and may be used as baitfish by anglers.
See: Minnow; Shiner.

SHOAL
(1) A shallow part of a body of water representing a submerged ridge, bar, or bank that consists of, or is covered by, unconsolidated sediment (mud, sand, gravel) and that rises near enough to the water surface to be a danger to navigation. A shoal is usually visible during low water and in the right daylight conditions and, if deep enough for a boat to pass over, can be observed on sonar. The area adjacent to a shoal may at times be attractive to fish.

(2) A school of fish, usually at the surface or in shallow water (a term used in Europe and sometimes in South America).
See: School; Schooling.

SHOCKING
A term for electrofishing *(see)*.

SHOCK TIPPET
A short length of heavy monofilament or wire that is added to the end of a fly fishing leader.
See: Tippet.

SHOES, WADING
See: Waders.

SHOOTING HEAD
See: Flycasting Tackle; Shooting Line.

SHOOTING LINE
A type of weight-forward fly line that is attached to a long, thin-diameter running line.
See: Flycasting Tackle.

SHORT STRIKE
When a fish strikes at a lure but misses it without contacting the lure, the fish has made a short strike. This often happens because fish are swiping at a lure to stun or cripple it, rather than to instantly

consume it. A short strike may be due to frenzied activity, cold water temperatures that make a particular species only moderately aggressive, or other factors. Using a trailer hook *(see)* with some lures will help catch such fish; making quick repeat presentations with the same lure or (often better) a different lure may get a hookup; and slowing the speed of retrieve may get a more solid strike.

SHORT STROKING
A term for the method of fighting big-game species used primarily in standup fishing *(see)*.

SHOT
A small round fishing weight.
See: Bulk Shot; Sinker.

SHOTTING
Balancing a float *(see)* with split shot.

SIDE CAST
See: Casting.

SIDECAST REEL
Similar in appearance to a fly reel, a sidecast reel is a revolving spool reel with adjustable spool positioning. The spool is turned perpendicular to the rod for casting and the line flows outward on a cast as it does on a spinning reel. The spool is turned parallel to the rod for retrieving line, and the line is wound on just as it is for a fly rod. Primarily made and used in Australia, this reel has such limited popularity that few anglers around the world are familiar with it or have seen one. Although it has good direct winching power, it has a very low retrieve ratio and thus slow line take-up.

SIDEPLANER
See: Planer Boards.

SIERRA LEONE
Situated roughly 7° north of the equator on the western coast of the African continent, Sierra Leone lies between Guinea to the north and Liberia to the southeast. Its coastal region faces the Atlantic Ocean. The country has a tropical climate, with a yearly average temperature between 82° and 90°F, and English is the official language.

Sierra Leone is renowned for exceptional tarpon fishing. Anglers fishing out of the Sherbro Fishing Club on Sherbro Island, approximately 100 miles south of the capital city of Freetown, have set many of the most significant world records for this species. Since 1991, 15 world records have been set in the Sherbro Island vicinity, and many of these fish weighed more than 240 pounds. The largest among them tied the all-tackle world record of 283 pounds. World records notwithstanding, fish in excess of 200 pounds are more than the rule here, and the first 300-pound tarpon ever known was caught in Sierra Leone waters. It's no wonder that Sierra Leone is known as "Tarpon Capital of the World."

The club at Sherbro opened in 1990 and accommodates 14 anglers. It has a small fleet of skiffs and provides tackle, although many anglers bring their own equipment, especially fly tackle.

The estuary at Sherbro opens out on the Atlantic Ocean, and the mouth of the Sherbro River constitutes a "pass" that funnels many smaller rivers into one big estuary. Drift fishing with rigged baits (mullet and bongas) is the principal technique, and tarpon are active throughout the area on favorable tides. Depths range from 12 to 25 feet in the Sherbro River, and at the end of low tide—weather permitting—it is possible to fish for tarpon out in deeper ocean waters.

The daily average tarpon strike ratio is around six, and all tarpon—except possible records—are released. The best fishing is from January through June, but February through May are peak.

Tarpon are not the only gamefish here; big snapper, barracuda, jacks, sharks, bream, and grouper are easily caught by anglers trolling up and down the river and the sea banks. As most of the coastal region is swampy, a number of short rivers drain Sierra Leone, most navigable only in the rainy season, which is primarily from May to October. These rivers are inhabited by crocodiles and hippos.

SIGHT FISHING
Some elements of sportfishing require a good deal of observation on the part of anglers. This takes the form of actually looking for fish and either stalking or hunting visible fish (almost always in shallow water), or looking for telltale signs of fish that cannot actually be seen.

General observation. Many anglers don't notice the little things that sometimes make a big difference in sportfishing. They don't see fish swirl after a lure. They don't see that quick moment when a fish spooks a bunch of bait and gives its presence away. They don't notice characteristics of the water that attract fish or stimulate activity.

Often this inattention is a matter of not being observant or of not knowing what some signs may mean. Observation is an important factor in fishing success. To some extent, on-the-water angling observation is a function of frequent fishing, but it is also a function of being in the right frame of mind and applying yourself to finding fish and thinking about what you're doing. This is especially so when the action is not fast and easy. Some anglers are simply not observant enough of natural signs because they rely on various gadgets, such as sonar and temperature gauges, a bit too heavily, forgetting that there are other aspects to fishing success besides the information gleaned from instrumentation.

Watching the water, for example, is very important in many ways, and helpful when pursuing many species of fish. Watching the water includes watching for reefs, rips, near-surface vegetation, current flows, shade, and water color.

Water color is an especially good example. The clarity of the water can be important to fish movement and/or location as well as to lure selection. If the water always looks the same to you in all places, you may not be looking closely enough at it.

Some species of fish are more likely to be in clear water (or the clearest possible) or are more prone to strike lures in clear water (because they can locate them better), and it would behoove you to look for such. The places where clear and turbid water mix—runoffs, creek mouths, tidal influxes, wind-affected edges, etc.—and the immediate environs around them, are sometimes the best locales to fish.

In certain instances, where dirty water, such as from a creek, enters a clearer body of water, the dirty water is carrying nutrients or small forage that attracts bait, and the bait in turn attract predators. Another good place to put a lure is where there are a lot of baitfish (or perhaps a place to not put a lure if there are none). When fishing for some species of fish at certain times of the year, especially in unfamiliar waters, it can be disconcerting if there is little or no sign of bait. That doesn't mean you won't catch fish; however, when you see bait flitting on or near the surface or in the shallows, that is often a sign directing you to the kinds of places to fish.

When the water is calm, you can spot bait or baitfish movement without much trouble by being attentive. When the water is roiled by wind and waves, it is much more difficult to make visual observations. The presence of some species of birds (see), incidentally, such as a shorebird like heron, can indicate an abundance of bait or small fish in an area.

When bait are schooled and being pushed aggressively by predators, it is quite easy to spot the action. Other times, just one fish is pursuing a single prey or a few fish, and the action is less obvious and perhaps more likely to be missed. Probably every angler has noticed a fish swirling and creating a commotion when it captured or chased some type of prey in either open water or the shallows; occasionally this activity results in a strike and hookup, although a gamefish may not even be responsible for the activity; people confuse the splash of a jumping mullet, for example, with feeding gamefish activity.

Nevertheless, fish that are stalking shallow water, that spook bait, or that capture some prey item on or near the surface, usually give away their presence and often are aggressive fish highly susceptible to capture at that moment. If you look for the signs of the presence of such fish, you'll probably be disappointed; but if you keep your eyes open and (just as important) listen while fishing, you will become aware of gamefish movement. This is especially true when casting and when fishing for most warm-water species of freshwater fish.

It is also true when fishing in coldwater streams. Both Atlantic and Pacific salmon, for example, will roll occasionally on or near the surface, sometimes in a very subtle manner. If you are unfamiliar with the water that you're fishing, this movement, though unrelated to feeding activity, will give you an indication of a fish lie and will point you toward an appropriate place to direct your efforts. Noticing a fish that jumps or rolls is obvious to many anglers, but not to all, especially when there is merely a rise on the surface that can be confused with the swirl of current.

Noticing bait that is in an agitated state is a subtlety that few anglers possess. Avid anglers describe this phenomenon as "nervous water," which is quite accurate although hard to convey. Nervous water is a surface patch, usually just a few yards across, where there is some slight rippling on the surface, distinctly different from that caused by current or light breezes. It happens when a pod of small baitfish is balled up and flitting about, neither feeding nor fleeing, but disturbed—usually because something is lurking nearby that means to maraud them shortly. If you see this action, work the area hard, keeping a lure handy that might imitate a small fish that is injured or struggling.

One of the easiest and best ways to enjoy more success through being observant is to watch your lures when you retrieve them, especially as they near the boat. Some fish are prone to swirl after shallow-running or surface lures and create a sizable boil in the water after they miss the lure in an apparent attempt to stun it. Anglers who aren't watching closely don't see those occasions when a fish strikes and misses the lure, and they cast elsewhere, though they might have been able to catch that particular fish or at least note its location for a later visit.

Wading the flats to cast to wary species is a game of spotting and stalking; this angler and guide are fishing on the south coast of Cuba.

Stalking shallow fish. On some occasions, you're able to see fish in shallow water that are not actually in the process of chasing bait but are foraging below the surface, or merely taking a feeding or resting position. Spotting such fish is certainly helpful for making the best presentation in the proper locale. Obviously some species of fish actively feed in shallow water, and they are primarily caught in those environs by stalking and sight-casting to them, often by intercepting them. This is the basis of most flats fishing.

The most common fish that are stalked by sight fishing in shallow water include tarpon, permit, bonefish, and redfish in saltwater, as well as other species, like sharks, cobia, and mutton snapper. In freshwater, various trout and Atlantic salmon are objects of stalking, as are certain members of the sunfish family—largemouth bass, smallmouth bass, and bluegills—especially in springtime when they are spawning. Other stalked freshwater fish include northern pike and, very rarely, lake trout in far northern areas when they are feeding in shallows.

When trying to spot shallow-water fish, look not at the surface but below the surface and at the bottom. Look for something that stands out as being different, whose movement contrasts with the bottom locale enough for you to detect it. Don't stare at one spot for long, especially when you're searching for fish, and try to bring your peripheral vision into play. When you see the wake of a moving fish, realize that the forward edge of the wake is behind the fish and take this into account when making a cast that is intended to intercept it.

Sometimes it's important to be able to see fish before you cast to them because you have to be able to approach them without alarming them. Other times, it's important to see certain objects that might be harboring fish. Polarized sunglasses are a big help here; those with wraparound side-view protection are best. A cap with a wide bill and dark underside is also a good aid. For difficult viewing, even with a cap or sunglasses, put your hands around the corners of your glasses and cup them to reduce side glare.

If you're fishing with someone else who sees a fish that you do not, use the clock system (the bow of the boat is 12 o'clock and the stern is 6 o'clock) to figure out the specific location of the fish by having your companion give you specific directions; if your companion says a fish is at 2 o'clock and about 60 feet away, you know where to be looking. These directions can be accompanied by rod pointing to help narrow down the positioning; you can point to the spot where you think the fish is, and your companion can tell you to point more to the left or right to zero in on it.

Remember that visibility is improved from high vantage points. Wading anglers (and those sitting in a kayak or canoe) rarely can see into the water the way someone fishing from a boat can. However, in freshwater, especially on salmon rivers, anglers will walk high banks to get a viewing vantage, and some have been known to climb trees (watching from bridges is also common).

A person sitting in a boat cannot see as well as someone standing, and a person standing in the well of a boat has inferior vision compared with someone standing on a deck. The best vision comes from standing on platforms *(see)* or towers *(see)*. Many flats guides, especially those who carry fly anglers, have transom platforms from which they pole, and these offer good visibility. Some flats boats have mini-towers over a center console; these are even better for visibility but are less conducive to fly casting, though fine for those using other types of tackle.
See: Finding Fish; Flat.

SIGHT INDICATOR
A visible lightweight object on the line used to detect subsurface strikes and monitor the position of the angler's offering (usually a nymph).
See: Strike Indicator.

SILICON CARBIDE GUIDE
Silicon carbide (SiC) is a material popularly used to form the ring in many fishing rod guides. Often called a ceramic, it is a hard material that resists abrasion well, although it can be brittle.
See: Rod, Fishing.

SILVERSIDES
Silversides are members of the Atherinidae family and occur throughout the world. Some are valued as food fish, and a few are caught for keeping in aquariums. They are important forage for larger predatory species, especially alongshore, in bays, and in estuaries.

All silversides lack a lateral line and have small, almost useless teeth. Their pelvic fins are located well behind the pectoral fins, and the small, spiny dorsal is well separated from the soft dorsal. The body is typically elongated. Some silversides live in freshwater; others are marine, found near shore. They are often called shiners but are more commonly referred to as "smelt," although they are not related to the true osmerid smelt *(see)*.

One of the most prominent silversides is the California grunion *(Leuresthes tenuis;* see: grunion, California), which grows to $7^1/_2$ inches in length and is famous for moonlight spawning runs and remarkable beach spawning. A similar fish is the gulf grunion *(L. sardina),* which is restricted to the Gulf of California.

California Grunion

Brook Silverside

Also prominent and frequently caught along Pacific piers is the larger (to $17^1/_2$ inches) jacksmelt (*Atherinopsis californiensis*; see: jacksmelt), which have small, unforked teeth in bands. This characteristic differentiates the jacksmelt from the California grunion and also from the topsmelt (*Atherinops affinis*), which grows to 12 inches but generally is in the same range as the jacksmelt. The topsmelt is most easily distinguished from the jacksmelt by its forked teeth set in a single row rather than in bands. These species constitute a sizable portion of the Pacific coast "smelt" catch.

Along the Atlantic coast, the tidewater silverside (*Menidia beryllina*), which grows to only 3 inches long, ranges from Massachusetts southward to the Gulf of Mexico. Although it is predominantly a saltwater species, it is also found in brackish water and freshwater. Other names frequently used for this species are whitebait and spearing. Several similar species occur in the same general range. These include the Atlantic silverside (*M. menidia*) and the Mississippi silverside (*M. audens*), a freshwater species.

The brook silverside (*Labidesthes sicculus*), which is 2 to 4 inches long, is also found only in freshwater, from the St. Lawrence River southward throughout the southeastern United States. Brook silverside schools are often observed skipping along the surface. This behavior has earned them the nickname skipjacks. Olive green above and silvery below, this species has a prominent silver stripe down each side. The snout is projected into a short beak, and the first dorsal fin is so small that it may go unnoticed. The brook silverside is sometimes used for bait but is not hardy.

SINGLE-ACTION REEL
A revolving spool reel whose spool revolves one time for every turn of the handle, resulting in a 1:1 retrieve ratio. The single-action reel, which is primarily used to store line, and which has been predominant in fly fishing, was the forerunner of all fishing reels, having been the only type of reel in existence until around the turn of the nineteenth century, when the multiplying reel came into existence.
See: Antique Fishing Tackle; Baitcasting Tackle; Flycasting Tackle.

SINGLE-FOOT GUIDE
A guide with a single attachment point to the blank of a fishing rod. A single-foot guide is advantageous for casting, and is primarily found on spinning rods, where it is placed on the underside of the rod.
See: Rod, Fishing.

SINGLE HAUL
Accelerating a fly line to load the rod either to help pick the line up off the water or to shoot out a greater length of it in the forward cast. Doing both of these during a cast is called a double haul.
See: Flycasting Tackle.

SINGLE HOOK
A hook with one point.
See: Hook.

SINKER
A metal fishing weight used to sink a lure or bait. There are many different shapes, sizes, and applications of sinkers. They are employed in freshwater and saltwater and primarily used for fishing with lightweight objects, especially natural bait.

Sinkers are made from a number of metals. They were once virtually all made of lead, and most sinkers in North America still are lead; however, an increasing number are being made from other materials due to toxicity concerns. Lead sinkers were banned years ago in Great Britain because it was believed that small sinkers (actually shot) were being swallowed by swans and killing them. This has led to the use of nontoxic metals, including brass, steel, tin, and tungsten, in small sinkers, although these were in somewhat scarce supply in the United States as of early 1999.

In North America, there has been a growing concern by environmental agencies about lead fishing sinkers (lead in shotgun loads was banned around water in the 1980s), and at least one state has enacted a ban on certain size lead sinkers and jigs due to loon mortality, while others have recommended that anglers voluntarily cease using small lead (in sinkers, jigs, and flies). This is likely to be a more widespread issue in the future, especially if the U.S. Environmental Protection Agency enacts regulations.

Naturally, these materials all differ in various ways, and both anglers and manufacturers are still adjusting to differences in densities, durability, cost, and other factors. Tin, for example, which is softer than other nonlead metals, is mainly being used in removable split shot. Steel, which is expensive but the most durable and noisiest metal, is being used in sliding and fixed sinkers. Brass is harder and noisier than lead but less so than steel; hard brass weights are less likely to be deformed, but poor quality control standards in production can lead to abrasive surfaces that will cut line.

Using sinkers. In an overall sense, there are fixed and free-sliding sinkers. Fixed versions attach directly to a fishing line or leader (dropper line) by being pinched, twisted, or tied; they move whenever the bait or lure moves and when a fish takes the bait or lure. Free-sliding, or slip, sinkers ride along the line; they are used almost exclusively with bait and allow the line to move when a fish takes the bait without moving the sinker, which provides less resistance than a fixed sinker and may be preferable for shy or light-biting fish.

Split shot, which are small pinch-on spheres that are commonly used in freshwater fishing, are usually attached firmly ahead of a hook and used with light line for suspending natural bait or drifting it along a stream bottom. Very light shot is also used with flies in trout fishing and with processed baits for coarse fishing. A rubber core sinker is fastened by turning the rubber core around the line ahead of the hook or lure; it is often used in trolling. Clinch sinkers are affixed like split shot. Split shot, egg, and pencil sinkers can be fixed to a dropper leader via a three-way swivel, which lessens hangups when fishing bait in fast water and facilitates unsnagging without losing the entire rig.

Obviously, heavier sinkers are needed the deeper you fish, the greater the wind pushes you while drifting, the faster you troll, or the faster the current. A golden rule for using sinkers is to use the lightest sinker that you can get away with and still fish in the necessary manner or place.

In addition to weight, sinker shape has an effect on casting, sink rate, and ability to hold bottom. Bulky sinkers are least castable and offer most air resistance; bottom-heavy sinkers offer the most accuracy because they don't roll over in the air.

Sinkers used in trolling include: torpedo (1), torpedo-style bead chain (2), keel-style bead chain (3), bottom-walking (4 and 8), planing (5), clinch (6), rubber-core (7), and bottom-bouncing (9).

Streamlined and compact sinkers have the best sink rate, which is of special interest in current and partially explains why split shot is so popular in rivers and streams. Split shot is also good for resisting snagging in current, because it rolls over rocky bottoms. In stillwater or where there is a soft bottom with light current, a sinker with a rounded bottom is adequate, but where there is heavier current or surf action, an angled sinker that digs into the bottom is necessary.

Trolling sinkers. Trolling sinkers include the torpedo sinker, which has minimal drag or water resistance because of shape; a torpedo-style bead chain sinker, which swivels and prevents line twist; a keel style, which tracks well with little swaying motion; a planing sinker, which dives to achieve depth; a clinch sinker, which is simple to add to or remove from fishing line; and a rubber core sinker, which is simple to use and has no abrasion. Many sizes and weights are available. These are all fastened in line, either being affixed on the main fishing line or tied to a leader. The bead chain styles are especially good for preventing line twist and, with a snap, aid leader and lure changing.

Slip sinkers. Sliding or slip sinkers include ball, egg or barrel, cone or bullet, and walking versions. Egg and ball sinkers slide freely on the line, are often stopped by a small split shot or a barrel swivel, and are preferred for open water. Cone shaped sinkers provide minimal drag, are relatively weedless, and are used with plastic worms. They may be pegged with a toothpick to keep them from sliding in heavy cover; some feature a corkscrewed stem that grabs the head of the worm and keeps the sinker and worm together. Walking sinkers are used with a stopper when casting or trolling with bait along the bottom; they remain upright when a fish runs with the bait.

Bottom sinkers. Bottom fishing sinkers include

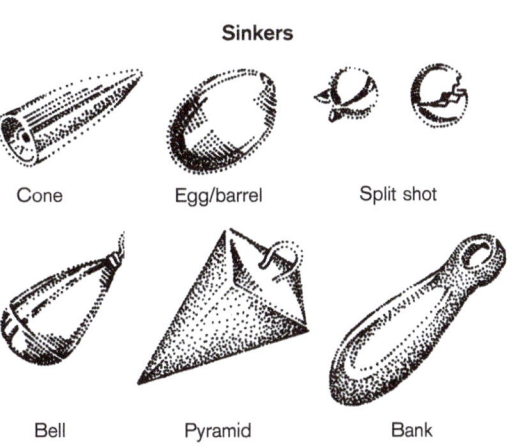

pyramid, bank, bell, and split shot. Choice depends on fishing conditions, including the species you seek, the depth to be fished, and such factors as current and wave action. Pyramid sinkers hold bottom especially well where there is much current or wave action and are especially useful where there is an undertow current. Bank sinkers are good in deep water and cast well. Split shot are preferred for light tackle. Dipsey sinkers are also used with light to medium tackle and where bait is suspended off the bottom above the sinker.

SINKING LINE
A fly line weighted to sink below the surface; there are full-sink lines and partial-sink lines, the latter sinking only at the tip.
See: Flycasting Tackle.

SINKING PLUG
See: Plug.

SINK-TIP LINE
A fly line with a floating body and a sinking tip section, also known as a floating/sinking line.
See: Flycasting Tackle.

SISCOWET
The siscowet, also known as siscoet, is a variety of lake trout (see: trout, lake) found in Lake Superior. It once existed in Lakes Huron and Michigan as well. It dwells at depths of up to 600 feet and was known to commercial fishermen as "fat trout" because of its high (70 to 90 percent) oil content, which made it mostly of value when salted or smoked. This fish lives and spawns deeper than other lake trout (which are referred to by some taxonomists as "lean" trout, in order to differentiate them from the siscowet) and may be genetically different or evolving. It is not a sport-caught fish.

Lake Superior also has a variety of lake trout known as the humper (also bumper, paperbelly, and bank trout), found on isolated offshore humps and reefs. It has a larger eye than the siscowet or the lake trout, a thin abdominal wall, a low fat content, and is small and long-lived.

SKAMANIA
A summer-run strain of steelhead (see).

SKATE
See: Rays and Skates.

SKATER
A high-floating dry fly, created with thick, long hackle. It is fished in a gliding (skating) manner in a river or stream. A skater is primarily used on Atlantic salmon but may also be effective on trout.
See: Fly.

SKEG
The lowest projecting part of an outboard or inboard/outboard motor, also known as the fin.

SKI BOAT
In North America a ski boat is any motorboat used to tow water-skiers. However, in South Africa, a ski boat is a small boat that is launched with great struggle and nerve from the beach to get through and fish beyond the surf line. Once very primitive, these boats, now equipped with two outboard motors and well-outfitted for angling, are launched from the beach as a necessity due to a lack of harbors and formal access sites. Up to four anglers may fish in ski boats, and they are used for inshore and offshore angling, sometimes for pursuing large pelagic species. Ski-boat anglers are numerous, and many ski-boat clubs exist.
See: South Africa.

SKIFF
This is a catch-all boating term, now used less frequently and primarily with regard to saltwater, which refers to small boats, usually not more than 16 feet in length, that are meant for all-purpose use, often in shallow and/or quiet waters. It may refer to a dory or small craft used as a tender to larger, moored boats, or a utility jonboat, or a small runabout. Generally, a skiff has a flat or slightly round hull and a pointed bow. It may be propelled by oars or a small outboard motor. Public rental boats at marinas are often referred to as skiffs.
See: Boat; Flats Boat; Jonboat.

SKIN CARE
See: First Aid.

SKINNING
See: Fish Preparation—Cleaning/Dressing.

SKIP CAST
A bounce cast (see).

SKIPJACK, BLACK *Euthynnus lineatus.*
Other names—little tuna, false albacore, spotted tuna, mackerel tuna, skipjack; Spanish: *barrilete negro, bonito negro, pataseca.*

A member of the Scombridae family of mackerel, bonito, and tuna, the black skipjack is commonly caught by anglers, usually while trolling or casting for other pelagic species. It is often used as a bait for big-game fish. Its food value has mixed ratings, although it is of some commercial importance. Its flesh is dark red and the taste is strong.

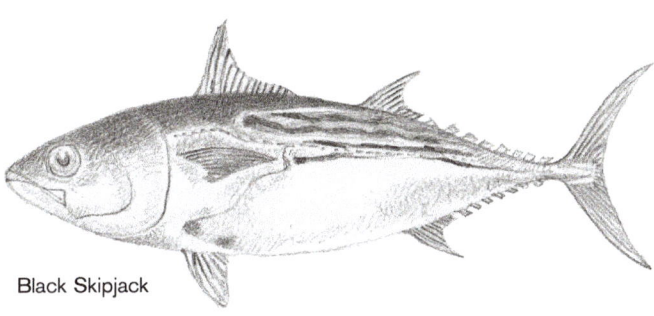
Black Skipjack

Identification. The dorsal fin of the black skipjack has 13 to 15 spines and is high anteriorly. This distinguishes it from bonito *(Sarda),* which have a relatively long and low first dorsal fin. The anal fin, which has 11 to 13 rays, is similar to the second dorsal fin in size and shape. The body lacks scales, except on the anterior corselet and along the lateral line. This is the only species of *Euthynnus* with 37, instead of the usual 39, vertebrae. Each jaw has 20 to 40 small, conical teeth. Bonito have fewer and larger conical teeth. Mackerel have flat, triangular teeth.

The black skipjack is distinguished from similar species by the four or five broad, straight, black stripes that run horizontally along the back and by its dark spots between the pectoral and ventral fins. In live specimens, stripes may be visible on the venter as well as on the back, which has frequently led to confusion with the skipjack tuna *(Katsuwonus pelamis).* The stripes on the belly rarely persist long after death in the black skipjack, however, whereas they remain prominent in the skipjack tuna *(see: tuna, skipjack).*

Size. Black skipjack are reported to attain a maximum length of 33 inches and a weight of 20 pounds, although they are usually encountered weighing several pounds. The all-tackle world record is a 26-pound specimen.

Distribution. This species occurs in tropical and warm temperate waters of the eastern Pacific Ocean from California to northern Peru, including the Galápagos Islands, and rarely the central Pacific.

Habitat. Like other pelagic and migratory species, the black skipjack occurs in schools near the surface of coastal and offshore waters. It sometimes forms multispecies schools with other scombrids.

Food. Black skipjack feed predominantly on small surface fish, squid, and crustaceans.

Angling. These fish can be hooked by trolling or casting small whole baits or strip baits, or small lures such as spoons, plugs, jigs, and feathers. They reportedly will strike lures trolled at speeds of up to 8 or 10 mph. Skipjack are usually caught deliberately for use as whole or cut baits, and fish caught incidental to other angling efforts are often kept for use as baits. Whole live skipjacks of several pounds are rigged and live-lined in some areas for marlin.
See: Bonito, Pacific; Mackerel; Tuna.

SKIRT
A dressing of synthetic material, hair, or rubber attached to a hook shank or lure body. Skirts are commonly made of silicone and Mylar, but may be rubber, vinyl, bucktail hair, squirrel hair, and other materials; they give body to a lure as well as action when retrieved. These may be used in some fashion and in varying lengths on most types of lures, but are especially common on spinnerbaits *(see)*, buzzbaits *(see)*, and jigs *(see)*.

SLAB
(1) A term for large panfish, usually crappie and occasionally bluegills.
See: Bluegill; Crappie, Black; Crappie, White.

(2) A flat wide-bodied lead spoon used by freshwater anglers for deep jigging.
See: Jigging; Spoon.

SLACK LINE CAST
An in-air flycasting maneuver that places slack in a fly line as it is laid on the water.
See: Mending.

SLACK TIDE
The state of the tide when tidal current velocity is near zero.
See: Tides.

SLEEPERS
Of little angling interest, sleepers are distributed in tropical and subtropical waters throughout the world. They are so called because of their habit of resting on the bottom as though "sleeping," rarely moving unless disturbed. If not resting on the bottom, they often remain suspended and motionless in the water, diving down to hide when frightened or in danger. Sleepers are closely related to gobies, although they lack the sucking disk that is customary in gobies and instead have separated ventral and pelvic fins. Most sleepers are fairly small, although the larger species have some food value. Sleepers are predatory in their feeding, hiding in weeds and crevices in wait for fish; they will strike live baits and are occasionally attracted by spinners, flies, and small plugs.

Bigmouth Sleeper

The fat sleeper *(Dormitator maculatus)* can reach 2 feet in length but is usually less than a foot long. It inhabits brackish waters and freshwaters through the Caribbean and the warm Atlantic northward to the Carolinas. Usually dark brown and mottled, it has a bluntly rounded head, a large mouth, no visible lateral line, and a rounded caudal fin. It bears a resemblance to a fat mullet, but its second dorsal and anal fins are large and of equal size. It makes a good aquarium pet because it can tolerate a wide range of water conditions.

The bigmouth sleeper *(Gobiomorus dormitor)* occurs along the Florida coasts, in the Caribbean, and also in freshwater. It can exceed 2 feet in length and is much thinner than the fat sleeper. It has a large, pike-like mouth and obliquely squared-off second dorsal and anal fins. The bigmouth sleeper has an olive green body and its first dorsal fin is outlined in black.

A 4-inch species, the blue sleeper *(Isoglossus calliurus)* inhabits the deep waters of the Gulf of Mexico; a 6-inch species, the emerald sleeper *(Erotelis smaragdus)*, lives off the southern coasts of Florida and in the Caribbean, where it blends with bright green algae. The blackfin dartfish *(Ptereleotris tricolor)* is also striking in color, with light green blue in front, purple blue from the second dorsal fins to the caudal fin, and a tail that is bright yellow in the center.

SLICK
An oily section of the water's surface, caused by oil seeping from chum *(see)* or by the residue of gamefish feeding on schools of bait.

SLIDER RIG
A slider rig is a lure that is affixed to a short leader and run down a fishing line while trolling. Also known as a "cheater," it's a means of fishing more than one lure on a single line attached to a downrigger *(see)*. This does not involve using two rods *(see: stacking)*.

To rig it, tie a snap swivel to one end of a 3-foot length of line and attach a lure, preferably a spoon, to the snap swivel. Tie a snap to the other end of the leader, then clip it to the line that is already connected to a downrigger release below the boat. With the boat moving forward, carefully toss the lure into the water behind the main fishing line and watch to make sure it isn't fouled. The slider rig will drift out of sight and ultimately stop well above the downrigger weight at a point where the main line is bowed most sharply in the water.

When a fish strikes the slider lure, it pulls back on the main fishing line and pops the release to which that line is attached. The rig slides down the main fishing line and stops at the snap or lure there (use a bead to keep the upper snap from marring the lower snap, knot, or line-tie area). The exact depth of the slider rig will be unknown, but you'll have two lures on one line and one downrigger.

Slider rigs probably are of little value when the

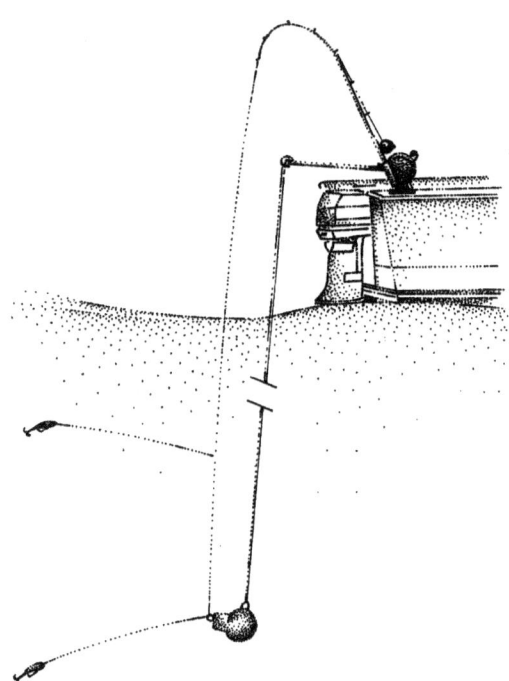

This depiction of a slider rig shows how it is possible to place the main lure at the same level as the downrigger weight, while placing a slider along the fishing line at a higher level; when a fish takes either lure, the fishing line detaches from the release clip at the weight.

main, or lower, lure is fished less than 20 feet down. If you drop the main lure down 12 feet and put a slider rig on, you'll see that the slider runs just below the surface; so at 20 feet, you might be getting the slider down only 8 feet or less, and there may be little reason to expect to get a fish on such a short line so close to the boat.

One drawback to slider rigs is that you lose a lot of fish that strike them because the hook doesn't get set into the mouth of the fish very forcefully. On the other hand, sliders give you the opportunity to put a different type and color of lure out. If a slider gets a strike or catches a fish, this may convince you to change the other lures or the depth at which you're trolling. Sliders are particularly useful when trolling deep, when fish may be scattered at all levels, when you are unsure of what depth to fish but need to scour a lot of water, or when you have no idea what color lure to use and need to try many different patterns.

There are some devices available that accomplish the same thing, but can be located more precisely on the fishing line, sliding down once a fish is on.

When using slider rigs it's possible to get double hookups (doubleheaders). This is interesting from both a fish playing and fish netting standpoint, especially when the catch is of decent size. Netting a double can be troublesome, because the fish caught on a slider rig will be several feet behind the fish on the main line. Once you net the lead fish, it's hard to get the trailing one; it's best to get the trailing one first, though this isn't always possible. Such problems aren't encountered that often, so it's something you can happily endure.

When using any type of slider rig, be careful not to exceed the number of lures, hooks, or hook points legally allowed per rod or per angler in the waters you're fishing. Be aware also of the number of rods allowed per angler. In Canada, only one rod is allowed per angler; in most states each angler can troll with two rods. American charter captains, many of whom fish out of 25- to 35-foot boats capable of holding five anglers plus the captain and mate, technically can fish two rods per person. Big-boat trollers may have as many as six downriggers; lines can be stacked on several of them to get eight or nine lures deep, and several of these will be equipped with sliders as well, so a veritable school of lures is swimming beneath the boat. Couple all of this with one or two rods on diving planers and/or flatlines, and you can see why it takes a good crew and a good boat handler to work all this without major problems.
See: Downrigger Fishing.

SLIP
A place at a marina where a boat is moored, usually between sets of pilings, piers, or floats; also referred to as a stall or berth.

SLIP BOBBER/FLOAT
Known as a slip bobber or slip float, this is a lightweight float *(see)* that slides along the fishing line, and is used in conjunction with some type of stop (a bead or thin line knot) on the line to position a bait at a certain level. This is usually used when the depth to be fished is greater than the length of the fishing rod (which is equal to the maximum that can be cast). In use, fishing line slips through or along the float until the stop halts the bait (or sometimes light jig) at the right depth.

SLIP CLUTCH
The drag mechanism on a fishing reel.
See: Drag.

SLIPPING
See: Backtrolling.

SLIP SINKER
A sinker *(see)* that slides freely on a line; this term is mostly associated with cone-shaped products used with soft worms *(see)*.

SLOT LIMIT
A restriction pertaining to the size of fish that may be kept, a slot limit prohibits anglers from keeping fish that are either outside of a specified range or within the specified range. If a slot limit is meant to protect fish of a certain size, then fish within that range have to be released, and fish outside that range may be kept. If a slot limit is meant to encourage harvesting fish of a certain size, then fish within that range may be kept, while fish outside that range have to be released.

Slot limits may be established for various species but are especially implemented for controlling largemouth bass populations. It is common for a slot limit to be established to protect fish of a certain size. For example, if a slot limit on bass prohibits keeping fish between 14 and 18 inches in size, then the effect is to aid the survival of fish in that range (presumably because there is a lack of such fish) in order to produce more large specimens; the larger fish will be effective predators and theoretically help control forage fish populations, including such species as shad and sunfish.

A slot limit, like a minimum length limit, must be tailored to a specific environment in order to respond to existing conditions. It is seldom a universally applicable regulation, and in order for it to be effective on a designated water, there must be angler compliance. For example, if there are few large bass in a given body of water as a result of high angling mortality, then a slot limit should help foster more big bass by protecting fish in the slot range and causing more mortality of smaller fish. However, if anglers treat the slot limit as a minimum length limit (for example, if a minimum length limit of 12 inches in a lake is changed to a slot of 14 to 18 inches because the lake has too many small fish and no large ones), the eventual result is a lot of small, medium, and large fish; and the impact on the forage base may be such that food becomes scarcer and growth rates decline, and the quality of the fish suffers. Therefore, anglers must keep fish that are under the size of this slot limit in order for the slot limit to achieve the desired goal, and especially for there to be a wide size range of fish that grow at desirable and sustainable levels.

A slot limit is seldom a permanent measure and usually changes over time to adapt to the changing status of both the gamefish and the forage species that they eat. It is a legal game regulation established by the fisheries agency that has jurisdiction over the location being fished, and enforced by fish and wildlife conservation officers.
See: Fisheries Management; Minimum Length Limit; Regulations.

SLOUGH
A marshy backwater; a small, fingerlike dead-end channel off a river or lake that often contains warmwater species, especially largemouth bass.

SLOVENIA
The southeastern republic of Slovenia, formerly a province of Yugoslavia, is a small country with an area of just 20,253 square kilometers. Mountainous

and heavily forested, however, Slovenia offers among Europe's best trout and grayling fishing.

Slovenia is bounded by Austria on the north, Hungary on the northeast, Croatia on the southeast, Italy on the west, and 47 kilometers of Adriatic coastline on the west. The best fishing is in the main rivers and tributaries of the Julian Alps in the northwestern part of the country.

Rivers and streams such as the Obra, Unec, Sava Bohinjka, Krka, Soca, and Iscica, and their tributaries, contain sizable populations of brown trout (locally called *poto na postrv*), rainbow trout *(arenka),* and European grayling *(lipan);* also present, in streams that flow to the Adriatic Sea, is the rare marble trout *(Salmo mormoratus),* and softmouth trout *(S. obtusirostris),* and huchen, which are found in streams that flow to the Danube River and eventually the Black Sea.

Snowcapped peaks and verdant valleys characterize Slovenia, and the rivers and scenery draw not only anglers but also rafters, kayakers, and others. All this attention makes some waters more difficult to fish in summer. April, September, and October are preferred for less crowded conditions, but summer fishing can be productive, especially for those who hike away from the more accessible areas. Snow runoff may prevent any fishing on some waters in spring. Nonetheless, most streams have good populations of fish, which are wary but beautifully colored and well marked.

The Obra is a meadow stream with beautifully marked brown trout and grayling; it is accessed about 10 miles from Postojna. The Unec is a spring creek also located near Postojna and is known for large grayling as well as brown trout. The Sava Bohinjka is a large, quick-flowing stream offering brown trout, rainbow trout, and grayling. The Krka, 25 miles south of the capital city of Ljubljana, flows through the village of Krka and has browns, rainbows, and grayling. The Soca has good numbers of these species, as well as marble trout; it flows from high peaks through gorges and villages and into the Adriatic. Its tributaries, the Tolminka and Idrijca, are also notable. The Iscica is a weedy, marshy stream about 6 miles from Ljubljana and harbors grayling and brown trout.

Fly fishing is the primary legal method for pursuing trout and grayling. Restrictions pertaining to barbless hooks, fish size, creel limits, and open seasons vary according to location along each river and from river to river. Fishing permits are necessary and can be obtained at tourist offices and major hotels.

SMELT

Smelt are small, silvery anadromous fish of the Osmeridae family that live primarily in the sea but make spawning runs into freshwater streams, as salmons do. A few smelt are strictly marine; others live only in large freshwater lakes and spawn in tributary brooks and streams. Some are marine

European Smelt

by origin but have adapted to a strictly freshwater environment; populations of some species live both in the sea and in freshwater. In all environments they are extremely important as forage for predators, including many game species.

All smelt inhabit the cool waters of the Northern Hemisphere in the Atlantic, Arctic, and Pacific Oceans and their drainages. The family is related to salmonids and contains 11 species in six genera, and is most generously represented in Pacific waters; many smelt species are so similar in appearance that they are difficult to distinguish. Most are harvested commercially. Smelt are among the top commercial fish exports of Canada, most of this going to markets in the United States. They are seldom pursued or captured on rod and reel by anglers but may be harvested recreationally in the winter and during spawning runs, often with a dipnet *(see).*

Like salmon and trout, smelt have a stubby adipose fin just in front of the tail. The lower jaw projects slightly beyond the tip of the snout. A lateral line is prominent, and there are no scales on the head. They are generally small (most growing to no more than 8 inches), schooling fish, often found in enormous numbers; in spring, great numbers move from their marine or freshwater habitats to tributary waters to spawn. Only one species, the anadromous Pacific longfin smelt *(Spirinchus thaleichthys),* spawns in late fall and early winter. All species spawn at night. In North America, the pond smelt *(Hypomesus olidus)* and the rainbow smelt *(Osmerus mordax)* are considered excellent food fish. In quantity, freshly caught smelt have an odor more nearly like cucumbers than fish.

The rainbow smelt, which is also commonly known as the American smelt, is the species most familiar to anglers and most common in North American fish markets. It ranges from Nova Scotia southward to Virginia along the Atlantic coast and also occurs in inland lakes. In the early 1900s, the rainbow smelt was introduced to the Great Lakes and other large, cold bodies of water to serve as forage fish. In nearly all instances, the smelt prospered, although the freshwater variety do not grow as large on average as the marine variety. This species is commonly caught by dipnetting in streams. The European smelt *(Osmerus eperlanus)* is similar in size and habits to the rainbow smelt. It is harvested in large numbers in northern European waters.

Among the other smelt species are the surf smelt *(Hypomesus pretiosus),* which, as its name suggests, spends most of its life in the surf and also spawns there. The closely related pond smelt *(H.*

olidus) lives wholly in freshwater ponds along the west coast of North America, apparently having become landlocked in the geologic past. The same species occurs also in Japan, where it is marine but enters freshwater streams to spawn. The delta smelt (*H. transpacificus*) is a species from both Japan and the eastern Pacific in California, where it lives in freshwater and brackish water. The whitebait smelt (*Allosmerus elongatus*), the smaller night smelt (*Spirinchus starksi*), and the longfin smelt (*S. thaleichthys*) are other Pacific species that are commercially fished to a limited extent and are used also as baits. The capelin (*Mallotus villosus*), which is circumpolar in arctic seas, is another prominent smelt, as is the eulachon (*Thaleichthys pacificus*), an oily fish found throughout northern Pacific waters.
See: Capelin; Eulachon; Smelt, Rainbow.

SMELT, RAINBOW *Osmerus mordax*.

Other names—American smelt, frostfish, leefish, toothed smelt, freshwater smelt; French: *éperlan du nord*.

One of the most prominent members of the Osmeridae family of smelt, the rainbow smelt is an important forage species for predatory fish and a principal target for inland and coastal commercial fishing. It is the subject of some recreational activity, particularly via dipnetting in the spring during spawning runs and ice fishing for landlocked populations in some lakes.

The rainbow smelt is a close relative of the eulachon *(see)* of the Pacific, the pond smelt (*Hypomesus olidus*) of the western Arctic, the capelin *(see)* of the Atlantic, and the European smelt (*Osmerus eperlanus*).

Originally an anadromous coastal species, rainbow smelt were first stocked inland in 1906, in streams and lakes feeding Lake Michigan in order to provide forage for salmonids. Eventually large rainbow smelt populations were found in all the Great Lakes, especially Lake Erie. There is some evidence that the rainbow smelt inhabiting Lake Ontario were not a result of these stockings but of an independent movement from Lake Champlain stocks.

Commercial fishing for rainbow smelt was primarily centered on the Atlantic coast until the middle of the twentieth century; in 1948, an experimental gillnet fishery was established in the Great Lakes and became increasingly successful. Gradually, the Great Lakes fishery exceeded Atlantic coast ventures in terms of the weight of total landings and their market value. Coastal anadromous rainbow smelt, however, are more highly valued—fetching more than twice the price—than inland smelt and are considered to be of superior food quality. Anglers target rainbow smelt strictly as a food fish, and this species generates extensive efforts in the Great Lakes and the coastal areas of the Maritime Provinces and the northeastern U.S.

Identification. The rainbow smelt is a slender,

Rainbow Smelt

silver fish, with a pale green or olive green back. Fresh from the water, the sides of the fish take on a purple, blue, or pink iridescent hue. The scales on the rainbow smelt are large and easily detached, and at spawning time those on the males develop small tubercles, resembling tiny buttons that serve as a mark of their sex. The lower jaw of the fish projects beyond the upper one, and the entire mouth extends beyond the middle of the eye. On the tip of the tongue are large teeth. One large dorsal fin is located about halfway along the back, and behind that is a small adipose fin.

Size/Age. Most rainbow smelt are less than 8 inches long, although some coastal specimens measuring 14 inches have been found in the coastal waters of the Maritimes and in Lake Ontario. They may live for at least six years.

Distribution. The rainbow smelt is widely distributed throughout eastern and western North America, inhabiting coastal waters as well as countless inland freshwater lakes. On the Atlantic coast they range from New Jersey in the south to Hamilton Inlet, Labrador, in the north. Their inland habitats include lakes in northeastern states and provinces, as well as throughout the Great Lakes from the St. Lawrence River to Lake Superior.

Populations of rainbow smelt also exist on the Pacific coast from Vancouver Island northward around Alaska and eastward along the Arctic coast at least as far as the Mackenzie River. The same species also ranges westward along the Arctic coast of Russia to the North Sea, including the White Sea. These westerly fish are identified by some taxonomists as arctic rainbow smelt (*O. mordax dentex*), whereas the easterly species is identified by those taxonomists as *O. mordax mordax*.

Habitat. The rainbow smelt is a pelagic schooling species, inhabiting inshore coastal regions and the midwaters of lakes. Because it is sensitive to both light and warmer temperatures, schools of rainbow smelt tend to concentrate near the bottom of lakes and coastal waters during daylight hours.

Life history. In the spring, both anadromous and landlocked adult rainbow smelt migrate upstream to freshwater spawning grounds. In some rivers, rainbow smelt begin their upstream migration before the spring thaw has begun. Spawners reach the tide head in the main tributaries when the water temperature is only 4° to 5°C. In the Great Lakes, migration begins shortly after ice out, when the water temperature is at least 8°C. They enter smaller streams when the temperature is 6° to 7°C. Anadromous rainbow smelt in the Gaspé Peninsula spawn in similar temperatures, although some land-locked populations in Lake Champlain and lakes in New Hampshire may spawn in temperatures as low as 2°C.

Rainbow smelt remain at spawning sites for a number of days. Larger smelt of all ages spawn first, and the average size of rainbow smelt on the spawning grounds decreases as the season advances. Shortly after spawning, many males die. Surviving males and females remain for about 5 to 10 days before migrating downstream.

Some rainbow smelt are mature at two years of age and all are mature at age 3. Fecundity varies from one area to another, and anadromous populations are more fecund than landlocked populations. A fully grown female rainbow smelt from the Miramichi River in New Brunswick will produce roughly 70,000 eggs, whereas a similar-size female from Lake Superior will produce roughly 31,000 eggs.

Spawning occurs mainly at night, typically over a gravelly bottom. The eggs are adhesive and stick to the gravel or other bottom objects. The time required for the eggs to hatch depends on the water temperature and can vary from 20 to 50 days. Fe-male rainbow smelt grow more quickly than males, attain a larger size, and live longer. Rainbow smelt restricted to small inland lakes are usually smaller than they are elsewhere, and often do not exceed 4 inches in length.

Food. Zooplankton, insect larvae, aquatic worms, and small fish constitute the diet of rainbow smelt, with zooplankton being predominant.

Angling. In some places, including northeastern Canada, rainbow smelt are fished with hook and line from docks during summer months. Fly anglers sometimes take smelt on artificial flies in summer, although these fish generally stay in deep, cool water. In winter, landlocked rainbow smelt in lakes are caught on hook and line through the ice. Thousands of people use dipnets and seines to capture rainbow smelt when they are abundant in spring, and regulations for this activity exist in all parts of their range.

Rainbow smelt dipping can be an extremely social activity and is usually done at night, wearing hip boots and carrying a lantern, a fine-meshed dipnet, and a bucket. Dipping usually commences once the first warm rain raises the water temperature above 39°F and continues for roughly two- to three weeks. Some people stalk rainbow smelt in the shallows and scoop them up one or two at a time as they see them in the light of their lantern. Others dip blindly in the deeper part of a stream, which can be arm-wearying when there are few or no fish but highly productive during peak run times (one to many dozen may be netted). Most dipping occurs in tributary streams, but in some places, especially the Great Lakes, it also occurs along the lakeshore and around sheltered points.

Rainbow smelt must be kept on ice and cleaned quickly to preserve their flavor; this is sometimes difficult in the middle of the night when you're tired and have a few quarts of fish to clean.
See: Smelt.

SMOKING

A term for the creation of a frothy, misty turbulence and silvery trail of bubbles, accompanied by an occasional roostertail, on the surface of the water as made by certain offshore trolling lures and teasers when running properly at a high speed.
See: Trolling Lures, Saltwater.

SMOLT

A young silvery salmon migrating from freshwater to the sea.
See: Salmon, Atlantic.

SNAG

(**1**) An obstruction on which a lure is likely to get stuck, especially a conglomeration of debris such as tree branches and brush.
See: Unsnagging.

(**2**) To deliberately hook a fish in any part of its body other than the inside of its mouth.
See: Snagging.

SNAGGING

Technically, snagging is the hooking of a fish in any part of its body other than the inside of its mouth. It may be called snatching and is also referred to as foul hooking, but, in a practical sense, foul hooking is considered an accidental or incidental hooking of a fish at a site other than in the mouth, whereas snagging has the connotation of being done deliberately. Snagging is commonly done by a rapid drawing motion, using a handheld rod and attached line with single or multiple fish hooks. Often the hook is weighted on the shank for casting and sinking purposes, and the gap of the hook is wide enough to permit the hook to sink more readily into the flesh of a fish. One of the reasons for regulations that set a maximum hook gap is to inhibit the ability to snag, usually in places where this activity has occurred frequently or was once permissible.

Fish that are the target of snagging may or may not be visible. It is not always necessary to use a rapid drawing motion to snag fish. Some snagging occurs when fish are crowded and a hook is retrieved slowly until it bumps a fish; then the fisherman instantly sets the hook as if responding to a strike. Also, fish that are crowded may be snagged while trolling with a multihooked lure, although this is usually an accidental occurrence.

Whether accidental or deliberate, snagging is generally prohibited except for certain nongame species, such as paddlefish, and for some Great Lakes fish, such as salmon, during their spawning runs. Fish that are accidentally snagged or foul-hooked by law must be returned unharmed to the water. In some places, it is legal to gather baitfish for personal use by snagging; small herring, bunkers, and other baitfish are sometimes snagged with small hooks and put in an aerated well for later use as live bait, especially for stripers.

Legal snagging of gamefish has generated controversy among anglers and nonanglers alike. It has been a hotly debated topic in places bordering the Great Lakes for many years. Some state fisheries agencies, responding to outcries, have outlawed snagging for salmon and trout in tributaries, although they once encouraged the practice to provide support for fledgling fisheries programs and as a means of harvesting fish that would die and be wasted. New York encouraged and permitted this practice as recently as the mid 1990s, at one time erroneously claiming that the migrating salmon could not be caught by means other than snagging. In Great Lakes tributaries, the crowding of rivers by people acting like game hogs and slinging leaded hooks in an attempt to snag big salmon brought out the very worst behavior and created a repugnant social fishing spectacle. Gradually this inappropriate activity has been curtailed and is less prevalent (legally) than it was in the 1970s and 1980s.

Snagging is still practiced in specific places and for certain species, and where legal it is considered a form of recreational fishing. However, snagging is not treated as sportfishing by the general angling community and is widely considered unethical and unsportsmanlike.

See: Foul Hook; Regulations.

SNAKE
A term, often derogatory, used for chain pickerel and small northern pike.

SNAKE GUIDE
The upper light-wire guides on a fly rod that aid the passage of fly line during casting and retrieval.
See: Flycasting Tackle.

SNAP
A metal connector between fishing line and a lure. Snaps are knotted to the fishing line and connected to the wire line-tie loop of a lure or to a split ring (see) that is connected to that loop.

In many cases, fishing line is tied directly to a lure. Lures that spin or roll when retrieved or trolled cause twist in the fishing line; twisting is countered by using some type of swivel (see). Lures that do not twist, which includes some spoons (see) and virtually all floating/diving plugs, do not need a swivel; they can be fished with a snap for two reasons, the most important of which is to enhance lure action. This is usually done with lures that do not have a split ring attached to the line-tie area. You can put a split ring there and tie the line directly to this, or you can use a snap; the snap should have a rounded bend to facilitate lure movement. The second, and subordinate, reason for using a snap is simply for convenience sake. A snap makes it easy to change lures quickly without having to retie knots. This may be especially useful with some lines that are difficult to tie knots in, such as thin-diameter microfilament lines (see: line).

Though convenient, snaps lead to problems and should only be used if really necessary. Poor quality snaps, or light snaps used with too heavy tackle, are the main causes of problems. They can be the weakest link in the angler-to-fish scenario due to their strength. If the rated breaking strength of a snap is 10 pounds, for example, and you're using 20-pound line, it's very possible that you could force the snap open, and lose the lure and/or fish, when maximum pressure is applied. It is unlikely that you'll know what the breaking strength of most snaps is when they are preattached to a lure or when buying them in bulk (though some have the strength noted on the packaging), but you can test the lighter ones with a heavy-duty spring scale.

It would be worthwhile to clip a few different snaps around a firm object, attach a reliable scale to the clips, and then pull on them until the clip breaks, noting how much pressure it takes to do so. The amount of force that it takes to open, straighten, or collapse a snap is a key to its usage.

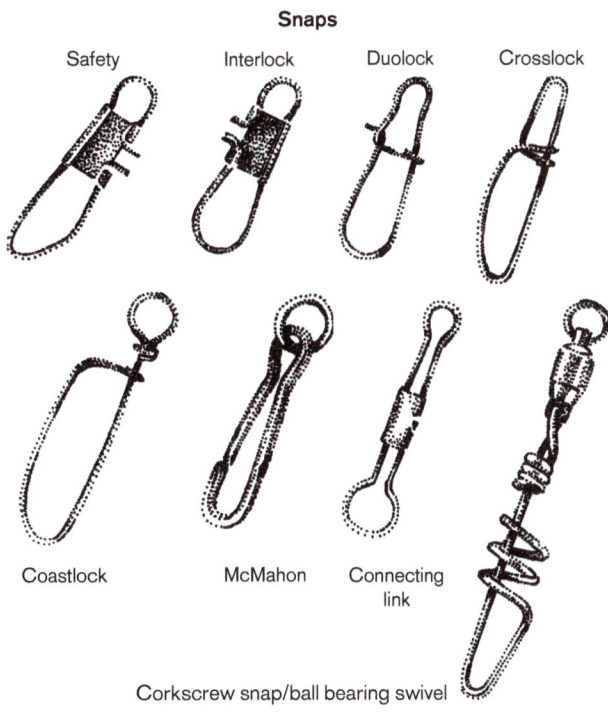

Snaps: Safety, Interlock, Duolock, Crosslock, Coastlock, McMahon, Connecting link, Corkscrew snap/ball bearing swivel

Though you should generally use the size of snap that complements the lure and line diameter, strength is a function of size and thickness of the metal, so take this into consideration. It is misguided economy to use thin metal snaps—especially the common two-piece safety snaps that are cheap and popularly used in freshwater—so avoid these or replace them on lures or rigs that come equipped with them.

Strength and ease of use are also functions of the locking design. The safety snap model, which has a sharp bend and doesn't really lock (the tag end sits in a guarded channel), is one of the poorest snaps but cheap and commonly used. A similar two-piece snap is the interlock (or lock snap) model, which is only slightly better because the tag end rests in a guarded channel and tucks around the edge for more holding power. Both of these are subject to failure after repeated opening and closing.

One-piece all-wire snaps in which the tempered wire wraps around itself are better than the previous items. The common duolock model has a double-end opening that allows attachment to two items with closed eye rings; this is a good, moderately priced, easy-to-use connector that is also found as part of light- to medium-duty snap-swivels. This snap is used by many freshwater anglers when tied to spoons and plugs, and is favored because of its rounded bend. Another popular and strong model is the crosslock, which has double ends that meet on the same plane and abut each other; the bend is less rounded, however, so it does not maximize action for some lures. Other types that are especially popular in saltwater include the coastlock snap, which has a single-opening end that is especially strong and common on many big-game swivels; the tournament snap, which is similar to but stronger than the coastlock; the heavy-duty corkscrew snap; and the McMahon snap, a dual grip model.

Other types of connectors that can loosely be considered snaps include a variety of lightweight light-wire models for fly fishing, some of which are really spring clips, and connecting links, which are double-looped wire with a sliding sleeve.

As for color or finish, some anglers prefer flat black; others silver and gold. The silver and gold colors sometimes help attract fish, which is viewed positively by many freshwater anglers and negatively by most saltwater anglers. Fish attracted to the snap may strike ahead of the lure instead of at the body of the lure where the hooks are; in bigger and toothier saltwater species, this may result in cutoffs.

SNAPPER

Snapper are members of the large Lutjanidae family of fish, which includes more than 100 species. These fish inhabit tropical or subtropical waters in the Atlantic, Indian, and Pacific Oceans. Most are schooling species, although sizes vary widely. Likewise they range by species from shallow nearshore and inshore waters to deeper shelf environs. They seldom inhabit estuaries and are generally demersal. Some snapper, especially larger-growing species, may be confused with grouper; however, they can be readily distinguished from grouper by one or two large canine teeth at the front of the upper jaw. Also, the rear end of the upper jaw slides under the suborbital rim instead of outside it. Snapper have a moderately large mouth and their dorsal fin is continuous or slightly notched.

Many snapper species are important commercial fish and high-quality food fish. Some, particularly reef-dwelling species, are popular with anglers. A few, notably dog snapper and cubera snapper, have been known to cause ciguatera poisoning.

See: Snapper; Snapper, Cubera; Snapper, Gray; Snapper, Lane; Snapper, Mutton; Snapper, Pacific Cubera; Snapper, Red; Snapper, Yellowtail.

SNAPPER, CUBERA *Lutjanus cyanopterus*.

Other names—Cuban snapper; Spanish: *cubera, guasinuco, pargo cabalo, pargo cubera*.

The largest of all the snapper and a member of the Lutjanidae family, the cubera is a hard-fighting gamefish as well as a fine food fish, although larger specimens may have coarse meat.

Identification. The head, body, and fins of the cubera snapper are silver or steely gray to dark brown with an occasional reddish tinge; the body is darker above than below, sometimes with a purplish sheen. Most young fish and some adults have irregular pale bands on the upper body. The cubera snapper has dark red eyes, thick lips, and a rounded anal fin. It also has connected dorsal fins that consist of 10 spines and 14 rays, and pectoral fins that do not extend as far as the start of the anal fin. The cubera snapper is often confused with the gray or "mangrove" snapper, although they can be differentiated by the number of gill rakers present on the lower limb of the first branchial arch; there are an average of seven to nine gill rakers on the gray snapper in contrast to five to seven on the cubera snapper. They can also be distinguished by the tooth patch on the roof of the mouth; the gray snapper has an anchor-shaped patch, whereas the cubera snapper has a triangular one that does not extend back as the anchor-shaped one does. In general, the canine teeth of the cubera snapper are enlarged and noticeable even when the mouth is closed. The cubera can lighten or darken dramatically in color.

Size. Although the cubera snapper commonly weighs up to 40 pounds, it can weigh more than 100 pounds and reach lengths of 4 or more feet. The all-tackle world record is a 121-pound, 8-ounce Louisiana fish.

Distribution. In the western Atlantic, cubera

Cubera Snapper

snapper occur from Florida and Cuba southward to the mouth of the Amazon in Brazil. They are very occasionally found north of Florida to New Jersey, are rare in the Gulf of Mexico, and are generally scarce in most of their range.

Habitat. Adult fish are found offshore over wrecks, reefs, ledges, and rocky bottoms; young fish sometimes enter freshwater or inhabit mangrove areas and grassbeds. Cubera snapper are solitary and are usually found in 60 feet of water or deeper.

Spawning behavior. In the Florida Keys, cubera snapper spawn during late summer and early fall during full moon phases.

Food. Cubera snapper feed primarily on fish, shrimp, and crabs.

Angling. Like grouper and other deep reef fish, the cubera snapper is primarily caught by bottom fishing methods at the right depth over irregular terrain. Off Florida, anglers catch them on wrecks with heavy tackle (50- and 80-pound two-speed outfits, as fish of 40 to 60 pounds are likely), using lobsters for baits on bottom rigs and often spotting moving fish on sonar while drifting. Strikes may be rather light, but the fish bulldoze to the wreck or reef quickly and must be outmuscled.

See: Grouper; Inshore Fishing; Snapper.

SNAPPER, GRAY *Lutjanus griseus.*
Other names—mangrove snapper; French: *sarde grise, vivaneau sarde grise;* Portuguese: *caranha, castanhola, luciano;* Spanish: *caballerote, pargo manglero, pargo prieto.*

A member of the Lutjanidae family of snapper and important commercially, the gray snapper is a good gamefish and also an excellent food fish. It is commonly referred to as the mangrove snapper and has white, flaky meat that is easily filleted and is marketed fresh or frozen.

Identification. The coloring of the gray snapper is variable, from dark gray or dark brown to gray green. The belly is grayish tinged with olive, bronze, or red, sometimes described as reddish or orange spots running in rows on the lower sides. A dark horizontal band occasionally runs from the lip through the eye, and some fish are said to have dark vertical bars or blotches along the sides. The tail may also have a dark margin, and the anal fin is rounded. There are two conspicuous canine teeth at the front of the upper jaw. The gray snapper can be distinguished from the cubera snapper by the shape of the tooth patch in the mouth, which is triangular in the cubera snapper and anchor shaped in the gray snapper. In general, the gray snapper resembles other snapper except that it lacks a distinct spot on the sides.

Size/Age. The gray snapper averages only about a pound in weight, although offshore catches commonly weigh 8 to 10 pounds; it reportedly may grow to 35 inches and a weight of 25 pounds, although fish exceeding 15 pounds are rare. The all-tackle world record is a 17-pound Florida fish. The gray snapper may live up to 21 years.

Distribution. In the western Atlantic, gray snapper extend from Massachusetts to Rio de Janeiro, occurring throughout the Caribbean Sea, the Gulf of Mexico, and Bermuda. Although rare north of Florida, they are common off southeastern Florida and around the Antilles. In the eastern

Gray (Mangrove) Snapper

Atlantic, gray snapper extend from Senegal to the Congo, including the Cape Verde Islands.

Habitat. Young gray snapper are mostly found inshore over smooth bottom in such places as estuaries, the lower reaches of tidal creeks, mangroves, and seagrass meadows; adult fish generally range offshore over irregular bottom in such places as coral or rocky reefs, rock outcroppings, and shipwrecks, to depths of about 300 feet.

Life history/Behavior. When gray snapper reach age 3 or older and a length of about 9 inches, they begin to spawn, usually at dusk in shallow water during full moon phases and between June and August. The female is courted by one or many males, and fertilized eggs settle to the bottom and remain unattended until they hatch. Gray snapper drift in small schools.

Food and feeding habits. Gray snapper feed primarily at night, leaving reefs late in the day for grassflats, where they consume plankton, small fish, shrimp, and crabs.

Angling. This species is particularly popular in Florida and around the Antilles, where it is caught by hook and line, by beach and boat seines, and in traps. Like other bottom and reef fish, the gray snapper is primarily caught by bottom fishing methods at the right depth over irregular terrain. Anglers fish for these and other reef fish from head boats and smaller private boats using manual and electric reels, sturdy boat rods, heavy monofilament line, and two-hook bottom rigs baited with squid and cut fish. In addition to fishing offshore, anglers also catch gray snapper in mangrove- and seagrass-dominated estuaries, using shrimp, clams, bloodworms, and occasionally artificial lures, especially small jigs.

See: Inshore Fishing; Snapper.

SNAPPER, LANE *Lutjanus synagris*.
Other names—Portuguese: *areocó*; Spanish: *biajaiba, chino, machego, pargo biajaiba, pargo guanapo, rayado, villajaiba*.

A member of the Lutjanidae family of snapper and highly regarded as a food fish, the lane snapper is caught commercially throughout its range and is marketed fresh and frozen.

Identification. The lane snapper is silvery pink to reddish with short, somewhat parallel pink and yellow stripes on its sides; there is often a faint greenish cast to the back and upper sides, which sometimes highlights a few light olive bands. The pectoral, pelvic, and anal fins are often yellowish, and the dorsal and tail fins are often reddish. The outer margin of the tail is black, particularly toward the center. A black spot about as large as the eye is present just below the rear dorsal fin and just above the lateral line, although it may be missing in rare cases; this spot is what distinguishes the lane from other snapper, in addition to an anchor-shaped tooth patch on the roof of the mouth, 18 to 22 gill rakers on the first arch, and a round anal fin.

Size. Usually weighing less than a pound, the lane snapper is ordinarily 8 to 12 inches long, sometimes reaching a maximum of 15 inches in length. The all-tackle world record is a 7-pound Alabama fish.

Distribution. In the tropical western Atlantic, lane snapper range from North Carolina to southeastern Brazil, including the Caribbean Sea and the Gulf of Mexico. They are most abundant around the Antilles, on the Campeche Bank off eastern Panama, and on the northern coast of South America. They are commonly found in Florida and only occasionally inhabit waters of the Bahamas and the Caribbean.

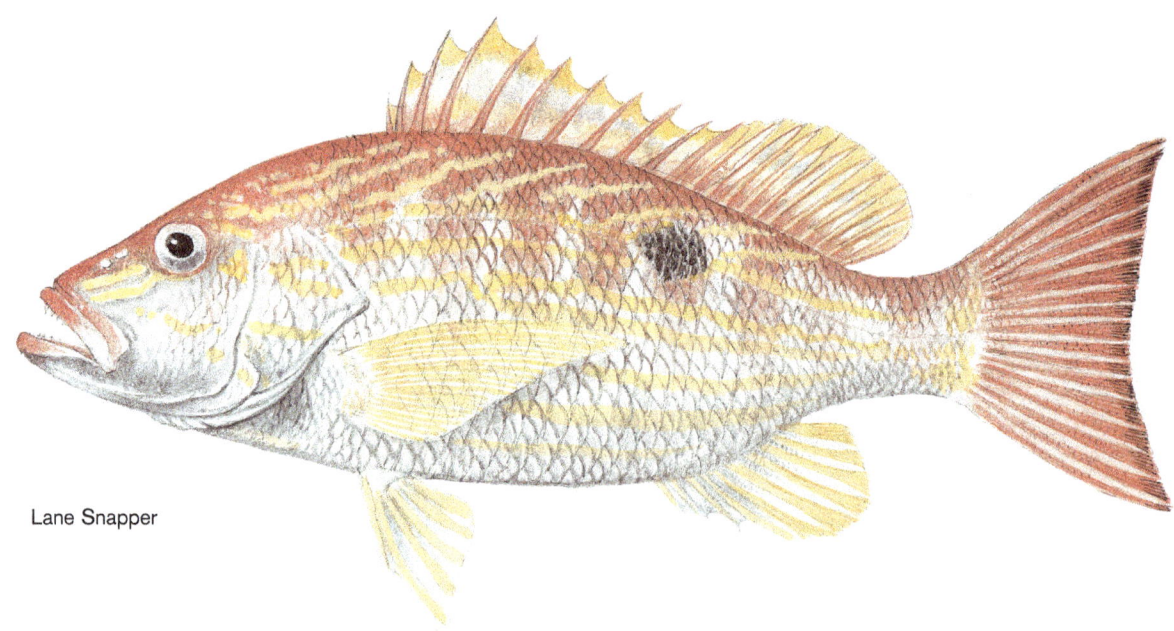
Lane Snapper

Habitat. Ranging from depths of 5 to 130 feet, lane snapper are found over all types of bottom, although they prefer coral reefs and sandy areas with vegetation; young fish stay inshore over grassbeds or shallow reefs, whereas adults move offshore, where they explore deeper reefs. Occurring in turbid as well as clear water, lane snapper often drift in schools, especially during the breeding season.

Spawning behavior. Becoming sexually mature when they are one year old and 6 to 7 inches long, lane snapper spawn from March through September. Spawning activity peaks from June through August. Depending on size, a female may lay 300,000 to more than 1 million pelagic eggs; young fish stay in grassbeds in estuaries, which serve as nursery areas until they reach 5 or 6 inches in length, when they migrate offshore.

Food and feeding habits. Lane snapper are opportunistic carnivores and primarily consume forage that is near or on the bottom, including anchovies and other small fish, crabs, shrimp, worms, and mollusks. They are fast enough to pursue and capture their prey, and they feed at night, moving off of reefs and onto grassbeds.

Angling. Because the lane snapper is small and occurs in shallow water, it is caught in baited traps and beach seines, as well as by hook and line. It is an excellent and fierce fighter on light tackle.

See: Inshore Fishing; Snapper.

SNAPPER, MANGROVE
See: Snapper, Gray.

SNAPPER, MUTTON *Lutjanus analis*.
Other names—Portuguese: *cioba*; Spanish: *pargo cebalo, pargo cebal, pargo colorado, pargo criollo, pargo mulato*.

Often marketed as "red snapper," the flesh of the mutton snapper is firm, white, and is an excellent food fish. It is a member of the Lutjanidae family of snapper.

Identification. The mutton snapper can be striking in appearance, varying from orangish to reddish yellow or reddish brown, or from silver gray to olive green on the back and upper sides. All the fins below the lateral line have a reddish cast, and the larger mutton snapper takes on an overall reddish color, which causes it to be confused with the red snapper. Young fish are often olive colored and may display dark bars. There is a distinct black spot about the size of the eye on the mid-body line below the rear dorsal fin, and of all the snapper with this type of dark spot, the mutton snapper is the only one with a V-shaped tooth patch in the roof of the mouth rather than an anchor-shaped one. There are also small blue lines below and near the eye, and the dorsal fin has 10 spines and 14 rays. Adults tend to develop a high back, and all fish have pointed anal fins.

The lane snapper *(see: snapper, lane)* is somewhat similar in coloring except that it has yellow streaks, and the mutton snapper has small blue streaks on a yellowish background, although these usually disappear with age. Another difference is that the lane snapper has squarish or even rounded anal and dorsal fins, whereas the mutton snapper has pointed anal and dorsal fins.

Size. Ordinarily 1 to 2 feet in length and 15 pounds in weight, the mutton snapper can reach weights of 25 to 30 pounds and lengths of 30 inches.

Mutton Snapper

The all-tackle world record is a 28-pound, 5-ounce Florida fish.

Distribution. In the western Atlantic, mutton snapper extend from Massachusetts to southeastern Brazil, including the Caribbean Sea and the northern Gulf of Mexico. They are most abundant around the Antilles, the Bahamas, and off southern Florida, and have been introduced into Bermuda waters.

Habitat. Young fish occur over soft bottoms such as seagrass beds, whereas adults are found over hard bottoms around rocky and coral reefs, as well as in bays and estuaries. They drift above the bottom at depths of 5 to 60 feet.

Spawning behavior. Spawning takes place from May through October with a peak of activity in July and August. Mutton snapper form small groups that disperse during the night.

Food and feeding habits. Mutton snapper feed both day and night on shrimp, fish, snails, crabs, and plankton.

Angling. Mutton snapper are strong fighters on light tackle and can be taken on natural baits or small lures fished vertically or slowly trolled near the bottom. They are primarily caught by bottom fishing methods at the right depth over irregular terrain but are sometimes taken on flats or lured to the surface and caught on a fly.

See: Inshore Fishing; Snapper.

SNAPPER, PACIFIC CUBERA *Lutjanus novemfasciatus*.

Other names—dog snapper, Pacific dog snapper; Spanish: *boca fuerte, huachinango, panza prieta, pargo jilguero, pargo moreno, pargo negro*.

The Pacific cubera snapper closely resembles the cubera snapper, the "river" or "mangrove red" snapper, and an African snapper; this resemblance involves habitat and behavior but extends as well to a similar appearance; they share deep reddish bodies, four large canine teeth, stubby gill rakers, and almost identical body and fin shapes. This seems to suggest that large cubera-type snappers may be more closely related to each other than are other members of the Lutjanidae (snapper) family.

Marketed fresh and frozen, the Pacific cubera snapper is an excellent food fish and is greatly prized as a sport catch.

Identification. The young Pacific cubera snapper is purplish brown with a light spot in the center of each scale, whereas adults and older fish are almost a deep red. Occasionally a blue streak is evident under the eye, as are roughly nine shaded bars on the flanks. The tail is very slightly forked or lunate (crescent shaped), the dorsal fin is made up of 10 spines and 14 soft rays, and the anal fin is rounded and has 3 spines and 8 rays. The pectoral fins do not extend to the anal fin or even as far as the vent in adults. The most distinctive feature of the Pacific cubera snapper is four uncommonly large canine teeth, two in the upper jaw and two in the lower, which are somewhat larger than the pupil of the eye. There is also a crescent-shaped tooth patch in the roof of the mouth.

Size. The Pacific cubera snapper is the largest of nine snapper occurring in its range, growing to at least 80 pounds. The all-tackle world record is a 78-pound, 12-ounce fish taken off Costa Rica.

Distribution. Pacific cubera inhabit the eastern Pacific from northern Mexico to northern Peru.

Habitat. Pacific cubera snapper are an inshore species, preferring rocky and coral reefs and caves in shallow waters with depths of 100 feet and possibly deeper. Young fish are found in estuaries near mangroves and the mouths of rivers.

Food and feeding habits. Carnivorous, Pacific cubera snapper prey at night on big invertebrates such as crabs, prawns, and shrimp, as well as fish.

Angling. This species is a strong fighter and a tough sportfish that can be caught on live baits, jigs, spoons, feathers, plugs, or pork rind fished or trolled at up to 5 mph. Where there are plenty of rocky pinnacles, reefs, and islands, anglers can land these fish by casting diving plugs and surface plugs, the latter creating some terrific explosions.

See: Inshore Fishing; Snapper.

SNAPPER (SQUIREFISH) *Pagrus auratus*.

Other names—cockney bream (up to 13 centimeters), red bream (at about 450 grams), squire (up to about 1.5 kilograms), old man snapper, pink snapper, tamure, squirefish (U.S.).

An Australian and New Zealand member of the Sparidae family of sea bream (formerly known as *Chrysophrys auratus*), the snapper is a highly valued food and sport species targeted by both recreational anglers and commercial fishermen.

Identification. Snapper are a handsome fish with a deep, elongate body that is strongly compressed. Some older fish (usually females) have a prominent bump on the head and a bulge on the snout, both thought to be developed as a result of nudging into reefs in order to obtain food. The mouth is of moderate size, and the teeth are large and peglike in front and molarlike on the sides.

Pacific Cubera Snapper

Their body coloring can vary, but is generally reddish pink with many bright blue spots on the sides. The fins are reddish or pink. The caudal fin is forked, and the single dorsal fin is not notched.

Size. Snapper are known to reach a weight of 19.5 kilograms and a length of 1.3 meters. An Australian record, taken at Whyalla, South Australia, in 1990, is listed at 16.4 kilograms; a 17.2-kilogram fish from New Zealand is the all-tackle world record. Most big snapper are taken close inshore, and the Spencer Gulf and Gulf of St. Vincent waters in South Australia are famous for large individuals. Large specimens have also been taken from the waters off Lord Howe Island, to the east of New South Wales.

Distribution. Snapper are found across the northern two-thirds of New Zealand, and in Australia from Barrow Island off the central coast of Western Australia, across the bottom of Australia, occasionally along the northern coastline of Tasmania, and up the East Coast as far north as Hinchinbrook Island in North Queensland. The predominant Australian angling areas are the inshore waters of Shark Bay in Western Australia, Spencer Gulf and the Gulf of St. Vincent in South Australia, and Port Phillip and Westernport Bays in Victoria. New South Wales anglers take fish along the entire coastline, whereas offshore reefs of southern Queensland appear to take precedence over other areas.

Habitat. Juvenile snapper, called cockney bream, inhabit estuaries and bays, where they live in and around seagrass beds, over sandy bottoms, and around any man-made or natural structures. Mature fish move out of the estuaries into offshore waters, where they stay close to both deep- and shallow-water reefs, bomboras, gravel beds, rocky headlands, and offshore islands. In South Australian waters, many snapper tend to remain within Spencer Gulf and the Gulf of St. Vincent.

Life history/Behavior. During the spawning season, which can vary with geographic location, snapper may spawn several times, usually well out to sea and when water temperatures range from 18° to 21°C. As young juveniles, they move close inshore and eventually make their way into the sheltered waters of bays, inlets, and estuaries. As they mature, they leave these waters and make their way to the open sea, where they find sustenance around islands and reefs, and along the rocky coastline. They are known to migrate for long distances, that is from the southern state of Victoria to the northern state of Queensland. Big snapper often seek the shelter of estuarine waters following coastal storms.

Food and feeding habits. The diet of the snapper is varied and includes small fish, mollusks, blue crabs, sand crabs, soldier crabs, squid, and prawns. It will also take strip baits of tuna, bonito, mackerel, mullet, octopus or squid tentacles, whole blue pilchards, and garfish. It tends to forage in deep water

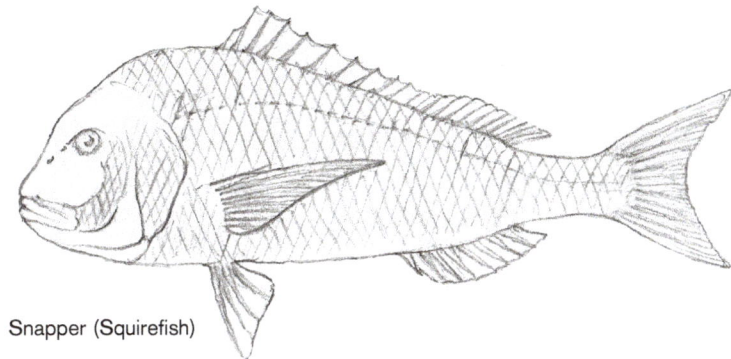
Snapper (Squirefish)

during daylight hours but will move into shallow water after dark.

Angling. A big old man snapper is a prize that many anglers strive for, yet the capture of any adult snapper from the red bream stage upward makes for a successful day. Tackle varies from 2-meter boat rods and reels spooled with 7-kilogram line to 3.5-meter rods and reels with 10- to 12-kilogram lines used by shore-based rock anglers. Long-handled gaffs to 6 meters are essential in shore-based situations, where anglers, perched high on a rock ledge, can be in danger from waves and swells if they clamber down to land a fish.

Heavy handlines (15 kilograms) are frequently used by Australian boat anglers, and jetty fishing is popular with shore-based anglers confined to bays and inlets. Most shore-based angling occurs at night.

Hook sizes vary from 3/0 to 7/0; ganged hooks (a series of four or five hooks joined eye to bend) to 5/0 are suitable for most baits. Chumming is commonly used and may consist of a mix of fish scraps, prawns, chicken pellets, and soaked bread sparingly distributed so as not to overfeed the fish. Baits are fished on bottom rigs with heavy sinkers for fixed positions, or allowed to sink naturally and drift. This latter method is popular with rock anglers using ganged hooks and unweighted baits. Boat anglers either drift over reefs or anchor upcurrent of a known reef and rely on chum to bring the fish around. Where snapper are attracted to the surface by chum, they can sometimes be tempted into taking a lure such as a soft plastic, feathered leadhead jig, or streamer fly.

Snapper are a favorite species for charter boat anglers. These craft leave for known snapper reefs early in the morning and can accommodate 20 or more anglers, who use rail-mounted winches or handlines. Charter boat skippers usually demand that rigs be identical in order to prevent entanglement, and sinkers to 500 grams are not uncommon where ocean currents are strong.

SNAPPER, RED *Lutjanus campechanus.*
Other names—American red snapper, northern red snapper, mutton snapper; Portuguese: *vermelho*; Spanish: *guachinango del Golfo, pargo colorado, pargo de Golfo.*

Snapper, Red

Red Snapper

The red snapper is one of the most valuable snapper for anglers and commercial fishermen; as a result, it has been severely overfished in American waters and is now closely protected. A member of the Lutjanidae family of snapper, it is one of the most highly coveted of all reef fish and is almost always the most expensive fish per pound on the market. The white meat of the red snapper is superb and is marketed fresh.

Identification. The red snapper is pinkish, scarlet, or brick red on its head and upper body, and silvery whitish below. It has a long triangular snout, a sharply pointed anal fin, and a distinctively red iris. Young fish of under 10 inches in length have a dusky spot below the soft dorsal fin at and above the midline, and the tail sometimes has a dark edge. Although the adult resembles the Caribbean red snapper, there are differences in ray and scale counts; the Caribbean snapper has eight soft rays in the anal fin, 50 to 51 scales in a row along the flank, and 10 to 11 scales between the beginning of the dorsal fin and the lateral line. The red snapper has nine soft rays, 47 to 49 flank scales, and 8 to 9 scales between the dorsal fin and the lateral line.

Size/Age. Commonly growing to between 1 and 2 feet in length, the red snapper can reach 3 feet and weigh more than 35 pounds. The all-tackle world record is a 50-pound, 4-ounce Louisiana fish. Adults can live for more than 20 years.

Distribution. Red snapper occur in the Gulf of Mexico and along the entire Atlantic coast of the United States as far north as Massachusetts but rarely north of the Carolinas. They are occasionally found in Florida but are absent from the Bahamas and the Caribbean.

Habitat. Adult fish are usually found over rocky bottom at depths of 60 to 400 feet, whereas young fish inhabit shallow waters over sandy or muddy bottoms.

Life history/Behavior. Red snapper spawn from June through October, and sometimes as early as April. They often intermingle with grunts and other snapper in schools. It takes three to four years for these fish to reach their spawning size of 15 to 16 inches.

Food and feeding habits. Red snapper are opportunistic bottom feeders that prey on fish, shrimp, crabs, and worms.

Angling. This species is caught commercially throughout its range, primarily with handlines, but also by using large electrically and manually powered reels to haul up line that has multiple-hook rigs.

Anglers use bottom fishing tactics over reefs, wrecks, oil rigs, and the like, usually fishing with stout tackle and lines in the 50-pound class. Consistently catching red snapper by hook and line is an art. Not only must one know where the best fishing grounds are, but also the bait must be presented in a manner that entices the snapper to bite. Although multiple-hook rigs similar to those used for other reef fish are effective, a favorite rig for large red snapper is a single 7/0 hook fastened to a 4- to 5-foot dropper off the main leader, which ends with an 8- to 16-ounce sinker. Selection of baits is critical. Squid heads with long tentacles, whole medium-size fish, and fresh bloody strips of little tunny or greater amberjack catch big red snapper. The fish seem to prefer a still or very slowly moving bait. Fishing from an anchored boat is productive, but when drifting, it can be beneficial to freespool the line for a few minutes before slowly retrieving the slack. As with many big snapper and grouper, gaining line quickly in the first few moments after the strike is critical. A hard strike and feverish winding is necessary.

Although many red snapper are caught right on the bottom, in some situations the larger fish are suspended off the bottom. These may be caught on heavy jigs, often tipped with a strip of bait, or by freelining baits at the proper upper level.

Artificial reefs have been built in the Gulf of Mexico to attract this species for sportfishing. Commercial shrimp fishing operations, accused of destroying young snapper through bycatch, is currently restricted.

See: Inshore Fishing; Snapper.

SNAPPER, YELLOWTAIL *Ocyrus chrysurus*.

Other names—Creole: *colas;* French: *sarde queue jaune;* Portuguese: *cioba, mulata;* Spanish: *rabirrubia.*

The yellowtail snapper is a member of the Lutjanidae family of snapper, a colorful tropical reef fish, and an excellent sportfish with superb meat that is marketed fresh and frozen.

Identification. The yellowtail snapper has a streamlined body that is olive or bluish gray above and silver to white below. It has fine yellowish stripes on the belly. Most striking is the prominent mid-body yellow stripe, which runs from the tip of the snout through the eye to the tail, widening as it extends past the dorsal fins. The tail is bright yellow and deeply forked, and the dorsal fins are mostly yellowish. There is no dark lateral spot, and the eye is red.

Size/Age. The yellowtail snapper usually grows 1 to 2 feet long and commonly weighs up to 3 pounds, although it rarely exceeds 5 pounds. It can reach 30 inches and 7 pounds, and a Florida fish that weighed 8 pounds, 8 ounces is the all-tackle world record. The yellowtail snapper can live for 14 years.

Distribution. In the tropical western Atlantic, yellowtail snapper range from Massachusetts and Bermuda to southeastern Brazil, including the Gulf of Mexico. They are abundant in the Bahamas, southern Florida, and throughout the Caribbean but are rare north of the Carolinas. They have also been found in the eastern Atlantic at the Cape Verde Islands.

Habitat. Inhabiting tropical coastal waters with depths of 10 to 300 feet, yellowtail snapper occur around coral reefs, either alone or in loose schools, and are usually seen well above the bottom. Young fish typically dwell inshore over grassbeds.

Life history/Behavior. Some yellowtail snapper are sexually mature at age 2; all are mature at age 4. Spawning occurs from April through August, and activity peaks in June and July. Yellowtail snapper move into deeper water, where they will produce from 11,000 to more than 1.5 million pelagic eggs.

Food and feeding habits. Yellowtail snapper feed mainly at night on benthic and pelagic animals, including fish, crustaceans, and worms. Young fish feed primarily on plankton.

Angling. Anglers use cut fish and squid to catch yellowtail inshore by fishing on the bottom from bridges and piers, and they catch them offshore by fishing over reefs from small private boats and party boats. These fish are attracted to chum and can be caught higher in the water column when they come into an established chum slick. They often do not take baits as aggressively as some other snapper or grouper do, however, and many are not hooked due to their small mouth (or too large a hook). They put a good bend in a light to medium-action spinning rod and make an excellent meal.

See: Inshore Fishing; Snapper.

Yellowtail Snapper

SNAP-SWIVEL
A terminal connection that combines a snap *(see)* and a swivel *(see)*.

SNELLED HOOK
A bait hook with an angled eye that is attached to the line by making a snell knot on the shank.
See: Hook; Knots, Fishing.

SNELL KNOT
A fishing knot for terminal connections.
See: Knots, Fishing.

SNOOK
Fat Snook *Centropomus parallelus.*
   Other names—Portuguese: *robalo;* Spanish: *robalo chucumite.*

Swordspine Snook *Centropomus ensiferus.*

Tarpon Snook *Centropomus pectinatus.*
   Other names—Spanish: *constantino, robalito, róbalos, robalos prieto.*

These three species of snook are all small, similar-looking fish with almost identical ranges and habits but are less prominent than their larger relative the common snook (*see: snook, common*). As members of the Centropomidae family, which includes the Nile perch (*see: perch, Nile*) and barramundi *(see)*, they are excellent table fish with delicate, white, flaky meat, and are good gamefish despite their small size.

There are believed to be 12 species of snook, 6 of which occur in the western Atlantic and 6 in the eastern Pacific, although no single species occurs in both oceans. A good deal is known about these three smaller Atlantic-occurring species, and about the common snook, but not about the others, especially those in the Pacific, which include such large-growing species as the Pacific black snook (*C. nigrescens;* commonly called black snook) and the Pacific white snook (*C. viridis*), as well as the smaller Pacific blackfin snook (*C. medius*).

   Identification. Snook in general are distinctive in appearance, with a characteristic protruding lower jaw and a particularly prominent black lateral line running from the gill cover to the tail.

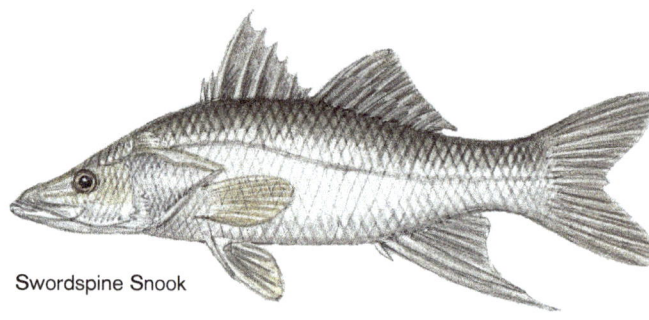
Swordspine Snook

The fat snook has a deeper body than the other snook, although it is not strongly compressed. Coloration varies depending on the area the fish inhabits, but the fat snook is frequently yellow brown or green brown on the back and silvery on the sides, and the lateral line is weakly outlined in black. The mouth reaches to or beyond the center of the eye, and it has the smallest scales of all the snook. There are 15 to 16 rays in the pectoral fin, 6 soft rays in the anal fin, and 10 to 13 gill rakers.

The swordspine snook is the smallest snook and is named for its very long second anal spine, which usually extends to or farther than the area below the base of the tail. With a slightly concave profile, it is yellow green or brown green on the back and silvery on the belly, and it has a prominent lateral line outlined in black. It has the largest scales of all the snook, as well as 15 to 16 rays in the pectoral fin, 6 soft rays in the anal fin, and 13 to 16 gill rakers.

The tarpon snook is distinctive, having 7 anal fin rays, when all other snook have 6. It also has a distinguishing upturned or tarponlike snout and a compressed, flat-sided body. The prominent black lateral line extends through the tail. The pelvic fin is orange yellow with a blackish edge, and the tips of the pelvic fins reach past the anus. There are 14 rays in the pectoral fin, 7 soft rays in the anal fin, and 15 to 18 gill rakers.

   Size/Age. The fat snook rarely reaches more than 20 inches in length, although it is said to attain a length of $2^{1}/_{2}$ feet. The swordspine and tarpon snook are usually less than 1 pound in weight or 12 inches in length. The all-tackle world records for the fat and tarpon snook are, respectively, 7 pounds, 4 ounces and 3 pounds, 2 ounces, both taken in Florida. Snook have a life span of at least seven years.

   Distribution. In the western Atlantic, all three species are present and are most abundant in south-

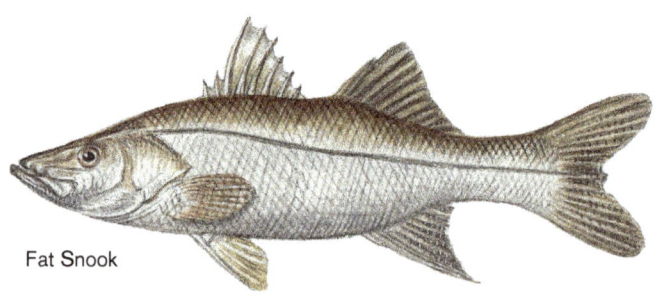
Fat Snook

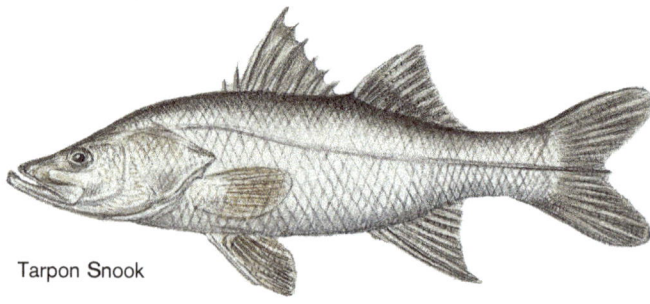
Tarpon Snook

A common snook from the surf near the Parismina River, Costa Rica.

The common snook is the most abundant and wide-ranging of the snook and is highly sought after because of its strength and acrobatics when hooked. It is a member of the Centropomidae family, which also includes such prized species as the Nile perch *(see: perch, Nile)*, although it is superior to the former as a sportfish, even though it doesn't reach the same monstrous proportions. It is also related to the barramundi *(see)*, with which it shares some appearance and behavioral traits.

In all there are believed to be 12 species of snook, 6 of which occur in the western Atlantic and 6 in the eastern Pacific, although no single species occurs in both oceans. Large-growing Pacific species with similar traits, although less common, include the Pacific black snook *(C. nigrescens;* commonly known as the black snook) and the Pacific white snook *(C. viridis)*.

The common snook was once a favored commercial species in Florida; it is now strictly a gamefish there but may be taken commercially in other parts of its range (Pacific snook are also commercially harvested). In the late 1970s and early 1980s, a severe decline in the Florida snook population occurred due to overfishing, loss of habitat, and pollution. Numbers have increased to safe levels, however, since the fish was given protected status in Florida in 1982. This effort established a legal size, a bag limit, and a closed season during the summer spawning period,.

Identification. A silvery fish with a yellow green or olive tint, the common snook has a body that is streamlined and slender with a distinct black lateral line running from the top of its gills to the end of its forked tail. It has a sloping forehead, a long, concave snout, and a large mouth with brush-like teeth and a protruding lower jaw. The fins are occasionally bright yellow, although the pelvic fin is usually pale, unlike the orange yellow, black-tipped pelvic fin of the tarpon snook *(see: snook)*. The common snook has a high, divided dorsal fin, as well as small scales that run from about 70 to 77 along the lateral line to the base of the tail. It has relatively short anal spines that do not reach the base of the tail when pressed against the body; there are usually 6 soft rays in the anal fin. There are also 15 to 16 rays in the pectoral fins and 7 to 9 gill rakers on the first arch.

Size/Age. The common snook grows much larger than other Atlantic-range snook, averaging $1^1/_2$ to $2^1/_2$ feet or 5 to 8 pounds, although it can reach 4 feet and 50 pounds. Females are almost always larger than males, although growth rates are variable. The all-tackle world record is a 53-pound, 10-ounce fish taken off eastern Costa Rica in 1978. Common snook can live for more than 20 years.

The Pacific black snook attains similar sizes and is believed to reach 60 pounds; a 57-pound, 12-ounce fish from western Costa Rica is the all-tackle world record for this species. The Pacific white snook also grows large, and a $39^1/_2$-pound

ern Florida, although swordspine and tarpon snook are rare on Florida's west coast. Fat and swordspine snook occur around the Greater and Lesser Antilles, whereas fat snook also extend down the southeastern coast of the Gulf of Mexico and the continental Caribbean coasts to Santos, Brazil. Swordspine snook occur down the continental Caribbean coasts of Central and South America to Rio de Janeiro, Brazil. Tarpon snook are found in the West Indies, and from Mexico to Brazil. They are also reported on the Pacific coast from Mexico to Colombia.

Habitat/Behavior. Snook inhabit the coastal waters of estuaries and lagoons, moving between freshwater and saltwater seasonally but always remaining close to shore and to estuaries. Fat and swordspine snook prefer very low salinity water or freshwater, whereas the tarpon snook is most common in shaded lakes with brackish waters. Fat snook occur more often in interior waters than other snook (instead of estuarine waters), and all three species use mangrove shorelines as nursery grounds. Snook are usually sexually mature by their third year.

Food. These species feed on fish and crustaceans.

Angling. *See: Snook, Common.*

SNOOK, COMMON
Centropomus undecimalis.
Other names—linesider, robalo, sergeant fish, snook; Portuguese: *robalo;* Spanish: *robalo, robalito.*

Common Snook

specimen from Cabo San Lucas, Mexico, is the all-tackle world record.

Distribution. In the western Atlantic, common snook are found primarily in southern Florida, as well as off the southeastern coast of the Gulf of Mexico, around most of the Antilles, and off the Caribbean coast of Central and South America extending southward to Rio de Janeiro, Brazil. They are also occasionally encountered off North Carolina and Texas. The largest snook in Florida, exceeding 30 pounds, are caught chiefly in east coast bays and inlets from Vero Beach south to Miami, but their most abundant populations are on the west coast from Boca Grande south throughout the Everglades region, including Florida Bay.

The range of the Pacific black snook is in the eastern Pacific, primarily from Baja California, Mexico, to Colombia, although it has also been reported from Ecuador and Peru. It is most common in Costa Rica and Panama. The range of the Pacific white snook is similar, extending from Baja California to Peru, including the Galápagos Islands.

Habitat. Snook inhabit warm, shallow coastal waters and are able to tolerate freshwater and saltwater. They are most common along continental shores, preferring fast-moving tides and relying on the shelter of estuaries, lagoons, mangrove areas, and brackish streams, as well as freshwater canals and rivers, usually at depths of less than 65 feet. Occasionally they occur in small groups over grassy flats and shallow patch reefs, and may be found at the mouths of tributaries and along the ocean side of shores near tributaries. Snook cannot tolerate water temperatures below 60°F; in winter, they stay in protected, stable-temperature areas such as those under bridges, in ship channels, turning basins, warmwater outflows near power plants, and the upper reaches of estuaries.

Life history/Behavior. Common snook congregate at mouths of passes and rivers during the spawning season, returning to the same spawning sites each summer. Spawning grounds include significant passes and inlets of the Atlantic Ocean and the Gulf of Mexico, such as Sebastian, Ft. Pierce, St. Lucie, Jupiter, and Lake Worth inlets on the east coast and Hurricane, Clearwater, and John's passes on the west coast. Common snook also spawn inside Tampa Bay around passes to the secondary embankments of Miquel Bay, Terra Ceia Bay, and Riviera Bay. The season extends from April through November but activity peaks between May and July; more intense spawning occurs during new or full moon phases. Females may spawn more than 1.5 million eggs every day in the early part of the season, with larvae drifting for 15 to 20 days after hatching. Young fish remain in the quiet, secluded upper reaches of estuaries until they reach sexual maturity, which males attain after two to three years and females after three to four years.

Common snook are protandric hermaphrodites—they can change their sex from male to female; this change usually happens between the ages of 2 and 7 and between the lengths of 17 to 30 inches. Within a group of common snook, sex reversal is brought about by a change in the size of individuals; that is, if a group that loses its largest fish has lost females, some males may undergo sex reversal to fill the absence, a process that takes from 60 to 90 days.

Food and feeding habits. Carnivorous predators that ambush their prey as currents sweep food into their vicinity, snook feed on both freshwater and saltwater fish, shrimp, crabs, and larger crustaceans.

Angling. Commonly caught in brackish water, snook are often found in the far reaches of freshwater rivers, as well as in lagoons and canals, often in the same cover-laden areas inhabited by largemouth bass where these species overlap. Their most common habitat, however, is inshore saltwater areas, particularly along mangrove-lined banks, as well as around such objects as bridges, docks, pilings, oyster bars and sandbars, along dropoffs and island edges, and in deep holes.

Renowned fighters, snook jump, run, dive deep, pull very hard, and are generally tough to land, especially in larger sizes. Many snook are lost by anglers. These fish have a penchant for heavy cover; when hooked, they repeatedly try to reach cover and get free by cutting the line, and they are often successful.

Although anglers must have a good reel drag, they also must be able to apply pressure to the fish to turn it and force it away from objects. The bigger the snook, the more of a challenge this becomes.

Casting or live-bait fishing are the primary means of pursuing snook. With the latter method, a small bait, such as a mullet, is livelined by anglers who stillfish or drift. Casters primarily work shallow nearshore areas, often casting into thick mangrove stands and up under the bank. Accurate casters who can pitch a plug into an opening or back under the brush will usually fare better than those whose casts repeatedly land on the edge of the cover and are always working away from, rather than through, it.

Although small spoons and flies or poppers are used, the favored snook lures are walking plugs worked rapidly on the surface, or darting shallow-running plugs worked in jerky, erratic motions just under the surface. A moving tide, usually the high ebb, produces well. Some sight fishing is done by anglers drifting and looking for cruising fish on cover laden flats or shores, but most angling is blind prospecting in likely places. Fly fishing is most prudent when the fish are visible, but it is also practiced in known snook-holding cover where fish aren't visible. Popping bugs and streamer flies are popular terminal items.

Snook are found singly or in groups, and the larger fish tend to be loners. Some fishing is done in deep holes with jigs or by trolling, too, although this is often in the winter when cold water makes snook sluggish. The better fishing time is during the spawning period. Some night fishing, primarily around bridges and piers, is also done for snook in the summer.

Although anglers need a stiff-tipped rod to properly work snook plugs, the tackle may be similar to that used in largemouth bass fishing. Baitcasting gear is better for accuracy and fish control, and 12- to 17-pound line is the norm.

See: Snook.

SOFT LURE

This is a catch-all term for a lure or body component of a lure that is made of a soft substance, as opposed to a lure made of metal (like a spoon or spinner), wood, or hard plastic (like a plug). Also called soft baits (as in artificial bait), these are primarily fashioned from soft plastic, but some are produced from soft processed natural food or a combination of both, and a few products are rubber.

Soft lures are not a category of lure per se; they are mostly found as artificial worms, as various body shapes for leadhead jigs, and as trailers or add-ons for a variety of other lures. Some plugs and surface lures have soft bodies as well.

Most soft lures exactly or closely represent some type of natural food. The list is headed by various

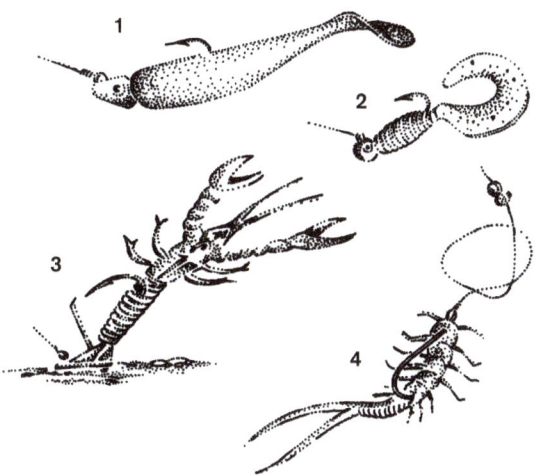

Popular soft lures include a so-called "shad" or fish-shaped body used on jigs (1), a curl-tail grub body (2), a crayfish imitation (3), and a hellgrammite imitation (4).

kinds of worms and small baitfish, and includes eels, leeches, salamanders (often called lizards), frogs, crayfish, hellgrammites, and mice. These are used in freshwater and saltwater; in the latter, most soft lures are used as jig bodies.

Soft lures have a feel that is unmatched by hard lures; in many cases, this means that they may be held by a striking fish for a moment or two longer than a hard lure. Since the strike and rejection of some lures happens in an instant, this extra holding ability can make a difference in catching fish. The use of scents with some soft bodies might have an added measure of appeal to certain fish. They also have the advantage of being relatively inexpensive and easily replaced; changing to a different color or style, or simply replacing a soft body, is easy and cheap. Some bodies also have a swimming action that is not only different, but better than that of most hard lures, and often can be fished effectively at a slower pace than hard lures.

There are various rigging methods for soft lures or soft bodies on lures. Methods of rigging worms or wormlike lures are described elsewhere *(see: soft worm)*. Standard means of rigging soft bodies on jigs follow, as well as a method of rigging an imitation hellgrammite for stream fishing.

Shad/Fish body on a jig. Fish-shaped soft baits, particularly those with a broad tail that shimmies widely, are often called shad baits and are fished on various styles of leadhead jig, with the larger bodies being used with blunt-end versions. The point and shank of the hook must be threaded through the middle of the soft bait to a location where, when the point is pushed out, the gap is about halfway exposed and the body of the bait is aligned with the leadhead and not bunched.

Grub on a jig. There are all kinds of soft-bait bodies, lumped under the category of grub, for use with leadhead jigs. The most common, used in various sizes for diverse species, is a curl-tail model. Rig this so the curled tail rides up vertically in the same direction as the hook, with the gap in the hook point halfway exposed and the body of the grub aligned and not bunched along the hook shank. Flat-tailed grubs should be rigged so that the tail is horizontal.

Crayfish standup jig. Some types of soft baits, especially the many-tentacled versions that might represent crayfish and those models that closely imitate these crustaceans, are effectively fished with a leadhead jig that allows them to either stand up or have a higher profile on the bottom. The hook is usually exposed on such a bait, although it may have a weedguard, and the extremities of the lure are free to move actively with every twitch of the rod tip.

Split shot bottom rig. When fishing in current, light round clamp-on split shot provides better movement through riffles and shallow runs than other types of weights. These can be fished at various distances, usually 8 to 18 inches, ahead of the soft lure. The lure body can be one of many different soft styles; it is fished with the hook point buried or exposed, the latter producing quick hookups but also more rock snags. A hellgrammite imitation, or something similar, is especially good in creeks and streams when bottom drifting for smallmouth bass.

See: Jerkbait; Jig; Lure.

SOFT WORM

An artificial wormlike lure made of supple synthetic material. Artificial worms are mostly made of soft plastic and commonly called plastic worms, but they may be made from other substances as well as imitate other food, such as leeches, snakes, eels, or salamanders.

Soft worms are perhaps the most productive of all artificial lures for freshwater bass; they are primarily used in fishing for largemouth bass but will catch other species, such as northern pike and pickerel, and are frequently used as components of jigs (see), spinnerbaits (see), and other lures. So popular are soft worms for bass fishing, it is possible that more of them are sold each year than all other bass lures combined.

What a soft worm specifically represents—earthworm, eel, leech, salamander, and so on—may be speculative, but there is no guessing about why it is successful. It looks like a fairly substantial morsel; it has a realistic feel; it has good action and moves enticingly and relatively naturally through cover; and, perhaps most importantly, it is worked effectively down at the level of the bass, which is to say the bottom and in protected hideaways. Moreover, one of the pleasant effects of successful soft worm fishing is a sense of accomplishment. Some lures require little more than accurate casting and routine retrieval to be effective, particularly when bass are active. But an artificial worm must be worked with your brain as well as your wrists; how you give it action, detect strikes, and react reflexively are major factors in its effectiveness.

Features

There are relatively soft worms and truly soft worms, versions that float and others that sink, and worms with all types of tail designs. They come in a whole spectrum of colors, and may sport light tails, light heads, light bellies, stripes, and polka dots. They are made in small, medium, large, and huge sizes. Some are scented, some are oiled, some come prerigged. In short, there is a veritable smorgasbord of soft worms.

The most important features of a worm, in descending order, are softness, buoyancy, size, body and tail shape, color, and scent.

Softness. Worms were once all made of rubber and very tough. Today, very few artificial worms are made of rubber (though some exist as prerigged worms on snelled hooks and leaders). The vast majority are made entirely of soft plastic. An increasing number are made of an amalgamation of soft plastic and processed natural foods that provide scent and flavor; these processed natural foods may be fish, crayfish, and other organisms and proteins. Thus, this category of lure transcends the use of plastic, and is chiefly categorized by its soft nature. In addition, advances in the chemical composition of certain plasticizing agents allow for manufacturing control over the suppleness of a worm, enabling some designs to deliberately be harder or softer in character than others.

Softness is a vital feature. A soft worm feels more lifelike and aids the angler in setting the hook. An artificial worm that is too soft is also fragile; it will tear when it comes into contact with objects and will barely hold a hook. A worm that is too hard feels unnatural and offers more resistance to hook point penetration, which at times is crucial in the timing of hooksetting. Most worm manufactur-

Tackle shops in largemouth bass country offer a huge variety of types, sizes, and colors of soft worms.

ers try to make worms that are tough enough to withstand reasonable use, but soft enough to aid fish catching, although for Carolina rigging, which will be explained shortly, worms should be a little tougher than the norm.

Buoyancy. Another prominent feature of worms is their degree of buoyancy. Better worms have a light enough density to float on the surface of the water without a hook in them. Some will even float with a 1/0 or 2/0 hook in them, which is useful for fishing a completely unweighted worm on the surface over thick cover.

A worm that floats has a better appearance in the water because when it rests on the bottom, the tail section rides up. This accentuates both the behavior of the moving worm and its stationary appearance. Some specialty worms, such as very large and pre-rigged versions, understandably do not float and are not meant to float.

Size. The size of worm to use can vary with fishing conditions and the size of bass that you expect to take in any particular water. There is often a corollary between the size of the worm and the size of the bass that are caught. However, large bass are caught on small worms and small bass on big worms, including some bass that are shorter than the length of the worm.

Choice of worm size also depends on what you're seeking. If you're expressly interested in a trophy-size bass, then you should fish with nothing less than a 7-inch worm. In places where 10-pound bass are possible, an 8- to 12-inch worm is usually the best bet; where bass over 6 pounds are caught infrequently, a 7-inch worm is usually as large as you need.

Most bass fishing is done with 6-inch worms. All but the largest bass are good candidates for this bait, and in waters that are heavily fished, this size worm is relatively unobtrusive and unalarming to fish that are probably well conditioned to the presence of artificial lures. In some places, like heavily fished, clear-water lakes, it's necessary to use 4- and 5-inch worms for regular success.

Body/Tail shape. The basic body shape of most worms is round and moderately tapered from head to tail. Some worms are flat on one side, which is not as appealing as fully round models and which doesn't produce as good an action or object resistance. (Some soft lures that suspend or sink slowly are vaguely wormlike in appearance but shaped more like fish and fished differently; *see: jerkbait*).

Most worms have circularly molded indented impressions along their length, much like an earthworm, though a few are completely smooth. It probably doesn't make much difference to a bass or to the action of the worm whether it is smooth or slightly rippled. Some worms have a series of raised rings along their body, which trap air between them and release bubbles as the worm is retrieved. These worms have a tendency to grab onto grass, pads,

In this assortment of soft worms, the horizontal group includes various jerk worms.

rocks, and limbs more so than other worms, which hampers their action and restricts their ability to freely move over objects.

Many worms are designed with straight tails, and an equal or greater number sport some type of curl tail. A few have beaver or paddle tails. Beaver-tailed models are bulkier than other worms, and you have to get used to the different feel of fishing them. They produce more action and vibration than a straight-tailed worm, and are effective in murky water, where added vibration for the large tail helps a fish locate the lure. They also make a nice trailer behind a jig, especially when flipping.

Curl tail worms include those with a simple J bend at the end as well as those with opposite curl features either at the end or two-thirds of the way through the body. Curl tails produce a nice swimming action with only the slightest assistance on the part of the angler.

It's worthwhile to experiment with different designs, just as it's desirable to have an assortment of different size and color worms. Many anglers eventually develop the most confidence in one particular design and use it for 90 percent of their worm fishing.

Scent/Color. Scent is also a matter of choice and personal confidence. Many worms are coated with some type of oil-like covering, which may or may not be scented; many others are imbedded with scents or derive scent from the processed natural materials they are made from. It is arguable what the value of this is and the extent to which it either attracts fish or makes them hold onto a lure. Scents may help mask human odors that are imprinted on soft plastic worms through hand contact, but it's hard to say that they contribute to the attraction of fish.

It is possible that fish will hold onto soft worms that are made with processed food a bit longer before rejecting them, providing a little more time to detect a strike and set the hook. Nevertheless, the most important factors for success are using a soft floating worm in the appropriate size and color and fishing it well.

Dark-colored worms are far more popular and successful than light ones, but there isn't a color or variation on color that hasn't been tried in soft worms. Some anglers are still partial to black and purple worms, and others to red, blue, grape, and motor oil, plus the two-toned shad colors and metal-flecked varieties. Many newer combination colors, like Fire and Ice, Junebug, tequila, electric blue, and red shad are also good.

Water color and visibility play a part in worm color determination, and at times one color outperforms another because it stands out better in a particular type of water. At other times, several colors are equally productive. More important than color, perhaps, is having confidence in your lure, fishing in the right places, and utilizing proper technique.

Some worms are better known by flavors than by colors. There is nothing to the flavor gimmick other than the fact that the impregnated smells help mask human odors, which may be imparted to worms when touched. Most worms are coated or otherwise treated with anise oil or some similar licorice-like smelling agent that keeps them moist and soft. Salt worms, which are impregnated with salt, are popular in some areas and are thought to induce bass to retain them longer than they might otherwise, but this advantage may be only psychological.

Firetail worms have merit when success is slow. Firetail worms are merely those with a light color blended into the tail section. Black, grape, blue, and purple worms with either a light pink or lime green tail are traditionally productive. Unfortunately, firetail worms also attract other species, including pickerel, bluegill, and rock bass, even more so than one-color worms. These fish can be a nuisance at times when you're seeking only bass.

Rigging

Texas rig. The Texas rig has been the standard worm-rigging method since suppliers stopped making worms out of hard rubber in preference for soft plastic. It can be used in almost any bass habitat, though it has limited value in really deep water and with heavy weights.

The Texas rig incorporates nothing more than a worm, slip sinker, and hook, with the hook point turned back and imbedded in the neck area

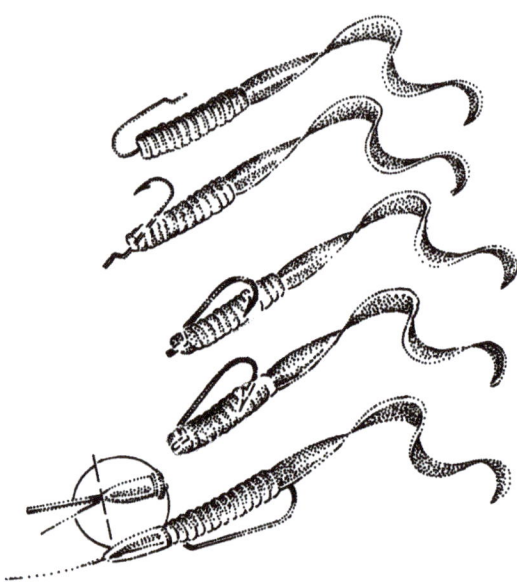

Shown from top to bottom are the steps for creating a Texas-rigged soft worm. If necessary when fishing in cover, a slip sinker can be pegged with the tip of a toothpick (inset) to keep it from moving.

of the worm so that it is essentially snag free. To accomplish this, put a cone shaped slip sinker onto your line, narrow end first, then tie the line to your hook. Take the point of the hook and imbed it into the center of the head of the worm up past the barb, then bring the point out the side of the worm. Pull the shank of the hook through this passage and rotate it 180 degrees. Bring the shank all the way out until the eye of the hook is secured in the worm head. Slide the point into the body of the worm so that it is firmly imbedded in it, yet has not pierced through it. Do not curl or rotate the worm but be sure that the hook and worm are aligned and that the worm is straight and not bunched up.

The slip sinker will slide freely on this rig, but there are times, such as when fishing in thick cover, when it is advantageous to prevent the sinker from sliding freely (and getting hung up). To do this, jam one end of a toothpick in the head of a sinker as far as it will go, and then break it off. Jam the other end into the back of the cone, and break it off. An alternative way of accomplishing the same thing is to use a slip sinker with a corkscrew stem, which holds the worm in place.

To use the Texas rigging style to place the hook further along the body of the worm, carefully thread the point and shank of the hook through it to near the midsection. This rig can be fished with either a very light slip sinker or without a sinker, and is employed when bass are taking a worm in the middle rather than head first. It is often used when bass are spawning, and thus called a bed, or spawning, rig.

The biggest problem experienced by users of the Texas rig is getting the worm curled or bunched up. This causes the worm to spin when it is retrieved, producing an unnatural, unappealing action and contributing to line twist.

The theory behind the unpegged Texas rig is that when a bass grabs the worm, it does not feel the hook and does not detect the weight, which slides up the line. Theoretically, this gives the angler an extra moment in which to react and set the hook. When the hook is set, it should freely pierce the worm, which is another reason why the worm should be relatively soft.

The size of slip sinker, which is also called a worm weight, varies from $1/16$-ounce to $1/2$-ounce and depends on depth, wind, and the general activity of the fish. They are still primarily lead, but that could change in the future to brass or stainless steel alloys. Some anglers like painted sinkers, but unpainted weights are overwhelmingly popular.

The lighter the sinker's weight, the more likely you are to have success. Sinker weight must be matched to the terrain and fishing conditions, but using the lightest sinker possible while still correctly fishing under those conditions brings the best results.

The primary reason for this is that the heavier the sinker, the larger it is and the more detectable it may be to a bass. This is particularly true when fishing pressure is intense or when the bass are sluggish. Another important reason is that the worm is moved more naturally with a light sinker than with a heavy one, where its actions are more dramatic and pronounced. A worm with a light weight swims more convincingly than one with a heavy sinker. Light weights don't hang up as much as heavy ones, and they aid in detecting strikes, so it's best to use the lightest slip sinker possible for the conditions.

Sometimes, strong winds or current make worm fishing very difficult, and you have to use a larger than customary weight to gain casting accuracy and to maintain a feel for the bottom. In shallow water you can usually get away with a light sinker, but as you fish deep, you may need to increase the weight of the sinker. You can cast small worms and light weights more effectively with spinning tackle than with baitcasting equipment. Light line is conducive to light sinker use, since it does not offer as much resistance as the larger diameter, heavier line.

Hooks vary from 1/0 to 6/0, depending on the length of the worm. A general guideline is: 1/0 or 2/0 with 4-inch worms; 3/0 with 6-inchers; 4/0 with 7-inchers, 5/0 with 8-inchers; and 6/0 with larger worms.

A number of worm hook styles are popular, and there's a dizzying array to select from now. Many anglers prefer a keel, or offset, hook shank with a wide, or so-called Southern, sproat. The offset shank retains the worm pretty well, and the wide gap gives plenty of room for hooking. You might try experimenting with various hooks that turn when you strike a fish, and also with hooks that have outside edge barbs. Make sure that the hook point is as sharp as it possibly can be.

Carolina rig. The Texas rig may be the most popular plastic worm rigging method, but it is not the only one. The Carolina rig, especially good for deep-water bottom fishing, features a floating worm that rises up unweighted. This rig sports a medium-weight sinker, followed by a barrel swivel, an 18- to 36-inch leader, and a hooked worm. The hook is generally no more than 1/0 size to give greater buoyancy to the worm and is usually exposed, though it can be imbedded into the worm Texas rig style when there are obstructions present. The sinker, which can be barrel-, egg-, or cone-shaped, weighs $3/4$-ounce to 1 ounce and slides freely to the swivel, so a fish can take the worm and move off without feeling resistance. The length of line between barrel and worm is somewhat

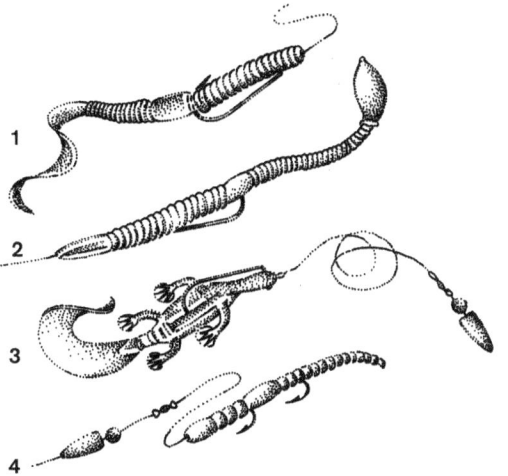

Soft worm rigs include: weightless floating Texas rig (1), mid-body Texas rig (2), Carolina rig (3), and an exposed-hook do-nothing rig (4).

arbitrary; 18 to 24 inches is the norm, but some anglers like to go with as little as 8 inches for swimming the worm through weed beds.

Other rigs. Another variation on this rigging method that is useful for unobstructed open-water fishing is the so-called Do Nothing rig. It features a heavy ($1/2$- to $1 1/2$-ounce) sliding slip sinker ahead of a barrel swivel, 3 to 5 feet of line between the swivel and worm, two panfish-size hooks, and a short straight worm. The hooks are rigged in tandem and are exposed; the worm is roughly 4 inches long. Some anglers use a small plastic bead between the sinker and swivel to prevent knot abrasion. A little tough to cast, this rig is fished in a slow, reel-cranking manner without any special rod or retrieval action. Despite its name, it is good enough to interest reluctant, bottom-dwelling bass.

The manner of hooking worms is often subject to experimentation. Setting the hook into the bony jaw of a bass is often difficult, especially if the hook point must first pierce the worm body; that's one reason super-soft worms are preferred by Texas rig users. Hooking variations, therefore, are usually directed at improving hooking efficiency. Some anglers put the hook through the head and leave the point exposed for fishing on the surface (without a weight), or they hook it in the collar or near the midsection for weightless, extremely slow, free-swimming simulation. A variation on the latter, with Texas-style hooking, is to thread the hook from the top of the worm down near the midsection, then bring the point out and imbed it into the worm. This is fished without a weight and has been called a spawning rig for bedding bass, which normally take a worm in the middle and swim off to remove it from the nest area.

Multiple hooking is another possibility, especially for short striking fish. Small worms can be rigged with one hook toward the rear by using a long, thin sewing needle to bring the line through the body, then tying it to the hook and inserting the shank of the hook in the worm. The hook can be exposed or it can be imbedded to make it weedless. A two-hook rig, in tandem and using snelled hooks, is a little tougher to execute, but many anglers prefer this. Such a rig enables anglers to catch bass that strike either the head or the tail of the worm. Worms can also be attached to jig hooks. Many anglers have summer bass success with 4-inch worms behind small jigs, fished on light line.

Fishing

When/Where. Bass are receptive to worms in relatively warm water. In warm water, worms are softer and feel more natural. In cold water, plastic worms harden and are more quickly rejected by bass. In temperatures below 55°F or so, worms don't seem to appeal to bass; from temperatures in the mid-50s to the mid-60s, they have some appeal; they are in their best range from the mid-60's on up.

When you want to cover a lot of territory fairly rapidly, a worm is not the best bait to use. If, however, in doing this while using another lure, you catch a couple of fish in one area, it may pay to switch to a worm in order to work that area more thoroughly and more productively.

Worms work well at any given time of the day, particularly during the summer, and at night. Summer is traditionally the best time to fish a worm, when the bass are well secured in or near some type of cover, and you need a worm to work that cover extensively. This is one of the true benefits of worm fishing: You cover the area well, and you fish it on the bottom, where the bass are. Though swimming a worm over cover may at times have merit, primarily you fish it on the bottom.

A plastic worm rigged in weedless fashion is at its best when used around typical bass holding objects like stumps, fallen trees, grass, pads, hyacinths, hydrilla, docks, milfoil, and the like. When making a cast to a particular object, such as a stump, for example, cast beyond and to one side of that stump (such as the shaded side) initially, working the worm slowly up alongside and then past the stump. Baitcasters should take care to cast beyond the area they want to fish a worm, as the worm does not drop straight downward, but usually falls on an angle toward the caster due to tension on the line. With a spinning reel, keep the bail open to allow the worm to fall relatively straight down from the place where it hits the water.

Retrieval. The strike of a bass on a worm has often been related as feeling like a double tapping at the end of the line; the first tap is what you detect when the bass makes the motion to inhale it, and the second is what you detect as it enters the fish's mouth. If you feel a third tap, the bass is probably expelling it.

Learning to detect a strike or to differentiate a strike from contact with underwater objects is the most difficult aspect of worm fishing. There is no shortcut to learning this. An ability to detect strikes and learn the "feel" of a worm comes through experience. The more you fish with a worm, the quicker you'll develop this feel.

Beginning worm anglers might try practicing in their backyard or in shallow water where they can see the worm. Drag it over rocks and logs and tree limbs. Crawl it on gravel surfaces. Watch it work in a clear pool. Simulate fishing conditions.

Another key to detecting strikes is closely watching your line. In the most radical instances, an eager bass may pick up a worm and immediately run with it, in which case the line noticeably moves off to the side or away. Sometimes you'll see the line move like this before you feel the strike. Usually, however, there is a barely perceptible flickering of the line, particularly the section nearest to the

When rigged to be snag-free, soft worms are great bass producers, fished in and around cover and on the bottom. They should be retrieved slowly, crawled along the bottom, and lifted and dropped over stumps, limbs, and other cover.

water, which is a result of the bass inhaling the worm and drawing it (and the line) inward. In time, you'll come to see and feel the strike at the same instant.

To retrieve a plastic worm, begin with the rod butt and your arms close to your body, with the rod held perpendicular to you and parallel to the water. Raise the rod from this position (we'll call it 9 o'clock) upward, extending it between a 45 and 60 degree angle, which would mean moving it from 9:00 to 10:30 or 11:00. As you raise the rod, the worm is lifted up off the bottom and swims forward, falling to a new position. Make this motion slowly, so the worm does not hop too far off the bottom and swims slowly. When your rod reaches that upward position, drop it back to its original position while at the same time retrieving slack line. Keep your motions slow. When you encounter some resistance, as would happen when crawling it over a log or through a bush, first gently try to work the worm along; if this fails, try to hop the worm along with short flickers of the rod tip.

Sometimes the slip sinker gets hung up under rocks, and if you jiggle your line, the sinker falls back and becomes free. Other times, the sinker will fall over a limb and slide down the line, while the worm stays back behind that limb. This makes detection and retrieval difficult and can be solved by pegging the slip sinker with a toothpick and breaking it off, thus preventing the sinker from sliding up the line. The sinker remains directly in front of the worm.

Pegging a worm is useful for fishing brushy areas, lily pads, hyacinths, moss, and grass as well as amidst stumps and trees, and it makes retrieval and strike detection easier. It goes against the theory of having a freely sliding slip sinker so a fish can pick up the lure and run off with it without detecting the weight, but this is minimized by a quick hook-setting reaction, a sensitive rod, and a sensitive line to detect strikes more readily.

Set the hook as soon as you can after detecting a strike. Remember that because the worm is rigged weedless with the hook imbedded in it, you can't simply rear back when you feel a strike, as you might when fishing a lure with exposed hooks. As soon as you detect a strike, lower the rod tip and extend it out and point it toward the fish. This momentarily gives the bass slack line. Quickly reel up the slack, and as the line draws tight, set the hook. Continue to reel in line to counteract the effect of stretch and to ensure that no slack is present. The whole maneuver is accomplished in an instant and appears to be one fluid motion. Removing slack line is critical, because your hook must penetrate not only the balled-up worm, but the cartilaginous mouth of the fish as well.

It is very difficult to fish a worm properly in wind. If you have a specific place that you wish to fish and it is buffeted by wind, you might anchor your boat in such a way that you can fish directly upwind or downwind of that spot. At other times you may elect to drift and fish, using an electric motor to either slow the drift speed or keep a desired position. If you have to drift, fishing in the direction the boat is headed is difficult, but may work because it allows you to fish a spot before the boat drifts over it. Where deep water is worked, it only makes sense to drift behind the boat.

Fishing against the wind can almost be like trolling and can be effective provided your boat is not moving too fast and your sinker is heavy enough to keep the worm down. One trouble with trolling a sinker-rigged worm is that bass strike and reject it quickly, but if you slow-troll it without a weight, it can be a different story; you might try this on shallow weedy lakes.

Occasionally, you may find it beneficial to swim the worm slowly just off the bottom. This works best in lily pads, in moderately thin grassy areas, and in similar spots. It's difficult to cast an unweighted worm with most baitcasting equipment, though not too difficult with spinning tackle.

Tackle. For worm fishing, use a good quality rod that has an even taper, with a strong butt and backbone and a "fast" or relatively limber tip. The disadvantage of a rod with a stiff tip is that it casts a worm poorly and is not sensitive enough for detecting strikes. Having a special "worm" rod to fish plastic worms isn't necessary. A graphite or good composite rod is strong and sensitive and is an advantage to an angler skilled at detecting pickups. The most popular rod choice is a $5^1/_2$-foot baitcasting model, but many anglers like 6-footers.

Spinning rods are not used as much for worm fishing as are baitcasting and spincasting rods, but they are perfectly acceptable if you have a fast-action rod that allows you to detect even faint strikes and to set the hook. Most people who fish worms on spinning rods use a rod that is too limber, and they are unable to set the hook.

There are no special criteria for reels where worm fishing is concerned. Line choice runs to the intermediate and heavy side, but 10- to 14-pound line is generally adequate for most situations, although it is worth noting that worms are fished in all manner of cover, so the line you use should be high quality and particularly resistant to abrasion and able to withstand sudden shock loading.

See: Jerkbait; Lure; Soft Lure.

SOLE

(1) Sole are flatfish *(see)* that typically have an extremely rounded to oval body. Their small eyes are close together, and most are right-eyed; like other flatfish, they undergo a unique maturation from egg to adult in which one eye migrates to the opposite side of the head. They live mainly in warm or temperate waters, and some species migrate into freshwater.

European Sole

True sole are members of the Soleidae family of flatfish, but the word "sole" has been widely used to refer to some flatfish that actually belong to other families. Species referred to as sole in North America are rarely seen by the recreational angler and are more common in cold European waters, where they are taken by both commercial and recreational anglers. European sole have been heavily marketed, and the term "fillet of sole," which was once specific to the common or European sole *(Solea solea),* is now applied to many other sole and indeed for many non-sole flatfish.

(2) Common Sole *Solea solea.*
Other names—European sole, black sole, Dover sole, parkgate sole, river sole, sea partridge, slip, tounge, true sole; Danish: *søtunge, tunge;* Dutch: *tong;* Finnish: *kielikampela;* French: *sole commune;* Icelandic: *sóikoli, sólflúra;* Italian: *sogliola;* Norwegian: *tunge;* Portuguese: *linguado legitimo;* Spanish: *lenguado común;* Swedish: *akta tunga, tunga, tungor, sjötunga;* Turkish: *dil, dil baligi.*

The common, or European, sole is a right-eyed member of the Soleidae family of flatfish *(see)* that has been commercially significant for European markets, where it is mainly caught by commercial trawlers.

Identification. The body of the common sole is oval; the eyed side is uniformly yellowish brown with dark blotches, and the blind side is creamy white. Distinguishing characteristics include a downward-curved mouth and a small caudal fin. The pectoral fins are well developed on both sides, and the anal and dorsal fins are tinged with white.

Size/Age. This species grows to 27 inches and 7 pounds but is commonly caught at 12 to 14 inches in length. It reportedly can live for 20 years.

Distribution. The common sole occurs in the eastern Atlantic southward from Trondheim Fjord, including the North Sea and western Baltic, and the Mediterranean Sea, including the Sea of Marmara, Bosphorus, and the southwestern Black Sea. Elsewhere, it occurs southward to Senegal, including the Cape Verde Islands.

Habitat. Common sole prefer water temperature ranging from 8 to 24°C and are located over sand and mud bottoms in varying depths, from near shore to 200 feet; they migrate to deeper water in winter.

Spawning behavior. Spawning occurs in spring and early summer in shallow water.

Food. The diet of sole consists of worms, mollusks, and small crustaceans. This fish is primarily a night feeder.

Angling. Bottom fishing with natural baits and metal jigs is the primary method of catching sole. Angling techniques are discussed in greater detail under other entries *(see: drift fishing; inshore fishing).*

Petrale Sole

SOLE, GRAY
A common name for witch flounder.
See: Flounder, Witch.

SOLE, PETRALE *Eopsetta jordani.*
Other names—sole, round-nosed sole, Jordan's flounder, California sole, brill.

A member of the Pleuronectidae family of right-eyed flatfish *(see),* the petrale sole is an occasional catch by anglers and a good sportfish, in part owing to its moderate size. It is an excellent food fish and is highly sought commercially, primarily by trawlers, and is marketed fresh or as frozen fillets. The liver of large specimens is known to be rich in vitamin A.

Identification. The body of the petrale sole is elongate, moderately slender, and compressed. The head is deep and the mouth large. The eyes are large, and the color on the eyed side is uniformly dark to light brown with dusky blotches on the dorsal and anal fins. It is white on the blind side.

The petrale sole are often confused with California halibut *(see: halibut, California)* because these species have a similar color and large mouths. Petrale sole, however, have an even, brown coloration and do not have a high arch in their lateral line.

Size. The average commercial catch is between 1 and 2 pounds, but this species can attain lengths to 28 inches and a weight of 8 pounds.

Distribution. The petrale sole ranges from the Bering Sea and Aleutian Islands throughout the Gulf of Alaska to the Coronado Islands of northern Baja California, Mexico.

Habitat. Petrale sole occur on sand and mud bottoms in waters from 60 to 1,500 feet deep, although they are most commonly found between 180 and 400 feet from April through October, and deeper in winter. Anglers on party boats are likely to encounter them at such depths on sand bottoms near rocky reefs.

Food. The diet of petrale sole includes crabs, shrimp, and fish such as anchovies, hake, small rockfish, and other flatfish.

Angling. In California, most of the petrale sole catch is made by anglers pursuing deep rockfish on party boats. Angling techniques for flatfish are discussed in greater detail under other entries *(see: drift fishing; inshore fishing).*

SOLUNAR TABLES *(Fish Activity Charts)*

Tables and charts that forecast periods of fish and game activity are commonly and generically referred to as solunar tables, partly because they are based on the location of the sun and moon in relation to the earth, but mostly because the first and most well-known of these was named and registered under the trademark of the Solunar Tables by its creator, John Alden Knight, in 1926. For decades, these solunar tables were the most prominently used forecasters of fish and game activity.

Today a number of fish and game activity forecasting tables (also called charts or calendars) are available. Magazines and newspapers publish various ones on a regular basis, including the original by Knight. Some people have a lot of faith in forecasting tables and use them to plan their local outings and major fishing trips; these tables are often popular with readers of outdoor publications, as publishers found out when the tables were stopped and protests poured in. On the other hand, many people think that forecasting fish and game activity is psychic babble, and never pay attention to the tables. Still others take the position that this business is like UFOs; maybe they exist and maybe they don't; neither side can unequivocally prove or disprove their validity.

Without getting into a long and tedious lesson in astronomy and related sciences, the nature of these tables can be summarized by saying that they are based upon the phase of the moon and the proximity of the sun and the moon to the earth on any given day. In most tables, the periods of peak activity, or "best" times to be afield, are forecast to occur during the full and new moon phases, and other, lesser periods of activity are forecast at times that coincide with quarter-moon phases and peak times of daylight or darkness daily. Activity periods are forecast to the exact minute of the day and are claimed (or implied) to be valid for all creatures, with appropriate time factoring for different geographic locations.

Some of the activity periods forecast by these tables coincide with tidal movement, and it is well-known to anglers that tide *(see)* has a significant bearing on fish activity in areas where it exists. It is also well-known to many serious anglers that low levels of light are prime for fish activity and fishing success, either because the predators that anglers seek can see their prey better or because they are simply more stimulated by the changing conditions.

Some producers of various forecasting tables make far-reaching claims about the validity of their information, even stating that it is based on proven scientific theories or facts, but there is no scientific proof that this information is correct. It's a theory. Nevertheless, some people who use activity periods to pick the times that they go fishing report dependability. Such a result is not scientifically valid, since the predetermined times influence when to focus efforts.

Many unbiased observers and anglers have looked at these tables after they have fished, or after compiling an array of detailed information about their own efforts, and have found that there were correlations between their better fishing results and the times that were forecast to be productive. Others have concluded that there was not enough of a correlation to be important.

Logically, one has to wonder how any fish and game activity forecasting table can be applicable for all species of fish (and game) in all habitats at all times and under all circumstances. So many intangible factors influence sportfishing that it is not only skeptical but reasonable to wonder how all fish activity can be pegged in such a way. Certainly the sun and moon do play a role in tides and in spawning for some species, and they are known to influence some insect hatches. But there is such great diversity in the rhythmic behavior of all fish, and especially the top predators that are sought by anglers, that forecasting, at least on an all-for-one basis, remains clouded in skepticism.

SONAR

Most anglers simply use the term "depthfinder" or "depth sounder" when referring to what is actually sonar equipment. At one time, sonar devices were also called fish locators, and are still sometimes called fishfinders. To much of the rest of the world, they are echo sounders.

The word sonar is an acronym for sound navigation and ranging equipment. This was applied by the military in World Wars I and II. Today's electronic depth finding and fish locating equipment helps anglers enjoy their sport and become more learned and proficient. Sonar is the boat angler's underwater eyes, and in some circumstances is viewed as being virtually indispensable. With it, the angler can find concentrations of migratory, suspended, schooling, and nomadic fish, and locate submerged habitat that may be attractive to particular species. With sportfishing sonar, an angler can become accurately acquainted with the beneath-the-surface environment of any body of water in significantly less time than without it. Additionally, the use of sportfishing sonar allows an angler to navigate more safely and quickly than he might otherwise, although it is not actually a navigational tool.

Locating fish with sonar is no guarantee that they are the kind of fish being sought. Sonar also can't ensure that you'll be able to catch the fish, regardless of the extent of your knowledge and experience. There is still no substitute for angling savvy, skillful presentation, and knowledge of fish behavior and habits. This notwithstanding, there are many times when even the most skillful anglers can find fish but not catch them.

While locating fish is an important usage of sonar (more for some species than others), trans-

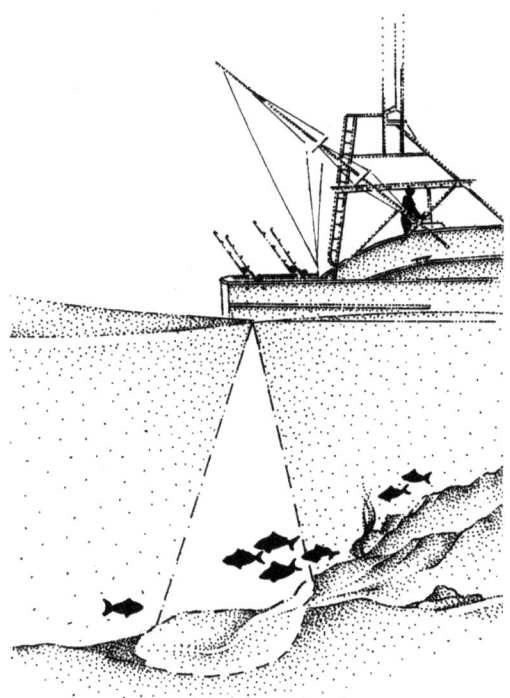

Although many people think that the primary usefulness of sonar is for finding fish, it is even more important for determining depth, finding contours and structures, and in general locating places that are likely to contain specific kinds of fish.

mitting depth information is its predominant function. Depth information is used consistently as an aid to determining where and how to fish, allowing more precise, and thus more effective, presentation of lures or bait than might be possible if the depth, bottom contours, and underwater habitat were unknown and constantly changing.

A basic key to catching fish is locating them or their preferred habitat and fishing appropriate lures or bait at the proper depths. If you're not familiar with the place you're fishing, chances are that without sonar you'll be largely unaware of the depths of the various areas, or would repeatedly have to drop a weighted line down to determine depth. This does not mean that you can't or won't catch fish. However, you may not be aware of certain characteristics of that body of water which might greatly aid your fish finding and fish catching efforts. If you learn to interpret the information that it provides, sonar can be one of the most important pieces of angling equipment. Skilled sonar users can predict with startling accuracy what species of gamefish are below and how catchable they are simply by noting how they relate to each other, to schools of baitfish, and to the bottom.

How Sonar Works

Sonar is essentially made up of a display unit and a transducer, which are connected by coaxial cable to each other. The display unit indicates the information that the transducer has provided by issuing signals through the water. Sound travels at about 4,800 feet per second through the water, which is four times faster than it travels through air. Sonar instruments issue signals (pulses or sound waves) from the transducer at extremely swift rates, actually many times per second. The greater the distance between transducer (the system component that sends the pulses out and receives echoes back from them) and bottom, the longer it takes for the pulses to reach bottom, and return echoes. Nonetheless, the speed of operation is amazingly swift, so swift that it is unlikely that a boat can outrun the signal. By measuring the time from the transmission of the signals until their reflected echoes are received, the sonar can determine the depth of underwater objects as well as the bottom.

Although, as previously noted, most anglers use the terms depthfinder, depthsounder, and fishfinder interchangeably when referring to sonar equipment, there is technically a difference. Most sonar used by anglers is very functional for determining depth and for determining the location of fish; however, there is some sonar, primarily digital numerical display units, that only provide depth information. These are primarily used by sailboaters and cruisers, and by design, they do not provide information about fish, suspended objects, and type of bottom. These are strictly depth-finding sonar, not sportfishing sonar. A digital depth readout is often included as a secondary feature on more sophisticated sonar units.

The two most popular operating frequencies for sportfishing sonar are 50kHz and 200kHz, although 120kHz, 455kHz, and other frequencies are also used. The lower frequency is meant for very deep water (beyond 300 feet) while the higher frequency is meant for shallower use, and some sonar features dual-frequency operation with corresponding transducers. Most anglers, especially freshwater anglers, use 200kHz units, or dual-frequency units that are primarily set for the higher frequency mode. Some dual-frequency models can display simultaneous information from both frequencies on the same screen or in a split screen presentation, enabling them to display and compare information.

The signal echoes that are returned to sonar instruments are presented via a liquid crystal display (LCD), cathode-ray tube (CRT), or light-emitting diodes (LED). The former provide picturelike representations on small rectangular screens while the latter appears as a flashing light on a circular calibrated dial. At least two manufacturers offer LCD screens that mimic the readouts of circular LED dial displays. Most sonar units used by anglers are of the LCD variety.

Transducers come in various sizes, mounts, and frequencies, and send out pulses in a three-dimensional cone-shaped wave. Cone angles range from narrow to extremely wide. The diameter of these cones influences how much detail will be seen. Unfortunately, there is no universally accepted "standard" method for measuring and rating cone angles in the sportfishing sonar industry. One manufacturer's 8-degree transducer may be the equivalent of another's 16-degree model, and so on. Generally speaking, high frequency (more than 100kHz) transducers come in "wide" and "narrow" cone angle versions. As a rule of thumb, you can quickly find the diameter of a transducer's coverage at any depth by dividing that depth by 7 for a narrow cone or by 3 for a wide cone. A narrow cone angle has about a 2-foot diameter at a depth of 15 feet; it has about a 4-foot diameter at a depth of 30 feet. A wide cone angle has a 5-foot diameter in 15 feet of water and 10-foot in 30. Most low frequency transducers have a cone angle of about 45 degrees, which covers a diameter about equal to the depth. Its diameter is about 15 feet at a depth of 15 feet and about 30 feet at a depth of 30 feet. As with all

cone angle is that it takes in so much information that you may trick yourself into thinking that fish it details are directly below the boat when they may be well off to the side. Some sonar sports dual transducer or single transducer housings with dual cone angle capability, so that you can switch back and forth.

Generally speaking, searching for fish with a wide cone cuts search time because a wider swath of water is scanned as the boat moves along. Once fish are spotted, switching to a narrow cone helps pinpoint their location. It's like searching for something in the dark. A floodlight will help you find

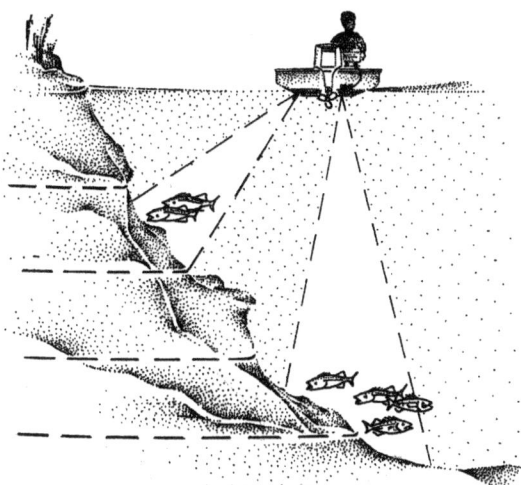

The majority of sonar devices only view what is directly below the boat, but some are designed to view out to the side, and a few can do both.

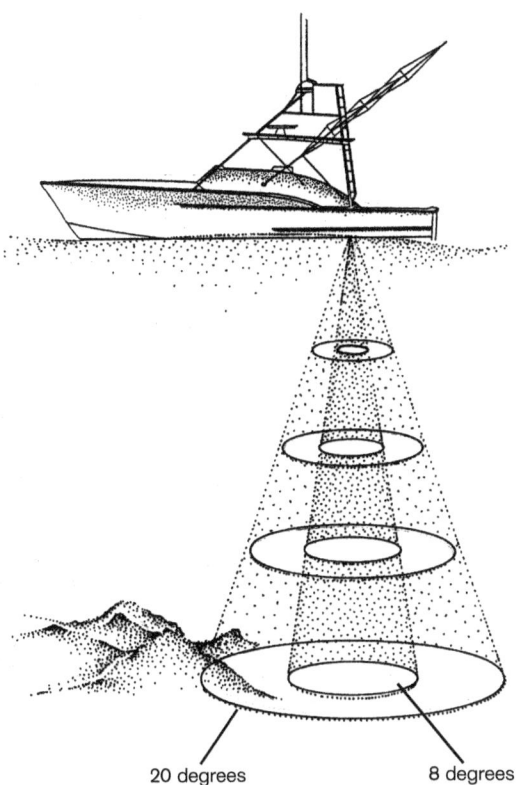

The diameter of the transducer cone angle affects coverage area.

rules of thumb, there are exceptions and a given unit's cone angle can be verified by checking the owner's manual.

The narrowest cone angles are most useful in extremely deep water, such as 150 feet or more. The widest cones enable you to see a lot more of what's beneath you, are especially useful for downrigger trolling and fishing directly below the boat, and work best at slow boat speeds. The medium-range cones are less specialized, have all-around functionality, and are best used in less than 100 feet of water. The only drawback to the super-wide

something faster than a spotlight; switching to the more concentrated power of a spotlight lets you examine it in better detail.

In addition to looking down, some units look to the side, either via a rotating transducer or a fixed mount, side-viewing transducer. The advantages of side-viewing are obvious: finding fish that are not below the boat, looking along a bank for fish to cast to, scanning through a river pool to see if it holds fish, and so on. Some anglers report success with side-viewing sonar and express confidence in it, but many anglers are not convinced that they reliably detect fish. Within the industry, there has been debate over the technological ability of sonar to reliably locate fish past the distance at which the upper edge of the horizontally aimed cone strikes the water's surface or the lower edge hits the bottom. Both the surface and bottom solidly reflect the transducer's sound signal and their massive echoes may mask the much weaker echoes from fish.

Nevertheless, more manufacturers are offering side-looking equipment each year. And many engineers, particularly those who in the past have worked on the design of anti-submarine, mine detection, and torpedo guidance systems are now working at sportfishing sonar development. This is an area in which there will likely be technological advances in the future.

Incidentally, some manufacturers offer an alternative for viewing areas away from the angler or the boat. This is a floating device that cradles the transducer, and which can be used to scan selected areas without the user being on top of them. The device, loaded with a transducer and connected to a readout unit via a long cable, can be tossed Frisbee-style into the water, or allowed to float downstream or offshore. This makes it possible for boat, bank, bridge, or pier anglers to scout an area within casting distance.

Another area ripe for improvement will be sonar that can unerringly determine the size of individual fish and distinguish between species. Manufacturers have made such claims in regard to existing equipment, but that era has not yet arrived. When sonar can truly indicate size and species (not leaving it up to individual interpretation and speculation), a whole new world will open up. Because anglers are frequently unable to determine the direction that deep fish are headed, as well as the distance they may be from the boat (at the speed traveled in passing over and beyond them), these issues, too, will change.

Types of Sonar

The sportfishing sonar field has changed radically since computer chips were integrated into marine electronics. Sonar today is incredibly sophisticated, with phenomenal abilities and incredible options.

Sonar evolved from flashers (LEDs) to paper chart recorders to LCDs and video sonar using cathode-ray tubes (CRTs). Chart recorders were once the premium sonar and the equipment that provided the best underwater detail; they are now obsolete and flashers are practically so, although some veteran sonar users still prefer flashers, which have enjoyed a minor resurgence, primarily among some bass and walleye anglers. Most sonar today features a liquid crystal display, and many people now use the terms sonar and LCD virtually synonymously. The better LCD sonar today gives as good detail as the premium paper chart sonar of old, and it's better in many ways than a flasher. Depending on the unit and optional accessories, sonar can also provide boat speed, distance traveled, and water temperature information, and can be integrated into other electronics, especially global positioning systems *(see: GPS)*.

Sonar is available in portable as well as permanent mount versions. Portable models work on almost any boat but are primarily used on small craft. The transducer is generally attached to a bracket and clamped to the gunwale or transom, or to a suction cup placed on the transom.

A fixed bow-mounted sonar is particularly helpful for freshwater anglers who spend much of their angling time in the bow, casting and running the electric motor to maneuver along likely fishing areas. Ideally, the transducer for this unit should be located on the bottom of the bow-mounted electric motor to give readings directly below the front of the boat. Remember that in water shallower than 15 feet a transducer's cone angle scans an area that may not be as wide as the boat. A trolling-motor-mounted transducer shows what's under the forward part of the boat, not what's under the transom 15 to 20 feet behind it.

A fixed console-mounted sonar is used by many boaters, sometimes as their only type of sonar, sometimes in conjunction with a bow-mounted unit. When it's the only sonar aboard, an accessory swivel bracket can let it be turned as necessary to be seen from anywhere in the boat. The transducer for console-mounted sonar (as well as for sonar located near the stern on a tiller-steered boat) is located on the transom, or, in a few cases, mounted in the sump or integrated into the hull during construction.

The basic types of sonar include the following.

Flasher. A flasher is an LED device with a flashing light on a circular calibrated dial. Flashers indicate everything that other types of sonar do, but they require extensive experience to interpret, especially in regard to the characteristics of the bottom. Although they depict the location of fish, that depiction is fleeting; thus, this type of sonar, less common than in previous years, is most useful in determining depth and bottom contour.

Flashers are simple units and deliver instantaneous readings without computer filtering or averaging. For this reason some experienced users who have multiple sonar on their boats still prefer flashers for tracking depth and spotting suspended fish at high boat speeds. When the flasher shows a string of blips, the user slows the boat, turns around, and reexamines the area with an LCD or video unit to identify what the flasher spotted.

Chart recorder. Also known as a graph recorder, this device uses a roll of paper upon which the images of fish, objects, and underwater terrain are displayed and permanently printed. These units have been made obsolete by liquid crystal displays and are no longer in production outside of the commercial arena, although some guides, charter boat captains, and avid anglers still retain and use them. Chart recorders are large and heavy, take up a lot space, and require some maintenance; however, they have excellent (some would say unmatched) detail and provide a permanent record for later review. They are most useful in shallow and moderate depths.

Video sonar. This device uses a cathode-ray tube (CRT) and displays images on a screen that looks much like a video monitor or television. Different colors are used to represent fish by size and distinguish objects and the bottom on color units. Monochrome units make these distinctions by displaying objects with different levels of image brightness rather than in different colors. They offer more screen detail and better visibility in sunlight than color units. Video sonar comprises a minor portion of the sportfishing sonar market, being used primarily on large sportfishing boats on the Great Lakes and in saltwater. A current a trend is toward increased use of monochrome video sonar by professional walleye tournament anglers. CRTs are also known as video sounders. They are generally more expensive, larger, heavier, and more fragile than other types. They are also harder to read in direct sunlight and use more battery power. However, some monochrome units offer excellent detail and target separation. They can be hard to match for spotting fish on the bottom or in weeds.

Liquid crystal displays. These units, known by the acronym LCD, are by far the most prominent sonar for anglers; they are also, but less commonly, referred to as liquid crystal recorders (LCR). There are digital readout models that only display numerical depth information and are of most use for routine boating. Most LCDs display fish, objects, and bottom information in a scrolling videolike manner via a grid of dots called pixels. The number of pixels in each vertical column on a screen determines its ability to display detail while the number of pixels in each horizontal row determines how long information stays on the screen before it scrolls off the edge. The greater the number of vertical pixels, the better the resolution or screen detail. The deeper the water you fish and the more screen detail you desire, the more vertical pixels you need for better images. The same is true for power; for deep water you need units with greater wattage.

The visibility of LCDs varies between products and in general has improved over the years, but is still an area of dissatisfaction for some users. Though easily read in some light conditions and from a position immediately in front of the unit, liquid crystal displays have been difficult to read from other angles, by viewers using polarized sunglasses, and in the dark with side- or backlighting.

Some LCDs have large screens and a split-screen zoom feature. This allows you to split the screen and show the normal image of everything in the water from surface to bottom on one side and a magnified portion of the water column on the other side. The zoom feature can be adjusted in size and magnification on better units. Some LCDs also have a three-dimensional viewing feature; however, many users may find this confusing and difficult to relate to for fishing applications. Three-dimensional viewing is offered as an option on some sonar, subordinate to conventional chart-style display.

LCDs do not produce paper records. Some have memory capabilities and can be linked to a home personal computer so that information can be stored and retrieved. This is undoubtedly an area that will become more prominent in the future. More technical information about the characteristics of LCDs and other sonar are contained in the following section.

More Technical Points

Although many advances are being made in sportfishing sonar, there are some underlying and unchanging fundamentals of sonar that affect performance no matter what new features may be added to this equipment. The technical information in literature provided by manufacturers includes a listing of operating frequencies, power, transducer cone angle, display resolution, and receiver sensitivity, all of which have an effect on the performance of sonar. If you were able to put sonar units side by side on the water and evaluate them, you'd see that some sonar units have better display capabilities than others, some can find and depict fish better than others, and some are easier to use than others. The following review of technical matters puts some of these performance aspects into perspective.

Frequency. Which frequency to use or which frequency sonar to purchase is one of the key issues that face anglers, and the choice depends on the application. There are advantages and disadvantages to both high- and low-frequency sonars for different applications.

The higher the frequency of the sound waves, the more quickly they fade and the shorter their useful range; low frequency sound waves don't fade as quickly as high frequency waves, and have a deeper useful range. Knowing a sonar unit's frequency, you can determine its useful range with any given output power and transducer cone angle.

High frequency sound waves have a shorter wavelength than low frequency waves; therefore, there are more cycles in a high frequency pulse than in a low frequency pulse of the same width or duration. The more cycles there are, the stronger the signal and the stronger the echoes. Therefore, a high frequency echo from a small object is stronger than a low frequency echo from the same object, and is more likely to be received by the sonar. This is relative only to the high frequency sonar's useful range.

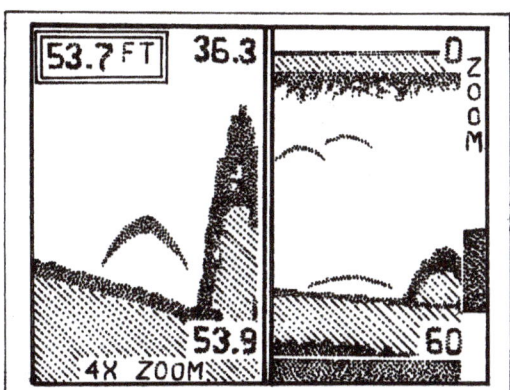

Split-screen sonar views, as depicted here, are very useful, allowing you to focus on a specific area in more detail.

The shorter pulse length of the high frequency can also be used for better target separation. From the instant a sound pulse begins to leave the transducer, it travels downward at the speed of sound through water. From the beginning to the end, the pulse takes up an area of depth measured in inches or feet. A pulse has a vertical thickness of about 1 inch for each 30 microseconds (millionths of a second) that the pulse lasts. The length of time a pulse lasts is usually computer controlled and varies with the depth range selected and the amount of filtering currently engaged. The deeper the depth range or the higher the level of filtering, the longer the pulse length. The thickness or width of this pulse determines how far apart objects must be before the sonar unit can see them as separate entities.

Sonar can see objects individually only if they are vertically separated by enough distance. Imagine a pulse that is 6 inches thick traveling downward toward two fish that are only 2 vertical inches apart. The leading edge of the pulse strikes the deeper fish before the trailing edge of the pulse clears the shallower fish. The transducer receives the sound reflected by both fish as a single, unbroken echo. As far as the unit is concerned there is only one fish. If the fish are 7 inches apart, the trailing edge of the pulse leaves the first fish, ending its echo, before the leading edge of the pulse strikes the deeper fish and begins returning its echo. Now, the transducer hears two consecutive shorter echoes instead of a single longer echo and the unit recognizes the fish as two separate objects.

The same is true for fish holding close to the bottom. If a fish is so close to the bottom that a pulse begins sending back a bottom echo before it stops sending the fish echo, the unit thinks the fish is a high spot on the bottom and blends it into the bottom reading.

The shorter the pulse length, the thinner the physical width of the pulse, and the closer things can be to each other on a vertical plane and still be seen by sonar as separate objects. High frequency sonar is capable of superior target separation and general screen detail because it can transmit short pulses with better results than low frequency sonar.

Whether high frequency sonar does detect smaller objects and have better target separation than low frequency sonar depends on other factors, such as receiver sensitivity and display resolution, and whether the sonar is capable of transmitting a short pulse. If the sonar doesn't have a highly sensitive receiver, it won't be able to receive the weak echoes from small objects. And if it doesn't have a good quality high-resolution display, or if you are not zoomed in very closely, it won't be able to show good target separation. If each pixel represents 12 inches of depth, for instance, two fish that are 6 inches apart can't be displayed separately regardless of the unit's pulse length.

The real benefit of low frequency sonar is that it has a deeper useful range. It can penetrate to deeper depths than high frequency sonar with the same amount of power. Imagine listening to an approaching band during a parade. The first instrument you hear is the low frequency sound of the bass drum. As the band gets closer, the last thing you hear is the high frequency notes of the flutes. Low frequency sound simply carries farther. Also, low frequency sonar has a wider coverage area than high frequency sonar. One of the main uses of the low frequency, wide-cone angle is tracking downriggers while trolling and being able to adjust their depth in relation to the depth of the fish that are also observed on the sonar. With high frequency sonar, the cone angle may be too small to see the downrigger weights because they do not drop directly beneath the boat. They usually swing out behind the boat and may swing out of the high frequency sonar's cone angle.

The difference between the two frequencies is most evident in different applications. One place where high frequency sonar would be preferable is in a lake where there is a lot of weeds or brush. In this situation, the longer pulse and broader cone angle of low frequency sonar would pick up so much of the brush or weeds that anything else in the area would blend into the echoes from the weeds. The shorter pulses and narrower cone angle of the high frequency would focus on a smaller area and be more likely to see a fish at or near the top of the weeds, possibly even allowing you to locate a fish in the weeds. If there is a lot of debris and turbidity in the water, the low frequency sonar will not pick up all the small particles in the water and can provide better information.

Power and sensitivity. Output power is a measurement of the strength of a sonar's transmitted signal, usually expressed as watts peak-to-peak, or as watts RMS. This can be confusing, but the peak-to-peak rating equals the RMS rating multiplied by 8. For instance, a transmitter rated at 400 watts RMS would have a peak-to-peak output of 3200 watts. Output power is usually constant at all depth-range settings and at all receiver sensitivity settings, although some units turn the output power down at shallower range settings.

Turning up the sensitivity doesn't increase the output power, as some think. Like the volume control on a radio, it simply makes the receiver more sensitive. The higher the sensitivity level, the weaker echoes can be and still be detected. Generally, the higher the output power, the stronger the sound waves transmitted and the deeper the sound waves will go; thus, the deeper the sonar's useful range. However, high power doesn't necessarily guarantee extreme depth readings. The receiver sensitivity also has to be good enough to receive weak signals from great depths. A low frequency sonar with low to medium power can read

---

Shark meat is palatable and nutritious if properly prepared; the fish in England's "fish and chips" is very often dogfish, a type of shark.

deeper and have a deeper useful range than a high frequency, high-power sonar.

Generally, the more levels of adjustment a receiver has, the more sensitive a unit is and/or the more it can be fine-tuned. Receivers with fewer levels of adjustment cannot be fine-tuned as well as those with more levels of adjustment. They can offer either too much or not enough sensitivity for present conditions and leave you wishing for an adjustment increment between the closest two that are available.

When trying to judge the effectiveness of a sonar's output power in terms of ability to detect fish, look at the maximum depth capability listed in the specifications. A good rule of thumb for judging how deep a sonar device will show you fish is to cut the maximum depth capability in half. The strongest echo will always be from the bottom. It is many times stronger than anything else. If a unit says that its maximum depth capability is 500 feet, you can trust it to depict fish that are as deep as 250 feet.

Whether it offers good performance in this area or not also depends on the cone angle of the transducer. A transducer is basically the sonar's antenna, and most are made up of crystals sealed inside a watertight plastic or bronze housing. The size and shape of the transducer crystal determines the pattern of sound waves the crystal will transmit. In each case, the pattern consists of one main teardrop-shaped lobe formed by most of the signal, and several smaller side lobes with small amounts of signal. Most manufacturers measure their cone angle at the minus 3dB or half-power point. Imagine measuring the sound volume directly below the transducer at a given depth, then moving horizontally in any direction until the sound volume decreases 50 percent. If you could mark that point in all directions, your marks would form a rough circle that indicates the area of sonar coverage for that depth. Some manufacturers may include the side lobes in their cone angle measurement and/or go far beyond the half-power point to measure the edge of the cone. This results in general confusion, and can make transducers appear to have greater effective coverage than they actually do, which means that in use the products do not provide the performance that is expected.

To further confuse matters, a transducer's effective cone angle is influenced by the sensitivity setting. The more you increase sensitivity, the farther off to the side fish and other objects can be and still be displayed. The more you decrease sensitivity, the closer to the center of the cone (where the sound power is strongest) these same objects have to be to appear on the display.

Display resolution. The resolution capability is one of the most important features of sonar. Liquid crystal displays are made up of a matrix of vertical and horizontal pixels; this provides resolution and is directly related to the detail that is displayed. The more vertical pixels there are, the better the resolution and the more detail that is provided. The more detail you see, the more you know about what is below and the better you're equipped to adjust fishing techniques. In a sense, it's like driving a car in the rain without windshield wipers: The poorer that you see, the less able you are to drive.

Each of the pixels in a vertical column represents a certain portion of the total depth. The more vertical pixels there are, the smaller portion of depth that each will represent, and the more detailed the picture. For instance, for a sonar with 100 vertical pixels set on the 100-foot range, each vertical pixel is covering 1 foot of water. In 200 feet of water, each pixel would be covering 2 feet of water. The 25th pixel down on the 200-foot range is covering from 50 to 52 feet. If a fish is at 51 feet, the corresponding pixel turns on to tell you there is an echo somewhere between 50 and 52 feet.

If a sonar had 100 vertical pixels and was used on a depth scale setting of 0 to 50 feet, it would provide a resolution of 6 inches per pixel. Yet, if there were two fish below and they were vertically less than 12 inches apart, they might be displayed as only one fish. The unit must be able to show a blank pixel between two darkened pixels in a vertical column to separately display targets. Depending upon how the unit's computer software fits each fish into the pixel grid, there might not be enough separation. If that sonar had 200 vertical pixels, then the resolution would be 3 inches per pixel, and two fish that were less than 12 inches apart could easily be displayed as two separate fish.

When the sonar transmits a sound pulse and receives echoes, it turns on the pixels in the vertical column at the right-hand edge of the display that correspond to the depth of the object returning the echoes. Then it moves that information one column to the left. It again transmits and listens for echoes and again darkens the pixels in the right-hand vertical column that correspond to the depth of the new echoes it receives. By doing this, the sonar screen constantly scrolls from right to left.

Many anglers mistakenly think that the whole screen renews with each sounding and shows a real-time picture of the underwater world, but the screen image is really built one vertical column at a time. What's happening right now between your boat and the bottom is shown at the far right edge of the screen and everything to the left is a screen history of past soundings.

In many LCD units, resolution can be enhanced further by using the zoom feature. Zoom allows you to magnify a small segment of the depth range currently on the display by applying the screen's full vertical pixel count to it. If, for instance, an entire 0 to 50–foot depth range is viewed on a display with 200 vertical pixels, there are four pixels for each foot of depth and each pixel represents about 3 inches. Zoom in on the depth segment from 40 to 50 feet and you apply all 200 pixels to only 10 feet of depth. Now, there are 20 pixels in each foot of depth and each pixel represents slightly more than half an inch. Since $1\frac{1}{2}$ inches of target separation is about the best that is claimed for an LCD sonar at this writing, that's better screen resolution than the unit's electronics are capable of using, so you'll get all of the detail the unit can produce.

Some of the confusion with regard to resolution centers on the manner of advertising the number of pixels. Some manufacturers talk about the number of pixels per square inch while others talk about the number of vertical pixels. These are not comparable figures, and a high pixels-per-square-inch count could mask a low vertical-pixels-per-column count, meaning that the unit may actually have less resolution than you think.

If you have a display grid that is 240 pixels tall and 100 pixels wide, you'll have great resolution because the vertical count is very high. A screen that is 100 pixels tall by 240 pixels wide has the same number of pixels per square inch but less than half the vertical resolution. Remember, the vertical columns of pixels represent the vertical water column between the boat and the bottom, and the higher the number of pixels in each column, the finer the detail it can display. The horizontal pixel count only determines how many vertical columns of screen history a display can show, and tells you how long information will stay on the screen before it scrolls off the left-hand edge.

Transducer Installation
Getting good readings from sonar is important to interpretation. Unfortunately, improper transducer installation leads to many problems and can hamper fishing efforts; it is the most common cause of poor sonar performance. Whether the transducer is mounted inside or outside the hull, it must be placed in a position that receives a smooth flow of water at all speeds. If it doesn't have a smooth flow of water, interference from turbulence can cause poor sonar readings or intermittent readings when the boat is under power. If you don't want to make the installation yourself, take the sonar and transducer to a boat dealer who has experience in rigging fishing boats.

If you're purchasing a new fiberglass boat, the absolute best thing to do is purchase the sonar before the boat is manufactured, send the transducer to the factory, and have them hand-lay it into the fiberglass when they build the hull. Some transducers installed by boat manufacturers and dealers shoot through the hull (but performance can suffer if there is air in the fiberglass or resin). Some boat builders mount the transducer face flush with the hull and you can't even tell where it's located. With some manufacturers, different transducers are required for different applications. In some boats, usually single-thickness fiberglass models, a shoot-through-hull transducer can be installed after the boat is built, but it may require a bit of experimentation to locate the best position. In any event,

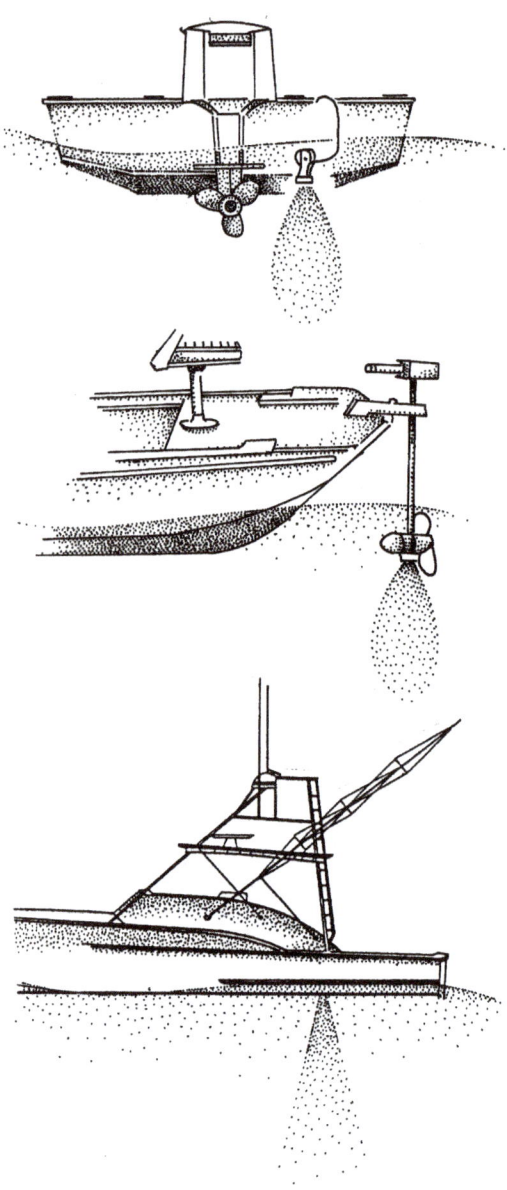

Depending on boat and fishing needs, sonar transducers are located on the transom (top), beneath an electric motor (middle), and in the sump (bottom).

some signal loss is likely to occur. Generally, the faster a boat can travel, the further aft and closer to the centerline the installation location should be, so that it stays in the water at high speeds.

If you can't install a shoot-through-hull type of transducer, you'll have to mount the transducer to the transom exterior. This is done for the vast majority of small and medium-size fishing boats and for virtually all aluminum boats. An outside transom mounting is difficult or impossible with high-performance fiberglass hulls that have stepped transoms or narrow pads. Be sure to read and closely follow the manufacturer's instructions pertaining to installation. On aluminum boats, be sure to install a transom mount transducer midway between the hull strakes to minimize the effects of turbulence when the boat is underway, and don't tighten the kickup bracket so much that it will not push back if you strike an obstruction.

If the bracket mounting holes are slotted for vertical adjustment, position the bracket according to the manufacturer's instructions, and then drill the mounting holes near the bottom of the slots. This leaves room to slide the transducer deeper than normal if necessary to get below turbulence. The more flexible or uneven the bottom of an aluminum hull is (or gets with age), the deeper a transducer needs to run to reach smooth water.

Position a transom-mount transducer so that no air bubbles will trail below it. Strakes, weld lines, and rivets, among other things, give off a bubble trail, especially at high speed. Find a location that permits clear water to flow below the face of the transducer, such as between strakes on an aluminum hull. Don't get so far from the centerline of the hull that the transducer might be out of water under certain conditions. If you get it too close to the propeller, it could cause prop cavitation. If there are heavy bubbles below a transducer, you'll get no readings.

Generally, however, to get the best readings of fish, the transducer should be level, on a horizontal plane, with its face looking straight down. Units capable of displaying fish as arches will only display a partial arch when going over fish if the transducer isn't facing straight down, and units that display fish as fish symbols or as pixel clusters will show small or weak signals. Transom mounting allows you to make adjustments to correct these errors. It should also be noted that sensors for speed and surface temperature readouts must be mounted outside in order to work, and they are sometimes available only as snap-on accessories for transom-mounted transducers.

The location and installation of the actual sonar unit and electrical and transducer wires should be well thought out. Other wiring and electronics may interfere with sonar and result in dots or lines appearing on the sonar screen. It may be necessary to keep the wiring from other electrical accessories away from the wires of your sonar to avoid interference. Rerouting wires may be necessary if you're experiencing problems caused by other electrical equipment.

There is one other location for mounting transducers: on the lower unit of an electric motor. This provides excellent and turbulence-free reading, but electrical interference from a trolling motor's pulse-modulated speed controller may cause interference at speed settings below wide-open. Don't worry about this unless you see interference spikes on your screen when the motor is operated. If you do have this problem, the customer service departments of your sonar and motor manufacturers can help you minimize or eliminate it.

Using Sonar

Many people have difficulty getting optimum results from their sonar, and a lot of units are returned for service when there is really nothing wrong with them. Most operator problems result from improper transducer installation and general misuse.

Today's electronics are so sophisticated and the operations manuals are so thick, they can be intimidating. Most people want to simply turn the device on and let it run, as if it were television. Thus, many people simply run their units in automatic mode and never get into the finer points of operation. Take the time to read every page of your manual. The place to do this is out on the water (not while fishing), so that you can go through the operations step by step, gain confidence in the unit, and actually see the machine do what it's supposed to do. It's a good idea as well to bring your boat over shallow water near shore, where you know the depth, and check to see that the sonar reads accurately. Find a stump several feet down, and see how it registers on your machine. Go over a sandy bottom, a mud bottom, a rocky bottom, and so on.

Sonar should be relatively easy to use, especially if you are already familiar with sonar in general and have used these devices before. Many better models of LCDs have on-screen menus and can guide you through their operation, letting you learn to use them without feeling like you need to enroll in an engineering course.

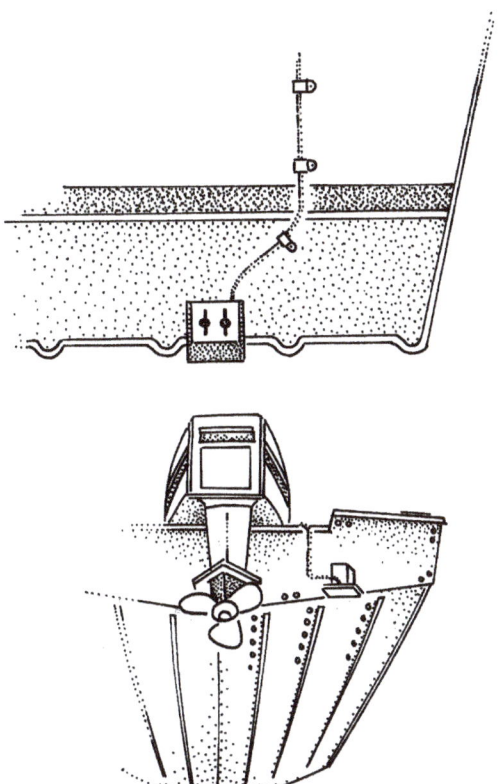

Shown is a transducer installation on a boat with a flat hull (top) and one with a modified-V hull (bottom); it is important with transom installation to get the transducer as shown, and situated between hull strakes and away from rivets.

A huge school of baitfish is displayed on sportfishing sonar.

Most anglers use sonar, especially LCDs, in the automatic mode. Although many units work adequately in automatic mode, you may get much better performance in the manual mode, where you control the sensitivity and range settings to get much finer detail. However, when most units are used in manual mode, the bottom setting does not change automatically, and it is a minor nuisance to have to do this whenever you move into deeper or shallower water. Depending on the unit, you may be able to work around this in automatic mode by zooming or by splitting the screen for two different views. In automatic mode, some units keep the bottom contour displayed in the lower third of the screen no matter how the bottom depth changes.

A lot of operational troubles center around the control functions, particularly sensitivity and suppression. The sensitivity control, which used to be called gain, is akin to the volume control on a radio. Many inexperienced sonar users keep this turned down too low, either because they are experiencing electrical interference or because they think a low setting is adequate. When the sensitivity is too low, sonar may fail to register key bait, fish, or bottom readings. Modern units run on automatic don't usually have this problem. However, more detail can be observed from higher sensitivity settings. Some cannot be adjusted in the auto mode, but if they can, turn up the sensitivity for trolling and fast moving. On the other hand, if you are merely looking for big fish and don't want to see every detail, you might want to lower sensitivity.

If you turn sensitivity too high, you might clutter the screen with a lot of nonfish debris. The best marriage is a high enough sensitivity to get a solid bottom reading with a distinguished bottom differentiation, some surface clutter (minute "scatter" near the surface), and a lot of detail in between. A good rule of thumb is to turn sensitivity up until you begin to see random dots of interference on the screen, then turn it down until they disappear.

Some sonars have a feature called grayline (or whiteline on some units) to help identify bottom hardness and to separate bottom-hugging fish from the bottom contour. It appears as a gray shading below a dark, sharply defined bottom contour line. Again, you may want to run sonar in the manual mode to get the best detail. If fish are holding tight to structures or the bottom, especially mud, the manual mode provides a better view. Some sonars also have advanced filtering features that clear out all or some of the clutter while having little or no influence on the fish and bottom readings.

If it's possible to adjust the scroll rate of your screen, crank that up, too, especially when you're on the move or when trolling. For many sonar instruments, there's a corollary between detail and a fast screen. A slow speed compresses readings horizontally, which hides important details. When you know what to expect, are continuously going over the same ground, or are interested only in depth, a slow speed might be adequate.

Many anglers want to see as much on screen as possible, including the latest split-screen features, which is why the narrow-screen sonars that were once prevalent have faded from popularity. By the time you studied the sonar, the information was off the screen. Units with wide screens (actual viewing area) and clear pictures are optimum. Sonar can be critical to fishing success, so the better you see below, the better you fish.

Illustrated is how a sonar unit might show a dense school of fish, a jigging spoon being fished above the school (the ragged line at 18 to 20 feet), and a fish that comes out of the middle of the school (the forward-slanting line) to look at the lure.

Most sonar today can show fish symbols in a so-called Fish I.D. mode. In standard mode (Fish I.D. turned off), sonar identifies fish as a series of dots (pixels) in a line or arch. It also displays surface clutter, temperature variations, minute particles, and thoroughly indistinguishable "stuff." Standard mode is preferable for serious fishing efforts because the sophisticated level of detail allows you to make your own determination of what you're seeing. However, many operators prefer the Fish I.D. mode in which only fish (in theory) are targeted; all other information is filtered out by the machine, and several sizes of symbols are used to correspond to the size of fish. Although Fish I.D. has some entertainment value, especially for youngsters and novice anglers, it is really not helpful. In fact, this feature may do more harm than good by blocking the display of scattered baitfish, downrigger weights, jigged lures, thermoclines, and other important information. Anglers should turn this feature off in deference to the more detailed hardcore view.

Most sonars also have fish and bottom alarms, and although these features may be useful, they are mostly regarded as an annoyance by avid anglers. The bottom alarm, however, can be very practical for high-speed navigation, boat operation in unfamiliar areas, and certain precise fishing methods (such as downrigger trolling).

Interpreting what you see on sonar is the million-dollar question. What signals are fish, what kind of fish they are, how big they are, what kind of bottom is below—these are the foremost puzzles.

Bottom characteristics are not as easy to distinguish as some anglers would like, perhaps in part due to the deficiencies of the unit or perhaps because of the settings employed. In manual mode, it is possible to fine-tune settings in order to get a clearer idea of bottom features. With LCD sonar, a hard bottom returns a strong signal, which on the display is seen as a dense, thick band.

If grayline is engaged, a hard bottom is shown as a thin black line with a wide gray band beneath. The harder the bottom, the wider the gray band. A soft or muddy bottom returns a weaker signal, and is displayed as a thinner, less dense band. With grayline on, it will appear as a dark band with little or no gray area beneath it. A rocky bottom produces a hard, thick signal with a ragged band. This is different with color video sonar, however, because different colors are used to indicate different echo strengths. Thus, on a color video sonar, a hard bottom appears as a wide band in the color reserved for the strongest echoes (red in some units), a mud bottom appears as a narrow band in a "weaker" color, and a sand bottom will be somewhere in between. On monochrome video sonars, the harder the bottom or the stronger an echo from suspended objects, the wider (top-to-bottom) and brighter the mark on the screen.

Fish signals often appear as arches on better units unless the fish are very small, the scroll speed is very slow, or the boat is moving very fast. This is because a fish is first picked up on the outer edge of the cone where it is farthest from the transducer; then, as the fish passes directly underneath the transducer, it gets closer so its reading curves upward. Because the sound is strongest in the center of the cone, the arch also gets thicker from top to bottom in the middle. The fish then gets farther away again as it passes through the opposite outer edge of the cone, causing its screen reading to curve downward again. A partial arch or diagonal line means that a fish was moving either into or out of the cone when you passed by. A fish that swims along under the boat prints as a solid horizontal line until it swims out of the cone. A school of bait shows up as a big pod, which may be vertical or horizontal depending on the school's orientation. Not all units depict fish in arches, however, and fish will not always appear as arches on any unit.

It is very difficult to tell the specific size of fish detected with sonar because this varies according to the species, the speed of the boat, the scroll speed, the sensitivity setting, and even where the fish is within the transducer's cone. If you catch a fish out of a school that you've just marked, you may have some idea how fish size compares to signal size, but if any of these factors change as you continue fishing, it's a new ballgame. Determining size of fish is somewhat possible but determining species is not, although educated guesses based on extensive experience and knowledge of individual species behavior and certain environments can be accurate.

Troubleshooting

It is common for the service departments of sonar manufacturers to receive units for repair that do not actually need repair. Therefore, it pays to consult your manual or call the customer service department of the manufacturer if you're experiencing difficulties. Poor operation often has to do with poor electrical connections, improper transducer installation, or interference due to other devices or other installation deficiencies. Here are a few tips on common problems:

If the unit does not turn on, check the power cable connections at the battery and at the unit, the in-line fuse, and the battery voltage to be sure it is above 10 volts.

If the unit freezes or operates erratically, it may be caused by electrical noise from the boat's outboard motor, electric trolling motor, an accessory, a cable connection to the back of the unit or to the battery, or a broken or pinched transducer cable.

If there's a weak bottom echo, erratic digital readings, or no fish signals, make sure the transducer is shooting straight down. If the transducer is shooting through the hull, be sure it is shooting through only one layer of solid fiberglass, and is bonded to the hull with hard two-part epoxy only. Never install a shoot-through-hull transducer with a flexible epoxy or spongy material like silicone sealant, because it can absorb up to half of the transducer's transmit power. Electrical noise from the boat's motor, trolling motor, or an accessory may be interfering with the sonar's electronics. The water may be deeper than the unit's limits with the transducer it is using. After a severe storm or flood, there may be enough debris in the water to mimic severe random interference until the junk settles to the bottom.

Also check battery voltage; if the battery voltage drops, the unit's transmit power is reduced as well. Be sure that control settings are proper.

If you're not getting proper fish readings, electrical noise from the boat's motor, trolling motor, or an accessory may be interfering. Also, the transducer may be cavitating; it has to be mounted where it has a smooth flow of water at all speeds. Cavitation or turbulence around the transducer will reduce the unit's ability to receive echoes from the bottom and other objects below the transducer.

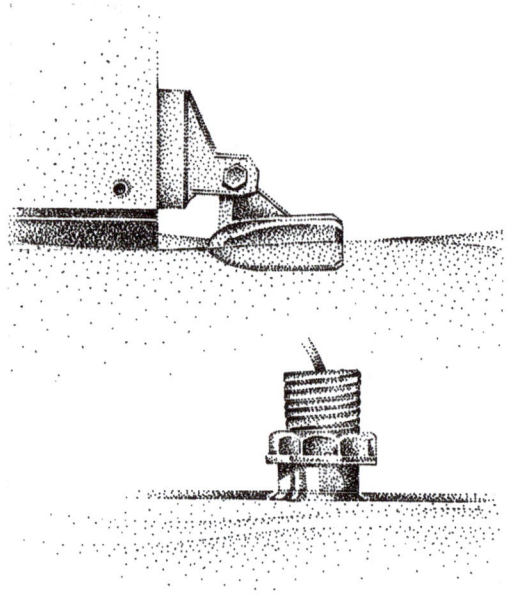

Shown is a transom installation for a high-speed transducer (top) and a through-hull installation (bottom) of a transducer as it would appear in the sump of a boat.

If there are gaps in the display reading when running at high speed, the transducer mount needs adjustment. Either the height or the angle needs correction. Gaps in the bottom reading on an aluminum boat may call for a deeper transducer running depth. If a transom-mounted transducer loses the bottom only at high speed, try tilting the rear end of the transducer's face 3 to 5 degrees downward. Make sure the adjustment doesn't cause the leading edge of the face to rise out of the water where it will catch air.

SORUBIM
A shovelnose catfish of South America, also known as tiger catfish and frequently misspelled "surubim."
See: Catfish.

SOUNDER
See: Sonar.

SOUTH AFRICA
South Africa sprawls over the southernmost tip of the African continent, covering a landmass that is greater than that of Great Britain, France, and Italy combined, and one-eighth the size of the United States. It takes in part of the Kalahari and Namib Deserts, has high peaks and expansive plateaus, and is swept by the cool waters of the South Atlantic and the warm waters of the Indian Ocean.

South Africa lacks any huge natural or man-made lakes, but it has many rivers and numerous impoundments. More freshwater fishing effort is expended on imported species—carp, trout, and largemouth bass—than on indigenous fish. The highland interior of the country, with its lofty altitude and numbers of fast-flowing rivers, provides excellent trout fishing. Significant trout fisheries range from the southern mountains of the Western Cape through the Cathcart and Hoggsback Districts of the Eastern Cape, and along the full range of the Drakensberg Mountains in Natal, with special emphasis on the southern Berg at Bergville to Himeville.

The country is blessed with 2,670 kilometers (1,725 miles) of coastline, yet that coastline has few bays or coves or natural harbors, and access to the sea is poor despite such length. Coastal fisheries are numerous, ranging from billfish and pelagic species offshore to a surfeit of species inshore, yet contrary currents on each side of the continent make the type and availability of species different, and far less numerous in the west than in the east. The warm Agulhas Current sweeping southward along the eastern coast provides different opportunities from those offered by the cool Benguela Current sweeping northward along the western coast. Nevertheless, saltwater fishing is well developed and avidly pursued, and South Africans as a whole are likely the most avid anglers on this continent.

Saltwater
The following review of the long South African coastline begins at the Mozambique border on the northeastern seaboard and follows the shoreline around the Cape of Good Hope.

Kwa-Zulu Natal. This rugged area is not only noted for its fishing opportunities, but for the adventure that is required just to get out on the water.

Northern coast. South Africa's only claim to tropical seas is the short segment of eastern coast nearest to southern Mozambique in the regions formerly known as Zululand. The clear blue waters here wash over coral reefs and into vast offshore trenches, drawing not only a good concentration of pelagic species, including billfish, but also the cream of South Africa's big-game anglers.

A vast section of the northern 120-mile-long coastline is a marine sanctuary. Anglers fishing from the beach and from boats, however, are permitted to target the abundant pelagic fish that migrate southward from the warmer northern tropical waters.

To access these waters, anglers use high-speed ski boats capable of being launched from the beach, as the only harbor is Richard's Bay at the southern extremity of the region. Launching through the surf line very often terrorizes the crew while exciting those watching from the beach, but these boats do allow anglers access to known fishing spots.

As this region falls within a wildlife conservation area, the only development surrounds the port of Richard's Bay and the tiny fishing hamlet of St. Lucia. Accommodations are in short supply, apart from these two venues, where hotels, lodges, and apartments are available. Most South Africans visiting this part of the Kwa-Zulu Natal coast prefer either caravans or tents for their coastal vacations. The board that manages the wildlife conservation area oversees numerous comfortable log chalets at selected venues, including Kosi Bay, Sodwana Bay, Cape Vidal, St. Lucia, and Mapelane. Restricted entrepreneurial development has taken place at Sodwana Bay.

Fish that predominate in this area are all tropical water species of the Indian Ocean, headed by the billfish family, of which the black and striped marlin are most common. Sailfish and an occasional (Pacific) blue marlin are also capt`ured in these waters.

The biggest black marlin caught in South African waters was captured in December 1984 at Sodwana Bay and weighed 938 pounds. The second largest fish, caught from a 20-foot boat at Sodwana in November 1981, was a 927-pounder. Many marlin of 900 pounds or more have been caught since then, and there's little doubt that a grander is waiting.

The marlin season commences in early November and peaks in late November, then tapers off to a conclusion at the end of April. Pacific sailfish are also captured in fair numbers, often by anglers targeting king mackerel. Sailfish visit these shores from October through April and range from 45 to 150 pounds. Releasing these and other billfish has become much more commonplace.

The main attraction is not billfish, however, but a plethora of other species that provide good light-tackle sport, especially king mackerel, and also queen mackerel, yellowfin tuna, bonito, dorado, and wahoo. Surf casting and fishing from rocky ledges also provide exciting catches, ranging from small bream to large sharks. Two tidal lake/estuary systems are found in the area. Anglers working from small craft and with light tackle are assured of good sport.

Southern coast. This stretch of coastline has fostered a fishing passion in many South Africans, as it is a holiday playground for most residents of the hinterland cities in the Pretoria-Witwatersrand region.

There is much diversity among the opportunities along the eastern seaboard in what was formerly `the Natal region, from small species in a rock pool to 400-pound marlin. Anglers pursue their sport from the protection of estuaries and bays, at rocky gullies, on ledges and high rock promontories, from long white beaches, and beyond the surf line in the deep sea.

The annual migration of vast shoals of sardines (pilchards) up the coast heralds the beginning of

A view of the coast along Sodwana Bay, where anglers launch boats directly into the surf.

another fishing year. During June and July, these little fish make their yearly appearance along the shore where the Natal coast stretches from the Umtamvuna River in the south to the Tugela River and the former Zululand boundary in the north.

The sardine run here is a fantastic annual phenomenon that brings gamefish in, and because this usually occurs during one of the premium holiday periods, many people are attracted to picking up rod and reel. The elf (bluefish) then makes an appearance and falls easy prey to the countless anglers who pursue these fish until August 31 each year. They are protected for spawning until November 30.

Surf and estuary fishing here is about as old as the Port of Natal, Durban. Historical records reflect that early settlers soon realized the potential of these waters to produce a harvest of fine table fare. It wasn't until just prior to World War II, however, that beach anglers—continually tempted by splashing and boiling shoals of fish just beyond casting range—effected an improvisation and paddled out beyond the big surf line aboard upgraded surfboards to catch these fish.

As the original surfboard was called a "crocker ski," the new craft is colloquially called a "ski boat"—a name that has been retained even for today's vastly different high-powered, sophisticated offshore fishing craft.

From this humble beginning, a new vista opened. Catches multiplied as king mackerel, Natal snoek (a barracuda-like fish), dorado, and a vast variety of reef fish added a new dimension to the sport of angling. Today, offshore angling is practiced extensively from this section of the South African seaboard. Ski-boat clubs have been formed from nearly every rocky promontory that affords some protection from the relentless surf line.

It is from these little bays, as well as from open river mouths, that ski boats negotiate the surf, permitting anglers to fish beyond the surf line.

The port of Durban is the only deep-water harbor along this 250-mile coastline. Therefore, it is the intrepid ski-boat skippers who break the barriers of the heavy surf who enable this sport to be enjoyed.

In summer, warm current makes its way close to shore and brings with it a concentration of various pelagic gamefish, including king mackerel, tuna, bonito, and dorado, as well as a fair number of sailfish and black, blue, and striped marlin. Reef fishing for species such as black and red steenbras, "kob" (kabeljou), yellowtail, and rock cod is a winter sport when the colder green water pushes in from the south.

Durban supports a fair number of offshore charter craft and private sportfishing vessels. Together with the high-class hotels, these operations offer visitors an opportunity to experience offshore fishing along this coast.

This area used to support a unique opportunity to fish for sharks off the southern breakwater of Durban Harbour, which was a whaling port until the early 1960s. A large number of sharks used to follow the whale carcasses as they were towed into port by whaleboats. These sharks were sought by a select band of anglers using heavy surf rods, wooden Scarborough reels, and 2,000 yards of 18-cord flex line and a chunk of whale meat as bait, to land numerous sharks exceeding 1,000 pounds. The heaviest recorded was a great white of 1,660 pounds in 1953. The end of whaling virtually put an end to this type of angling, and today it is only the odd shark that is caught.

Wild Coast and border. The lack of coastal development and beautiful but rugged nature of this 300-mile stretch of oceanfront gave it the name "Wild Coast." Extending roughly from west of Port Edward to just east of Port Alfred, this area features varied species and angling conditions.

From the northeast corner and down the coast past the port city of East London to the Great Fish River, there's an abundance of estuaries, rarely more than 5 or 6 miles apart. For the first hundred miles, the green rolling hills slope steeply from 300 or 400 feet down to the sea and are interspersed with short stretches of sheer cliffs, sandy beaches, and estuaries. At one beautiful spot near Msikaba, a waterfall tumbles over the cliff face and into the sea.

From the central Transkei region southward, the high green hills make way for heavily wooded sand dunes and long stretches of beach again broken by the estuaries, some of which are open to the sea only for short periods in the rainy season. Nevertheless, they harbor many saltwater fish and prawns. Several of the estuaries feature hotels that cater to visiting anglers, whereas other estuaries lack facilities and are accessed only via four-wheel-drive vehicles. The steep banks of the estuaries are heavily forested and are home to an incredible array of birds. This backdrop makes fishing here an unforgettable experience.

The warm Agulhas Current (up to 26°C in summer) sweeps down the length of this coastline. Close to shore in the north, it meanders as it nears East London, sometimes moving in close, sometimes moving 12 miles offshore, depending on the prevailing winds. At its strongest near the continental shelf, the current allows little sand and silt to settle, which results in large areas of prime reef fishing.

The Agulhas brings pelagic fish south almost year-round. Regular catches include black and striped marlin, yellowfin tuna, record-size kawakawa, skipjack tuna, king mackerel, queenfish, kingfish, dorado, and wahoo.

A prime attraction for reef anglers on this 300-mile stretch is the giant, endemic snapperlike fish called the red, or copper, steenbras. These magnificent fish grow to 130 pounds, and strict management measures have been implemented to limit the catch, as their numbers have been reduced. Numerous other reef species here make bottom fishing attractive.

The Agulhas also provides shore anglers with a variety of warmwater fish interspersed with cooler-water fish when the current meanders offshore. Garrick are prized targets at some deeper-water shore spots like Brazen Head, Poenskop, Mbolompo, Mazeppa Bay, the East London Harbour breakwater, and Cove Rock. Tuna are sometimes taken from these ledges. Some marlin have also been hooked and lost. Yellowtail, elf, and kob constitute the bulk of the catches.

A variety of breamlike fish are still reasonably abundant, as are sharks and rays, which, on a tag-and-release basis, make up the bulk of the catches in competitions. Estuarine angling is good for kob (which grow to more than 100 pounds), spotted grunter, river snapper, garrick, and small kingfish. A popular light-tackle fish is the tarpon relative called the skipjack, which performs spectacular aerobatics when hooked. Although saltwater fly fishing is still in its infancy in South Africa, many anglers have recorded good catches of all these fish in the estuaries.

With the exception of the East London Harbour, all boats launch through the surf from estuaries, semi-sheltered bays, or open beaches. This coast is extremely popular with South African anglers, and a growing number of visitors are sampling its unspoiled beauty and variety of fish.

Eastern Cape. The Eastern Cape has a well-deserved reputation for exceptionally varied and versatile angling. The offshore grounds are a short distance away, bottom fish are plentiful, rock and surf angling exist along many miles of unspoiled and uninhabited beaches, and opportunities to cruise up one of numerous rivers or estuaries are also available. Many angling clubs exist in this region, and given the area's well-controlled launching areas, much of the excellent fishing is accessible.

Most anglers work the inshore reefs and target bottom fish, which include kob reaching 60 kilograms, and black and red steenbras, among many other species. The region is of foremost renown for garrick, a great gamefish prized for its excellent displays on light tackle. The Eastern Cape boasts what is likely the best garrick angling in the world, and many world records have been captured here.

Yellowtail inhabit the inshore reefs, and shoals half the size of a football field are not uncommon. The banks at Struisbaai are especially known for such shoals. The winter run of yellowfin tuna, following the sardine migration northward to Natal, can provide outstanding action. Sometimes fast-moving fish, ranging from 15 to 50 kilograms, are observed chasing food. Masses of birds mill overhead, forming the backdrop to a spectacle that can produce scores of tuna.

The Eastern Cape has a high success ratio for the popular, speedy, and powerful mako shark. Although makos here are usually small, ranging from 30 to 100 kilograms, an angler is virtually assured of catching one on the offshore reefs with relatively light tackle when the water is clean. The far offshore environs also produce hammerhead sharks, some large, and occasionally broadbill swordfish. The largest broadbill docked at the capital city of Port Elizabeth was caught accidentally by a commercial boat more than a decade ago and weighed an incredible 650 kilograms.

The Eastern Cape has spectacular and extensive unspoiled beaches and cliffs. One can travel for miles up the beach in a four-wheel-drive vehicle, meeting only the occasional angler. The Tsitsikama coastline, which stretches from Port Elizabeth to Knysna, has breathtaking and untouched rock angling. Tsitsikama forest reaches the cliff face, and the ocean melts to incredible depths at one's feet. As a result, large black and red steenbras, which are traditionally caught only out at sea, are landed from these rocks.

With numerous rivers and estuaries entering the sea here, excellent light-tackle angling is available amidst tranquil and varied settings. A wide variety of fish thrive in these rivers and estuaries, and excellent catches of kob, grunter, steenbras, skipjacks, and other species are the norm. Some rivers stretch inland for up to 30 kilometers, and, when venturing by boat (the only method), an angler can be virtually guaranteed of memorable exclusivity. It is not uncommon to stop the boat to view wildlife in or near the water. The flats and inaccessible dense bush are home to a multitude of birds and game. Many upriver trips have been rewarded with glimpses of the shy and elusive bushbuck ram and other seldom-seen animals.

Western/Southern Cape. This vast region has an incredibly diverse array of sportfish.

Cape Agulhas to Cape Point. Just east of Cape Agulhas, Africa's southernmost point, lies the small coastal town of Stiruisbaai, arguably the capital of nearshore boat angling in the region known as the Western Cape. This is served by a small but functional harbor that is home to a sizable commercial fleet and is frequented in season by many recreational ski-boat anglers. The huge shelf of nearby Agulhas Bank supports a variety of bottom-feeding as well as pelagic species, desirable both as sport and food fish.

Fed from the east by the tropical Agulhas Current and the nutrient-rich cool Benguela system in the west, this continental shelf area extends as far as 120 miles offshore, in places, to the dropoff. The bank is home to many sought-after species, most prominently the southern yellowtail. Present year-round but most abundant in summer and autumn when they average 6 to 15 pounds, the strikingly hued yellowtail offers a combination of dogged fighting spirit, attractive appearance, and excellent edibility that encourages many here to consider it the prince of ocean pelagic species.

A productive method of capture includes drifting over pinnacles with weighted lines placed between midwater and the bottom, and baited with squid, sardines, or Japanese sauries. Another successful procedure is to cast metal spoons (called spinners) at shoals of yellowtail feeding on the surface with birds, usually terns, overhead.

Another favorite species here, the kob is similar to the red drum. Favoring reefs surrounded by sand, this species is generally similar in size to yellowtail, but 100-pounders are fairly common. The South African record weighed more than 150 pounds. Sometimes occurring in large shoals, the bottom-feeding kob is most abundant from December through June and feeds during dark hours, particularly at dusk and dawn.

Similar at first glance to the kob but sleeker and more sporty is the geelbek (Cape salmon), primarily a night feeder. Reaching 40 pounds but averaging about 10 pounds, this species is a relative of the American white seabass and is an excellent gamefish. Although normally caught near the bottom, geelbek often come to within a few yards of the surface, particularly at night.

A number of bottom-feeding redfish species also occur in this area. The largest is the famous red steenbras, which attains 150 pounds but is commonly around 30 pounds. This species is a powerful and aggressive member of the snapper family, sometimes occurring in schools. With its large canine teeth, it is striking in appearance; the pinkish blue of the juveniles changes to an orange yellow to copper coloration, sometimes with dark markings, in the adults.

Other popular redfish include the red stumpnose and the red roman, reaching 20 and 10 pounds respectively. As with most redfish, these species are all prized table fare. Another common fish is the elf, which averages about 2 pounds and rarely exceeds 10 pounds. This species never reaches the size of its North American equivalent, although it is an esteemed food fish.

Occurring occasionally along the surf line and over reefs is the garrick, also known locally as the

Sharks are said to have existed 200 million years before dinosaurs; the power of a 6$\frac{1}{2}$-foot dusky shark at the tip of its teeth was measured at 22 tons per square inch.

leervis. Although never common, this hard-fighting gamefish is highly sought by a select band of anglers and is most often caught in the summer.

Rock and surf angling are popular and rewarding pastimes here. Anglers land numerous species of sharks from these sites, and they take kob and elf regularly. White steenbras are also targeted.

Huge shark specimens thrive in this region, among them duskies, ragged-tooth, mako, and the occasional hammerhead, but the most impressive is the great white. This species is at times abundant on the reefs and is a bait-stealing nuisance to anglers. Always commanding respect when encountered, the great white is occasionally caught by recreational anglers, mainly for tagging and release.

Moving west from Cape Agulhas toward Cape Point, the coastline consists of rocky sections interspersed by long, white sandy beaches. Gansbaai and Hermanus are the only two harbors of note in this area. Although mainly used by the commercial fishing sector, these harbors do have some facilities for the recreational angler. Recreational-boat angling in this area is not common, but rock and surf angling are popular.

Species encountered along this coast are the same as those in the Cape Agulhas area, both at sea and from the shore. Another species that shows itself at certain times of the year, mainly in winter, is the snoek. This barracuda-like fish has a vicious set of teeth; although normally caught commercially, it is a popular recreational catch. Averaging 5 to 9 pounds and growing to 20 pounds, the snoek offers excellent sport on light tackle.

At the western end of this section of coastline is the large, shallow, semi-enclosed body of water known as False Bay, which is up to 30 miles long and 35 miles wide and hosts a variety of species. The more common are yellowtail, kob, geelbek, elf, and snoek, and bottom-feeding redfish also occur regularly. This bay was famous for summer catches of bluefin tuna in the 1960s, but these fish were heavily depleted and have not been encountered in this location for many years.

False Bay is serviced by two excellent harbors, Gordon's Bay on the eastern side and Simonstown on the western side. A number of excellent slipways for trailer-borne craft are located here. Because of its sheltered waters and variety of fish, False Bay is an excellent and popular boating venue, with hundreds of boats at sea on good days.

Cape Point to Table Bay. Although not the southernmost point of Africa, Cape Point is generally accepted as a meeting place of the warm, subtropical Agulhas Current and the cold, Antarctic-influenced Benguela Current. Consequently, the inshore waters of the coastline between Cape Point and Table Bay are cool, averaging 12°C, but the Agulhas Current has a continuing effect as one moves farther offshore, where the water reaches 22°C in summer.

Due to the mixing of currents and the presence of two large undersea canyons in this area, conditions are often ideal for big-game species, particularly tuna. Albacore, or longfin tuna as the fish is known off the Cape, are at times extremely abundant and support a large commercial fishery. Cape Point is famous for producing big catches of this species and for having large specimens, many of which have made the record books over the years.

Albacore are abundant off the Cape in spring (September and October) and in autumn (April and May); shoals normally move north with the prevailing southeast drift in the hot summer months, when the water temperature climbs to more than 20°C. With the onset of northwesterly winds in autumn, the cool subtropical water is displaced by warmer, temperate water, and the albacore return.

Another common tuna species here is the yellowfin. These fish are caught up to 200 pounds, and the average catch off Cape Town runs between 80 and 120 pounds. Often occurring in great shoals, this fish is an exciting quarry. Trolling plastic lures and diving plugs is the common method of catching tuna off the Cape, but chunking and drifting with bait is also popular and effective. Anglers often use the latter technique in conjunction with casting a metal spoon.

Many large offshore sportfishing vessels operate in this area and are berthed either at Simonstown in False Bay or at Hout Bay on the western coast of the Cape Peninsula. In addition, many trailered boats launch from Hout Bay or False Bay and make daily runs to the tuna grounds anywhere from 10 to 50 miles offshore.

Other area species include skipjack tuna, yellowtail, dorado, bigeye tuna, striped and black marlin, and swordfish. Also common but not normally fished for are a number of shark species, including makos, blues, duskies, and great whites.

Marlin are rare visitors to Cape waters and are normally found during summer, when water temperatures are highest. Although rarely deliberately fished for by anglers because of their scarcity, some large specimens have been landed, mainly by commercial vessels. The largest of these was a 1,338-pound black marlin. Swordfish have been more abundant than previously estimated, and some Cape anglers have caught them using night fishing techniques.

Inshore angling in the cooler waters is confined mainly to snoek in autumn and winter. No other significant sportfish are caught with rod and reel, but a popular fishery using ring nets exists for the delicious Cape rock lobster.

West coast. Due to the influence of the cool Benguela Current, recreational angling off the west coast of the Cape and farther north is limited and consists mainly of snoek. A commercial fishery exists for this species, particularly around Dassen Island and St. Helenabaai.

The Cape rock lobster is also abundant and provides a substantial recreational fishery. Tuna

---

Pearl essence is the silvery substance in the skin of herring and other fishes, and it is essential to the manufacture of lipstick, nail polish, paints, ceramics, and costume jewelry.

are prolific off the west coast of the Cape Peninsula but are normally encountered too far offshore for recreational boats to reach. At times, however, shoals move to within striking distance of small boats, and some good catches have been made during the summer.

A large estuary known as the Langebaan Lagoon at Saldanha Bay is a popular area for water sports. Again due to low water temperatures, the variety of fish in this area is restricted. Anglers use light tackle to land kob, elf, and yellowtail, as well as a number of bottom-feeding species, plus sharks and rays. Leaping thresher sharks are much sought after, as are tope, duskies, and cow sharks, and the occasional great white. Large skates are also landed.

Freshwater

South Africa has few natural lakes but numerous small to midsize impoundments and many rivers. A few of the rivers are large, many are shorter tributaries to the larger flows, and some are intermittent. Angling for coarse species is popular in warmwater rivers and lakes, and in lakes for bass, whereas trout fishing in the scenic mountainous regions is excellent, unsung, and lightly publicized.

For the traveling angler, the tourism infrastructure in South Africa is excellent. Numerous dams have been built in nearly every river system, and resorts offer accommodations ranging from well-appointed chalets and rondavels to high-grade caravan and camping parks.

Because of its year-round mild climate, the region east of Pretoria offers traveling anglers good fishing during summer and winter, with mid- to late summer possibly the best time.

South Africa has only three natural lakes that offer sportfishing: Barberspan in the Western Transvaal, Groenvlei in the Southern Cape, and Zeekoeivlei in the Western Cape. The more famous dams (reservoirs) visited by thousands of anglers every year include Loskop in the southeastern Transvaal, Fanie Botha near Tzaneen in the northeastern Transvaal, Hartebeespoort near Pretoria, Vaal Dam south of Johannesburg, Koppies in the Orange Free State, Chelmsford in Natal, and Sterkfontein near Harrismith in the eastern Free State.

In total, more than 130 dams are under the control of the Department of Water Affairs, and all are open to anglers, although the directorates of nature conservation in each district provide fisheries control and management.

The biggest man-made lake, with some 130 kilometers of navigable water, is Hendrik Verwoerd on the Orange River. This impoundment holds significant populations of enormous yellowfish and catfish, and has become more popular in recent years; previously it was regarded as too far from either the Cape or the huge Pretoria-Witwatersrand-Vereeniging area (which holds some 70 percent of the country's population). It is, however, just about in the center of the country.

Anglers take a limited number of tigerfish from the eastward flowing rivers of Mpumalanga Lowveld and northern Kwa-Zulu Natal. The fish are rather small, but a few impoundments do contain larger fish. The Pongola Dam in northern Kwa-Zulu Natal, for example, has produced tigerfish up to 8.3 kilograms.

Coarse species, especially carp and catfish, are the primary freshwater fishing interests of South Africans. Freshwater coarse fishing is a large industry in its own right, and because most of the dams are within nature reserves, anglers have the opportunity to get close to nature on every outing.

Bass and coarse species. In terms of hours spent in pursuit of various fish, carp are the most heavily favored freshwater species. Introduced here by British colonials evidently as early as 1859, they have thrived throughout the land and been widely distributed. The generally warm and discolored rivers and dams, as well as abundant natural vegetation, have contributed greatly to their success. The most popular angling technique for carp is similar to that for coarse fish in Europe: using long, supple rods and mushy corn baits that are cast great distances from shore. The rods are then set in rod rests to await a bite. This activity attracts tens of thousands of anglers to riverbanks and dams every weekend. At Hartebeespoort Dam, for instance, some 7,000 to 10,000 people congregate on its banks during summer weekends, nearly all in search of a big carp.

The current South African all-tackle carp record is a 21.98-kilogram fish, caught in 1988 in the Transvaal Lowveld. The previous record was a specimen of 21.85 kilograms, caught at Hartebeespoort. Carp fishing throughout South Africa is very good, and anglers have also perfected techniques for catching carp from boats, which has generated a healthy inland fishing industry among boaters.

The second most popularly targeted fish is the sharptoothed catfish *(Clarius gariepinus)*, popularly (but incorrectly) termed "barbel." These are South Africa's largest indigenous sportfish and grow to large sizes; the current South African all-tackle record stands at 31.805 kilograms. Catfish occur throughout the region, with the exception of the southern Cape Province.

The third most popular fish is the blue kurper (called bream in Zimbabwe). These are known elsewhere as tilapia and are excellent table and sportfish, occurring mostly in the warmer regions. They are a particular target of boat anglers.

Highly regarded indigenous sportfish also include the largemouth yellowfish *(Barbus kimberleyensis)*, with a record of 22.20 kilograms, and the smallmouth yellowfish *(Barbus aeneus)*, with a record of 7.837 kilograms. The big yellows are most often caught during cold winter months on the Transvaal and Orange Free State Highveld and, according to popular legend, bite best "at 2 o'clock on a winter's night with a rising moon and the temperature below freezing."

Many of the dams in South Africa, particularly in the Transvaal, Kwa-Zulu Natal, and Cape Provinces, have populations of black bass. Largemouth and smallmouth bass are found here, as is the occasional spotted bass. Largemouth bass were imported to South Africa in 1928 and smallmouth bass in 1937; these species, as well as the less common spotted bass, have been transplanted extensively. The Natal Parks Board began experimenting with Florida-strain largemouth bass in the early 1980s, and these fish were also stocked in many waters.

Largemouths seldom exceed 10 pounds in South African waters, but they have been caught in the 12- to 13-pound range, usually those of the Florida strain. Waters in Mpumalanga produced a 13-pound, 6-ounce bass in 1997. A catch of five bass weighing a total of 52 pounds was made in Kwa-Zulu Natal.

Anglers have organized bass fishing clubs, which have been very active in recent decades, holding competitions on various waters. Much more water for bass fishing is being developed as a result. The best angling times are from late winter to midspring during the spawning period, but bass are caught year-round. Catch-and-release is particularly popular for this exotic species.

Trout. South Africa has an underestimated trout fishery. Rainbow and brown trout are underutilized resources here, and competition for these fish is generally light. This fishery consists of miles of rivers, and plenty of small still waters, many of them in beautifully scenic country.

Eastern South Africa is divided from its vast interior by the Drakensberg Mountain range, which stretches from the Eastern Cape in the south to the Transvaal in the north. To the trout angler, the mountains are a godsend. Close to the coastal plains these mountains rise steeply to more than 10,000 feet, causing a massive upwelling of moist air and heavy rain on the eastern slopes in summer (December and January). Thus, they are the birthplace of countless trout streams flowing east into three prime trout areas: the midlands of Kwa-Zulu Natal, the Eastern Transvaal, and the Eastern Cape around the towns of Barkly East and Lady Grey. At the farthest tip of Africa in the Western Cape, trout thrive in the high mountains a short distance inland of Cape Town, where the climate is Mediterranean and offers clear sun-filled days in summer.

Apart from these main locations, there is good trout fishing in the independent Kingdom of Lesotho, a landlocked mountainous country crisscrossed by bright, clear streams, most of them rising more than 8,000 feet above sea level. Food is more abundant in these high streams, and the mayfly populations are particularly dense. The condition and average size of the trout are exceptional. The area is accessible with four-wheel-drive vehicles, but travel

Fishing for trout on the Holsloot River in the South African mountains.

by plane or helicopter makes the trip much more comfortable. Lesotho is unlike most of South Africa, where rivers and lakes can be reached with ease.

Trout were first introduced to South Africa in the late 1890s, coming from Loch Leven brown trout stock imported from Scotland. These browns did well in their environment, and rainbows were introduced a decade or so later to complement them. Still, most of the rivers today retain a clear one-species identity, rarely holding both species simultaneously. South African trout waters are small by international standards, more like streams than rivers, yet the average size of the trout caught is large. Most of the rivers produce fish of up to 4 or 5 pounds, and in the Barkly East area, river fish up to 9 pounds are encountered.

Trout proliferate in the upland sections of most rivers, and the waters tend to become overpopulated. Natural predation is fairly significant, especially from otters and white-breasted cormorants, but, as with most exotic species, the trout generally has an easy passage in this country's waters. High midsummer water temperatures, hail storms, flash floods, extended periods of drought, siltation, and the predations of humans do more damage to the trout populations than their rivals in the animal kingdom. Because trout were once alien to South Africa, some naturalists think trout should be outlawed. Fortunately, most conservationists have decided that trout play an important role in recreation and tourism.

If Africa in general, and African trout fishing in particular, has an Achilles heel, it is drought. Good trout fishing is dependent on good rainfall, and a season or two of poor rains sets the sport back a notch or two. Although South Africa is a dry country, droughts are less common in the eastern highlands than in the interior, and often less devastating. Equally problematic are flash flooding and siltation. On the other hand, given a spell of good rainfall, such as might happen over a several-year period, the country is a veritable trout fishing paradise.

South African trout water is largely in the hands of private riparian owners. Public fishing is available, primarily in the Western Cape and in Kwa-Zulu Natal, but as the sport has grown in popularity, more water has been reserved for private use. Farmers owning stretches of the famous rivers guard their asset jealously, and syndication of fishing rights to groups of anglers, once a rarity, is now the norm. A few commercial operations make excellent fishing available to visitors, arranging safaris to some of the best trout rivers and still waters in South Africa and Lesotho. Most anglers fish these rivers by wading.

To compensate for the relative uncertainty of river water and the fact that rivers are not always easy to access, South African trout anglers have taken to stillwater fly fishing in a big way. All of these stillwaters are man-made impoundments, and they average 10 to 20 acres. Most are remarkably fertile, and the growth rate of the fish in them is phenomenal. Trout up to 10 pounds have become commonplace, and the best exceed 14 pounds.

Most stillwater anglers fish from float tubes, using floating lines with nymphs and dry flies. The rewards are great catches of rainbows and browns. The sport is exciting and all but totally independent of the vagaries of the weather.

The trout season generally starts in September and runs through the end of May. Many stillwaters, however, have no closed season. The best fishing is in spring (September and October) and in autumn (from late March through May). During these months, the water is cooler and the trout feed more actively.

Although these waters are fertile, hatches are not predictable. In fact, most are sporadic, so dry flies are not used as extensively as they are overseas. The fish are consequently less likely to be selective feeders, and, in the main, nymph anglers do best. Most fly anglers fishing on stillwaters and in rivers use 4- or 5-weight outfits, with 8- to 9-foot rods. The fish are hardly ever consistent surface feeders.

The mountain streams of the Western Cape are a notable exception, where free-rising trout come to the dry fly smartly, just as they do in the upland streams in Lesotho.

SOUTH CAROLINA

Thanks to geographical diversity, a comparatively small population density, a long coastline, and an abundance of streams, lakes, and ponds, South Carolina has a great deal to offer anglers. The variety of fish, the types of fishing available, and a plethora of easily accessible destinations make South Carolina angling broadly appealing to residents and visitors alike.

The Palmetto State is home to a dozen large man-made lakes with a total surface area of some 463,000 acres. In addition, 16 state-owned lakes are intensively managed for angling. Many public and private waters offer angling opportunities in all of South Carolina's 46 counties. Altogether, some 1,400 such small lakes and ponds—all larger than 10 acres—offer a total surface area of almost 500,000 acres. Thousands of miles of free-flowing streams, ranging from Appalachian trout streams to coastal blackwater rivers, add to the delightful mix, as does a hefty chunk of Atlantic coast.

The state's freshwater lakes and streams offer a smorgasbord of species. Rainbow, brown, and brook trout exist in a handful of counties; all three species reproduce naturally in some streams and are stocked in others. Trout grow fairly large in the cold, clear waters of Lake Jocassee, which is also home to smallmouth bass. For the most part, though, the state's featured freshwater species are of the warmwater variety. These include largemouth, hybrid, and striped bass; various panfish, including bluegills, shellcrackers, redbreasts, warmouth, and perch; black crappie; white crappie; channel, blue, and flathead catfish; pickerel; and nongamefish species like gar and mudfish. Popular saltwater species include seatrout, redfish, amberjack, grouper, sea bass, sea bream, cobia, and tarpon.

Freshwater

South Carolina's inland topography falls into three distinct regions—the Upcountry, the Piedmont, and the Lowcountry—and each has its own distinctive features. The state's large lakes, with the noteworthy exceptions of Lakes Marion and Moultrie (often called Santee-Cooper after the rivers impounded to create them), are all in the Upcountry and Piedmont regions. In addition to the major waters noted in these areas, South Carolina has plenty of small and generally unpublicized bodies of water, many of which offer exceptional fishing opportunities.

Upcountry. The northwesternmost portion of South Carolina, a sort of rough triangle formed by the state's borders with North Carolina and Georgia, is locally known as the Upcountry. It is home to a number of trout streams and three large lakes—Jocassee, Keowee, and Hartwell. Although South Carolina's stream fishing for trout cannot rival that found in neighboring North Carolina, the Department of Natural Resources (DNR) does stock large numbers of fish each year; these are raised at a hatchery in Walhalla.

There is limited natural reproduction in several remote streams, most notably those flowing into Lake Jocassee. The best trout streams include the upper reaches of the Chattooga and its East Fork, plus the Chauga, Whitewater, Eastatoe, and Saluda Rivers. For those who enjoy getting back of beyond, some of the feeder streams, along with creeks that can be reached by hiking the Foothills Trail, are inviting destinations.

The tactics that take trout in this area range from dry-fly fishing to the plying the waters with natural baits. For fly anglers, the emphasis is on good presentation rather than selecting the best fly pattern. Streams are relatively low in fertility, so the trout are opportunistic feeders. Among consistently productive dry-fly patterns are the Adams, Royal Wulff, Thunderhead, Elk-Hair Caddis, Adams Variant, and Yellow and Royal Humpies. In late summer, flies that imitate beetles, jassids, and hoppers are productive. The nymph angler will score well with bead-head versions of Tellico, Gold-Ribbed Hare's Ear, and Prince patterns, whereas favored streamers include Muddler Minnows, Matukas, and Black-Nosed Dace. For those using ultralight spinning gear, the smallest spinners are effective, as are such live baits as crickets, spring lizards, red worms, and nightcrawlers.

For the stillwater angler, all three of the area's large lakes have much to offer. Keowee, and particularly Jocassee, have good populations of brown trout. These stay mostly quite deep; in warmer weather, trolling with downriggers is effective. Jigging with large spoons, or using threadfin shad or blueback herring, both of which inhabit the reservoirs, are other favored techniques.

Some smallmouth bass live in these lakes, and largemouth bass are plentiful. Panfishing for black crappie and various species of bream is also available, although lakes with warmer water elsewhere in the state are better.

Although located in the Upcountry region, sprawling Lake Hartwell's 56,000 acres (shared with Georgia) offer fishing similar to that found in the Piedmont. The northernmost impoundment in a chain of dams on the Savannah River, Hartwell is one of the state's better crappie lakes. It has plenty of largemouth bass as well, although they tend to run smaller on average than those in South Carolina's favorite bass fishing destinations. Spotted bass are nearly as abundant here as largemouths. Hybrid striped bass, and—to a lesser degree—pure-strain stripers, are Hartwell's featured species, and the lake is generally lightly fished.

Piedmont region. Overall, the Piedmont region of South Carolina offers the state's finest fishing. This is due in large part to the area's seven major lakes: Thurmond and Russell on the Savannah River, Wylie and Wateree on the Catawba River, and Greenwood, Monticello, and Murray.

Lake Wylie splits the North Carolina–South Carolina border. It's a prime crappie and largemouth reservoir, and an overlooked hotspot for bullhead and channel cats. Large catches of crappie are regularly taken using small minnows or jigs, and most of the fish linger around numerous brush piles placed by anglers around docks and piers. Largemouth bass get a lot of pressure, but the lake is sufficiently fertile to withstand constant attention. Both crappie and bass fishing are best in spring and fall, although mild temperatures here as well as in the Lowcountry mean viable fishing throughout the year.

The height of summer is prime time for Wylie's plentiful catfish, most of which are in the 1- to 5-pound class. Stinkbaits, including a local favorite, "aged" mussels taken from the lake's sandy shorelines, can be fished off gradually sloping points. There are some white bass in Lake Wylie as well, and bluegills are exceptionally plentiful.

Lake Wateree is very similar, with the one notable difference that the reservoir has striped bass. These do not normally run as large as in other lakes where size limits are in effect, but the fish are plentiful. Crappie in Wateree run large, and in the lake's long, straight main channel, anglers troll with several rods using jigs to catch this species in great numbers.

Lake Murray has long enjoyed a richly deserved reputation as a hotspot for big largemouth bass. This fame was at least in part a product of the reservoir's having extensive areas of grass. The grass was killed in the late 1990s, however, so this fishery is likely to experience some decline. On the other hand, thanks to the implementation of a 21-inch minimum size limit for stripers and the presence of plenty of the baitfish favored by rockfish, action for this species improves a bit every year. A return to the glory days of the late 1960s (stripers were first stocked here in 1961, after South Carolina biologists became the first to determine how to raise and stock them in landlocked situations) is a distinct possibility. With 525 miles of shoreline and extensive development, including the construction of numerous docks and piers, Murray has plenty of the shallow-water structure and cover in which crappie and bream thrive. Both are here in great numbers.

Lakes Russell and Thurmond (also known as Clarks Hill Lake) are shared with Georgia, and the two states enjoy a reciprocal licensing agreement. Russell is a sprawling reservoir of some 27,000 acres, 1,500 of which were left with standing timber when the gates on the dam first closed. Buoys mark this prime fish-attracting cover. The lake's most popular species is white bass, although it is also noted for yellow perch, catfish, and rainbow trout.

Thurmond Lake, with its 71,000 acres, 1,200 miles of shoreline, and scores of islands, is one of the largest man-made bodies of water in the country. The lake is renowned for its striper and hybrid bass fishing, and blueback herring are the natural baits of choice. The humble but popular crappie is this reservoir's number one fish; anglers creel between 200,000 and 300,000 pounds of slabs in an average year. An ideal way to access this impoundment—also true of most other large lakes in South Carolina—is via one of the state parks located on its shores. Here, as elsewhere, these parks normally include camping areas, launch sites, bait and tackle stores, and other facilities.

Like Thurmond, Lake Greenwood is considered a crappie hotspot. In most years it ranks tops in South Carolina for the number of this species caught per acre. It is also known as one of the state's better largemouth bass lakes, and the nature and configuration of its many fingers and small side channels make Greenwood a structure-fishing dream.

Monticello is relatively small at just under 7,000 acres, but in quantity, it ranks as South Carolina's top catfishing destination. It features a 300-acre sub-impoundment (also called Monticello) that is intensively managed. This sub-impoundment is but one of a number of state-managed lakes in the Piedmont. Most have stricter creel limits and more rigid size restrictions than do waters open to the general public, and they also are restricted to electric (or in some cases, small gasoline) motors on boats.

The Piedmont region has fine moving-water fishing in larger rivers (mostly navigable with jonboats and canoes) and medium-size streams that are easily waded. Many of these waterways are underutilized because they're not suitable for modern, high-powered boats—the choice of anglers who fish the state's larger waters. Yet rivers such as the Catawba, Broad, and Wateree hold good populations of bass, channel cats, and panfish. They also feature false springtime spawning runs by stripers. The Saluda River tailrace near Columbia offers all these species as well as trout.

Lowcountry. The Palmetto Lowcountry is an area rich in history, with stately homes sitting atop river bluffs, and remainders of rice dikes dotting the landscape. Much of the finest fishing here is a throwback to yesteryear, when large impoundments and powerful boats were unknown. Blackwater rivers weave their way seaward like so many laughter lines on an old man's face, and their inky waters, stained dark by decomposing leaves and other vegetation, are as rich in fish as they seem steeped in mystery.

The best way to fish most of these streams, especially over the many miles between the fall line and the high-tide mark, is by drifting. Jonboats, canoes, and tiny one- or two-person craft—manufactured locally and known as strip boats—are ideal for this type of fishing. Bigger boats can be used on the lower reaches of some of the larger blackwater rivers. Largemouth bass, redbreasts, crappie, and catfish inhabit these streams, and some local anglers concentrate on less-esteemed species such as bowfin, gar, and grinnel (technically, bowfin and locally known as "swamp lawyers").

Among the better blackwater rivers are the Black, Edisto (famed for its redbreast fishery, although monster catfish have made inroads on

Santee Cooper is South Carolina's most prominent place for stripers and big catfish.

the populations of this popular panfish), Ashepoo, Santee, Ashley, Combahee, Lumber, Waccamaw, and Pee Dee. Also deserving of angling attention is storied Wambaw Creek, which figured prominently in the tales of the late and renowned writer Archibald Rutledge, and Four Holes Swamp, which links a number of natural lakes before eventually emptying into the Edisto River.

The most noted angling destination in the Lowcountry is the vast, interlocking complex formed by Lakes Marion and Moultrie and their connecting diversion canal. Commonly known as Santee-Cooper, this vast inland sea of 171,000 acres features a mixture of flooded timber, cypress swamps, and huge stretches of open water. Over the years, world records for several species of fish, including striped bass, channel catfish, blue catfish, and warmouth, have been produced here.

That in part explains the presence of dozens of marinas around the lake. In addition to offering record-breaking fish, Marion and Moultrie are also first-rate largemouth bass and crappie lakes. When it comes to big catfish, Santee-Cooper may be in a class by itself. It takes specimens above 50 pounds even to raise eyebrows, and every year whiskered giants in the 80-pound range are landed. In winter, smaller cats—mostly channels and blues—are caught in large numbers around the riprap at the base of the dam.

For largemouth anglers, vast areas of flooded timber and cypress swamps offer ideal topwater or shallow-running lure fishing in the spring and fall. The plentiful structure also lends itself to prime bream and crappie fishing; the latter usually spawn in late March and April, whereas bream go on the beds in May. Striped bass fishing peaks in the spring when the linesiders head to the diversion canal in spawning runs, but action can also be fast and furious in late fall and winter, when schooling fish "herd" baitfish to the surface and then smash them in savage flurries of feeding. Circling sea gulls are a visual index to such frenzies.

Saltwater

Saltwater fishing in South Carolina has many faces. Inshore, surf casting and pier fishing have long been popular, and public beaches, state-operated piers, and daily-fee fishing piers line the coast. In recent years, fly anglers have discovered that coastal waters offer action on redfish (usually called spottail bass, or just spots, in South Carolina), trout, and channel bass, among other species. Fly fishing has become particularly popular in and around Charleston Harbor. There is less sight casting than one encounters in crystal clear flats—thanks to waters that are normally murky—but shrimp, minnow, or crab patterns can be effective.

Snapper, sea bass, sea bream, cobia, grouper, and sharks, among other species, are the available inshore species. A recent angling dimension of recent vintage is spadefishing with jellyfish as baits. Mullet, spots, and sheepshead are regularly caught from the many piers that dot the more developed portions of the coastline; flounder, croaker, and whiting are the favored species. The most popular enticements for inshore species are live shrimp or shrimp-imitating jigs, but fiddler crabs are the offering of choice for the shell-cracking sheepshead. Minnows (or minnow-imitating streamers for fly anglers) are preferred for flounder.

In the northern coastal area, where the Gulf Stream comes a bit closer to shore, regular charter and head boats sail out of Myrtle Beach and Little River for mackerel, bluefish, tuna, and billfish. In recent years, increasing numbers of tarpon have shown up during the summer. Farther south, numerous wrecks and some jetties were built specifically with the angler in mind. Among the fish regularly taken on the wrecks are Spanish and king mackerel, albacore, false albacore, amberjack, bluefish, cobia, and bonito. Sharks can be caught almost anywhere if you can find a deep hole not too distant from shore.

SOUTH DAKOTA

Most people don't know that more cattle than people live in South Dakota. Nor do they know that you can cast flies on a mountain stream for wild trout in the western region, fish for bass on nearly every body of water in the central region, catch jumbo yellow perch well over 2 pounds through the ice in the eastern region, and catch many (and large) walleye along the vast stretches of the Missouri River. And all of these activities can be enjoyed without seeing very many cattle or people.

The most prominent angling attention in South Dakota is garnered by the Missouri River system, which in this state encompasses four large dams that were built between the late 1940s and early 1960s. These dams have spread water over 900 square miles and have divided the system into four reservoirs that range from large to enormous.

Beginning at the North Dakota border and ending at Nebraska, the South Dakota's fisheries are home to walleye, chinook salmon, northern pike, rainbow trout, brown trout, lake trout, smallmouth bass, largemouth bass, blue catfish, channel catfish, flathead catfish, white bass, crappie, tiger muskies, paddlefish, and sturgeon. The northernmost and largest reservoir, Lake Oahe is also the most attractive body of water and produces football-shaped walleye that are esteemed by even the most well-versed walleye anglers throughout North America. Because Oahe is so popular for producing sizable and numerous walleye, the other reservoirs in the system receive comparatively less pressure, even though they potentially host equal fishing opportunity.

The Black Hills region in the far western part of the state is South Dakota's taste of Montana. Full of trout fishing possibilities in countless streams surrounded by scenic landscape, it is also the home of three large reservoirs that offer a diversity of species and fishing prospects.

The Glacial Lakes region, in the eastern part of the state, consists of a series of relatively small and shallow lakes that are similar to a dishpan in structure. Good walleye, northern pike, and perch fishing is present in nearly every body of water. Anglers enjoy stable and sometimes abundant fishing opportunities when water levels are high due to above-normal precipitation. The glacial lakes are famous for producing abnormally large perch, and ice fishing here draws anglers from afar. In winter, it's not uncommon for more than 500 vehicles to be parked on one body of water when there is a good perch bite on.

There are several public and private stock ponds that start near the Missouri River in the central part of the state and spread west, some of which have not been tested with a lure in years. Top-quality bluegill and largemouth bass fishing are available for those who know where fish have been stocked, and for those who are willing to find out.

Missouri River System

One hundred years ago, the Missouri River flowed almost uninterrupted through South Dakota. Paddlefish, catfish, sauger, and sturgeon were among the most abundant native fish that survived in the flowage of the muddy Missouri. But today, four dams block the flow of water and have created four impressive reservoirs, often referred to as the "Great Lakes of South Dakota," that provide superb sportfishing.

Lake Oahe. Covering 256,000 acres in South Dakota and stretching 232 miles from Bismark, North Dakota, to the dam near Pierre, Lake Oahe (pronounced oh-wha-hee) is by far the largest and most prominent reservoir in the system. In terms of size and population of walleye that live in a reservoir, Oahe is among the best in the nation. The mother reservoir is also home to chinook salmon, northern pike, rainbow trout, brown trout, lake trout, smallmouth bass, catfish, white bass, yellow perch, and crappie.

Walleye move into the larger creek arms and rivers in the spring to spawn. The Grand River near Mobridge and the Moreau River near Akaska are two significant tributaries on the upper reservoir, and these are prominent spawning areas for walleye. Anglers fish light jigs tipped with a minnow, keying on points, flats, and dropoffs near these large creek arms. It is difficult to catch pre-spawning walleye on Oahe; however, after spawning, walleye will hold in spawning areas and can be caught in relatively shallow water. On warmer spring days, anglers work fairly shallow waters, ranging from 1 to 15 feet deep, casting a light jig tipped with a minnow or chub up into shallow dirty water. By late April, walleye begin moving back downstream.

Summer is also a good time on Lake Oahe for walleye. As the water temperature increases, fish can generally be found anywhere from 15 to 25 feet deep. Most anglers switch to fishing live nightcrawlers or leeches behind a bottom-bouncing rig on points, colored water, flats, and dropoffs near the main river channel. Generally the lower third of the lake, from the Cheyenne River area to the dam, produces the biggest fish. Eight- to 10-pounders are more likely there than in the upper reaches, although numerous fish frequent the upper two-thirds of the lake.

Anglers in the northern reaches of the lake continue to take walleye through the ice during the winter. A cold winter is needed to freeze the lower end of the lake, but anglers can have success ice-fishing for salmon, walleye, pike, and smelt when ice is present.

The smallmouth population at Oahe is very respectable but underfished, because walleye receive most of the attention. Smallmouths are fairly predictable and easy to find here; the action center predominantly on rocky points, sunken islands, submerged vegetation, and dropoffs. With roughly 2,251 miles of shoreline, Oahe offers many locations to seek smallmouths.

Lake Oahe has produced healthy populations of large northern pike over the years, some of which have weighed in at over 30 pounds. Fifteen- to 20-pound fish are common. However, consistent availability of quality spawning cover necessary for natural reproduction causes the pike population

A fall fishing scene on Lake Oahe.

to be cyclic. Anglers can expect good pike fishing when the water levels at Oahe are high enough in the spring to flood vegetation near the edges of the reservoir.

Most anglers fish for pike during the spring, when they move into the creek arms to feed and spawn, often spawning under the ice-covered bays. Most pike are taken using a stationary dead smelt rig. Casting spoons and assorted plugs will produce fish on warmer spring days. Shore-based anglers often do better than boaters in the spring, although the latter can reach bays that are harder to access by land. Some of the better pike locales on the lake are Cow and Spring Creeks near Pierre, West Whitlock near Gettysburg, and Blue Blanket and Swan Creeks near Mobridge. Fishing is also productive from mid-October through the fall.

Chinook salmon were introduced to Oahe in 1982. These powerhouse fighters can grow at a rate of 5 pounds a year here, feeding mainly on rainbow smelt and lake herring. Lake herring were stocked in Oahe in an attempt to take pressure off the smelt, an important forage base for walleye. Much like chinooks introduced into the Great Lakes, Oahe salmon have failed to prove they are an easy fish population to manage, even when conditions appear to be in their favor. The Oahe salmon population is cyclic and cannot be considered a dependable fishery. When all the pieces fall into place, however, anglers can enjoy reeling in a fish that never would have survived in the middle of South Dakota without the construction of the dams. Salmon exist throughout the lake, but most angling occurs near Oahe Dam and north from Spring Creek to the Cheyenne River.

Lake Sharpe. Lake Sharpe is an 80-mile-long 55,000-acre reservoir between the towns of Pierre and Chamberlain. Although it is not likely to raise a big population of large fish, such as the state-record 15.3-ounce walleye that was pulled from its waters, Sharpe is unique its consistent spawning success. Walleye, catfish, northern pike, crappie, white bass, perch, and large- and smallmouth bass are other gamefish available in the lake.

A large portion of the lake's walleye population winters in the tailwaters below Pierre down to the Antelope Creek area. Following an upstream migration of walleye that begins in September, most anglers do well in late fall and early winter below Oahe Dam in the tailrace. Walleye fishing is best from late April through roughly mid-June, when the fish are in a serious feeding mode following the spawn. Walleye inhabit the West Bend and Joe Creek areas around Memorial Day, and most are caught by anglers drifting with nightcrawlers.

Trout are stocked below Oahe Dam, where fly anglers find the fish in slack water. Three- to 9-pound rainbows are common in the spring. White bass are also caught in abundance as they make their way upriver in the spring to spawn.

Lake Francis Case. The next reservoir in the system, and second largest at 100,000 acres and 107 miles long, is Lake Francis Case. Several catchable species exist in the lake, along with a few that may accidentally show up on the end of the line. With a lake of such large proportions and connected to other large bodies of water, there is always a chance of catching the unexpected, such as a shortnose gar. More likely angling targets, however, are catfish, northern pike, crappie, white bass, perch, large- and smallmouth bass, and tiger muskellunge.

Anglers can catch good numbers of walleye and consistent sizes year-round; the average walleye is 14 to 17 inches. The forage for walleye primarily consists of emerald shiners and gizzard shad; neither of these are comparable to the high-energy rainbow smelt forage in Lake Oahe, which prevents the fish in Francis Case from growing as large as the walleye in Oahe.

Walleye are caught at the upper end of the lake near Ft. Thompson in coldwater conditions in January. Anglers then use light line and a jig tipped with a minnow to catch sluggish fish. This prespawn bite will usually run from January through April, weather permitting.

When a lake is capable of producing smallmouth in the 5- to 6-pound class, it is destined to develop a reputation, and this has happened to some degree at Lake Francis Case. Smallmouth fishing, however, is overshadowed by the interest in walleye. Points, dropoffs, and rocky areas are key places to locate smallmouth.

The northern pike in this lake do not hold a strong tradition, but they do in other reservoirs along the river system. Catfish are caught throughout the reservoir and can grow to fairly good size. Using a stationary bait rig to catch cats is the most popular and successful technique. Francis Case produced the state's 54-pound flathead catfish record, and also the 33-pound tiger muskellunge record.

Lewis and Clark. The smallest of the four main-stem Missouri reservoirs, Lewis and Clark covers 32,000 acres and is probably the most underfished reservoir in the state. It is the only one, however, that boasts smallmouth bass as its prime fishing attraction. This lake produces top-quality smallmouth angling, with a high average daily catch. The upper section of the lake, along with that portion of the Missouri River between Springfield and Fort Randall, has good largemouth fishing and the best smallmouth action in the state. Large stands of bulrushes and winding sandbars create a series of chutes and back bays that harbor plentiful bass.

There's also a good population of walleye and sauger. Because of its smaller size, relatively shallow depths, and high water-exchange rate, the reservoir has had fishery problems, and fish populations fluctuate.

Below Gavins Point Dam is the only place in South Dakota where you can legally take paddlefish. Anglers are required to apply for a tag for this activity, which takes place during a set season.

Glacial Lakes Region

The Glacial Lakes Region stretches from the town of Aberdeen in northeastern South Dakota over to Watertown and down past Sioux Falls. Glaciers carved out roughly 200 lakes here thousands of years ago. The lakes range in size from a few acres to several that cover 16,000 acres (including Thompson, Poinsett, and Waubay Lakes).

Three relatively small rivers drain much of the eastern part of the state. The James River runs a course through both North Dakota and South Dakota and eventually feeds into the Missouri near the southern part of the state. Any fish found in the Missouri are also found in the James.

Most of the lakes provide walleye and saugeye. Saugeye, which are the offspring of a female walleye and male sauger, grow larger than pure sauger; they reach an average size of 5 pounds and inhabit turbid waters.

Many anglers wear waders to cast the shorelines in the spring and fall. When water temperatures are cold enough, walleye cruise and feed in the shallows during the morning, evening, and at night. The best action for wade fishing is usually during May.

Opportunity exists to catch yellow perch that average over a pound in size; some are in the 2-pound class and a few push the 3-pound barrier during a good cycle. Excellent water conditions and a broad-based forage cycle contribute to the abnormal size.

The quality of the Glacial Lakes' yellow perch fishery, and the overall fisheries, is directly related to high-quality water that provides excellent breeding conditions. A low water level and declining water quality will take their toll on these relatively shallow lakes. Lakes Waubay, Thompson, Henry, Whitewood, Preston, and Cattail are a few of the jumbo perch producers.

Northern pike also exist in many of the lakes, but Waubay has the most noted fishery for this species. In early spring, once the ice starts to leave the lakes, anglers can catch pre- and post-spawn pike with spoons and quick-strike dead smelt rigs.

Smallmouth bass were stocked in many eastern South Dakota lakes during the 1980s, and self-sustaining populations are found throughout the region. Popular smallmouth lakes are Clear, Enemy Swim, Pickerel, Poinsett, Kampeska, and Amsden. Amsden is also the only lake in South Dakota that possesses pure-strain muskellunge.

Ice fishing. A particular fishing activity in the Glacial Lakes region happens during the winter after the lakes ice over. Excellent walleye, pike, perch, and crappie angling attract people who might not fish at all during the open-water season. Once the ice is roughly 12 inches thick, anglers drive vehicles onto the frozen lakes, punching holes and searching for fish. A few vehicles fall through the ice nearly every year, and some fatalities occur because of accidents. Ice fishing requires prudence.

As to fishing tactics, anglers use stationary live-bait setups tipped with a minnow, chub, or wax worm, depending on the species they seek. Jigging is also a popular method, used to both attract and trigger fish into hitting the jig or a nearby baited line.

Black Hills Region

The Black Hills region, where roughly 400 miles of streams are actively managed for trout, holds trout promise for South Dakota anglers. Wild brook and brown trout, plus a few rainbows, have acclimated and maintained a self-sustaining population in some streams, although these species were not native to the area. Gold miners brought the fish to the Black Hills from Colorado in 1886.

Castle, Spring, Rapid, and Box Elder Creeks are the principal coldwater streams that not only feed the large lakes but also provide outstanding stream trout fishing. Two stretches of Rapid Creek, one in Rapid City, receive special management and are maintained as "blue-ribbon" fly fishing areas.

Beaver ponds in many of the tributaries in the Black Hills region provide additional remote fishing opportunities for anglers wishing to be absolutely alone. Immeasurable miles of streams run through the Black Hills, where stream anglers can fish for brookies and rainbows away from popular access areas.

The major mountain lakes provide opportunities for trout fishing as well, especially in Pactola, Sheridan, and Deerfield Lakes. Rainbows are a top attraction at Deerfield, which is near Hill City. The dam face and deep channel running parallel to it offer the best shot at splake. Most splake and rainbows in Deerfield average 12 inches long, although there's always a shot at a big splake. Pactola offers excellent opportunity for cutthroat fishing. Sheridan Lake has superb angling for northern pike, yellow perch, and largemouth bass, in addition to trout. For a measure of seclusion, anglers can ply the smaller trout lakes, such as Mitchell Lake, Horsethief Lake, and Slate Creek Dam.

West River Dams

Publicly owned dams on the West River prairie are managed for largemouth bass and panfish. West River stock dams (farm ponds) have produced South Dakota's biggest largemouth bass. The main problem with catching them is finding the waters and the people that own the water. Most of western South Dakota is privately owned. Bass in the 3- to 5-pound class are common, however. Privately owned waters here can sometimes be accessed simply by driving up and asking area ranchers if they have any ponds with fish in them and if they would allow you to wet a line.

Numerous small stock dams on private land throughout the state have been stocked by the Game, Fish and Parks Department under Fish Management Agreements. Permission must be obtained from the private property owner to fish such waters.

Dams also exist on the various National Grasslands, and some hold fishing opportunities; there are several on the Fort Pierre National Grassland. A float tube or small boat has become a common way to fish these small waters.

SOWBUG

Sowbugs are small freshwater crustaceans of the order Isopoda that are a favorite food of trout and other fish. Also known as pillbugs, they are mostly terrestrial or marine. Approximately 130 freshwater species occur in North America. Large numbers of sowbugs are often an indication of organic enrichment.

Sowbugs are dark brown to gray in color and up to 3/4-inch long. They are flattened dorsally and much wider than they are high, with seven pairs of legs and two pairs of antennae, one of which is usually much longer. They move by slowly crawling over surfaces and are sometimes confused with scuds, but they are wider than scuds and walk instead of swim.

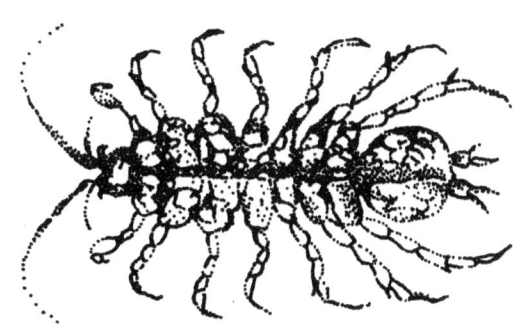

Sowbug, greatly enlarged.

SPADEFISH

Spadefish are distinctively shaped members of the Ephippidae family of mainly tropical and subtropical species. Their bodies are very flattened and nearly as deep as they are long. The first, or spiny, dorsal fin is separate from the second, or soft-rayed, dorsal, which has exceptionally long rays at the front and is matched in size and shape by the anal fin directly beneath it. The body is silvery and has four to six black bands that may be absent in older fish. The broad caudal fin has long rays at the tips of the upper and lower lobes so that the fin is concave. The mouth is small. Juvenile spadefish are black and are known to lie on their side to mimic floating debris.

Species that occur in North American waters and are occasionally encountered by anglers include the Pacific spadefish (*Chaetodipterus zonatus*), which ranges from Southern California to Mexico in the eastern Pacific, and the similar Atlantic spadefish (*C. faber*), which ranges from Massachusetts to Brazil in the western Atlantic and is more abundant in the Caribbean and Florida. The latter is sometimes mistakenly called angelfish; they are also known in Portuguese as *enxada* and in Spanish as *paguara*.

Spadefish travel in large schools, spawn in spring and summer, feed on shrimp and crustaceans, and are found inshore or in nearshore environs, especially around navigational markers, along sandy beaches, in harbors, or over wrecks. They may grow to 15 pounds but usually weigh less than 2 pounds. These fish are good table fare.

SPAIN

Some of Europe's most diverse fishing exists in the southwest, in Spain, where anglers will find a good array of trout fishing in the mountains, some salmon and sea-run trout, and a potpourri of coarse species in many river systems. These offerings are rounded out by opportunities to catch black bass, zander, and pike. In addition, the Canary Islands are home to perhaps the most internationally renowned fishery for big-game species.

With a richly varied topography among its 194,885 square miles, Spain offers more freshwater fishing opportunities than most nonresidents realize. Some 76,000 kilometers of river water courses through Iberia, and many of the waterways have been impounded for hydroelectric purposes, creating large reservoirs. The primary freshwater fish for anglers is brown trout (*trucha común*), but others include Atlantic salmon (*salmón*); sea-run brown trout (*reo*); rainbow trout (*trucha carco iris*); largemouth bass (*perca negra*); pike (*lucio*); zander, or pike-perch (*lucioperca*); carp (*carpa*); tench (*tenca*); barbel (*barbo*); and chub (*cacho*).

Salmon numbers and runs are modest and are concentrated in the Asturias region in the north, fronting the Atlantic. The Eo, Porcia, Esta, Narcea, Sella, Cares, Deva, and Piloña Rivers contain salmon and are accessed through specific reserves, where beats are controlled and hard to access. The season varies according to location but generally runs from early or mid-March through early July.

Sea-run trout are also modest in numbers and found in the northeast in a few rivers in the Galicia region. The Mandeo, Tambre, Sar, Mero, Jubia, and Sor Rivers are most notable; the season is generally from early March through mid-August.

Although trout are the main angling attraction, their populations are widespread. Rainbow trout have been introduced in various waters, but brown trout are more numerous. Most rivers and streams across the northern section of the country, including the Galicia, Asturias, Castilla, Pais Vasco, Navarra, Aragon, and Cataluna regions, support trout. These regions encompass many mountainous areas, including the Cordillera and Cantabrica ranges of the Pyrenees, which extend for some 270 miles and also form Spain's northeastern border with France.

Although the entire northern region is the most prominent brown trout area, two other regions host significant populations of these fish. One is in the middle of the country in rivers and streams emanating from the Sierra de Gredos, Sierra de Guadaramma, and Sierra de Albarracin ranges, respectively northwest, north, and northeast of the capital city of Madrid. Most of these flow to the Duero River, a large waterway that flows westerly to the Atlantic. The second region is in the mountainous area of southern Spain, especially in the many flows between the cities of Granada and Albacete in the Sierra de Segura range.

Fishing for coarse species is particularly popular among Spaniards and occurs especially in the central tableland in slower rivers and stillwaters. Waters in the vicinity of Madrid, south of Cuenca, north of Granada, near Linares, and north and west of Ciudad Real are the focal points.

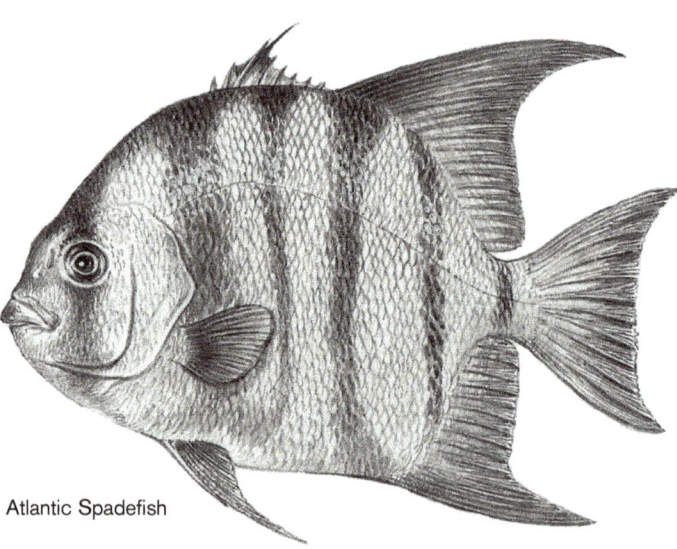
Atlantic Spadefish

Spaniards are showing a growing interest in largemouth bass, which were introduced to Spain and have flourished in many impoundments. Large lakes with bass include Ricobayo north of the city of Zamora, Almendra northeast of Salamanca, Alcántara north of Caceres, Orellana west of Ciudad Real, the backwaters of the Rio Guadalquivir southwest of Sevilla, Mequinenza and Ribarroja south of Lerida, Alarcón and Contreras south of Cuenca, and Entrepeñas and Buendía east of Guadalajara. Numerous smaller bass waters exist, including some near Madrid and Granada.

Roughly 88 percent of Spain is bordered by saltwater. This includes the Bay of Biscay on the north, some 770 kilometers of the Atlantic on the west and south, and some 1,660 kilometers of the Mediterranean on the south and west. Although opportunities for sportfishing exist, there is little to attract the visiting angler. The narrow coastal plain has many rocky headlands and few good harbors, the exceptions being Barcelona along the Mediterranean and several places along the Galician coast on the Atlantic. Thus saltwater angling efforts are directed primarily at the Canary Islands.

Canary Islands

The Canary Islands are situated roughly 80 miles off the northwest coast of Africa in the Canary basin of the eastern Atlantic, which is at roughly the same latitude as Daytona Beach, Florida, in the western Atlantic. There are seven islands in all, and they aren't far from the Madeiras and the Azores, which have produced monster blue marlin, yellowfin tuna, and bigeye tuna throughout the 1990s.

The Canaries, of course, are better known for sun, fun, and frolicking than they are for fishing. They do not offer a large fleet of modern sportfishing boats, but they do have some of the large blue marlin (and blues of a large average size), for which this region of the North Atlantic is noted. This is because the Canaries are situated on a shelf where the water drops off to awe-inspiring depths. The drop is steep not far from shore—there's a 1,200-foot dropoff about 5 miles out—and creates an upwelling. These shelves and the upwelling, coupled with the Canarian Current, attract pelagic species to these waters. June through October is the preferred fishing period, and the island of Lanzarote provides chartering opportunities.

As with other places in the eastern waters of the North and South Atlantic, where local fisheries concentrate on inshore waters and traditional commercial pursuits focused on sustenance, there is much less effort devoted to rod-and-reel clashes with the big, speedy, powerful denizens of the deep than there is in many other waters. But these trends have slowly been changing, and big-game sportfishing is on the rise here.

The record books show that the Canary Islands currently possess three line-class bigeye tuna records. The largest is a 363-pounder taken on 130-pound tackle. In addition, the waters have produced a record 897-pound bluefin tuna on 50-pound line, one Atlantic blue marlin line-class record, and five Atlantic bonito and two albacore records (including the all-tackle record-holding 88-pound albacore).

How big the marlin actually get is anyone's guess, but reports say that blues of 1,300 and 1,600 pounds have been registered by commercial fishermen, as well as bluefin to 1,200 pounds and a broadbill swordfish of 691 pounds. Anglers do encounter yellowfin and bigeye tuna in the 200-pound class, sometimes in schools, and some success has been registered with smaller swordfish at night, although the angling is often spotty, with streaks of activity for both tuna and billfish.

In September 1987, the Canaries produced their first 1,000-pound blue marlin on rod and reel, and since then numerous 800- to 1,000-pounders have been tagged and released, and a few granders landed. The average size of these blues approaches the 500-pound range.

SPAWN BAG

A mesh enclosure for a small group of fish eggs. Also known as a spawn sack, it is commonly used in river fishing for coho and chinook salmon and steelhead.
See: Natural Bait.

SPAWNING

The reproduction activities of fish.
See: Fish.

SPAWNING RUN

The migratory movement of fish related to spawning, mostly used with reference to fish that move up rivers and streams.
See: Fish.

SPEARFISH

Longbill Spearfish *Tetrapturus pfluegeri*.
   Other names—longnose spearfish, Atlantic longbill spearfish; French: *makaire becune;* Japanese: *kuchinaga, kuchinagafuura;* Portuguese: *espadim bicudo;* Spanish: *aguja picuda*.

Shortbill Spearfish *Tetrapturus angustirostris*.
   Other names—shortnose spearfish; Arabic: *kheil;* Hawaiian: *a'u;* Japanese: *fûraikajiki*.

Mediterranean Spearfish *Tetrapturus belone*.
Other names—French: *aguglia impériale;* Italian: *acura imperiale, aguglia pelerana*.

   These species are lesser-known and small members of the Istiophoridae family of billfish that are also referred to as slender spearfish. They are pelagic, offshore, deep-water fish that appear

Longbill Spearfish

to be available all year in small numbers but are infrequently encountered by anglers in most parts of their range. They are of some commercial value, usually as incidental catch, and are fairly good eating, although the flesh is dark.

Identification. Spearfish can be distinguished from other billfish by a slender, lightweight body, short bill, and a dorsal fin that is highest anteriorly (higher than in marlin and lower than in the sailfish). The vent is located well in front of the anal fin; in all other billfish, the vent is located close to the anal fin. The bill of the shortbill spearfish is barely longer than its lower jaw, whereas in the longbill spearfish it is about twice as long, but it is still noticeably short when compared to that in other billfish. The pectoral fins of the shortbill and Mediterranean spearfish barely reach to the curve of the lateral line. In the longbill spearfish, they extend beyond the curve. The longbill spearfish has more elements (45 to 53) in the first dorsal fin than any other Atlantic billfish, although it may appear similar to the white marlin *(see: marlin, white)*. The shortbill spearfish of the Pacific has approximately the same count (47 to 50 elements), but the Mediterranean spearfish has fewer (39 to 46). The lateral line is single and arches above the pectoral fins. The dorsal fin is bright blue and has no spots. The vertical bars on the body are never as prominent as in other billfish and may show only slightly or not at all.

Some scientists believe that a fourth species of spearfish *(Tetrapturus georgei)* exists. Called the roundscale spearfish *(marlin peto* in Spanish), it occurs around Sicily, Portugal, and Spain and is said to resemble the so-called hatchet marlin. The hatchet marlin, which has not been named scientifically, has not yet been proven to be a separate species and is presently considered a variation of the white marlin, which may also be the fate of the roundscale spearfish.

Size/Age. Available data indicate that the longbill spearfish matures by the age of 2 and rarely lives past age 3. Its maximum longevity may be age 4 to 5. The all-tackle world record for the longbill spearfish is a fish of 94 pounds, 12 ounces, and for the Mediterranean spearfish is 90 pounds, 13 ounces.

Distribution. Spearfish are cosmopolitan but nowhere are they abundant. The longbill spearfish is known to occur in the northwest Atlantic from New Jersey to Venezuela, including the Gulf of Mexico. Japanese longliners have also recorded its occurrence in the north-central Atlantic, in the south Atlantic, and off South Africa. The shortbill spearfish is known in the Pacific and Indian Oceans. It is not reported to occur in the Mediterranean but has been captured in the Atlantic Ocean west of the Cape of Good Hope, South Africa. The Mediterranean spearfish is known to occur only in the Mediterranean Sea. The Canary Islands and Hawaii have produced a number of record-setting specimens.

Food and feeding habits. Spearfish feed at or near the surface, mainly on small and medium-size fish and squid, including dolphin, sauries, flyingfish, and needlefish.

Angling. The fishing methods to use for these species are the same as for other billfish, although lighter tackle, as would be used for white marlin or sailfish, is more appropriate. Most catches are incidental.

See: Big-Game Fishing; Billfish; Offshore Fishing.

SPEARFISHING

(1) The taking of fish with a handheld spear or spear gun by a snorkeler or diver while swimming in the water. Spearfishing is generally legal in saltwater; the legality varies in freshwater. Where allowed, spearfishing is regulated by fisheries agencies, usually requires a fishing license, is subject to seasons, and is usually restricted to certain species. Although spearfishing is popular with some snorkelers and divers and, where legal, is considered a form of recreational fishing, it is not widely practiced and is not treated as sportfishing by the general angling community.

(2) An alternate term for spearing *(see)*, the taking of fish with a handheld prong, harpoonlike device, or spear.

SPEARING

Taking fish with a handheld prong, harpoonlike device, or spear, any of which may also be known as a gig. These devices are meant to spear or impale fish by means of a pronged or barbed instrument, which is attached to a rigid object such as a pole. Also known in some places as gigging, spearing is primarily a freshwater activity and one that has been practiced traditionally to procure food. The legality today varies in freshwater and is regulated by fisheries agencies; it usually requires a fishing license, is subject to seasons, and may be restricted to certain species. In some locales, a spear must be attached to a tethered line.

Eels and suckers are among the fish subject to spearing in streams and creeks, but spearing is also practiced for other species, especially rough fish such as carp, buffalo, and bullhead. It is also practiced in northern locales during the winter, usually on frozen lakes in small shanties (fish houses or dark houses) that have been darkened to enhance visibility through the water. Although spearing is still practiced and, where legal, is considered a form of recreational fishing, it is not widely employed and is not treated as sportfishing by the general angling community.
See: Spearfishing.

SPEARING
A term for silversides (see) of the Atlantic coast.

SPECIES
A group of similar fish that can freely interbreed; similar species make up a genus.
See: Fish; Fisheries Management.

SPECIMEN
A term predominantly used by British coarse anglers to refer to a large or trophy-size representative of a particular species. Specimens are fish that are above average in size, and people who specialize in pursuing such individual fish are called specimen hunters.

SPECK
A term primarily used in southern parts of the United States for crappie (see), which are often also called speckled perch, although they are not a true perch.

SPECKLED PERCH
A term primarily used in southern parts of the United States for crappie (see), which are not a true perch. They may also be called specks.

SPECKLED TROUT
(1) A term primarily used in northeastern parts of the United States and eastern Canada for brook trout. They may also be called squaretails.
See: Trout, Brook.

(2) A common alternative term for spotted seatrout.
See: Seatrout, Spotted.

SPEED GAUGE
Although a speedometer measures the velocity of a moving boat, it is often not precise enough for fishing usage, especially trolling, or not capable of depicting slow-speed measurements. Anglers who troll use various instruments, referred to as speed gauges, speed sensors, or speed indicators, to accomplish this. These include electronic instruments fitted with a paddlewheel, which is secured to the boat transom flush to the hull; global positioning (GPS) navigational devices, which measure speed via distance traveled over time; and by nonelectronic drag-weight gauges, which measure speed relative to markings on a plate. They may also include a standard tachometer, which measures engine rpm, and which can be used to gauge relative speed, although this is very imprecise. Additionally, there are devices, attached to downrigger weights, which measure via paddlewheel the speed of the lure at the depth of the downrigger weight. This is sometimes different than surface speed.

The most common dedicated speed gauges are electronic models that measure surface speed; these are either stand-alone products or accessory elements incorporated into sonar instruments. They are not generally accurate above about 50 mph but are excellent for measuring trolling speed. As a boat moves over the water's surface, the drag of the water turns the unit's paddlewheel, which is mounted on the transom of the boat. One of the wheel's paddles contains a piece of magnetic metal that triggers a sensor on the wheel's stationary frame with each revolution of the wheel. The electronic speedometer simply counts the number of times its sensor is triggered and uses the wheel's rpm to calculate speed.

The mounting position of the paddlewheel sensor is critical. Like a sonar transducer, it must receive an uninterrupted flow of smooth water, free of turbulence and air bubble streams at all speeds. Don't mount it behind hull strakes or ribs, or directly in front of the engine's lower unit. The prop may pull extra water past the wheel giving an artificially high speed reading. Mounting the wheel's bracket too high or low will also cause inaccurate readings.

Maintaining a consistent boat speed can be critical to trolling success, and even with these potential problems, the electronic speedometer is hard to beat. Conventional boat speedometers measure water pressure picked up by a tube mounted on the transom or built into an engine's lower unit. They don't generally work below 5 to 10 mph and are useless for trolling. Even the speed-over-ground readings of nondifferential GPS may not be as accurate as a paddlewheel-driven electronic speedometer at trolling speed. If, for instance, you're trolling north at $1^1/_2$ mph and the GPS system's selective availability feature is falsely moving your position south at 2 mph, speed accuracy is out the window (see: GPS).

Nevertheless, dedicated paddlewheel speed gauges vary from one brand to the next, although some can be calibrated. Boat speed is influenced by a host of factors, making exact speed comparisons between boats with paddlewheel speed gauges difficult, no matter which gauge is used. Incidentally, since accuracy is dependent upon the speed differential between the boat's hull and the surface of the water, things that make the surface of the water move can cause erroneous speed readings. Wind actually moves the surface of the water and a boat traveling with the wind will show a slower speed than a boat moving against it at the same true speed over the bottom. A boat moving with a river's current will also have a slower speed reading than when moving against it. It is possible to be moving with a swift current downriver and yet show no reading on the speed gauge because the paddle is either not turning forward or barely turning.
See: Trolling.

SPENTWING
A dry fly that imitates a mayfly spinner that has fallen on the water with its wings outstretched.

SPEY ROD
A long, two-handed fly rod, named after Scotland's River Spey, preferred by some European casters; this type of rod may also be called a Euro rod or salmon rod.
See: Flycasting Tackle.

SPIDER HITCH KNOT
A double-line knot primarily associated with saltwater fishing, especially the use of heavy leaders and big-game angling, and used as a quick-tie replacement for the Bimini Twist.
See: Knots, Fishing.

SPIKE
A rod-holding tube, also known as a sand spike *(see)* and pointed at one end for insertion into the sand, used by surf anglers to secure a rod.
See: Surf Fishing.

SPINCASTING REEL
See: Spinning Tackle.

SPINCASTING ROD
See: Rod, Fishing; Spincasting Tackle.

SPINCASTING TACKLE
Spincasting tackle is arguably the easiest type of fishing tackle to learn to master. While suited to a variety of light- to medium-duty fishing applications, sizing practicalities of the spincasting reel ultimately limit the application of the tackle due to line capacity constraints and mechanical disadvantages.

Spincasting tackle, which is often referred to as spincast tackle, is characterized by a front-cover reel with a hole or opening through which line passes. Line is wound on a stationary spool under the cover or hood, and a button is used to release the line. This is distinctive from other tackle forms, whose reel design and geometry overcome the line capacity restraints characteristic of spincasting products. Those forms include baitcasting tackle *(see)* and conventional tackle *(see)*, both of which recover line via a revolving spool; spinning tackle *(see)*, which features a stationary spool and a revolving line winding bail; and flycasting tackle *(see)*, which has a revolving spool but a much narrower application. The spincasting reel is also distinctive from other tackle forms in that its design and geometry inherently lacks cranking power, although this limitation is not serious for the typical light- to medium-duty applications for which this style of reel is intended.

This is reflected in the fact that spincasting tackle is widely used across North America, and ranks first in total number of units sold annually, Nevertheless, it is the stepchild of fishing equipment. It is seldom given serious consideration in popular publications and virtually overlooked by avid or broadly experienced anglers, some of whom have never used it. Yet beginning anglers of all ages, as well as casual anglers, are drawn to spincasting tackle, largely because it is the simplest of all tackle types to use. A five-year-old can learn to use spincasting tackle in a short time but would have problems with another type of tackle. People are also drawn to it because it is durable, adequate for the majority of their angling activities, and relatively inexpensive. The fact that most spincasting reels come pre-spooled with line eliminates the most basic rigging problem.

Mostly employed in light freshwater fishing applications, spincasting tackle, to many people, is associated with less arduous and less intense fishing activities, particularly stillfishing *(see)*. Some people believe—erroneously—that this gear is only meant for panfish and catfish angling, or for fishing with bait and a float. Usage really depends on the individual's abilities and preferences, and on the grade of equipment.

Despite their popularity for freshwater fishing, very few spincasting reels are used in saltwater. Spincasting reels targeted for saltwater applications are really high line capacity freshwater reels whose metal components have been replaced with stainless steel components to prevent corrosion. The fact that most spincasting reel components are enclosed makes cleaning the reel with freshwater a challenging task. Additionally, relatively low line capacities and reduced crank power make them a rarity for saltwater applications.

In part, the lesser esteem that has befallen spincasting tackle is due to the fact that the spincasting reel of the past had modest to poor cranking power, inferior drag capability, and perceived limited casting accuracy and range. That has changed somewhat with today's higher-end products. Many of the elements of today's better spincasting reels now rival spinning and baitcasting reels in the quality of features and in their applicability to varied freshwater fishing activities.

Nevertheless, a primary constraint to the spincasting reel category is relatively low line capacity. Spincasting tackle is limited to reels that hold less than 150 yards of 25-pound line; most, in fact, hold far less line of much lighter strength, and their limits in this regard in part explain why spincasting reels are typically pre-spooled by the manufacturer. Baitcasting and spinning reels are available that operate with much greater line capacities. Additionally, the spool of a spincasting reel, which is enclosed by the front cover, makes the reel easier to use but also creates a misperception that the line cannot be easily feathered on the cast to control accuracy. Furthermore, because the line on the spool is not in constant view of the angler, several line-related functional problems can unknowingly develop. Too much line, too little line, tangled, frayed, or twisted line are more difficult to detect with spincasting reels than in reel types with open spools.

The gearing system on spincasting reels is similar to the gearing system on spinning reels. Both transfer crank handle rotational forces through a 90-degree bend to the reel's mechanism that wraps line on the spool. This is accomplished through a gear system capable of converting motion between two 90-degree shafts. In comparison, baitcasting reels transfer motion from the crank handle directly to the revolving spool through two parallel shafts. Of the three categories of fishing equipment, spincasting reels display the most inherent limitations in gearing efficiency, and many anglers feel that it is more difficult to retrieve identical weights with a spincasting reel than with a spinning or baitcasting reel. These constraints are further explored in the gearing section that follows.

There are some other limitations to spincasting reels. Spincasting reels have more areas that come in contact with the line during casting than spinning or baitcasting reels. These contact areas impart friction to the line, thus reducing the potential casting distance. Line flows freely off the end of a spinning reel, only hitting the front flange of the spool before reaching the first line guide (stripper guide) on the rod. In contrast, line on a spincasting reel comes in contact with similar components, plus the inside surface of the front cover and the edges of the protective front cover line guide as it exits the reel. This friction reduces casting distance and cranking power. Thus, casting distance is generally greater on spinning reels than spincasting reels. Spincasting and spinning reels both inherently have the capability to cast further distances than baitcasting reels—compliments of a stationary spool versus the revolving spool on baitcasting reels.

There is a perception among anglers that accuracy with spincasting tackle is not very good, but this is often a function of poor casting technique, mismatched tackle, or both.

Some exhibition casters are remarkably accurate with conventional spincasting tackle, more so than they would be with other equipment, simply because they've mastered all of the elements of the spincasting game and have properly matched gear. And some of the best European match tournament anglers use specialized spincasting reels with rods worth thousands of dollars, because of the ease with which the reel can be controlled. The typical angler, however, uses spincasting tackle primarily in situations where accuracy and distance are not critical, and where the species of fish sought are usually small, which tends to reinforce the perception that accuracy is not an attribute of this equipment.

As with any type of tackle, accuracy is really a function of practice and using the right technique. In theory, baitcasting reels are the most accurate because the angler can easily be in constant contact with the revolving spool which controls the line. The spool can be slowed or stopped at any point. The spincasting reel has the capability of being the next most accurate—by using the forefinger to contact the line as it exits the front cover, an angler is in almost constant contact with the line. Because the line is making a loop as it exits the front cover, in theory, the angler may not be in constant contact with the line as would be possible when using a baitcasting reel. In addition, hand position on most spincasting reels is the same as it is on baitcasting reels, making the transition from using spincasting tackle to baitcasting tackle easier. The third most accurate gear, in theory, is the spinning reel. Although the line departing a spinning reel can be feathered with the angler's forefinger, that line is traveling in a larger loop than on a spincasting reel, therefore, the angler is not in contact with the line as continuously as on spincasting reels, which have a much smaller line loop.

Rods play an important part in matching fishing application. Given a proper matching of rod, reel, and line diameter for the intended lure size, spincasting anglers have the equipment to rival even the most skilled baitcasting angler in casting accuracy, and they have little difficulty casting ultralight lures for trout and panfish.

As with most other tackle types, spincasting gear varies widely in quality; some models are better suited to certain fishing activity than others. Some reels sport features that make them suitable to achieving casting distance, reducing line twist,

Some prehistoric sharks had bizarre features; Stethacantus had a brush of external teeth on a rigid massive dorsal fin, while Damocles serratus had a rigid, serrated, forward-pointing dorsal spine.

making fast or slow (power) retrieves, instantly engaging the anti-reverse, back-reeling, being able to indicate strikes, and having interchangeable right or left retrieves. Some hybrid models even reside under the rod, featuring a casting trigger instead of a button, making them more like a spinning reel. These products are used on spinning rods instead of spincasting rods.

A product of the mid-twentieth century, spincasting gear is the youngest of all types of tackle. It fills an important role in the marketplace, and deserves more respect than it is usually accorded.

It was fisherman R. D. Hull who, in the fall of 1947, convinced the Oklahoma-based Zero Hour Bomb Company, a firm that was in need of new direction after World War II and which manufactured explosive timing devices used in oil production, to tool up to produce his new type of fishing reel. A west Texas watchmaker, Hull was said to be frustrated with backlash problems in baitcasting reels, and allegedly got the idea for the prototype of a spincasting reel while in a grocery store, observing a clerk wrapping a meat package. The string for wrapping the package was pulled from a stationary spool. Hull created a contraption that looked like a tin can with a hole in both ends.

The contraption was designed with a fixed spool in mind, so that line would come off it much the way that the wrapping string came off its spool in the grocery store, and, most importantly, wouldn't backlash.

It is not known whether officials at the Zero Hour Bomb Company were anglers, but they decided to produce Hull's new reel under the acronym ZEBCO. In June of 1949, 25 handmade Zebco Standards—the first spincasting reels—were built on the first day of production. The manufacturer ceased building explosive timing devices and concentrated on fishing reels.

With a good deal of promotional help over the following decade, the spincasting reel surged in popularity. In 1955, Zebco began production of their now infamous 33 model spincasting reel (then called a closed-face spinning reel). It was priced at $19.95, a hefty sum at a time when gasoline was about 25 cents a gallon and soda pop was 5 cents a bottle. That model reel is still in production today, and still costs under $20. In 1961, Zebco produced one of its other infamous spincasting models, the 202, which is also still in production and believed to be the largest selling reel in the history of fishing, with over 50 million sold. The company that allied itself with R. D. Hull and the contraption that would be known as a spincasting reel was turning into one of the giants in the world of sportfishing tackle.

The spincasting reel, which did not use a revolving spool for casting or line retrieval, came along at the same time that the previously invented European spinning reel was emerging in North America, and concurrent with the development of nylon monofilament fishing line *(see: line)* and the evolution of fiberglass fishing rods. It offered easier use for casters than the baitcasting (levelwind) reels then available, which at that time caused an annoying and frustrating backlash (line tangling) for most anglers on every fourth or fifth cast.

At the time of the emergence of both spinning and spincasting tackle, anglers primarily used levelwind or baitcasting gear, flycasting tackle, and conventional or big-game tackle for respective applications. But there was a lack of equipment that was easy for anyone to use and which could handle varied angling activity, especially the casting of various weighted objects. Both spinning and spincasting reels filled that void, and eventually played a huge role in a fishing participation boom that has extended to the present day.

In the early 1950s, the reels that are presently referred to as spinning models were then called open-faced spinning or, less often, open-faced reels. The reels that are referred to today as spincasting were then called closed-faced spinning, or closed-faced reels. This terminology has caused some confusions in literature, although the intentions are understandable; the early nomenclature was arguably more appropriate than what is used in today's parlance.

Spinning reels all feature an exposed stationary spool and an exposed line pickup and line-winding

The contraption nailed to this board in 1947 was the prototype of the first production spincasting reel, which is shown in the lower right and was made in 1949.

bail arm; thus, it was common in the early days of their existence for these to be called open-faced reels. Spincasting reels all feature a stationary spool, a line pickup, and a line-winding mechanism that are covered by a cone or hood; thus, it was common for these to initially be called closed-face reels. Both types of reel feature a spool that remains stationary when line is wound, or spun, around it, and when it is unwound during casting. However, during the operation of the drag, the spools on both categories of reels generally rotate. This is different than baitcasting and conventional reels, whose spools turn and cause the line to wind and unwind. Essentially, any reel with an exposed stationary spool is a spinning reel, and any reel with a covered stationary spool is a spincasting reel.

Over the years, covered stationary spool reels became predominantly known and categorized simply as spincasting (or spincast) reels. Perhaps this was an outgrowth of the use of the word baitcasting to describe levelwind revolving spool reels. If this seems confusing, it is.

At the risk of further confusion, it should be pointed out that another distinguishing difference between spinning and spincasting reels is that the former always sit underneath the rod seat, while the latter usually sit atop the rod seat. Some hybrid spincasting reels sit underneath the rod handle, but they have a covered stationary

This Zebco reel is typical of spincasting reels; note the star drag on the handle shaft, the conelike hood, and the pushbutton line release.

spool, and otherwise basically function like a conventional spincasting reel. These may actually be easier for many people to use than the conventional spincasting reels, and are similar in operation to spinning reels.

Finally, it is worth noting that a major difference between spincasting and other reel types is the ability to change line. Although changing line on a spincasting reel is not actually difficult, it is less easy with this reel than with spinning or baitcasting products because the others have easier access to the spool. On spincasting reels, the spool is shrouded by a spinner head and both are underneath a front cover. To get to the spool you have to remove the cover and raise the spinner head (which might also be referred to as an internal rotor). This is one reason all spincasting reels come from the manufacturer pre-spooled with an appropriate strength and length of line. Another reason is that performance is greatly affected by line limpness and diameter. The spincasting reel is the least tolerant of all reel types in this regard and can fail to function with improper line. Yet another reason for pre-spooling, and one that plays to the greatest strength of spincasting reels in the marketplace, is that it makes them more appealing to the less experienced angler. There are virtually no spinning or baitcasting reels pre-spooled with line by the manufacturer. This interesting difference says a lot.

General Operation

Spincasting reels range from ultralight models weighing a few ounces and used with 4-pound line, to heavy freshwater and light saltwater models weighing between 15 and 17 ounces and used with 20- to 25-pound line; they generally work best when the terminal gear weighs between $1/4$ and $3/4$ ounce. They are also known as American spinning reels, spincasting reels, spincast reels, spin-cast reels, and closed-face spinning reels, and they generally mount on top of the rod handle (rod seat), similar to baitcasting reels. This is evidently due to the fact that when spincasting reels were first created, most nonfly and nonconventional casting rod handles were of the recessed-seat type suitable for use with revolving spool reels. Those reels sat atop the rod and had a right-handed retrieve. Spincasting reels followed suit.

The spincasting reel usually has a pushbutton that controls the release of line, a stationary spool that line is wound around by a spinner head with a line pickup pin, and a round or cone-shaped cover with an opening for line to pass through. It also has an adjustable drag that is controlled mostly by a thumb wheel or star wheel, and either a single or dual grip handle.

In use, with the back of the reel facing the angler, the pushbutton is depressed by the thumb, which releases the line for casting yet holds it in place until the thumb is removed from the button. When the button is released, line flows off the spool, through the opening in the reel hood, or cover, and out through the guides, carried by the weight of the object at the terminal end of the line. To retrieve the line, the handle is rotated forward, which causes the pickup pin to turn and catch the line under the hood, winding it around the concealed spool.

These are the basic elements of operating a spincasting reel, although drag and anti-reverse features come into play as well, and the general design, style, and feel of each product has relevance to its use.

Casting/Line Release Features

Pushbutton. The operation of a spincasting reel essentially starts with depressing the pushbutton, a component that is usually touched with the thumb and frequently called the thumb button. This releases the line and allows it to come off the spool. As long as the pushbutton is fully depressed, it acts as a brake and keeps the line in place. When tension on the button is released, the line flows unimpeded off the spool, through the opening in the cover, and out the line guides of the rod. A pushbutton should be easy to activate, with little force necessary, and virtually all of them are.

In spincasting reels, when you press the pushbutton, the line is compressed between the inside of the cover and the external surface of the rotor (spinner head). The line is sandwiched between these two components until the pushbutton is released. On some higher quality reels, a brake ring is located on the external surface of the rotor or spinner head. On these models, the brake ring holds the line against the front cover instead of the surface of the spinner head itself. The brake ring is typically molded from a softer rubber or plastic material. Material selection for this component is very critical. A soft material is best so that the line is not damaged when it is pressed against the front cover, yet the material must also resist being cut or permanently deformed by the line. Those spincasting reels without a brake ring have metal to metal contact between the spinner head and front cover, which compresses the line and has the potential to damage it.

When the pushbutton is pressed, it also causes a line pickup pin to drop out of the way. The pickup pin winds line onto the spool. As long as the pin is extended in the retrieve position, it holds line in place and you can't cast or let line out (except when the drag functions). Thus, pressing the pushbutton causes the pickup pin to drop out of the way, moves the spinner head forward, and sandwiches the line between the spinner head and the inside cover, so that in the casting motion the lure doesn't drop to the ground. When you release the pushbutton, the spinner head drops back, which allows the line to flow freely off the spool. Naturally, this works the same when you are simply releasing line rather than casting, as might be done when lowering bait or a jig; you just press the pushbutton and let go of it to let line flow from the reel. At this point, and until you turn the handle, line is free to flow off the spool, and the reel is said to be in freespool.

Freespool is a term commonly used to refer to that state when line is able to freely unwind from the spool; it does not literally mean that the spool of the reel can freely rotate. The term is something of a carryover from the use of baitcasting and conventional tackle. In these types of tackle, the spool does revolve to release line, and freespool really does indicate that the spool is free to rotate to easily release line. With spincasting reels, in freespool the gears are engaged and the pickup pin has just been moved out of the way so that line can flow off the spool. In some of the very early model spincasting reels, the gears actually did separate or disengage from each other in the cast position.

Although the pushbutton is by far the typical means of changing the reel from the retrieve to the cast position, there are some variations. A common one in use today is a trigger release, which is used on spincasting reels that mount under the rod handle, facing away from the angler, and are cast more like a spinning reel than a conventional spincasting reel. These operate somewhat like pushbuttons, except that a trigger, which is pulled by the index finger, performs the function of a button. Pulling the trigger up is like pushing a thumb button in. This variation makes a spincasting reel with a trigger release something of a crossover between a spinning reel and a spincasting reel. Although most of this type of tackle is very good quality and very easy to use, there is not a big market demand for it.

Another version of spincasting reel, virtually unknown in North America but used by expert match tournament anglers in Europe, also mounts under the rod handle and has a button on the front nose that releases the line; the button is touched by the forefinger. Old spincasting reels had a post on top of the reel that you pushed down to disengage the gear set (this post, or button, really did disengage the gear sets; thumb buttons and triggers today do not); when you cast the reel, the center shaft gear still rotated. Instead of line just coming off the spool, the center shaft gear rotated and there was a flywheel on the back of the reel so you could feather the flywheel. To engage it, you pushed the handle in toward the reel. The thumb button is a little bit different than the original approach to line release in spincasting reels, but an easier one.

Cover/Hood. When making a cast with a spincasting reel, it is important that as the line comes off the spool and heads out the rod, it does not touch very many components. Each component it touches adds friction and decreases distance.

Most spincasting reels feature a rounded or cone-shaped hood or front cover that encloses the line spool and other parts. When the line comes off the fairly narrow spool, it forms a loop. Most rounded and cone-shaped front covers have a hole at the front of the reel for line passage. It is important that as the line comes off the spool the loop is necked down quickly to form a straight or nearly straight stream as it goes through this hole and out to the first rod guide. The large first guide on a spinning rod serves this necking-down function, and the design of most spincasting reel covers does the same thing.

Some spincasting reels have a rounded cover with a large open area at the front of the reel. This allows the line to come off the spool without encountering the inside of the cover. The larger coils of line that flow off the reel have to be necked down at the first rod guide, much like a spinning reel. If the line is properly controlled between the reel exit and the first rod guide, this system has the potential to generate longer casts than other types of front covers. However, to realize this increased casting distance, the rod line guides would have to be of the large variety associated with those found on spinning rods. If they are not, having a large line exit on the cover is counterproductive. In reality, properly shaped front covers, with small holes for the line to exit, work best with today's casting rods, which sport smaller line guides.

Spool size/Capacity. The amount of line on a reel spool, in addition to the size of the spool, are also key factors in casting. Spool size on spincasting reels is primarily governed by line capacity and practicality of the overall reel size. As line capacity is increased, the reel becomes longer to compensate for a wider spool, or bigger in diameter to compensate for a bigger diameter spool. If a longer spool is used, a spool oscillation system is required—like spinning reels—to evenly lay the line across the width of the spool. An oscillation system makes the reel even longer. Additionally, the bigger diameter spools have a limitation. Line must travel from the center hub of the spool over the front flange of the spool and out the reel. As this distance increases, friction on the line increases, dramatically decreasing casting distance.

Overall reel sizing is more a concern with spincasting reels than spinning reels because of the balance issue. With a spincasting reel perched on top of a rod, gravity causes the reel and rod to naturally rotate so that the reel is upside down. The larger and heavier the reel, the more difficult it is to comfortably balance the reel right side up. Spinning reels are naturally positioned underneath the rod, so that this tendency to rotate is avoided.

Spincasting reels generally have less line capacity than spinning reels for the reasons already listed. Most spincasting reels hold a maximum of 100 yards of the recommended line diameter. Typically, a spincasting reel user does not cast a distance of more than 30 yards, and more frequently only 15 to 20 yards. However, when the line gets low on a spincasting reel, which happens through regular use (breaking some off, retying knots, and so on), an angler may not realize it as readily as when using other types of tackle with constantly visible spools. Obviously, the cover can be removed to readily check line capacity, but many people just don't do this and can suddenly discover that they are so low on line that they cannot cast a proper distance (or would be subject to a crisis if they caught a large fish that took line off the drag).

Spincasting reel spools are narrow and shallow, and the line lays fairly uniformly on them. A few spincasting reels have over-wrapping or oscillating line-winding to keep more line on the top surface near the edge of the spool. European match reels are almost always of this variety, as are some of the higher quality spincasting reels in the North American market.

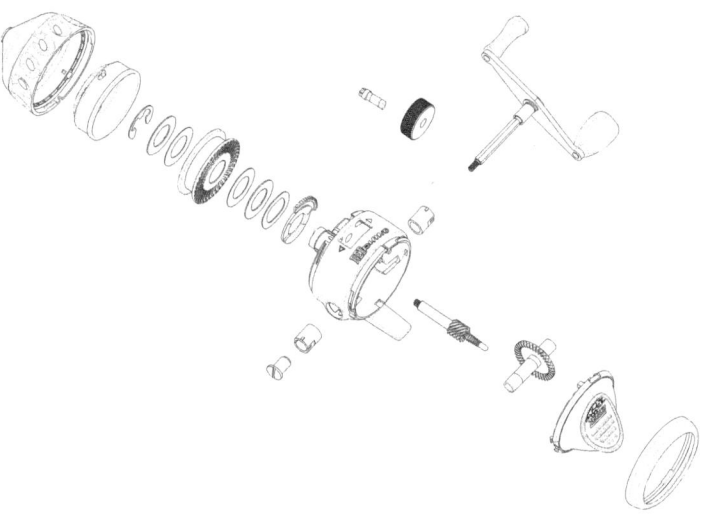

All of the parts of a Zebco Red Rhino spincasting reel are shown here; this product features a soft-touch thumb pad release, large helical gears, and continuous anti-reverse.

When a spool is wider, which means that more line is near the surface, it casts better, because the line won't have to make as sharp an angle as it comes off the spool. If you have a thin, deep spool, and you cast 30 yards off the spool, the line pulls down deeper as it comes off the spool than it would with a wider spool. Naturally, this is compensated to some extent by how full the spool is with line to start. Some spincasting reels oscillate the spool to lay line more evenly, as is done on spinning reels, but the value of this is dubious in spincasting reels due to their generally shallow and narrow spools. It does put more cost into the reel, and the gain in casting distance is not likely to be that significant or of that much value to spincasting tackle users.

Retrieving/Line Recovery Features

Line pickup. When you turn the handle on a spincasting reel, the gears rotate and cause the internal rotor, or spinner head, to revolve. This allows a line pickup pin to wind line on the stationary spool. Some reels have multiple pins to hasten pickup.

The pickup pins on some reels are ceramic, and on others stainless steel. Ceramic (the same type of material used for most rod guides) has a low friction surface and does not get cut by line. Fishing line can pick up assorted matter on its surface and is extremely abrasive. Held under tension, and pulled back and forth across a surface, it can cut a groove in brass, soft steels, and other materials. Some stainless steel holds up pretty well, although it is not as smooth as ceramic. Some manufacturers use hard chrome-plated spinner heads and ceramic pickup pins to help prevent the line from cutting those mechanisms and to help reduce some of the friction in the retrieve.

One of the things that is important in the start of the retrieval motion is how fast the pickup pin engages. This is generally measured by the degrees of rotation the handle must be rotated through before the reel reengages and line starts wrapping on the spool. A faster engagement is an advantage in certain fishing situations. If a fish strikes when the reel is not in the retrieve mode, the speed at which it can be converted to the retrieve mode may be the difference between catching and missing the fish. The less rotation there is before engagement, the better.

Engagement speed is partly affected by numerical gear ratio. The faster the gear ratio, the faster the pickup pin is going to reengage. It is also affected by the number of cams on the top surface of the spool boss. In spincasting reels, there is a cammed surface on the end of the spool boss (a cylindrical extension of the body around which the spool rotates). One surface of the pickup arm is in continuous contact with the outer surface of the spool boss. When this surface of the pickup arm is in contact with the outer surface of the body's spool boss, the pickup pin (connected to the end of the pickup arm) is positioned to wrap line on the spool. In the cast position, this surface of the pickup arm is pushed above the spool boss, allowing the pickup pin to retract within the outside diameter of the reel's internal rotor. As the rotor is turned, the critical surface of the pickup arm engages cammed surfaces on the end of the body's spool boss. These surfaces direct the pickup arm back to the outer surface of the spool boss, and thus position the pickup pin in the retrieve position. Hence, the more cam surfaces on the end of the spool boss or the more pickup arms in the reel, the faster the reel will convert from the cast position to the retrieve position. Having only one cam or only one pickup pin isn't bad, just slower to convert the reel from the cast to retrieve position.

If you must retrieve a lure the minute it hits the water, pickup speed can be very important. Ditto for striking a fish that hits the moment a lure or bait lands down. For many people, however, line pickup speed is not much of a factor. In baitcasting reels, this is more of an issue. Flipping switches were designed for these products specifically for this reason. Anglers can flip or short-cast a lure and have the reel gears engaged the moment the lure hits the water, without having to manually make this adjustment.

Gears. The gear set in a spincasting reel is less efficient than in a baitcasting reel, but comparable to that in a spinning reel. Both spincasting and spinning reels have a right-angled gear set, which means that the equipment is trying to transfer the rotation force input at the crank knob through a 90-degree bend to the shaft that rotates the spinner head or rotor. Baitcasting reel gears, by contrast, simply transfer rotation force between two parallel shafts, having the advantage of no lateral forces like a right-angled gear set.

In spincasting reels, the gear sets are composed of a small pinion gear on the center shaft (connected to the spinner head) and a drive gear on the drive shaft (connected to the handle). These gear sets can be on-center or off-center gears. Most spincasting reels, and especially the less expensive models, have on-center gears. This means that if the shafts were extended, they would eventually intersect inside

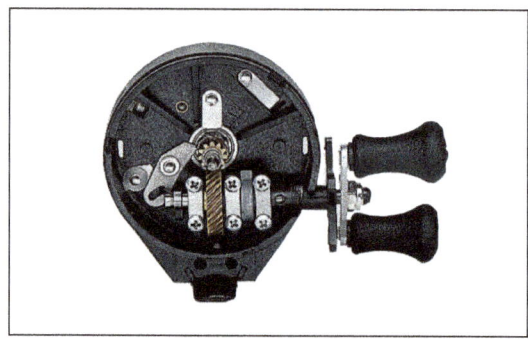

This internal view of a spincasting reel reveals the connection from handle to gear shaft, as well as this product's brass worm gears.

the back of the reel. In off-center gears, the crank shaft is "off-center" from the center shaft. The shafts can be extended inside the back of the reel without intersecting. The pinion, or small gear, is always located on the center shaft. The drive gear is always located on the drive shaft, which attaches to the handle.

It should be noted that in most gearing applications, gears are used to allow a small force to move a big object (for instance, as in a winch). In these applications, gears act as speed reducers, reducing the speed and increasing the torque. In most fishing reels, this function is reversed. It is speed of retrieve that the gears are used to maximize, not torque. Thus, the drive gear is on the crank shaft and the pinion on the center shaft. Winches have the opposite approach.

The better quality, and more expensive, reels often have off-center gears. In these higher quality reels, the gear teeth are cut at an angle, called a helix angle. Helix angles for spincasting reels can range from around 20 degrees to 45 degrees. Helical gears permit higher gear ratios in smaller spaces. Additionally, helix angles on gears allow more of the drive gear tooth's surface to remain in contact with the pinion gear tooth's surface. The more area of the teeth that remain in contact, the quieter, smoother, and more durable the gear set.

One of the advantages to off-center gears is that the crank shaft can be run all the way through the reel and be supported on both ends. This is not possible with an on-center gear set because the crank shaft is blocked by the center shaft. With the off-center gear supported at both ends, it is much more solid and durable and can support heavier loads. This type of gear support typically results in a sturdier feel for the user. With an on-center gear set, the drive gear is only supported on the handle side. Putting a heavy force on the crank handle can tend to cause the drive shaft to twist, putting undo wear on gear support components. This condition is eliminated by supporting the drive shaft on both ends.

Another advantage to the off-center gear design is that it permits higher helical angles, therefore higher gear ratios and smoother and quieter gears. This is a price-driven aspect to spincasting reels from the standpoint of the manufacturers; off-center gear systems are more expensive but meant for those who expect more and are willing to pay for it.

The material of the gears, incidentally, is extremely important. The drive gear in spincasting reels can be created from a die cast or powder metal process. Most are die cast of zinc or aluminum alloy materials. Some stainless steel powder metal spincasting drive gears are also used. In some spinning reels, the drive gear may also be forged. Die casting is a process used to form molten metal into complex, predetermined shapes. Powder metal is a process that starts with very small particles of a metal, forms them to a predetermined shape under pressure, then sinters the particles together so that a solid component is formed. The pinion gear can be die cast, machined, or powdered metal. The same materials are used if the pinion is die cast or powdered metal. Brass is typically used if the gear is machined. Machining (gear hobbing) creates a more precise gear, yet is also more expensive. Proper material selection between the gears results in a gear set that exhibits even wear. Due to the gear ratio, the pinion gear rotates more times in one revolution of the crank handle than the drive gear. For this reason, it is generally important to make the pinion gear of a more durable material than the drive gear. So the gear sets on more expensive spincasting reels will be offset, usually with high helix angles and brass pinions.

The average spincasting reel user has little understanding of this. Most people don't relate to what mechanisms in a reel make up their fishing experience. Manufacturers feel that the average spincasting reel user is looking for reliability, durability, and ease of use, all at an attractive price level. But if you have the opportunity to use spincasting reels of different quality, you will quickly see the difference. The question is whether the differences are important for your fishing experiences and expectations.

Left/Right retrieve. This is not generally an element of spincasting reels because of the dominance of on-center gear sets, which by their nature prohibit convertibility. Therefore, the majority of spincasting reels are set up for right-handed cranking. However, spincasting reels with off-center gears can have convertible right or left retrieves. These are always the higher end products, and include models that sport line-release triggers and sit under the rod handle.

Gear ratio/Cranking power. Engineers can talk in technical terms about the cranking power of a reel, about torque, and about how you can theoretically convert the force at the handle knob to the force on the line. But what anglers relate to in the simplest terms is how fast the reel is (retrieve speed) and how easy or difficult it is to retrieve a set weight (including an object that offers a lot of resistance). There are various factors that come into play to optimize both areas.

The components that directly relate to the retrieve speed of the reel are the reel's gear ratio and the diameter of the spool. Any reel's gear ratio can be exactly determined by dividing the number of gear teeth located on the drive gear by the number of gear teeth located on the pinion gear. With everything else being the same (handle length, spool diameter, number of ball bearings, and so on), a reel with a gear ratio of 3:1 (read three to one), can more easily retrieve a set weight than a reel with a 6:1 gear ratio. However, the reel with the 3:1 ratio will retrieve less line with one revolution of the crank handle than the reel with the 6:1 gear ratio.

While many anglers look for reels with specific gear ratios, their desire is really to optimize retrieve speed and crank power. A lower retrieve speed is typically optimal for crankbaits, while a faster retrieve speed is typically required for buzzbaits. Numerical gear ratio is an indication of retrieve speed, but the spool diameter is just as important. The larger the spool diameter, the more line that is wrapped on it for each turn of the crank handle. The larger the gear ratio, the more revolutions of the spinner head (spincasting reels), rotor (spinning reels), and spool (baitcasting and conventional tackle), thus the more line that is wrapped on the spool.

Because both factors are important for retrieve speed, it is possible for a large spincasting reel with a 3.5:1 gear ratio to have a faster line retrieval than a baitcasting reel with a gear ratio of 6:1. This really describes the number of inches of line that is retrieved for one revolution of the crank handle. This is typically measured as IPT (inches per turn). Because anglers can obviously rotate the crank handle at different speeds, manufacturers utilize IPT to distinguish between slow, cranking reels and faster reels.

Many spincasting reels have a low gear ratio, ranging from 2.5:1 to about 4:1. Some of the models intended for use with artificial lures have a higher gear ratio. The gear ratio is usually marked on the reel packaging, but may not be noted at all. In comparison to the gear ratios on other types of tackle, spincasting reel gear ratios are generally numerically low. However, spool diameters are typically larger. Therefore, manufacturers tend to optimize gear ratios and spool diameters to produce products for specific fishing conditions. In reality, it is not fair to compare the performance of a spincasting reel sto that of other types of tackle based solely on respective gear ratios.

Anglers can't quickly determine line recovery when evaluating a reel they might purchase because specifications on the circumference of the spincasting spool aren't provided on the reel or in the packaging materials. Although with a 4:1 ratio reel, for example, you know that one revolution of the handle wraps four revolutions of line on the spool, if you don't know how much line is gained with each complete wrap, then you don't know the actual recovery. (Of course, in a reel that you own, you can determine the gain by marking the line and measuring it.) For a greater discussion of this subject, see: Gear Ratio and Line Recovery.

Although line recovery is not quite as big an issue in spincasting reels as it is in spinning reels, it is nevertheless a factor that anglers should be aware of. The generally low rate of line recovery of spincasting reels, particularly less expensive models, is one of the reasons that some anglers do not use them, or don't use them for certain species of fish or methods of fishing (like trolling). While most consumers have a notion that gear ratio is of primary importance, there are other factors that go into this, and line recovery is a major one. Remember, however, that reels with low gear ratio do better the greater the load and the more resistance offered by lure or fish. Many components affect the relative ease or difficulty with which a reel retrieves a set load. These include easily measured items such as gear ratio, spool diameter, and handle length, as well as less tangible items that tend to reduce frictional loss in the gearing system (efficiency of gear sets, ball bearings, and lubrication).

The length of the handle has a bearing on this issue because that length controls the leverage that you can put on the handle. The longer the handle, the more leverage and the easier it is to retrieve a set load. It is essentially the same principle used in wrenches; it's easier to loosen nuts with a long-handled wrench than with a short-handled one. Spinning reels, because their handles are very long, tend to have a better advantage in terms of cranking power than spincasting reels. Because spinning reels hang underneath the rod and have a long stem, there is room to put a long handle on them, which adds more leverage advantage than can be obtained with most spincasting reels. Long handles on a spincasting reel tend to interfere with the rod. You can replace a short handle on a spincasting reel with a longer one, but it will look a little funny, and it may interfere with the gripping of the rod.

Ball bearings/Bushings. Ball bearings and bushings provide a way to minimize friction on rotating shafts. There are well-engineered plastics today that provide very low friction. If there is a very good surface finish on these, and close tolerance between the bushings and the shafts, the reel will perform well.

Ball bearings are typically viewed as more durable and more reliable products, and usually employed in higher end reels, although there are different grades of ball bearings. There is a performance difference in these grades, although the average consumer does not know which grade is in the reel.

Spincasting reels usually have either no ball bearings or one, typically on the center shaft. Some may have three, but it is doubtful that there is much performance gain from the extra ball bearings. Spincasting reels with three ball bearings usually have one on either side of the crank shaft and one on the center shaft. For a more detailed review of ball bearings and bushings, see: Reel, Fishing.

Depth locator. Some spincasting reels have a depth locating feature that is meant to allow an angler to repeatedly let out the same amount of line, usually in order to lower a bait or lure to the same depth. This is often used in panfishing, especially for crappies, and may be known as a crappie locator or crappie finder.

Usually this feature is activated by a lever on top of the reel. The lever is attached to a pin, which is pushed forward by the lever and which lays across the spool. When you start retrieving, the recovered line goes over the pin. When you release the line, it goes out until it reaches the pin and then stops; line cannot be pulled from under the bottom of the pin with ordinary tension (although in some models the depth locating selector switch automatically releases when there is heavy pressure, as might be applied suddenly by a large fish). Now you have a preselected depth to fish or the amount of line to set out. This is most commonly used in crappie fishing for returning to the same depth, and the lever can be pressed either when you're fishing at a certain depth, or at the exact moment that you receive a strike at a given depth. This feature has a niche application and performs the same purpose as using a tiny stopper on the line of a spinning reel, which some anglers employ for selecting depth. However, in spinning reels, a tiny stopper can travel onto the reel without much problem, whereas such a stopper is likely to catch on the pickup pin of a spincasting reel.

Strike detector. A few spincasting reels have an audible clicking mechanism, which may be known as a strike detector or bait clicker, to alert you to activity when the reel is in the cast or freespool mode. This can be important when a rod is left unattended or out of reach, usually when fishing with bait and when the reel is in freespool (anti-reverse off). If this feature is activated, it will produce an audible clicking sound when a fish strikes and the line starts running. Then you can pick up the reel, convert it from the cast to the retrieve mode, and set the hook. A selectable anti-reverse is important here; you should disengage the anti-reverse so that the line will come freely off the reel and the clicker will sound.

Drag Features

Common drag factors. As with the gear sets,

the drag systems in spinning and spincasting reels are also similar. Most spincasting and spinning reel drag systems operate on the same principle. When tension on the fishing line exceeds a preset limit, the spool slips (rotates counterclockwise) and allows additional line to unwrap off the spool. When that tension drops below the preset drag level, the spool stops rotating counterclockwise.

In most of these products, there are drag washers on either side of the spool. Compressing the drag washers against the spool makes the spool more difficult to rotate, resulting in stronger drag tension. Decreasing pressure on the drag washers makes the spool easier to rotate, resulting in lighter drag tension. However, it is the mechanism that controls pressure on the spool that is the significant difference between the drag on a spincasting versus a spinning reel. In most spinning reels, there is more uniform pressure on the spool than there is in a spincasting reel. Additionally, multiple drag washers may be used on either side of the spool in spinning reel drag systems. Nevertheless, there are certain things to look for when evaluating the drag systems of these, as well as other, reels.

The measure of a drag system is determined by smoothness and adjustment range. Technically, smoothness is a measure of line tension variation measured at the reel. If the desired line tension is 4 pounds, the drag should allow additional line to be released from the spool when line tension immediately reaches exactly 4 pounds. In actual practice, additional line can be released from the spool when line tension is less than or more than 4 pounds. Typically, this is measured by manufacturers as percent of drag variation. With the drag set at 4 pounds, the drag may actually release line when line tension reaches 10 percent above or below the actual setting, or 20 percent, or 30 percent, and so on. The lower the drag variation number (percent), the smoother the drag.

Variations to this include the "breakaway" force, which is the force required to start the drag releasing line. In some reels, with the drag set at 4 pounds, a higher line tension is required to get the drag started. Once started, it may release line at 4 pounds. In some reels, this breakaway force is close to the original drag setting. In other reels, this breakaway force might be twice as high as the original drag setting, or even higher. Drag variation may also be influenced by the speed at which line is pulled from the reel. On some reels, allowable line tension may vary, depending on whether line is pulled rapidly or slowly from the reel. Drag variation differs with the drag setting. It is easier to achieve a low drag variation at a low drag setting (1 or 2 pounds). Generally speaking, as the drag setting is increased, most drag systems are not as smooth. The best reels display a breakaway force equivalent to the drag setting, a consistent line tension at all speeds, and drag settings within 10 percent to 20 percent of the actual drag setting.

It should be noted that in fishing conditions there are many variables that affect the smoothness of a drag system: those mentioned here that apply directly to the performance of the reel, plus other variables, such as the stretch in the line, the amount of line out, the limberness of the rod, the type of line guides used, and so on. Another variable obviously is the friction material; for example, Teflon is often used in light-duty drags because it has the same static and kinetic friction coefficient, which means that it takes the same force to start it moving as to keep it moving. In other materials, it takes more force to start movement than to maintain it.

Adjustment range is the second measure of a drag system's performance. In spincasting reels, there are two basic types of actuators used to increase or decrease the drag setting. Drag stars are typically located near the reel handle. Drag wheels typically extend through the body of the reel. Both are rotated clockwise to increase drag force and counterclockwise to decrease drag force. In theory, anglers desire great flexibility in adjusting the drag setting. The best drag systems allow some type of correlation between the degree of rotation of the drag actuator and the increased or decreased line tension. For instance, 90-degree drag actuator rotation may equate to a $1/4$-pound increase in allowable line tension. Ideally, drag actuators should be limited to between two and three complete revolutions. Additional revolutions become somewhat cumbersome. Fewer revolutions provide an inadequate amount of flexibility in drag settings. The drag actuator should be easy to rotate to its maximum setting; at this setting, the drag force should be adequate to break the recommended line weight for the reel.

In typical freshwater fishing situations, anglers set the drag at 30 to 50 percent of the breaking

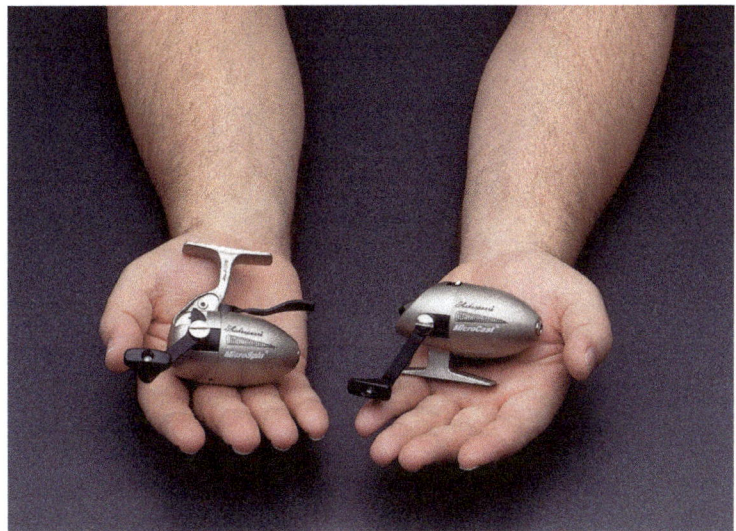

These two diminutive Shakespeare spincasting reels exemplify a trigger-release model (left), which mounts under the rod, and a pushbutton-release model (right), which mounts atop the rod.

strength of their line; most, if they have a 10-pound line, for example, set the drag by feel at between 3 to 5 pounds, meaning that it will take 3 to 5 pounds of tension to cause line to slip (5 pounds may actually be too much for some situations). This is measured with a short length of line on a straight pull off the reel.

To optimize ease of use, manufacturers should strive to allow plenty of adjustment for the drag setting in this range. If you consider line tension in terms of revolutions of the thumb wheel or the star wheel, you'll see that it is desirable to ramp up the drag very rapidly to get to 30 percent of the line's breaking strength. Few people are going to set their drag tension at less than 30 percent of the line strength. Ideally, the first quarter-revolution should get you up to that 30 percent number. Then, for the 30 to 50 percent breaking strength range, there should be a lot of adjustment; it may take two revolutions to cover that range and fine-tune the drag. Then, after reaching 50 percent of the breaking strength, the drag should ramp up very quickly to a full lock-down position with a short revolution of the control wheel; this is in case you have to break off, pull on a snag, or have more tension for a strike in heavy cover. Thus, the important aspect of drag range is how many rotations it takes to get to the lock-down point, and where is the most adjustment range for fine tuning.

Some of the greatest interest among anglers comes from being able to readily get maximum force, which locks the reel down and completely prevents the drag from slipping. This maximum force is seldom beneficial for most fishing activities, including playing large or strong fish, unless you are using very heavy line. Where it is most likely to be useful, however, is when a lure or hook gets snagged and cannot be freed; this situation may require you to lock the reel down, point the rod directly at the snag, and pull back to free the hook or break the line *(see: unsnagging)*. However, this may bury the line on the spool and put a severe strain on the reel. It might be better to wrap the line around another object before pulling on it. If the drag cannot be locked down completely, line will slip off, and it may be harder to free the hook.

Many people mistakenly think that they need to set the drag very tight for effective hooksetting. Once you have 20 yards of line out and you have rod flex, line stretch, and the dampening effect of the water to contend with, you don't need very much drag force at the reel. You cannot exert the maximum pressure when you set the hook. But when you set the drag pressure at or near maximum force, when the fish is close to the boat and less contribution is made by line stretch, rod flex, and water, having the drag locked down may mean that the line cannot absorb the sudden shock of a quick run, even from a fish whose weight is less than the breaking strength of the line. People are often amazed that a 5-pound fish can break 14-pound line, but that does not happen if the drag is set properly and the washers are allowed to slip freely when necessary.

Drag systems. The purpose of the drag function on any reel is to let line slip from the reel at varying pressures when force is applied to the line. It serves as a sort of clutch, or shock absorber. It is especially important when using light line, when playing large and strong fish, and when fish make strong and sudden surges while being landed. If an angler never catches large fish, only uses heavy strength line, and is content to wind fish in, then it is conceivable that his drag will never be used. But heavy line is not suitable for many species and many methods of fishing, and it is practically inevitable that at some time, even with moderate-strength line, an angler will catch a fish that weighs more than the actual breaking strength of his line, and which requires some finesse, rather than brute strength, to land. This means that the drag will come into play, because if it doesn't, the force will exceed the strength of the line and the line will break.

When the drag comes into play, it allows the fish to continue applying force, but at a pressure that is less than the breaking strength of the line, because when the force reaches a certain level (usually less than 50 percent of the line's breaking strength), a properly set drag mechanism allows line to slip from the reel.

Understanding how to use drag, and how to set drag, is one of the most important aspects of sportfishing, and is reviewed in detail elsewhere *(see: drag)*. Clearly, however, the functioning of a drag is a critical element of every reel, and the quality of reel drags vary considerably.

The drag mechanism on spincasting reels, as on most smaller reels for various fishing applications, used to be fair to poor at best, but these systems have changed markedly since anglers started using all of the various equipment types for more challenging fishing, and placed greater demands on the rod, reel, and line. While the lowest priced spincasting reels (toddler or kiddie versions) do not have sophisticated drags, most medium and higher quality models have reasonably good drags, and a few excellent ones.

Approximately three types of drag systems are used in spincasting reels today. The most simple is one that uses a drag wheel and features a spring arm that puts pressure on the edge of the spool. As the drag wheel (commonly called a thumb wheel and located on the body of the reel) is rotated, it puts more or less pressure on the edges of the spool. This system is composed of the spool, the spring arm, and the adjustment wheel, and is reasonably effective for modest fishing applications.

The more common system has a threaded shaft that, when rotated by means of the drag wheel, puts pressure on the clutch plate. The clutch plate is located between the spool and the body of the

---

The first known conservation measure in the new world was enacted in the Massachusetts Bay Colony in 1639; it forbade using striped bass and cod as ground fertilizer.

reel. As pressure is applied to the clutch plate, it exerts pressure on the drag washers, thus making the spool more difficult to rotate. This type of drag system has the ability to produce extremely smooth drags at low tension settings. One variation of this type of drag is when the clutch plate is raised or lowered by means of a drag star instead of a drag wheel.

In another variation, the clutch plate rotates instead of being pushed forward when the drag wheel rotates. This features a drag wheel and a clutch plate with cams. As the wheel is rotated, it turns a little gear that is keyed to a clutch plate that has cams on its bottom surface. These cams are like small opposing ramps, and they start to engage when the drag wheel is rotated. This pushes the clutch plate forward. As more pressure is applied to the spool, it becomes harder for the spool to rotate. This method provides more uniform pressure against the drag washers and against the spool than the previously mentioned systems. Those systems produce side load, whereas this system moves the entire clutch plate forward, resulting in a more uniform center loading of the drag washers and spool. The result is a drag that is smoother at higher loads, puts less wear on the other parts, and produces less stress on the other components of the reel.

These drag systems rely on the spinner head remaining stationary and the spool rotating to release line. An advantage of this is that line exits the spool in a fixed location; it comes off the spool at the position of the pickup pin and flows through the front cover. Because the line is not traveling around the spool, as it would if the spinner head rotated, a loop, such as the one generated in the casting mode, is not produced. The absence of this loop contributes to reduced drag variation, and thus, a smoother drag.

A disadvantage of a stationary spinner head and rotating spool is that if the reel handle is rotated when the drag is slipping, line twist is introduced into the reel. If not remedied, this line twist can cause line tangling problems on subsequent casts. For this reason, many spincasting reels have a spool clicker built into the reel. When the spool turns backward, releasing line, a clicking sound is heard, indicating that the drag is functioning. This is an audible reminder not to rotate the reels handle until the drag stops slipping. Unfortunately, many people (using this type of reel as well as others, especially spinning reels) inadvertently put twist in their line by continuing to reel when the line is slipping via the drag. This is especially likely to be done by inexperienced anglers.

Finally, another unique type of drag system found in spincasting reels functions with a slipping gear instead of a slipping spool and has the advantage of producing less twist in the line, regardless of the level of expertise of the angler. In this type of reel, the spinner head is allowed to rotate backward, unwrapping line from the spool much like back-reeling. This is accomplished by a floating drive gear. The drive gear is not rigidly attached to the drive shaft, but is actually sandwiched between drag washers. This type of system is only actuated with a drag star. As the drag star is rotated, additional pressure is applied to the drive gear. When line tension exceeds the drag setting, the spinner head rotates backward, causing the center shaft to rotate backward, which, in turn, causes the drive gear to slip. Because the drive gear slips on the drive shaft, the reel handle does not rotate backward.

In this system, rotating the handle while the drag is slipping has no effect on line twist. It is the drive gear that slips, not the spool. However, because the spinner head unwraps line from the spool, a loop (like that generated when casting) is formed. This loop results in drag variations much higher than that found in other spincasting reel drag systems. Additionally, the anti-reverse mechanism on this type of reel must be between the reel handle and the drive gear. Shock loads imparted by fish or other solid objects are transmitted through the gear set to the anti-reverse device. Thus, the gear set is more exposed to damage in such a system. In drag systems characterized by a slipping spool, anti-reverse mechanisms can be located between the spinner head and the pinion gear. Shock loads are absorbed by the anti-reverse, instead of being transmitted through the gear set, thus protecting the gear set from potential damage.

Drag washers. Ideally the drag in any reel operates smoothly, without hesitation. In other words, it starts immediately when needed and maintains a constant rate of tension as line flows continuously off, and it keeps the same level of tension as it is periodically called upon during the time it takes to play and land a strong fish. The less variation in the performance of the drag, the better. Some of this performance is affected by the type of drag system and the range of adjustment it is capable of, as well as the amount of force it can apply. Some of this is affected by the number and material of the washers.

Drag washer material is really most critical in the setup stage of drag usage. One of the problems with drags and the materials from which they are made is that they are being asked to do something very difficult. It is desirable to have a drag that slips freely yet creates a high amount of pressure. It has to be able to slip, yet sustain a high load, perhaps even a compete no-slip lockdown load. Thus, you're looking for two opposite attributes in a washer to accomplish these needs.

Drag washer materials in spincasting reels, like those in other reel types, have evolved over the years. Phenolic washers were used in the past, as were various fibrous washers, and some people replaced their washers with leather versions. Today, the primary drag washer material in better quality spincasting reels is Teflon or polyethylene (specifically, ultra-high molecular weight polyethylene). In spincasting reels, these materials do a reasonable job of satisfying the two opposite demands.

There is a correlation between the size and the surface area of the drag washers and their ability to function at higher forces. The total force is more a function of the maximum diameter of the washers instead of the total surface area. A large diameter washer, even if it covers only a small surface area, can produce a greater force than a small diameter washer with a lot of surface area.

Anti-Reverse Features

When the handle of a spincasting reel is turned forward, line is wound onto the spool. If the handle can be wound backward, in reverse, line unwinds from the spool. Some reel handles cannot be turned in reverse. Most, however, can be turned in reverse by the operation of a switch on the outside of the reel. This switch, known as the anti-reverse, allows anglers to put the reel in reverse by turning it to the off position, or to keep the anti-reverse constantly out of use by turning it to the on position.

When the anti-reverse switch is in the off position, the handle and the rotor can be moved forward and backward; line can come off the spool when the handle is turned backward and also when the drag slips. When the anti-reverse switch is in the on position, the handle and rotor can be turned forward but cannot be turned backward; line can only come off the spool when the drag slips. A reel with this switch is said to have selectable, or selective, anti-reverse, while one without it is said to have nonselectable anti-reverse.

At one time when reel drags were poor and often unreliable, it was useful to have a reel with a selective anti-reverse feature. Anglers felt more comfortable when playing a strong fish if they could reel backward to let line out to play the fish. Many were accustomed to doing this with baitcasting, or levelwind, reels, which initially had direct drive, and had to be back-reeled, or wound backward, when a strong fish put a lot of pressure on it. The trouble with back-reeling is that it is rare to be able to reel backward quickly enough to keep up with a rapidly turning handle when a fish speeds off; therefore, you have to let go of the handle, which usually spins wildly and which may cause a snarl, backlash, or overrun upon completion of the swift back-reeling. When an angler tries to grab the rapidly turning handle, it often smacks his fingers, which caused the old reels to be called knuckle busters.

Today, reel drags are quite reliable and efficient, especially when properly set, and there is no reason to back-reel, even if a reel has the ability to do so. Today's reels do not need selective anti-reverse, but most of them have it to give anglers the option of using it. Probably the only time that the average angler uses this feature is when line is accidentally wound around inner or outer parts of the reel and needs to be worked free.

What is more important for anglers, however, is how the reel operates when the forward-turning motion is stopped. There is a natural tendency to pull up on the handle when not reeling, whether to set the hook or to momentarily stop while retrieving. In older models of reels, and in some lesser quality current models, there is considerable play in the handle and rotor when the reel stops, and the handle may actually turn backward slightly before engaging. This tendency produces a feeling of sloppiness or instability, and if there is too much backward movement of the handle, it may adversely affect hooksetting and may allow a loop of slack line to appear on the spool in some retrieval motions, which may eventually impair casting. Ideally, the reel should engage instantly and firmly, and the better spincasting reels have features that provide this. It is usually called continuous anti-reverse or infinite anti-reverse and should keep the drive gear from moving even the slightest bit backward.

One thing that governs how quickly the drive gear engages is how many ratchets there are in the system. The ratchets are little stops for a pawl; when the pawl hits a ratchet, it causes engagement. The more stops there are, the quicker it engages.

Most anti-reverse systems in spincasting reels are built into the drive gear. One method of doing this is with a walking pawl system. As the drive gear turns forward, a small pointed pawl slides over the ratchets, creating a clicking sound, but does not engage them; as the gear tries to rotate backward, the point catches the ratchets and stops the gear from turning in reverse. This is a two-piece system, and the most simple one.

Another anti-reverse system features a little actuating piece on the crank shaft with a small pawl that engages the ratchets on the back side of the drag. As the handle rotates forward, the actuator keeps the pawl out of the way. The pawl sits up at an angle, so that, as the actuating piece starts to rotate backward, it kicks the pawl up to engage the ratchets. There is no clicking sound in this reel because the pawl is always disengaged completely, and the anti-reverse is considered silent. When the anti-reverse is in the off position, it keeps the pawl out of the way and the crank shaft can always turn backward.

Both of these systems are located on the drive gear. A disadvantage to this is that when there is a shock load on the line, that shock load gets transferred through the gear set to the anti-reverse, which can be damaging to the gear set. If the anti-reverse system were in front of the gear set, between the shock load and the gear set, then the anti-reverse system would absorb the load before it got to the gear set.

In a few high quality spincasting reels as well as some spinning reels, the anti-reverse system is in front of the gear set. This may be accomplished with a one-way clutch, or a more conventional pawl and ratchet setup. It should also be noted that, with the anti-reverse located on the center shaft, a five-tooth ratchet will engage much faster than a five-tooth ratchet located on the drive shaft. The center shaft rotates much faster than the drive shaft due to the gear ratio; therefore, a much smaller amount of rotational motion is required to engage the anti-reverse located on the center shaft than is required if it is located on the drive shaft.

The one-way clutch device is a part that came from printers, where it is used to control the location of print on paper and the rotation of parts. In reels, its job is to completely prohibit backward travel of the shaft. It does this very well on most reels, and if it doesn't do it as well on some as on others, it is because of different tolerances in the other components. This system results in a (silent) continuous or infinite anti-reverse.

Ergonomics and Appearance

Shape. In a sense, many spincasting reels today are very similar in outward appearance to the early versions, particularly with respect to the cone-shaped covers. Reels with these and similar large covers are adequate for people who hold a spincasting outfit with their hand on the rod itself, and mainly touch the reel when they grab the handle or press the pushbutton. For such users, the pushbutton must be located low and close to the rod for easy use. Some people wrap their hand around the rod and reel, in effect palming it. For these users, a low-profile reel that sits closer to the rod is more desirable. Some spincasting reels have a pushbutton that extends off the right side of the reel; these are very easy for palming and pushbutton actuation, but they are far less common than those with centrally located buttons. The smaller housing and less boxy contour of most spincasting reels are more conducive to a wraparound hand grip. Whichever system is preferred, the reel should have a smooth design and surface on the side that is held with the hand or in the palm. Any projections will cause discomfort.

Naturally, the pushbutton (or trigger) should be easy to depress, and a thumb wheel drag should be easy to reach and finger. Reels with convertible left or right retrieve need a large drag wheel that is centered so it can be easily reached no matter which hand is used. The more casting the user does, the more important are ergonomic matters. A person who mostly stillfishes and places the rod in a holder is less concerned about this than someone who will be holding and casting the reel continuously.

Handles. Handles and knobs are largely a matter of personal preference. There is no benefit in terms of reel function or technical performance for having a dual-knob rather than single-knob handle, but some people prefer two knobs, in part because they feel that it is easier to grab one of them quickly, as when they aren't looking at the reel. There is no strength advantage to having dual knobs because, as noted earlier, strength and cranking power are governed by the distance from the crank shaft hole to the knob, not from the distance between two knobs. But for many people there seems to be a better balance to spincasting reels with dual-knob handles.

Many spincasting reels, especially in the lower price range, feature a single-knob handle, while many of the more expensive reels feature a dual-knob handle. It is interesting to note that virtually no baitcasting reels with a single-knob handle are sold in North America, while nearly all spinning reels have a single-knob handle, and some have a counterbalanced handle.

Handles are mostly made from stamped aircraft-grade aluminum. Some are made from plastic to achieve better aesthetics and to reduce cost. The knobs vary in material, although most anglers prefer a soft material that is easy to grip, especially when wet, and that may be contoured for comfort. On higher end reels a soft rubber is used on the knobs rather than hard plastic. If the handle and the knobs are not large and comfortable enough for the user, they will be fatiguing and perhaps counterproductive.

Appearance. Overall appearance is largely a subjective matter. Manufacturers feel that the average spincasting reel user needs a reliable and durable product. They may use metal on higher end products to convey a tough image, but this is not necessarily a performance factor or an ergonomic one. Weight may be a factor to some people but not to others, and the materials used will have some impact on that. Size should be relative to application. Color is trend driven and tends to parallel what is popular in the automotive industry, because it is industrial designers who pick colors. In spincasting reels, there are colored plastics, metals, painted plastics, and a variety of decoration approaches, none of which have functional significance and are mainly geared toward aesthetics.

The materials used on spincasting reel parts vary. Metal exteriors are stainless steel or aluminum. Stainless steel is strong and forms easily; aluminum is softer and bends easily and is not as tough as stainless steel. The spinner heads are typically plated brass or stainless steel. Various plastics are used for different parts, primarily glass-reinforced nylon, ABS, polystyrene, or polycarbonate. The reel foot may be glass-filled nylon because this material is very stiff and very strong. ABS and polystyrene are typically used for covers; these are lower cost materials and not as stiff or strong as others, but in many spincasting reels those values aren't needed in that component.

Rods

Spincasting rods are mostly similar to those used in baitcasting and fairly uncomplicated. The guides are mainly mounted atop the rod, and guide rings are generally small, unlike those used with spinning tackle, because lines come straight out of the nose

 Scientists say that sharks have changed little in the past 360 million years; the first shark-like scales were discovered in Mongolia and aged at 420 million years.

cone of the spincasting reel. (An exception to this is the hybrid spincasting reel sporting a trigger release, which mounts under the rod rather than on top of it, and is used with a spinning rods.)

Reels mount a little higher on top of the rod's reel seat and above the rod, which used to be facilitated by a handle with an offset seat (when the rod blank fit into the handle as a separate, rather than integral, component), providing more comfortable use. However, refinements in reel design, including the placement of the release button, and rods featuring blank-through handle construction, have virtually done away with this offset design, meaning that spincasting reels today are used with rods having standard straight and pistol grip (especially popular) styles of handle. Pistol grip handles, and some straight grip handles, have a trigger grip on the underside of the rod opposite and at the lower end of the reel seat.

Spincasting rods usually aren't as stiff as baitcasting rods, having generally lighter action for use with light lines and lures. They are made in one- and two-piece models, and a few are telescopic. Lengths are shorter than most baitcasting and spinning rods; they range from $4^1/_2$ feet to 6 feet, with 5- and $5^1/_2$-footers the norm, and some shorter rods available for youngsters. Most rods marketed specifically for spincasting use are made of fiberglass, usually E-glass *(see)*, but a few feature composite construction, with graphite used in the material or the resin.

Unlike reels, many of the issues pertaining to spincasting rods—functions, materials, components, and so on—are similar to those of other rods, and these are more fully detailed elsewhere *(see: rod, fishing)*.

Using Spincasting Tackle

Line. Six- to 10-pound nylon monofilament line is most commonly used on spincasting tackle and is the choice of many anglers who do varied and general fishing, although some models handle line up to 25-pound strength. Whatever the strength, line is pre-spooled on spincasting reels by the manufacturer. It is possible to use lighter line, such as 2- through 4-pound test, on ultralight models, but few people use 2-pound on spincasting tackle, and a minority use 4. When you change the line, it is best to use the same strength of line if it is of the same or similar diameter, although you can make some changes. If you go to lighter line, you may find that the finer diameter is so thin that it gets hung up because the reel tolerances are not adequate for that diameter. On the other hand, you can go up in strength but keep a similar diameter. For example, if you had a spincasting reel spooled with conventional diameter 8-pound line, you might replace this with a 12-pound line of thin diameter. This could give you a line with a diameter equivalent to a 6- or 8-pound conventional nylon monofilament line, but with the strength of 12-pound line, and offer some species and condition advantages that you might not have had with the original line *(see: line)*.

Although it is possible to use other types of line with some spincasting reels, nylon monofilament is the best choice. A good monofilament with controlled stretch to help buffer the drag, the actions of the angler, and the actions of the fish, is more forgiving and less prone to problems than a braided or microfilament product.

Refilling the spool. The various aspects of properly filling a reel spool are detailed elsewhere *(see: line)*. Putting line on a spincasting reel spool is slightly more complicated than other reel types only because the spool is under the cover. To get to it, remove the cover, and take off whatever old line remains on the spool. Because spincasting reels do not have large line capacities, it is usually best to refill the entire spool so that you have a continuous unknotted section of line. If you choose, you can tie a line-to-line knot and replace only that portion of the spool that is missing. However, there's a good chance that this knot will catch on the pickup pin or the inner edge of the front cover opening, and cause some difficulty, unless it is very small and the ends are clipped off perfectly. It is generally best to replace all of the line rather than put a knot in it that may cause trouble.

When you refill the spool, start by putting the tag end of the line from the filler spool through the rod guides and then through the front cover opening, and tie it to the spincasting reel spool. It has to come through the reel cover opening for you to put the cover back in place and then wind line on. Make sure that you wind the new line on under tension, and fill the reel spool to within $1/_8$-inch of the top of the reel spool lip.

If you overfill the spool, or have excessive line slack, you may encounter a situation when the line gets under the spinner head. You'll know when this happens because the line will stop dead right in the middle of a cast. This is an infrequent occurrence, especially in better quality spincasting reels, but when it does occur you can fix it simply by removing the front cover of the reel, pressing the pushbutton or trigger, and removing line from underneath the spinner head. The line usually comes free by unwinding it several turns. If this does not work, you will have to take the spinner head off to get the line out. Check to see that the line is not frayed before reusing.

Line twist. Line twist is commonly associated with the use of both spinning and spincasting tackle. This issue is discussed in greater detail under other entries *(see: line; spinning tackle)*. However, some general observations are in order here.

As twist accumulates in nylon monofilament line, it causes damage by building up ever greater stresses. Under load, as when fighting a fish, these stresses may weaken the structure of the line and can lead to breakoffs. A twisted line is like a loaded spring. When tension is released on a cast, the

---

The enormously popular brown trout is not a native American fish; 80,000 brown trout eggs were shipped from Germany to America in February 1883.

line tends to balloon outward from the axis of the line flow. This increases line-to-guide friction and reduces casting distance. It is also why some line twist disasters (a wad of mangled line) tend to wrap around the first rod guide. Twist causes almost no problem when line is kept under tension. The stored spring energy due to twist is evident only when tension is released. Then, a snarl can almost instantly appear.

Twisted line is not difficult to cure if you're in a boat or near running water. Line will untwist itself if you let a long length of it out behind your boat, with nothing attached to the end of it (no snap, swivel, split shot, hook, or lure), and drag it along for a few minutes. The faster your boat travels, the faster the line unravels. Reel the line back in and you're ready to attach terminal gear and fish. You can achieve the same effect on moderate to fast flowing water by letting the unweighted line float downstream and then holding it in the current for several minutes. This has the same effect as dragging it behind the boat.

Line twist can occur when using spincasting (as well as spinning) reels, and it may cost valuable angling time, cause otherwise unnecessary replacement of line, and contribute to lost lures and breakoffs. To a large extent, it can be overcome or prevented by putting line on correctly, reeling it in under tension, using a swivel with lures that are likely to spin in the water, playing large fish properly, and, especially, by not reeling against a slipping drag.

As previously explained, some spincasting reels have a drag system that is built into the drive shaft; in this configuration, reeling against the drag does not twist the line. However, for all other types, when the handle is turned as the drag slips, line twist occurs.

One of the absolute worst causes of line twist is turning the reel handle while the drag is releasing line. Excited anglers continue to quickly crank the handle, typically against a drag that is set too light, while no line is retrieved. Each turn of the handle puts multiple twists in the line in a direct relationship to the gear ratio of the reel. High gear ratio reels add more twists than low gear ratio reels. You can minimize this by being conscious of what the drag is doing at all times while fighting a fish, or using a slightly tighter drag. If the reel has a drag clicker, whenever it starts to sound, you should stop reeling, and learn to pump-and-reel, which requires proper rod manipulation *(see: playing fish)*, rather than to crank and crank and crank. Some drag types are better at reducing or preventing twist than others, and while some do a good job of eliminating twist even when an angler reels against a slipping drag, the best solution is not to reel when this is happening, and to take measures to reduce other means of creating twist.

This includes trying to maintain some tension on the line when you are reeling in under ordinary circumstances, as when retrieving a light-tension object. This tension can be applied by letting the line flow through the thumb and forefinger of the hand that holds the rod and reel. This may require holding the outfit slightly forward of the top of the reel and/or in the back of your palm, which may feel slightly awkward or uncomfortable to people with small hands and no wrist strength. Using your fingers for moderate tension should only be done when retrieving lures or hooks that offer little or no tension; it should not be done when playing a fish. Remember that the purpose of this is to try to control slack line and keep whatever spring may have built up in the line from unloading.

Matching and selecting. As with any type of fishing tackle, the issue of matching the right reel to the right rod is an important one, but in these times, it is a relatively easy one. A lot of spincasting tackle is sold in matched combinations of rods and reels, and the manufacturers have already done the job of putting the right reel with the right rod. Naturally, many of these items, and especially the upper end products, are also sold separately. Fishing rods are virtually all labeled by line classifications and by weight of objects to be used, which practically assures that you don't put a light-duty spincasting reel, for example, loaded with 6-pound line, on a medium-heavy rod that is rated for 10- to 14-pound line use. What you might do is look for a rod with a specific type of action, say one that had a fast taper for casting light lures, and look for this in the length that you prefer for your most frequent tackle use.

When selecting tackle, as well as matching a rod and reel, you have to take into consideration the kinds of fishing that you expect to do. A beginning angler may be unsure what to select without any prior fishing experience. Guidance from a knowledgeable salesperson could be very helpful; such a person is more likely to be found in a specialized store (a sporting goods dealer or bait and tackle shop). You might also seek guidance from an acquaintance or relative who has experience with this type of equipment and some knowledge of the fishing that a beginner is likely to do. Some manufacturers provide equipment guidelines on their packaging or display materials to provide general direction for appropriate usage, and this can be helpful.

In a general sense, selecting tackle starts with a determination of the size of fish that you are likely to catch and evaluating the conditions under which you will be fishing. The larger and stronger the fish, the stronger the tackle necessary for beginners, until you get the experience to use lighter gear. Fishing where there are a lot of obstructions usually requires medium or heavy grades of tackle. Small fish, fewer obstructions, and clearer water usually are suitable for lighter tackle. Most selection thus starts with a determination of the line strength necessary for the conditions, and having the appropriate rod and reel. You should also give some attention to line capacity. If you will be fishing in a way or under circumstances that require a lot of line, then you will need an appropriate amount of line on the reel. Spincasting reels seldom have more than 100 yards of line capacity, and many smaller models have only 60 or 70 yards. This is significantly less than the capacity of spinning reels. If you expect to go trolling, for example, the smaller line capacities will not be adequate.

Again, in a general sense, spincasting tackle in the 4- to 8-pound class is suitable for all types of panfish (including crappie, bluegills, and yellow perch) as well as small trout, small bass, and small catfish or bullheads. Tackle in the 8- to 14-pound range is heavy for most panfish, but adequate for bass, walleye, pickerel, some trout fishing, and some pike and catfish angling. Heavier tackle is suited to fishing for larger fish (trout, pike, catfish, bass, and stripers) and in places where there are a lot of obstructions. Six- to 10-pound line is most commonly used on spincasting tackle and is the choice of many anglers who do varied and general fishing.

It is commonly believed by manufacturers that spincasting tackle is purchased largely according to price, and evidently sales patterns bear this out. Generally, spincasting tackle is less expensive than other comparable types of tackle, and it represents a good value for the expense. For a little more money, you usually can step up to better equipment, especially a better reel, and the kind of features that the best spincasting reels have (ceramic pickup pins, dual-grip handles, helical gears, continuous anti-reverse, and so on) certainly provide elevated performance and, in most cases, greater useful life.

When purchasing spincasting tackle, you should obviously take into consideration the species that you will be targeting, the places that you will fish, and your own level of experience. If you purchase the tackle from a store, you will have an idea of how well it fits your hand, how comfortable it is, and whether the weight and general feel are to your liking. It's a good idea to mount it on the rod that you intend to use with it, to make sure that it sits securely in the reel seat and that it is at the proper height for comfortable handle turning as well as line flow to the guides.

Setting up. Prior to making that first cast, you must set up the rod and reel. Attaching the reel to the rod is a simple and straightforward matter of placing the reel so that the cover opening is facing the first rod guide (otherwise it would be backwards!), nestling it in the reel seat of the handle, and tightening it so that the reel is firmly in place. Ideally, it should be snug and have no wobble. Tighten the retaining mechanism by hand so that it is snug but not so tight that you can't undo it by hand.

On a new reel with pre-spooled line, the tag end of the line is attached to a ring that is outside the front cover opening, which is there to keep the line from slipping under the front cover. Put the reel in freespool (press the pushbutton or trigger), clip the ring off, run the line through the rod guides, and attach it to a lure or, preferably, a practice casting weight. If the line is not attached to a ring but inside the cover, take the cover off (usually by unscrewing it or twisting and lifting), place the end of the line through the opening in the cover, put the cover back on, and feed the line through the rod guides with the reel in freespool.

Holding the rod and reel. Most spincasting reels have only right-handed retrieve. This means that regardless of which hand you prefer to reel with, with a right-hand-retrieve model you hold the rod and reel with your left hand and reel with your right hand. In those models that have convertible retrieve systems, you can set the handle up to retrieve from whichever side you prefer. Normally, it is beneficial for people who are right-handed to reel with their left hand and for lefties to reel with their right hand, so that the dominant hand is the one that holds the rod and is used to play the fish or direct the retrieve. Because the dominant hand is used to cast the rod, there is no need to take further action after casting to start using the reel; the other hand is immediately placed on the reel handle grip and it starts turning the handle. This is how most people use a spinning reel, the difference being that a spinning reel is under the rod handle instead of on top of it. This is also how most people use a trigger-release spincasting reel, which also mounts under the rod.

Whether out of habit or because it feels better, most right-handed anglers who use mount-on-top spincasting (and baitcasting) reels, cast with the reel in their right hand, then switch the reel over to their left hand and grab the handle (located on the right side of the reel) with their right hand. This means that they have their dominant hand reeling and subordinate hand holding the rod, and they must make the extra step of switching the rod and reel from one hand to the other every time they cast. By contrast, using a mount-on-top spincasting reel with a right-sided cranking handle, a left-handed person would cast with the rod in their left hand and then simply grab the reel handle with their right hand. Thus, the rod is in the dominant hand, the reel handle is in the subordinate hand, and there is no switching of rod and reel from one hand to the other. This is clearly the proper way to do things for most anglers, and yet, most do it backward, perhaps because of custom or habit, or because they have a right-hand-retrieve model that requires them to cast with their right hand and reel with their right hand.

If you do this, and are happy and comfortable with it, fine. But if you are a beginning spincasting reel user, you should learn to cast and hold the reel in your dominant hand, and reel with your subordinate hand. This will soon feel completely natural and comfortable to you, and you'll wonder

Spincasting Tackle

Spincasting tackle is easy enough for young children to use.

how anyone could do it otherwise. Because many spincasting reels have only right-handed retrieve, a beginning angler who is right-handed should consider a trigger-release model with left retrieve, or a pushbutton model with convertible retrieve.

No matter which hand you use to hold the reel, two-handed casting is best for the sake of both learning and accuracy. The preferred hand holds the reel with the thumb actuating the pushbutton; the other hand is wrapped around the reel cover with the thumb and forefinger properly positioned to feather the line. This is an important point for people who are learning to use this tackle, as it will lead to greater accuracy with practice.

You may choose to palm the reel and rod handle in your hand, or you may hold the rod handle without palming the reel. Whatever feels best for you is right, provided that you are comfortable casting and holding it that way for long periods, and can readily access the pushbutton or trigger with the same hand that holds the rod for easy one-handed operation.

Casting technique. The actual method of casting is accomplished by pressing the pushbutton with your thumb (or the trigger with your forefinger) and holding it throughout the backcast, then releasing it at the optimum point of rod flex in the forward motion of the cast. When the button is released, line flows off the spool, through the opening in the reel cover, and out through the guides, carried by the weight of the object at the terminal end of the line. When you are not casting, but simply letting line out, as might be done when lowering a weighted bait or lure directly below, you simply press the button or trigger and let go of it to release the line. The released line can be stopped altogether by pressing it firmly. To convert the reel to the retrieve position, turn the handle, and the pickup pin will gather the line and begin to wind it on the spool.

Before making a cast for on-the-water fishing, you should set the drag to the proper amount of tension, and then adjust the position of the lure at the rod tip. The lure should hang a few inches below the rod tip. You can get it to this position by reeling in the line until the lure is a few inches from the tip guide; if the reel is right at the tip, pull a few inches of line off the reel drag, which will cause the lure to hang a few inches below the tip.

Assuming that you are right-handed, place the rod and reel in the palm of your left hand so that the handle of the reel is up and facing you. Extend the left forefinger to trap the line against the opening of the spool. Depress the pushbutton with your right thumb and point the rod tip at your intended target. Lift the rod back toward you swiftly, using your wrist and forearm (not the whole arm), and allow the weight of the plug to flex the rod. In a continuous and unhesitating motion, still using the wrist and forearm, bring the rod forward in an accelerated motion. Release the line and the pushbutton at the same instant during the forward stroke to cast the plug toward the target. While the casting plug is in the air, the line should flow across the tip of your left forefinger. To put the plug right where you want it, increase upward pressure with the left forefinger. With a bit of practice, you will learn at exactly what point in the forward stroke to release the line and the pushbutton, which is a major element in attaining the proper trajectory for accurate placement.

Although explaining this belabors the act of casting, it is really a simple technique that almost anybody can master in a short period of time. You'll quickly learn to feather the line with your left forefinger to drop the plug right where it needs to be. This does involve the use of both hands, but for most people that shouldn't be an issue. Your right hand still executes the casting stroke. The only function of the left hand is to get your left forefinger out where it needs to be to control the line.

When you are learning, and whenever striving for accuracy, get the rod and reel out in front of your body with both hands and make the rod follow an imaginary line from your nose to the target. Always remember the most important single phase of the spincasting technique is to have the line flowing over your left forefinger while the plug is in the air. Once you get the feel for the control you have over the lure by simply lifting the forefinger slightly up against the line, you're on your way.

Although most people do not rate spincasting tackle very highly in the accuracy department, some of the best exhibition and trick casters can do things with spincasting tackle that are truly amazing, so obtaining accuracy is partly a matter of how far you are willing to take the practice element, and using the right rod and weight of lure. It is true, however, that when using lures and fishing in cover, baitcasting tackle (once you have mastered spool control) is an easier type of tackle to consistently obtain accuracy with. For many spincasting tackle users, achieving casting accuracy is not a big issue. A lot of spincasting reel users do not need accuracy in their fishing, because they primarily employ this tackle while using bait and bait rigs, especially from a dock or shore, and in relatively open water. For more information on all aspects of casting, *see: Casting.*

Setting/Checking drag. The drag on a spincasting reel is adjusted by turning the drag wheel or star wheel. When either of these wheels is facing you, turning them to the right increases tension, and turning to the left decreases it. If a reel is used infrequently, it is a good idea at the end of each outing to back the drag tension off to relieve pressure on the drag washers. Before starting a day of fishing, you should check and adjust the drag tension setting before making a cast. Many an angler has neglected this and found upon hooking the first fish of the day that the drag was so weak it impaired hooksetting, or so tight that it adversely affected fish playing.

To test the drag on a spincasting reel, pull line off it at various drag tension settings. Most people, especially if they have fishing experience, test the drag by pulling the line by hand directly ahead of the reel, and making necessary adjustments by feel, starting with a light drag setting and testing and adjusting until they reach a tension setting that feels right. For most fishing situations, especially in freshwater, this is adequate, and anglers wind up putting somewhere in the neighborhood of 30 to 50 percent of the maximum breaking tension on the line. This "by feel" adjustment is a somewhat imprecise method of doing things, but adequate for the vast majority of spincasting reel users. Using and setting drag is covered in more detail elsewhere *(see: drag).*

If you want a general evaluation of how smooth the drag on a given reel is, run the line from the reel through the rod guides and attach it to a scale. Angle the rod tip up and pull on the line while you check what happens to the rod tip. If the tip remains in place, the drag is smooth, which is good. If it moves up and down, the drag is erratic, which may cause problems.

Maintenance and repair. Many people do very little, if anything, to maintain their spincasting reels other than removing tangled line from them. This may be all right if the reel is only used occasionally. Common sense dictates that if the reel has any loose part, which is most likely to be the retaining nut on the handle, it should be tightened as soon as you notice it, and that you should rinse any reel that has encountered sand, dirt, mud, or saltwater. Use a fine spray of freshwater, rather that a hard stream, to clean the reel and do so as soon as possible after use. Cleanse it of dirt or sand whenever it gets dirty, and give the reel a chance to dry out completely when it gets wet. It's a good practice to reapply lubricant to the areas recommended by the manufacturer's literature after cleaning a reel, subjecting it to a lot of moisture, or submersing it.

Details on reel maintenance are discussed elsewhere *(see: tackle care/maintenance/repair).* Manufacturers recommend that infrequently used reels be cleaned and relubricated annually, and that reels that are used several times a week be attended to monthly. Periodic maintenance means lightly oiling and greasing accessible parts. Some reels come with small oil or grease tubes, and these can be purchased from tackle suppliers or obtained from the manufacturer. A thorough cleaning requires disassembling most of the reel, scrubbing or rinsing most of the gunk from the parts, drying, and then relubricating.

SPINNER

(1) A term for the sexually mature, or imago, stage of an adult mayfly *(see).* Spinners sometimes appear in great numbers over the water; they mate in the air and females fly down to the water's surface to lay their eggs.

(2) A metal lure with a blade that revolves around a central shaft and spins when retrieved.

Probably no type of lure is sold in such quantity and with such international reception as the spinner. Its origins in history are uncertain, and what it represents is more the suggestion of something to eat rather than a duplication of it, but through its flashy appearance and movement, and in a variety of models and sizes, the spinner has been a perennially popular freshwater lure. It is seldom used in saltwater (due mainly to strength and corrosion concerns), and would be a rare sight among the tackle of a veteran saltwater angler, even though some models will surely catch certain marine species.

A spinner may not be the best lure to use for all freshwater fish, or to use in every possible circumstance, but in the right size and fished in the appropriate place, it is a lure that will catch most species of freshwater fish. The basic small to intermediate size spinner is of foremost appeal in angling for stream trout and salmon, which probably see more spinners (in $1/30$- to $1/4$-ounce sizes) than all other species of fish combined. Smallmouth bass, panfish, pickerel, pike, and muskies (large bucktail versions for the latter) are also favorite targets.

Most spinners are used for casting, but some are trolled. They are relatively uncomplicated to use and, in most sizes, hook fish fairly readily. The blade is central to the effectiveness of the spinner, not only because of the visual appearance it has when moving, but because it generates a good deal of vibration, which can be detected by fish in murky water where visibility is limited. The blade vibrates differently from one style to another.

There are essentially two types of lures that fit this well-established lure category: in-line spinners, and weight-forward spinners. A spinning blade of some type is also used in combination with a variety of lures, including spinnerbaits *(see)*, buzzbaits *(see)*, and tailspinners *(see)*, although usually not in an in-line fashion, and may be an add-on to plugs, plastic worms, and jigs.

In-Line Spinners

In-line spinners feature a freely rotating blade (or blades), mounted on a single straight (in-line) shaft. Behind the blades are beads or bodies of lead or metal, which provide the lure's basic weight and make it castable. Skirts of feather, hair, or plastic tubing, may be added to the hook to increase the spinner's appeal, but many hooks are unadorned.

These lures are available in weights from $1/32$ ounce to several ounces; with single, double, and treble hooks; with blade lengths from $1/2$ inch to several inches; and with assorted types of tail material. Squirrel and bucktail hair are traditionally favorite hook garnishes, but soft plastic bodies are increasingly used on single-hooked spinners, and some feature rubber or plastic minnow bodies.

Assorted spinners, from top to bottom, include small versions for trout and panfish, midsize versions for bass and walleye, and bucktail spinners for larger fish, including pike and muskies.

A majority of spinners are equipped by manufacturers with a treble hook, but some have single hooks, and a few feature an interchangeable hook (others are not interchangeable, meaning that when you must use a single hook, two points of the treble have to be snipped off). The $1/16$-, $3/8$-, and $1/4$-ounce sizes are best for bass fishing; the smaller sizes are used in panfishing; and the biggest models are fished for large pike, muskies, and possibly striped bass.

The blade design controls the action and the angle of blade revolution. Blades that are attached to the shaft via a clevis are mainly of Colorado, Indiana, French, or willowleaf shape, although there are variations on these and some nonconformist styles as well. The willowleaf, which is the narrowest blade, has less water resistance, so it rotates closest to the shaft, and thus, spins faster. The Colorado is the broadest blade and has the most water resistance, so it rotates farthest from the shaft and spins slowest. The others are in between these two. Another style, the so-called sonic blade, is somewhat like a broad willowleaf; it is concave at one end and convex at the other, mounts directly on the shaft (which runs through the lure), and has a narrow rotation to make it work well in fast current. In a properly designed spinner, the blade spins even at a slow retrieval speed, so water conditions and current flow, if present, help determine which style to use.

The actual spinner blade is available in many colors, but the blade's color is not nearly as important as its visibility under fishing conditions. A good reflective quality is desired. Spinners also give some vibration when retrieved, a fact that is important to the fish and which probably accounts for the success of spinners when used at night and under very poor water clarity conditions.

Factors like blade design, weight, and surface area are related to how the lure is retrieved. A spinner does not begin working until it is being retrieved. The blade does not spin when the lure is falling, meaning that this is not a lure for jigging. If a spinner is fished too slowly, the blade may not spin or may spin erratically, but if it is retrieved too quickly, the blade cannot catch the water, and it will fall flat against the lure's body, keeping the blade from rotating and probably causing the whole lure to spin, which will not catch fish. Therefore, it's important to get the right speed to work the blade properly; this is usually not much of a problem because these lures generally accommodate a range of normal swimming speeds.

In moving water, you generally don't fish a spinner directly downstream, but cast it upstream at a quartering angle. The lure is tumbled by the swift water and also reeled forward at the same time, or it is fished like a spoon *(see)* with rod tip held high and the lure retrieved just slowly enough to let the blade turn while the spinner swings downstream. Fish a spinner as slowly as you can under the circumstances; you should be able to feel the blade revolve with a sensitive rod. The depth of retrieve can be altered by raising or lowering the rod, or changing the speed of retrieval. Hanging the spinner directly downstream in the current can also be effective, as long as the current has enough force to turn the blade freely.

Though spinners may often hang up, this may be due to poor use. In streams, it's important to get the lure working the moment it hits the water. Hesitation often means hung spinners, particularly when casting across a stream in a fast flow. Matching the size and weight to the water is also important.

In lakes and ponds, small and intermediate size spinners are mostly fished fairly close to the surface or relatively shallow and on a straight retrieve. In deeper water, they are worked by counting the lure down to a specific level (you must predetermine the sink rate) and retrieving slowly. Because lighter spinners don't have the weight or lure action to stay at one level, they angle upward on the retrieve; a long cast, an unimpeded freefall to deeper levels (keep an open bail on a spinning reel), and a low-angled rod help lengthen the time that the lure is in the right zone. Although a steady retrieve is often productive, it pays to vary a straight retrieve occasionally by hesitating the lure, twitching it quickly, and otherwise briefly altering its movement, which may cause a following fish to pounce.

Large spinners with bucktail hair dressing are known as bucktails and stand out from all other spinners in terms of their application, although they're fished similarly to smaller spinners in most respects. These weighted spinners sink quickly and are strictly cast for muskies and pike, generally being fished over the top of submerged grass (in which case you can't let the lure sink too far on the initial drop), along weedlines, and around cover or structure.

Spinning tackle and light lines are best for most in-line spinner use, although baitcasting tackle is preferable with large bucktail spinners. The majority of spinners are fished with light line, usually in the 2- to 6-pound range, and sometimes from 8- to 12-pound line. For stream fishing, light tackle, light line, and small spinners are the rule. Heavier line is used with the largest spinners.

It is always necessary to use a swivel or snap-swivel with these lures to counter the tendency of the rotating blade to turn the lure over repeatedly and cause line twist. A few spinners are very good at resisting line twist, and bending the upper shaft may help avoid it, but line twist is such a serious problem with spinners that you should not take a chance in going without a good quality swivel or snap-swivel.

Twist can also be caused by debris on the lure, especially on the clevis. Debris tends to get on spinners fairly readily, as these are not very weed-free lures. This or anything else that causes the blade not to spin freely deserves attention.

Weight-Forward Spinners
Weight-forward spinners are long-shanked lures with a lead weight molded to the shaft ahead of a spinner blade, which in turn is ahead of a single hook. The hook is primarily supplied bare and impaled with a live worm. Some have a single or treble hook that is dressed with hair, fur, or a soft plastic body such as a grub.

These spinners are used for slow trolling, drifting, and casting in freshwater, and are mainly popular for smallmouth bass and walleye fishing on northern lakes, especially when garnished with a live worm and drifted across rocky reefs. Simpler versions, which feature a long-shanked hook and a single rotating blade with beads along the shaft, have long been known as June Bug spinners.

Weight-forward spinners exist in small to intermediate sizes and with a variety of weight and blade shapes. The positioning of the weight on the lure causes it to sink headfirst, meaning that, unlike in-line spinners, the blade can spin on the descent and possibly catch fish. Narrow weight shapes allow a weight-forward spinner to sink quickly, and are good for fishing in current and deep water. Wider weights have more water resistance, and are preferred for shallow-water use. The head is usually preceded by a long wire shaft (sometimes removable), to foil bite-offs from sharp-toothed fish, and the twist-free nature of the lure allows usage without a swivel or snap-swivel.

Unlike in-line spinners, weight-forward spinners stay at a deep level when retrieved slowly. They should be counted down to the proper level when fished high in the water column, and allowed to reach bottom when it's necessary to crawl deep. To start the retrieve, snap the rod tip up to help get the blade turning. These lures catch fish on both a routine uninterrupted retrieve, and when the lure is hesitated and jerked occasionally during a normal retrieve However, they are prone to fouling when cast. To minimize this, bring the rod tip back gently and lob the lure forward instead of making a standard rod-loading cast; also, pull the rod tip in as the lure hits the water to turn it toward you and straighten it out. Avoid a snap-swivel or snap to further decrease fouling.

SPINNERBAIT

A spinnerbait is an unusual looking lure in a V-like configuration if viewed from the side. The lower arm of V-shaped wire sports a tapered lead headed hook usually garnished with a skirt or soft-bodied grub, and the upper arm features one or two freely revolving spinner blades. When the lure is retrieved steadily, the blades and upper arm run vertically above the bottom part of the lure. Viewed from the side, the ensemble resembles an open safety pin, which prompted some early users to dub it a safety pin spinner. It is not a true spinner *(see)*, in the on-line sense of that lure, but is referred to as a spinner by some anglers, and an overhead spinner by others.

A spinnerbait is one of the favorite lures of bass anglers and one of their most popular offerings for springtime and shallow-water angling. Although it is thought of almost exclusively as a freshwater lure for bass fishing, and is primarily available in sizes appropriate for largemouth and smallmouth bass, a spinnerbait can be very effective for chain pickerel and northern pike, and may be useful for catching some panfish and the occasional muskie. Strictly a casting lure that is primarily used on largemouth bass and secondarily on smallmouth and spotted bass, a spinnerbait is seldom deliberately employed for, or effective on, such species as trout, salmon, or striped bass, although it will catch peacock bass.

A relatively easy lure to fish, the spinnerbait is remarkably weed- and tangle-free when fished around cover and obstructions. It can be an exciting lure to retrieve in shallow water and in water that is clear near the surface, because it's possible to watch fish rush after it and strike. Because they are fairly large and bulky lures, spinnerbaits cast very well, although models with large blades and with tandem blades can be more air-resistant and are subject to swaying from the intended trajectory or target; this may be countered by making low-angle presentations, such as casting underhanded or side-armed.

Spinnerbaits come in a variety of configurations, with differing blades, lead heads, and body colors.

What a spinnerbait is supposed to look like is uncertain. Obviously, its shape does not imitate a particular natural food, yet it possesses certain qualities that attract fish, especially bass in the spring and fall. Through blade color and movement, a spinnerbait certainly offers visual flash and auditory vibration. Fish can both see and hear it well. With a good skirt on the hook shaft, a spinnerbait also offers pulsating movement and the impression of having plenty of substance. Add to this the fact that it can be effectively fished in all but the thickest cover and can be fished in intermediate and deep water, and you have the elements of a unique but effective type of lure.

Sizes, Bodies, Colors

Spinnerbaits are available in a wide range of sizes, from micro to maxi models. The lightest ones, in $1/16$- to $3/16$-ounce sizes, are used with light line and light spinning tackle, primarily for bluegills and crappie, but also for smaller specimens of largemouth and smallmouth bass, plus white bass. Small spinnerbaits usually feature a single blade on the overhead shaft and a soft grub-shaped body rather than a multi-tentacled skirt. For the most part, these are fished in shallow areas and near the surface.

The largest versions, which weigh in the $1\frac{1}{2}$- to 2-ounce range and sport thick gauge wire and huge blades, can be employed in muskie and northern pike fishing, but are not heavily favored for the former, where in-line bucktail spinners predominate. These lures must be used with heavy-action tackle and rods whose tip can respond quickly and with authority to punch a lure home.

Bass-sized spinnerbaits primarily range from $1/4$- to 1-ounce, with $1/2$- and $5/8$-ounce models being especially popular. Many bass anglers seldom use less than a $1/2$-ounce spinnerbait, and a few may use magnum models (up to $1\frac{1}{2}$ ounces) for deep-water work. Though by many standards these are large lures, such sizes are readily accepted by largemouth bass, although the smaller models are usually more appropriate for smallmouths; the intermediate sizes are so favored by bass anglers that they constitute the bulk of the spinnerbait market.

The weight of a spinnerbait is, in large part, determined by the size of the head on the lower shaft. This is essentially a lead jig head, and is usually tapered to facilitate swimming. On small spinnerbaits, that head may be rounded, like a ball-head jig, but for most bass models, it is shaped more like a cone or bullet. Some heads may be turned up slightly to resist diving and enhance upward or shallow movement, especially on a fast retrieve.

The main part of all spinnerbaits is the wire used to form the upper and lower arms. The thickness of the wire in these arms has some bearing on how the lure fishes and how durable it is. Thin wire produces a good feel and good lure action but can snap under the strain of a big fish, and, in general, will not withstand as much use as thicker arms. Yet, wire arms that are too thick detract substantially from lure action and feel, and are thus undesirable for most fishing. When using a good spinnerbait, the angler can usually feel the vibration of the turning blade, which produces a thumping sensation. When a spinnerbait is not visible, strikes are often detected when that thumping ceases. If the wire arm on a spinnerbait is too thick, the angler cannot constantly feel the lure working, and is thus more likely to not detect some strikes, or to be delayed in setting the hook upon receiving some strikes. But if the wire is too thin, the angler may not be able to drive the hook well enough when he gets a strike, or the lure will be easily deformed after a bit of use.

Spinnerbaits that are used for pike fishing, however, should be made of a heavier gauge wire to take the extra twisting, thrashing, and strain that pike inflict on a lure. Most spinnerbaits designed for bass fishing do not hold up well to repeated northern pike catching. Also, spinnerbaits used for pike fishing are better if they have a fixed line-tie point rather than an open one. Most spinnerbaits have an open crook at the tip of the lure where the upper and lower arms converge, which is where the fishing line is directly tied with a nonslip knot. However, in pike fishing, wire leaders are often employed, and a snap is used at the front end of that leader to connect to a lure. When a snap is connected to a standard spinnerbait, there is nothing to prevent that snap from sliding along either shaft, which it will do when cast, when fluttered into deep water, or sometimes during the fight with a fish. This can cause you to lose a fish, to lose the lure, or to damage the lure. A better style for this usage is a spinnerbait with a circular loop bend at the line-tie point; a snap cannot wander from that type of connection.

Some spinnerbaits feature overhead blade arms that extend well beyond the hook on the bottom arm. This is of some help in preventing hangups,

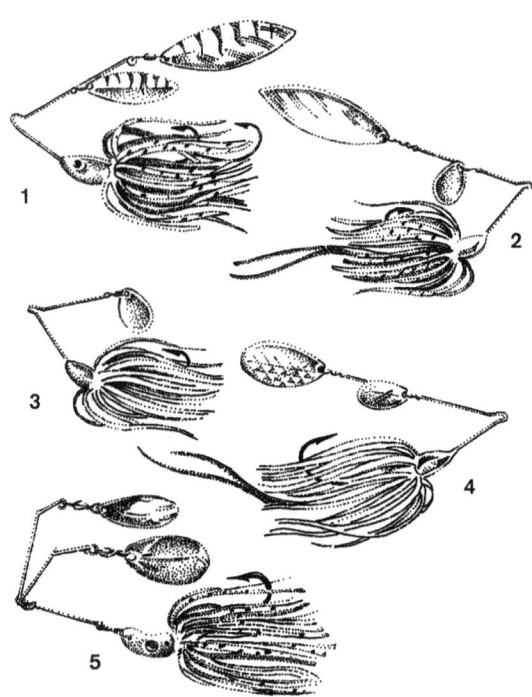

Spinnerbait styles are numerous and generally defined by their blade configurations, arm length, and arm number. Popular single-arm arrangements include twin willowleaf (1), willowleaf and Colorado (2), single Colorado on a short arm (3), and twin Indiana (4); the twin spin (5) is distinguished by its double overhead arms, usually with Colorado or Indiana blades.

but it sometimes hampers hooksetting. Spinnerbaits with a long arm and a jumbo willowleaf trailing blade are used to create a large look when targeting big fish. The majority of spinnerbaits primarily have a medium-length overhead arm in which the blade assembly is directly above the hook, which is thus unobstructed, or which extends just a tad past the hook but no further than the end of the skirt. A combination of blade types and sizes is used on these. Some spinnerbaits have short arms and usually a single Colorado or Indiana style blade. These produce a lot of vibration and are good for deep fishing.

Arm length can be a two-edged sword. Short-armed spinnerbaits hang up frequently in thick brush and stumps and timber. If you need to roll such a lure over a log, it often won't make it, because the overhead shaft is too short to afford any protection. If you take a short-armed spinnerbait that is attached to fishing line and gently try to pull it over your arm, you'll get the picture; if the hook pricks your arm, it will stick in a log. For such times, a longer-armed spinnerbait is best.

Incidentally, there is a now relatively obscure type of spinnerbait called a twin spinner that features two overhead arms instead of the normal one, with each possessing a single blade. The overhead arms are fairly short and lay off to an angle instead of being directly in line with the lower arm, so that the blades on each (Indiana or Colorado versions) can spin freely. These are very snag-resistant lures, and they can be worked well at slow speeds, which may be good for inactive fish. Also, the larger models with smaller blades can be good for deep-water probing.

Spinnerbaits have to be periodically tuned to keep running properly. When retrieved at a normal pace, a good spinnerbait runs straight, without twisting 360 degrees or leaning off to the side. It should be able to do this at slow as well as high speeds. You can adjust a spinnerbait so that the blades and hook run vertically in the water by bending the entire overhead shaft arm in the opposite direction from which it is running astray. Bend the arm slightly, and then test the lure; keep adjusting in increments until you get it right.

The primary aspect of a spinnerbait's body is its type and color. Although soft plastics and bucktail hair may be used on the shank of the hook for body, greater bulk and action is had with other materials, so soft bodies and bucktails are not that prominent on spinnerbaits. Most bodies feature a skirt that has been evolving over the past few decades in material from vinyl to rubber to synthetics and in appearance from monochrome to multicolor to an ultra snazzy potpourri of colors and enhancements.

White has long been a preferred skirt color, especially for the early season and in murky water; all chartreuse and chartreuse/blue (or black) combinations have been preferred in clearer water. Variations of these, with sparkle or iridescent enhancements, are still very popular, but you can find a host of colors and local preferences now, just as you can for fishing other types of lures, and opinions on skirt and overall lure color vary widely.

On many occasions, the color of skirt makes no difference in the number or size of fish caught. This is especially true when the lure is fished in water that is extremely turbid, at night in the dark, and in very deep water. There are many contradicting beliefs among anglers as to body color, just as there are as to blade color, blade size, and even the number of blades.

Most spinnerbaits today are equipped with silicone skirts, but they used to be primarily dressed with vinyl, hair, or rubber skirts, and some are still available in these materials, particularly rubber. The newer synthetics hold up well in cold water and offer good body swimming action. The disadvantage with rubber is that the tentacles have a tendency to stick together in the tackle box; you can avoid this by sprinkling some talcum powder in the compartments that house your spinnerbaits and by using trays that allow you to store spinnerbaits with the skirts hanging loosely rather than bunched up. If the legs melt together, pull the skirt off and replace it with a fresh one. Synthetic skirts, some with elaborate colors and designs, have become much more prevalent, and it's now possible to create a pop art look with spinnerbaits. Metal flake and iridescent skirts make the older types and colors look especially drab. By changing skirts, you can readily mix and match body and head colors. Most anglers believe that the jig head and body should complement each other in color, but that is not an absolute necessity.

To apply a skirt, hold it up so that the tentacles hang straight down, then turn it upside down so that the tentacles come out and over the stem of the skirt, resembling small streams of water being shot out of a fountain; thread the stem over the hook point and the shank until it fits snugly on the base of the lead head. This backward skirt produces far more pulsating action than a straight-back skirt would.

It's a good idea to dress up spinnerbaits still further, especially large ones, by adding a curl-tailed soft worm, grub, or pork chunk to the main hook. Some anglers are partial to 3-inch, twin-tailed, soft plastic trailers, which swim feverishly just behind the skirt, and give a valuable extra dimension to the look of the lure. A short plastic worm with a twisted or curled tail is also good, and provides nice additional motion. Slender pork rind or other materials are also possibilities. Remember that many of these add a little more weight as well as bulk. Keep long plastic trailers from extending too far behind the lure in pike and pickerel country or they will be snipped off.

A trailer hook is a good idea for bass fishing, except when the cover is so thick that the extra hook causes hangups. Spinnerbaits account for a lot of fish and one of the beneficial aspects about using them is that their single main-body hook permits relatively quick unhooking and near zero chance of hurting yourself (similar to jigs but unlike multihooked plugs). However, they are often subject to swiping or short-striking by bass, and a trailer hook can account for many bass that would otherwise be lost. It is not necessary to use a trailer hook all the time, but it doesn't hurt, especially if the fish are visibly striking short or hitting merely to stun. The trailer hook should ride up like the spinnerbait hook, and should not be imbedded in any skirt or body material. To keep the trailer hook from sliding off, block it with a small piece of surgical tubing. Place a small ring of this material over the eye of the trailer hook, then bring the point of the spinnerbait hook through the eye and tubing, and secure it.

Another addition sometimes made to a spinnerbait is a small rattle. Some lures have a receptacle for a rattle that is on the hook shank underneath the forward part of the skirt. A rattle may be added using pieces of surgical tubing as well, usually on the hook shank but sometimes in front of the head on the lower wire arm. The purpose of this obviously is to add more noise to the lure, which may be most appropriate in spinnerbaits that do not produce a lot of vibration, like a smaller lure with a short willowleaf blade.

 A bathyscape 7 miles deep in the ocean receives more than 8 tons of weight per square inch, yet there are various fish at this level that live in equilibrium by equalizing internal and external pressure.

Blades

Spinnerbaits are available in single and tandem blade versions. Tandem blades on the overhead arm of the spinnerbait usually feature a small spinner followed by a larger one. These are predominantly for shallow fishing, but this is just a generality. Single blade spinnerbaits can also be effective when fished shallow, although they are thought to be a better lure style for deeper retrieves. In actuality, although some anglers have strong preferences for when and where to use single or tandem blade spinnerbaits, they can be used in a broad range of conditions that are equally affected by the overall weight of the lure and the size and shape of the blades.

Spinnerbaits principally feature Colorado, Indiana, and willowleaf design blades, or hybrid versions of these basic styles. The Colorado is between round and pear-shaped and is generally believed to produce the most vibration, although

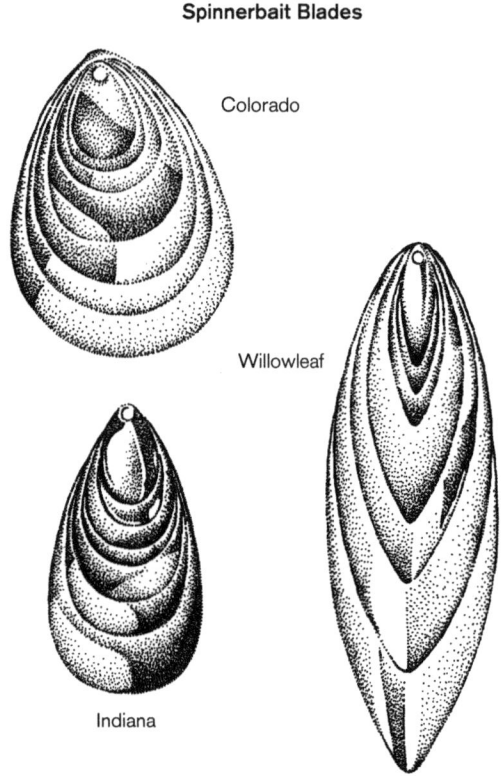

Spinnerbait Blades

Colorado
Willowleaf
Indiana

this is a function of how much it is cupped. The more cupping there is to the blade, the greater the vibration. The common size is No. 4, which is roughly the size of a quarter, but the range is from No. 2 to the magnum No. 8. Colorado blades are often found on single blade spinnerbaits. They are good for slow retrieves, murky water, and dark conditions. A small Colorado may precede a larger willowleaf blade on a tandem spinnerbait.

Indiana blades are teardrop-shaped and produce good vibration, too, though they spin faster, and work well on tandem blade lures. They, too, are used in combination with other blade types, either in front of a willowleaf or behind a Colorado. Willowleaf blades, shaped as the name implies and coming to a sharply tapered tail point, were less commonly used in the past but are now extremely popular. These long blades are mainly used on a tandem rig with a big No. 4 or 5 willowleaf, usually in silver or copper, behind a smaller Indiana blade; however, willowleaf blades can be used in tandem, or as a single, and are preferred in the magnum sizes (up to No. 8) for big fish. The willowleaf doesn't offer as much vibration as other types of blades, but it revolves freely and produces a lot of flash. It is an attention getter, especially when hammered or fluted or spiced with light-bouncing colors.

Spinnerbaits with big blades are generally reserved for waters with distinct big-fish potential. This is not to say you won't catch big bass on smaller lures, but the probability is that you'll catch fewer small bass with an oversized bait. They are also used for deep-water fishing, where flash may not be a factor, but where a heavy dose of vibration is essential. Smaller blade sizes, especially the willowleaf, are necessary when the primary forage is small, and it may be necessary to try to match the size of blade to the size of baitfish currently available where you're fishing.

There are also hybrid blade styles that don't fit generic descriptions. The most prominent of these are jointed oval-shaped blades, which wave rather than spin and are usually found on short-armed spinnerbaits. There are also winged blades, spiral blades, and blades with various intentional deformations that change or exaggerate a basic shape. Additionally, there may be a difference in action as well as vibration among blades of the same overall design due to the amount of cupping in the blade. The greater the cupping, the more the blade pulls water. With a pair of pliers you can increase the cupping or decrease it, even flattening it in the latter case.

Spinnerbait blades come in different colors and impressions. Nickel (silver) and copper have traditionally been most popular, followed by gold, and painted white, chartreuse, and orange. However, multicolored blades and paintings have made great inroads, and the standard metal finishes may now be much more diverse than polished older versions, including hammered design, horizontal bars, fluted patterns, diamond patterns, and more. Most are intended to reflect light rays and create flash.

Copper, which historically has been the favorite of most anglers, is good for slightly turbid and off color water. Silver works well for most of the year, especially in the spring and in clear water. Painted blades, most notably chartreuse, work well when murky green water conditions are present, and are preferred by some anglers in clear water because they are more subtle overall, do not produce as much flash, and provide something of a three-dimensional appearance. Many newer blades are painted with various patterns and with sparkling, flashy designs. They look great, but it is unclear whether this produces a practical effective advantage, although there may be a psychological benefit if the appearance causes the user to retrieve it more attentively. Some anglers believe that painted blades, combined with reflective painted skirts, many of which are garnished with sparkles or a prismatic finish, imitate a school of baitfish and appear more attractive to fish than more traditional looking spinnerbaits.

Because spinnerbaits are very popular lures, and used in common bass haunts on many heavily pressured waters, it is reasonable to wonder if bass do not become accustomed to seeing certain colors of these lures and thus more wary of them, which leads to a rise in the usage of newer and formerly less popular colors. To some extent, this may be true with all types of lures. The point is that colors on all lures, especially spinnerbaits, run in fads among anglers, and it may well be worthwhile to use colors that differ from the norm on heavily pressured lakes, or to return to colors that were once popular but which have fallen out of favor, and thus are no longer being seen so often by the fish.

The style or combination of blades you use may be a reflection of where and how you fish. Tandem spinnerbaits are generally meant for speedy retrieval. A twin willowleaf combination is the best for pure quick retrieving, and a willowleaf-Colorado combination is for more intermediate retrieval. To get a slow retrieve, especially in shallow water, you need a blade that grabs a lot of water and spins well. This might be a Colorado combination, or more likely a single Colorado blade, perhaps of large size. Although some anglers use tandem blades for deep fishing, their effectiveness there is primarily when being retrieved rather than when falling, because the blades usually get tangled on the drop and don't rotate. If you consider this issue in terms of water condition, try spinnerbaits that produce more vibration when the water is turbid (fish rely more on sound than sight) or when it is cold (sound coaxes better than flash), and spinnerbaits that produce more flash when the water is clear (sight is most important) or when it is warm (the fish are active and more aggressive).

Spinnerbait Fishing for Bass
A spinnerbait evidently appeals to the predatory, reflexive instincts of bass as much as to its hunger instincts. A bass must strike a spinnerbait because it grabs its eye and looks like something vulnerable, or because it produces vibrations that sound like something it ordinarily eats or might eat.

Spinnerbaits are versatile lures, as might be inferred from the wide assortment of blades, colors, and sizes available. A spinnerbait is a good lure for fishing in and around cover; lily pads, grass, stumps, brush, treetops, boat docks, rock piles, logs, and similar fish holding places can all be

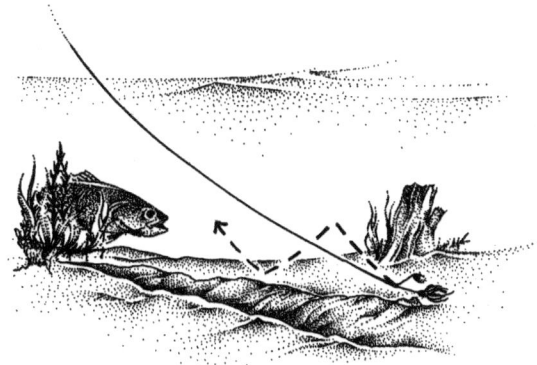

Although most anglers retrieve spinnerbaits shallow, these lures can be very effective when crawled across the bottom, and fished in a slow, deep, lift-and-drop manner.

effectively worked. A spinnerbait is primarily fished on a standard cast-and-retrieve, usually in shallow or intermediate depths, where it is most productive for the average angler. But it can also be fished in deep water, although the methods in each case are quite different.

The most common technique of fishing a spinnerbait is to retrieve it from within a few inches to several feet beneath the surface; if the water is clear enough, you can see and watch the lure coming through the water on the retrieve. It is not only beneficial, but highly enjoyable, to watch a spinnerbait when it is being retrieved this shallow. Nearly every time, if you can see the lure, you will see the fish strike it. Sometimes, a bass seems to dart out of nowhere. Other times, it comes from right where expected. This is very much like surface fishing; the excitement of anticipating and seeing the strike is always present. Even when the water is murky and you can't see the lure, you usually know about where it is located as it swims, and the strike may create a splash or boil on the surface. Spinnerbaits are usually struck from the side, suddenly forcing the lure sideways as if it were hit by a gust of wind. When this happens, jam the hook home fast. Another distinct advantage of this technique is that you can see the fish that attempt to strike the bait. You can often see if a bass misses the lure, hits short, or is merely taking a close look. Sometimes, these fish can be caught with another cast of that spinnerbait in the same area, or with an alternative lure that works more slowly.

It is also beneficial to watch the lure as it is retrieved right to the boat. Sometimes, particularly on shallow, stumpy flats, a fish may come from almost under the boat after the lure, yet turn away at the last second as the lure nears the boat. Chain pickerel and northern pike characteristically follow this lure right up to the boat, sometimes striking at boatside. If you see this, you can be prepared.

It is important to begin retrieving a spinnerbait the moment it hits the water for maximum effectiveness when working the shallows. With spinning tackle, this is no problem, but right-handed baitcasters will have to switch the rod to their left hand during the cast so they can engage the reel as the lure hits the water, or their lure may get fouled initially or fall too deep to fish the nearby cover.

Sometimes, bass are holding by objects at a level deeper than your lure is being retrieved and will not come up for it, even though you're fishing in what is generally considered shallow water. If you're fishing a spinnerbait close to the surface with poor results, try letting it sink out of sight to a depth of between 4 and 8 feet, and retrieve it steadily at that depth. Occasionally, you'll have to fish a spinnerbait out of sight right along the bottom like this, in intermediate or greater depths.

The shallow cover places where most anglers successfully use a spinnerbait necessitate getting as close to the particular object as possible. Do this by casting the lure beyond the target and bringing it back into contact with it, then continuing on. Make several casts to each object, from every angle, paying particu-

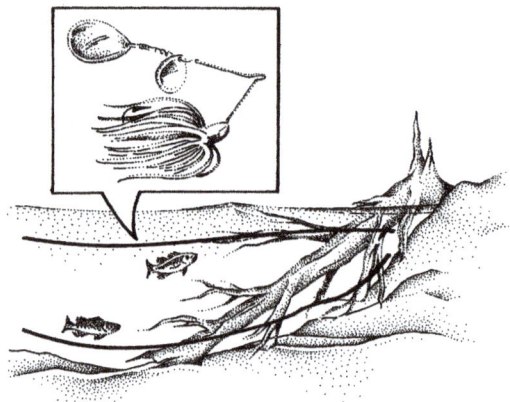

When cast into cover along the bank, a spinnerbait can be retrieved shallow at a moderate pace (upper dark line) through the top layer of water, or more slowly and deeper (lower dark line) through the lower layer.

lar attention to the deep and shady sides.

An effective method for working weed beds and weedlines is to crawl a spinnerbait slowly over the top of grass that is submerged a few feet. For grass beds with definable weedlines, however, it may be better to cast parallel to the edge or bring the lure over the top and let it flutter down the edge. For lily pads, it's best to work the channel-like openings, but don't be afraid to throw into thick clusters and far back into pockets, then ease it over the pads and drop it in another pocket.

Perhaps the most reliable pattern for spinnerbait fishing, especially in the spring, is working the wood. This includes stumps, logs, and stickups. Make sure your spinnerbait is close to these objects; in fact, bump them with the lure at times. The momentary fluttering of the bait's blades and the object contact seem to produce strikes. Stickup trees, bushes, and floating logjams (as often found in coves) also are productive for spinnerbait users.

In these locales, you should get your bait as far back in them as possible before commencing the retrieve. Boat docks and houses, too, fit in this category.

Spring and early summer are prime times for spinnerbait use. In spring and early summer, spinnerbaits allow you to cover a lot of ground effectively and quickly, while you watch your lure work and see strikes. Midsummer is generally not considered a very good spinnerbait time, but this is all relative. Smallmouths in deep water are very susceptible to spinnerbaits fished at night in the summer, and many northern waters, where the water stays warm and fish are relatively shallow, can provide spinnerbait action that rivals that of early season. In some well timbered lakes where bass remain in shallow to intermediate depths through summer, spinnerbaits are quite effective. As the water cools in early fall, spinnerbaits again become primary bass lures, and when fished slowly and deep in the winter or early spring, they are also productive.

Although it has been long taken for gospel that spinnerbaits are only for fishing in water that is as deep as your fishing rod is long, or where you can see the lure from the time it hits the water until the time it gets back to the boat, this is not the case, as some savvy anglers have discovered. Deep fishing with spinnerbaits is something that many anglers have overlooked in the past, preferring to use a deep-diving plug or a Carolina rig worm for probing the nether regions of bass lakes and reservoirs. However, the vibration of big-bladed spinnerbaits in deep water can be enticing to larger bass. Spinnerbaits do indeed have merit for fishing along sharply sloping shorelines, dropoffs, rocky ledges, and among deep timber, whether on a lift-and-drop motion, in a series of short hops, or on a straight retrieve at a deeper than normal level.

Where there is submerged cover in deeper water—points, open-water humps, stumpy flats or ridges near deep water, ledges, and assorted vegeta-

Shallow grass and bushes are excellent places to fish a spinnerbait for largemouth bass.

tion—you can make a long cast and either let the lure fall to the bottom, or count it down to the proper level, before beginning the retrieve. Watch the line for indications of a strike as the lure is falling, and after it reaches the desired level, start a slow steady retrieve. If you crank the reel handle too fast, the lure will rise and lift away from the bottom of the desired zone, so be sure to reel slowly to keep the spinnerbait in the right place.

You may need a very heavy spinnerbait for this, one in the 1-ounce range, to get and keep it at the right level. This is harder to cast than smaller spinnerbaits and may require the use of a two-handed rod, both for casting and retrieving comfort. If you can't find such a heavy spinnerbait, or are pressed to use a lighter one, then try putting a rubber-core sinker onto the shaft of a lighter lure, camouflaged by the skirt.

There are different opinions about using single or tandem blades in deep water. Most people are likely to find a single large Colorado blade very effective, especially in the dark and dirty depths. In addition to producing a lot of vibration, the single Colorado also spins when the lure is on the descent, which can provoke strikes on a falling spinnerbait (say one that is dropped off a deep ledge), or when it is retrieved in a short-hopping motion rather than on a steady retrieve. When short-hopped, a deep spinnerbait is worked more or less like a jig, but if the blade doesn't spin on the descent as well as on the ascent, then it's not that effective. Tandem blades often do not do that.

Keep in mind when fishing a spinnerbait deep that the size of your line may be an important factor. In shallow water, line diameter is not that critical to spinnerbait success or to effective action, but in deep water, a line with a heavier diameter may not fall as well as one with a smaller diameter, and thus tends to ride up. Also, using a short-armed spinnerbait has an advantage for blade action as well, again especially on the drop.

Because heavy spinnerbaits are required for deep water, a fishing rod should be stout enough to make long casts, set the hook when a long length of line is out, and move a good-size fish off or out of cover if necessary. A 7-foot medium-heavy action rod fills that bill, provided it can also transmit the feel of the lure working.

In general, baitcasting tackle is best for spinnerbait use, except when using the lightest versions for small fish. A baitcasting reel does not need a lot of line capacity for spinnerbait use, but it should be filled to capacity for the sake of casting efficiency as well as retrieval. Because it is common to fish a spinnerbait at a fast retrieve, especially in shallow water, reels with a medium or fast retrieval ratio work fine; however, a high-speed reel can lead to fishing a spinnerbait too fast on those occasions when it is necessary to fish a spinnerbait slowly. For really slow fishing, a slower retrieval ratio is advantageous, as it is difficult to deliberately fish a high-speed reel in a slow mode for long periods.

There are a lot of good spinnerbaits on the market, including many that are made and sold within a localized area, so you shouldn't have to look far to find variety. If you keep a supply of extra blades, barrel swivels, trailer hooks, and skirts to be able to modify your spinnerbaits as necessary, you'll be able to enhance the lure's effectiveness and increase your angling success.

SPINNER-JIG
A spinner with a small spinner blade on it.
See: Spinner.

SPINNER RIG
A slow-trolling device, also called a nightcrawler harness, comprised of a Colorado or Indiana spinner, five or six plastic beads, and two short-shanked snelled bait hooks that are impaled in a whole live nightcrawler. This rig is used in freshwater for catching walleye, perch, and smallmouth bass.

SPINNING REEL
See: Spinning Tackle.

SPINNING ROD
See: Spinning Tackle.

SPINNING TACKLE
Spinning tackle is a type of multipurpose fishing equipment characterized by a reel with a stationary spool around which line is wound. This is distinctive from other multipurpose tackle forms, which feature a reel with some type of revolving spool, particularly baitcasting *(see)* and conventional tackle *(see)*, and from flycasting tackle *(see)*, which has a much narrower purpose.

Spinning tackle is related to spincasting tackle *(see)*, which has a stationary spool and is the easiest type of tackle to learn to use. Spincasting reels have a housing over the spool that caused them to be known at one time as closed-face spinning. The reels that are now known simply as spinning were once called open-faced spinning. These terms are used with decreasing frequency in North America today.

Spinning tackle is extremely popular and widespread in use across North America and Europe. Spinning reels have long ranked second among the various reel categories both in terms of the value of the units sold (behind baitcasting) and total number of units sold (behind spincasting). There is some irony to this because the stationary-spool spinning reel is the second most recent tackle type to be developed and to become widely available (spincasting is even more recent). In

North America, spinning began its ascendancy after World War II; it exploded as a popular tool for casting small- to medium-size lures and fishing with bait in freshwater when nylon monofilament line was introduced. At that time, revolving spool reels were widely employed but difficult to cast and use with small or light terminal gear, and flycasting tackle was (and essentially still is) being used strictly for casting super-lightweight objects.

Today, the boundaries between application by type of tackle have blurred due to improvements in all categories of reels, rods, and line. Baitcasting and conventional tackle, for example, have progressed markedly, and some of this equipment is today suitable for use with small terminal gear. Yet spinning has retained a strong following because there is a fairly short learning curve for using it, it is economically priced, and it is suitable for a diverse range of species and angling techniques, particularly in freshwater. Spinning tackle has become a preferred equipment choice for young anglers and one that anglers continue to employ to some degree as they progress from novice through more experienced stages and expand their interests and activities.

Spinning tackle has had a greater following in freshwater than in saltwater, in part because of the differences in conditions, techniques, and size of fish. Spinning gear was once relegated to specific applications, but refinements in equipment have resulted in models of spinning tackle that can be used in applications ranging from ultralight panfishing to offshore billfishing (as in sailfish and white marlin). Appropriate models of spinning reels with corresponding rods can be used for virtually all fishing methods, including casting, trolling, and fishing with bait, but not all spinning reels are up to all tasks, and the factors that go into the selection and use of this or any type of fishing tackle are many and varied.

Reels

The development of the spinning reel is generally credited to British caster Alfred Holden Illingworth, who may have taken a cue from the loom spindles and bobbins used in the cotton mills owned by his family. In 1905, he designed and patented a mechanical means of retrieving line and rotating it around a handheld stationary spool. Anglers had previously hand-wound fishing line around stationary objects and used a weight to propel them. There were earlier attempts at achieving what Illingworth perfected, but none offered the advantages of his device.

In the March 21, 1908, edition of the British publication *Fishing Gazette,* an advertisement by The Light Casting Reel Company for the Illingworth Casting Reel depicted the product mounted underneath the rod, with a left-retrieve handle and looking like a husky flycasting reel. The advertising copy listed among the reel's advantages: "extremely simple in use; no over-running; will cast the lightest bait; does not kink the line; the speed of winding is rapid; the line needs no guiding when winding in as it is automatically spread with precision; proficiency is rapidly acquired . . ." To prove at least one of his points, Illingworth used his invention to take first place in the 3-gram ($1/10$-ounce) distance casting competition at the International Casting Tournament of 1908.

Although Illingworth's reel could cast light objects ($1/16$- to $3/8$-ounce in particular), it was not as proficient at casting heavy objects as the American multiplier, or baitcasting, reel. Yet it was ahead of its time. The rods of that day were ill-suited to casting lightweight lures. There wasn't enough interest yet in lightweight lures for many to be produced, and the gut or braided silk lines of the day were woefully inadequate. These factors combined to make the early spinning reel more novel than utilitarian.

The first spinning reel to be commercially distributed in the United States was the French-made Luxor, which was introduced by New York importer Bache Brown in 1938. Like Illingworth's reel, and unlike other types of fishing reels of the day, it did not use a revolving spool for casting or retrieving line. Yet that reel, and the principle behind it, went virtually unnoticed until 1944, when Brown used the Luxor patent to design a new model named Airex and built in the U.S. Nylon line (braided at first) was just becoming available; rods, mostly made from bamboo, tubular steel, or tubular aluminum, were getting better. Many more lightweight lures were being made, and the public was hungry for an alternative to the stiff and difficult-to-use baitcasting tackle and the flies-only capability of flycasting gear. Six million Airex reels were reportedly sold by 1950, and many other companies joined in the manufacture of what was then called a fixed-spool reel. In the 1950s, fiberglass rods and nylon monofilament line became available, and spinning was on a fast track to increased sportfishing interest.

Although created decades earlier, the spinning reel burst into popularity just ahead of the spincasting reel. Until both spinning and spincasting tackle emerged, anglers primarily used levelwind or baitcasting gear, flycasting tackle, and conventional or big-game tackle for respective, and at that time somewhat specialized, applications. There was a lack of easy-to-use equipment for varied angling activity, especially the casting of different weight objects. As Illingworth's invention promised in 1908, the new fixed-spool, or spinning, reel offered easier casting than the baitcasting (levelwind) reels then available, which at that time generated an annoying and frustrating backlash for most anglers on every fourth or fifth cast. The spinning reel was also capable of casting lightweight lures (which eventually led to casting a range of lure weights).

Both spinning and spincasting reels eventually played a huge role in a fishing participation boom that has extended to the present day, and spilled over into the improvement of all other tackle types.

In the early 1950s, with the emergence of spincasting reels, which also had a stationary rather than revolving spool, the terminology used to describe these products was slightly different. Reels that are presently referred to as spinning models were then called open-faced spinning or, less often, open-faced reels. The reels that are referred to today as spincasting were then called closed-face spinning, or closed-face reels. This terminology has caused some confusion in literature, although the intentions are understandable; the early nomenclature was arguably more appropriate than what is used in today's parlance.

Spinning reels all feature an exposed spool that is stationary during the casting and retrieving processes; thus, it was common to call these open-faced reels in the early days of their existence. Spincasting reels all feature a stationary spool, a line pickup, and a line-winding mechanism that are covered by a cone or hood; thus, it was common for these to initially be called closed-face reels. Both feature a spool that remains stationary (fixed) when line is wound, or spun, around it, and when it is unwound, although the spool does revolve when the drag feature is called upon. This is different from other reel types, whose spool revolves and in so doing causes the line to wind and unwind. Essentially, in the modern vernacular, any reel with an exposed stationary spool is a spinning reel, and any reel with a covered stationary spool is a spincasting reel.

At the risk of further confusion, it should be pointed out that another distinguishing difference between spinning and spincasting reels is that the former always sit underneath the reel handle, while the latter usually sit atop the reel handle. Likewise, baitcasting reels are always mounted on top of the rod handle.

The fact that spinning reels are mounted underneath the rod handle no doubt contributes greatly to their prominence. To most people, especially those who have never used fishing equipment before, it seems natural, and feels more comfortable and balanced, to hold a fishing outfit in which the reel is positioned underneath the rod rather than one in which the reel is atop the rod. This placement reduces the type of arm fatigue that is associated with frequent, if not constant, casting, and the fact that spinning reels are convertible to either right- or left-handed retrieve assures that the rod is held in the dominant hand, which is often not the case when using spincasting or baitcasting tackle.

Spinning reels today are used in freshwater and saltwater, although more commonly in the former, primarily because freshwater anglers outnumber saltwater anglers, freshwater fish are smaller and less punishing on tackle, and more casting is generally done in freshwater. They range from small-profile

There are many spinning reels with various features available.

ultralight models for use with 2-pound-test line to large-profile saltwater heavyweights for use with up to 30-pound line. Despite the improvements that have been made to other equipment, spinning reels are generally considered the most versatile reels.

Spinning reels have undergone many changes over the years, perhaps the most significant being in drag and casting features, as well as in line twist reduction aspects. Spinning (and spincasting) reels have long been products that were conducive to producing line twist through angler misuse or through the activation of the reels themselves. Twisted line hampers casting and general fishing effectiveness and may result in damaged line, so it is a problem to be avoided and corrected. Therefore, reducing or eliminating twist, from whatever source, has been a major focus of spinning reel manufacturers, and continues to be a work-in-progress, notwithstanding advertising claims to the contrary.

General Operation

In the most basic sense, spinning equipment works much like all other tackle except flycasting in that a weighted object, when cast, pulls line from the spool. The spool of a spinning reel is stationary during the cast, which means that there is little chance of a backlash (see) forming, as happens when a moving spool turns faster than the line is carried off that spool.

The spinning reel has a line roller that controls the release and retrieval of line. The line is guided by the bail to the line roller. When the handle is rotated, the line roller wraps line around the stationary spool. It also has an adjustable drag mechanism and usually a single-grip handle. When the bail is opened, line may flow freely off the spool.

In use, with the reel under the rod handle and facing away from the angler, the bail is opened and the line is held, usually by the index finger of the hand that holds the rod handle, to prevent the line from coming freely off the spool until released by the finger. When the finger is removed, released line flows off the spool and out through the rod guides, carried by the weight of the object at the terminal end of the line.

To retrieve line, the gears are engaged by rotating the handle clockwise (forward). This rotational movement is transferred to the rotor, with a simultaneous axial movement (forward and backward motion) transferred to the spool of better quality reels. As the line roller, which is connected to the rotor, rotates around the spool, line is wrapped on the spool. The spool's axial motion causes it to move toward the front of the reel and then toward the back of the reel. This motion, coupled with the rotor motion, causes line to wrap onto the spool in an equal layer instead of piling up in one place.

These are the basic elements of operating a spinning reel. Some models have different bail-opening, line-holding, drag, anti-reverse, spool oscillation, and other features. The general design, style, feature selection, and feel of each product also has relevance to its intended use.

Casting/Line Release Features

Bail. The bail on a spinning reel is an important component of both line release and line pickup, and is a standard feature on virtually all present-day reels.

Early spinning reels did not possess a bail as such. These models all featured a roller mounted to a bracket on the edge of a revolving housing. The line was directed to the roller by finger so that it could be captured for spool winding. The angler used the tip of the index finger to lift line off the roller preparatory to making a cast; to retrieve, the line was caught at the spool lip by the tip of the index finger and placed on the roller. This system was referred to at the time as a manual pickup. Because there were no moving parts, it was mechanically reliable, but becoming adept with it took practice.

Some adroit anglers, who found this system quick and certain if the line was kept under tension, stayed with it even when a quasi-pickup bail, in the form of a metal finger, evolved. This bail forerunner was a short outward curved arm that cocked open for casting and tripped closed for retrieval and automatically caught and secured the line. Known at the time as an automatic pickup, it was easier to use than the manual version, but did not always catch the line instantly.

That lead to the development of a more efficient auto-pickup system that featured a curved and longer wire arm hoop fixed to opposite sides of the housing. When tripped over the top of a reel, this arm always scooped in the line and became known as the pickup bail, or simply the bail. The bail and its anchor points to the rotor became known as the bail assembly.

Naturally, the functioning of a pickup bail today is more elaborate than it used to be, and so reliable that it is a rarity to find an angler who uses a spinning reel without a bail (the metal arm can be removed from some bails, however, to permit manual finger pickup, and a bail-less reel is favored by a small number of surf anglers). Virtually all spinning reels feature a bail, and the process of opening it in modern reels is accomplished either by manual or automatic means.

Bail opening systems. Because the bail holds line in place, it must be opened to cast or to allow line to flow off the reel without casting. There are several bail opening systems in spinning reels. No matter which system is used, the lure must first be placed in the proper casting position relative to the rod tip before the bail is opened.

For conventional spinning reels the best way to do this is to turn the handle and reel the line in until the lure is near the rod tip and the line roller is just under the index finger so that it is convenient to grab the line. With the lure in proper casting position, generally 3 to 6 inches below the tip of the rod, and the line roller correctly positioned directly below the rod, the line can be grabbed. If the line roller is not correctly positioned, strip line off the reel by pulling on it above the reel (which uses the drag to allow the spool to slip backward). Pull just enough off the spool so that the lure is the right distance below the rod tip. Once the lure and line roller are at the proper casting point, the bail is opened and the line held.

The manual and customary manner of opening the bail is to grab the line by the roller with the tip of the rod-holding forefinger, then flip up the bail with your other hand. Keep tension on the line with your finger until the cast is made. This is how the vast majority of reel bails are opened.

As inventors improved the original spinning reels by adding a bail to automatically direct the line to the line roller, improvements were also made in the line pickup area. Most of these improvements were intended to make it easier and faster to open the bail and capture the line before casting. The vast majority of these systems still require that the line roller be positioned directly in line between the spool and the rod.

Automatic bail opening is another system that has evolved as a means of simplifying basic spinning reel operation. This was first manifested in line pickup via a trigger positioned directly above or beside the line roller. Early trigger systems simply opened the bail as the trigger was pulled by the index finger, with the line being captured by that finger as it pulled the trigger.

In this system, positioning of the trigger in relation to the line roller was critical so that the index finger captured the line and pulled the bail-opening trigger at the same time. As the trigger is pulled and the bail opens, the index finger continues its upward motion to capture the line against the rod. The reel can then be cast in the customary manner. This mechanism made for a little faster casting, and eliminated the need for the user's free hand to open the bail.

A major improvement in automatic bail opening occurred in the early 1980s with a system that used a pin to capture the line. In this system, as the trigger is pulled by the index finger, the bail opens and a special "firing pin" simultaneously captures the line. The line is firmly held by the pin until the trigger is released. With this more user-friendly system, the index finger simply pulled the trigger to open the bail and capture the line during the back cast. As the rod is brought forward through the casting motion, the trigger is released, causing the pin to release the line and the line to freely flow off the end of the spool. The caster never has to touch the line.

A drawback, however, is that the line roller has to be positioned directly underneath the index finger before the trigger can be actuated. This problem was overcome in the early 1990s with the development of a reel with a trigger that extends from the base of the reel stem instead of being attached to the rotor. Because the trigger is not attached to

This Zebco reel has an automatic bail-opening feature in which a pin captures the line when the trigger opens the bail; the empty spool helps illustrate this process.

the rotor, it can be actuated regardless of the position of the line roller relative to the user's index finger. As the trigger is pulled—even if the line roller is directly beneath the reel, instead of being positioned between the spool and rod—the casting mechanism still functions. In this system, the bail opens, and the firing pin captures the line until the trigger is released. When the trigger is released, the firing pin drops the line, which flows freely off the end of the spool. This system is currently the ultimate evolution of "one-handed" casting systems for spinning reels.

While changes were evolving in casting systems, they were also evolving in the anti-reverse area. In conventional spinning reels without a trigger bail, the user rotates the handle until the line roller is visually in the correct casting position. This requires taking your eye off the surrounding fishing area for a few moments and takes a few seconds longer to correctly position the line roller.

To address this, manufacturers developed anti-reverse systems with on-, off-, and self-center positions. With the reel in the self-center setting, the spinning reel handle can be rotated in reverse for up to one full revolution. The internal anti-reverse mechanism engages, thus stopping the counterclockwise revolution of the handle exactly at the point where the line roller is located in the proper casting position.

With this self-centering anti-reverse system, you can turn the handle backward, and when it stops, the line roller—and optional trigger system—is always correctly positioned for casting. Visual alignment of the line roller is not required. While this is an advantage in casting, it is something of a hindrance when setting the hook on a big fish because the line roller can travel up to one complete revolution before encountering the anti-reverse stop. Not only does this allow excess line to play out while trying to secure a big fish, it creates a significant amount of shock loading on the anti-reverse single stop. Most, if not all, reels that utilize a self-centering bail anti-reverse system, also have a full on setting for the anti-reverse. From a mechanical point of view, the best operating condition is to turn the anti-reverse setting to the self-centering position immediately prior to casting, and switch it to the full on position as soon as the cast is completed. Obviously, this is not convenient.

While there is a more in-depth discussion of anti-reverse systems later in this text, it should be noted that continuous anti-reverse mechanisms, which are very popular in better quality baitcasting reels, are also employed in better quality spinning reels. However, only one series of spinning reels currently on the market incorporates the advantages of a fully functional continuous anti-reverse system with a casting mechanism that is always correctly positioned for the next cast.

Spinning reels that have bail triggers can definitely make it easier and faster to cast. If time and number of casts are an important element of an angler's fishing activity, a bail trigger should be beneficial. While the species pursued and the angling circumstances are critical factors, the result of being able to cast quickly can be greater or more efficient water coverage, and more opportunities to catch fish.

For most people, making more casts in a shorter time is less significant than ease of use. Reels that automatically align the line roller with the stem of the reel certainly facilitate line pickup, and grabbing a bail trigger is indeed simple.

Although automatic bail-opening reels do enable one-handed operation, they have been modestly received by anglers. This may be due to the fact that many spinning reel users have been accustomed to manual bail operation for so long that they do not view that method as being difficult, and are reluctant to change.

Another factor is that many trigger-equipped reels have a somewhat narrow area between the rotor housing and the stem, which people with large fingers find problematic. A thick-fingered person may get knuckles wrapped by a spinning trigger or find that there isn't enough area for the trigger to open because it pinches against the fingers when pressed. These are ergonomic design issues that may be flaws for some, but insignificant to others. It is possible to remove the trigger assembly on some reels without adversely affecting other aspects of performance.

The repeated opening of a spinning reel bail is something that frequently used to cause trouble. A lot of that had to do with broken springs, a problem that has been virtually eliminated today with over-center design. The modern bail spring, which may be called a lever spring or an arm lever spring, works in a simple in-and-out mode that helps flip the arm open and, in most models, allows the bail to be closed manually as well if desired, in lieu of closure by turning the handle. Bails may still be problematic if they are damaged in such a way that the inner surface area is made coarse and causes line to snare, which is uncommon, or if they are bent or broken as the result of a mishap, which is fairly common. Occasionally, a bail will fail to close when the rotor is turned, and if this begins to happen frequently, the reel should be serviced.

The unplanned and unanticipated closure of a bail when casting is occasionally a problem. Older spinning reel bails locked in place, but lever spring bails do not. Stronger springs have largely eliminated that, but when a spring goes bad, it is possible for a bail to close unexpectedly, often when a forceful long-distance heave is made.

Spool type. Another aspect of spools that has a bearing on casting, and is today mostly an historical footnote, pertains to the design of the rotor and position relative to the spool. Until the 1960s, spinning reels all featured a rotor that moved around the outside of a spool; the lower portion of the spool moved back and forth inside the rotor. This was standard operating procedure for many years; today, a spool that moves within the rotor is known as a cupped or internal spool. This design produced a reel with a somewhat large diameter frame or housing, which did nothing for comfort or performance. More significantly, however, was the irritating fact that line frequently got caught between the lower portion of the spool and the interior of the rotor, and was swept under the spool, causing it to be wrapped around the gears or the gear shaft. Most of the time, the spool had to be removed to

Most spinning reel spools are easily removed and feature a skirt that covers internal components; the majority, including this one, are aluminum.

get to the trapped line, which had to be unwound and usually had gear grease on it or was damaged. This process required unscrewing the drag retaining knob, which may have caused the loss of washers in some products, and always required the resetting of drag tension later.

This issue was changed by skirted spool reels, which became popular in the mid-1970s. In these, the rotor revolves around the inside of the lower portion of the spool; in effect, the lower portion of the spool is like a flange and shrouds the moving rotor like a skirt. This virtually eliminates the problem of line slipping under the spool and wrapping around the shaft, and it helps reduce the overall profile and bulk of a reel. The net result is more trouble-free casting.

Such a spool is now predominantly called a skirted spool, also known as an external spool. Skirted spools are found on nearly all modern spinning reels. Some anglers continue to use older reels with internal spools, and a few internal-spool reels are still being produced, but they make up a small percentage of the spinning reels in current use. Modern reels with internal spools generally have tight machined tolerances to minimize the line-under-spool problem, and they also have a pop-off spool button that makes it possible to remove the spool without altering the drag setting or losing parts, so they are not quite as problematic as in the past.

Spool flange and material. Factors affecting casting efficiency include the design and material of the front spool flange (lip), the material of the spool, its diameter, and the ratio of the front spool flange diameter to the spool hub diameter.

The flange obviously has to help retain or catch line when tension is momentarily relaxed, but it cannot impede the flow of line off the inner spool when a cast is made. When line is low on the spool, it is more likely to contact that flange, which increases friction and reduces distance, so the problem becomes amplified. Therefore, the design of the spool flange can have a significant influence on casting distance.

Spinning reels that have a big, broad radius on the lip certainly hold the line against the spool as you cast, but they also funnel the line down into a small cone pattern, which constricts the line coming off the spool. A very sharp radius on the edge of the spool tends to explode the line off the spool. It will actually make the line blow off as it heads toward the first rod guide. Some manufacturers say that the sharp edge can provide 10 to 15 percent additional distance. This is not something that you can see very well with your eye by watching repetitive casts, although it can be revealed by high-speed photography.

The material of the front spool flange also has some influence on casting distance or casting ease, and this boils down to friction. Aluminum and stainless steel spools produce less line friction and are preferable for top performance. Spools made of synthetic materials, including graphite, composites, or different plastics, are usually found on lower priced reels. These materials are used primarily for economic reasons. Such spools are easily made, but the material has a relatively high coefficient of friction in relation to nylon monofilament line, so it causes a noticeable loss in casting distance. A lot of manufacturers upgrade synthetic material spools by putting a metal rim, mainly aluminum, stainless steel, or even titanium, over the flange.

Spool width and diameter. The size of the spool is an element of casting, especially with regard to the width relative to the depth of the spool. Many spinning reels now have relatively large width-to-depth ratio spools, much more so than spincasting reels. In a very narrow spool (small width-to-depth ratio), line pulls from deeper in the spool and makes a sharper angle as it comes off. On a wider spool (large width-to-depth ratio), referred to by marketers as longer and resulting in the term "long-cast" spools, more of the line remains closer to the top of the spool flanges. When casting, the line doesn't make as dramatic an angle as it passes over the spool flange as it does on a narrower spool. This is the premise behind long-cast or long-stroke reels. Such spools also usually have a fairly large arbor diameter, which cuts back on total line capacity, but also means that there is less deep line to flow off a reel. Naturally, this is compensated to some extent by how full the spool is with line to start, and it reinforces the point that a filled spool aids casting.

Overall, spool diameter has an influence on casting distance also, not to mention its effect on line retrieval. In the distant past, spinning reel spools had a larger overall diameter than they do today. In broad terms, the larger the diameter of the spool, the better the casting distance. If you had a spool that released line at a rate of one wrap per foot instead of at a rate of three or four wraps per foot, there would theoretically be much less friction per wrap from the spool and, therefore, greater distance achieved.

However, it is rather unwieldy to have a light-action reel with a very large spool diameter, say one of 3 to 4 inches. To get this, you would have to compromise weight and styling. Designers have moved toward lighter and more streamlined spinning reels for many years, and this styling is not conducive to overly large diameter spools. In fact, spool diameters have shrunk on all but heavy-duty models (mostly for surf and other saltwater fishing applications). Although these reels represent a numerically small portion of the total spinning reel market, line capacity as well as extreme casting distance are important issues for the saltwater market. With the majority of spinning reels used in freshwater, and in circumstances where casting a normal distance is acceptable, manufacturers have enhanced casting distance with spool lip design, optimized spool width-to-depth ratio, and especially the method of winding line on the spool.

Line winding. While line winding is an aspect of reel operation accomplished during retrieval, it directly affects casting performance. The more even the winding lay, the better the line comes off the spool when cast. The ideal is a system that puts line on a spool as evenly as possible and allows line to come off the spool as cleanly as possible. The methods of moving the spool back and forth to get an even line lay are generally called line winding, and, in the case of spinning reels, oscillation. There are four oscillation systems or methods of line winding, and each as described here provides progressively better performance. These systems relate to the gears, which will be reviewed in more depth shortly, but this information will explain the relationship of line winding to casting function.

In general terms, the line winding operation is accomplished by turning the rotor, which drives the spool back and forth, revolves the bail assembly around the spool, brings line across the line roller, and lays it on the spool.

The most basic line winding method is a locomotive system, which operates on the same principle as a steam locomotive. The gear has an eccentric cam, and as it turns, the yoke moves back and forth. The yoke is attached to the center shaft, which in turn is attached to the spool. As the yoke moves back and forth, the center shaft and spool duplicate the motion. This is normally used on inexpensive reels, and it does not provide a very even line lay.

The Scotch yoke system is a variation of the locomotive; it utilizes an off-center pin on the backside of the crank gear, which rides in a groove on the yoke that is attached to the center shaft. As the crank gear turns, the pin moves up and down the groove in an eccentric circle and pushes the center shaft back and forth.

These systems simply move the spool back and forth and put parallel wraps of line on the spool. The wraps often bury themselves amongst each other so they do not come off the spool as easily as do better systems, and when they are put on the spool under intense pressure, they may become so deep-seated that the line jams and will not freely come off the spool under a cast, or experiences distance inhibiting pinching. If light line is employed, this pinched wrapping could lead to snapping off a lure during a cast, or it could mean that the line doesn't flow off the spool when the drag is needed for fighting a strong fish, causing the fish to be lost. In addition, these systems have a tendency to pile line up in the middle of the spool, which also impairs casting.

A variation of the Scotch yoke is the S-curve system, which provides a longer stroke (the spool travels forward and backward over a longer distance). This type of oscillating system is an integral part of achieving spools with larger width-to-depth ratios that hold a significant amount of line and cast smoothly. This oscillating method features an S-shaped groove in the yoke, and there is a pause at each end of the stroke so that the line will lay on the edges of the spool as well as in the middle. The S-curve system reduces midspool bunching and produces more even line distribution than the previously noted systems, but with some reels, there is a tendency for line to bunch at the top or (most likely) the bottom edge of the spool.

Currently, the most efficient line lay system features a helical gear or worm gear system, similar to what exists in baitcasting reels. Oscillation is achieved by a pawl connected to the center shaft that follows a groove cut in the worm gear. This method permits smooth line lay without dwelling at each end of the stroke, and permits an even longer stroke than the S-curve system. This system is more efficient at distributing line and preventing both line bunching and parallel wrapping.

Unfortunately for new reel buyers, when you look at a spinning reel in a store, it is difficult to tell which line winding system the reel utilizes. The information provided with higher priced reels usually contains some descriptive information; in the case of worm gears, this is almost always pointed out. If you compare two reels of similar size, the main difference will be in the width of the line-holding area of the spool. A greater gap indicates a long stroke and either an S-curve or worm gear system. If you turn the handle of a reel, you should notice a difference in smoothness, with worm gears having the smoothest operation. A reel with a locomotive system is fairly apparent because this produces a pretty rapid back and forth movement of the spool, and it is fairly jerky.

Retrieving/Line Recovery Features

Line is retrieved by rotating the handle, which in turn rotates the rotor and drives the spool back and forth. As the rotor rotates, the bail assembly revolves around the spool, brings line across the line roller, and lays it on the spool. The process of retrieving begins with closing the bail, and performance is greatly affected by how the line moves over the roller and is wound onto the spool, as well as by the gear type and operation.

Line pickup/Bail closure. There are manual and automatic means of closing the bail to begin picking up line. Manual closure is possible due to a reliable lever spring in the bail assembly; it exists on many reels in conjunction with automatic closure, but allows you to close the bail without turning the handle. To manually close the bail, you simply flip it down by hand. This feature is often used in live-bait fishing when it is necessary to let a fish move off before setting the hook; the angler opens the bail after detecting pickup of the bait, waits for the fish to move off, then, at the appropriate time, closes the bail manually and sets the hook when the line draws tight.

Automatic bail closure is found on all spinning reels and is activated by turning the handle, which instantly flips the bail down. To automatically pick up line when the bail of a spinning reel is open, move the handle forward, which turns the rotor and causes the bail to trip closed and directs the line to the line roller.

There are internal and external bail trip mechanisms. Internal trip bails are more common and work inside the reel so that you don't see any of the mechanism. When the bail is opened, it moves an internal pawl into a position where it will strike a ramp inside; when the rotor is turned, the pawl strikes the ramp and forces the bail to close.

External trip mechanisms operate by having some part of the open bail strike a ramp or plate on the stem of the reel handle. It may be a pawl or the back of the arm lever that makes contact; when the rotor is turned, the pawl or lever strikes the ramp or plate and forces the bail to close. In effect, this system knocks the bail down; some operate fairly noisily and with varying degrees of jarring. Various shapes and surfaces are used at the stem contact point to aid smooth operation; some, like a plastic roller, work better than others.

Although mechanically there is no advantage to either method, as a general rule the internal trip operates a little more easily and quietly than the external trip, which is why it is preferred by most anglers. However, an external trip provides more internal room for design freedom; for example, it permits the use of a larger clutch mechanism.

In practical use, the bail closure needs to operate as smoothly, quickly, and effortlessly as possible. The greatest irritation with automatic bail closures is tight operation, which for many spinning reels is the result of the positioning of the trip mechanism relative to the striking ramp or plate.

When the bail is open, the farther the strike mechanism is from the ramp or plate, the more momentum is built up when the handle is first turned and the more force is generated as that mechanism hits the ramp or plate. But if the strike mechanism is close to the ramp or plate when the handle is first turned, there is little or no momentum in the rotor, so the trip mechanism binds at the ramp or plate, particularly the latter, and more force has to be applied to turn the handle and move the rotor in order to trip the bail. The design of the part that actually causes the bail to trip, whether internal or external, has some bearing on the fluidity of this operation. Some (like the roller part on the stem) make it easier to force the handle than others.

Many high-end internal trip spinning reels have a smooth closing reel because of the location of the internal trip in relation to the normal position of the bail roller when the line is picked up. Line is usually picked up when the bail roller is close and slightly to the right of the reel stem; this provides more than 180 degrees of rotor revolution before the bail trips, which generally makes for consistent performance. Ironically, although there are disadvantages to reels with self-centering bail triggers, these have a fairly trouble-free internal trip bail closing, also because the rotor makes half of a rotation before striking the ramp that closes the bail.

Naturally, the ease or difficulty of bail closure is related to speed of overall operation. If you have to fight with the reel to close the bail, you may lose precious seconds, like when you're trying to keep your eyes on the fishing action but have to look down at the reel, or when you have to retrieve a lure the minute it hits the water.

Some people manually close the bail with their hand not holding the rod at the end of a cast. With practice, this becomes a very natural motion, avoiding the inconvenience of trying to rotate the handle to close the bail.

Because a reel is likely to be cast many times in the course of a day, this most basic aspect of spinning reel usage is very important. When purchasing a reel in a store, you can assess this feature by holding the reel and repeatedly opening and closing the bail, alternating the location of the bail each time it is opened to simulate in-field use. This is one aspect of a reel that you can seriously evaluate and compare before buying; you can assure yourself beforehand if bail closure on a given reel operates smoothly, quickly, and effortlessly, or at least more so than other products.

Left/Right retrieve. Although there are a few exceptions, virtually all spinning reels today have convertible retrieve systems, so you can set the handle up to retrieve from whichever side you prefer. Normally, it is beneficial for people who are right-handed to reel with their left hand and for lefties to reel with their right hand, so that the dominant hand is the one that holds the rod and is used to play the fish or direct the retrieve. Because the dominant hand is used to cast the rod, there is no need to take further action after casting to start using the reel; the other hand is immediately placed on the reel handle grip, and it starts turning the handle. However, anglers who are used to fishing with baitcasting or spincasting tackle may wish to maintain the same standard by placing the spinning reel handle on the right side.

This retrieval convertibility is made possible by the type of gears in spinning reels, and separates them from most spincasting and baitcasting products, which are primarily designed for right-handed cranking, or in a few cases left-handed cranking, but not convertible cranking.

Gears. The most basic part of the operation of a reel is the gear set, which in a spinning reel is less efficient than in a baitcasting reel, but better than that of most spincasting reels. Both spinning and spincasting reels have a face or right-angled gear set. The drive gear shaft is at a right angle to the pinion gear shaft. Rotational motion at the handle is transferred through a 90-degree angle by means of the gear set to the pinion or center shaft. Baitcasting reel gears, by contrast, are in-line and have parallel gear sets, which has the advantage of no lateral thrust forces on the right-angled gear set.

Spinning reels may have on-center or off-center gears. Whereas most spincasting reel gears are on-center, the vast majority of spinning reel gears are

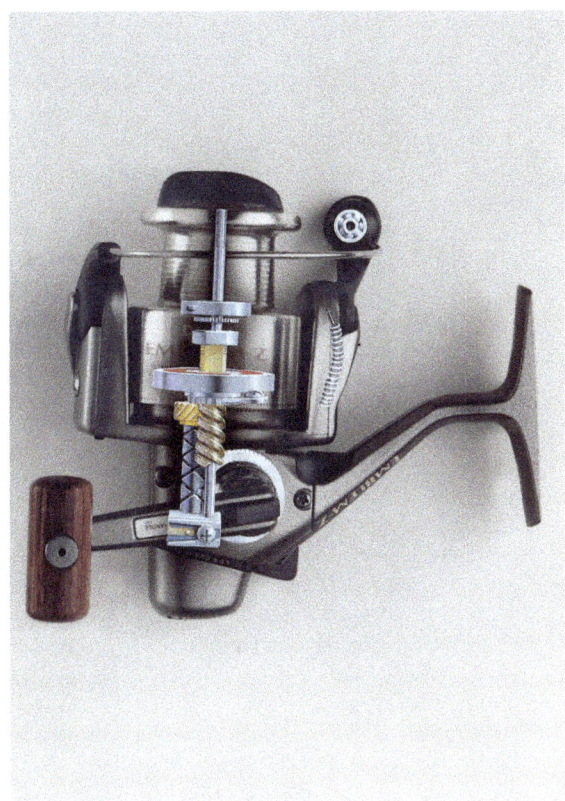

This composite image reveals the gears and some internal components of a Daiwa spinning reel.

off-center, which means that the axis of the crank shaft is above or below the axis of the center shaft. Because spinning reels have off-center gears, the crank shaft runs all the way through the reel and is supported on both sides. This gear set allows for convertible right- or left-hand cranking, and is durable with less motion, or play, in the operation of the reel. It also produces a much sturdier feel than on-center gears.

The least expensive spinning reels use a zinc diecast face gear and a straight-tooth zinc diecast pinion gear. The next step up is a zinc diecast face gear and a diecast helical pinion with a fairly low helix angle. There is a limit to how high a helix angle can be diecast, but this does provide a better gear feeling. The next grade up is a zinc diecast face gear and brass pinion, which is by far the most universally used combination. This provides strength and durability as well as smooth gear meshing. Most of the better reels that have a reputation for being smooth use this system. For other applications, like heavy-duty saltwater, the gears are made out of stainless steel. The face gear is powdered metal (processed into a die and pressed under extreme pressures), and the pinion is a cut gear. Aluminum forged gears are also used in some of the more expensive reels in freshwater applications, primarily for longevity and strength.

In almost any simple gear set, one gear material is normally harder than the other. This both directs and controls the action of the two parts throughout their life and actually keeps the gears running smoothly for a longer period. Two hardened gears running together would amplify even the smallest machining imperfection or piece of grit on the gear teeth.

It is common in spinning reels for the pinion gear to be brass. This is a hard material, and it allows for the more intricate machining required in this smaller part as well as absorbs the greater anticipated wear in this gear with its fewer teeth. The corresponding drive gear is most often made of aluminum in quality reels, and is sometimes made of easily diecast zinc. In either case the gear teeth should be machined as precisely as possible to assure smooth operation and long life.

Almost all reel gears in better quality spinning reels are fabricated with helical gear teeth. This means that each gear tooth is curved, rather than straight, on the gear circumference. Helical hobbing results in greater strength, thicker cross section, and a high degree of inherent smoothness. The major benefit is that, unlike straight-hobbed gears where only a single gear tooth is fully engaged at one time, helical gears allow at least partial engagement of several gear teeth at all times, spreading the load and potential wear.

Very few of the spinning reels constructed today don't use the face gear system mentioned earlier. Some older reels (especially Zebco's Cardinal models) in the past used a cross-helical gear system (which was erroneously called a worm gear) and were widely considered to be the smoothest reels ever made. Both gears in those reels were cut gears similar to the gearing in a baitcasting reel; having a perfect tolerance was critical. This method is not nearly as forgiving as the other systems, and everything has to be aligned very precisely. Such a system is expensive to manufacture, however, and reels that had it have been out of production for a long time. Those reels were prized by many avid anglers and are still in use by owners who have taken good care of them. Despite their smoothness, however, they had relatively slow gear ratios as compared to today's reels.

Gear ratio/Cranking power. Engineers can talk in technical terms about the cranking power of a reel, about torque, and about how you can theoretically convert the force at the handle knob to the force on the line and the center shaft. But what anglers relate to in the simplest terms is how easy or difficult it is to retrieve a heavy weight, or an object that offers a lot of resistance. Reels that can easily handle a heavy load are said to have a lot of cranking power. Various factors come into play here.

The length of the handle has a bearing because that length has to do with the leverage that you can put on the handle. The longer the handle, the more leverage and the easier it is to retrieve a set load. If you make a handle longer, you reduce the force at the crank knob. It is essentially the same principle seen in wrenches; it's easier to loosen nuts with a long-handled wrench than one with a short handle. Spinning reels tend to have a better advantage than spincasting reels in terms of cranking power because their handles are very long. Because spinning reels hang underneath the rod and have a long stem, there is room to put a long handle on them, which adds more leverage advantage.

The gear set itself is also a big factor with regard to cranking power. If you have a reel with a gear ratio of 4:1 (read four to one), it's easier to retrieve a load because this is a low gear ratio. If you have a reel with a gear ratio of 6:1, which is considered high, it's a lot more difficult to retrieve a load, although you get more speed. If you're retrieving something that offers very little resistance, the high gear ratio is okay. But you need a lower gear ratio for something that offers more resistance. Thus, the lowest gear ratio reels have the greatest cranking power and the highest gear ratio reels have the least cranking power.

There is a wide range of gear ratios in spinning reels. Many have a high gear ratio in the 6:1 to 7:1 range. The gear ratio is usually marked on the reel packaging and sometimes on a sideplate decal, but may not be noted on some at all. Gear ratios are much higher on spinning reels than they are on spincasting reels, which average below 4:1. Manufacturers tend to refer to a reel with an upper-end gear ratio as a "high gear ratio" or a "fast-retrieve" reel, but this is all relative. A 5:1 reel might be called high, and in comparison to a 4:1 spincasting reel, it would be high, but it is clearly lower than some other spinning reels. And in any event, gear ratio does nothing more than designate the mechanical gear action of the reel, which is not the whole story about true speed.

No matter what the gear ratio is, the evaluation of a reel's ability to retrieve line should boil down to something engineers call Inches Per Turn of the handle, or IPT. This is the amount of line recovered per turn of the handle, or, simply, line recovery. That is a better measurement of retrieval ability than gear ratio. Line recovery is determined by spool diameter, which is a key dimension for any reel and which sets the circumference of the line level on the spool and the amount of line wound onto the spool with each turn of the reel handle. A 6.2:1 ratio reel with a 1.5-inch diameter spool, for example, will recover about 11 inches of line per handle turn. A 6.2:1 gear ratio reel with a 2-inch diameter spool will recover almost 19.5 inches of line per handle turn. This is the true measurement for anglers interested in retrieve speed.

Anglers cannot quickly determine line recovery when evaluating a reel they might purchase because specifications on the circumference of the spool aren't provided on the reel or in the packaging materials. In a 6:1 ratio reel, for example, you know that one revolution of the handle puts six wraps of line on the spool, but if you don't know how much line is gained with each complete wrap, you don't know the actual recovery. (Of course in a reel that you own, you can determine the gain by marking the line and measuring it.)

For a greater discussion of this subject, *see: Gear Ratio and Line Recovery.* While most consumers have a notion that gear ratio is of primary importance in retrieval, and some think that the higher the ratio the better, there are other factors that go into this, and line recovery is a major one. Remember, however, that reels with low gear ratio do better the greater the load and the more resistance offered by lure or fish.

Line winding/Twist reduction. The impact of line winding on casting as well as its relationship to the gears was previously detailed, but in terms of retrieval and overall fishing performance, line winding is equally important, especially with regard to its affect on line twist, which is the most common difficulty incurred with this type of tackle. Although improper use of fishing equipment is the major cause of line twist *(see: line)*, the normal operation of a spinning reel may promote line twisting.

In an effort to reduce line twist when winding line, much attention has been paid to the bail roller. Rollers used to be primarily ceramic; most today are made of chrome plated brass and some have a tungsten coating. An important aspect of the line roller mechanism is dissipating the heat to prevent the line from breaking down. A line roller that actually rolls is important for this. Some bails have either no roller or a stationary roller. Most line rollers actually turn as the line comes in to reduce friction on the line.

This is a magnified view of a twist-reducing line roller on the bail of a Daiwa spinning reel.

Some higher priced reels have a ball bearing in the roller to help make it turn easier. The downside to this is that grit and water can get to this spot, so it requires regular lubrication to prevent destruction of the ball bearing. Most ball bearings aren't designed for use in places where there is a lot of water, as happens on the bail roller when line constantly pulls water across it.

The size and shape of the line roller are factors that affect twisting. Although line rollers have to move the line from the bail to the spool, the problem is that twist can occur if the line turns over on itself while moving from the bail to the spool. The different systems in use now have sharp roller slopes and grooves in the roller to help prevent twist. They are built to even larger diameters, they keep the line in one spot on the roller and prevent it from moving around, and they eliminate slack line movement on the roller surface. These components by themselves do not prevent twist, but they do help keep the line in such a position that it does not spin over.

Another key to preventing twist is the proper alignment of the line roller and the spool. If the system is aligned properly, there won't be line twist that is attributable to the line roller. In order to put line on a spool in a controlled even manner and to eliminate line twist, the line roller and the bail arm have to be positioned precisely in relation to the spool. The manufacturer has to design the reel so that the line roller is perpendicular with the axis of the spool, which allows for proper line placement. Another factor is the distance between the line roller and the surface of the spool. Rollers mounted close to the spool form sharper angles at extreme oscillation points and contribute to rollover twist formation.

A recent innovative reel system eliminates criti-

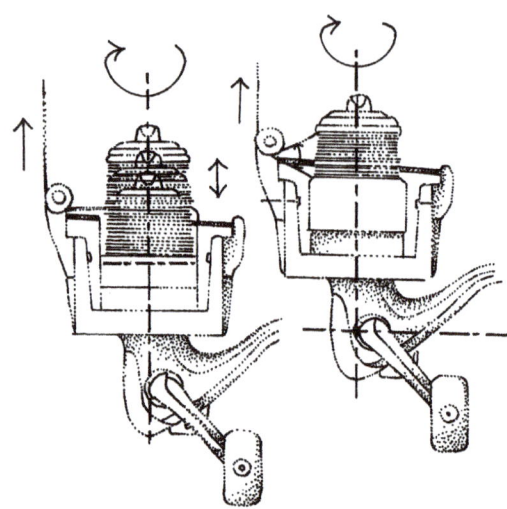

In most spinning reels, when line is pulled off the spool and across the roller, the spool simply turns clockwise without the spool moving up and down (right); this repeatedly changes the angle of line from spool to line roller and increases its tendency to twist. In an oscillating spool reel (left), in addition to turning clockwise the spool moves up and down on the shaft when line is pulled off the reel; this provides a constant angle from spool to line roller, thereby helping to prevent twist.

cal angles and prevents twist by oscillating the spool both during the retrieve and when releasing line under drag. It moves the mechanism that drives the spool oscillation from the body of the reel up, under the spool itself. Here, a worm drive, similar to the levelwind on a baitcasting reel, is connected to the pinion gear/rotor assembly and oscillates the spool. It allows the spool to rise and fall as a pawl travels through the endless worm track. This true spool oscillation design permits the spool to oscillate during the retrieve and, unlike other reels, also when the spool is releasing line via the drag.

With this design, the line is continuously fed straight from the spool to the roller guide at all times, no matter how far a fish runs or what the line level on the spool is. Critical angles are completely eliminated. This means that the drag force on the line does not vary due to changing line feed angles. This prevents twist caused by line rollover when the line feeds from the spool to the roller, and eliminates line damaging friction.

Handle/Rotor. As previously noted the length of the handle affects cranking power, and longer handles provide more cranking power than shorter handles. Some handles seem longer than they actually are because they have a counterbalance on the nongrip side, but this is simply an optical illusion. Length is really measured from the handle grip to the crank shaft. Obviously, handles that are too short decrease leverage, and those that are too long are awkward.

Nearly all spinning reel handles have a single grip, but there has been a trend toward adding a counterbalanced extension to them. Although found on higher priced reels, the value of this is arbitrary, especially in lightweight reels. Admittedly, a counterbalanced handle feels good in a store when a person takes a reel and gives the handle a wild spin. Likewise, a balanced rotor gives the reel a stable feeling, too. When you spin such a reel in a store, and it has no wobble whatsoever, you'll likely say it "feels good." However, an angler never spins the handle wildly like this when fishing, and seldom turns the handle this fast when retrieving or fighting a fish, particularly when using the smaller models and angling for the average freshwater fish. You can't make your hand turn the handle this fast. When you're cranking at most normal rates of retrieve, you will never notice whether the spinning reel handle is balanced or not.

There is more merit to having a balanced rotor than a counterbalanced handle, as sensitivity is enhanced with a waver-free action. Theoretically, a smoother working reel with less wobble or vibration makes it easier to detect a light strike. Conventionally designed spinning reels are somewhat unbalanced because the rotor has a heavy bail mechanism on one side. If the weight of the entire rotor is balanced, you get a smoother retrieve, and it feels better when you're cranking it.

Manufacturers of better spinning reels use computers and design software to balance by weight, adding or adjusting weight in the required spots when they are designing the reels to get the rotors perfectly balanced. Rotors balanced in this fashion use the required functional components placed at the proper positions of the correct mass to cause the rotor to be "balanced" while it is rotated. This is a relatively new technique, one that was developed as a result of new computer-aided design (CAD) technology utilized by engineers. Some manufacturers still rely on balancing rotors by adding coun-

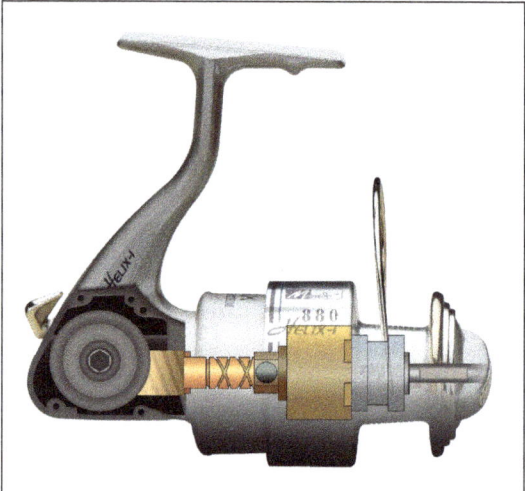

This computer-generated illustration represents the interior of the unique Marado Helix spinning reel, in which a worm drive, connected to the pinion gear/rotor assembly, oscillates the spool both during the retrieve and when the spool is releasing line via the drag.

terweights at the appropriate location, much as car tires are balanced today.

Ball bearings/Bushings. Bearings and bushings provide a way to minimize friction on rotating shafts. Bushings don't spin as freely as ball bearings, which are typically viewed as durable and reliable and a way to add rotational freeness to the system. They are usually employed to differing degrees in medium- and high-end reels; they may also appear in some lower priced reels, but keep in mind that there are different grades and materials of ball bearings. There is a performance difference in these grades, although the average consumer doesn't know which grade is in a given reel. Some lower grades of ball bearing actually add noise to a reel.

Spinning reels may have from one to nine ball bearings, although it is debatable as to whether having more than four or five of these adds significant performance advantages. What the added ones seem to be is a marketing ploy, and a supplemental cost factor.

The most important place to have a ball bearing is under the pinion gear. When a reel is advertised as having one ball bearing, it will always be under the pinion. The second most important spot is behind the crank, or drive, gear. On a two–ball bearing reel, the second ball bearing is usually on the left side of the crank gear, because most people reel with their left hand, and this side experiences the most load. A reel with three ball bearings often has a bearing on the other side of the crank shaft as well so that both ends of the main gear are supported with a ball bearing. On an oscillating worm gear system, a ball bearing may be placed on each end of the worm shaft.

These are all useful bearings and do improve performance of the system. The continuous anti-reverse clutch is counted as a bearing by some manufacturers, and this feature is seldom found on a reel with less than two ball bearings.

When you add more ball bearings than these you have to look for creative places to put them, and most of these are of dubious value, like on the handle knob, in the bail assembly, in the drag system (front and/or rear), and possibly in the line roller. A ball bearing on the line roller is even of dubious value because it is exposed and potentially subject to fouling. In the primary places, however, ball bearings do result in smoother operation and greater reel longevity. For a more detailed review of ball bearings and bushings, *see: Reel, Fishing.*

Drag Features

The purpose of the drag function on any reel is to let line slip from the reel at varying pressures when force is applied to the line. It serves as a sort of clutch, or shock absorber, and only works when the anti-reverse mechanism, which will be explained shortly, is employed (which it is virtually all the time). A properly set drag is especially important when using light line, when playing large and strong fish, and when fish make strong and sudden surges while being landed. If an angler never catches large fish, only uses heavy strength line, and is content to wind fish in, then it is conceivable that his drag will never be used. But heavy line is not suitable for many species and many methods of fishing, and it is practically inevitable that at some time, even with moderate strength line, an angler will catch a fish that weighs more than the actual breaking strength of his line, and which requires some finesse, rather than sheer strength, to land. This means that the drag will come into play, because if it doesn't, the force will exceed the strength of the line and the line will break.

When the drag comes into play, it allows the fish to continue applying force, but at a pressure that is less than the breaking strength of the line, because when the force reaches a certain level (usually less than 50 percent of the line's breaking strength), a properly set drag mechanism will allow line to slip from the reel. The way it allows line to slip from the spool is by turning or revolving the spool. A spinning reel spool (as well as a spincasting reel spool) is stationary when the line is cast and when it is retrieved; the spool moves back and forth when line is retrieved, but it does not turn. However, when there is sufficient force to activate the drag, the spool turns in a clockwise rotation, which allows line to come off under tension. Thus, although spinning reels are said to have a stationary spool, that spool will revolve when the drag is employed.

Understanding how to use and set drag is one of the most important aspects of sportfishing and is reviewed in detail elsewhere *(see: drag)*. Clearly, however, the functioning of a drag is a critical element of every reel, and the quality of reel drags varies considerably.

The drag mechanism on spinning reels, as on most smaller reels for various fishing applications, used to be fair to poor at best, but these systems have changed markedly since anglers started using all of the various equipment types for more challenging fishing, and placed greater demands on the rod, reel, and line. While low-end spinning reels do not have sophisticated drags, most medium and higher quality models have reasonably good drags, and many of

Bearings in a top-quality spinning reel may include, clockwise from top: a continuous anti-reverse clutch bearing, a bail roller ball bearing, and five standard ball bearings.

the higher priced ones have very good drag systems.

Common drag factors. While the gear sets in spinning and spincasting reels are comparable, the drag systems are a little bit different. They basically work off the same principle in that they're adding pressure to, compressing, and causing resistance on, the spool. In most spinning reels, there is more uniform pressure on the spool than there is in a spincasting reel, perhaps making some of the drags a little bit smoother as well as more controllable. There are certain things to look for when evaluating the drag systems of these, as well as other, reels, and although this information is supplied elsewhere in slightly different form, it bears inclusion here because of the great importance that the drag feature has in practical fishing.

The first item to look for in a good reel drag is variation. If you set the drag to create 4 pounds of tension on the line, you want it to stay at 4 pounds. If it varies to 5 and 6 pounds, that is not particularly good. Influencing factors include how fast you pull on the line, and where you set the drag. If you have 10-pound line and you set the drag at 2 pounds, you'll have less variation than if you set it at 8 pounds. With lower force, it is easier to control variation.

Another aspect is maximum drag force. Ideally, you should try to set the drag at 30 to 50 percent of breaking strength. If you could only set it at 4 pounds for a 10-pound line, that's probably not enough for some fishing situations. So you should check the maximum force you can obtain on the reel before using it to make sure that it will be adequate for your needs. However, achieving absolute maximum drag force—where the drag doesn't slip at all—is not as important for actual fishing as many anglers believe.

Some anglers are very interested in being able to readily get maximum force, which locks the reel down and completely prevents the drag from slipping. This maximum force is seldom beneficial for most fishing activities, including playing large or strong fish, unless you're using very heavy line. Where it is most likely to be useful, however, is when a lure or hook gets snagged and cannot be freed; this situation may require you to lock the reel down, point the rod directly at the snag, and pull back to free the hook or break the line *(see: unsnagging)*. If the drag cannot be locked down completely, then line will slip off, and it may be harder to free the hook.

Many people mistakenly think that they need to set the drag very tight for effective hooksetting. When you have 20 yards of line out, and you have rod flex, line stretch, and the dampening effect of the water to contend with, you don't need very much drag force at the reel. You cannot exert the maximum pressure when you set the hook. But when you set the drag pressure at or near maximum force, when the fish is close to the boat and there is less contribution made by line stretch, rod flex, and water, having the drag locked down may mean that the line cannot absorb the sudden shock of a quick run, even from a fish whose weight is less than the breaking strength of the line. People are often amazed that a 5-pound fish can break 14-pound line, but that does not happen if the drag is set properly and the washers are allowed to slip freely when necessary.

In typical fishing, anglers set the drag at 30 to 50 percent of the breaking strength of their line; most, if they have a 10-pound line, for example, set the drag by feel at between 3 to 5 pounds, meaning that it will take 3 to 5 pounds of tension to cause line to slip. This is measured with a short length of line on a straight pull off the reel.

Another important aspect of drag is range of adjustment, or how many revolutions you can turn the control mechanism on the reel. If you consider line tension in terms of revolutions of the drag knob, you'll see that it is desirable to ramp up the drag very rapidly to get to 30 percent of the line's breaking strength. Few people are going to set their drag tension at less than 30 percent of the line strength. Ideally, you should get up to that 30 percent number with just a short revolution of the knob. Then, for the 30 to 50 percent breaking strength range, there should be a lot of adjustment available to cover that range and fine-tune the drag. After reaching 50 percent of the breaking strength, the drag should ramp up very quickly to a full lockdown position; this is in case you have to break off, pull on a snag, or have more tension for a strike in heavy cover.

Thus, the important aspect of drag range is how many rotations it takes to get to the lockdown point, and where is the most adjustment range for fine-tuning. Some spinning reel drags, usually on the lowest-end models, have a small rotation from no drag to maximum drag. That might encompass one full, 360-degree, rotation of the adjustment knob. The best drags allow more than two, and usually up to three, full rotations of the drag knob, meaning that they will rotate 720 degrees or more. This maximum adjustment range is accomplished through the spring system that applies the load to the drag stack.

The problem with adjustment range comes from conflicting demands. Some anglers want a wide range of adjustment while others want to get maximum force. These differences require tradeoffs in design elements. There's a point where smoothness versus lockdown just aren't compatible.

Normally a reel is designed for an average weight of line. If, for example, a reel is designed for 10-pound line, a normal drag setting for that would be about a third of the line weight to prevent line breakage. So 3 to 4 pounds would be the medium range. But it still has to be able to achieve lockdown pressure while maintaining a smooth drag. For anglers who need a range of adjustments, the best system for this 10-pound-rated reel is one that can actually break 10-pound line yet have a smooth range of adjustment and smooth drag performance throughout that range.

Another element of drag performance is the amount of force required to start the drag slipping. On some drag systems, this force (called breakaway force) can be significantly higher than the actual drag setting. This condition is especially found in reels where the drag has been tightened and left to sit for several days. The drag washers and drag lubrication tends to take a "set." The next time the drag is called on, additional line tension is required to overcome this "set" before line tension returns to the intended setting. Many a big fish has been lost by the angler who forgot to loosen the drag before storing equipment for the next trip, or who didn't check the drag setting before beginning to fish.

Drag systems. Spinning reels have either front or rear mounted drag systems. Front mounted drags were the norm for many years, then rear mounted drags became overwhelmingly popular, and then there was a move back to front drags in better quality reels and virtually all saltwater models. Today there is a mix of both in the marketplace, with many experienced anglers preferring front drag because of smoother performance.

Both systems feature one or more discs or washers that direct adjustable tension on the spool shaft by turning an adjustment knob. Generally, both systems include hard metal washers on the extremity of a stack or series, and soft or nonmetallic friction washers on the inside of the series. Tension on the main shaft is increased by turning the knob clockwise and decreased by turning it counterclockwise.

On a front mounted drag the adjustment knob is at the very top of the spool, and for many such reels, the spool is actually removed by turning the knob counterclockwise until it is completely free of the center shaft. On some of these reels, there is a pop-off button in the middle of the knob, which is pressed to free the spool from the shaft, allowing the drag adjustment to be unaltered when the spool is removed.

On a rear mounted drag, the adjustment knob is at the very bottom of the reel and is generally circular. A screw in the middle of the knob holds it fast to the center shaft so that the knob cannot accidentally be removed. Turning this knob completely counterclockwise does not remove the knob and has no bearing on spool removal. The spool on such a reel is simply removed by pressing a pop-off button at the top of the spool, regardless of the drag tension setting. Such easy spool removal is an advantage to rear mounted drag reels, although spool removal is not a frequent necessity for many anglers.

There are other advantages and disadvantages to both systems. It is possible, for example, that the drag control knob on some front mounted drag reels will become so loose that the knob will fall off and be lost, which ends fishing with that reel until a new knob is obtained. That cannot happen with a rear mounted drag reel.

Rear mounts are also somewhat easier to adjust during the act of fishing because they keep hands away from the line. Adjusting drag tension on a front mounted drag while playing a fish means that your hand may get in the way of the line. On a reel with top mounted drag, the line extending from the bail roller, which is usually under a lot of tension, is often in the way when a quick adjustment is necessary. This is generally viewed as a disadvantage to top mounted drags, although for many anglers it is seldom necessary to increase or decrease drag tension during the act of fighting a fish, and, in fact it should not be adjusted if it has been set properly.

Drag tension should be checked and adjusted before using a reel for the first time, at the beginning of each new fishing session, after a spool has been removed, and whenever the tension setting has been increased or decreased while the reel is in use. In theory, the majority of tension setting adjustment takes place when the reel is not actually being fished, and seldom when a fish is being played, so the location of the drag adjustment knob may not be that critical.

What is most critical, in fact, is the smoothness of the drag, or its ability to perform without erratic motion over a wide range of adjustment. The smoothness of a drag is controlled by the materials, the way they are assembled, and the size of the washers. Front drags are thought to be smoother than rear drags. Many, although not all, are smoother, mostly as a result of larger components in the drag system.

It is important for drag washers to dissipate

This exposed view of a Fin-Nor Ahab spinning reel reveals a very large drag disc in a front-drag system that allows two-way access to the drag; the spool can be rotated counterclockwise and removed without affecting the preset drag setting.

heat, which builds up rapidly in a reel when the drag is under a lot of pressure. The size of the washers is a major element of this, with spool material also being a contributing factor. Aluminum dissipates heat more efficiently than synthetic spools. Therefore, aluminum spools are a better choice for reels expected to handle long runs by strong fish. Smaller washers build up heat more quickly and dissipate it less efficiently than larger washers. Poor dissipation causes erratic drag performance. The design and placement of front mounted drags allow for the use of larger washers, which is one reason they perform well. A rear drag can be every bit as smooth as a front drag but has difficulty maintaining that smoothness at higher line tension settings unless it uses the same size drag washers as the front drags. When large washers are used in a rear drag reel, the body starts getting bigger, which to some people is less aesthetically attractive. Because the trend in most reels has been to smaller overall size, rear drags have had correspondingly sized washers. Front drags, however, allow for small overall body size but larger washers. In compa-rable quality front and rear drag reels, the washers are of similar quality, but the size differs. So many, if not most, rear drags aren't as smooth as front drags because of design constraints.

Incidentally, research and development personnel say that it is not the overall size, or outside diameter, of a drag washer that is critical to obtain maximum line tension, but the mean diameter. That is a calculation of the inside diameter and the outside diameter. If you take a large outside diameter and a small inside diameter, the mean diameter is actually closer to the inside than it is to the outside, so in order for drag washers to be more efficient, they should have a large inside diameter as well as a large outside diameter to obtain maximum drag lockdown.

Naturally, the washers in a stack or series should be as close as possible to each other in size. Large diameter front and rear washers promote smoothness. Some reels have large diameter washers in the front of the stack and smaller washers in the rear of the stack. It's best if the stack is tailored front and back on the spool to make it efficient.

Drag washers. Ideally, the drag in any reel will operate smoothly, without hesitation. In other words, it will start immediately when needed and maintain a constant rate of tension as line flows continuously off, as well as keep the same level of tension as it is periodically called upon during the time it takes to play and land a strong fish. The less variation that there is in the performance of the drag, the better. Some of this performance is affected by the type of drag system and the range of adjustment it is capable of, as previously noted. Some of this is affected by the number and material of the washers.

Drag washer material, which is usually the same whether in front or rear drag systems, is really most critical in the setup stage of usage. One of the problems with drags and materials is that they are asked to do something that is very difficult. It is desirable to have a drag that slips freely and yet can create a high amount of pressure. It has to be able to slip, yet sustain a high load, perhaps even a complete no-slip lockdown load. Thus, you're looking for two opposite attributes in a washer to accomplish these needs.

Drag washer materials in spinning reels, like those in other reel types, have evolved over the years. Phenolic washers were used in the past, as were various fibrous washers, and some people replaced manufacturer-supplied washers with oil-soaked leather, composition cork, and other materials. Felt, nylon, cork, and metal have been common in many spinning reel drag washers. The primary material in modern high-end spinning reels, most of which have very smooth drags, is Teflon or a proprietary synthetic composite, including a material called TDM, which is a mix of fiberglass, graphite, and Teflon; in spinning reels, these materials do a reasonable job of satisfying the two opposite demands. Teflon, for example, has a very low coefficient of friction, which allows the spool to turn while providing a smooth slip surface; it has the same static and kinetic friction coefficient, which means that it takes the same force to start it moving as it takes to keep it moving. In other materials, it takes more force to start movement than to maintain it. A material that does not have a low coefficient of friction produces a jerk or spurt in spool momentum as the line pays off. This smoothness, incidentally, can be aided by lubricants. Many of the lubricants used by manufacturers are also proprietary, and some are Teflon impregnated greases; they help considerably to smooth the drags out.

There is a co-mingling of different material washers in many drags. Because heat dissipation is one of the most important elements to deal with, metal washers, which dissipate heat well, are used in conjunction with washers made from other materials, which provide the smooth slip surface. In better quality reels, for example, Teflon may be used with stainless steel.

The drag system in most midpriced spinning reels is generally of fairly good quality while the drag in most high priced models is good to excellent. The majority of spinning reels sold are used for light and medium-light applications in freshwater and, for the majority of users, the drags are actually over-built. Freshwater anglers, for the most part, do not require exceptional drag performance unless they use the reels for such species as steelhead, salmon, striper, and big trout. Many freshwater anglers catch relatively small species on average, and fish that do not require a lot of drag usage except during extraordinary circumstances. Then there is the average bass angler, who wants to lock the drag knob down so that a fish can't run into cover. As a result, many freshwater anglers do not appreciate or understand the drag function, and barely pay attention to it, even if they have a spinning reel with a good drag. That is why the drag is overbuilt for them.

Saltwater anglers, on the other hand, frequently need and really test the performance of a spinning reel drag. Thus, drag performance and drag components are mainly significant to people who catch fish that will put some pressure on a reel. The irony is that in freshwater or saltwater, you never know when a fish will come along that does just that, so if you do understand drag and prepare for fighting a strong fish, you'll be covered.

Combinations/Levers. Some spinning reels have sported combined drag systems in which there are both front and rear drags, the front drag being the primary one for fish fighting and the rear drag being a means of releasing tension on the line while the bail is closed. The rear drag is small and has a very light setting, so if a fish takes live bait, for example, it can move off under minimal resistance. When ready, the angler engages the main system and uses it to play the fish. Generally, there is a lever to engage or disengage the main drag; in some systems, the main gear is engaged automatically when the handle is turned. The idea is to have a preset main drag as well as a lightly adjustable secondary drag so that it's possible to quickly switch between them. It is primarily an advantage in fishing with bait; if you tried to accomplish the same thing with an open-bail reel, extra line could wind off the reel (especially if drift fishing in current) and possibly delay hooksetting.

There have also been some spinning reels that featured a lever or trigger that was used to apply supplemental pressure to a spool. The lever is mounted on the stem and activated by the index finger; this is similar in location to, but different in operation from, a bail trigger, which opens the bail. In operation, when the spool is turning under preset drag tension, additional pressure is applied to the revolving spool by pulling the lever. Theoretically, this allows you to have a light preset drag, yet provides additional pressure if needed when fighting a fish.

This feature is one that has not caught on with anglers and which has some serious practical drawbacks. Gauging the right amount of supplemental pressure to apply via the lever is probably the biggest problem, because you must use an appropriate amount of pressure to correspond to the strength of the line and the circumstances, and it is easy to apply too much additional pressure. The possibility of grabbing the trigger accidentally and applying unnecessary additional pressure exists, as does the possibility of inadvertently holding onto the lever for too long a time when you really need to completely let go.

Anti-Reverse Features

When the handle of a spinning reel is turned forward, line is wound onto the spool. If the handle can be wound backward, in reverse, line unwinds from the spool provided that there is tension on the outgoing line. Some reel handles cannot be turned in reverse. Most, however, can be turned in reverse by the operation of a switch on the outside of the reel. This switch, known as the anti-reverse, allows anglers to put the reel in reverse by turning it to the off position, or to keep the anti-reverse constantly out of use by turning it to the on position.

When the anti-reverse switch is in the off position, the handle and the rotor can be moved forward and backward; line can come off the spool when the handle is turned backward and also when the drag slips. When the anti-reverse switch is in the on position, the handle and rotor can be turned forward but cannot be turned backward; line can only come off the spool when the drag slips. A reel with this switch is said to have selectable, or selective, anti-reverse, while one without it is said to have nonselectable anti-reverse.

At one time when reel drags were poor and often unreliable, it was useful to have a reel with a selective anti-reverse feature. Anglers felt more comfortable when playing a strong fish if they could reel backward to let line out to play the fish. Many were accustomed to doing this with baitcasting, or levelwind, reels, which initially had direct drive, and had to be back-reeled, or wound backward, when a strong fish put a lot of pressure on it.

There are some anglers who back-reel for freshwater fish and advocate this on its own or in conjunction with using the drag. Many do so because they do not want to rely on the drag, or have a reel with a poor drag system, or simply do not set the drag properly (usually they tighten it too far). The trouble with back-reeling is that it is hard for many people to reel backward quickly enough to keep up with a rapidly turning handle when a strong fish speeds off; therefore, they have to let go of the handle, which usually spins wildly, and which may cause a snarl, backlash, or overrun upon completion of the swift back-reeling. When anglers try to grab the rapidly turning handles, they often smack their fingers, which caused the old reels to be called knuckle busters. Another problem is that you have to gauge the action of the fish in order to reel quickly to keep up with it. It is possible to back-reel small fish, like 2-pound bass, as long as the drag is a good one and properly set, but it is better to keep the anti-reverse engaged, especially for stronger and harder-fighting fish.

Today, reel drags are quite reliable and efficient, especially when properly set, and there is no reason to back-wind, even if a reel has the ability to do so. Today's spinning reels do not really need selective anti-reverse, but most of them have it in order to give anglers—especially competitive bass anglers who insist on cranking the drag tension up high—the option of using it. Probably the only time that

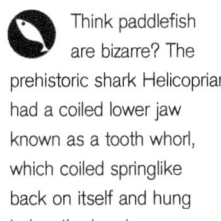

Think paddlefish are bizarre? The prehistoric shark Helicoprian had a coiled lower jaw known as a tooth whorl, which coiled springlike back on itself and hung below the head.

the average angler uses this feature is when line is accidentally wound around inner or outer parts of the reel and needs to be worked free.

What is more important for anglers, however, is how the reel operates when the forward turning motion is stopped. There is a natural tendency to pull up on the handle when not reeling, whether to set the hook or to momentarily stop while retrieving. In older models of reels, and in some lesser quality current models, there is considerable play in the handle and rotor when the reel stops, and the handle may actually turn backward slightly before engaging. This tendency produces a feeling of sloppiness or instability, and if there is too much backward movement of the handle, it may adversely affect hooksetting and may allow a loop of slack line to appear on the spool in some retrieval motions, which may eventually impair casting. Ideally, the reel should engage instantly and firmly, and better spincasting reels have features that allow this, which are usually called continuous anti-reverse or infinite anti-reverse reels. These should keep the drive gear from moving even the slightest bit backward.

In today's spinning reels, there are two major variations on spinning reel anti-reverse systems. The continuous anti-reverse system, or one-way clutch, as some people call it, is used in most higher end spinning reels. This system provides seemingly immediate engagement of the anti-reverse system, allowing instantaneous bone-jarring hooksets. This system is composed of a device underneath the pinion, which looks like a roller bearing (it may be called a one-way roller bearing and really is a bearing, except its configuration allows it to only turn in one direction). This is a part that is most commonly used in the printer industry to control the location of ink on paper and the rotation of parts. In reels its job is to completely prohibit backward travel of the shaft. It does this very well on most reels, and if it doesn't do it as well on some reels as on others, it is because of different tolerances in the other components. This system results in a continuous or infinite anti-reverse.

The second type of anti-reverse system is the pawl and ratchet system. This system is similar to the anti-reverse system on winches on the front of a boat trailer. A metal pawl engages gear teeth or ratchets to prevent backward rotation of the rotor. A finite number of teeth or ratchets translate to some backward rotation of the rotor before the pawl engages. The number of teeth on the ratchet plate really determine how fast the anti-reverse system will engage. The more teeth, the faster the system will engage. As with all things, optimizing one feature often creates other problem areas. To add more teeth, either the ratchet plate has to become bigger in diameter, or the teeth must become smaller. Obviously, with a bigger diameter plate, the reel itself must become larger. And with smaller teeth, the anti-reverse system becomes weaker.

Actuating the ratchet plate can be accomplished in several different manners. One of the most common is to utilize a small slider or actuator (generally plastic) on the crank gear shaft. The actuator contacts a pawl in such a fashion that when the crank shaft is rotated forward, the actuator keeps the pawl from contacting the ratchet gear located on the center or pinion shaft. When the reel is cranked backward, or when the rotor rotates backward, the slider actuator forces the anti-reverse pawl into the anti-reverse ratchets, thus preventing backward rotation of the system. This system does not produce a "clicking" sound, because the slider actuator keeps the pawl away from the ratchet teeth, except when the rotor turns backwards. When the anti-reverse is in the off position, the selector switch prevents the slider actuator from forcing the pawl into contact with the anti-reverse ratchets. In this condition, the rotor is allowed to freely turn forward or backward.

Manufacturers have compensated for the inherent limitations of the typical pawl and ratchet system in better spinning reels by installing continuous anti-reverse devices or moving the anti-reverse into the rotor itself. Most anti-reverse systems are located on the gear shafts inside the body of the reel. Recently, manufacturers have found a way to move the pawl and ratchet anti-reverse system to the rotor of the reel. In this position, a bigger diameter is available for the ratchet plate. In some reels, ratchet teeth are actually located on the inner diameter of the rotor. As noted, this bigger diameter ratchet plate allows more teeth on the ratchet, providing a more immediate stop on pawl and ratchet systems. Some reels actually have 60-point anti-reverse systems, which is a tremendous improvement from the less than 20-point systems obtained when the anti-reverse is in the reel's body.

In considering these anti-reverse systems for speed of engagement, it is also important to consider where the anti-reverse mechanism is located in reference to the gear set itself. In spinning and spincasting reels, the gear ratios are arranged so that the pinion gear, and thus the center shaft, rotate faster than the drive shaft. A low speed rotation at the reel handle is translated to a faster speed at the device

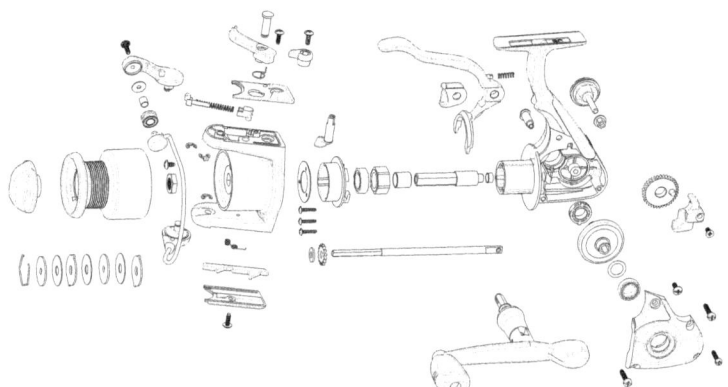

Shown are all of the parts of a Quantum Hypercast spinning reel, which includes a bail trigger, counterbalanced handle, front drag system, and continuous anti-reverse.

that winds line on the spool. This is important to note, because it requires more efficient anti-reverse mechanisms, whether pawl and ratchet or continuous anti-reverse, to be placed on the center or pinion shaft. A more immediate stop is achieved when the anti-reverse is actuated from this shaft instead of the drive shaft. An additional advantage is that the jarring forces producing a radical hookset are absorbed in the anti-reverse mechanism instead of being transmitted through the gear set before the anti-reverse engages. In the latter condition, more wear and tear is passed on to the gear teeth, potentially causing preliminary gear roughness, and perhaps even broken gear teeth.

As discussed earlier with regard to bail opening systems, there can be several settings for anti-reverse systems. These settings are generally selectable by means of a lever or sliding switch at the rear or along the bottom side of the reel. If the reel is equipped with a selectable anti-reverse system, it will have a combination of either an on-off setting, or an on-off–self center setting. In the on setting, the anti-reverse system is in fully functional mode. In the off setting, the anti-reverse is turned off and the reel handle will freely rotate backward to release line from the spool with the bail closed. The self-center position allows the angler to rotate the handle backward to a degree. Backward rotation will stop when the line roller, and in most cases casting trigger, are positioned correctly directly underneath the rod for the next cast.

Most modern spinning reels have silent anti-reverse, which means that when the anti-reverse is engaged, there is no noise in the system. Some low-end units, and much older reels, have an audible anti-reverse, so there is a constant clicking sound when you turn the handle, which is due to the fact that the pawl is forced into the ratchet constantly, and as you turn the handle, the pawl bounces up and down on the ratchet. The same thing happens when the drag is used and the spool revolves to let out line under tension, which, incidentally, is what used to produce the phenomenon of "screaming reels" that some writers prosaically described. Now when the drag is used on most reels, there is no sound.

Ergonomics/Convenience Features
Weight/Body materials. The issue of ergonomics is fairly simple in a spinning reel, and boils down to a comfortable fit in the hands, easy access to features, and overall weight.

Spinning reels sit under the rod handle; the stem of the reel has a foot that is seated in the handle so the outfit is held by wrapping your fingers around the reel foot, with the stem laying between the fingers. Most people place the stem between their middle and third finger. A minority place it between their third finger and little finger. In each case, it is held close to the base of the fingers, and this contact with the stem, as well as the separation between the fingers and the weight that sits there, may be uncomfortable, especially if the reel is held for long continuous periods.

Obviously, this part of the reel needs to be as comfortable to hold as possible. The thickness and width of stems vary on reels, and preferences among anglers do as well. A thin stem is generally viewed as being more comfortable, as is a perpendicular stem in the area where it is held, but to some people, a wider stem, which puts more surface area between the fingers, provides greater support than one that is thinner and narrower. Some reel stems have been padded for cushioning or contoured to relieve pressure points. The design of the stem becomes more important as the weight and the amount of continuous use increase.

Another factor, especially for cold weather anglers, is how the stem feels when the reel is cold and handled with bare hands. Metal is colder than composite materials, so the latter feels better in cold weather and a padded area may offer some warmth. A bit of electrician's tape or some type of padded tape wrapped tightly and evenly around the handle stem can help ward off the cold contact. There are a lot of good lightweight gloves that can be worn without sacrificing finger movement, so this may be the best route to take, especially if you need the strength of a metal frame and stem for the type of fishing done.

An especially important practical and ergonomic issue is that the distance from the foot to the spool or bail roller has to be such that the line or bail trigger can be readily grabbed with your index finger. For people with small hands, including children, this may be a problem, especially with larger reels. People who have large hands or thick fingers often have a problem with lighter spinning reels, which seem to have a clearance between the foot and bail assembly or trigger that was designed for small or thinner fingers. Thus, when they press the bail trigger, it pinches against their fingers, or when they turn the handle, the bail assembly smacks their knuckles. This may not only occur to people with large hands or thick fingers, but to others with normal size hands who hold the reel between their third and little fingers, primarily when using bail triggers. That type of hold, while it is comfortable to those who prefer it, places two fingers above the stem, so that when the trigger is pressed by the forefinger, there is less room for it to lever back, meaning that it pinches against the middle finger and may not open. This requires people to change their hold, which can be disrupting, sort of like having to hold your pencil differently than you've always been accustomed.

Weight, of course, has an influence on comfort for nearly everyone except those with the strongest hands and wrists. While both anglers and manufacturers would like reels to be as light as possible—after all, rods are much lighter than reels—there are trade-offs to going light. Lighter reels are comfortable to hold, but they cannot be so light that they lose durability and strength. Reels can be punished not only through the torque and pressures of playing a fish or unsnagging, but also from abuse, like being dropped or banged or stepped on.

Spinning reel housings used to be made solely out of diecast aluminum, which provided plenty of strength but was heavy. When plastics and various composite synthetic materials became available, people didn't trust them, and only the cheaper reels used them.

It should be noted that plastics can offer significant advantages, not only in the tackle industry but many other places. Complete experimental car engines are currently being produced from plastic resins. Proper selection of engineering grade resins today for fishing reel components provides a combination of strength, durability, corrosion resistance, and economic price unparalleled by any other class of materials. In fact, design engineers claim gear sets could be made of plastic resins that would be quieter, smoother, and more durable than conventional diecast or brass gear sets. Yet, would the public be willing to take a chance on these gears? Many gear sets in handheld portable power drills, and screwdrivers are molded from plastic today.

Eventually more expensive reels used the better synthetic components and they became much more accepted. Then aluminum bodies became preferred again on better reels because of their durability. Mostly these changes evolved because of marketing and an understanding of the demands that tough fishing placed on reels.

Certainly aluminum didn't get any lighter, although some synthetics did get better. Nevertheless, even with the advanced state of synthetics today, aluminum is more durable. It moves less and is less prone to allowing misalignments in the system under pressure. A strong reel has a stable mounting system, so gears maintain their strength and don't wear out as fast. The stronger the housing, the more stability for the gears.

A lot of force is applied to a reel under heavy use, and in a spinning reel, it is applied to the gears in a manner that is opposite to the norm. A small gear normally drives a large gear, so you put a small force in and get a large force out. In a spinning reel, however, a large gear drives a small gear, so the forces are reversed, and it takes a lot more pressure on the crank gear to turn it under a load. This is why higher gear ratios have less cranking power. There is a speed increase instead of a power increase. Consequently, the forces generated in the gear teeth are substantial and resistance to turning in the rotor forces the gear teeth apart. If the housing or frame is made of stiff materials to back the gears up, spreading can be kept to a minimum and the system lasts longer.

Most freshwater anglers don't put substantial force on their reel when retrieving or playing a fish, but they do when they are snagged on some object. Wrestling a hook or lure off the bottom is typically how the average freshwater angler generates a lot of force. In saltwater, where more large fish are caught, it is more likely that an angler will put substantial force on a reel when retrieving or playing a fish.

Handles. Handles and knobs are largely a matter of personal preference. Nearly all spinning reels have a single-knob handle, and some have a counterbalanced handle. Strength and cranking power are governed by the distance from the crank shaft hole to the knob, not from the end of the counterbalance to the knob or, in the case of two-knob handles, the distance between the knobs.

There is no benefit in terms of reel function or technical performance for having a dual-knob rather than single-knob handle, yet dual-knob handles are popular on mid- and top-range spincasting reels and on virtually all baitcasting reels, in part because people feel that it is easier to grab either one of them quickly, as when they aren't looking at the reel. There is no strength advantage to dual knobs, and since spinning reels are mounted under the rod rather than on top of it, most people are happy to do without the extra weight and awkward look of a dual-knob handle.

Handles on spinning reels are made from engineering grade plastic resins, zinc, and aluminum diecast alloys. The knobs vary in material, although most anglers prefer a soft material that is easy to grip, especially when wet, and that may be contoured for comfort. On higher end reels, a soft rubber is often used on the knobs rather than hard plastic, and they are more flat and paddle shaped than round. If the handle and the knobs are not large and comfortable enough for the user, they will be fatiguing and perhaps counterproductive.

Appearance. Overall appearance is largely a subjective matter with no practical bearing on performance. Spinning reel design has steadily favored smaller and more streamlined bodies, and the styling (and color) follows automotive trends with rounded smooth contours, which are more pleasing to the eye than the shapes that used to prevail. Some popular reels get a body face-lift after a few years to keep up with trends, but they may not be much different internally.

Spool features. Being able to change a spool quickly is a nice feature for those who might use a supplemental spool filled with a different type or strength of line. Spool removal is easy on rear drag reels, all of which have a front pushbutton spool release. Some front drag reels also have a pushbutton release, but most feature a drag adjustment knob that must be wound off to release the spool, which is a bit less convenient. One of the newer innovations in top saltwater spinning reels is a spool that can be removed simply by pushing down on the spool and rotating it counterclockwise. This is done without touching the drag adjustment knob, so the drag tension remains where it was.

Some spinning reels come with a spare spool, and if they don't, a spare can readily be purchased from the manufacturer. Spares are generally the same size as the original spool, but there may be some that have a smaller or larger arbor diameter, or it may be possible to get an arbor spacer, which snaps around the spool arbor and decreases line capacity. It is seldom possible to mix and match spools from various reels, although it would be nice to put a larger diameter (outside diameter, not arbor) spool on a reel whose original spool diameter was small. This is not possible on current reels, but there was once a product that sported different screw-on rotors with different diameter spools. It never caught on, probably because people decided that they could just as well buy another reel with a larger diameter spool, if they could find one.

Many spinning reel spools, especially smaller models for freshwater use, sport a tab or clip that can hold line when the terminal tackle has been removed and the reel is being stored. This keeps loose line from spiraling off the spool and is a nice feature, provided that the tab is slightly recessed on the spool exterior. If the line keeper tab is not recessed, and protrudes just a smidgen past the spool surface, it will occasionally catch a spiral of line and the tab will have to be cut off.

Other convenience features on some spinning reels include: a switch on the rotor or bail assembly that allows the bail to collapse for compact storage; a lever, button, or other means of folding the handle easily for storage; line size and capacity information on the surface of the spool.

Saltwater features. Although most of the issues previously reviewed are relevant to any spinning reel, the products that are intended for saltwater use have a few different elements that are worth mentioning. This is not to infer that a spinning reel that is primarily used in freshwater cannot also be used in saltwater, provided that it has an appropriate drag mechanism and line capacity; it certainly can, but the reel will need daily and careful washdown maintenance to help avoid corrosion, and it must be very sturdy if it will be used on really tough fish.

Reels that are going to be used regularly in saltwater need to have more built-in corrosion resistance, very sturdy components, and a top quality drag. Most saltwater angling entails encounters with larger and tougher fish than found in freshwater, and the environment is far more punishing, so reels that will be used regularly in saltwater have to withstand the environment and the application. These are built heavier, with more substantial components, including beefier drags and more corrosion protection through the use of stainless steel and/or anodized coatings. Naturally, they are heavier reels, and they often have large spools to accommodate 200 to 300 yards of line. These spools should be forged rather than diecast and the spools should preferably be made from a high grade of stainless steel. Graphite spools may do for light saltwater fishing, but not where heavier lines and intense pressure are involved. Super-heavy pressure on a graphite spool will break it, especially if a person puts stronger line on the reel than what it is designed for.

Virtually all saltwater spinning reels have a multi-element top mounted drag system and most have large drag washers, at least two or three stainless steel aircraft grade ball bearings, and a very sturdy handle; there are no bail opening triggers and few folding bails. The retrieve ratio is usually in the 4.5:1 to 5.1:1 range, with a few slightly higher, but not in the ultrahigh ranges that are found in many freshwater spinning reels. The reason—lower gear ratio for cranking power—is obvious and especially acute for saltwater fish. Even reels that are designed for saltwater need to be properly cleaned after each use and periodically maintained.

Rods

Spinning rods are different in one important and distinguishing respect from baitcasting rods and most spincasting rods: The guides mount under the axis of the rod and thus are placed under it, and the reel sits under the handle rather than on top of it. This also occurs with flycasting tackle *(see)* because these products are theoretically geared more to casting functions than to fish fighting functions. This doesn't mean that they do not fight fish well if properly designed, just that casting is generally their greatest attribute.

The rings on spinning rod guides are also larger than they are with other tackle, in order to accommodate the large spirals of line that come off the spinning reel spool when casting, and to minimize the effects of coiled or possibly twisted line rapidly funneling through the guides. A single foot is standard for the guides, meaning that there is just one attachment point for the rod to the blank, which improves rod action. In addition, spinning rod guides are designed so that they extend a greater distance from the rod shaft than with other types of rods in order to help reduce line slap, which is the tendency of line that is cast from a spinning reel to strike the rod shaft, thereby increasing friction and reducing casting distance.

Spinning rod handles are straight, with fixed or adjustable (ring) reel seats, and both one- and two-piece models are common. Handle length and overall rod length vary widely according to application, ranging from 4-foot ultralight models to some surf fishing versions in the 14-foot class. Shorter models exist for ice fishing (jigging).

Action, taper, and material construction vary considerably. Spinning rods are commonly made of graphite and a mix of graphite and other materials, and many models are specifically tailored to special uses and styles of fishing.

nlike reels, many of the issues pertaining to spinning rods—functions, materials, and components—are similar to those of other rods, and these are more fully detailed elsewhere *(see: rod, fishing)*.

China's Fan Li is believed to be the first person to breed and raise fish (reportedly common carp); he wrote the first known document on fish culture, a book entitled Fish Breeding, in 473 B.C.

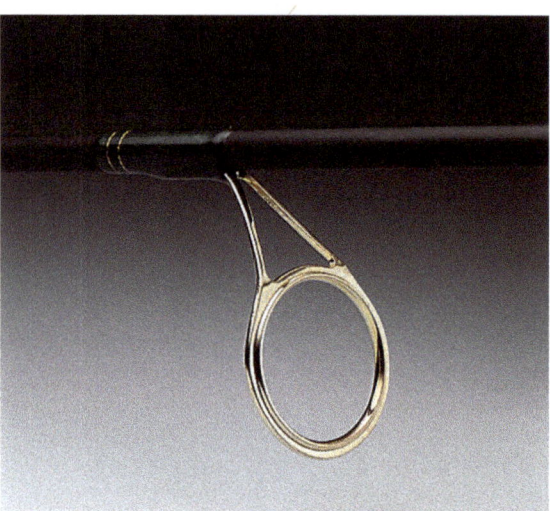
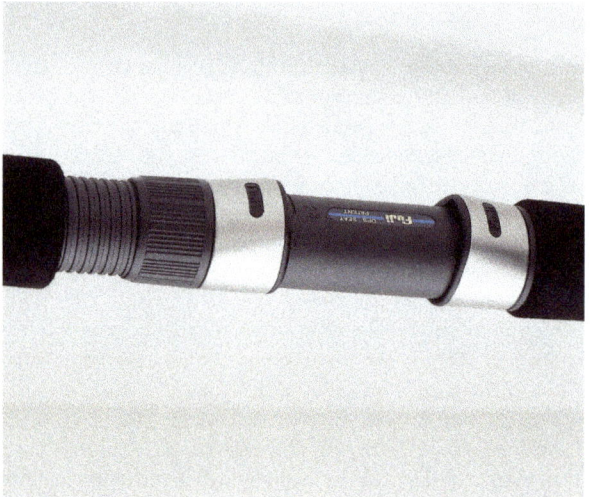

The single-foot guide (left) and fixed reel seat (right) are common on spinning rods.

Using Spinning Tackle

Line. Although all of the various line strengths from 2 through 30 pounds are employed with spinning gear, 6, 8, and 10 pounds are certainly the most commonly used strengths and are a choice of many anglers who do varied and general fishing. For light-tackle fishing 4- to 6-pound line is popular, although 8 pounds might be light for some circumstances and species; 2- and 4-pound strengths are ultralight for most circumstances, with more people using 4 than 2. Exceeding 12-pound strength is less common in freshwater and more common in saltwater, and the heaviest strengths are seldom used in freshwater but often in saltwater, especially for surf fishing and offshore use.

Fishing line is rarely pre-spooled onto a spinning reel, although with some lower priced models and some start-up combinations, it may be. Users make their own selection of line type, strength, and brand, usually purchasing it separately and either spooling it on the reel themselves or having it done by a tackle dealer.

Nylon monofilament is the overwhelming choice of line type for spinning reels, and there is some usage of microfilament line for freshwater use. Lead core, wire, and braided Dacron lines are more suitable for levelwind or baitcasting reels, and are seldom employed on spinning reels of any size. The better nylon monofilaments for spinning reel use are those that are supple rather than stiff. Stiff, wiry lines tend to coil more and spring off the spool. Lines with low memory cast better on spinning reels. Some nylon monofilaments have less memory than others. Braided and fused microfilament lines, which have very low memory as well as little stretch, cast well on spinning reels and are compatible with both wide and narrow spools.

Spinning reels are designated for certain line strengths or diameters. Most reels indicate the strength of line they are intended for, and some also give a diameter. Diameter is as important as strength (or more so); there are many lines with a thin diameter but conventional strength. Thus, if a spinning reel holds 150 yards of conventional diameter 8-pound line, it will take much more yardage of an 8-pound line with a 4-pound diameter. The labeling on a box or spool of a good quality line should not only denote strength, but also diameter, and if you know the diameter, you will have a clearer picture of how much line to put on the spool.

Generally, it is best to keep within the recommended line strengths when filling a spinning reel. If the manufacturer recommends using 6- and 8-pound line with the reel, that recommendation is based upon a standard 6- or 8-pound line with a conventional diameter. You can probably use conventional diameter 4- and 10-pound line as well, but it would not be worthwhile to use much higher line. Not only are spool size and capacity issues, but this reel is not meant to handle the greater stresses that might be generated with much heavier line. So, for example, putting 15-pound line on that reel could be problematic.

However, and this is where things get tricky, there are 15-pound lines that have the diameter of a conventional 8-pound line, so you can get it to lay on the spool quite nicely. Nevertheless, it is still line with a 15-pound breaking strength (and some 15s actually break much higher); this may be capable of overpowering the reel. If the rod is up to handling a lot of stress, and the line is rated to break at a minimum of 15 (often more) pounds, and the reel is meant for up to 8-pound line, then the forces generated on the reel by maximum pressures could be harmful to some parts (handle, gears, crank shaft, bail) of the reel.

On the other hand, you might use an 8-pound line with a diameter of conventional 4, and achieve much greater line capacity on the reel at a line strength that the reel is rated for. Or, you could "cheat" a little bit and use 10-pound line that has a diameter of conventional 6-pound line, if that benefited your fishing situation *(see: line)*.

This is a grossly misunderstood aspect of spinning reel usage that has largely been brought about by the emergence of thin diameter lines (nylon monofilaments, braids, and microfilaments). Remember that, although reels are primarily designated according to line strength and general application, many good reels also bear line diameter ratings.

Filling/Refilling the spool. The various aspects of properly filling a reel spool are detailed elsewhere *(see: line)*. Putting line on a spinning reel spool is less complicated than putting it on a spincasting reel because the spool is open and accessible whereas the spool on a spincasting reel is under the cover.

If you are a new angler or new to the use of spinning reels, the fastest and easiest way to fill a reel is to have it wound on by a linewinder, which is a professional machine. Many tackle dealers offer this service to their customers, although it is seldom available from a mail order supplier or mass merchant.

In brief, the spooling process entails mounting the reel on the rod and running line from a service spool through the rod guides beginning at the top of the rod. Open the bail and tie the line to the arbor of the spool, snip off the tag end excess, close the bail, and reel the line on under tension. It is important to avoid or at least minimize twisting of the line during the spooling process, as detailed elsewhere *(see: line)*. Fill the spool to within $1/8$-inch of the lip, but do not overfill, which may cause line to coil off the spool and tangle.

When the line gets low on the spool, or when it is old and needs replacement, you have the option of completely refilling the spool, or refilling only part of the spool. If a spinning reel holds 150 yards of line, economically it makes sense to refill with just 60 or 80 yards of line rather than the full 150, depending on a number of factors.

When you partially refill the spool, you have to tie a line-to-line knot *(see: knots, fishing)*. The weakest portion of a line is usually the knot, so this connection must be a good one to maintain the basic strength of the line, should that knotted section come under pressure. If you never use more than the first 30 or 40 yards of line on a reel, then such a knot is unlikely to come under pressure. If you tie a perfect line-to-line knot, it shouldn't matter if and when it does come under pressure.

The line-to-line knot must be small and smooth, however, for it to lay on the reel without interference, and to minimize friction when it comes off the spool lip and through the rod guides. Some people tie a bulky line-to-line knot that gets in the way.

Of course, the line that stays on the back of the spool, to which the newer line is connected, must be in a usable condition and of the requisite strength for your fishing needs. That line, which is usually referred to as backing when another section is tied to it, has to hold up to the demands of the fishing situation when put under pressure. If it does not have the proper strength, it needs to be replaced, and the entire spool should be refilled.

Line twist and its prevention. Line twist has been an inherent problem in spinning reels since they were introduced and is somewhat analogous to the problem of backlash in baitcasting tackle in terms of causing line tangles and irritation. There is no spinning reel user who has not experienced some degree of line-twisting trouble when using either their own or someone else's spinning gear, and, unfortunately, some anglers experience far more line twisting than others. There are anglers who have given up on this tackle because of line twisting trouble, but there are ways to deal with twist, and manufacturers have in recent times produced spinning reels that are much less likely to instill twist than older products. Giving up on spinning gear because you've experienced twist is not a good idea, as this tackle serves a useful purpose and can perform some functions better than any other tackle type when used properly.

Although twist can occur when using other types of tackle, it is more prevalent with spinning gear, and line twist does cost spinning tackle users valuable angling time, induces frustration and irritation, and may cause otherwise unnecessary replacement of line. It may also contribute to lost lures and breakoffs. Therefore, spinning tackle users need to know what causes line twist and how to avoid as well as cure it. The general phenomenon

Twisted loops often form on the spool of a spinning reel and generally cause further problems; a loop like this should be removed as soon as possible.

of line twist has been addressed elsewhere *(see: line)*, so this section will address specific issues relative to spinning reels because of the significance this issue has with these products.

Line twist damages nylon monofilament line by building ever greater stresses as it accumulates in the line due to a variety of causes. Under load, as when fighting a fish, these stresses may weaken the structure of the line and can lead to break-offs. A twisted line is like a loaded spring. When tension is released on a cast the line tends to balloon outward from the axis of the line flow. This increases line-to-guide friction and reduces casting distance. It is also why some line twist disasters (a wad of mangled line) tend to wrap around a spinning rod's gathering guide. Twist is of little problem when line is kept under tension. The stored spring energy due to twist is evident only when tension is released. Then, a snarl can almost instantly appear.

Technique is one of the agents of these snarls. A semi-slack slow-retrieve application with lures that have minimal water resistance, for example, does not provide constant tension, and if a line is predisposed to twisting due to other factors, such tackle usage may foster twist and line snarls, which they would not in applications with more water resistant lures and under constant retrieve speeds that maintain tension on the line. But, if you need to use a semi-slack retrieve, then that's what you have to do, and because that does not cause line twist in itself, you have to address the root problems.

No matter what steps you take, however, you must realize that most spinning reels, especially older models, actually put a twist in the line just by virtue of their design, which is a root problem that is not experienced with revolving spool tackle.

Reel manufacturers have devoted a great deal of effort and research time to analyzing and attempting to eliminate line twist from spinning tackle. Among the many discoveries made by the best known producers of quality spinning reels is the fact that it is impossible to totally eliminate all of the causes that contribute to line twist in spinning reels. Some advertising claims would lead you to believe that certain reels eliminate twist; actually they may minimize twist (in some cases to a significant degree), but they do not entirely eliminate it, and they cannot eliminate twist that is caused by improper angling use.

As previously noted in the review of spinning reel components, some twists are caused by the physical design factors built into the reel. For example, as the rotor and bail of a spinning reel rotate, line is put under tension that draws it to the low point of the typical roller on the bail arm. This line movement happens when the line rolls over the guide surface until it reaches the low point. The rolling action causes the line to twist. Each time slack is allowed to form in the line, through rod action, for instance, the line can move on the roller. When tension is reapplied, the line can again roll and twist. These many small twists are cumulative and eventually become a problem, especially when combined with other causes.

The twist problem is compounded by nylon monofilament line, which has a memory and tends to retain its coiled shape after it has remained on the spool for a while. These coils can help twist-induced spring to tangle the line more easily. Luckily, after several casts the line absorbs some water, softens, and loses some or all of the coil. This is why some spinning reel users soak their line, preferably in warm water, to relax the memory before starting to fish with it.

One of the absolute worst causes of line twist is turning the spinning reel handle while the drag is releasing line. Excited anglers continue to quickly crank the handle, typically against a drag that is set too light, while no line is retrieved. Each turn of the handle puts multiple twists in the line in a direct relationship to the gear ratio of the reel. A 4.4:1 ratio reel puts over four twists into the line per turn of the handle. High-ratio reels add even more twists. Being conscious of what the drag is doing at all times while fighting a fish, or using a slightly tighter drag, can minimize this.

Wide- or long-spool reels that increase distance between the front and rear spool flanges have also contributed to line twist. Through spool oscillation on the retrieve, the line is wound onto the spool in a straight line from the line guide to the spool. But when the drag is employed, and line is taken off under tension, for example with the spool at the full extension of its oscillation stroke, the line wound onto the top of the spool forms a sharp, critical angle on its travel to the line guide on the bail. Tension on the line pulls the line downward along the spool and causes it to roll over the surface of the remaining line. This rolling action creates twist in the line and under tension creates friction that can result in damage and wear. While this phenomenon is at its worst in long-spool reels, it does occur to a lesser degree in traditional size spools.

Another factor that adds to this problem is the distance between the line roller on the bail and the line surface on the spool. This distance has an effect on the angle formed in the line at extreme oscillation points and contributes to roll-over twist formation. Rollers mounted close to the spool form sharper angles and can add to the twist problem.

Designers and engineers over the years have provided partial solutions to the overall problem through new mechanisms and parts refinements. Some of the early successes were the introduction of the roller line guide, which lowered friction and strain and increased the diameter of the guide. Reels were even designed to allow the entire rotor and bail to rotate backward when line was released to the drag. This had the same effect as the back-reeling technique, which literally unwinds and untwists the line as it is released. This design proved to prematurely wear out drag parts and caused the occasional

---

The vast majority of living fishes are derived from species that first appeared in the Triassic Period, at the same time that dinosaurs first appeared.

knuckle smacking. Another manufacturer deliberately created a very wide diameter spool with a short distance between the spool flanges to minimize oscillation induced twist under drag release.

More recently, reel makers have concentrated on the line twist induced by the line roller. These parts are now built to even larger diameters with integral ball bearings. This reduces friction and stress on the line. It also allows the more important design addition of a narrow slot that instantly captures the line and eliminates the possibility of twist caused by the line rolling over the surface of the roller, as well as eliminates slack line movement on the roller surface. Removal of this almost unnoticed contribution to line twist has been a remarkable improvement.

Spools are also reaching a realistic compromise in geometry. Extremely long flange to flange distances have been reduced while spool diameters have increased to the point where oscillation strokes are shorter and line memory is reduced. This, in turn, decreases the critical angles formed under drag release and reduces the tendency of the line to roll over itself, inducing twist. Some reels help prevent line twist by eliminating critical angles as a result of oscillating the spool not only during the retrieve, but also when the spool is releasing line through the drag. The line is continuously fed straight from the spool to the roller guide at all times, no matter how far a fish runs or what the line level on the spool is. Therefore, there is no twist from line roll-over when the line feeds from the spool to the roller.

Obviously some degree of line twist may be inevitable when using spinning reels, but a great deal can be done to reduce it to acceptable levels. As noted elsewhere *(see: line),* among the root problems, or contributing to them, is the way that your equipment has been used. Line twist can be reduced by using a good quality ball bearing swivel with lures that rotate or spin in the water. Incorrectly filling the reel from a bulk line spool can result in a tremendous amount of line twist even before the first cast is made. These are basic line-use issues that you can control.

You can also control how you play fish when using spinning gear. Try to fight all fish with the spinning reel spool in the center of its oscillation stroke. In this way, when the drag releases line, feed angles are reduced and so is twist. Try to maintain some tension on the line at all times to control slack line situations and keep the spring from unloading. If there is any twist in your line at the end of a day's fishing, cut off the lure and hardware and trail an empty line through the water to remove the twist, then reel it back on the spool under moderate finger tension.

Untangling line. There are two types of tangles that occur with spinning reels when a loose coil or loop of line is covered by a tight wrap of line. One is the obvious snarl that catches in the rod guides or slips through the rod guides. The severity of this varies, and most can be untangled by patient manipulation and reverse picking of the various coils and strands. In bad cases, the line will have to be cut, which means that the lure or hook has to be retied and also that a certain amount of line will be lost on the edge of the spool. If this happens a couple of times, the line level on the spool may be reduced to the point where casting performance is adversely affected.

The other type is the obvious appearance of a loose coil on the spool itself. This loose coil is what leads to the bird's nest tangle that comes off a reel, and if you notice this, you should address the problem by removing the spool rather than by casting the line again or pulling it off the top of the spool. If you remove the spool from the reel, you can pull line off from the back of the spool, over the skirt or flange, until you get to the problem loop or coil. Wind the line back onto the spool and then put it back on the reel. This is more easily accomplished on reels where the spool can be removed without unwinding the drag adjustment knob.

Try to address what causes these snarls or loops in order to prevent their occurrence. The problem occurs when line is retrieved on little or no tension, and gets placed onto the spool in a loose loop, which is then covered by other loops. Often a stop-and-go type of retrieve, such as the motion used in slowly working a jig, causes this. Make sure that line retrieval is accomplished under tension, and keep an eye on the spool to spot a loose loop before it becomes a major snarl.

Matching and selecting. As with any type of fishing tackle, the issue of matching the right reel to the right rod is an important one, but in these times, it is a relatively easy one. Some spinning reels and rods are sold in combination, although these are usually of lesser quality with minimal features, and more geared to light and beginning usage. Most of the time, a reel is purchased separately from a rod. Matching these up used to be referred to as balancing, and properly paired outfits were referred to as "balanced tackle." This simply meant that the rod and reel felt right when used together; the outfit was not overly butt heavy due to a large reel paired with a lightweight rod, or tip heavy due to a small reel paired with a medium or heavy action rod.

Fishing rods are virtually all labeled by line classifications and by weight of objects to be used, which practically assures that you don't put a light-duty spinning reel, for example, loaded with 6-pound line, on a medium-heavy rod that is rated for 10- to 14-pound line use. What you might do is look for a rod with a specific type of action, say one that has a fast taper for casting light lures, and look for this in the length that you prefer for the most frequent uses that you'll put the tackle to.

Spinning tackle is often classified by the manufacturers as being in a certain category and for a certain type or range of usage. Reels, for example, might be classified as ultralight, light, medium-light, medium, medium-heavy, and heavy, but the exact definition of this can range from one manufacturer to the next and, in any event, is most likely to be found by the line capacity information on the reel or in the packaging literature. A reel that is designated as medium freshwater/light saltwater is pretty self-explanatory. Anglers, of course, have different definitions of what a light, medium, or heavy rod is, too, and so there is often some confusion in terminology. A rod and reel for use with 6-pound line, for example, is light to most people, yet classified as medium by others. Like describing the weather as partly cloudy or partly sunny, it all depends on your point of view, and, of course, conforms to the size of the species you'll catch and the conditions you'll face.

When selecting tackle, as well as matching a rod and reel, you must take into consideration the kinds of fishing that you expect to do. A beginning angler may be unsure what to select without any prior fishing experience. Guidance from a knowledgeable salesperson could be very helpful; such a person is more likely to be found in a specialized store (a sporting goods dealer or bait and tackle shop). You might also seek guidance from an acquaintance or relative who has experience with this type of equipment and some knowledge of the fishing that a beginner is likely to do. Some manufacturers provide equipment guidelines on their packaging or display materials to provide general direction for appropriate usage, and this can be helpful.

In a general sense, selecting spinning tackle starts with a determination of the size of fish that you will be likely to catch an evaluation of the conditions under which you will be fishing. The larger and stronger the fish, the stronger the tackle necessary for beginners, until you get the experience to use lighter gear. Fishing where there are a lot of obstructions usually requires medium or heavy grades of tackle. Small fish, fewer obstructions, and clearer water usually are suitable for lighter tackle. Most selection thus starts with a determination of the line strength necessary for the conditions, and having the rod and reel appropriate for this. You should also give some attention to line capacity. If you will be fishing in a way or under circumstances

General Guidelines for Matching Spinning Tackle

Line Strength	Lure Weight	Reel Type	Rod Type	Fish Species
2–4 lbs.	1/16–1/4 oz.	ultralight	ultralight; 4–6 1/2 ft.	stream trout, small bass, panfish, white bass
4–8 lbs.	1/4–3/8 oz.	light	light; 5–7 ft.	freshwater: panfish, trout, largemouth and smallmouth bass, white bass, pickerel, shad, walleye, small catfish; saltwater: small bonefish, redfish, striped bass, other inshore species
8–12 lbs.	3/8–5/8 oz.	medium	medium; 6–7 1/2 ft.	freshwater: catfish, walleye, pike, salmon, striped bass, large bass and trout; saltwater: most small to midsize bay and inshore species, smaller offshore species
14–17 lbs.	1/2–1 1/2 oz.	medium-heavy	medium-heavy to heavy; 6 1/2–9 ft.	freshwater: large catfish/salmon/striped bass/pike/muskie/lake trout; saltwater: tarpon, striped bass, larger inshore species, midsize offshore species
20–30 lbs.	1–3+ oz.	heavy	heavy and ultraheavy; 9–13 ft.	freshwater: very largest species; saltwater: surf fishing, largest inshore species, offshore species

that require a lot of line, then you'll need an appropriate amount of line on the reel. The preceding table provides a general guide to matching fishing tackle, but is by no means an absolute definition.

For some people, spinning gear is purchased strictly according to price; in other words, you have a certain amount of money to allocate to the purchase. Generally, spinning tackle is less expensive than baitcasting tackle but a bit more expensive than spincasting tackle, and the lower-end items have fewer features and a lower performance factor. For undemanding fishing activities, and as an entree into the game, these rods and reels are fine. You get more features, better materials, and improved performance as you move up in price, especially in regard to reels. Higher priced reels should provide not only elevated performance, but also greater useful life if you take care of them.

If you purchase the tackle from a store, you'll have an idea how comfortable it is between your fingers, and whether the weight, general feel, handle knob, and general operation are to your liking. Make sure that there is enough room for your fingers between the handle and the bail or bail trigger; you don't want to find out later that either of these smacks your fingers. It's a good idea to mount the reel on the rod that you intend to use with it, to make sure that it sits securely in the reel seat; this is seldom a problem, but it could be, especially if you're using it with an older rod.

The purchase of fishing equipment relies a lot on word-of-mouth or the advice of in-store sales personnel, who are expected to know the value of certain features or the differences among various products. This is a problem, because many such personnel do not know enough about these matters to be really helpful. Also, manufacturers generally do a mediocre job of fully explaining features in their own literature and ads. While they are quick to point out benefits or claims, such as that a certain reel casts further, they seldom explain exactly how this is accomplished, or how much further it will cast. Many of the points that were reviewed earlier have emphasized issues that a prospective purchaser should be aware of and should consider in the selection process.

Holding the rod and reel. Most spinning reels have a convertible retrieve system, so you can set the handle up to retrieve from whichever side that you prefer. Normally, it is beneficial for right-handed people to reel with their left hand and for lefties to reel with their right hand, so that the dominant hand is the one that holds the rod and is used to play the fish or direct the retrieve. Because the dominant hand is used to cast the rod, there is no need to take further action after casting to start using the reel; the other hand is immediately placed on the reel handle grip and starts turning the handle. This is how most people use a spinning reel.

As for the actual grip on the rod and reel, this is

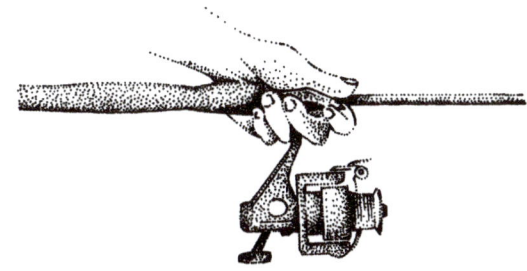

The most common means of holding a spinning outfit is by wrapping the middle fingers around the reel foot and stem, as shown; some people prefer to hold it between the middle finger and forefinger. The reel is always underneath the axis of the rod, never on top of it.

again personal preference. Because spinning reels sit under the rod handle and the stem of the reel has a foot that is seated in the handle, the outfit is held by wrapping your fingers around the reel foot, with the stem laying between and close to the base of the fingers. Most people place the stem between their middle and third finger. A minority place it between their third finger and little finger. Whatever feels best for you is right, provided that you're comfortable casting and holding it that way for long periods, and can readily access the bail roller or trigger.

Casting technique. The actual method of casting is accomplished in the following manner.

Begin with the reel under the handle and facing away from you. Adjust the drag to the proper tension level. Hang the casting plug (or lure or weight when fishing) from 3 to 6 inches below the tip of the rod and turn the handle to bring the bail roller close to the reel stem. If the lure is not in this position, reel it up to the tip and strip line off the reel by pulling on the line above the reel. Pull just enough off the spool so the lure is the right distance below the rod tip, while at the same time bringing the bail roller close to the reel stem and extended index finger. The bail roller must be properly positioned to allow the finger to easily grab the line and to touch the lip of the spool.

To open the bail manually, grab the line at the roller with the tip of your forefinger and flip up the bail with your other hand. To open the bail automatically, depending on the reel, either extend your forefinger over the roller and grab both the line and the trigger, or simply grab the trigger.

Keep tension on the line with your finger; this will be released at the optimum point of rod flex in the forward motion of the cast. When this tension is released, line flows off the spool and out through the guides, carried by the weight of the object at the terminal end of the line.

To execute the cast, the reel should face away from you and you should be looking at the back of your hand. Point the rod tip at and slightly above your intended target. When you are learning, and whenever striving for accuracy, get the rod and reel out in front of your body and make the rod follow an imaginary line from your nose to the target.

Bring the rod back sharply, using your wrist and forearm (not the whole arm), and allowing the weight of the lure to flex the rod. In a continuous and unhesitating motion, and still using the wrist and forearm, bring the rod forward in an accelerated motion, releasing the line with your forefinger during the forward stroke when the rod tip is pointing above the target.

The amount of flex in the rod depends on the rod design and material, with pure graphite rods only requiring a short hammering type of stroke, and more parabolic composite or fiberglass rods requiring more of a back-and-forth motion. With a bit of practice, you'll learn what adjustment to make for the rod action as well as for different lure weights, and you'll learn at exactly what point in the forward stroke to release the line, which is a major element in attaining the proper trajectory for accurate placement. If the lure goes too high in the air, the line was released prematurely; if the lure lands a short distance in front of you, the line was released too late. It shouldn't take too long to get the hang of it, which is one of the key benefits of using this type of tackle.

The released line can be moderately controlled

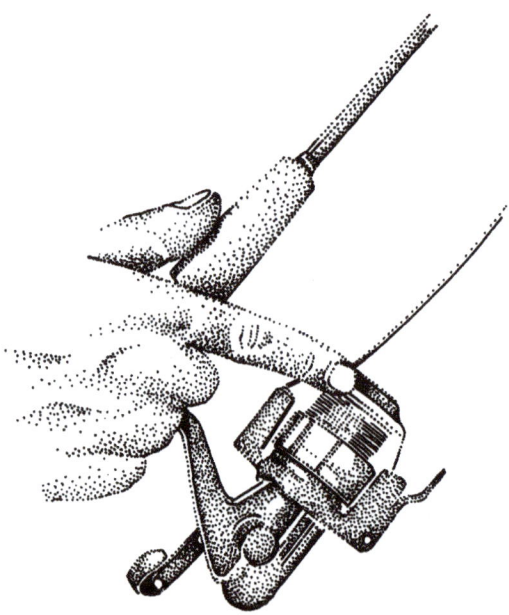

To feather line for accuracy when casting with spinning tackle, place your forefinger near the lip of the spool to contact outgoing line.

during a cast by allowing it to brush against an extended index finger from the rod-holding hand; the finger should be held near the spool lip. This is called feathering and is the most common method of controlling line that is cast from a spinning reel, although it is only moderately effective at achieving accuracy. Better accuracy can be obtained by allowing the outgoing line to brush against the forefinger of the noncasting hand, although the open bail wire may make this difficult. To do this, the front of the reel has to be in the palm of the other (usually left) hand; extend the left forefinger out and press it against the lip of the reel's spool, keeping it there during the casting motions. When the cast is made and the weight released, keep the left hand in place and control the line by applying slight pressure on it with the left forefinger. This method puts your left forefinger on top of your line as it peels off the spool during the cast.

On some reels, the location of the open bail arm sometimes makes this two-handed method of line control a little difficult, but it can nevertheless be done. An improvement upon this is removing the bail arm, as described later.

In lieu of feathering the line in either of these manners, many spinning reel users simply stop the cast altogether by pressing the extended index finger against the spool; by closing the bail; and by the end of forward momentum when the lure or weight reaches its target. Abruptly pressing a finger against the spool and closing the bail may cause the plug to stop abruptly and even lurch back toward you; allowing the lure to stop when it loses its own momentum is only suitable for open-water situations and cannot be used when obstructions are present or when pinpoint accuracy is necessary. These acts are not conducive to pinpoint casting, although they may be acceptable in situations where it is not necessary to place a lure or bait in an exact spot.

Achieving accuracy is largely a matter of practice, reflex, and timing. This is greatly aided by feathering the line to control speed and distance, although it is still necessary to have the right rod speed and lure trajectory. Mastering this takes times and practice.

Although most people do not rate spinning tackle very highly in the accuracy department, some anglers are able to be extremely accurate, so obtaining accuracy is partly a matter of how far you are willing to take the practice element, and using the right rod and weight of lure. It is true, however, that when using lures and fishing in cover, baitcasting tackle (once you have mastered spool control) is easier for most people to consistently obtain accuracy with. For some spinning tackle users, achieving casting accuracy is not a big issue because they do a lot of open-water casting with this equipment.

Achieving distance is an issue that many spinning tackle users dwell on, and which is repeatedly emphasized by reel manufacturers in touting the benefits of their products. This deserves a thorough review, since it has relevance to other tackle and fishing techniques as well. For more information on this and all aspects of casting, including other methods of achieving accuracy, *see: Casting*.

Setting/Checking drag. Before making a cast for on-the-water fishing, it is vital to set the drag to the proper amount of tension. Issues pertaining to drag in spinning reels were reviewed earlier in this section, and using and setting drag is covered in more detail elsewhere *(see: drag)*. Briefly, however, the drag on a spinning reel is adjusted by turning the front- or rear-mounted drag knob. Turning this clockwise increases tension, and counterclockwise decreases it. If a reel is used infrequently, it is a good idea at the end of each outing to back the drag tension off to relieve pressure on the drag washers. When starting a day of fishing, you should check and adjust the drag tension setting before making a cast. Many an angler has neglected this and found upon hooking the first fish of the day that the drag was so weak that it impaired hooksetting, or so tight that it adversely affected fish playing.

To test the drag on a spinning reel, pull line off it at various drag tension settings. Most people, especially if they have fishing experience, test the drag by pulling the line by hand directly ahead of the reel, and making necessary adjustments by feel, starting with a light drag setting and testing and adjusting until they reach a tension setting that feels right. For most fishing situations, especially in freshwater, this is adequate, and anglers wind up putting somewhere in the neighborhood of 25 to 30 percent breaking tension on the line. This "by feel" adjustment is a somewhat imprecise method of doing things, but adequate for the vast majority of spinning reel users.

If you want a general evaluation of how smooth the drag on a given reel is, run the line from the reel through the rod guides and attach it to a scale. Angle the rod tip up and pull on the line while you check what happens to the rod tip. If the tip remains in place, the drag is smooth, which is good. If it moves up and down, the drag is erratic, which may cause problems.

Maintenance and repair. Many people do very little, if anything, to maintain their spinning reels. This may be all right if the reel is only used occasionally. Common sense dictates that if the reel has any loose part, which is most likely to be a sideplate screw, it should be tightened as soon as you notice it, and that you should rinse any reel that has encountered sand, dirt, mud, or saltwater. Use a fine spray of freshwater, rather that a hard stream, to clean the reel and do so as soon as possible after use. There is nothing wrong with dipping a reel in freshwater if you have to cleanse it of dirt or sand, since it is likely to be exposed to wet and rainy conditions while fishing; just don't make a habit of it, give the reel a chance to dry out completely, and keep it lubricated.

Details on reel maintenance are discussed elsewhere *(see: tackle care/maintenance/repair)*. Manufacturers recommend that infrequently used reels be cleaned and relubricated annually, and that reels that are used several times a week be attended to monthly. Periodic maintenance means lightly oiling and greasing accessible parts. Some reels come with small oil or grease tubes, and these can be purchased from tackle suppliers or obtained from the manufacturer. A thorough cleaning requires disassembling most of the reel, scrubbing or rinsing most of the gunk from the parts, drying, and then relubricating.
See: **Baitcasting Tackle; Reel, Fishing; Spincasting Tackle.**

SPINY WATER FLEA
Bythotrephes cederstroemi.
An exotic species in North America, the so-called spiny water flea is not an insect but a tiny crustacean with a long, sharp, barbed tail spine. A native of Great Britain and northern Europe east to the Caspian Sea, the spiny water flea was first found in Lake Huron in December 1984. It is believed to have arrived in freshwater or mud in the ballast of ocean-going freighters, similar to the manner in which other exotics, particularly zebra mussels, were inadvertently imported. By 1985, it had spread to Lakes Erie and Ontario, by 1986 to Lake Michigan, and by 1987 to Lake Superior. It has since spread throughout the Great Lakes and into some inland waters, and has evidently established itself as a permanent part of the North American ecosystem, carving out a niche for itself at the expense of existing lake fisheries.

The quick success of the spiny water flea in colonizing all of the Great Lakes raises the possibility that it may become even more widespread over the years. Because these animals compete with native organisms, including young perch and other small fish, for food, and because they reproduce rapidly, they pose a threat to native species that is not yet fully understood and may become more significant in the future.

Unique body. The spiny water flea is easily recognized by its unique body shape. As an adult, the spiny water flea is no longer than $3/8$ inch. The tail spine is its distinguishing feature and separates it from all other free-swimming lake invertebrate animals, or zooplankton. That spine is proportionately long, often comprising more than 70 percent of the animal's length, and contains from one to four pairs of thornlike barbs. The head consists primarily of a single large eye filled with black pigment. Also present are a pair of sickle-shaped

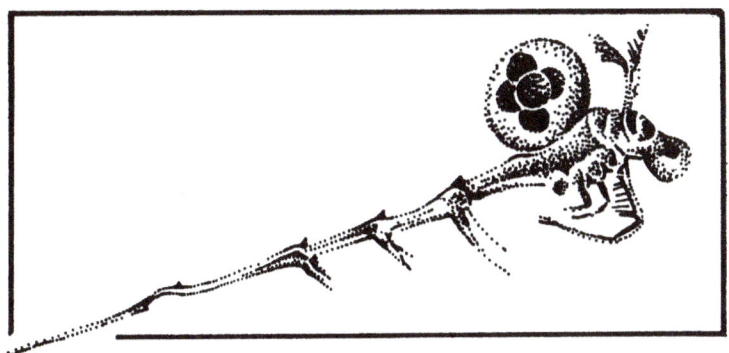

These tiny crustaceans (adults are $3/8$ inch long) exist in clusters that look like bristly gobs of jelly with black spots.

mandibles, or jaws, used to pierce and shred prey. These animals possess four pairs of legs; the first pair is much longer than the others and is used for catching prey, whereas the other pairs are designed for grasping prey to be consumed. Just behind the head is a pair of swimming antennae, which propel the animal through the water. Spiny water fleas are good swimmers, moving several times their body length in a second. The ability to swim, as opposed to merely drifting with the current, helps them encounter prey and to move between shallow and deeper lake waters.

Like all other crustaceans, its outer shell is molted during growth phases. The spiny water flea is unique because it sheds only the outer shell that covers the tail spine. The animal is never without its long stout spine; this fact suggests to biologists that the tail serves a vital protective function.

Unusual reproduction. The spiny water flea has a remarkable influence on biological communities in large part due to its rapid reproduction. Reproductive females carry their offspring on their backs in a balloonlike brood pouch, which can be filled either with developing embryos or resting eggs. Most of the time, females exhibit a rapid and unusual method of reproduction known as parthenogenesis, or asexual reproduction. By this method, females produce from 1 to 10 eggs that are able to develop into new females in the absence of mating or fertilization. The new females are genetic replicas, or clones, of the mother.

The generation time of this life cycle (embryo to adult females) varies with water temperature, because rates of metabolism rise and fall with temperature. During the summer when the surface water of the lake is warm, spiny water fleas can produce a new generation without fertilization in less than two weeks. Since males are not needed for this method, they are rarely found when food is plentiful, or when environmental conditions favor rapid population growth.

In spiny water fleas, the sex of offspring is not determined genetically but by environmental factors. So, when food becomes limited or when the lake cools in the fall, males begin to appear. Declining environmental quality can be sensed by adult females, who respond by producing male rather than female offspring. These males are able to mate with surviving females, producing resting eggs. The resting eggs are first carried as orange brown spheres in the female brood pouch. They are later released and fall to the lake bottom, where they can survive the cold winter. In spring or early summer, these eggs hatch into juvenile females that begin parthenogenic reproduction again. Resting eggs can remain dormant for long period, which may explain their arrival in North America and which may be indicative of their ability to be spread through innocent means to other waters via such carriers as boat wells and wet grass on boat trailers.

Disrupting the balance. Spiny water fleas eat smaller herbivorous crustaceans, including the common zooplankton, Daphnia, which is an important food item for small, juvenile fish. Thus, they compete directly with young fish for food. Because of their unique reproductive pattern, spiny water fleas can reproduce many times faster than fish. Rapid population growth enables them to monopolize the food supply at times, to the eventual detriment of other species.

Although the spiny water flea can fall prey to fish, its spine seems to frustrate most small fish, which tend to experience great difficulty in swallowing the animal. Fish usually manipulate food in their mouths before they swallow it, but the awkwardly shaped spiny water flea is difficult for small fish to ingest, although they have no trouble capturing it. Laboratory experiments show that small fish spend 8 to 10 percent more time eating spiny water fleas than other prey, and eventually learn to avoid it.

In Lake Michigan, spiny water fleas have rarely been found in stomachs of fish less than 2 inches in length, although fish of that size avidly consume Daphnia when that food item is available. There are indications that the growth rates and survival of these young fish may be adversely affected by the presence of spiny water fleas in the ecosystem, owing to competition for food. In general, the more abundant the spiny water flea becomes, the less food remains available for juvenile fish.

In European lakes, populations of spiny water fleas are often suppressed as the result of predation by larger fish. The large black eye and full brood pouches make adult females fully visible to fish, and fish prefer them over smaller species of zooplankton. In addition, because of their size, they provide more protein. Scientists have found large numbers of spiny water fleas in the stomachs of adult fish in the Great Lakes, but the benefits of this food to older fish may be outweighed by the tendency of small fish to avoid it, and by the fact that it competes for the food eaten by small fish.

Faced with possible predation by fish, the spiny water flea has been found to adopt a behavior called diel (daily) vertical migration. Adult females move deeper in the water during daylight hours, where less light penetrates and visibility to fish is reduced. At night, they move closer to the surface, where there is abundant food and the warmer water helps to quicken metabolism and growth.

Studies of the offshore waters of Lake Michigan found that spiny water fleas were mainly found in depths of 33 to 66 feet during the day, while at night the majority of the population occupied the water from the surface to 33 feet.

Avoid spreading. Spiny water flea adults as well as their eggs may wind up unseen in the bilge water or well water of boats, as well as in bait buckets. In areas of high infestation, fishing lines and downrigger cables may become coated with both eggs and adults. To avoid spreading these animals, precautionary steps should be taken while fishing and after fishing, especially when a boat or bait container is transported from one place to another. Therefore, it is important to remove any aquatic hitchhikers from your boat, boat trailer, fishing tackle, and accessory equipment before leaving the water, and to clean all equipment with hot water and dry it later on.

Drain all water from the boat (bilge and livewells or baitwells) before leaving the area. Do not transport water, fish, or baits from one place to another. Empty a bait container on the land, not in the water. Wash your boat, trailer, and gear with hot water if possible at home and flush the engine with water. Let everything dry for three days. Be advised that in many places it is illegal to transport exotic species.
See: Exotic Species.

SPLAKE *Salvelinus namaycush x Salvelinus fontinalis.*
Other names—wendigo.

A member of the charr group of the Salmonidae family, the splake is a distinctively marked hybrid fish produced in a hatchery by crossing a true lake trout female *(S. Namaycush)* and a true brook trout male *(S. fontinalis).* This interbreeding does not occur in nature but is initiated by humans, and results in a fertile hybrid species capable of reproducing. The name "splake" is a combination of the words "speckled" from speckled trout, which is an alternate common name for brook trout *(see: trout, brook),* and "lake" from lake trout *(see: trout, lake).*

The splake has been stocked in various lakes across the northern United States and Canada. Because of the splake's fast growth rate, resiliency, and adaptability, it has viewed as an excellent candidate for restocking waters where lake trout have been decimated by the sea lamprey, or for providing trophy fish potential in waters that cannot support lake trout. Splake are aggressive fish and excellent to eat. They are a popular ice fishing target in lakes that contain them.

Identification. The splake is difficult to identify externally because it resembles different aspects of both parents. The body shape is intermediate between the heavier lake trout and the slimmer brook trout. The shape of the tail is also intermediate. It is not as deeply forked as that of the lake trout, and more closely resembles the slightly indented tail of the brook trout. In coloration and markings, the splake more closely resembles the brook trout. It has vermiculations like brook trout, red orange ventral fins, and yellowish spots along its flanks. Dead specimens can be positively identified by the number of pyloric caeca, the wormlike appendages on the intestinal tract right after the stomach. The brook trout, which is the smaller parent, has only 23 to 55 (usually less than 50) pyloric

Splake

caeca, whereas the intermediate-size hybrid has 65 to 85, and the lake trout, the larger parent, has 93 to 208 (usually 120 to 180) pyloric caeca.

Size. Splake do not grow as large as lake trout, but they do grow larger than brook trout. Most splake weigh a few pounds, although those from bigger waters with a large forage base may be in the 8- to 12-pound class. The all-tackle world record is a fish from Ontario's Georgian Bay on Lake Huron; it weighed 20 pounds, 11 ounces and was caught in 1987.

Distribution. Splake inhabit Lakes Superior and Huron in the Great Lakes, and various midsize lakes in selected states from Colorado, Utah, and Idaho in the western U.S., to northern New York and Maine in the east.

Life history/Behavior. Although they can reproduce, not all splake do, and some populations lack suitable habitat for spawning, which is generally rocky reefs near deep water. They also are capable of back-crossing (hybrids mating with parent species), which has occurred in hatcheries but evidently not in the wild. Spawning occurs in fall, usually in October, on rocky reefs. In spring, splake are often near tributaries or on gravel shoals, and in summer they seek deep water.

Food. This omnivorous species eats smelt, white perch, yellow perch, crayfish, insects, sculpin, and other fish.

Angling. Due to its initial fast growth rate and game nature, the splake is highly regarded by anglers, who pursue these fish by using shallow and deep lake techniques similar to those employed for its parents, especially lake trout. Spring, when the fish are shallow, is generally best for open-water success, but fall fishing on reefs, when the fish are spawning, can also be good. Working near bottom along the edges of dropoffs while ice fishing is most popular in many splake waters.
See: Charr.

SPLIT RING

A small steel ring with two spiral turns. Similar to a key ring but smaller, split rings are primarily used to connect the closed eye of hooks to a closed wire loop on a lure and to serve as a line-tie connector to certain lures. In the latter capacity, split rings are used with many spoons *(see),* being connected to the line tie hole at the head of the lure, and with most floating/diving plugs *(see: plug)*, being connected to the wire loop at the head or on the lip. Split rings are used in place of open rings, where a gap in the ends can allow a hook eye to slip out, and in place of solid rings, which prohibit easy hook changing.

Anglers often add split rings to some lures that don't have them in the line-tie area to improve their action; this is best for lures that don't incur twist and for which the line can be directly knotted to the split ring. Split rings are also changed when lure hooks are changed or if the ring spirals spread apart under pressure. To give added action to a lure or to move the hook a little farther away, you can add one or two split rings between the hook eye and the body wire loop.

When the spirals on a split ring are out of alignment, the ring has lost its strength and should be replaced; you're likely to lose the lure to a strong fish or a snag unless you change the ring. Split rings are available in a range of sizes and should be used in a size that complements the lure and hook. However, a split ring can be the weakest link in the angler-to-fish scenario due to its strength. If the rated breaking strength of a split ring is 12 pounds, for example, and you're using 20-pound line, it's possible that you could open up the spirals of the ring, and lose the lure and/or fish, when maximum pressure is applied. It is unlikely that you will know the breaking strength of most split rings when they are pre-attached to a lure or when buying them in bulk, but you can test them with a heavy-duty spring scale.

Changing split rings can be difficult with standard pliers that have a large grip area. Needle-nose pliers with a good tip grip work well for intermediate and large split rings, but split ring pliers, which have a beaklike tip to separate the spirals, are best, and eliminate the chance of weakening a ring by spreading the spirals, which is especially likely in smaller split rings.
See: Snap.

SPLIT SHOT
A small round fishing weight split in the middle.
See: Sinker.

SPOOL
(1) The part of a reel that holds fishing line.

(2) A manufacturer's storage device (usually round and with a large arbor) that holds fresh line for use on a fishing reel. The capacity and purpose depend on whether such a spool is classified as a tippet or leader spool, a reel-filler spool, or a bulk spool.

(3) The act of putting line on a fishing reel; one might say, "the dealer spooled my new reel with 6-pound line."

(4) Depleting line on a reel when accomplished by the actions of a large and powerful fish; one might say, "the fish spooled all of the line off the reel and just kept going."
See: Line.

SPOON
A sinking, wobbling lure, primarily made of hard metal. Spoons are used for casting, trolling, and jigging in freshwater and saltwater; they can be fished with many types of tackle and are used at all levels in the water column, from just under the surface to the bottom.

Julio T. Buel of Whitehall, New York, is credited with inventing the fishing spoon; he fished with his own creation as early as 1821, reportedly was issued a patent in 1834, and began the commercial manufacture of spoons in 1848. Whether it was derived from an actual utensil or merely had a vague resemblance to one, the lure he created did prove attractive to gamefish, imitating through its action, flash, and size the movement and appearance of prey fish. This, plus being relatively simple to fish, is still the main attribute of a spoon, although it is available in a multitude of shapes and styles to suit particular applications.

Spoons are unlike other lure forms in that the bladelike metal body wobbles but doesn't spin, is not attached to a center shaft, and generally suggests an injured or fleeing baitfish through a range of retrieval speeds. These are popular lures that have international appeal and at some time or another will likely catch nearly any species of fish, although they are more preferable for some species than for others, predominantly employed in freshwater, and most useful in clear water due to their visual appeal.

Trout, salmon, and charr species are the primary targets for spoon use, but northern pike, largemouth bass, smallmouth bass, striped bass, and walleye are also susceptible to specific types of spoons. Smaller predators are generally not good targets for these active lures, except for the smaller jigging versions.

Most spoons are metal and generally slender, with a slight curvature that provides swimming action when retrieved and a flashy appearance that complements its movement. There are wide-body models, flat-sided models, a few plastic spoons, and in general greater diversity in appearance and application than most people realize.

Spoons can be divided into two basic yet vastly different categories. The first and foremost are casting and trolling spoons, all of which have a curved body; the second is jigging spoons, which generally have a flatter and thicker body and a more focused application.

Casting and Trolling Spoons
This is the standard category of spoons, and it includes a wide array of lures, some of which are used strictly for trolling, some strictly for casting, and

some for both. Those used strictly for casting can be subdivided into weedless and nonweedless models.

The design of the metal body and the overall weight govern what can and cannot be cast, as well as the overall action and working speed. In a general sense, these can be separated into thin- or thick-bodied lures. An assortment of thick-bodied spoons are used in both casting and trolling. These range from tiny $1/32$-ounce versions used for panfish and trout to objects 9 inches long weighing several ounces and used for large lake trout and muskies. Wafer-thin spoons, which are too light and too air-resistant to be cast, are used in trolling, where a weighted line, a sinker, a downrigger, or some other device is employed to get the lure down to the desired fishing depth.

No matter what the application, casting and trolling spoons are made of hard metal, usually brass or steel, and have a curved body (one side is concave). This curvature causes the lure to drag and wobble as it moves through the water. Generally, the longer the lure, the wider and slower the wobbling action; the shorter the lure, the narrower and quicker the action. Likewise, the more pronounced the curvature, the more resistance the lure has and the more accentuated its action; spoons with little curvature have less water resistance and a narrower and less pronounced action.

Thick-bodied spoons have more weight and cast better than lighter and thinner models, provided they aren't too heavy. Some compact aerodynamic models can be cast a country mile on light line and long rods, which is very beneficial for shore-based anglers. This distance cannot be achieved with most other lures, especially air-resistant plugs. However, because long, wide-bodied spoons have more air resistance, it's harder to achieve distance and accuracy with them.

A thick body also has the advantage of sinking faster, which is a factor in both open water and river fishing. In a slow moving river, a thick body might sink too fast and invite snagging on the river bottom; however, in deep and swift flows, a thick-bodied spoon is better for getting down in the water as soon as it lands and staying deeper and closer to the fish upon retrieval.

The surface of the spoon has a lot to do with its effectiveness and complements its action. This is more than a matter of mere color, although all types of colors and combinations (sometimes with prism tape in dots, stripes, and other patterns) are used. Most casting and trolling spoons have an unpainted polished side, which reflects light and helps make the lure, or at least the flash from it, visible from a good distance. Others have a plated or hammered surface that also has good reflection qualities. Lesser quality spoons have a duller and less reflective surface, and older tarnished or scarred spoons are less effective (they can be restored with polish and spruced up with prism tape).

Spoons always have a hole at their front end for

Spoon types, from top to bottom, include weedless, jigging, casting, and trolling versions.

attachment to the fishing line. Line should never be tied directly to this hole but instead to a snap or, preferably, a snap-swivel; the latter will minimize or prevent line twist. Some spoons are preassembled with a swivel, snap, or metal split ring. Line can be tied directly to the swivel, but a snap-swivel should be used with the others.

Virtually all spoons have one hook, a single or treble version, on their back end. Trebles are more common than singles, especially on lightweight spoons; most hooks are attached via a split ring to the back of the lure, but a few (weedless versions) have single hooks that are integral to the metal body. It is generally the manufacturing norm that spoons intended mainly or solely for casting have treble hooks, and that lightweight trolling spoons have single hooks, but there are exceptions, and many anglers replace the treble hooks on their spoons with singles; this usually doesn't impair action (it may improve it) and aids hook removal (it may be mandated in some places).

Incidentally, spoons are generally fished far enough off the bottom in lakes that they don't get snagged, although they often get snagged in rivers. Single hooks help avoid snagging and, on spoons, are equally effective at hooking fish (which often hook themselves when they strike a trolled lure).

The most important factor in using casting and trolling spoons is achieving the right retrieve or trolling speed to get the proper action out of a particular spoon. Some spoons swim lazily and sink too deep when worked too slowly; or they swim too rapidly and rise too high when worked too fast. You should always swim a spoon near you and observe it to determine the best speed for using it.

In trolling, there are two main approaches to fishing a spoon. Lightweight spoons are used with some device for getting deep. Heavier spoons are generally flatlined, mostly on nylon monofilament but also on lead-core and wire lines. Determining the depth of flatlined spoons is critical to fishing at the right level. Trolling is discussed in greater detail in a separate entry *(see: trolling)*. Remember to alter the behavior of a spoon when trolling; this can be done by letting it flutter down when the boat slows or rise briefly when the boat speeds up, and by jerking the rod tip periodically to dart the spoon forward like a struggling or fleeing baitfish. This tactic is highly effective when trolling a spoon.

When casting in current, you normally cast up and across stream or directly across stream, reel in slack line, keep the rod tip angled up, and allow the spoon to drift downstream with the current (sometimes reeling it very lightly), then lower the rod tip and reel it in with a slow, steady retrieve, a jerk-reel motion, or a combination of both. You can also fish it directly downstream for a sustained period, keeping the rod tip high and allowing the movement of the water to activate the lure; this is best with a thin or intermediate thickness spoon.

When casting in lakes, let the lure sink after it enters the water, perhaps counting it down to a certain level (you have to predetermine sink rate) to reach the desired depth before beginning the retrieve. A straightforward retrieve sometimes does the job, especially if fish are numerous and aggressive, or a stop-and-go or jerking retrieve may be better. It usually pays to put a twitch or jerk into a straight retrieve to stimulate a strike.

Spincasting, spinning, and baitcasting tackle are appropriate for casting with spoons, depending on the weight of the lure used. Spinning, baitcasting, and light conventional tackle are better for trolling, also depending on lure weight as well as other factors. Thin diameter lines bring out the best action in casting and trolling spoons because they have less water resistance.

Weedless models. Weedless spoons are used for bass, pike, and pickerel fishing in and around thick vegetation, such as lily pads, bulrushes, sawgrass, and milfoil. They are generally not 100 percent snag-free, but will usually get through most vegetation with the aid of their incorporated wire hook guard. These lures are best used with a rippled pork rind, soft plastic curl tail, or rubber skirt trailer to spice up their swimming action, and some anglers like to garnish this with a pork chunk. Good colors vary with species, but silver is a perennial favorite for bass, pike, and pickerel. Orange with red diamonds (the five of diamonds), red-and-white, and chartreuse-and-red are very popular for pike. Gold, black, chartreuse, and frog green are good for bass as well. Sizes range from $1/4$ ounce to 1 ounce, with the largest models intended for pike fishing.

The basic technique for fishing a weedless spoon is to cast it far back into the vegetation and work the lure slowly over and through it, allowing it to ease into and flutter down every little opening possible. When fishing thick lily pads, for example, you would cast back into the pads and slowly reel the lure up to an opening, let it slither off a pad into a pocket, and ever so slowly bring it through that pocket and then over or through more pads to the next pocket.

The important point about weedless spoons is that you must fish them slowly and pick your way through the vegetation. Also, you must delay a moment in setting the hook when a fish strikes. Numerous missed strikes or "boils," especially by bass, on these lures are due to the nature of the cover, so you must be sure a fish has your lure before you try to hook it.

A sometimes useful modification of this type of lure for bass is the placement of a spinner blade in front. This is accomplished through a short wire shaft ahead of the basic lure, around which a small silver or gold blade revolves. This combination provides added flash and attraction that will bring the lure to the attention of reluctant bass when the lure appears in holes or openings of thick grass or lily pad clusters.

Jigging Spoons

Jigging spoons are thick-bodied lures made of hard metal or lead that lack a curved profile. Though somewhat spoonlike in appearance, they don't have a distinctive wobble when retrieved, which makes them suitable for vertical jigging. Their action is essentially one of darting upward and fluttering backward. Most jigging spoons, especially those used in freshwater, have a flat, compressed, two-sided body, but others, especially large versions used in saltwater, have a three- or four-sided profile that tapers at either end; the so-called diamond jig of saltwater prominence has four sides and is wide at the middle and tapered to a point at either end.

Jigging spoons used in freshwater vary in shape and size; they are commonly used in $1/4$- to $1/2$- ounce sizes for black bass, white bass, and stripers, and mainly employed for vertical jigging in situations where fish may be schooled or suspended. However, smaller models are used to catch panfish and for ice fishing, and larger models (up to 2 ounces) are occasionally used for striped bass and deep bottom fishing for lake trout. Many versions are long, narrow, and tapered, but others are wide and squat (called slabs or slab spoons). The former usually have a plain or hammered plated finish while the latter are painted, generally in white, yellow, silver, or gold. In saltwater, jigging spoons are usually larger and commonly fished up to several ounces in inshore waters, though versions up to 16 ounces (more of a lead lure with a hook than a spoon) are used on appropriately heavy tackle for the greatest depths.

Jigging spoons have an integral line-tie ring or hole at the head, and some are equipped with a split ring. Nearly all have a treble hook attached to the rear via a split ring. The trebles are likely to get hung up a good deal, but their weight helps unsnag them fairly easily if you have a direct line of pull overhead. Fishing line should be tied directly to the

---

How did we get the term blue ribbon trout streams? Perhaps from the use of the color blue to depict the best trout streams in a Montana survey report, akin to the first-place ribbons awarded at country fairs.

lure or to a split ring; avoid using a snap or snap-swivel, which increase hook fouling.

In vertical jigging look for fish that are near or on the bottom around specific structure, or for suspended fish that are at various levels in the water column. To use these jigs, lower them either to the bottom or to a specific depth, jerk your rod up, and let the lure flutter down. Repeat this procedure for a while at the same depth. The lure jerks up and flutters back, and should rise a foot to a foot and a half with each upward motion, then be allowed to sink back slowly as you keep gentle contact with it (if the line is tight on the fall the lure will not flutter properly). Most strikes come on the fall back, and feel like a faint tap or simply stopping of the lure. Microfilament or other low-stretch lines are especially good for this work because of their high sensitivity, which telegraphs a strike. Spinning and baitcasting tackle (or conventional tackle for heavyweight jigging spoons in saltwater) are good, and rods should have a stiff butt section and fast taper; a limber tip decreases sensitivity and makes both strike detection and hooksetting more difficult.

Jigging spoons can also be used for casting to (and rapidly retrieving through) schools of surface-breaking fish because great casting distance can be achieved. Their main attribute is that they can be cast a long distance, and vaguely look like fleeing baitfish. Jigging spoons lack wobbling action on a straight retrieve, so they should be retrieved in a quick jerk-and-reel manner for schooling fish.

Other jigging lures. A few lures are a cross between a spoon and a leadhead jig, and are mainly used for vertical jigging, though they are sometimes cast. A few of these are primarily thin metal bodies, and called blade baits by some anglers; they may be vertically jigged or fished on a cast-settle-jig-settle-jig manner for white bass, smallmouth bass, largemouth bass, and panfish. Likewise, some lures, called tailspinners (see), have a rounded lead body and a spinning blade on the tail; they are fished similarly to the thin-bodied baits. As a group, these lures are sometimes called jump baits, meaning that they are primarily used in quick-casting to schools of surface-feeding white bass, largemouth bass, and striped bass, although the same can be said for various spinners, casting spoons, and vertical jigging spoons.

There are also some balanced jigging lures, made of metal and used for vertical fishing in a different manner than jigging spoons. The lead bodies of these lie horizontally instead of vertically in the water when fished. One type is a heavy lead body mainly used in saltwater with treble hooks on the tail and under the belly and a forward slanting head; the line tie is on top just behind the head, and the lure is weighted so that the tail sits slightly down and the lure darts upward when jigged.

Another type that is favored in freshwater for ice fishing (see), but sometimes used for open-water deep jigging, is a balanced lead minnowlike lure that has a single hook at each end, a treble hook under its belly (in larger models), a small plastic lip on the tail, and a centered topside line-tie. This lure swings out and up to either side of a vertical position when jigged, always with the body staying horizontal.

See: Inshore Fishing; Jig; Jigging.

SPOONPLUG

Spoonplugs are specialized metal lures used occasionally in flatline trolling in freshwater. These uncommon lures are stamped from brass into a slightly arched position with upsweeping sides, and are generally used on a low-stretch line. There used to be seven models, all used solely for bottom bumping. Spoonplugs can take a lot of abuse; they can be run into all kinds of objects but still hold their form without needing tuning adjustments.

As with other trolling baits, the size of the lure and the length and strength (diameter) of line out determine how deep it will run. Spoonplugs are intended for relatively high speed trolling, particularly by anglers who are new to a lake and are both scouting for fish and trying to learn the bottom contours and structures.

There are very few practitioners of spoonplugging today outside of the upper Midwest, in part because of the evolution of deep-diving plugs, thin diameter low-stretch lines, and other methods of getting deep.

See: Flatlining.

SPORTFISH

In the broadest sense, sportfish refers to freshwater and saltwater fish sought by recreational anglers using sporting equipment. In some quarters, "sportfish" is used interchangeably and synonymously with the term "gamefish" (see), although there is a subtle difference. In a sense, the sportfish could be narrowed to species with characteristics that are especially favored by anglers, such as size, strength, ability to sustain resistance to capture, feeding methods, jumping ability, etc. However, that would leave out many species that are very popular with anglers and caught for recreational enjoyment and/or for food, some of which do not have much fighting endurance or have good endurance but are not as exciting to catch as others. Certainly some sportfish are more flamboyant or more vigorous than others, but sporting virtue is in the eye and definition of the beholder; some of the most difficult fish to entice, such as carp, are highly prized by one segment of the angling population yet disdained by another segment, even though they are tenacious fighters.

See: Sportfishing.

SPORTFISHERMAN

(1) A person who catches or tries to catch fish for personal use, fun, challenge, and leisure by using sporting methods and sporting equipment, essentially some type of rod, usually but not always equipped with a reel, to which a line and a hook or lure are attached. "Sportfisherman" is used interchangeably with "angler." It has a more specific meaning than "fisherman," although both words may connote the same thing when used in reference to the employment of sporting equipment.

Although sportfisherman has a masculine gender, it is often used in a generic sense throughout the recreational and fisheries management communities, the sportfishing equipment industries, and the boat and motor manufacturing industries to imply female as well as male anglers. That generic usage appears often because of its overwhelming dominance in everyday language and also because the alternative, "fisher," which is an archaic although non-gender-specific version of "fisherman" *(see)*, may also refer to an individual engaged in commercial or recreational activity.

See: Angler; Angling; Commercial Fisherman; Fishing; Recreational Fisherman; Sportfishing.

(2) A large boat, also referred to as a sportfishing boat or offshore boat, that is usually over 35 feet long, outfitted with big-game fishing equipment and set up for angling, and capable of cruising many miles offshore in the primary pursuit of pelagic species. Such a boat is designed with accessories and an interior layout that facilitate sportfishing activities and needs; it would be used to fish off all coastal areas and far from the coastline, as well as in such big bodies of freshwater as the Great Lakes.

See: Sportfishing Boat.

SPORTFISHERY

All aspects of catching or trying to catch fish for personal use, fun, challenge, and leisure by using sporting equipment; the proceeds are released or kept for personal use and not sold. This term includes fisheries resources, anglers, and businesses providing goods and services.

See: Sportfisherman.

SPORTFISHING

The act of catching or trying to catch fish for personal use, fun, challenge, and leisure by using sporting methods and sporting equipment, essentially some type of rod, usually but not always equipped with a reel, to which a line and a hook or lure are attached. "Sportfishing" is used interchangeably with "angling" but is more often associated with saltwater angling, especially the type of offshore activities characterized by the use of a vessel, called a sportfisherman *(see)*, outfitted for big-game fishing.

"Sportfishing" has a more specific meaning than "fishing," although both may connote the same thing when used in reference to the employment of sporting equipment. It is distinguished from commercial or recreational fishing by virtue of the equipment employed, an implicit understanding of fair chase, and the exercise of sportsmanship. Sportfishing also implies the intent to keep fish (if fish are kept) for personal use rather than for sale or trade, although some saltwater fish that are caught by sporting means may legally be sold.

What constitutes sport or sporting equipment is open to individual interpretation and encompasses a wide range of equipment and circumstances. Even anglers disagree as to whether certain tactics, tackle, and techniques exclusively used in sportfishing actually qualify as "sport." This is a debate grounded, in part, in attitudes and ethical considerations that defy settlement and muddy any attempt at strict definition.

See: Angler; Angling; Commercial Fisherman; Fishing; Recreational Fisherman; Sportfish.

SPORTFISHING BOAT

The term "sportfishing boat" is used in the angling and recreational boat manufacturing world synonymously for midsize to large boats used for inshore and offshore fishing in saltwater, or in large bodies of freshwater, and specifically outfitted for fishing applications as opposed to general-purpose use or recreational cruising. Technically, any boat that is designed precisely for fishing (as opposed to cruising, water-skiing, or running about), with accessories and interior layout that exclusively accommodate angling activities and needs, is a "sportfishing" boat, but in common parlance, this term has become associated with the type of craft (a minority of which are trailerable) that might be used to fish off all coastal areas and far from the coastline, as well as in such big bodies of freshwater as the Great Lakes.

Sportfishing boats can be loosely grouped into offshore and inshore categories, although there is much that is common between the two, and considered in terms of outboard, inboard, and inboard/outboard power, as well as by interior and hull configuration.

Offshore Boats

Modern offshore boats provide more speed, comfort, and standard fishing features than ever before. The higher speeds are made possible through the use of high-tech coring materials that reduce weight, and also due to the revolution in marine power. Engines produce more horsepower with less weight these days, providing more speed.

The comfort aspect came about as boat builders discovered that women fish and boat, too, and so the Spartan finishing work of yesteryear has given way to fishing boats that can be downright plush.

And fishing features have grown as competition for sales has intensified and features were added to enhance sales. Yesterday's option is often today's standard equipment.

There are more types of boats available to the consumer, too. A walk down the aisle of a boat show will expose you to a dizzying variety of sizes, hull types, construction materials, power options, and, of course, prices. But even with all of the evolution in the boat marketplace, there are still some basic choices that must be made when considering a sportfishing boat.

The first is a major choice of power options: inboard, outboard, or inboard/outboard, the latter being a hybrid of the others. In the past, any boat over about 30 feet was sure to be built around inboard power, but that's no longer true. Modern outboards, with their vastly improved reliability and economy, are now commonly found on the transoms of boats up to 35 feet long.

This 27-foot sportfishing boat has twin outboard motors mounted on a transom bracket.

Outboard models. Outboard-powered fishing boats come in several different configurations. The center console is arguably the most common, and it's easy to see why. With the helm located roughly amidships, the center console design offers unparalleled fishing room and access, with a spacious cockpit and an open bow. You can generally fight a fish 360 degrees around the boat without running into an obstacle, and that can come in handy when the fishing action is fast and furious.

Some people prefer the cuddy cabin design, with a spacious cockpit aft and an enclosed cabin forward. Cuddy designs offer at least minimal bunk space so you can spend the night aboard, but most people use the cuddy for lockable storage and for temporary shelter in inclement weather. Lockable storage can be very important when you have lots of tackle aboard and you have to leave the boat unattended in remote or unfamiliar areas.

The third design type combines some of the best features of center console and cuddy cabin boats; this is the walkaround, and it's a style that seems to be growing in popularity. The walkaround has a cabin forward, but, like the center console, it generally also has some space forward, at the bow. This space is accessed via walkways between the cabin sides and the gunwales. You give up a little bit of cabin area with the walkaround, but you get easier access to the bow for fishing, anchoring, docking, sunbathing, or whatever.

Another major choice involves hull design. Offshore boats generally have either a modified-V or a deep-V hull. Modified-V hulls have less than 18 degrees of transom deadrise and tend to be more stable while at rest or when trolling. The downside to the modified-V is that it tends to pound more in a head sea.

The deep-V hull has 18 degrees or more of transom deadrise and usually a sharper entry at the bow. Deep-V hulls were developed for the offshore racing circuit and slice through waves better than their flatter counterparts, enabling higher speeds in choppy conditions. However, deep-V hulls tend to roll more at rest (a phenomenon known as being "tender").

All of the aforementioned boats are mono-hull designs. Perhaps the hottest trend in outboard-powered boats is the rise in popularity of the catamaran. Cats, as they are known, have two hulls connected by a deck. They ride very differently from a mono-hull because most cats use semi-displacement rather than planing hulls. It should be noted, however, that several builders do use twin planing hulls for their cats.

Either way, the cats offer a substantially smoother ride in choppy conditions. The twin hulls have much less forward surface than mono-hulls, so when they meet the face of an oncoming wave, they cut through it rather than slamming into it. A cat's bow rises gently with the waves rather than reacting quickly. This gentle motion is preferred by many people who are tired of being pounded in a chop. Cats also ride level at virtually any speed, so when things get really rough, you can throttle back and still maintain decent headway and not worry about the boat's trim. Mono-hulls often struggle at slow speeds in rough water conditions, as they fall on and off plane.

You also must consider power requirements when choosing a hull type. Deep-V hulls have more wet surface than modified Vs, and therefore require more power to push them. They are also somewhat harder to get onto plane. Catamarans also require quite a bit of power to push them through the water. In the old days, offshore boats all had flat bottoms so they would run well with the relatively weak engines that were then available. In the 1950s and '60s, boats were slow, so they didn't need deep-V hulls to cut waves.

That's no longer the case. Modern outboards (and inboards) have improved radically and can push most any kind of hull with ease, so the choice really gets narrowed down to one of personal preference based on how the boat will be used. If you tend to make long runs in rough water, a deep-V or catamaran will most likely be necessary. If you don't often run in rough stuff, however, or if you anchor or drift a lot, a modified-V may be the ticket.

In mono-hull designs, a sturdy and well designed offshore boat should have a wide chine area for a dry ride. The chine is where the hullside meets the bottom of the boat. Sportfishing boat builders usually put in a flat chine section of a few inches to throw spray out and away from the boat, rather than allowing it to travel up the hullsides, where it will most likely blow in your face. Many builders utilize a reverse chine design which actually angles downward to deflect spray even further.

Most offshore hulls (especially deep-V hulls) also use lifting strakes to get the boat out of the water at speed. Strakes are the lengthwise ridges molded into the bottom of the hull. They force water down and out, creating lift and helping to throw water out to the side where the chines will theoretically knock it down. Too many strakes, however, adds even more wet surface and slows the boat down. This was a problem with older hulls that had strakes placed all over the place in the days when designers were experimenting with different designs.

Today's designers, of course, benefit from the wonderful world of computers. CAD (computer-assisted design) systems enable naval architects to study hydrodynamics in much more detail, and everyone benefits from this as hulls evolve and become much more suited to specific tasks. Furthermore, computerized manufacturing systems let boat builders (at least the bigger ones) turn out well-fitted boats with tight manufacturing tolerances, boats that should provide many years of reliable service.

Having said all of that, it should be pointed out that many, if not most, boat companies do not have such computer systems, and simply make it up as they go along. This isn't necessarily bad, but the point is that you should do your homework when looking at sportfishing boats and know how the boat you are looking at was designed and built.

As mentioned, modern outboard sportfishing boats are finished to a much higher standard than they were 20 years ago. Sub-console head compartments, freshwater showers, tackle storage lockers, livewell systems, and other goodies are now standard on many boats. That was unheard of even a few years ago. Fishing features have proliferated as well.

Rod storage used to be a problem on outboard-powered sportfishing boats, but there are well thought-out storage solutions on lots of boats these days. Livewell systems are now ubiquitous, and come in a wide variety of configurations and sizes. No matter what your live-bait needs, you can certainly find a boat with a well that suits you.

Modern sportfishing boat builders have also finally gotten around to dealing with the issue of fish boxes. It used to be that if you caught a lot of fish, or a few big ones, you had no choice but to store them in large coolers on the deck, and that took up a lot of precious fishing room. Nowadays, however, boat builders have devised some clever ways to build in fish boxes beneath the cockpit sole of many boats. Just be sure that these boxes drain overboard either directly or through a macerator pump, because many builders drain their boxes into the bilge. That transforms a fish box into a mere storage compartment.

Another modern trend in outboard sportfishing boats is the transom configuration. The outboard sportfishing boat building world has almost completely switched over to a modification of the transom bracket known throughout the industry as the integrated transom system, or the "Euro transom." This design places a transom wall between the cockpit and the engines, creating an engine platform. Livewells, fish boxes, sinks, and bait rigging trays are often built into this transom wall, providing a convenient location for them right in the middle of the fishing action.

Other builders utilize actual engine brackets that are bolted onto a flat transom. One of the advantages of these transom styles is safety; a full transom effectively prevents waves from sloshing into the cockpit and increases performance. Another advantage is that by mounting the engine(s) farther aft and slightly higher, there is less drag in the water, and the boat runs faster. It also gets weight farther aft, which increases performance as well.

Some hard-core anglers, however, still prefer the old notched transom design in which the outboards are simply bolted to the back of the boat with some sort of splashwell or transom gate in front of them. These people feel that the integrated transom system places the engines too far aft, making it difficult to fight a fish around the engines. With the notched transom, you generally can walk right up to the front of the engines and fight the fish around the lower units without being cut off by having the line nick the skeg or propeller. Once again, the choice comes down to personal preference.

Indeed, preference means a lot in the sportfishing boat market. Modern outboard sportfishing boats have the fuel capacity, construction integrity, and enough comfort features to make them viable for serious duty far from the sight of land. They are the boat of choice for many offshore anglers because of their speed, maneuverability, and relatively low initial cost. That's also why you see more and more outboard sportfishing boats at major offshore tournaments these days.

Inboard models. There are circumstances where only an inboard boat will suffice, however, and once again, technology has provided a tremendous range of options. Inboard-powered boats have benefited from major advancements in engine technology, primarily in the development of high horsepower, low weight diesel engines. Gasoline inboard power has improved rapidly, too, with the development of sophisticated new fuel injection systems that have remarkably improved both efficiency and reliability.

For sportfishing boats over 35 feet (often called "sportfishermen"), inboard engines are still the standard. The same hull considerations discussed with outboard boats also hold true with inboards, and again you must weigh modified-V versus deep-V considerations. But with the wider beams normally found in inboard boats, tenderness can be less of a problem, as beam adds stability.

In days gone by, almost all inboard boats were made of wood; indeed, many of the super expensive custom sportfishermen still are. Wood is still one of the lightest, yet strongest, materials available, but building a wooden boat is obviously labor intensive and therefore expensive. Aluminum boats can still be found offshore, but fiberglass boats are far and away the most common.

Inboard boats come in two basic configurations: flybridge and express. Flybridge boats have the helm placed on top of a salon area, where it is normally accessed by either a ladder or steps. Flybridge boats are often referred to as "convertibles," an archaic term meaning they can do double duty as both cruising and fishing boats. Flybridge boats do offer more comfort amenities on the whole when compared to express boats. The salons they provide often are a combination living room, dining area, and galley, and there are usually additional staterooms below.

Express boats have the helm on a raised bridge deck, forward of and just slightly higher than the cockpit. The bridge deck is where the salon would be on a flybridge boat. Express boats can be fished with a smaller crew than flybridge boats because the captain is just a few steps away from the action and can help wire, tag, or gaff a fish at boatside. Whereas you may need a crew of at least three to effectively fish a flybridge boat, an owner can fish with one other person or even alone on an express boat.

While the high-tech construction methods briefly mentioned earlier are important with smaller outboard boats, inboard boats have benefited the most from the use of new and lighter materials. Solid fiberglass hulls were once the norm, but they were heavy, hard to push, and therefore usually slow. Lightweight materials began showing up in the 1980s as core materials in decks, hullsides, bulkheads, and even stringers. Nowadays, lightweight coring is standard all over inboard boats, even in many hull bottoms. This has allowed larger boats to shed thousands of unnecessary pounds and helped bring about much higher speeds.

New high-power diesel engines have helped push the speed envelope, too. New turbocharging technology has allowed engine manufacturers to squeeze more and more power out of smaller blocks than ever before. This has caused many boat

A 40-plus-foot sportfisherman, with a 12- to 14-foot beam, is capable of taking large parties offshore.

builders to offer inboard diesel power as an option in smaller and smaller boats. It's sort of the opposite of the trend toward outboards on larger boats, but, once again, it's indicative of the amount of choice available.

Inboard sportfishing boats, whether of the express or flybridge design, should have a large cockpit, although one regrettable trend these days involves sacrificing cockpit space in some flybridge boats for the sake of enlarging the salon. All things are tradeoffs on boats, and if you make one thing bigger you must take away from something else. To many serious offshore anglers, lots of cockpit space is important.

Cockpits should provide an uncluttered working area, with storage for gaffs, tag sticks, mops, shore power cords, and so forth. There should be ample fish box volume, and if you normally boat big fish, some sort of transom gate is nice, too. Padded cockpit coaming is great on any size boat. A sportfisherman shouldn't have too much freeboard at the cockpit; it should be easy to reach the water's surface when leaning over the side.

Fighting chairs are mounted in the center on many cockpits. These specialized chairs have a rod gimbal that receives the butt of a rod and allows it to pivot freely in a fore-and-aft motion while fighting a fish. The chair is mounted on some sort of pedestal, or it can be freestanding, but it must be able to rotate so you can follow a fish with the rod tip during a fight. Some chairs have a footrest that gives the angler leverage during the fight.

Chairs on a centerline pedestal should be mounted so that there is plenty of room for the mate to walk between the footrest and the transom, and chairs must be securely fastened to the deck. Several unlucky anglers doing battle with a huge marlin or tuna have suddenly found themselves in the water when their fighting chair ripped loose and went overboard! Chairs should ideally be mounted with the pedestal securely bolted to the keel, but oftentimes that's not possible because fuel tanks are under the cockpit sole. In that case, a large backing plate should be used to spread out the load.

Inboard sportfishermen, with either gas or diesel power, are sensitive to loads, and ideally should be designed with a specific table of weights and balances. In smaller inboards, it's hard to get enough weight aft, especially on flybridge boats with their forward superstructure. That's why fuel tanks are placed as far aft as possible. It is wise to pay close attention to how a boat rides at cruising speeds. It should ride proud, with the bow high, but without squatting at the stern. Beware of a boat that runs bow down, even with a full load of fuel. It is bow-heavy and may have handling difficulties, especially in a low fuel situation.

Inboard/Outboard models. Inboard/outboard sportfishing boats, or simply "I/Os," have been around for a long time, but they never really took off with the fishing crowd. I/Os are a combination of inboard and outboard technology, with a lower unit like an outboard, coupled to an inboard engine. The engine sat under a hood right in front of the transom, where many anglers perceived it was in the way.

Things are changing with this system too, though. The explosion of new high-horsepower, lightweight diesel engines has caused many people to reconsider I/Os. Builders are now experimenting with jackshaft technology, placing the engines forward where they would normally sit in an inboard application, and connecting them to the drive unit via a long drive shaft. This gets weight forward and frees up the cockpit area for fishing.

I/O boats offer several major advantages over both outboard and inboard versions. They offer competitive performance with outboards but much better efficiency, especially when diesels are used. The longevity of these engines is better as well. Because all of the underwater running gear associated with a straight inboard is eliminated, drag is reduced substantially with an I/O too, and performance is greatly enhanced. For some people, I/Os may truly offer the best of both worlds.

Inshore Boats

General-purpose inshore boats may be the most popular type of fishing boat available because of their versatility. As opposed to flats boats *(see)* or skiffs, which are designed and built for a very specific purpose, inshore boats can be fished in a wide variety of situations.

Inshore boats typically have more freeboard than flats boats, so they can be used in rougher waters. This makes them perfect for bays, rivers, and limited coastal use, all of which are situations where running across open water is always a possibility. And even though the higher hullsides add weight, these skiffs still have relatively shallow drafts, with either modified-V or flat bottoms.

Most inshore boats are laid out in some variation of the center console design. Again, this provides optimum fishing space and room to move around, and lets you carry lots of gear. A well-designed inshore boat should have lots of rod storage, including extended tubes for fly rods, as well as plentiful dry storage.

These boats usually lack big fish boxes, but they often come with large livewells. The livewells are usually placed aft, but sometimes builders will put a smaller well forward for storage of "pitch baits." These are baits that are kept handy to pitch to a passing fish. Just note that wells placed forward bounce more than wells placed aft and will be pretty hard on the bait.

A rugged nonskid surface on all walking areas is a must, especially on raised casting decks. These decks can be found both at the bow and the stern of many boats, both with and without toe rails that help keep you from sliding overboard. Hand rails should be placed in strategic locations, too.

Because almost all of these boats are outboard powered, it really comes down to a choice of style and options. Inshore boats can probably be considered to be 22 feet or less, but most will probably be 18 to 19 feet long. Hull styles include V-hulls and cathedral hulls, with V-hulls riding better in a chop, but cathedral hulls providing better stability and a wider bow.

Some inshore boats are of the rolled-edge skiff design, basically a one-piece boat where the tops of the gunwales roll outward. Others are conventional hull-and-cap designs, with a separate molded hull and cap that are bonded and screwed together. The one-piece rolled-edge design is light and very cost-effective, but many people prefer the additional fit-and-finish to be found only with the two-piece design.

Inshore boats are pretty simple, and by carefully analyzing your individual needs, you'll soon find a style that fits your fishing requirements like a hand in a glove.

See: Bass Boat; Boat; Inshore Fishing; Jonboat; Navigation; Offshore Fishing; Trailer; Walleye Boat.

SPOT *Leiostomus xanthurus.*
Other names—Norfolk spot, spot croaker; French: *tambour croca;* Spanish: *verrugato croca.*

A member of the Sciaenidae family, the spot is an important commercial fish. Its migration habits bring it to shore in schools, enabling both recreational anglers and commercial fishermen to catch

Spot

spot in large numbers. Much like its cousin, the Atlantic croaker *(see: croaker, Atlantic)*, the spot is a small and flavorful fish.

Identification. The body of the spot is deep and stout, and the tail is slightly forked. The soft dorsal fin has more than 30 rays, and the anal fin has more than 12 rays. Its coloring is gray to silver with a gold tint on the sides and 12 to 15 dark lines extending from the dorsal fins to the lateral line. There is a round black spot about the same size as the eye above each pectoral fin. The fins are pale yellow, except the dorsal and caudal fins, which are milky. The spot's color and lack of chin barbels distinguish it from other sciaenids.

Size/Age. The average spot weighs a ½ pound, and these fish rarely reach 2 pounds, making them the proverbial saltwater panfish. They can live for five years.

Distribution. Spot occur from Massachusetts to Mexico, inhabiting roughly the same range as the Atlantic croaker. Although a western Atlantic fish, at least one spot was discovered in Tokyo Bay, Japan, in the late 1980s, although it is believed that it was transported in the ballast water of a ship.

Habitat. Spot inhabit estuaries and coastal saltwaters, generally roaming over sandy and muddy bottoms. They may frequent waters as deep as 60 meters but usually remain much shallower.

Life history/Behavior. Spawning occurs at sea in the fall and winter, in water temperatures of 59° to 79°F. The spot is capable of producing as many eggs as the Atlantic croaker, nearly 1 million. The eggs are pelagic and carried shoreward by wind and currents. Juveniles move into less saline estuary areas, sometimes even to freshwater, until they are old enough to return to saltwater. Growth is rapid for the first few years, due to the abundance of food in estuaries. They reach maturity at age 3. The spot is a schooling fish and travels in groups of 100 or more.

Food and feeding habits. Spot consume small crustaceans, detritus, worms, and small fish.

Angling. Spot are found over mud and sand bottoms, and shell reefs. They are often caught accidentally by anglers pursuing other species, but they are best deliberately pursued with light line, small hooks, and pieces of clams and cut fish, or worms, presented on the bottom. Spot are not viewed with great enthusiasm by anglers but can be a fortuitous catch on days when nothing else is happening and some food is expected.

SPREADER BAR

A stainless steel bar, also called a spreader rig, that contains a number of teasers mounted in a pattern and trolled either alongside or directly in front of flatlined baits or lures to resemble a large school of baitfish. A spreader bar is used in offshore fishing, especially for marlin and tuna.
See: Trolling Lures, Saltwater.

SPREADER RIG

To flounder anglers, a spreader rig is a wire bar used for fishing two baits on the bottom. It consists of a coat hanger–like wire with two loops in the middle, the upper of which is attached to the fishing line, and the lower of which supports a bank sinker, and two short leaders at either end, both attached to snelled bait hooks. It is hard to detect light strikes with this rig, and many anglers prefer to fish their line direct to a sinker, without the spreader, using one or more hooks up above.

This term is also used by offshore anglers for a spreader bar *(see)* for trolling multiple teasers.
See: Inshore Fishing.

SPRING TIDE
See: Tides.

SPUD
A heavy long-handled metal bar with a chisel blade for chopping holes in ice for fishing.
See: Ice Fishing.

SQUARETAIL
A term primarily used in northeastern parts of the United States and eastern Canada for brook trout *(see)*, which may also be called speckled trout.

SQUAWFISH, NORTHERN *Ptychocheilus oregonensis.*
Other names—squawfish, Columbia River dace, Columbia squawfish; French: *sauvagesse du nord.*

The northern squawfish is a large-growing member of the Cyprinidae family of minnows that is often caught in northwestern North America trout and salmon waters. Yet it is not actively sought and is viewed as a threat to more popular species. Related fish include the Colorado squawfish *(P. lucius)*, the Sacramento squawfish *(P. grandis)*, and the Umpqua squawfish *(P. umpquae)*, which have limited distribution in their respective river systems. The Colorado squawfish, which is

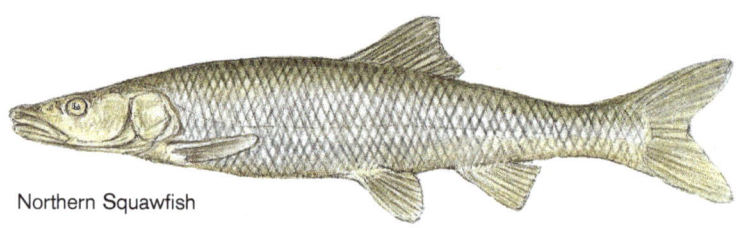

Northern Squawfish

endangered, is North America's largest native minnow and can grow to 6 feet.

Identification. The northern squawfish's mouth is terminal and large, extending back past the front edge of the eye. The head is somewhat conical and flattened between the eyes, and the body is slender and barely compressed. All fins are clear, with no spots or coloration, and there are 9 to 10 rays in the dorsal fin and 8 rays in the anal fin. The caudal fin is deeply forked. Its coloring is usually dark green or greenish brown above and lighter and often silvery on the sides, and it has a whitish belly. Spawning males take on a yellowish or yellow orange color and develop tubercles on the head, back, and some fins.

Size/Age. This species can live 10 years and grow to 25 inches, although it has been reported to attain lengths between 3 and 4 feet. Common sizes are in the 7- to 10-inch range.

Distribution. Northern squawfish occur in North America in the Pacific drainages from the Nass River in British Columbia to the Columbia River in Nevada, in the Harney River basin in Oregon, and in the Peace River system (Arctic basin) in British Columbia and Alberta.

Habitat. Northern squawfish inhabit lakes, ponds, and runs of small to large rivers.

Food. The diet of northern squawfish is terrestrial insects, aquatic insect larvae, plankton, crustaceans, small fish, and fish eggs. Large individuals especially prey on small fish and are considered serious predators of juvenile salmonids. In the Columbia River, fisheries managers undertake efforts to control squawfish numbers to minimize this problem.

Angling. This and other squawfish species are generally viewed with disdain or at least dissatisfaction by anglers, in part because of their threat to trout and salmon, although larger specimens can be extremely sporty on light tackle and are readily caught on small lures and flies. Squawfish are edible and may be smoked, although their (bony) flesh is not especially sought after.

See: Minnow.

SRI LANKA

A pear-shaped island approximately 45 kilometers from the southeast tip of India, Sri Lanka is engulfed by the vast Indian Ocean on the south and the Bay of Bengal on the east. It is separated from India by the Palk Strait and the Gulf of Mannar.

Covering an area of 65,663 square kilometers, Sri Lanka boasts a coastline that features lagoons, inlets, and sandy beaches. The central region is covered with hills that spew 16 rivers into the broad plains of the north and the narrow plains of the south. The largest of these is the 333-kilometer Mahaweli Ganga, which enters the Indian Ocean south of Trincomalee; the smallest is the 107-kilometer Gal Oya. The rivers tumble over rocks in the hilly section, forming waterfalls, and are broken by rapids. Other prominent rivers include the Kelani, which reaches the sea near Colombo; the Kalu, which reaches the sea near Kalutara; and the Aruvi Aru, which reaches the sea near Mannar.

The climate of Sri Lanka is equatorial and tropical; thus it is mostly hot and wet. Temperatures vary by region; when it is 37°C or higher in the northwest, it can be around 10°C in the hills. Days are unpleasant because of high humidity, but evenings are cool. The cooler months of December and January are best for outdoor activity; March and April are the hottest months, and May through August are wet due to monsoons. These storms bring very heavy rains, although the monsoon season varies by region.

There is much commercial fishing along the coastlines, but very little sportfishing. The successive Portuguese, Dutch, and British dominance over this land for 500 years left no mark on the local population with respect to inducing interest in angling as a hobby. As such, very few people in Sri Lanka fish for pleasure. Fishing is predominantly a matter of subsistence, and commercial fishing is an important industry. Freshwater fisheries have started recently with the help of Japanese experts, but local anglers are poor and generally use crude equipment. Nevertheless, the freshwater, brackish, and marine habitats in the country support quite a few good gamefish.

The major rivers of Sri Lanka host appreciable stocks of the khudchee mahseer *(Tor khudree)* of the family Cyprinidae, which attains a length of 1,447 millimeters; the mulley *(Wallago attu)*, a catfish of the family Siluridae that grows to a length of 1,828 millimeters; and several murrel (snakehead catfish), of the family Channidae, including ara *(Channa marulius),* which grows to 1,219 millimeters, *C. punctatus,* which grows to 304 millimeters, and *C. striatus,* which grows to 914 millimeters; and rainbow trout, which were introduced and attain a length of 381 millimeters.

The khudchee mahseer is taken on spoons or paste baits, and is a noted fighter. The mulley is caught on live ground bait, whereas murrel are caught on natural baits like live frogs or small fish. The trout are caught on flies and various lures. Local anglers are known to uniformly use gram-flour paste as bait for most of the fish they target.

The brackish waters of Sri Lanka support two members of the family Plotosidae, the keengar *(Plotosus canius),* a gray eel-catfish that grows to 914 millimeters, and the striped eel–catfish *(Plotosus lineatus),* which attains a length of 304 millimeters;

as well as the ilish *(Tenualosa ilisha),* an anadromous fish of the family Clupeidae and also known as Hilsa shad, which grows to 457 millimeters.

Marine anglers target several sea catfish of the family Ariidae, including soldier catfish *(Osteogeneiosus militaris),* which grows to a length of 355 millimeters, and *Hemipimelosus jatius,* which grow to a length of 304 millimeters; ladyfish of the family Elopidae *(Elops machnata),* which grow to a length of 457 millimeters; Indo-Pacific tarpon *(Megalops cyprinoides),* which grow to a maximum size of 457 millimeters; whitings *(Sillago sihama)* of the family Sillaginidae, which grow to 304 millimeters; threadfins *(Eleutheronema tetradactylum)* of the family Polynemidae, which grow to 1,828 millimeters; and the most relished silver pomfret *(Pampus aregenteus),* which grow to 304 millimeters, and black pomfrets *(Parastromateus niger),* which grow to 609 millimeters. Both are in the family Stromateidae.

In addition to these species, the offshore and inshore waters are also known to host wahoo, trevally, pompano, dolphin, grouper, snapper, croaker, barramundi, cobia, mackerel, amberjack, albacore, yellowfin tuna, marlin, and sailfish.

There are very few anglers in the open seas because Sri Lankans cannot afford to own or use seaworthy boats. A small number of anglers, who fish from the beach, land only small-size fish. The rugged northeastern coast contains Trincomalee Harbor, which is an excellent natural harbor and provides some opportunity for offshore and inshore boat fishing. Other harbors of prominence are at Colombo and Galle on the southwestern coast.

(*Note:* many of the species mentioned here are not listed individually in this book because very little information about them is available.)
See: **India.**

STACKING
This is a means of fishing with multiple rods on a downrigger *(see)*. It is especially useful on boats equipped with just one or two downriggers and allows you to control the depth at which two lures are fished.

To employ a stacked system, set the first line as you would conventionally. Once the first line has been placed in the release next to the weight, lower the weight 10 feet and attach a stacker release to the downrigger cable. Put the second lure out the desired distance, and set the line in the stacker release. Place both reels in rod holders, and leave on the freespool clickers; then place the boom in the proper position (if applicable), and lower the weight to the desired depth. The two lines are now spaced 10 to 12 feet apart.

Be sure to place the rods in holders so that the lower line will not tangle with the upper line if a fish strikes and immediately comes toward the surface. The setback for the upper line should be shorter than for the lower line to minimize interference if a fish strikes the lower line.

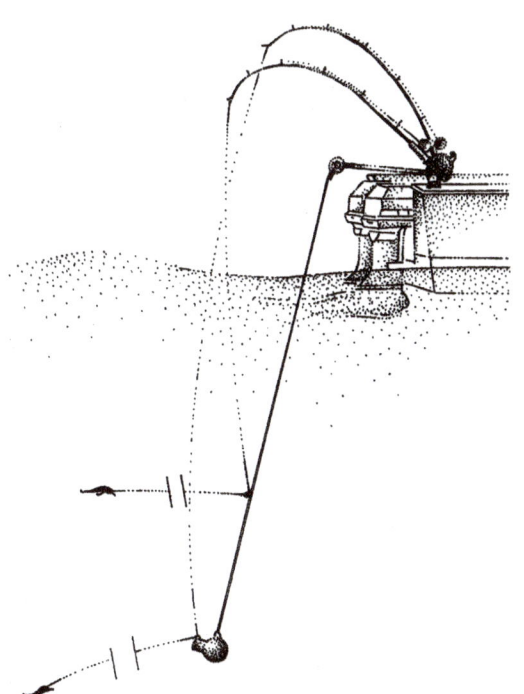

Two rods can be fished off one downrigger by stacking as shown, resulting in two lures being placed at different depths.

The vertical distance between the two lines is optional, although it shouldn't be less than 10 feet to avoid tangling from erratic action or turns. Where very deep water is fished or where you're scouting at various depths, a difference of 30 to 50 feet may be useful. You might encounter this situation when trolling near the bottom for one species of fish (lake trout, for example) while running a second line off the same downrigger for a different species (such as chinook salmon) that might be considerably higher in the water column and near the thermocline.
See: **Downrigger Fishing.**

STAMP
(1) Used and issued by fisheries management agencies, a stamp is a form of fee-based permit (usually in freshwater) supplemental to a resident or nonresident fishing license. It allows the holder to angle for, and possess, a particular species or group of (usually related) species. The revenue derived from the sale of a stamp is directed to a specific program and used for purposes that are specific to the management of that specie(s), instead of being put into general fisheries management coffers.
See: **Regulations.**

(2) Issued by government postal services, stamps depicting fish have been used to reflect art, history, and prominent natural resources, as well to document the payment of a postal fee. Because fish have been important natural resources in numerous countries, and in some cases are very colorful, they have graced stamps in many countries. A stamplike article that depicted cod was issued in 1755 in the then-colony of Massachusetts, and the first gummed stamp depicting a fish, again cod, was issued in 1865 in Newfoundland. Today there are many colorful stamps of fish issued by countries around the world, and tropical philatelists have devised a system of classifying postal fish stamps based upon their prominence in the design of the stamp.

STANDARD LENGTH

The length of a fish as measured from the tip of its snout to the hidden base of the tail fin rays.
See: Measuring Fish; Regulations.

STANDUP FISHING

Standup fishing is a saltwater angling technique in which anglers stand up while utilizing relatively short rods and repeated short-pumping strokes to fight offshore fish. It is differentiated from standard big-game or offshore fishing in which conventional rods are longer and the angler sits in a fighting chair equipped with a between-the-legs gimbal.

Standup tackle and fish-fighting methods evolved in the 1980s in response to the needs of Southern California offshore anglers who were primarily tangling with monstrous yellowfin tuna on long range party boats. These boats were not equipped with fighting chairs, and dozens of anglers on a single long-range boat at anchor labored with heavy conventional big-game tackle and long rods while standing up to fight tuna and, occasionally, billfish. With their knees locked against the railings, and their backs and shoulders under a lot of strain, they struggled to maintain their balance and keep from joining their quarry in the briny far below their high deck perch.

An entire tackle and fishing system for these anglers emerged. Short, sturdy rods with short butts were rediscovered and further developed to provide incredible leverage when nestled in low rise, custom gimbal belts. As rod butts were shortened, fore grips were lengthened. Matching kidney harnesses in a variety of sizes and shapes to match the range of body shapes and sizes of the anglers soon followed. A multitude of modifications to fine-tune the system appeared next, and short, powerful, "Stroker" rods were soon joined by equally short graphite composite rods with excellent recovery power.

Because much of the success of the standup system depended on the fit of the harness employed, harness systems were the next component to upgrade. Borrowing from improvements in sit-down harnesses, more comfortable standup harnesses with sophisticated padding and bracing appeared. Nylon and space-age plastic replaced the old canvas and leather contrivances from the early days when anglers did battle with giant Nova Scotia tuna from makeshift barber chairs. Strap lengths were altered to accommodate the special needs of the standing position, and then harnesses that allowed the gimbal belt to be clipped onto the harness itself developed, thus reducing the number of belts encircling the angler.

Standup systems spread east, and Northeastern tuna anglers began to adopt the San Diego gear on forays to far off canyons of the Western Atlantic. In many situations, especially on smaller skiffs, the California tackle seemed custom designed for their needs as well, and bigeye, bluefin, and yellowfin tuna fell to standup anglers in yet another ocean.

Standup systems offer several advantages not afforded big-game anglers anchored to a chair. The most significant of these is mobility. The standup angler is able to rove about the cockpit whenever the fish surges or changes direction, which in turn increases the odds for successfully landing a powerful fish. This is especially true near the end of the fight. When a large billfish or tuna is brought to the boat, the seated angler can do little to prevent a cutoff if his quarry suddenly charges beneath the boat. The mobile angler can more easily handle any situation by following the fish around the cockpit, can keep the rod tip pointed at the fish more easily, and can often prevent catastrophe when a green fish is brought to the boat.

Many people feel that greater pressure can be exerted on a gamefish with a short standup rod and a quick pumping action, which in turn reduces the fighting time. Marlin experts have tallied innumerable marlin catches using the standup "short stroke" technique to support such a contention, while many California tuna anglers fighting straight down monsters from high decks certainly concur. However, this is not necessarily the case; in some instances, using standup tackle to land big fish may take longer. This depends upon the physical condition of the angler, having the appropriate tackle, and properly employing effective technique.

Many anglers find greater satisfaction in fighting a big fish while standing up than while seated in a large chair that has to be moved by an accomplice. They feel that they get to see more of the action, especially right after the hookup, when their seated counterparts are busy settling into fighting chairs and adjusting seat harnesses. Some even consider the standup catch a greater accomplishment than catching the same fish from a fighting chair.

There is yet another advantage offered by standup systems. The small-boat angler with a limited budget quickly discovers the difference in cost between an expensive fighting chair and a standup harness. The harness doesn't deflate the tackle budget the way a fighting chair does.

As the early enthusiasm for standup fishing spread from West Coast tuna anglers to Northeast

With a short standup rod and quick-pumping motion, an angler can catch large fish without an overly long endurance contest.

tuna anglers and marlin anglers in the Atlantic and Caribbean, it was unfortunately not accompanied by a clear understanding of either its practical applicability or of the necessity for proper choice and fitting of rods and accessories. Even now, many newcomers to standup fishing do not realize the tremendous force that can be generated by the leverage of short rods, and are not setting the drags on their reels accordingly. In short, they are not considering their own physical limitations or even those of their gear. They run the risk of placing themselves in jeopardy of either being pulled overboard or hurled backwards if the hook pulls.

There's a big difference between a fish simulating machine at a sport show, which is where many anglers get their first exposure to standup gear, and the tossing deck of a sportfishing cruiser. The machine doesn't always surge and run like a real life giant gamefish, and the line never seems to break on a simulator. It's an interesting exercise, but there's more to preparing for standup fishing.

Although standup tackle was geared originally at tuna anglers, it has broadened to a base that includes billfish and shark anglers as well, plus any small-skiff anglers without a chair. An angler fishing from a small skiff without a chair is in much the same position as the angler in the party boat: He can't sit down. When fishing for billfish with 20- to 50-pound class tackle, he is not handicapping himself at all with standup gear. Multiple hookups, which can often occur when seeking sailfish, are more easily handled by the standup angler, especially if the boat is equipped with a rocket launcher. This multiple rod holder can actually provide the standup angler an advantage over his compatriot who chooses to fish from a fighting chair, and multiple hookups can more often result in multiple catches.

Indeed, most billfish that can be handled on tackle up to and including 50-pound class, can be taken standing up with the right rod and fitted harness system, and some practice. Although the amount of pressure that can be applied to the fish is limited by the drag setting of the reel commensurate with the line class (whether standing or sitting), many offshore anglers feel that they can more easily apply maximum pressure with a good standup system. In either case, the experienced angler usually adds additional pressure on the line or spool with a gloved hand when the situation calls for it.

There is no doubt that fighting a large gamefish from a standing position can sometimes offer advantages and thrills not possible for the seated angler. However, this has to be put into perspective as an option.

The angler fishing from a skiff or sportfishing cruiser replete with a fighting chair has choices. The advantages of fighting a truly large billfish or shark, or a giant bluefin tuna with a longer conventional trolling rod from a fighting chair give the seated angler a decided edge. Such fish require 80- and 130-pound class tackle, which is just too heavy in the true conventional design for standup fishing. It isn't possible for most people to exert enough pressure while standing up with such tackle to wear out monster fish. However, standup tackle is often used to take yellowfin tuna as large as 400 pounds on long-range boats, as well as giant bluefin tuna in the 200- to 500-pound range; the tackle employed for this is generally 50-pound class (the wide-spool models for greater capacity) and sometimes 80-pound class, equipped with 100- to 130-pound line.

However, those fish that are not truly monstrous in size are certainly fair game for standup fishing, and this tackle is preferred by many people over heavier conventional gear used in fighting chairs. Thus, standup tackle has become popular not only for midsize tuna and billfish, but sharks, wahoo, amberjack, yellowtail, and large bottom fish, including halibut and lingcod.

Tackle

The rod and the gimbal harness are at the heart of the standup system. Most standup fishing, especially for deep and hard-fighting species, is done with big-game reels and special standup rods, although some standup spinning tackle is available for lighter work. Standup rods are made by most leading rod makers and are generally 5 to 6 feet in length. Some are lighter than others, with graphite offering the most strength per weight. Many standup rods are made from fiberglass, but some are made from graphite or from composites. Although graphite offers the advantage of lighter weight without a commensurate sacrifice of strength, the advantage of its greater recovery power is lost when fishing from a standing position because standup anglers depend less on the tip of the rod to fight their fish than do seated anglers. The pumping strokes (called short stroking or short pumping) that are most effective when standing, are short and rely little on the recovery power of the rod. They need the strength of a strong butt. Short stroke pumping gains line a little at a time; this, not the gradual recovery of the rod itself, is what whips the fish.

Anglers should follow a number of simple, mostly common sense, guidelines when shopping for their own standup system.

Because people are built differently, not every standup rod or rod butt length fits every angler. Choose a rod with enough backbone to handle about 18 to 22 pounds of drag without exploding. There are a multitude of short rods available that have been developed specifically for standup fishing pressures. Avoid simply a short blank; most standup rods are 5 to 6 feet long with $5\frac{1}{2}$ feet a favorite, and whatever you select should have been specifically designed for the rigors of standup fishing. An aluminum butt and full set of roller guides are favored for the most arduous work, but some standup rods combine roller and stainless steel ring guides. The overall length as well as butt length should be matched to your stature. The fore grip should be long and extend well up the rod from the reel seat, but how far can only be determined by trying on the whole system. An extra long fore grip is essential because it provides the angler with greater leverage if you hold it as far forward on the grip as possible. A long fore grip also allows you to fully extend your arms in comfort, so you don't tire as quickly.

Most standup rods are rated by line class, but this is not as closely followed when matching reels and line as it is in conventional offshore fishing. For example, a rod might be rated as 80-pound class, but used with a 50-pound class reel spooled with 50- or 80-pound line. One hundred and 130-pound line is used on some outfits.

The harness system is every bit as important in standup fishing as the rod and reel. Much of the advantage of the short rod is lost if the harness and gimbal belt do not fit properly. When fighting a large fish with standup tackle, one is constantly on the edge of a fine balance. If the reel drag should grab, or if the harness straps are not adjusted properly, you may find yourself on the verge of going overboard as you rock back and forward to pump your fish. The harness must allow your center of gravity to be precisely where it should be, tipping you neither too far forward nor backward. If you have to lean forward all the time, you're in trouble. Just any old harness with a high riding gimbal belt will not do. Ideally, you should shop for the entire system—harness, gimbal belt, and rod—at the same time.

The padded harness should fit snugly across your hips, not above the hip bones. This is most important. It should definitely not be situated beneath your buttocks or across the back of your legs where it would force your center of gravity, under load, much too far back for safety.

The gimbal belt, either attached to the harness by clips or snaps, or belted separately around your body, should be situated across the top of your legs. It should not be down around your knees or up around your belt line. For comfort, its width should be dictated by the width of your upper legs. If it's too narrow, you'll realize your error 5 minutes into a tussle with your first large fish, and then it's too late for exchanges.

Once you've taken these factors into consideration, hook up everything together: rod and reel, harness, and gimbal belt. Adjust the straps so that your arms reach well up on the fore grip with the harness and gimbal belt placed as previously noted. Break your knees only enough to settle your weight onto your heels. Your body should be leaning slightly forward, much like the posture of a skier. A skier (like a standup angler) must maintain balance without either pitching forward or falling backward, especially when encountering bumps and holes in the surface of the snow (analogous to a pitching deck or surging gamefish). Neither skier nor standup angler should hold his shoulders back or settle into a seated position with his center of gravity behind his heels. Nor should he force himself into a weight-forward position, where a sudden bump could pitch him face first into the snow (or a surging fish yank the angler headfirst over the transom and into the ocean).

The triangle formed between the point where your outstretched hand grasps the rod high on the fore grip, your armpit, and the end of the gimbal rod butt where it rests in the gimbal belt, should be equilateral and each of these three angles should approximate 60 degrees. The dimensions of rod and rod butt, along with the fit of the harness and gimbal belt, should allow you to assume such a posture comfortably. If it doesn't feel right, try a longer or shorter butt, or look for a longer fore grip until you find what fits your height, weight, and torso and arm length.

Next, try an exercise that will confirm that the entire system fits you, and allow you to make a dry run to make sure that the system is adjusted according to your own physical limitations. First, tie the end of the line to an immovable object. Then, assume the position outlined above with your weight on your heels and your body in the "skiing position." Tilt back a bit, lowering your center of gravity and applying pressure on the bent rod. While in that position, set the strike drag on the reel to a comfortable point. Regardless of the line test, set it so that you pull line off the reel against the drag at a point that is both comfortable and realistic for your own strength and balance. You should not be able to lean backward with all your weight without pulling line against the drag. For the average angler, the reel's strike drag setting should probably never exceed 18 to 22 pounds. This is no time for machismo. To be on the safe side, try maintaining the pressure on the bent rod for at least 15 or 20 minutes, and then see how you feel. You may decide to lighten the drag still further.

That "safe" drag setting, which you can record afterwards using a hand scale, should be your reference point for your standup tackle system. It becomes your safety factor and helps prevent accidents. Remember, the breaking strength of your line is a consideration secondary to your own physical capacity and safety. While heavier line provides more abrasion resistance, line diameter must also be considered in terms of reel capacity. If you're after trophy gamefish you must first match your choice of reels (including considerations of line capacities and drag systems) to your chosen line test, always remembering the drag setting limit imposed by your physical capacity. As a standup angler, you're operating under a whole new set of rules from the seated angler, whose chair takes much of the heavy pressure. Your personally fitted harness system, along with a sensible drag setting and a balanced, rather than exaggerated, stance will help prevent a nasty accident should you pop the line or pull the hook on a large fish.

Little has been said here about reels, but that's because special types of reels expressly for standup fishing are unnecessary. Most standup anglers after big game prefer lever drag reels, and many use models with two-speed features. Star drag reels are still widely used and can do the job, but have the disadvantage of not being able to be readjusted accurately during the fight. The drag on lever reels, however, can be preset so that the angler can always return to his preset strike position and know how many pounds of drag his reel is exerting at a variety of settings. Drag is an important element of this system, however, for obvious reasons. There is a lot of pressure applied on big fish, and when they surge, it's essential that the drag not only be properly set, but smooth. If it surges, the angler can lose balance and be in danger of falling. At the very least, it will hamper fishing efforts and increase the length of the fight.

Line capacity, of course, is a factor when fighting big fish in a broad offshore ocean, but all of the common big-game reels (see: *big-game tackle*) have plenty of capacity, especially if used with thinner diameter line. A full reel is important, however, as it means that more line is recovered with each turn of the handle. Many anglers fill their reels with a greater line strength than the customary rating for the reel (for instance, filling a 50-pound IGFA-class reel with 80-pound line).

Accessory tackle items that many standup anglers employ, especially those on long-range party boats where they fish over railings, is a forearm pad and knee pads. The forearm pad protects

Standup fishing is a necessity on long-range boats.

the arm when it brushes against the rail, and the knee pads protect the knees against railings and gunwales. On boats with high gunwales or rails, many anglers plant their feet squarely on the deck with their knees against these objects, so the pads provide some comfort.

Technique
When using standup tackle on a deep fish, begin with your left hand on the rod near the top of the fore grip and right hand on the reel handle, and lift up. Some anglers lift up with their arms, but many prefer leg-hip-pelvis action in conjunction with the harness. When you use your arms you're putting a lot of stress on back and shoulder muscles; there is more power in your legs. Therefore, you should stand with your feet well apart for comfort and stability, then make a dipping and pumping motion by bending your knees and thrusting the gimbal on your pelvis forward as you pump the rod upward. This is followed quickly by using your legs to rise up while lowering the rod a short distance and winding a few inches of line rapidly and evenly onto the reel spool. Lowering the rod only a short distance produces just a few inches of line at a time, but the idea is to keep this up and make many line-gaining strokes per minute, giving the fish no chance to get its head or have a moment of recovery.

In the real world of pitching decks and surging big gamefish, much has been made of this standup fishing technique, referred to by some as a "pump and grind" burlesque motion. No matter how it looks, when used sensibly it allows the angler to apply maximum pressure on a fish, especially when the fight is straight up and down (and close to that), or when the boat is backing down. If the feet are planted too far apart, or the angler exaggerates the pumping action to the point of leaning too far forward or backward at either end of the stroke, the angler can place himself in jeopardy.

This can be especially true when a fish is pulling hard far from the boat horizontally. At such times, the rod is bent less than when the fight is more up and down, and the chances of pitching forward when the boat rolls or the fish suddenly surges harder, or of crashing backwards if the line snaps or the hook pulls, are greater. When a fish is close to the boat, with the rod sharply bent by a fish bulldogging below, you can maintain better balance while at the same time applying greater pressure. The leverage becomes greater because the fore grip-to-rod-tip distance is shorter when the rod takes a deep bend. It's also easier to maintain a steady balance when the pressure of the fish is down, rather than out.

At such times, there is little doubt that a short stroke pumping action, with only a quick turn of the reel handle at each short stroke, applies maximum pressure on a fish. This technique was developed many years ago by anglers fighting giant bluefin tuna in the Bahamas, who used a short stroke, even though fishing from a fighting chair using long trolling rods, to land many giant tuna in a day. But the average angler is often unable to do that, especially with long rods, and he has a tendency to tire himself out and give the fish too much opportunity to recoup some energy.

When standup fishing, the same principal can work as well, the difference being that the short rod aids pumping and pressuring, enhances mobility, and can be employed more effectively by more anglers. It is important to realize that this short-rod/short-pumping technique avoids the long strokes from conventional tackle that often permit a fish to get its head on a downstroke even though it appears that the angler is making progress.

There are some formulas that explain the difference in mechanical advantage of a long rod versus a short rod when fighting fish that are deep, but the bottom line is that there is a mechanical advantage to the shorter rod and more efficient use of the angler's energy because he can handle the pressure more easily.

The basic method of fighting a large fish on standup tackle, called short stroking, is more than just a continuous series of short rod jerks. However, it does involve short rod lifts followed by rapid cranking of the handle, with attention paid to maximizing effort in the power zone and being careful not to lift the rod too high. Bringing the rod tip up high (above horizontal in the case of standup fishing) places too much pressure on the rod tip and not enough on the butt. Properly designed standup rods have a fast rod tip recovery, but gain most of their muscling ability from a powerful butt; the lower two-thirds of the rod provide great

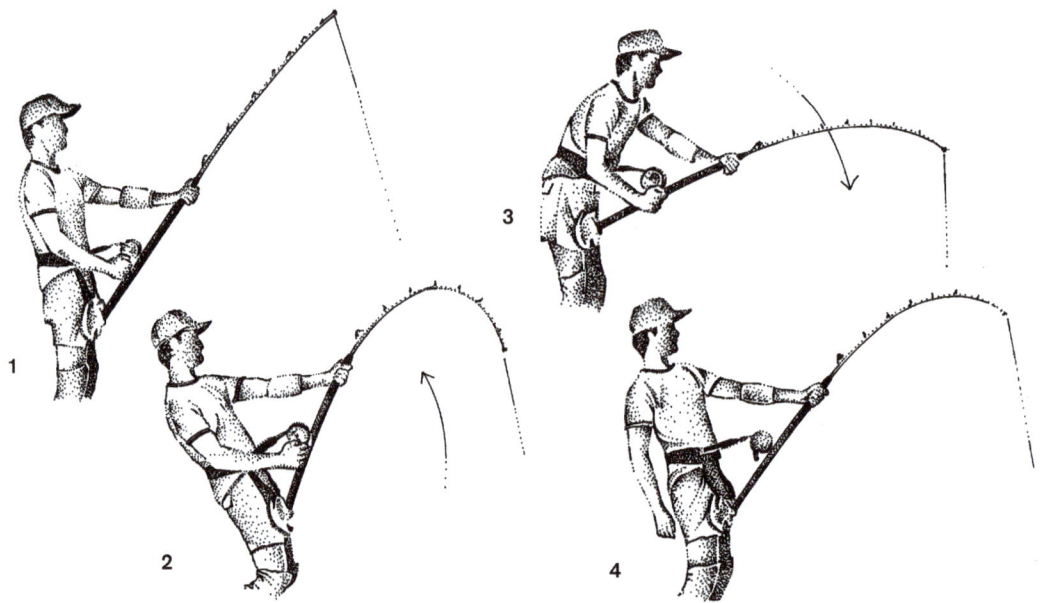

This angler is using standup tackle with a properly adjusted rod belt and harness, and knee pads for bracing. Playing a fish begins with the left hand gripping the rod near the top of the fore grip (1). Working a deep fish requires lifting, which is best done by dipping the knees and hips and leaning back (2), then simultaneously lowering the rod and turning the handle to recover line (3). Continue this until the fish is brought to landing position. When a fish runs off and takes line during a battle, or when you need to rest briefly, maintain pressure by leaning slightly back to keep the rod tip up, and hold the rod in hand without pulling on it (4). Alternate hands for holding the rod if necessary, but recover line whenever the opportunity exists.

lifting ability, and this is diminished when the rod is raised above the horizontal level. Therefore, the correct technique is nonstop short cycles of lifting and retrieving.

With the knees bent, the reel in low gear (assuming a two-speed reel), and the rod doubled over to the water, begin by raising the rod up to horizontal position; this is called the upstroke. You should start cranking the reel handle a fraction of a second before lowering the rod and continue until the downstroke is completed. The distance move may be so slight that only a fraction of a turn of the handle is completed. As soon as the downstroke is completed, the upstroke begins, and the cycle is repeated. Most of the time, you make progress in short increments, but it is important with large fish that you keep it up. Keeping the short-stroking action up does not allow a fish to rest for a second, and directs its head upward.

Remember that the greatest advantage is for fish that are not close to the surface, and that the best scenario is not when a fish is directly below your boat at a 90-degree angle, but out a bit so that the line points to the fish at a lesser angle. When a hooked fish is far from a dead boat and the angle of the line is shallow or closer to horizontal, be careful not to exaggerate the pumping motion. Although short pumping works here, it is in such situations that the beginning standup angler must remember the guidelines on drag setting and stance. When the pull is nearly horizontal, the risk of pitching forward or backward are greatest, and an exaggerated short stroke can get you into trouble. Also note that the motion of some standup experts, when tested against a machine, produces a pull that exceeds the preset drag setting of the reel. Although this translates into greater pressure on a fish, it also carries implications in terms of the safety factor of drags set according to the physical limitations of the individual angler.

It is generally helpful if anglers maintain a steady rhythm when pumping fish using standup tackle and are careful not to overdo it. Some anglers get excited and forget about their own comfort and safety, which they will likely pay for later. Rest when the fish is taking line, and cradle the rod in your hand rather than wrapping your thumb around it; this avoids the "death" grip and lessens hand cramping and fatigue. When there are swells, you can also use the motion of the sea to your benefit, pulling on a fish as the boat lifts upward, and reeling in line as the boat descends.

Although standup fishing has become a popular technique for big-game anglers, and has actually prevented many of the aches and pains that were incurred by anglers who fought large tough species while standing up with older gear, there are some physical limitations to it and not everyone can do this. This technique is not recommended for children or for adults with a bad back or in a physical condition that would prevent them from maintaining their balance and strength during the course of a fight.

This does not mean that standup fishing is only for athletic muscle-bound gym rats. On the contrary, proper technique rather than plenty of muscle is the key, provided that you have the right equipment.

Incidentally, this system of equipment and technique is still evolving, and anglers are finding ways to merge the best aspects of standup fishing with the virtues of a fighting chair. Remember that standup tackle has limitations when the fish are too large and heavier equipment than can be held is necessary. What if you're using standup tackle for midsize fish and along comes a monster? Suddenly it's obvious that the fish on the other end of the string should best be fought from a fighting chair. To address this, some chairs now have a double-ended gimbal; turned one way the gimbal fits long butt conventional trolling rods and turned over it accommodates short standup rod butts in such a position that the reel handle can be cranked without banging your thighs. There are also rod holder inserts designed specifically to handle standup rod butts.

Short standup rods, when placed in conventionally situated fighting chairs, have the disadvantage of being too short for the line to clear the gunwale or covering board, and the angler in a chair with a short rod runs a great risk of abrading his line during the fight. However, if the chair is mounted on a platform high above the covering board, where the line could clear either corner of the boat, the angler could gain tremendous leverage advantage from the short rod with its long fore grip. At the same time, the pressures normally absorbed by his body when standing would be transferred to the gimbal in the chair itself when seated. This could be the best of both worlds.

See: Big-Game Fishing.

STARBOARD
The right side of a boat facing the bow.

STAR DRAG
A mechanism for adjusting the spool tension on certain types of fishing reels. Also known as a star wheel, this multispoked wheel is located at the handle, and is rotated to increase or decrease drag tension.

See: Baitcasting Tackle; Conventional Tackle; Spincasting Tackle.

STEAKING
The cutting of large fish into steak-size portions.
See: Fish Preparation—Cleaning/Dressing.

STEELHEAD *Oncorhynchus mykiss.*
Other names—steelhead trout, steelie, sea-run rainbow.

There is a lot of confusion among the non-angling public about this fish. The term "steelhead" refers to the anadromous form of rainbow trout *(see: trout, rainbow)*, and the fish known as steelhead bears the same scientific name as rainbow trout. Most scientific evaluations of rainbow trout list the steelhead as a form of rainbow trout. There are no major physical differences between a steelhead and rainbow trout, although the nature of their differing lifestyles results in subtle differences in shape and general appearance and a greater difference in color. Technically, the steelhead is a rainbow trout that migrates to sea as a juvenile and returns to freshwater as an adult to spawn, a process known as anadromy. Pacific salmon *(see: salmon, Pacific)* do this too, although steelhead (and rainbow trout) are positively separated from the various Pacific salmon species by having 8 to 12 rays in the anal fin.

"Anadromous" refers to fish that live a good portion of their lives in saltwater and spawn in freshwater; steelhead, which are endemic to the Pacific coasts of North America and Asia, have been successfully transplanted to inland environments, especially the Great Lakes. They live their entire lives in freshwater, residing in the lake but migrating up tributaries to spawn (which they accomplish more successfully than other introduced trout or salmon). Thus, steelhead may exist both in coastal environments and in large inland lake-river systems. The appearance and behavior of both forms of steelhead is largely the same.

The scientific classification of steelhead/rainbow trout, and the terminology that has been used for decades by the public, also led to confusion. Anglers view steelhead/rainbow trout as a type of "trout," as that is how scientists viewed them for more than two centuries. Steelhead/rainbow trout were placed in the trout genus and called *Salmo gairdneri* until late in the twentieth century, when both were reclassified and incorporated into the genus of Pacific salmon. This change resulted in the current scientific name, *Oncorhynchus mykiss.*

Unlike Pacific salmon, the steelhead/rainbow trout has 8 to 12 rays in the anal fin, does not always die following spawning, may spawn more than once, and returns to the sea after each spawning.

No matter what it is called or where it is found, the steelhead is one of the most coveted fish for anglers, both in freshwater lakes and in rivers or streams. It is frequently acrobatic, grows to large and challenging sizes, and is a strong battler. Some anglers consider it the best of all freshwater sportfish, and most would rank it among the top three or five.

The coastal steelhead is also a target of commercial fishing. Its flesh is bright orange or red, delicious, and marketed both fresh and frozen.

Identification. Generally speaking, steelhead are more slender and streamlined than rainbow trout. As with rainbow trout, the coloration on the back is basically a blue green shading to olive with black, regularly spaced spots. The black spots also cover both lobes of the tail. The black coloration fades over the lateral line to a silver white coloration that blends more toward white on the stomach. Steelhead fresh from the ocean or an inland lake are much more silvery than the resident rainbow. On steelhead, the typical colors and spots of the trout appear to be coming from beneath a dominant silvery sheen. This sheen gradually fades when the fish are in rivers, and steelhead become difficult to differentiate from resident rainbow trout as the spawning period approaches.

Steelhead and rainbow trout lack the red slash on the underjaw characteristic of cutthroat trout, but they do have white leading edges on the anal, pectoral, and pelvic fins. Spawning steelhead and rainbow develop a distinct pink to red striplike coloration that blends along the side, both above and below the lateral line. On steelhead, the rainbow trout coloration gradually fades following spawning to the more characteristic silvery color that the fish display during their ocean and lake journey. The distinct and beautiful coloration of steelhead during the spawning period is apparently important for mating and reproductive process. The silvery sheen and streamlined shape of ocean- or lake-bright

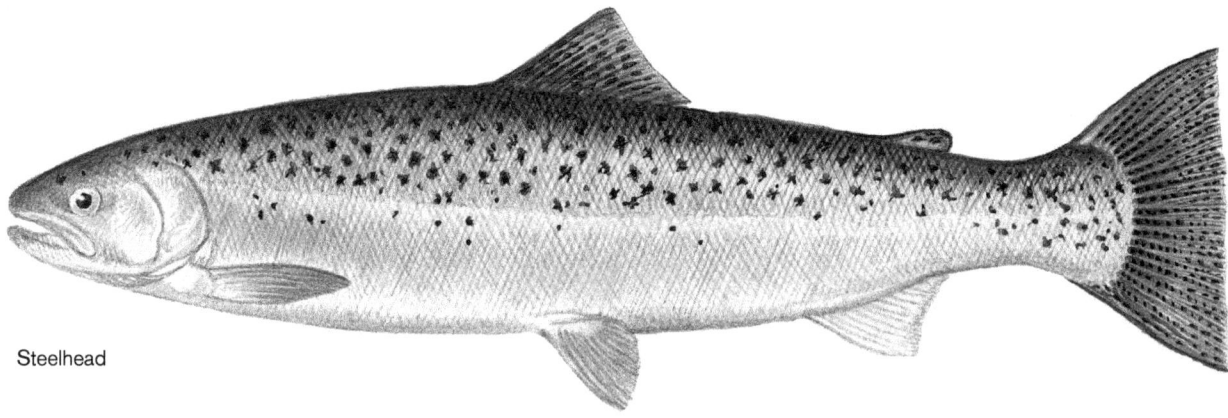

Steelhead

steelhead is essential to survival in the large-water environment.

Juvenile steelhead trout are identical to rainbow trout until the period prior to their ocean migrations. Young trout and stunted adults have 8 to 13 parr marks on their sides. There are 5 to 10 parr marks between the head and dorsal fin. Prior to migrating to the sea, juvenile steelhead become very silvery and resemble miniature adults. They are called smolts during this life phase.

Size/Age. Steelhead grow much larger on average than rainbow trout and are capable of exceeding 40 pounds. The all-tackle world record is for a 42-pound, 2-ounce Alaskan fish caught in 1970. Steelhead are typically caught from 5 to 12 pounds, and fish exceeding 15 pounds are not uncommon in some waters. Most fish returning to rivers are five to six years old, and they can live for eight years.

Distribution. The original steelhead range in North America extended from Alaska's Kenai Peninsula to the Baja Peninsula in Mexico, and far inland in coastal rivers. Northern California, Oregon, Washington, southern Alaska, and especially British Columbia have had significant steelhead populations. Overfishing, pollution, dams, other habitat alteration, and additional factors have adversely affected many native runs of steelhead, as they have impacted Pacific salmon stocks. Some coastal runs are depressed if not threatened. Steelhead are also native to the eastern Pacific and portions of Asia, and have been widely introduced throughout the Great Lakes in North America, where they are primarily supported through hatchery production, as well as to other waters in North America and on other continents.

Life history/Behavior. When compared to the mundane habits of rainbow trout that spend their entire lives in streams and lakes, steelhead lead a complicated and dangerous life. Each spring thousands of 6-inch steelhead smolts leave the streams to begin their ocean journeys. Few survive to return; in Alaska, for every 100 smolts that reach the sea, only 5 to 10 return as a first-spawning adult.

Over a period of one to three years, steelhead move hundreds of miles or more from their parent stream. Many steelhead from Washington and Oregon are known to migrate far at sea to areas off the Alaskan Peninsula. A steelhead tagged south of Kiska Island in the western Aleutians was recovered roughly six months and 2,200 miles later in the Wynoochee River, Washington. Some fish from Alaska migrate to areas west of the Aleutian Islands and are routinely caught in net fisheries off the coast of Japan. Large numbers are intercepted in high-seas fisheries.

Most populations of steelhead appear in rivers in the fall; called fall-run steelhead, they enter freshwater systems as adults from August into the winter. Some river systems have spring-run steelhead, which end their ocean journeys in mid-April, May, and June; bright, shiny spring-run fish may

A steelhead from the North Fork of the Lewis River, Washington.

be mixed with well-marked resident rainbows that have spent the entire winter waiting for the spring spawning period. Still other populations return to their home stream in July and are known as summer steelhead. Spring and summer runs are much less common.

Spawning takes places in winter and spring. A male may spawn with several females, and more males than females die during the spawning period. Unlike salmon, steelhead commonly spawn more than once, and fish exceeding 28 inches are almost always repeat spawners. The ragged and spent spawners move slowly downstream to the sea, and their spawning, rainbow colors of spring return to a bright silvery hue. Lost fats are restored and adults again visit the feeding regions of their first ocean migration. On rare occasions, a fish will return to the stream within a few months, but most repeat spawners spend at least one winter in the sea between spawning migrations.

Generally, juvenile steelhead remain in the parent stream for roughly three years before migrating out to saltwater. If all steelhead left the stream at the same age, returned after the same length of time in the ocean, and died after spawning, the adults in a given stream would be of similar age. But they don't. In some Pacific coast rivers, summer-run, spring-run, and fall-run fish appear at the same time, greatly complicating matters.

Steelhead of the Great Lakes and inland systems have a similar life history, although their appearance in or near tributaries varies depending on their origins. Most migrate into tributaries from late fall through early spring, spawning in late winter or early spring. Summer-run fish, called Skamania steelhead, appear near shore and in tributaries in summer months.

Food and feeding habits. Steelhead in the ocean consume squid, crustaceans, and small fish. In large lakes, they primarily consume pelagic baitfish such as alewives and smelt. When making spawning runs in rivers and streams, they do not feed.

Angling. Steelhead in the ocean are seldom deliberately pursued by anglers; most of those taken are caught incidental to salmon fishing efforts, and are spawning or post-spawning migrants. There is a significant fishery for lake-dwelling steelhead in the Great Lakes, which are caught in a manner similar to salmon and brown trout, primarily by trolling. Spawning-run steelhead in rivers and streams are eagerly pursued throughout winter and spring by anglers using flies, spinners, spoons, diving plugs, and natural baits, especially salmon or trout roe and crayfish tails; they like fast, deep, running water, often gathering in deep holes, in fast whitewater areas, and behind rocks and logjams. Angling techniques in general are similar to those for chinook salmon *(see: salmon, chinook)*.
See: Trout.

STEEL ROD
A fishing rod made from solid or tubular steel, and mounted with a handle, reel seat, and guides. Steel and split-cane bamboo were the primary rod materials until the development of fiberglass and the perfection of rods manufactured from those materials.

Now antiquated, steel rods are no longer used for either mass or custom rod construction. Some older versions may be collectibles.
See: Antique Fishing Tackle; Rod, Fishing.

STEERING DEVICE, REMOTE
For big-boat skippers, particularly those who spend a lot of time at the stern tending rigs and lines, who frequently fish alone, or who don't have a mate, remote control steering is very helpful. There are two ways to accomplish this, the most common being an auto-pilot, which works on a preselected course bearing and maintains a specific heading. This is primarily used for navigation as opposed to boat handling while rigging lines or fighting fish. A better way is with a wired or wireless control that allows for remote and constant positioning and repositioning as circumstances dictate. These help maintain boat control and are especially useful for keeping the boat straight when you set lines, fish alone, fight a big fish, or when you maneuver to adjust lines. Remote control steering doesn't work as well in rough water, in saltwater (due to corrosion of electronic parts), or when you're headed into the wind because many small steering adjustments must be made constantly.

STERN
The rear part of a boat.

STERN DRIVE
A term for inboard/outboard motor and the boats powered with such a motor.
See: Boat; Sportfishing Boat.

STICKBAIT
A long, generally slender, plug without a lip or concave head, used for surface fishing.
See: Plug; Surface Lure.

STICKLEBACKS
Sticklebacks are small, slim members of the Gasterosteidae family that are rarely more than 3 inches long and are confined to the Northern Hemisphere, occurring most abundantly in North America. They are primarily freshwater fish, but some occur also in brackish or shallow inshore waters of seas. The family contains seven genera, nine species, and several subspecies; they are of minimal forage value for predatory fish and little used as baits, but they have a distinctive appearance and unusual courtship and spawning behaviors.

Sticklebacks get their name from the short, stout spines in their first dorsal fin, the number of spines generally identifying the species. Family members have from 3 to 26 well-developed isolated dorsal spines preceding a normal dorsal fin having 6 to 14 rays. Most also have a spine at the leading edge of the anal fin and each pelvic fin. The body lacks scales, but in most species it is armored along the sides with bony plates.

Several species of sticklebacks are kept in aquariums. They swim with short spurts of speed, then pause. This makes them interesting to watch, as does their spawning ritual, which people are unlikely to observe in the wild. At spawning time, the males adopt courtship colors, with the belly bright red in some and velvety black in others. Each male builds a nest among the stems of aquatic plants; the nest is hollow inside but completely covered on the top, bottom, and sides with stems held together with a secretion of sticky threads. Once the nest has been built, the male searches for a female and drives her toward the nest, nipping at her fins and chasing after her if she turns the wrong way.

As soon as the female has laid her eggs, she leaves the nest, sometimes squirming out through the bottom. The male enters the nest immediately and fertilizes the eggs. Often he may go out again and get one or two other females to lay eggs in the nest. Some males build several nests at the same time. The eggs hatch in a week or less. While the eggs are incubating, the males of most species aerate them by fanning currents of water through the nest (the male of one species builds a nest with two holes in the top, and sucks water from one of the holes to cause circulation over the eggs). After the eggs hatch, the male tends the fry for several

Ninespine Stickleback

days, generally trying to keep them near the nest.

One of the common species in North America is the brook stickleback *(Culaea inconstans)*, found in streams from southern Ohio westward to Montana and northward, and throughout southern Canada from Nova Scotia to eastern British Columbia. It is generally less than $3^1/_2$ inches long. The five or six spines on its back are completely separate from one another rather than joined by a membrane, and the caudal peduncle is especially slender. Like most sticklebacks, it is quarrelsome and guards its territory, particularly its nest, from intruders.

The three-spine stickleback *(Gasterosteus aculeatus)* occurs in northern Eurasia and North America, living in both brackish water and freshwater. A number of subspecies are recognized. The ninespine stickleback *(Pungitius pungitius)*, found in northern Europe, China, Japan, and northern North America, is dark brown, and the male becomes a rich black during the courtship and spawning periods. The fifteen spine stickleback *(Spinachia spinachia)* is a Euro-pean saltwater species restricted to northwestern Europe. The four-spine stickleback *(Apeltes quadracus)* is found only along the eastern coast of North America, from North Carolina to the Gulf of St. Lawrence. The blackspotted or two-spine stickleback *(G. wheatlandi)* is another western Atlantic species.

STILLFISHING
A somewhat antiquated term for any activity in which the angler fishes from a stationary position, usually with bait and float or bobber. This term commonly refers to a person in a boat that is anchored or otherwise stationed in a fixed place, but it may also refer to fishing from a fixed shore or bank position.
See: Float.

STILLWATER
A broadly used term, more prevalent in the United Kingdom, to classify and include any body of water that is not a river, stream, or tributary. To the British, stillwaters include a lake, reservoir, pond, or canal. To North Americans, they mainly refer to small lakes or ponds.

In a technical sense, stillwater means a body of water without current; however, many reservoirs, and some lakes, can have movement, either as a result of wind, inlets and outlets, or, in the case of man-made sites, as the result of water being used for irrigation or water supply or power generation.

STINGER HOOK
See: Trailer Hook.

STINGRAY
See: Rays and Skates.

STINKBAIT
A dough, paste, dip, or other prepared and foul smelling product that is applied to a hook and used for catfishing. Stinkbaits may be commercially manufactured or devised in home kitchen or home workshop experiments.

For more details and fishing information, *see: Catfish*.

STOCK
(1) A grouping of fish usually based on genetic relationship, geographic distribution, and movement patterns. This term is used more often with respect to saltwater species, especially in regard to a harvested or managed unit of fish. It is slightly different from a "population" of fish, a term that is used more commonly with respect to freshwater species and in regard to a group of individuals of the same species living in a specified area.
See: Fisheries Management.

(2) To place into a waterway fish that have been raised in a hatchery or other breeding area or that have been captured from some other location.
See: Hatchery.

STOCK DAM
A small pond, often called a tank or stock tank, possibly used for watering farm animals.

STOCKING
The introduction of fish (and other organisms) into a body of water. Stocking is usually considered to be an activity carried out deliberately or inadvertently by humans, although it can occur through natural means. With regard to fish, stocking may refer to the transfer of naturally grown specimens from one body of water into another, or it may refer to the introduction of hatchery-reared fish, in either case to introduce a new species or to supplement an existing population of that species.

The deliberate transfer of naturally grown fish is generally a prohibited activity, or one that can be done only with a permit from an appropriate management agency. The purpose of such a restriction is to prevent the spread of undesirable species, to control fish populations, to protect existing strains of fish, and in general to leave the management of aquatic resources to professionals. Anglers can inadvertently spread game and non-gamefish species, as well as aquatic plants and other animals, via the water in their boats and bait containers. The introduction of some species into a new environment can have adverse impacts upon fish populations and other resources.

The stocking of hatchery-reared fish occurs on several levels. A small number of federal hatcheries exist, usually for the purpose of helping to restore native fish populations (such as naturally spawning lake trout in the Great Lakes) by raising and stocking native species. There are many privately owned and operated fish hatcheries, some of which are now also called fish farms, that supply fish for stocking purposes, primarily to individuals and groups with private waters. This is almost entirely freshwater fish, particularly bass, trout, catfish, and panfish.

Most stocking of fish into public waters is carried out by state fisheries agencies, primarily for freshwater fish. The majority of their stocking effort is focused on popular and prominent species, some of which have been depressed in number on specific waters because of overfishing, pollution, environmental changes, or other reasons. Various species of trout and salmon, plus striped bass, are among the most commonly stocked fish, but bass, walleye, and muskellunge are stocked as well.

Stocking is one of the tools that may be used by fishery biologists to manage fisheries. Stocking is subject to controversy and expectation; the rearing and stocking of some species of fish (like striped bass and chinook salmon) have provided enormous sportfishing opportunity, but the introduction of others (like various species of carp) has been ill advised and detrimental in assorted ways.

See: Exotic Species; Fisheries Management; Hatchery.

STOCKING FOOT WADERS
See: Waders.

STONECAT *Noturus flavus*.
The stonecat is a widely distributed and relatively common member of the madtoms *(see)*. It represents one extreme of madtom life histories, including the largest madtom in body size, the species with the longest life span, and a lower relative fecundity than other madtoms. It may be used for bait, especially in bass fishing.

Identification. Stonecats are olive, yellowish, or slate colored on the upper half of their bodies and are the only madtoms that exceed 7 inches in total length. As a member of the *Noturus* subgenus, the stonecat has backward extensions from the sides of the toothpatch on the roof of its mouth.

The stonecat has two forms. In the Cumberland drainage in Tennessee, a scientifically undescribed form of the stonecat possesses two light bars (perpendicular to body length) on its nape. In other areas, there exists a patch in place of the bars. In both forms, the stonecat has a white spot at the rear of the dorsal fin base and one on the upper edge of the caudal fin. There are either no or a few weak teeth on the rear of the pectoral spine.

Size/Age. Of 261 specimens collected from Missouri and Illinois streams, the largest specimens were a male 7.0 inches and a female that was 6.4 inches. Growth is fastest in the first year of life. Individuals up to 5.3 inches are at least three years of age. Individuals greater than 6.5 inches are four years and older. One-year-old specimens average 2.0 inches. The largest and oldest stonecat ever collected was 12.25 inches in total length and nine years old.

Distribution. The stonecat has a widespread distribution. It exists in the Great Lakes, the St. Lawrence River, drainages of Hudson Bay, and the Mississippi River basin. It can be found from the Hudson River drainage of New York west to the Red River drainage of Hudson Bay. It is found in drainages of the Mississippi River basin from Quebec to Alberta, southerly to northern Alabama and Mississippi, and westerly to northeastern Oklahoma.

Habitat. Generally, the stonecat inhabits riffles of medium to large rivers in places with many large rocks. It also occurs in lakes where currents or wave action produce streamlike conditions. In the main channels of large rivers, it has been found in swift water over sand substrate.

Food. Mayfly larvae is an important food item for all sizes of stonecat. Excluding those specimens greater than 4.7 inches in standard length, all stonecats consume stonefly, caddisfly, and midge larvae. Stonecats less than 3.1 inches in standard length consume blackfly larvae, whereas larger stonecats consume more crayfish. Like most typical madtoms, stonecats consume a variety of organisms that are only infrequent prey, including fish eggs, worms, amphipods, and chilopods.

Spawning behavior. Females mature at three to fours years of age and a mean standard length of 4.7 inches. Clutches are guarded by males under large, flat rocks in pools or crests of riffles. Rocks used as spawning cover averaged 200 square inches and were found in water averaging 34 inches deep. Nest-guarding males were a minimum of three years of age. Clutches contained 104 to more than 306 eggs.
See: Catfish.

Stonecat

STONEFLIES
Stoneflies belong to the scientific order Plecoptera, a term derived from *pleco*, meaning folded, and *ptera*, meaning wing, owing to the fact that their wings are folded down along the back when at rest. They are well-known aquatic insects *(see)*, some species of which are also called salmonflies, and they include nearly 500 species in North America, all of which

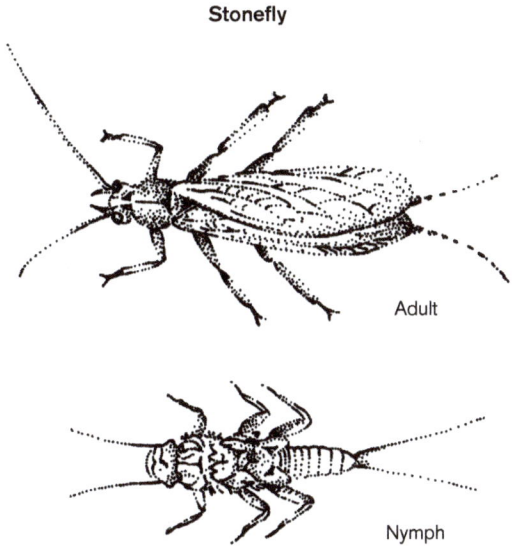

Stonefly — Adult, Nymph

have aquatic larvae and all but one of which are terrestrial (nonaquatic) as adults. Their life cycle consists of egg, nymph, and adult stages, with most of this being in the nymph, or immature, form.

The larval development period depends on species and local climate but can last underwater from three months to three years. During a given year, the larvae of different stonefly species hatch into adults at different times. Stonefly larvae are either predators or they feed on fungi and bacteria associated with leaf debris.

Generally, stoneflies are flattened and have legs that end with two hooks which allow them to maintain themselves in fast-moving current. Typically, stonefly larvae are found in cool clean streams with high levels of dissolved oxygen, and are very sensitive to pollution.

The life cycle of stoneflies is very similar to that of mayflies *(see)*. Nymphs are timid and become active upon maturity. Unlike mayflies, when stoneflies are ready to hatch, they crawl out of the water onto the streamside and shed their nymphal skin out of the water on logs, stones, or tree branches. Although they are food for fish in the nymph form, they become especially significant food when migrating to the shoreline to hatch.

Some adult stoneflies fall or are blown into the water after hatching, and some fall in while flying, because they are awkward and weak in flight. They mate in flight, and females deposit their eggs on the water, bouncing like bombers along the surface. Both sexes fall spent to the water after. This mating stage is when stoneflies are most available to fish; they may be present in great numbers, which is referred to as a hatch and which may provide spectacular surface feeding by trout.

Stonefly larvae are mostly distinguished by these characteristics: two long antennae, much longer than the head; two hairlike tails; gill filaments that are often located on or behind each leg; three pairs of segmented legs (six legs total) on the middle section of the body that each end in two hooks; and four wings that are folded back and flat on top of each other when the insect is at rest.

Stonefly larvae are similar to mayfly larvae; however, mayflies have platelike or feathery gill tufts along the sides of their abdomen, and stoneflies have none (rarely, stonefly larvae have fine gill filaments on some of the abdominal segments). Mayfly larvae usually have three tails (although some have two), whereas stonefly larvae have only two hairlike tails. Also, the antennae of mayfly larvae are much shorter than those of stonefly larvae. Further, mayfly larvae have only one hook at the end of each leg and stonefly larvae have two hooks.

Damselfly larvae can also superficially look like stoneflies, but damselfly larvae have three (not two) oar-shaped tails and short antennae.

STONEROLLER, CENTRAL *Campostoma anomalum*.

Other names—stoneroller, minnow, hornyhead, knottyhead.

The central stoneroller is a member of the Cyprinidae family of minnows. It is a hardy species that provides important forage for gamefish and is commonly used as bait.

Identification. The central stoneroller has a thick and barely compressed torpedo-shaped body that is dull gray with a brassy tint and a pale golden stripe along the upper side. It has an unusual appearance due its subterminal mouth and a hard cartilaginous ridge on the lower jaw. The mouth formation and lower ridge enable the central stoneroller to scrape algae and other minute organisms off rocks. There are dark brown to black blotches on the back and side of large specimens, the caudal fin is moderately forked, and the lateral line is nearly straight. Breeding males exhibit large tubercles on the top of the head and the upper scales almost to the base of the tail, and there are small tubercles on the pectoral rays and the first dorsal ray; they also have an orange cast, with orange and black anal and dorsal fins.

Size. This species grows to $8^{1}/_{2}$ inches but is usually 4 to 6 inches long.

Distribution. The central stoneroller ranges widely in the eastern and central United States and southern Canada in the Atlantic, Great Lakes, Hudson Bay, and Mississippi River basins, from New York to North Dakota and south to Georgia

Central Stoneroller

and Texas and northern Mexico. It is least common in the Great Plains.

Habitat. Central stonerollers prefer clean riffles, runs, and pools with current in streams, creeks, and small to medium rivers.

Spawning behavior. The male central stoneroller primarily builds pit nests by carrying pebbles in its mouth or disturbing the upstream gravel to float pebbles downstream. Nests are communal and constructed in gravel areas at the top of riffles. They are relatively shallow and are built in quiet areas or those with moderate current or where there is overhanging protection. Spawning occurs in spring, and males defend their territories and aggressively challenge other males.

Food. The diet of central stonerollers is algae, insect larvae, and other bottom organisms. This fish has an unusually elongated gut that winds around the swim bladder to facilitate the digestion of algae.

Angling. Because it is hardy and lively on a hook, the central stoneroller is often used as bait.
See: Minnow.

STRAKE

Longitudinal ridge along the bottom of a boat hull that ends at the stern. These are usually multiple strakes on either side of the centerline, and they help lift the boat when running.
See: Boat.

STRATIFICATION

The temperature layering of lakes in temperate climates. The water temperature in shallow lakes is generally the same, or not very different, from top to bottom, through the season. However, deep lakes stratify because the density of water changes as its temperature changes.

Water is most dense at 39°F. Above and below that temperature, water expands and becomes less dense. This means that in the spring, just before the ice melts, the water near the bottom will be at 39°. Water above that layer will be cooler, approaching 32° just under the ice. As the air temperature rises, the ice melts and the surface waters begin to heat up. Wind action and increasing density cause this surface water to sink and mix with the deeper water; this process is called spring turnover, and the entire lake is essentially a uniform 39°.

As long as the weather remains windy, the lake will continue to mix. When a calm period occurs, the lake water will stratify thermally, separating into layers of different temperature. The warmer, lighter surface water becomes segregated from the colder, heavier bottom water.

As summer progresses and the temperature difference between top and bottom increases, stratification becomes more stable, and water layers are isolated from each other. The surface layer, or epilimnion, is well mixed and of nearly uniform temperature. Below that is a transition layer, called the thermocline or metalimnion, where the temperature drops at least a degree per meter. The bottom layer, containing the coldest water, is the hypolimnion. Significant differences may exist in the water chemistry between the three layers and are most pronounced by mid- to late-summer. One of the most important things that also happens at this stage is that new oxygen *(see)* usually remains in the upper layers, being prevented by the thermocline from reaching the deeper levels; oxygen is not replenished in the deeper cold levels, and the lack of replenishment can be a problem in some waters.

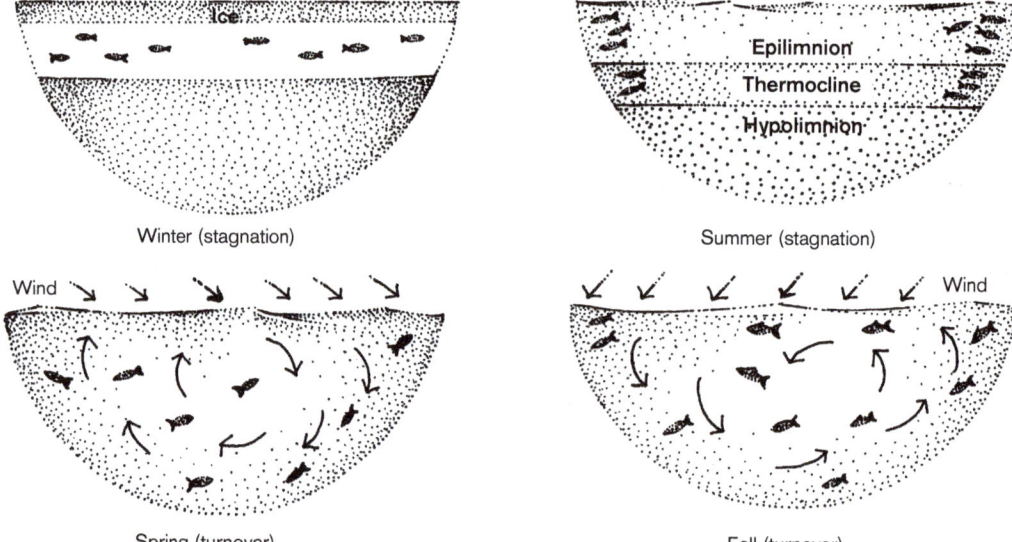

Seasonal Water Conditions

The turnover phenomenon occurs twice yearly after periods of stagnation.

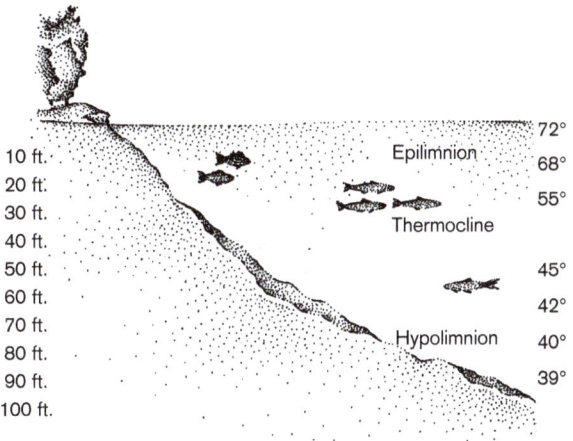

In lakes where a thermocline is established, that zone is usually rich with oxygen and fish.

As air temperature drops in the fall, the surface water temperature declines. Gradually the thermal gradient is broken down and the lake water again becomes all the same temperature; this process is called the fall turnover. As water temperature continues to drop, the lake mixes until it reaches a uniform 39°. Once the lake surface has reached 32°, a cold, calm night can leave a sheet of ice on the surface, leading to increasing ice thickness.

The stratification of a lake has important implications for anglers from spring through fall, especially those who seek coldwater species. Early in the season, the warming upper layers become most attractive for the widest variety of species and are most accessible to anglers, which in part explains why spring fishing is very popular. In the warmer weather when the upper layers have warmed, coldwater fish will generally be in the deeper levels that correspond to their preferred temperature zone, which is usually also the same zone that their primary forage inhabits. This is usually just above, in, or just below the thermocline, the depth of which varies depending on the body of water. In the fall, the reverse scenario occurs, although the location of coldwater fish may now also be influenced by spawning (and movement to tributaries).

Gamefish that do not prefer colder water are generally in the upper layer of a lake and along the margins throughout the seasons, and in the warmest water available in winter.

STREAMER FLY
A sinking artificial fly with feathers that represents specific or generic baitfish as well as such assorted prey as leeches, worms, eels, and so forth.
See: Fly.

STRIKE
(1) The actual, or attempted, assault of a lure, fly, or hooked natural bait by a fish; also called a "bite" with reference to natural bait.

(2) The reaction of an angler when a fish takes the lure, fly, or bait, generally known as "setting the hook" *(see)* but also referred to as striking the fish.

(3) A preset drag position on a lever drag reel *(see)*.

STRIKE DRAG
The basic drag position on lever drag (big-game) reels used for most fish fighting activities. This is preset to desired levels of tension, usually 25 percent and sometimes up to 33 percent of the wet breaking strength of the line.
See: Big-Game Tackle; Line.

STRIKE INDICATOR
(1) Also known as a bite indicator, a strike indicator is any small object, usually one that floats, which is used to indicate a bite, or strike, by a fish on some form of natural bait. All floats and bobbers are types of strike indicators, although not actually called such.
See: Bite Indicator; Bobber; Float.

(2) A visible object that is attached to the leader when fly fishing to help show leader movement when a fly has been taken by a fish in moving water. By watching this object, which is primarily used in nymph fishing, the angler knows when to react quickly to a strike. A strike indicator may be a white swatch of deer hair, a colorful adhesive-backed piece of foam, or floatant-dressed yarn, and is attached to the leader an appropriate distance above the fly in accordance with the depth of water to be fished.
See: Fly.

STRINGER
A rope, chain, cord, line, or similar device for tethering fish. Fish may be retained on the main strand of the stringer, or on plastic or metal clips that are spaced along the stringer. A stringer is usually placed in the water to prevent exposure to sun, wind, dirt, and other elements, and is intended for retaining fish that will be kept, not later released. Further information about stringers and the proper care and storage of fish is contained in other entries.
See: Catch-and-Release; Fish Preparation—Care.

STRIP BAIT
A strip of meat from a fish, clam, squid, or other bait impaled on a fish hook.

STRIPPING
The act of manipulating a fly and retrieving line and fly by pulling on the fly line.
See: Fly; Flycasting Tackle.

STRIPPING BASKET

A basketlike container, also called a shooting basket, for holding fly line that is retrieved (stripped) after a cast. The basket, which may be fastened to the waist of an angler by a belt, or placed on the ground or boat floor, should be completely smooth inside and with rounded edges. In addition to being a convenient place to stow fly line, it keeps that line from getting tangled on loose objects so that it can flow readily (shoot) through the rod guides when executing a cast.

STRIPPING GUIDE

The lowest guide or guides, closest to the reel on a fly rod.
See: Flycasting Tackle.

STRIPPING LINE

An important element of fly fishing and flycasting in which a fly is retrieved or manipulated by stripping it in with your free hand; fish may also be played by stripping line in, as opposed to reeling it onto the spool of the fly reel.
See: Flycasting Tackle.

STRUCTURE

In the broadest sense, structure is any object that provides shelter or feeding opportunity to gamefish; this term is especially used by bass anglers in freshwater and covers a wide array of natural and man-made objects where bass are caught. In coastal waters, a structure is a man-made object, primarily a gas or oil rig or platform, which tends to concentrate species much like a natural or artificial reef (see).

STURGEON

Sturgeon are large, slow-maturing, long-lived, and primitive fish found in large inland and coastal rivers, as well as in some lakes. They are contemporary species of ancient lineages; fossil remains of sturgeon and related paddlefish (see) have been dated to early in the Triassic Period of the Mesozoic Era (230 to 265 million years ago), making them contemporaries of dinosaurs and causing them to be referred to as "living fossils." Of the relatively few bony fish that can be characterized as living fossils, such as the coelacanth (see), only sturgeon and paddlefish are represented by more than one or two living species.

Green Sturgeon

Best known for the black caviar made from their eggs, sturgeon and paddlefish are members of the order Acipenseriformes, but at some distant point they separated from a common ancestor. As a result, sturgeon are members of the family Acipenseridae, and paddlefish are members of Polyodontidae. Both are considered bony fish; however, they have a mostly cartilaginous skeleton. Their closest living relatives are gar (see) and bowfin (see).

Like paddlefish, sturgeon are distinctive in appearance. Both possess a heterocercal tail (the upper lobe is larger than the lower), a spiral valve intestine, a spiracle (aperture for breathing), an upper jaw that is not fused with the cranium, and a cartilaginous backbone as adults. Sturgeon have five rows of bony scutes (scalelike plates), a bottom-oriented extendible hoselike mouth with fleshy lips, four barbels; an extended snout, and a teardrop-shaped body.

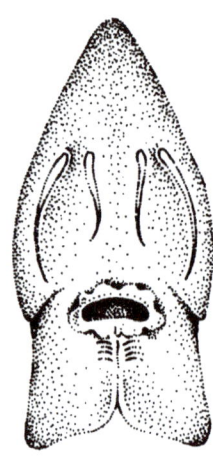
The mouth and barbels of a shovelnose sturgeon.

Most sturgeon are good to eat, although many people have never had the opportunity to taste them, or only associate them with their roe, which is the only true form of caviar (because paddlefish are related to sturgeon, there is some debate over whether their roe can be called caviar; but all other fish eggs are simply fish eggs, even if creative marketers call them caviar). In North America, in their days of abundance, sturgeon were highly marketable, particularly the flesh of the white, lake, and Atlantic sturgeon. Sturgeon is compared to beef or veal (the flesh of Atlantic sturgeon from New York's Hudson River was called "Albany beef"), and there was once a booming market for it when smoked. Smoked lake sturgeon helped fuel the economy of some Ohio towns along Lake Erie in the late 1800s.

Sturgeon have been steadily declining in numbers due to overexploitation; habitat changes, especially the construction of dams; and pollution, especially from chemicals that threaten the viability of eggs. In North America, a federally threatened or endangered sturgeon occurs on every coast and in the Mississippi River drainage. Populations of North American sturgeon that can sustain fishing pressure exist in only a few localities.

The situation is even more critical in Eurasia, where poaching has augmented the problems caused by dams, pollution, and overfishing. Several species are on the verge of extinction, several are unofficially endangered, and all of the rest are threatened or virtually endangered.

Species
Estimates of the number of sturgeon species worldwide range from 23 to 30. Ichthyologists generally recognize four genera of sturgeon: *Acipenser, Scaphirhynchus, Huso,* and *Pseudoscaphirhynchus.* All are found only in the Northern Hemisphere, throughout Eurasia and North America, and they are remarkably similar across this range.

In North America, there are nine recognized species in two genera, *Acipenser* and the endemic genus *Scaphirhynchus*. White sturgeon *(Acipenser transmontanus)* and green sturgeon *(A. medirostris)* occur on the West Coast of North America. White sturgeon occur in lower and upper waters, sometimes hundreds of miles inland. Green sturgeon are usually found in the lower areas of estuaries (this species is also found in China, Japan, Korea, and Russia). Atlantic sturgeon *(A. oxyrinchus oxyrinchus)* and shortnose sturgeon *(A. brevirostrum)* live on the East Coast. The lake sturgeon *(A. fulvescens),* occurs in the Great Lakes and the upper Mississippi river system. Shovelnose sturgeon *(Scaphirhynchus platorhynchus)* and pallid sturgeon *(S. albus)* are found in the Mississippi River system. The Alabama sturgeon *(S. suttkusi)* is endemic to the Mobile River drainage in Alabama. The gulf sturgeon *(A. oxyrinchus desotoi),* a subspecies of the Atlantic sturgeon, occurs frequently in all gulf drainages from Tampa Bay, Florida, west to Mermantau River, Louisiana.

The best-known North American sturgeon are the Atlantic, lake, and white species. The white is most popular with anglers, largely due to its size and greater abundance within its range. Accounts of historic landings of white sturgeon report maximum weights between 1,300 and 2,000 pounds, and lengths of 20 feet. At least three white sturgeon caught in the nineteenth century reportedly weighed more than 1,500 pounds, and the largest-known rod-and-reel catch was a Columbia River specimen of 1,285 pounds. They are not known to attain such sizes today.

Sturgeon have historically been especially prevalent in the territories of the former Soviet Union, especially in the Volga River and the Caspian Sea into which it drains, as well as the Black and Adriatic Seas. The best known of the Eurasian species are the endangered beluga sturgeon *(Huso huso),* which produces beluga caviar; the endangered stellate or starry sturgeon *(A. stellatus),* which produces sevruga caviar; and the critically endangered European, or osetr, sturgeon *(A. sturio),* which produces golden brown osetr (or ossetra) caviar.

The beluga sturgeon is the largest fish known to inhabit freshwater, although accounts of its enormity vary widely; it has been reported to grow to lengths up to 20 feet and possibly 28 feet, and to reach a maximum weight of $1^1/_2$ tons. Reportedly a 3,359-pound beluga sturgeon was at one time captured; a 2,707-pound female caught in 1924 reportedly yielded 542 pounds of roe. A 2,645-pounder was reportedly netted in the Ural River in 1986. Another species, the sterlet sturgeon *(A. ruthenus),* which is near extinction, produces a legendary roe described as the "gold caviar of the Czars."

Life History
Members of the genus *Scaphirhynchus,* and the lake sturgeon, are potamodromous. They live in rivers or lakes, respectively, and migrate upstream into smaller tributaries or rivers to spawn. Their migratory patterns are similar to those of paddlefish.

Adult sturgeon of the genus *Acipenser,* with the lone exception of lake sturgeon, are anadromous. They typically winter in the ocean, migrating into coastal rivers as the water warms above 12°C. Sturgeon also use peak river discharge in the spring as a cue for migratory behavior. Most sturgeon stage in brackish water for a few days before migrating upstream, or out to the ocean. Staging in brackish water allows their body to adjust to the difficulties of regulating mineral concentrations in saltwater to the often extreme opposite problems of attaining balance in freshwater. They then migrate hundreds of miles upstream to reach gravel bars and spawn in high-velocity currents. Several males spawn with each female, and the eggs adhere to the gravel. The eggs hatch and the fry are carried downstream to areas with slower water velocity. Adults then move downstream to summer habitats where they remain until the fall. For many sturgeon species, summer habitat may be a refuge from high water temperatures.

In the fall, adults migrate downstream, stage in brackish water, and then migrate out to the ocean. Juvenile sturgeon remain in freshwater for several years. During the fall, they may migrate downstream until they reach brackish water, overwinter there, and migrate upstream in the spring.

Early growth is rapid, and juveniles may reach their adult size in as few as 3 years. Sturgeon often do not mature until 6 years of age, and in some areas they do not mature until age 10 or 12. Sturgeon spawn intermittently, every 2 to 6 years depending on the species.

The longevity and maximum size of sturgeon vary with local conditions and according to large-scale geographic patterns. Members of *Acipenser* are the largest and longest-living North American sturgeon, easily reaching a length of 4 feet and a weight of 100 or more pounds. Most species frequently will live 30 years and have been aged at more than 100 years. *Scaphirhynchus* are smaller (slightly under 3 feet), sometimes reaching a weight of 70 pounds, and, typically, older individuals have been aged at 25 to 30 years old. All North American sturgeon species have been overfished, however, and it is likely that the oldest and largest individuals may have been removed and that, for various reasons, the individual species do not attain weights approaching their historic highs.

Most sturgeon are opportunistic feeders. Juveniles primarily eat aquatic invertebrates, whereas sub-adults may also consume mollusks, fish, and crayfish. Some species such as white sturgeon are good predators and willingly prey on other fish. Migrating adults of *Acipenser* typically do not feed while in freshwater, except white and lake sturgeon. Feeding occurs year-round in saline waters, but diets are relatively undescribed for most species.

Sturgeon are benthic and are most often found on or near the bottom. They are typically concentrated in deep pools that occur in river bends. During migration (spring and fall), juveniles and adults inhabit deep pools that occur in brackish water along the freshwater-saltwater interface of coastal rivers.

Threats

North American sturgeon were commercially important in the nineteenth and early twentieth centuries for caviar, oil, and food. These products were largely exported to Europe. Overfishing and pollution led to rapid population declines by the early 1900s. The construction of dams and the loss or alteration of habitat throughout the twentieth century, as well as increased and different types of pollution, contributed to further decline.

The slow growth, long periods of sexual immaturity, and intermittent spawning of sturgeon exacerbates recovery of their populations, as does the continued effects of habitat alteration, pollution, and locks and dams that prevent access to spawning sites. Consequently, most sturgeon are rare throughout their range, and either declining or holding at current levels, although at one time they were all common and abundant.

Currently, shortnose sturgeon, white sturgeon in the Kootenai River, and pallid sturgeon are federally listed as endangered species. The gulf sturgeon is federally protected as a threatened species. Federal protection has been proposed for the Alabama sturgeon. Every sturgeon, except for the green sturgeon, is protected by state laws in at least one state within its distribution. Because shovelnose sturgeon are nearly identical to pallid sturgeon, a federally endangered species, some localities do not allow commercial or recreational fishing for shovelnose.

Although many states have limited the commercial and recreational harvest of their respective sturgeon species, because these fish cross so many jurisdictional boundaries, including the U.S.–Canada border, a coordinated management and recovery effort is difficult and is further hindered by a lack of awareness among the general public regarding the history and status of these species.

Sportfishing

In the United States, anglers can potentially participate in three fisheries for sturgeon. In the Northwest and in Northern California, anglers can catch white sturgeon, and deliberate efforts at catching this species on rod and reel occur mostly in the Columbia and Snake Rivers as well as in San Francisco Bay. Lake sturgeon are caught in Wisconsin and Michigan; an ice fishing spear fishery for lake sturgeon exists in Lake Winnebago. In the Mississippi River drainage, it may be legal to catch shovelnose sturgeon in some areas.

Sturgeon are an infrequent accidental catch for anglers fishing for other species. Unlike paddlefish, it is illegal to snag them in most areas where they occur. Anglers should check regulations regarding these species; you may be required to release any sturgeon caught. Large fish that may legally be kept are best released to help benefit the recovery of the species. Because of their bottom-feeding habits and due to pollution (especially chemical) in some bodies of water inhabited by sturgeon, there are often health advisories about consuming these species.

Sturgeon are still part of legal commercial fisheries in some states, and they were once important, and in some cases still are important, components of indigenous fisheries.

See: Sturgeon, Atlantic; Sturgeon, Lake; Sturgeon, Shovelnose; Sturgeon, White.

STURGEON, ATLANTIC *Acipenser oxyrinchus*.

Other names—sturgeon, common sturgeon, sea sturgeon, Albany beef; French: *esturgeon noir d'Amerique*.

The Atlantic sturgeon is a member of the Acipenseridae family of sturgeon and primarily a fish of the East Coast of North America. It has been used as a high-quality food fish and as a source of caviar since colonial days; it was so abundant in portions of its range that, in 1675, canoeists in Delaware Bay were warned to beware of 14- to 18-foot sturgeon that floated like submerged logs in tidal tributaries.

Although of traditional value to aboriginal people, Atlantic and other sturgeon primarily became highly prized in the nineteenth century for meat and roe, and as a source of isinglass, a gelatin obtained from the lining of the swim bladder and used as a clarifying agent and as an adhesive in glue. Caviar and smoked meat from Atlantic sturgeon were important exports (if processed correctly, the caviar from Atlantic sturgeon can be equal to that from Eurasian sturgeon), and restaurants characterized the meat of Atlantic sturgeon from

Atlantic Sturgeon

the Hudson River as "Albany beef." The head, skin, and backbone were boiled for oil. By the late nineteenth century, the numbers of Atlantic sturgeon, as well as those of shortnose sturgeon *(A. brevirostrum)*, a smaller species that shares much of the same range, had dramatically declined. Near the end of the nineteenth century, commercial landings of East Coast sturgeon, believed to be a mix of Atlantic and shortnose, were in excess of 7 million pounds a year. Landings throughout the twentieth century were only incidental.

Like many other sturgeon, the Atlantic is anadromous, living much of its life in brackish or saltwater and spawning in freshwater rivers. This species, and other sturgeon, are relatively slow growing and mature late in life, making them vulnerable to overexploitation. Dam construction, water pollution, and other changes in habitat, in addition to commercial overfishing, caused continued declines throughout the twentieth century. The Atlantic sturgeon is a threatened species today, and the shortnose is federally listed as endangered.

The decline of both species has left only remnant populations. Today, the lack of fish-passage facilities at dams, as well as poor habitat conditions, continues to impede the reestablishment of many sturgeon populations.

There is virtually no sportfishery for Atlantic sturgeon, due to their low numbers and harvest restrictions. If populations were high, a recreational fishery would undoubtedly exist, similar to that for the white sturgeon (see: sturgeon, white) in the Pacific Northwest, as catching hard-fighting specimens of the largest species in freshwater would appeal to many anglers. A limited directed commercial fishery still occurs for them, however, and a large portion of the landings are bycatch due to developing ocean fisheries. These practices continue to threaten recovery efforts.

Most fisheries are now closed in compliance with the Atlantic sturgeon management plan of the Atlantic States Marine Fisheries Commission, but the outlook is still poor, and much needs to be done to bring about even a modest growth in populations. Minimum size limits, harvest restrictions, and closed seasons exist in some states.

Identification. The Atlantic sturgeon is dark brown or olive green with a white belly. The head is protractile and has a long flat snout with four barbels on the underside. Five rows of scutes (bony scalelike plates) extend along the length of the body; one is along the back, and two each are along the sides and belly. The centers of the scutes along the back and sides are light, making them stand out in contrast to the darker surrounding color. These scutes are set extremely close together, and the bases of most overlap. The Atlantic sturgeon is distinguished from the similar shortnose by a longer snout.

Size/Age. Atlantic sturgeon may live as long as 60 years. They can attain a size of 14 feet and weigh more than 800 pounds. An 811-pounder is the largest known specimen. Fish exceeding 200 pounds, however, are rare today.

Distribution. This species ranges along the northwestern and western Atlantic coast in North America from the Hamilton River in Labrador, Canada, to northeastern Florida. It is currently more populous in the Hudson River, New York, than in other parts of its range, although it is not abundant there.

Habitat. The habitat of Atlantic sturgeon is primarily the estuaries and bays of large rivers, and deep pools of rivers when inland; in the ocean it inhabits shallow waters of the continental shelf.

Life history/Behavior. Spawning migrations to freshwater last from late winter through early summer, occurring later in the year at higher latitudes. Although it matures late in life, the Atlantic sturgeon is highly fecund, with total egg production proportional to its body size (a 9-foot, 245-pound female, about 30 years old, produced 61 pounds of roe). Nevertheless, it has a low reproduction rate, as females spawn only once every 3 to 5 years, and juvenile mortality is high. Furthermore, females do not mature until ages 7 to 10 in the southern part of their range, and ages 22 to 28 in the most northern part of their range; these late maturations complicate management efforts, especially because the fish are at sea for long periods, until they return to natal waters to spawn.

Juvenile sturgeon remain in freshwater for their first summer of life and then migrate to deeper more brackish water in winter. The juveniles migrate to and from freshwater for a number of years before joining the adult migration pattern. Tagging studies have demonstrated that Atlantic sturgeon migrate extensively both north and south of their natal river systems.

Food and feeding habits. Juveniles and adults are bottom-feeding scavengers, consuming a variety of crustaceans, bivalves, and worm prey, as well as insect larvae and small fish.

See: Sturgeon.

STURGEON, LAKE *Acipenser fulvescens.*
Other names—sturgeon, red sturgeon, rock sturgeon; Cree: *nameo, nemeo.*

A member of the Acipenseridae family of sturgeon, the lake sturgeon was an important part of aboriginal culture in North America. In some cultures, spring ceremonial festivities were held at lake sturgeon spawning sites. In the early 1800s, lake sturgeon (and other sturgeon) were important as a source of isinglass, a gelatin obtained from the lining of the swim bladder, which was used as a clarifying agent in wine, beer, and jelly and as an adhesive in glue. Around 1855, a market for caviar was developed that in turn spurred a market for smoked fish around 1860. Caviar and smoked meat from lake sturgeon were also important exports to Europe. By 1910, however, lake sturgeon fisheries had been overexploited through the Great Lakes region. Overfishing, coupled with dams, habitation alteration, and pollution have since impeded the lake sturgeon's recovery in most areas.

Currently, there are minor sport fisheries (hook and line and spear fishing) for lake sturgeon in Wisconsin and Michigan, including Lake Winnebago, the Menominee River, and other areas. Recent commercial fisheries existed in the Moose River, Ontario, and St. Lawrence and Ottawa River systems in Quebec. In some fisheries, research indicated that stocks were experiencing too much fishing pressure, and new regulations to prevent damage to these self-sustaining populations were suggested.

For waterways with declining or extirpated populations (that is, Lake Winnipeg, Lake Erie, and Lake Ontario), lake sturgeon are being successfully raised in hatcheries for stocking. Current research shows, however, that brood stock should be taken from the water body where hatchery raised fish will be released; yet brood stock is also rare in areas where stocking may be helpful. These populations will require a great deal of time and improved conditions before they can recover fully. Lake sturgeon have responded positively to changes in dam discharges that facilitate or imitate run of river conditions. Signs of this include increased spawning activity.

Identification. The somewhat torpedo-shaped lake sturgeon has a spiracle, and the upper lobe of the caudal fin is longer than the lower lobe. The anal fin origin is behind the dorsal fin origin. The fish exhibits an olive brown coloring, and the scutes (bony scalelike plates) on the back and along the side are the same color as the skin. There are 9 to 17 scutes on the back, 29 to 42 scutes along the sides, and 25 to 30 anal rays. There are 4 barbels on the underside of the mouth.

Size/Age. Lake sturgeon may reach 9 feet in length and have been reported to weigh between 200 and 300 pounds, although fish of 100 pounds are extremely large today, and most are in the 40-pound range and about 4 feet long. The life expectancy of lake sturgeon varies according to different reports, but at one time it was believed to be 80 to 100 years or more. A specimen caught in 1952 was reputed to have been 152 years old, but older specimens of the modern era have only ranged to 38 years old.

Distribution. Lake sturgeon occur in the St. Lawrence waterway and the Great Lakes. They are found in the Hudson Bay and Mississippi River basins from Quebec to Alberta and southward to Alabama and Louisiana, including Lake Winnipeg, Manitoba, and its tributaries. They are rare in the Ohio and middle Mississippi River basins. Lake sturgeon numbers are a fraction of what they once were throughout this range, and the species does not occur in some parts of its former range; some stocking efforts are undertaken.

Habitat. Lake sturgeon are primarily freshwater fish, occurring in large lakes and rivers, usually 15 to 30 feet deep. They are found over mud, sand, or gravel bottoms but may (rarely) occur in brackish water.

Life history/Behavior. Males mature around 14 to 16 years of age and females near 24 to 26 years of age. As adults, lake sturgeon migrate as far as 125 miles to spawn. They sometimes leap out of the water during spawning, and fall with a loud splash.

Spawning sturgeon migrate in the fall and then overwinter at the spawning sites. Spawning peaks in April at temperatures of 48° to 58°F; a secondary spawning probably follows in May. They spawn on gravel bars, or below dams or other obstructions, in swift, shallow water, sometimes in a spectacular commotion of thrashing, rolling, and leaping. Six to eight males spawn with each female. They broadcast their eggs and sperm over large substrate such as boulders, and the eggs adhere to the substrate. Eggs hatch at 8 to 14 days of fertilization and drift downstream to more placid waters during the night. As is typical for most sturgeon, early growth is rapid. Mature females spawn only once every several years.

Lake Sturgeon

Food and feeding habits. Lake sturgeon feed in freshwater, typically on the bottom. In Lake Winnebago, young lake sturgeon feed primarily on midge larvae, larvae of some moths with aquatic life phases, and water fleas. Mayfly nymphs and mollusks are also important components of the lake sturgeon's diet. The amount of fish consumed by lake sturgeon varies by location, ranging from little or none to 25 percent of the diet. In some areas, small fish are a preferred bait.

Angling. *See: Sturgeon, White.*

STURGEON, SHOVELNOSE *Scaphirhynchus platorinchus.*

Other names—sturgeon, hackleback sturgeon.

A member of the Acipenseridae family of sturgeon, the shovelnose is a small species and the most abundant sturgeon in the Mississippi and Missouri Rivers and tributaries. The shovelnose is rarely encountered by anglers but has historically had commercial value. Because shovelnose sturgeon are nearly identical to pallid sturgeon *(S. albus)*, a federally endangered species, some localities do not allow commercial or recreational fishing for shovelnose.

Identification. Shovelnose sturgeon have a broad, flat head with an extended spadelike snout. There are four barbels under the snout, the two middle ones being almost as long as the outside barbels. All four are located in a straight line in front of the mouth. The body is brown to gray in color, with five rows of scutes (bony scalelike plates). The upper lobe of the caudal fin is longer than the lower lobe and has a threadlike extension, which may be worn off in older individuals. There are scales under the body and also on the caudal peduncle.

Size/Age. The average size of adult shovelnose sturgeon is about 20 inches and $1^{1}/_{2}$ pounds. A large specimen is about 5 pounds; they rarely exceed 3 feet or 6 pounds in weight but reportedly may grow to 10 pounds. The shovelnose is smaller than the pallid sturgeon, which is also found in the Mississippi River system.

Distribution. The shovelnose occurs in much the same range as the lake sturgeon *(see)*, although not in the Great Lakes. Its range is the Mississippi River basin from western Pennsylvania to Montana and south to Louisiana; the Mobile Bay drainage in Alabama and Mississippi; and the upper Rio Grande in New Mexico.

Habitat. This species prefers the fast currents of large rivers with sand or gravel bottoms but can live in muddy waters.

Spawning behavior. Spawning begins at five to seven years of age and occurs over sand and gravel in large channels with fast currents.

Food. The shovelnose feeds entirely on the bottom on the larvae of aquatic insects, which constitute the bulk of its diet. It may occasionally eat small fish.

STURGEON, WHITE *Acipenser transmontanus.*

Other names—sturgeon, Columbia sturgeon, Oregon sturgeon, Pacific sturgeon, Sacramento sturgeon; French: *esturgeon blanc.*

A member of the Acipenseridae family of sturgeon, the white sturgeon is the largest fish occurring in freshwater in North America. In some areas, populations have recovered sufficiently since their decline in the early 1900s to support important recreational and commercial fisheries. Fisheries for white sturgeon occur in California, Washington, Oregon, and Idaho. Regulations vary from catch-and-release to slot limits. Peak fishing seasons vary among locations and span the entire calendar year. White sturgeon are listed as federally endangered in the Kootenai River, where the population has declined to critical levels due to dam operations and poor water quality from mining operations. Recent improvements in dam operations and water quality have allowed white sturgeon to begin spawning again in that river, and it is hoped that this population will not be extirpated.

Identification. White sturgeon have a moderately blunt snout as adults, barbels closer to the snout tip than to the mouth, and no obvious scutes (bony scalelike plates behind the dorsal and anal fins. The fish is gray to pale olive on its upper body and white to pale gray on its ventral side. It has 28 to 30 anal rays, 11 to 14 scutes on its back, and 38 to 48 scutes along the sides.

Size/Age. White sturgeon have been reported at more than 100 years old; most of the oldest individuals of the current era are roughly 40 to 60 years old. Accounts of historic landings of white sturgeon report maximum weights of between 1,300 and 2,000 pounds, and a length of 20 feet. At least three white sturgeon caught in the nineteenth century reportedly exceeded 1,500 pounds, and the largest-known rod-and-reel catch was a Columbia River specimen of 1,285 pounds. Fish under 6 feet long and weighing 60 to 70 pounds are commonly caught today, and fish from 6 to 9 feet long and weighing 200 to 500 pounds are possible, certainly in the Hell's Canyon section of the Snake River.

Shovelnose Sturgeon

White Sturgeon

Distribution. White sturgeon are limited to the Pacific shores of North America from the Aleutian Islands, Alaska, to Monterey Bay, California, although they move far inland to spawn. In Canada, this fish is found in the Fraser River system; the Columbia River above Revelstoke, British Columbia; Duncan Lake, Vancouver Island; and possibly Okanagan Lake and other coastal drainages. The white sturgeon is landlocked in the upper Columbia River drainage and Montana. In Idaho, the white sturgeon occurs in the Snake River downstream from Shoshone Falls and in the Clearwater and Salmon Rivers. An isolated stock occurs in the Kootenai River drainage. In Montana, the white sturgeon appears in the Kootenai River. Genetic studies of Northwest populations have suggested that distinct subpopulations may be present within the species range. Some of the most reliable sportfisheries occur in the lower Columbia River, in the Snake River in Idaho, and in California's San Francisco Bay.

Habitat. The habitat of white sturgeon is primarily the estuaries and bays of large rivers, and the deep pools of rivers when inland.

Life history/Behavior. White sturgeon are anadromous, migrating from the ocean into freshwater to spawn; populations that are landlocked due to dams also show seasonal movements. Spawning typically occurs from April through early July, when water temperatures are 50° to 64°F, during the highest daily flows of the river. Spawning occurs in swift water. When hatched, yolk-sac larvae drift to deep water with slower currents where they grow rapidly, sometimes 15 inches or more in the first year. Females typically mature when 16 to 35 years of age, at roughly 47 inches in fork length.

Food and feeding habits. Young-of-year fish prey on amphipods, chironomid larvae, eulachon eggs, and other benthic organisms. Juveniles additionally consume bivalves. Adults are piscivorous and do feed in freshwater. Common baits include pile worms, ghost shrimp, grass shrimp, squawfish, and carp.

Angling. Sportfishing for white sturgeon (and other sturgeon for that matter) is strictly a bottom-working proposition, often with heavy tackle. The tackle must be matched to the water conditions and potential size of fish to be encountered. Light level-wind outfits and 17- or 20-pound line, for example, might be used for 60-pounders in the relatively slow and open water of San Francisco Bay, but heavy-duty lever-drag ocean reels with 40- to 80-pound line or more, and a capacity of 200 to 300 yards, might be used in the swift water of upper rivers where much bigger fish are a possibility.

Contrary to some beliefs, sturgeon are not idle squatters waiting for the current to bring them food; they meander about using their sensory abilities to locate prey or a scent trail that leads them to food. As a consequence, bait is the ticket to catching fish, and the possibilities are broad, depending on circumstances. Favorites include assorted fish (carp, squawfish, whitefish, herring, shad, and the like), both whole and cut in halves or chunks, as well as roe or spawn in bags, nightcrawlers, eels, and scented bait concoctions.

Hooks need not be especially large for smaller fish; 1/0 to 4/0 short-shanked models do the job, although larger versions, like 8/0 or 10/0 sizes, are necessary where big fish are likely. Sinkers are heavy, however, as most sturgeon fishing is done below high falls and dams, with slip, three-way, or walking sinkers in 3- to 10-ounce sizes, and sometimes a pound or more in serious current. Recently, white sturgeon anglers have taken to using microfilament line for its sensitivity, as the take of a sturgeon is extremely subtle. Sturgeon don't grab and run, so you look for a slight tap and then wait for the fish to steadily move off with the bait before setting the hook sharply.

When seeking sturgeon, fish large, deep holes directly below dams and falls, downstream from rapids, along the outside edge of a bend, and in the main channel. They also hold directly downstream from areas where the river bottom shallows up and there is a hard rock area. In smaller rivers, if the shallows are 2 to 4 feet deep, fast, and running over rock and gravel, look for sturgeon to hold about 50 yards downstream from structure, where the surface water visibly smoothes out. Here, the water should be about 8 to 10 feet deep.

When fishing a slow-moving, mud-bottom river that has a number of slowly twisting turns, look for sturgeon to hold along the outside edge of a bend. Investigate places that are at least 2 feet deeper than other areas in the river channel. Stick to the center of the river channel if the river has few or no bends.

Where the river bottom consists of mud and loam, keep your bait slightly above bottom by using a floating jig tipped with a leech or nightcrawler or

A white sturgeon from the Columbia River, Washington.

a tiny crappie float tied between sinker and bait. In fast rivers, fish channel areas with deep drops.

In tidal bays, either side of a tide change is good for fishing along dropoffs and by bridge abutments, on points, at bay mouths, and along breakwalls with baits, using a bottom rig with plenty of weight.

Sturgeon look like plodders, but they are strong, fast swimmers when hooked, and the battle can last a long time. They can provide exhilarating moments, sometimes leaping out of the water.
See: Sturgeon.

SUBSPECIES

A recognizable subpopulation of a single species *(see)*, usually with a particular geographic distribution.

SUBSTRATE

The base on which an organism lives or grows; the sea or lake bed.
See: Bottom.

SUCKER

Suckers are medium-size fish that are well known to many anglers for their large lips. They belong to the family Catostomidae, which is closely related to the minnows. Their closest relatives are actually a group of fish from Southeast Asian rivers known as loaches. Suckers and related groups belong to the Ostariophysi order, a successful group with several physiological advancements for life in freshwater.

Suckers are widespread, distributed all across North America and into Russia and southern Asia. In North America, they occur from the Arctic Circle down well into Mexico and from the East Coast to the West Coast. The white sucker *(Catostomus commersoni)* is one of the most widely distributed fish in North America.

There are 75 species in the family Catostomidae, and they are distributed among three subfamilies: Ictiobinae, Cycleptinae, and Catostominae. Ictiobinae, the buffalofish, are the biggest suckers and are widely distributed across the Great

Northern Redhorse Sucker

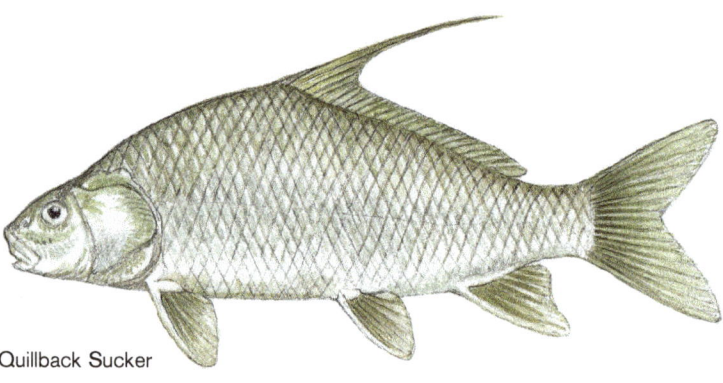
Quillback Sucker

Plains, the Mississippi Valley, and the Gulf Coast of North America. They are distinguished from other suckers in North America by their very long dorsal and anal fins *(see: buffalo, bigmouth; buffalo, smallmouth)*. The subfamily Cycleptinae has two members; one is in Southeast Asia, and the other, the blue sucker *(Cycleptus elongatus)*, is in North America. Catostominae is the most wide-ranging of the three subfamilies. This group, primarily inhabiting North America, is composed of two tribes, Catostomini (the fine-scaled suckers) and Moxostomatini (the redhorses). Representative of the latter is the northern redhorse *(Moxostoma macrolepidotum)*, which ranges across most of the northern United States and is characterized by red fins, especially the tail fin.

Suckers are most easily distinguished by their inferior mouths and large fleshy lips. They have no barbels like catfish, no hardened spines in their dorsal or anal fins like perch and sunfish, and no adipose fin like trout. Suckers are robust fish, slightly laterally compressed. Most suckers are medium-size fish, but they range in adult size from only 6 inches (Roanoke hogsucker, *Hypentelium roanokense*) to more than 33 pounds (buffalo).

Most suckers are not bright or distinctive in color. Many have an almost metallic sheen in shades of gold, green, purple, or white. Their coloration becomes more intense during reproduction, when many species darken in color and develop lateral stripes. Reproductive adults also develop hardened tubercles on their anal and caudal fins and heads. Young suckers typically have a more distinct color pattern, with several saddles on their backs and dark blotches on their sides for camouflage.

Many suckers get their names from their appearance, behavior, or habitat. The hogsuckers (genus *Hypentelium*) are named for their piglike heads and snouts. The quillback sucker *(Carpiodes cyprinus)* has extended narrow fin rays in its dorsal fin that are similar in appearance to porcupine quills. Buffalofish are named for their thick heads and steep foreheads that liken them in appearance to the American bison. The jumprocks (genus *Scartomyzon*) are so named because some species jump out of the water while spawning. The torrent sucker *(Thoburnia rhothoeca)* is named for the fast-moving, turbulent riffles that it inhabits in Appalachian mountain streams.

Life history. Suckers inhabit all types of freshwater habitats, including rivers, lakes, and small streams. Most river species live in moderately fast-run habitats with moderate depths. The biggest suckers live in large lakes and deep pools in larger rivers. Among the three subfamilies, Ictiobines and Cycleptines are specialized for life in large rivers and lakes, whereas the Catostomines inhabit a wide range of habitats. Most suckers live in waters with moderate velocity, although some mountain suckers in the Appalachian region inhabit very fast riffles. Because of their large size, suckers do not need to seek cover from predators, so they often coexist with bass and trout in deep pools. Despite popular belief, suckers are not fish that inhabit dirty, silty waters. In fact, most suckers require very clean substrate and are not tolerant of low dissolved oxygen.

With inferior mouths and large, fleshy lips, suckers are well adapted to feeding on the bottom of streams or lakes. Most species suck up substrate and sift out small invertebrates and other organic materials. The most common foods are insects and worms, although some suckers are specialized for feeding on snails, vegetation, or crustaceans. Several species will also feed on detritus, and scrape algae from rocks. Suckers that feed on detritus, like the white sucker *(see: sucker, white)*, are the most widespread and abundant. Chubsuckers (genus *Erimyzon*) are midwater plankton feeders.

Many sucker species congregate in schools in deep habitats. Most of these species are large, and it is not believed that the schooling behavior is a mechanism for avoiding predators, but for feeding and reproducing. Many sucker species are thought to be nocturnal, feeding on other organisms that are most active at night. Their fleshy lips have sensory organs that allow them to seek out food at night.

Most suckers are moderately long lived; most species average a life span of 8 to 15 years. They become sexually mature at 2 to 3 years.

Spawning behavior. A majority of suckers spawn in early spring, although some species continue into early summer. Many larger species make long migrations to the headwaters of rivers to spawn. They may come from farther down in the river or from adjacent lakes. These species spawn upstream, then the larvae hatch and drift downstream to recolonize lower stream reaches. Suckers typically need clean gravel substrate in which to spawn. This type of habitat usually occurs at the tail ends of pools, in riffles, and in gravel bars.

Most sucker species spawn in large aggregations. Several males may spawn with the same female at the same time. Many suckers spawn in a trio, with a female flanked by two smaller males. The males align next to the female in a suitable location in a riffle or pool tail. Then all three individuals shake violently as sperm and eggs are released. This shaking allows the fish to dig down into the substrate and bury the newly deposited eggs. Only one species of sucker, the river redhorse *(Moxostoma carinatum)*, actually prepares a redd like trout, but many do move around much gravel as they dig into the stream bottom. Suckers produce many small eggs and provide little or no parental care.

Value. Suckers are often labeled as trash fish and are badly maligned by many anglers. This most likely results from a misunderstanding of their life history and value. It is thought by some that suckers feed on trout eggs and pose a threat to trout populations. This is not true, as most suckers and trout that live in the same streams are adapted to living with each other and trout reproduction is not hindered. They certainly do not specialize on trout eggs, and there is little evidence that they regularly feed on trout eggs at all.

Suckers are also not commonly thought of as gamefish, although there are substantial commercial and recreational fisheries for them in certain regions of the country. Large species are often snagged or dipnetted as they make their large spawning runs in early spring. Also contrary to popular belief, suckers have very tasty flesh, although it is somewhat bony.

The real value of suckers is in their ecological role. They utilize food resources such as snails, detritus, and algae that would otherwise go largely unused. This gives them an important role in the ecosystems in which they live, processing nutrients and resources that benefit other species. Their usefulness as pike and muskellunge bait is also a testament to their value as prey for these large gamefish.

Angling. Although not a gamefish per se, suckers are pursued by a small number of anglers every year, especially in the spring when these fish ascend tributaries and rivers to spawn.

Suckers are found in most watersheds in creeks, streams, rivers, lakes, reservoirs, clear backwaters, and ponds. They will eat just about any fresh, natural baits found in their locale, but they aren't crazy about artificial lures and are not prone to chase after lures, although they may occasionally be caught on a slowly worked spinner or a jig tipped with bait, usually by an angler fishing for some other species. They are bottom feeders, and offerings should be presented on bottom or within a few inches of bottom. A host of sinker styles do the job, and the desired sinker weight varies according to depth and current.

Garden worms and bits of nightcrawlers work on suckers better than anything else. Don't put an entire nightcrawler on the hook when fishing for suckers; this is simply a way to feed these hard-to-hook creatures. Use about a third of a worm at a time and bunch it on the hook. A single, No. 2, turned-up-eye hook with a short shank is good for sucker fishing. There should be at least 24 inches between the hook and the sinker. In slow water, or no current, the length may be shortened.

Avoid setting the hook prematurely. Most anglers set the hook when they feel the initial tap of a sucker, but they miss the fish. Let the fish tap your bait about three times. After the third time, point the rod tip directly at the fish, pick up slack line, and then set the hook hard; in this way you'll hook about 85 percent of your strikes.

When fishing rivers, work the flats where current flows over rocks and gravel. It is the same structure where you might find catfish or walleye. Try eddies, small pools below islands, currents behind stumps, pockets downstream from large rocks, holes below bridge abutments, and small-stream channel areas where there is a gradual slope into deeper water. Cast bait downstream and allow it to rest directly below you.

See: Hogsucker, Northern.

SUCKER, WHITE *Catostomus commersoni.*
Other names—black sucker, black mullet, brook sucker, carp, common sucker, common white sucker, eastern sucker, mud sucker, fine scaled sucker, grey sucker, mullet; French: *meunier noir, cyprinsucet.*

This is one of the most widespread and abundant suckers, found only in North America.

Identification. White suckers are inconspicuously colored, usually in drab hues of white, yellow, and pink. The upper half of the fish is typically more darkly colored than the lower half. Although adults have little dark pigmentation, juveniles have three lateral black blotches halfway up the side of the body: one between the dorsal fin and opercle, one below the dorsal fin, and one on the caudal peduncle. The body is elongate and nearly circular in cross section. They have rather small scales that get larger near the posterior.

Age/Size. The white sucker is a medium-size fish reaching up to 18 inches or more in length and up to 8 pounds in weight. The largest individuals may be as old as 17 years, but the normal life expectancy is between 12 and 15 years. Sexual maturity is reached at about the same time in both sexes. The first spawning occurs between 3 and 5 years of age, depending on the region.

Distribution. The white sucker is one of the most widely distributed suckers in North America. It ranges from Canada south to the southern Appalachian Mountains and west into Utah and Idaho. Its range has expanded from bait bucket transfers when anglers release unused baitfish.

Habitat. The white sucker is a habitat gener-

White Sucker

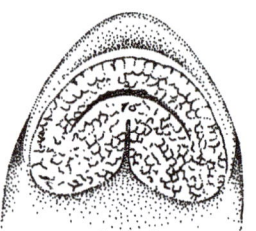 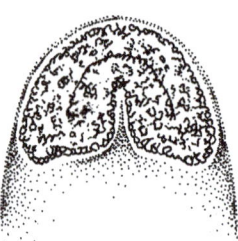

Sensory pores around the mouths of suckers, including the white sucker (left) and northern sucker (right), help these bottom scroungers find food.

alist, living in all types of freshwater environs. It occurs in lakes, rivers, ponds, reservoirs, and even some small streams. It can exist in fairly degraded systems, being tolerant of some turbidity, pollution, siltation, and eutrophication. In rivers, adults frequently inhabit deep pools, whereas juveniles live in stream margins and backwaters.

Life history/Spawning behavior. White suckers make long upstream spawning migrations in early spring. The spawning season may extend from late March into early July in some areas. Upstream migration may be triggered by increasing water temperature or stream flow that occurs during this time of year. The suckers move into deep pools and congregate before spawning. They then gather and spawn in areas of clean gravel substrate. Males and females line up next to each other on the bottom of the stream, then shake violently, releasing eggs and sperm as they bury the eggs in the substrate. In lakes, they perform this activity in shallow shoals or may move upstream into rivers. White suckers darken in coloration during spawning. The males become olive colored on the upper portion of the body and may develop a pinkish lateral stripe.

Food and feeding behavior. Like most suckers, this species feeds on a variety of benthic organisms and organic nutrients. Its primary diet includes burrowing insect larvae that are sucked up and sifted in its gill rakers. Midge larvae, small crustaceans, algae, and detritus are the most common foods.

Angling. The white sucker is not a commonly sought after gamefish, though it is occasionally taken with spears and snags during its spawning runs. It is not a common commercial fish either because of its soft and bony flesh. It is, however, widely utilized as bait. The value of white suckers as bait for large muskellunge and pike is well known. See: Sucker.

SUMMERKILL
See: Fishkill.

SUNFISH
Scientifically, sunfish are members of the Centrarchidae (meaning nest building) family. Although this family is typically categorized as including sunfish only, some scientists include sunfish and bass. The terminology and cross-usage of some words attributed to the various species has made for a good deal of confusion among nonscientists.

Centrarchids number some 30 strictly freshwater species of North America and include three generalized subdivisions: black bass, crappie, and true sunfish. All of these are warmwater species with similar or overlapping habitats. They have rough scales and two dorsal fins that are united, the first of which is heavily spined. Their anal fins all have three or more spines, and their tail is typically broad. Nearly all are nest spawners, with nests built by the males, who also guard the nest and the young briefly. All are carnivorous, and the larger members prey on small fish.

Black bass *(see: bass, black)* belong to the genus *Micropterus*; they have more elongated bodies than other centrarchids and include the largest and most famous family member, the largemouth bass *(see: bass, largemouth)*. Crappie belong to the genus *Pomoxis*; they have a longer anal fin, generally equal in length at the base to their dorsal fin, than any of the other centrarchids, and are capable of larger growth than most of the sunfish. There are two species of crappie; however, a smaller crappielike species, the flier *(Centrarchus macropterus)*, is sometimes lumped with crappie by ichthyologists even though it is generally grouped with sunfish by the public.

Bluegill

Pumpkinseed Sunfish

On sunfish, the markings and shape of the gill covers are key identifiers.

A float-fished cricket nabbed this bluegill at Lake Okeechobee, Florida.

The largest group of centrarchids is the true sunfish. Most of the species are small and not of much angling interest, although they are of great importance in their respective environments as forage for larger predators and for the foraging they do themselves. True sunfish do not include the pygmy sunfish of the Elassomatidae family.

The larger-growing and more widely distributed sunfish are extremely popular with anglers throughout the United States, and provide countless hours of angling enjoyment. They are widely valued for their excellent, white flaky flesh. Their abundance and high rates of reproduction generally allow for liberal recreational harvest; commercial fishing for these species is illegal in all places where they are found.

The various sunfish and crappie are all considered panfish *(see)*, which is a nontechnical generic group term for small freshwater fish that are widely utilized for food as well as sport.

The most wide-ranging and best known true sunfish is the bluegill *(see)*; it and many others species of sunfish are colloquially known as "bream." Other popular species of sunfish are the green *(see: sunfish, green)*, pumpkinseed *(see: sunfish, pumpkinseed)*, redbreast *(see: sunfish, redbreast)*, and redear *(see: sunfish, redear)*; the warmouth *(see)*; and the rock bass *(see: bass, rock)*. In some places, anglers may encounter such sunfish as the Sacramento perch *(Archoplites interruptus)*; the Roanoke bass *(see: bass, Roanoke)*; the orangespotted sunfish *(Lepomis humilis)*; the mud sunfish *(see: sunfish, mud)*; and the spotted sunfish *(Lepomis punctatus)*.

Sunfish are tolerant of diverse and warm environments, and have proven very adaptable. They have been widely introduced elsewhere in North America, sometimes deliberately and others by accident, and have also been introduced to Europe and Africa. In some places they are kept in balance by angling and natural predation, but in others they become overpopulated, resulting in stunting.

The generally shallow nature of true sunfish permits angling by shore-based anglers, making them collectively the number-one warmwater pursuit of nonboating anglers. They are characteristically strong, although not flashy, fighters for their size, making them a pleasing catch on light spinning, spincasting, and fly tackle, as well as with reel-less poles.

SUNFISH, GREEN *Lepomis cyanellus.*
Other names—green perch, black perch, pond perch, creek perch, sand bass, blue-spotted sunfish, rubbertail.

The green sunfish is a widespread and commonly caught member of the Centrarchidae family. It has white, flaky flesh like other sunfish, and is a good food fish.

Identification. The green sunfish has a slender, thick body, a fairly long snout, and a large mouth with the upper jaw extending beneath the pupil of the eye; it has a larger mouth and a thicker, longer body than most sunfish of the genus *Lepomis*, thus resembling the warmouth *(see)* and the smallmouth bass *(see: bass, smallmouth)*. It has short, rounded pectoral fins and, like other sunfish, it has connected dorsal fins and an extended gill cover flap, or "ear lobe." This lobe is black and has a light red, pink, or yellow edge, and the body is usually brown to olive or bluish green with a bronze to emerald green sheen, fading to yellow green on the lower sides and yellow or white on the belly. Adult fish have a large black spot at the rear of the second dorsal and anal fin bases, and breeding males have yellow or orange edges on the second dorsal, caudal, and anal fins.

Green Sunfish

There are also emerald or bluish spots on the head, and sometimes 7 to 12 indistinct dark bars on the back; these are especially visible when the fish is excited or stressed.

Size. The average length is 4 inches, ranging usually from 2 to 8 inches and reaching a maximum of 12 inches, which is extremely rare. Most weigh less than a half pound. The all-tackle world record is a 2-pound, 2-ounce fish taken in Missouri in 1971.

Distribution. In North America, green sunfish occur from New York and Ontario through the Great Lakes and the Hudson Bay and Mississippi River basins to Minnesota and South Dakota, and south to the Gulf of Mexico. They also occur from the Escambia River in Florida and Mobile Bay in Georgia and Alabama to the Rio Grande in Texas, as well as in northern Mexico.

Habitat. Green sunfish prefer warm, still pools and backwaters of sluggish streams as well as ponds and small shallow lakes. Often found near vegetation, they are known to establish territory near the water's edge under brush, rocks, or exposed roots. They often become stunted in ponds.

Spawning behavior. This species becomes sexually mature at two years old or as small as 2 to 3 inches long, spawning from April through August, when water temperatures range from 68° to 84°F. Males build saucer-shaped nests in water usually less than 1 foot deep, and often in areas sheltered by rocks or logs. The yellow, adhesive eggs are guarded by the male until they hatch in three to five days. Green sunfish spawn simultaneously with other species of *Lepomis*, and hybridization is not uncommon; crosses between bluegills and green sunfish occur most frequently, producing sterile offspring.

Food. Green sunfish prefer dragonfly and mayfly nymphs, caddisfly larvae, midges, freshwater shrimp, and beetles, and will occasionally eat small fish such as mosquitofish.

Angling. These fish are a common catch, taken with standard panfishing methods.

See: Panfish; Sunfish.

SUNFISH, LONGEAR *Lepomis megalotis.*
Other names—longear.

Similar in size and general appearance to the pumpkinseed (*see: sunfish, pumpkinseed*) and a member of the Centrarchidae family of sunfish, the longear sunfish is a small, excellent gamefish on light tackle, although in many places it is generally too small to be avidly sought. The white and sweet flesh is excellent to eat.

Identification. With a stout body, the longear sunfish is not as compressed as the bluegill (*see*) or the pumpkinseed, its close relatives. It is one of the most colorful sunfish, particularly the breeding male, which is dark red above and bright orange below, marbled, and spotted with blue.

Longear Sunfish

The longear generally has a red eye, orange to red median fins, and a blue black pelvic fin. There are wavy blue lines on the cheek and opercle, and the long, flexible, black ear flap is generally edged with a light blue, white, or orange line. The longear sunfish has a short and rounded pectoral fin, which usually does not reach past the eye when it is bent forward. It has a fairly large mouth, and the upper jaw extends under the eye pupil.

Size. The longear sunfish may grow to $9^1/_2$ inches, averaging 3 to 4 inches and just a few ounces. The all-tackle world record is a 1-pound, 12-ounce fish taken in New Mexico in 1985. Males grow faster and live longer than females.

Distribution. Similar in range to the green sunfish (*see: sunfish, green*), the longear sunfish occurs in east-central North America, west of the Appalachian Mountains from southern Quebec and western New York throughout the Mississippi Valley and westward through Minnesota and Nebraska and south into Texas, as well as along Gulf Coast drainages to western Florida.

Habitat. This species inhabits rocky and sandy pools of headwaters, creeks, and small to medium rivers, as well as ponds, bays, lakes, and reservoirs; it is usually found near vegetation and is generally absent from downstream and lowland waters.

Spawning behavior. Spawning takes place from late May to mid-August, when water temperatures range in the upper 70s and lower 80s, with longear sunfish that are at least one to two years old moving to gravel bottoms. Males build shallow, saucer-shaped nests in water 8 inches to 2 feet in depth, guarding the eggs until they hatch about a week after being deposited. Many nests are usually found close together, and the number of eggs laid during the season by one fish ranges from the hundreds to thousands depending on the size of the fish.

Food. Longear sunfish feed primarily on aquatic insects, but also on worms, crayfish, and fish eggs off the bottom.

Angling. Longears are caught with standard panfishing methods, and are especially caught on live worms and crickets.

See: Panfish; Sunfish.

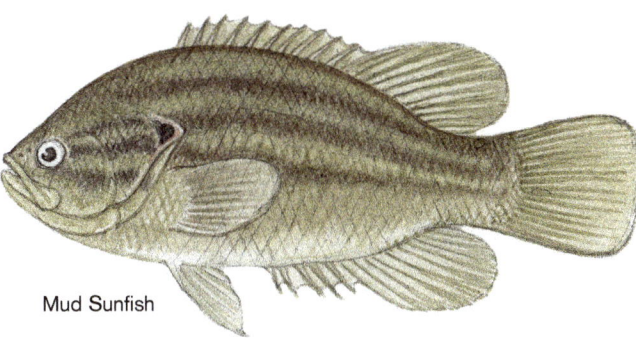
Mud Sunfish

SUNFISH, MUD *Acantharchus pomotis.*
Strongly resembling the rock bass (*see: bass, rock*) in general color and shape, the mud sunfish is not actually a member of the *Lepomis* sunfish family, although it is called a sunfish. It has a rectangular, compressed body that is dusky reddish brown on the back and pale brownish underneath. The lateral-line scales are pale, and along the arch of the lateral line is a broad irregular stripe of dark scales about three scale rows wide. Below the lateral line are two straight dark bands, each two scale rows wide, and an incomplete third, lower stripe one scale wide. It is distinguished from the similar rock bass by the shape of the tail, which is round in the mud sunfish and forked in the rock bass. Also, young mud sunfish have wavy dark lines along the sides, whereas young rock bass have a checkerboard pattern of squarish blotches. The mud sunfish may reach a maximum of 6^1/$_2$ inches.

In North America, mud sunfish are widely distributed in the Atlantic Coastal Plain and lower Piedmont drainages from the Hudson River in New York to the St. Johns River in Florida, and in Gulf Coastal Plain drainages of northern Florida and southern Georgia from the Suwanee River to the St. Marks River. They usually occur over mud or silt in vegetated lakes, pools, and backwaters of creeks and in small to medium rivers. Adult fish are frequently seen resting head down in vegetation.

This species is generally an incidental catch for anglers.
See: Panfish.

SUNFISH, OCEAN *Mola mola.*
Other names—headfish, moonfish; Danish/Swedish: *klumpfisk;* Dutch: *maanvis;* Finnish: *m hk kala;* French: *môle commun, poisson-lune;* German: *mondfisch;* Greek: *fegaró psaro;* Icelandic: *tunglfiskur;* Italian: *pesce luna;* Norwegian: *månefisk;* Polish: *samogłów;* Portuguese: *lua, peixe-lua;* Spanish: *mola, pez cabeza, pez luna, pez sol;* Turkish: *pervane.*

A relative of the puffers, triggerfish, and porcupinefish, the giant ocean sunfish is listed in the *Guinness Book of World Records* as the heaviest bony fish and the one with the most eggs. Ocean sunfish are exceptionally strong swimmers, and most records of this fish are based on sick specimens, which are easily captured. Occasionally caught with harpoons, ocean sunfish are utilized fresh and in Chinese medicine.

Identification. Appearing to be all head, the ocean sunfish is characterized by its much-reduced and rudderlike caudal fin, which is gently curved and sturdy; it also has a high soft dorsal fin and anal fin that it swims with by sculling. It lacks a spinous dorsal fin or pelvic fins, and it is dark brownish gray or gray blue. It has no scales, a small terminal mouth, leathery skin, and a poorly developed skeleton.

Size. The ocean sunfish can grow to 10 feet long and 11 feet high (including dorsal and anal fins) and weigh up to 4,400 pounds.

Distribution. Found in all oceans except polar seas, the ocean sunfish ranges in the eastern Pacific from British Columbia to Peru and Chile. In the eastern Atlantic, it occurs from Scandinavia to South Africa (occasionally in the western Baltic and Mediterranean), and in the western Atlantic from Canada to northern South America.

Habitat. Often drifting at the surface while lying on their sides, ocean sunfish may also swim upright and close to the surface with their dorsal fin projecting above the water. They are sluggish in cold water.

Food. Ocean sunfish feed on zooplankton, eel larvae, small deep-sea fish, as well as on jellyfish, crustaceans, mollusks, and brittle stars.

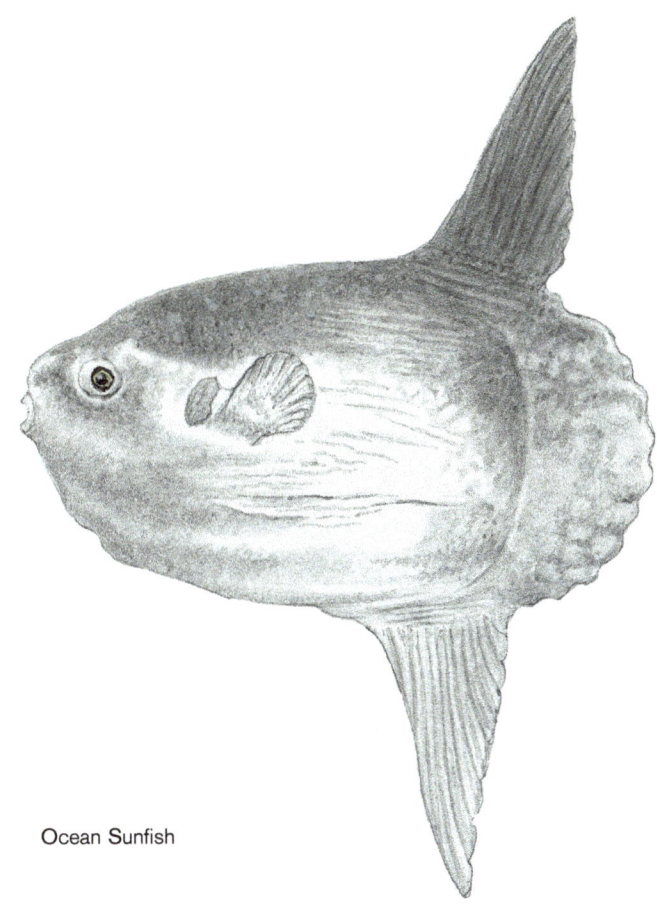
Ocean Sunfish

Angling. The ocean sunfish is not an angling target, but it may occasionally be observed by offshore anglers.

SUNFISH, PUMPKINSEED *Lepomis gibbosus*.

Other names—bream, common sunfish, round sunfish, pond perch, pumpkinseed, punky, speckled perch, sun bass, sunfish, sunny, yellow sunfish.

The pumpkinseed is one of the most common and brightly colored members of the Centrarchidae family of sunfish. Although small on average, it is especially popular with young anglers because of its willingness to bite on worms, its wide distribution and abundance, and its close proximity to shore. Its flaky white flesh is also good eat.

Identification. A brilliantly colored fish, the adult pumpkinseed is olive green, spotted with blue and orange as well as streaked with gold along the lower sides; there are dusky chainlike bars on the side of juveniles and adult females. A bright red or orange spot is located on the back edge of the short, black ear flap. Many bold dark brown wavy lines or orange spots cover the second dorsal, caudal, and anal fins, and there are wavy blue lines on the cheek. The pumpkinseed sunfish has a long, pointed pectoral fin that usually extends far past the eye when bent forward. It has a small mouth, with the upper jaw not extending under the pupil of the eye. There is a stiff rear edge on the gill cover and short thick rakers on the first gill arch.

Size/Age. Although most pumpkinseed sunfish are small, about 4 to 6 inches, some reach a length of 12 inches and are believed to live to age 10. The all-tackle world record is a 1-pound, 6-ounce fish taken in new York in 1985.

Distribution. Although pumpkinseeds occur from Washington and Oregon in western North America to New Brunswick, Canada, they are most abundant in the northeastern United States. Their range extends as far south as Georgia on the east, and includes most of the United States except for the south-central and southwestern regions. It includes Ontario and southern Quebec. They have been introduced to Europe but are considered a nuisance there.

Habitat. Pumpkinseed sunfish inhabit quiet and vegetated lakes, ponds, and pools of creeks and small rivers, with a preference for weed patches, docks, logs, and other cover close to shore.

Spawning behavior. Males and females reach sexual maturity during the second year of life, spawning during the spring and summer when waters are in the mid-60°F range. The males construct nests in water of less than 5-foot depths, often near shore and aquatic vegetation; the circular nests are 4 to 16 inches in diameter and are built separately or in small groups. The number of eggs produced by a female varies with age and size, and they hatch in about three days, the male guarding the young for a week or more. After the young leave the nest, the male often clears it in preparation for a second spawning. More than one female may lay eggs in a single nest, and because several species of sunfish often spawn in the same area at the same time, there is frequent hybridization between this and other fish in the genus *Lepomis*.

Food. Pumpkinseed sunfish feed on a variety of small foods, including crustaceans, dragonfly and mayfly nymphs, ants, small salamanders, mollusks, midge larvae, snails, water beetles, and small fish.

Pumpkinseed Sunfish

A pumpkinseed sunfish from a New York reservoir.

Angling. These fish are a common catch, taken with standard panfishing methods, although their small mouths make them nibblers, requiring small hooks and baits.
See: Panfish; Sunfish.

SUNFISH, REDBREAST *Lepomis auritus.*
Other names—longear sunfish, redbreast bream, robin, redbelly, sun perch, yellowbelly sunfish.

The redbreast sunfish is the most abundant sunfish in Atlantic Coastal Plain streams. Like other members of the Centrarchidae family of sunfish, it is a good fighter for its size and excellent to eat.

Identification. The body of the redbreast sunfish is deep and compressed but rather elongate for a sunfish. It is olive above, fading to bluish bronze below; in the spawning season, males have bright orange red bellies while females are pale orange underneath. There are several light blue streaks radiating from the mouth, and the gill rakers are short and stiff. The lobe or flap on the gill cover is usually long and narrow in adult males, actually longer than in the so-called longear sunfish *(see: sunfish, longear).* The two species are easily distinguished because the lobe of the redbreast is blue black or completely black all the way to the tip and is narrower than the eyes, whereas the lobe of the longear is much wider and is bordered by a thin margin of pale red or yellow around the black. The pectoral fins of both species are short and roundish in contrast to the longer, pointed pectoral fins of the redear sunfish *(see: sunfish, redear),* and the opercular flaps are softer and more flexible than the rigid flaps of the pumpkinseed sunfish *(see: sunfish, pumpkinseed).*

Size. Redbreast sunfish grow at a slow rate and may reach lengths of 6 to 8 inches, although they can attain 11 to 12 inches and weigh about a pound. The all-tackle world record is a 1-pound, 12-ounce fish from Florida in 1984.

Distribution. Generally occurring in rivers across the United States and Canada, the original distribution of redbreast sunfish is the Atlantic slope of North America from New Brunswick, Canada, to central Florida, and westward to the Appalachian Mountains; the range now extends to parts of Texas, Oklahoma, Arkansas, and Kentucky. They have been introduced to waters in Mexico, Puerto Rico, and Italy, where they are considered a nuisance due to stunting.

Habitat. Redbreast sunfish inhabit rocky and sandy pools of creeks and small to medium rivers. They prefer the deeper sections of streams and vegetated lake margins.

Spawning behavior. Redbreasts spawn in spring and summer when they are two to three years old and as small as 4 inches long; this may occur as early as April in the southern part of their range. Spawning peaks in June or when water temperatures range from 68° to 82°F. Males build nests in water 1 to 2 feet deep near stumps, logs, rocks, or other protected areas over sand or gravel bottom; the nests are 30 to 36 inches in diameter and 6 to 8 inches deep. Redbreast sunfish often occupy nests that have been abandoned by other sunfish. The number of eggs laid ranges in the thousands to tens of thousands, varying with the age and size of the female.

Food. Their primary food is aquatic insects, but redbreasts also feed on snails, crayfish, small fish, and occasionally on organic matter from the bottom.

Angling. These fish are a common catch, taken with standard panfishing methods.
See: Panfish; Sunfish.

Redbreast Sunfish

SUNFISH, REDEAR *Lepomis microlophus.*
Other names—shellcracker, stumpknocker, yellow bream, bream.

The redear sunfish is a popular sportfish because it fights hard on light tackle, reaches a relatively large size for a sunfish, and can be caught in large numbers. Like other members of the Centrarchidae family of sunfish it is an excellent panfish, with white, flaky meat.

Identification. Light golden green above, the redear sunfish is roundish and laterally compressed; adults have dusky gray spots on the sides, whereas juveniles have bars. It is white to yellow on the belly, with mostly clear fins, and the breeding male is brassy gold with dusky pelvic fins. The redear sunfish has a fairly pointed snout and a small mouth, with blunted molaform teeth that make shell cracking possible. It has connected dorsal fins and long, pointed pectoral fins that extend far beyond the eye when bent forward; the latter distinguish it from both the longear *(see: sunfish, longear)* and redbreast *(see: sunfish, redbreast)* sunfish, which have short, roundish pectoral fins. The ear flap is also much shorter than in the other two species and is black, with a bright red or orange spot or a light margin at the edge.

It can also be distinguished from the pumpkinseed sunfish *(see: sunfish, pumpkinseed)* by its gill cover flap, which is relatively flexible and can be bent at least to right angles, whereas the flap on the pumpkinseed is rigid. The redear sunfish is somewhat less compressed than the bluegill *(see)*, which contrasts with the redear sunfish by having an entirely black ear flap without any spot or light edge.

Size/Age. The redear sunfish can become rather large, reaching weights of more than $4^1/_2$ pounds, although it averages under a half pound and about 9 inches. The all-tackle world record is a 5-pound, 3-ounce fish taken in California in 1994. It can live up to eight years.

Distribution. Native to North America, redear sunfish are found from about the Savannah River in South Carolina to the Nueces River in Texas north toward the Mississippi River basin to southern Indiana and Illinois, with some populations in western states. They have been introduced to waters in Africa and Latin America.

Habitat. Redear sunfish inhabit ponds, swamps, lakes, and vegetated pools of small to medium rivers; they prefer warm, clear, and quiet waters.

Spawning behavior. Some redear sunfish are able to spawn when they are only 5 inches long and one year old, although most do so after they are age 2 or older. Spawning occurs when waters reach 70°F, which may be as early as March in Florida, and extends through early fall. Males build and guard shallow circular nests, which hold tens of thousands of eggs; nests are often built in colonies near vegetation, in 2- to 8-foot depths.

Food. An opportunistic bottom feeder, the redear sunfish forages mostly during the day on aquatic snails, which gives it its common name, "shellcracker." These fish also feed on midge larvae, amphipods, mayfly and dragonfly nymphs, clams, fish eggs, and crayfish.

Angling. Shellcrackers are taken with standard panfishing methods.
See: Panfish; Sunfish.

Redear Sunfish

SUNGLASSES

Sunglasses are one of the most important accessories that any angler can have for two important reasons: eye protection from sun and wind, and improved visibility.

From a medical standpoint, protecting your eyes takes precedence over other concerns, and in this regard, it is necessary to wear sunglasses that block 99 to 100 percent of ultraviolet radiation to reduce sun exposure that can lead to cataracts and other eye damage. Because exposure to ultraviolet radiation can occur even when the sun is not shining, it's a good idea to wear sunglasses even on cloudy days; as a general rule, if you can see any shadow, then wear sunglasses. For maximum protection, sunglasses that offer side shielding are even better, and because they block out light just as if you cupped your hands around the edges of your face, they also improve visibility.

From an angling standpoint, improved visibility is an important reason to wear sunglasses. Visibility can be improved in a number of ways, the most important of which is reducing glare. This is reflected light that occurs from all directions and is present even on cloudy or hazy days and can be very uncomfortable and fatiguing to the eyes as well as a reason for preventing visibility into or through the water.

Another aspect of improving visibility by wearing sunglasses is enhancing depth of field to see close and distant objects better, distinguishing colors in the environment (a contrast issue), and being able to look into the water to see fish and objects. Seeing fish is especially important in sight fishing activities where you must see a fish in order to be able to make a proper presentation to it, but also in other activities, such as wading to see objects that should be avoided, and when fishing in clear offshore waters to spot either gamefish or baitfish that are attracted to your boat. Sunglasses should be polarized to reduce glare and improve through-water vision; side shielding is also very helpful.

Polarized lenses are a necessity for fishing and boating activities because they are the most effective means of eliminating glare and preventing light absorption, meaning that they allow your eyes to be more comfortable and more contracted, which means greater distant vision. To make sure that sunglasses you are considering purchasing are, in fact, polarized, you can take two pairs of sunglasses that are believed to be polarized and hold them parallel to each other (one in front of the other) and then rotate one lens 90 degrees; if they are polarized the lenses will become dark.

Many different lens colors are available. Dark gray and dark brown lenses are preferred by most anglers, although not all are the same or of equal quality; dark gray lenses are considered best for very bright conditions, although dark brown is generally more versatile. Light brown or nearly amber lenses are also popular and provide very good contrast, and are also helpful for spotting fish. The wild colors, including mirror lenses, may look cool, but they are not a benefit for fishing.

Anglers who do not wear glasses, or who wear contact lenses, have an extensive array of good sunglass choices, but eyeglass wearers have a much greater problem. Some eyeglass wearers have polarized prescription lenses, which are costly; many use polarized clip-ons, which are cheap, do not offer side protection, and may not fit all eyeglass frames or thickness of lens. Some eyeglass wearers prefer lightweight, polarized, supplemental sunglasses that fits over their prescription lens; these are economical and moderately priced, and many offer full wraparound protection as well.
See: First Aid.

SUNSCREEN
See: First Aid.

SURFACE
The uppermost part of a body of water. The most favored manner of fishing is probably fishing with lures or flies that float on the surface (also referred to by some anglers as topwater fishing) or that are trolled across the surface (standard big-game procedure) in order to receive visible strikes, although this method is not suitable to all conditions or all species.
See: Dry Fly; Surface Lure.

SURFACE FILM
See: Surface Tension.

SURFACE TENSION
A skin of hydrogen-bonded molecules formed on the surface of a liquid over the freer-moving molecules within the liquid. Because of this bonding, the surface of water has a tendency to contract, drawing taut like the rubber of an inflated balloon and being much like a skin. When observed under calm conditions, it may be referred to as the surface film. Surface tension may cause a free-floating object on the surface to move in a different manner or speed than if it were below the surface.

The surface of water is able to support small objects and organisms; this is how water spiders are able to run across the surface of a pond. Surface tension is a barrier to some organisms, namely insects, some of which want to pass into the water below it and some of which want to pass into the air above. The surface tension is too great for some insects to break, and it is an element for others to avoid; they can become trapped while gliding across the surface to lay eggs or to feed. When an insect is caught in the surface tension, it may struggle and become easy prey for fish, especially trout. The imagoes (sexually mature adults, or spinners) of mayflies and caddisflies struggle to escape the surface tension and emerge from the water. These elements are all at work on artificial flies, and all have a bearing on angling activities.

SURF CART
A manufactured or homemade device, often with low-pressure balloon tires for wheels, used by surf anglers for toting equipment.
See: Surf Fishing.

SURF CASTING
See: Casting; Surf Fishing.

SURF FISHING
Fishing from the beach—minus the pier or bridge—is the saltwater angler's answer to freshwater fishing from the bank. Known as surf fishing, it brings forth a vision of an angler with a long rod, braving large breaking waves and casting a heavily weighted bait great distances over the roiled and foamy water, mostly on a deserted stretch of beach, at dawn or at night. However, angling in or from the surf not only refers to this conventional view, but also to fishing accessible coastal beaches, in protected backwaters or in locations where the surf ripples instead of pounds, with a variety of fishing equipment for any number of inshore species, at all times of the day.

Fishing from the surf may be the venue of choice for anglers without boats or for those who prefer to be on *terra firma* (sometimes not so *firma*, how-ever, along the beach). It may be preferred by those who simply like the sights, sounds, challenges, and camaraderie provided, notwithstanding some disadvantages in mobility. And surf fishing has been an angling mode since before there were boats with motors; in the United States, it really blossomed after World War II, when new rods, reels, and lines made casting easier and when surplus Army Jeeps made it possible to access then undeveloped beach areas.

Surf fishing has experienced some cyclic levels of activity, particularly along the Atlantic seaboard where landforms make it a readily available angling option in virtually every coastal state. Relatively high fish population levels generated a lot of surf fishing activity from the 1950s through the 1980s. Striped bass, bluefish, and weakfish were the mainstays along the Northeast and Mid-Atlantic states. Red drum, channel bass, spottail bass, puppy drum, and redfish had a large following along southeastern and Gulf Coast states. And on the West Coast, the previously transplanted striped bass drew many anglers to the rocky shoreline.

But surf fishing fortunes took a nosedive in the late 1980s as striped bass, weakfish, bluefish, and red drum populations suffered because of commercial overfishing, poor reproductive rates, and myriad environmental problems. These fisheries reemerged in the mid- to late 1990s, and the number of surf anglers concurrently blossomed.

All surf anglers aspire to the lofty goal of catching a trophy specimen of one of these popular species, but most are happy with a bucketful of spot, croaker, trout, flounder, perch, or any of the various small species that are common along the surf line. And although specialized attention is devoted to some species, especially when fishing with lures, a majority of the effort is directed at catching anything that is available.

Certainly the tackle and the techniques that are devoted to surf fishing for particular species vary according to the habits of the fish as well as the conditions, but certain similarities are evident no matter where it is enjoyed.

Surf fishing pits angler against fish in a place where almost everything favors the fish. It is an act that requires total confidence in the ability to pick the exact spot along thousands of miles of coastline where a fish will find the angler's single offering. More often than not, the choice is wrong, but it is a tremendous thrill to stand in the surf with spray on your face and a big fish on the line, knowing you did it all by yourself.

Basic Outfits

Surf anglers are often pictured as lone wolves patrolling the high surf with long rods, tossing heavy baits or lures and landing 50-pound stripers or drum through the breakers. Indeed, that is how most surf anglers picture themselves. In reality they spend most of their angling time pursuing much smaller fish with much lighter tackle. The average surf caster will carry some heavy artillery but will also have a variety of smaller outfits that in some cases are light enough to be at home on freshwater trout streams.

Selecting a surf fishing outfit, particularly the magnum versions, requires an examination of several factors, beginning with the size and strength of the individual. A big person can usually handle a much heavier outfit than someone small in stature. This does not mean that these two people couldn't fish side by side and have an equal chance of success; they just need tackle to match their physical capabilities.

Heavy gear. The heaviest outfit in common use by today's surf caster is one called the Hatteras

Heaver. Developed along the Outer Banks of North Carolina, this rod-and-reel combination is designed to toss a 6- to 12-ounce sinker and a big chunk of cut mullet or menhaden into the teeth of a gale.

The rod will be 10 to 12 feet long with a heavy action and will have a tip whose diameter is equivalent to the business end of a pool cue. Most Hatteras Heavers are made of graphite, but some anglers prefer heavier fiberglass models that are less likely to be damaged by rough handling. Such big rods call for big reels and heavy line. Conventional reels having a capacity of at least 300 yards of 20-pound line or 200 yards of 30-pound, and sporting ball bearings on the drive shaft, are very popular. These are filled with 20- to 30-pound line (primarily conventional-diameter nylon monofilament) that is usually knotted to a 50- to 80-pound shock leader. Spinning reels are not as common on heavy-duty rods as they are on lighter gear, but some mega spinning reels, which hold a similar amount of line and have high-strength gears, will handle the load. Spinning tackle users may fill up with 30-pound line, but 25 is more common, again tied to a 50- to 80-pound shock leader.

Hatteras Heavers generally find limited use, although fishing a drum run on a place like Hatteras Point without one puts the angler at a great disadvantage.

Medium and light gear. A more practical outfit that will serve all but the most severe fishing operations is a 10- to 12-foot medium-action rod that will handle 4 to 6 ounces of weight. A conventional reel, or a spinning reel, filled with 15- to 20-pound line and matched to the rod, completes the package.

Fiberglass, graphite, and a blend of both fibers are currently used for these rods. A fiberglass surf casting rod is heavier and less expensive than graphite, although the latter is more powerful, meaning that it transfers more energy from the rod to the object being cast. A rod made with both fiberglass and graphite combines the best properties of both and has more durability than an all-graphite product.

Most rods used by surf anglers are longer than those used by saltwater anglers who fish from boats. Long rods are needed to overcome the height of the waves and to attain greater casting distance. While long is good, longer is not necessarily better. Once a rod surpasses 12 to 13 feet in length, effectiveness drops off dramatically. Long-distance tournament casters use 12- to 13-foot rods, and if they could get another inch of distance out of a longer stick, they would use 30-footers. Even 12-footers may be too much for some people, so this is where you need to evaluate rod length in relation to your own stature and strength.

Older two-piece surf rods were made of fiberglass and had metal ferrules. These behaved like two separate rods, one short stiff piece that held

An angler fishes a nearly calm surf at sunset.

the reel and one long thin piece running out from the ferrule to the tip. The metal ferrule not only made an unyielding connection but also had an annoying habit of becoming a permanent connection. Dissatisfied with these, hard-core surf casters turned to one-piece rods that were lighter and more powerful but created serious storage problems. Eventually rod designers began to build two-piece rods that behaved like one-piece models by making the ferrule part of the rod blank; this has made storage and transportation of rods much easier for surf anglers.

Although this is the conventional medium-weight tackle for surf fishing, some situations require slightly different approaches. For example, anglers who fish for snook in the surf in some parts of their range may use 7- to 9-foot rods equipped with medium-weight baitcasting reels and spooled with 12- to 17-pound line. To the hard-core surfcaster, this is a lightweight rig, one that would not do for heaving heavy weights with bait; but these anglers are more concerned with getting some distance on their casts to get lures out into the proper depth of water and portion of the surf, as well as having some leverage for playing fish. They may use the same tackle inland or inshore for non–surf fishing activities. So surf tackle is relative to the situation, and some situations may dictate still lighter tackle yet.

In addition to the standard medium-action outfit, most surf anglers will also have at least one smaller setup. This will be used, for example, when working a slough for small bottom feeders or when tossing light lures for trout, blues, and drum.

A 7-foot rod matched to a reel holding 10- to 15-pound line will handle bottom fishing and will cast all but the smallest lures. Speckled trout anglers and anglers fishing for small stripers often toss small jigs or lightweight plugs, and they will step down to much lighter rods and reels using 6- to 8-pound line. These smaller outfits are also utilized by pompano anglers who cast light weights and small baits just beyond the surf line.

The choice between a spinning or conventional reel for medium or light surf gear is primarily decided by personal preference and experience. Many anglers like the ease of operation provided by a spinning reel, whereas others feel they have more control with the revolving spool on a conventional reel *(see: baitcasting tackle; conventional tackle; spinning tackle)*. In the hands of a good caster, the modern conventional reel works well and offers less line-twisting trouble.

Nylon monofilament remains the line of choice for the vast majority of surf fishing situations. Braided and fused multifilament lines with a thin diameter aid casting and reel capacity, but their low abrasion resistance can cause problems in the tough conditions of surf fishing.

Shock leaders. Shock leaders are required in most surf fishing situations. A shock leader absorbs the wear on the line created by constant casting with heavy weights or lures. It should be long enough to wrap two or three times around the spool while the lure or bait rig hangs close to the first guide up from the reel. This heavy leader also comes in handy when trying to pull a big fish in through the breakers. As a general rule the shock leader should be twice as heavy as the running line. Use a Blood Knot for tying a 50- to 80-pound leader to 20- or 30-pound fishing line, and an Albright Knot for a heavier leader *(see: knots, fishing)*. The knot is the weak link in the entire rig, so it must be properly tied, trimmed off as closely as possible, and regularly checked for wear.

Accessories

Surf fishing can be a very simple sport requiring only rod, reel, line, hook, sinker, and bait. But surf anglers, like most other anglers, are drawn to accessories; some may be as simple as a canvas bag to carry spare tackle or as elaborate as a four-wheel-drive truck with a fully equipped slide-in camper.

One thing that most dedicated surf anglers agree on is that it is false economy to go fishing with only one rig or lure. Even the most experienced surf caster will snap off the occasional rig, and it may take only one nasty bluefish to render that lure inoperable. You need to be prepared.

Transporting gear. Since you need more than just one easily carried outfit, the problem becomes transporting extra gear from the point of departure to the surf line. Certainly the most convenient and comfortable method of conveyance is a four-wheel-drive vehicle, but many beaches are closed to vehicles and many surf anglers are not willing to devote a considerable amount of capital to the sport. Enter the 5-gallon bucket. A surf angler can pack everything needed for a day at the beach in a 5-gallon spackle bucket, which is readily available at many construction sites.

Clean the bucket and modify it as necessary. Holes drilled around the lip will serve as places to store lures and will prevent horrible tangles on the bottom of the bucket. An old bicycle tire stretched around the outside will keep exposed hooks from finding waders or body parts. Small tackle boxes filled with hooks, snaps, and various hardware can be placed inside, along with bait, bait knife, cutting board, sand spikes, and something to eat and drink. Expeditions of more than a few hours require a small cooler to keep bait fresh, and this means more to carry; if you're planning to keep some of your catch, consider that you will be more burdened on the return trip.

Although most surf anglers set up shop and stay in one place, others prefer to walk the beach, fishing as they go. These anglers must travel light but still have the tackle they need. A surf bag made from canvas or nylon, carried on a shoulder strap or wader belt, becomes the tackle box. The interior of the bag is divided into compartments that hold lures or rigs, and the outside has small pockets that separate the snaps, swivels, and leaders.

A surf cart is a device that makes life much easier for the walk-on angler. Carts are made from a variety of materials including wood, plastic, and aluminum. Style and design reflect the builder's personal choice and encompass everything from a flat piece of plywood to an elaborate cart complete with rod holders and tackle drawers. Some manufactured carts use low-pressure balloon tires for wheels, similar to those used for beach wheelchairs, with rod holders along the sides and enough storage to accommodate an extended stay.

At the optimum end of the transportation scene is the convenience offered by a four-wheel-drive vehicle, traditionally called a beach buggy by surf fishing enthusiasts. Many people who live near the beach or who fish the surf regularly have four-wheel-drive trucks or sport utilities that they use for getting to a parking place close to the fishing spot; in a few cases, it is possible to actually drive onto the beach, but this is now becoming less of an option. Naturally, such transportation is expensive, especially when the vehicle is new and deluxe. Used four-wheel-drives can be found, but careful inspection is needed to weed out the ones that have led a rough life.

These vehicles are usually outfitted to varying degrees to facilitate hauling tackle and accessories.

Accessories for surf fishing are very popular in places where vehicles can access the beach; this is a scene from Montauk, New York.

Most beach buggy owners will add a rod-holding rack on the front to store rods, with reels on them, in a vertical position; a front cooler rack can hold waders, rods, sand spikes, buckets, and other items.

The interior of some beach buggies can be customized with tackle lockers, coolers, rod holders, stoves, bunks, portable toilets, and any number of other accessories to make life and fishing more convenient while on the beach.

It would be nice to have a vehicle just for surf fishing, but most anglers must use their beach-access vehicle for everyday driving as well, so the surf fishing accessories should be removable when not in use.

Waders and wet suits. Fishing the surf without getting into the water is almost impossible. In areas where the weather and the water are warm, anglers may wade in shorts or a bathing suit. Northern climates require more protection from the elements, except during midsummer.

A set of good-quality chest waders (see) is the best protection from cold water. Some are made from rubber, and the newer models are constructed from neoprene and are preferred by many surf anglers. Inexpensive and poor-quality waders will not hold up under the constant abuse delivered by pounding waves and abrasive sand, so it's smart to get a good pair from the start.

Chest waders must be worn with a tightened belt to seal off the top in case the angler takes a tumble in the surf. Without this protection, the waders can fill up, pulling the angler under the water. As an added precaution, and for additional protection against rain and surf spray, a foul weather jacket is worn over the waders and is also belted at the waist.

A few surf anglers in certain places are not satisfied with casting from shore and feel compelled to swim to an offshore rock or sandbar in an effort to reach fish feeding beyond the range of shore-bound casters. These anglers are in the water for long periods of time and require the protection of a wet suit. They may find themselves exposed to stinging jellyfish, curious and possibly hungry sharks, and strong currents. Their rods and reels are designed to operate under water. Most use spinning reels with holes drilled in the back plates so that the water pressure doesn't pop off the spools. The rods are graphite to save weight, and other tackle is kept to a waterproof minimum. Obviously this activity is not for the average person and doesn't appeal to everyone, but in certain locations it can be the means to success.

Footwear. When fishing warmwater areas where waders and wet suits are not required, the surf caster should always have some type of footwear protection. "Wet shoes" (shoes made to be worn in water), an old pair of canvas deck shoes, or even a pair of high-sided rubber boots will work. It's important to protect your feet from the many sharp objects found in the sand. A cut on the bottom of the foot may end a day at the beach, and a severe cut may be an inconvenience for many days to come.

In many areas, jellyfish are common in the surf, and they will make it very uncomfortable for the unprotected wading angler. A pair of long pants provides some protection, but stings may still occur. Meat tenderizer, incidentally, is the best remedy for jellyfish stings. Rub a liberal amount of tenderizer on the injured area to relieve the pain.

Many surf anglers not only fish from the beach proper, but also walk the beach and stop to fish from jetties (see). Because jetties are wet and often moss-coated, they are slippery, and firm-gripping soles are a must. Standard rubber soles and felt soles will not suffice unless the jetty is dry. Many jetty anglers use manufactured creepers, which are devices that strap on over other footwear (they must be sized accordingly) and have spikes on the soles for gripping. The creepers can be slipped over canvas boat shoes in warm climates or over waders in cold areas. A more expensive solution is a pair of creepers custom-made from stainless steel or aluminum. On the less expensive but temporary side, a pair of discarded golf shoes will work; however, they soon fall apart under the ravages of saltwater, sand, and rocks.

Sand spikes. Sand spikes are devices employed by surf anglers to hold their rods while baiting up or changing rigs. They also hold the rod as the angler waits for a fish to take the bait. Most sand spikes are made from plastic pipe, but a few are constructed from aluminum tubing. Aluminum sand spikes are custom-made by shops that specialize in cooler racks and other accessories for surf fishing vehicles.

Plastic sand spikes may be 3 to 5 feet long and made from heavy PVC pipe or very light plastic tubes. A 3-footer is well suited for the walk-on angler because of its light weight. Longer and heavier sand spikes made from schedule 40 PVC are used when the surf is high. They may be hand carried, but the extra weight and length make this a burden.

Other gear. For the angler who is wading in the surf or standing on a jetty, landing a big fish can be difficult, and a gaff (see) is often indispensable. Beach anglers can use a short-handled or release gaff placed under the fish's lower jaw, but jetty jockeys need a longer tool and placement is not always as accurate. Jetty gaffs are normally custom-made from 5- to 6-foot rod blanks. The gaff is epoxied into the small end, and the butt is wrapped with cork tape. A bungee strap is used to hold the gaff across the angler's back until needed.

Many surf anglers patrol the beach at night, which is sometimes a delicate and dangerous job, complicated by the fact that any light shown on the water will probably spook the fish. Most after-dark surf anglers carry a small flashlight with a narrow beam that is usually held in the mouth when a light is needed to tie on new rigs or untangle lines. A miner's light worn around the head is another option.

Several tools should be a part of every surf angler's kit; the most important tool is a pair of high-quality fishing pliers. These are invaluable for cutting line and leader, removing hooks, crimping wire leader sleeves, and many other uses. A multipurpose tool is equally valuable for a variety of purposes, many of which cannot be anticipated. A knife for cutting bait or cleaning and filleting fish is also necessary.

Like all other anglers, those plying the surf should have raingear (at least a jacket for rain, surf spray, and wind), polarized sunglasses, a long-billed hat, sunscreen, and possibly insect repellent.

Bait

In most surf fishing situations, bait will outproduce artificial lures, but there is more to bait fishing than simply tossing a hunk of meat into the ocean. The angler who presents the proper bait in a natural manner will consistently bring fish to the beach. An effective presentation requires consideration of both the proper bait to use and the way to use it, as well as the bait rigs.

Bait rigs. A typical surf bait rig consists of a hook and sinker held together by a section of monofilament leader material. For big fish, such as trophy-size red drum or striped bass, you need 50- to 100-pound leaders. Small bottom fish, however, can be taken on leaders as light as 10 pounds.

Rigs can be purchased in local tackle shops, and these shops usually stock all the various types of rigs popular in the area. Tackle shops also carry the locally favored baits. When fishing an unfamiliar area, you should begin by purchasing local rigs to match whatever has been catching fish in that location even if you prefer to make up your own rig, as many surf anglers do.

Effective bait rigs do vary from one location to another, but most fall into one of three categories: top/bottom, single hook, and fishfinder.

Top/Bottom Rig

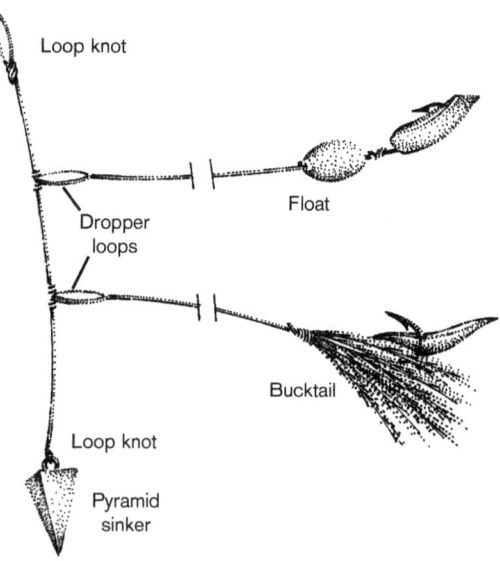

The top/bottom rig, which is primarily used for small bottom fish, features a sinker and two hooks, spaced 5 to 12 inches apart, decorated with beads, spinner blades, bucktail hair, soft grubs, floats, or any other device that you believe will attract fish. Some species, such as pompano, prefer to take their bait from a plain hook.

In most applications, the drop from the leader to the hook will be quite short. Long leaders will foul when they're cast or as they're tossed about in the surf. Short leaders keep the hook close to the line for a better hookset. A top/bottom rig made from wire with 3- to 4-inch standoffs is popular in a few areas. Snelled hooks are looped over the ends of the standoffs.

Single-hook rigs are used when bigger fish are sought. Leaders may be 12 inches or longer and are made from heavy nylon monofilament or braided wire; the latter is reserved for such toothy critters as big bluefish, and the monofilament is used in all other cases.

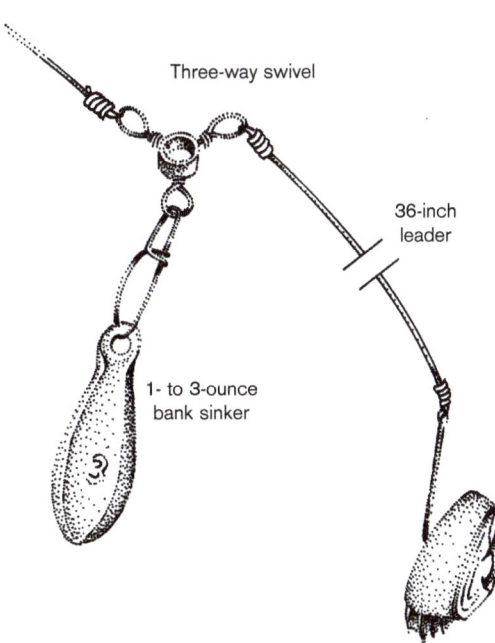

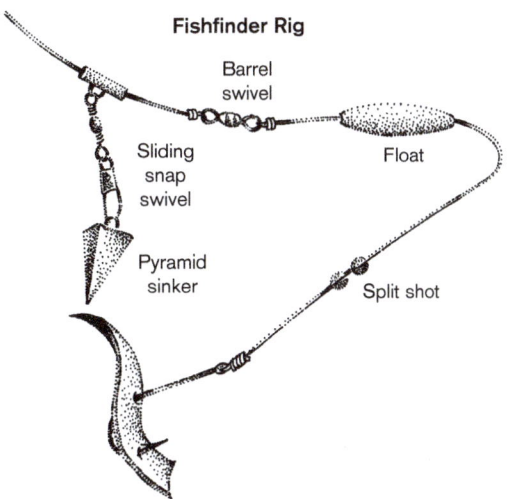

Known as a fishfinder rig, this is a basic setup for surf fishing.

The heart of the single-hook rig is a three-way swivel. The leader is attached to one eye, a sinker snap to the second eye, and the running line to the third eye. In most cases, the hook is left undecorated, but a large cork float, known as a fireball, may be added when sight feeders are the target.

A fishfinder rig is a single-hook rig that moves along the line. The running line or shock leader is threaded through a sleeve, usually made from plastic, and then tied to a large swivel. The leader is tied to the other end of the swivel. A sinker snap is attached to the plastic sleeve to secure the sinker, which will rest on the bottom. When a fish picks up the bait, it can move away without feeling the weight of the sinker. This is important when using live baits or when the target species needs a bit of time to get the bait well into its mouth.

The length of the leader on a fishfinder rig is a matter of some disagreement among anglers. A long leader, up to 36 inches, is favored by some, but it is very difficult to cast. Short leaders of 12 inches or less are easier to cast but provide little protection to the running line or shock leader. One variation is to put the plastic sleeve on the leader; this restricts the amount of line a fish can take but allows the sinker to slide down within 6 inches of the hook when casting.

Surf anglers seek all types and sizes of fish and utilize all types and sizes of hooks. The Chestertown is popular for small bottom feeders; the wide-gap Siwash works well on larger fish such as trout or flounder; and the offset Beak is often used for big drum or striped bass. In recent years, the Tuna Circle hook has gained popularity as catch-and-release *(see)* fishing has become more common. The Tuna Circle usually hooks a fish in the corner of the mouth, causing little if any injury to the victim. It is easy to remove once the fish is landed but has excellent holding power while the fish is being played.

Sinkers are needed to anchor each of these rigs to the bottom. They basically are found in pyramid and bank styles, with the former more common along the beach. A pyramid sinker has four angled sides that meet in a point. The eye is on the flat base, causing the sinker to dig into the sand and hold the rig. A bank sinker is shaped like a teardrop and will not dig into the sand or hold a rig in one location. It is used when the angler wants the bait to move across the bottom as the angler slowly cranks the rig back to the beach.

Various modifications have been made by anglers in an effort to build a better sinker for surf fishing. The Hurricane sinker is a pyramid with rounded sides that is supposed to cast well into a wind. A bank sinker with stiff wires molded into the end has less wind resistance than a pyramid. The wires turn over and dig into the bottom to hold better than the standard bank sinker.

Modifications are common not only on sinkers but on every aspect of surf fishing tackle. Surf anglers are an inventive lot. Many make their own rigs, build their own rods, and pour their own sinkers. Some create new products, but very few of these inventions make their creators rich.

Surf bait basics. The most important consideration when using bait is its condition. Fresh bait is vital to success and must be selected with the same care used to buy fish for the table. Look at the gills of prospective baitfish; they should be red, and the eyes should be clear, not pink. The flesh should not be soft, and the fish should have a clean smell. Frozen fish will work as bait, but fresh (unfrozen) is preferable. Frozen shrimp and crabs are useless. Frozen squid, however, seems to work as well as the fresh product.

Buying good bait is the first step, but it must be properly stored to keep it in prime condition. A cooler should be dedicated just for bait and set up to keep bait and ice separated. Most bait will lose color and turn to mush when submerged in ice water. Plastic containers that seal out air and water are excellent for keeping bait in a cooler. They also separate the different types of bait you might use, making it convenient to find what you want in the bottom of a crowded cooler.

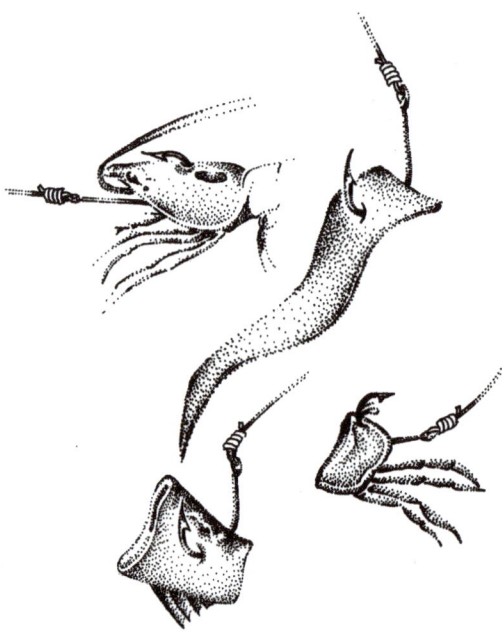

Shrimp, strips of fish or squid, crabs, and chunks of fish are among the top baits for surf fishing.

All efforts to keep bait fresh will be wasted if it is cut up and left out for sea gulls, flies, and hot sun to spoil. Cut the bait into whatever size is appropriate, take what you need to put on the hook, and return the rest to the cooler.

Fish used for bait in surf angling come in all shapes and sizes. In most cases, fish will be cut into pieces, but small specimens such as finger mullet may be used whole. Depending on the target species, fish bait is cut into fillets or chunks. Chunks are used when you need a tougher bait for long casts or bigger fish. Fillets are used when you want a thin bait that will move in current. Fillets may be whole or cut into strips. Strip baits are effective when trying to imitate small thin baitfish, whereas whole fillets imitate larger species.

Fish baits should be cut with care. Try to make strips wide at the hook end tapering down to a point. Fillets should be cut to the shape of a fish; a sharp knife will split the tail for a very lifelike presentation. Chunks should be cut from the back of the head to the tail. The size of the target species determines the size of the chunk. For some reason, many anglers discard the head and tail, forgetting that fish eat the whole thing. In all cases it's a good idea to remove the scales from fish bait; this is easy to do and makes hook insertion much easier.

Baits should be hooked through the thickest part, chunks through the back, fillets and strip baits through the wide end. Put the hook all the way through the bait, and leave the point exposed. It is hard enough to drive a hook into the fish's mouth; you don't want to be driving it through the bait as well.

Squid is cut into strips or small pieces. The strips work well when small, thin baitfish are in the surf. Pieces are just right for bottom feeders that prey on small invertebrates. The head of a squid makes an excellent bait for larger gamefish, and the tentacles can be threaded onto a Chestertown hook in place of a worm.

Sea worms are great baits for a surprising number of fish. Striped bass and weakfish are very fond of worms, especially in the spring. Sea mullet and spot will take a worm in place of anything else. Whole worms are hooked through the head or tail and allowed to stream out in the current. At times you may need several worms on the same hook to attract attention. Worms cut into bite-size pieces and threaded onto the hook are the ticket for bottom feeders who suck the bait into their mouths. A bit of worm left dangling from the end of the hook will add some moving enticement to the bait.

Fresh shrimp may be fished whole or cut into small pieces. They are very expensive bait and are saved for situations where only shrimp are effective. Pompano and speckled trout do show a definite preference for shrimp, but both will often take less-expensive offerings.

Crabs come in two stages: hard and peeler. A hard crab has a hard outer shell; a peeler crab has a soft shell under a hard outer shell. A peeler, which is also called a shedder, is getting ready to shed the outer shell and emerge as a soft-shelled crab. The soft shell variety is defenseless and is easy prey for all types of eager predators.

When fishing with either type of crab, remove the hard outer shell and cut the crab into sections with a pair of heavy-duty shears. Place the hook through a leg hole, not through the shell. Crabs do not stay on the hook very well and are often secured with rubber bands or dental floss.

Red drum are very fond of peeler crabs, especially in the spring when crabs are shedding. Unfortunately, every other fish in the ocean shares this craving for peeler crabs, and baits do not last long in the water.

Peelers can be expensive bait. Try to get the largest peelers you can, and cut them into as many pieces as possible. Trout will take a single section, but red drum require at least a quarter of a crab to attract their attention. A small piece of peeler on a bucktail will give the appearance of a larger bait.

Hard crab is a poor substitute when fish are feeding on peelers. The two baits evidently smell and taste different because fish can certainly tell them apart. Hard crabs become more acceptable later in the season when peelers are scarce. Cut hard crabs in small sections for big fall-run spot and croaker, and use half of a crab for drum and striped bass.

Live bait is used by surf anglers, but it does require a special container to keep the bait alive. Carrying a large container full of water and bait is not practical for a walk-on angler. A four-wheel-drive vehicle is needed to move a heavy livewell and provide the power to aerate it.

A large cooler can be converted into a portable livewell (see) or bait tank. A 30- to 50-quart cooler will suffice, but some anglers use a big 120-quart cooler. Obviously the larger the cooler, the more baitfish it will support, but a 120-quart cooler full of water weighs about 240 pounds and requires a big pump to keep it properly aerated.

A 50-quart cooler and a bilge pump that moves 800 gallons per hour will keep three or four dozen baits alive all day. Mount the pump in the bottom of the cooler, and run a hose up to a piece of PVC pipe hanging just below the hinge. The pipe should be between 18 and 24 inches long with $1/2$-inch holes drilled at 1-inch intervals. A cap seals one end with a 90-degree elbow on the other end. The hose from the pump attaches to this elbow.

The pump and the pipe can be permanently attached to the cooler with clamps and screws, although this will make it difficult to use the cooler for anything but a live bait tank. If the pipe hangs down from the hinges on heavy monofilament and the pump just sits on the bottom, the whole rig can be removed when not in use.

Live baitfish are deployed with a fishfinder rig. When live bait is taken, the fish will swim off while turning the bait around to swallow it head first. This procedure takes a few seconds, and the fish may drop the bait if it feels the weight of the sinker. Exactly how much time you should allow for the fish to have the bait before you take up the slack and set the hook depends on the size of the bait, the species of fish, and your own judgment, keeping in mind that a longer wait usually means a more deeply hooked fish, which is more difficult to release unharmed.

Fish used as bait are best hooked through the lips or eye sockets. This allows them to swim in a somewhat natural manner while anchored to the bottom or while being slowly retrieved. Eels are also fished alive but require different treatment and handling. Store eels in a small cooler with a mixture of ice and water. By keeping the eels as cold as possible, they will be much easier to handle when the time comes to put them on a hook. A damp rag will allow the eel to be handled without getting slime on the angler and the tackle.

Hook the eel through the lips or the eyes. Use a single-hook rig with a 3-foot leader tied to a drail heavy enough to cast the bait beyond the breakers. A slow retrieve back to the beach keeps the eel moving and prevents a seriously tangled leader. Eels that are cast out and allowed to sit on the bottom will get into all sorts of curled and line-wrapped mischief.

Salted eels are fished with a swimming lip. Although technically they are dead baits, rigged eels are worked like a lure. Cast them out and retrieve them so that they swim just above the bottom. A rigged eel is deadly on striped bass, especially at night or on overcast days.

An angler prepares a bait rig for surf fishing off of a Virginia barrier beach.

In most coastal areas, there is a favorite bait and favorite way of fishing it. If you are a traveling angler, check with local tackle shops and follow local guidance until you find something that works better.

Sitting versus fishing. Most surf anglers leave their rods in a sand spike while their bait soaks somewhere offshore. Spiking the rod and soaking bait allows the angler to enjoy the social side of surf fishing while still catching the occasional fish. In some cases, you want the bait to stay in one place, such as at the edge of a bar when you're waiting for a big drum to pass by. Nearly all surf anglers in drum country, while sitting in a beach chair with rod securely spiked and a cooler of refreshment nearby, will assure you that they really are drum fishing. But if you want to catch more than the occasional fish, you need to work at it. Get your rod out of the sand spike, and tend to business by replacing old bait with fresh bait, repositioning the bait, and covering various areas of the surf.

Certain situations clearly dictate a more active approach to surf angling than the chair and cooler method. Flounder, for instance, prefer a moving target, so you must keep the bait moving over the bottom. Several fish species cruise the inshore side of an outer bar looking for food washed over by the wave action. The best way to capitalize on this is to cast a bait onto the bar and allow it to wash down the dropoff. It takes some practice to reel in just enough line to keep in touch with the rig while letting it drop in a natural manner. You don't do this once and then stop; you keep trying.

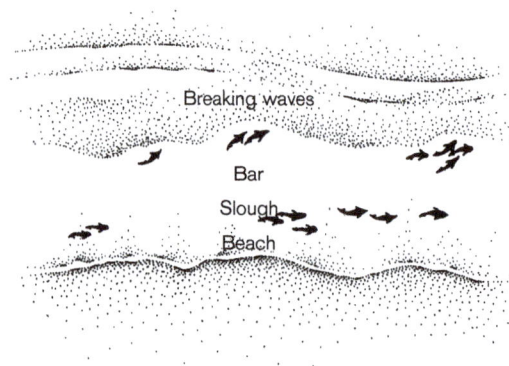

Where there is an outer bar that receives breaking waves, fish hold close to the inner side of the bar and also lurk in the deeper water of the slough.

Using very light tackle and small rigs for pompano requires similar techniques. The small sinker will not hold bottom and will be swept along the beach. You must watch the angle of your line, moving it inshore while the current takes it parallel to the shore. The strike will come just beyond the breaker or in the white water after the wave breaks. Once the rig has passed these spots without notice, slowly reel in and try again.

Lures

The successful surf angler will choose the appropriate bait or lure to match current conditions. Although fishing with bait is generally preferred in the surf, lures are used in many locations on a wide variety of fish, and at certain times they will outproduce live or dead baits. Certain species, like Spanish mackerel, for example, are seldom taken on bait but will hit a well-placed metal lure. When bluefish are blitzing the beach, a surf bait will work, but a big surface popper provides more exciting action.

Three basic types of lures are used in the surf: metal lures, plugs, and leadhead jigs. Each has a specific use, but most fish will take all three under varying conditions.

Metal lures. Because surf angling requires casting a good distance and letting a sinking lure settle into and work through roiling water, surf anglers often prefer a thick-bodied metal lure. Metal lures for taking fish from the surf began with the heavy-bodied and so-called tin squids (see) that were hand-cast on tarred line coiled at the angler's feet. Now metal lures are made from lead or stainless steel and are tossed by rods and reels. These are straight, heavy-bodied products that are primarily used for casting.

There are several well-known brands of stainless steel models that cast like a bullet and work with either a fast or a slow retrieve. Thin and thick versions are used when you're matching thin or fat baitfish, respectively. Lead models also come in various sizes, with smaller ones working on Spanish mackerel and small bluefish, and larger ones on trout and striped bass.

Smaller metal lures are cast to breaking fish and retrieved rather quickly. The strike often comes as soon as the lure hits the water, so the reel must be engaged upon impact. If the fish fails to make contact immediately, you must crank the lure quickly to keep it working close to the surface. At times a slight pause to let the lure drop a bit may induce a strike. Larger, heavier lures are fished along the bottom with a hopping, jigging action to imitate a sand eel. Sometimes it's good to let lure sink into the sand and then jerk it out by quickly raising the rod tip.

Spoons are sometimes also used in the surf, but their wide surface area and generally light weight make them less aerodynamic and more difficult to cast. Under favorable conditions, the heavier, thicker metal spoons can be employed as is. Lightweight spoons can be effective when accompanied by a drail, which is tied 12 to 18 inches above the spoon to add the weight necessary to cast beyond the breakers. Allow the rig to sink; then use a moderate retrieve to keep the spoon just above the bottom. Trout, stripers, drum, and other bottom feeders may find this technique irresistible.

A few manufacturers still produce lures made from tin, and more may do so if regulations prohibit lead lures. Tin is more expensive than other metals, but it does have a special glow when polished in the wet sand.

Plugs. Saltwater surf plugs had their roots in freshwater and really got started in the 1940s with models that were introduced and used successfully for stripers on Cape Cod. Then, as now, a surf fishing plug must be heavy enough and have the proper shape to cast well, plus have a slow to moderate swimming action. Most surf plugs are shallow-swimming models; deep divers have little merit in the shallow intertidal zone of the surf.

Swimming plugs for surf use come in various styles. The most popular plugs have a slow side-to-side action and can be worked in different sea conditions. Darting versions have a long, angled face and will swim in a wide side-to-side motion. They can be very effective in a rip at the mouth of an inlet or at the end of a point or bar. Cast the plug upcurrent, and allow it to sweep past with little or no retrieve. The force of the current will cause the plug to work.

The breaking waves and cross currents will contribute to the action of most swimming lures, and you must adjust the retrieve to compensate for these factors. Plugs should be cast just beyond a wave that is about to break. As the wave rolls toward the beach, the plug is retrieved at the proper speed to keep it working in the whitewater but ahead of the next wave that would tumble it head over tail. The plug should give the impression of a baitfish caught up in, or struggling against, the waves and thus be easy prey.

An exception to this retrieval tactic are needlefishlike plugs that are long and thin and without inherent action. These are slowly retrieved without any movement of the rod tip so that they come through the water in a straight line. These plugs are basically like a stick with hooks, but they have accounted for many big stripers. Some other straight-running plugs are used in the surf with a bit of rod-tip movement.

Surf anglers can also double-up when using a plug by placing a second lure on a dropper line ahead of the plug. This second lure may be a small fly, a soft grub, or a small bucktail jig, each of which acts like a baitfish trying to avoid a predator (the plug). Quite often a strike will come on the dropper lure.

Cross currents or rips at the end of points leave eddies of slower-moving water where gamefish wait for bait to tumble past. A plug cast up and across the current will sweep by this eddy and may attract a strike. Slow-swimming lures that will work with little more than the pressure of the current are particularly effective in these rips. Plugs worked in the roiled surf along jetties, causeways, and pilings are also likely to bring strikes, since the flash of these lures where waves wash up and roil can be an attractant.

Occasionally a surface plug has merit in the surf, although this is usually when a school of gamefish has pinned a school of bait against the beach or is chasing bait to the surface. At such times, almost any lure that will reach the fracas will be effective, but a surface lure that pops, chugs, and spits water is most exciting to fish.

Not all surf fishing occurs along open beach, as this scene at an old gun-mount structure in Cape May, New Jersey, attests.

Many topwater surf plugs are weighted for long casts but sit very low once they are in the water. A constant, fast retrieve is needed to keep them working on the surface. Plugs that float high can be retrieved slowly; allow them to rest a bit between pops. This style of plug can be effective at night on calm waters.

The pencil-style popper has a unique design and action. Weighted at the stern, it rides in the water with the top pointed up and the rear pointed down. Work the popper with a slow retrieve combined with a fast and furious action from the rod tip. This is best accomplished with the rod butt placed between your legs while you work the tip with your hand placed above the reel. This position is rather awkward looking but very effective when you want the plug to jump up and down in one place like an injured baitfish.

Leadhead jigs. The most versatile weapon in the surf angler's arsenal is the leadhead jig, known to many simply as a leadhead. Dressed with bucktail hair, a soft-bait tail, or a strip of bait, this lure will imitate the food of most gamefish.

Leadheads come in a variety of head shapes, with the rounded, bullet, and Upperman styles very popular with surf casters. A surf jig must cast well and sink fast, and these particular shapes have low resistance to both air and water.

Larger jigs are usually shaped like a bullet and may be adorned with glass eyes or a smiling face. A few leadheads are shaped to impart a swimming action. The lip used ahead of a rubber or plastic eel is an example of this style of leadhead. The boxing glove style makes the jig wobble slowly from side to side as it falls through the water column. Most strikes occur when a jig is dropping, so this style can attract more fish. It does have a higher wind resistance than most jig heads but can still be effective when worked along the beach on a still, warm summer evening. Turbulent waters in the surf make it difficult to maintain control of a jig. Light line will aid in both casting distance and control, with the jig tied directly to the main line without benefit of leader or hardware.

Bucktail jigs will catch just about anything that swims in the ocean at one time or another, and they are the preferred surf jig. The hollow deer hair of a bucktail adds buoyancy and a breathing action unlike any other lure. Worked with a jigging motion that allows the bucktail to rise and fall, the hair will compress and expand, imparting a lifelike action.

Select the size and color of the bucktail to match the size and color of local baitfish. Also consider contrast. A dark lure works better against a light background like sand, and a light color stands out more against a dark background like rocks. A bucktail with white hair and a red head is a popular all-around pattern.

Tie a bucktail directly to the line or leader with an Improved Clinch or Loop Knot. The Improved Clinch keeps the jig working in a vertical direction, and a loop allows it to swing from side to side. Bucktails can be worked fast, slow, shallow, and deep. A fast retrieve just below the surface can be deadly on Spanish mackerel or bluefish. Working it slowly along the bottom is good for speckled trout, flounder, or striped bass.

Threading a soft-tail bait onto the hook shank makes a leadhead jig even more versatile. Large soft-tail leadheads are deadly on drum, striped bass, and flounder. Smaller versions are used for speckled trout, puppy drum, and a wide variety of other small bottom feeders. Some have a curled tail and a swimming action; others impart little motion or only a small wag. The speed of retrieve is generally slower for soft-tailed jigs. A straight retrieve works best on swimming models, whereas a hop-and-skip action can make the straight runners come alive. Tying two jigs 8 to 10 inches apart improves casting distance and may make the lure more appealing.

In all cases, a jig should be worked all the way through the surf line. Gamefish may follow a jig to the water's edge before deciding to eat, so an early end to the retrieve may take the bait out of the water too soon.

Sweetening a jig with some sort of natural bait is a common practice along the surf. Tough baits such as squid or shark belly hold up well and may be added to a naked jig or one dressed with bucktail hair or a soft tail. Pork rind can add life to any leadhead; the long, thin strips imitate such natural food as spearing, and they are deadly on flounder and trout. They also work for bluefish and hold up against their sharp teeth. White seems to be the favorite and most productive color in the surf, but pork rind is available in many hues.

The prudent angler will carry a selection of leadhead jigs in a wide variety of colors. The same is true of soft tails. Surf fish can be finicky, and the angler who can present the lure *du jour* will look like an expert angler.

Casting

Obviously, surf fishing is dependent on casting to get the bait or lure into the strike zone. The angler who can cast the farthest will often, but not always, catch the most fish. However, this is all relative. Casting far does not usually mean launching a lure or bait more than 150 feet. This distance may seem extreme to some anglers, particularly those used to fishing in freshwater, but it is not that far by saltwater standards, and some anglers are able to cast several times that distance at the beach. Fortunately, most fish feed close to the beach, and a super long heave is not required. A simple overhead cast will put the bait in the strike zone most of the time. Try to place such a cast just beyond the breakers or just inside the outer bar.

Proper tackle selection goes a long way toward making a good surf cast, especially one of moderate to long distances. A graphite rod combined with a conventional reel is a good beginning. Using the lightest line practical, in combination with a shock leader tied with a low-friction knot, also aids distance. Although thick-bodied metal lures and weighted surface plugs produce long casts, they may not always produce fish. Sometimes only a big hunk of cut bait will catch a fish. The problem with casting a heavy sinker and a big hunk of bait is trying to move two different objects in the same direction at the same time. The sinker sits at the very end of the line and by itself would be easy to cast. Add a second weight that has completely different aerodynamic properties and is dangling from a leader offset from the main line, and you encounter a problem.

Technique. To begin the most basic cast, start with the bait and sinker lying on the beach behind you. While facing the ocean, point the tip of the rod directly at the rig, take out all line slack, and then bring the rod tip up sharply over your head, stopping at an imaginary 10 o'clock position as you release the line. Many beginners have a problem releasing the line at the proper time. Releasing it too early will cause the rig to fall behind you; releasing too late will cause it to fall short and the line may cut your finger. Practice will overcome this problem.

Small rigs with one or two hooks are much easier to cast. Some rigs currently on the market have a release system that holds the hook tight to the line but lets it swing free when the rig hits the water. This produces an aerodynamic packet that should go farther toward the horizon.

For extreme distances, you might try the pendulum cast, which was introduced to American surf anglers by John Holden in the 1970s. This technique is a bit complicated and involves swinging a single weight around, behind, and over your head to load the rod with the maximum amount of energy. Long-distance casters can exceed 700 feet in competition, using special equipment and this technique. Beach casters may top 600 feet with outfits capable of bringing in a fish. To practice this cast, you will need a very long practice field with plenty of room on all sides because a breakoff will often travel to the right or left of the caster.

A modified version of the pendulum cast will do the job in most fishing situations. Hold the rod over your shoulder, and let the rig swing just above the ground. Push the rod back until the rig swings straight out, loading the rod. Come around in a side-arm fashion, and release the line when you feel maximum load. For more information, *see: Casting*.

Conventional reels permit longer casts than spinning reels because their revolving spools actually push the line off the reel, and there is less coiling and friction from the departing line. If left uncontrolled, the line will overrun the spool and create a backlash *(see)*. Expert casters control the line with light thumb pressure on the spool; most people rely on counterweights or magnets to do this job, in some cases with a moderate amount of thumb pressure. These cast control mechanisms cut down on maximum casting distance, however, especially when dealing with such forces and distances as are required for surf fishing.

Remember that a longer rod does not always result in a longer cast. A 7- to 10-foot rod will work well up to 150 feet. An 11- to 13-foot rod will cast as far as anyone needs to go if it is well matched to the angler. Anything over 13 feet will only get in the way.

Be practical and safe. When trying to get a lure or bait into distant water, you do not need to start running from the base of the dunes to just short of the water's edge before making a cast. Forward body speed is not carried over to the cast. This is not javelin throwing. Stay in one spot and concentrate on making a good casting motion, using the rod to maximize leverage.

Also, it does little good to wade out up to your armpits, make a cast, lock the reel in gear, and drag your rig back to the beach. Leave the reel out of gear until you're back on dry land; then lock it down and crank out the slack.

Always look behind you before making a cast. Fellow anglers, children, bathers, and pets may stroll behind you, and they may take exception to being hooked or whacked with a bait or heavy sinker. You should also be mindful of your own safety. If waves are crashing over the jetty, for example, wait for the tide to subside so you don't take an unnecessary risk.

Picking a Spot

The surf line is a constantly changing mix of sand, mud, rock, or any combination of materials. Surf anglers must use experience and knowledge to pick a spot where the fish will be active during their time on the beach. Anglers working from boats not only have greater mobility, but also have electronic aids, which are of no value to surf casters. Most surf anglers are on foot and thus have limited mobility. While it is always possible that the inexperienced angler may stumble onto a fishing hotspot, those who study the surf and learn about tides and currents will know where to be and at what preferred

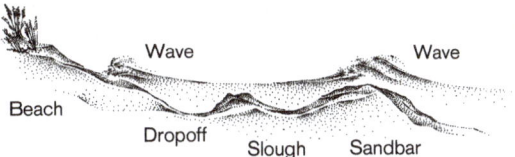

This cross-sectional view of the beach and surf helps to illustrate the features that impact on site selection and fish presence.

times, and will do better over the long haul.

Sand makes up most of the beaches where surf anglers congregate, and it moves about with the tides and currents. This movement creates bars, sloughs, washouts, runouts, holes, channels, and other formations that may combine some or all of the above. The surf angler must look at the surface of the water and figure out exactly what lies underneath, be aware of the present stage of the tide and current, and have some knowledge of what the existing or predicted winds will do to the waves. It is also helpful to know when the target species is likely to stop by for a meal. This sounds like finding a needle in a haystack, but it is not that complicated.

According to oceanographers, a wave will break when the water below it is twice as deep as the wave is high. In other words, a 1-foot wave will break in 2 feet of water. Thus, waves break in shallow water but hold together over deep water.

A natural beach allows the wave to break gradually, dissipating its energy over some distance. As the wave rolls in, it begins to break offshore on the outer bar, churning sand from the bottom and pushing it back to the bar. A smaller wave now rides across the deeper water of the slough before breaking onshore. As this wave breaks on the beach, it scours out a dropoff at the edge of the white water. This dropoff moves in and out with the tide, but the outer bar remains somewhat stationary.

The distance from where the surf caster stands to the outer bar can vary considerably. In some places the bar will come to the beach forming a point, but a little farther up or down the shoreline the bar will be a distance of at least two and a half casting lengths offshore.

Because of varying combinations of wind, tide, and current, deep holes form along the beach. Some may come and go on a single tide, and others stay around until the next big storm. Washouts, runouts, and breaks in the outer bar are channels created by currents moving back and forth on the tides. Not only are these channels deeper than the surrounding water, but they act as highways for fish and bait to move from offshore to inshore and back offshore.

Low tide is the best time to figure out what type of structure lies below the water. When the depth of the water is at its lowest point, the difference between shallow and deep water is apparent. Waves will be breaking on the shallow areas, some of which may be completely exposed. Deeper water will be calm and should appear blue or green rather than white.

An offshore wind will create problems as it pushes more water toward the beach and increases the size of the waves. Deeper water and higher waves can disguise bottom structure; if the wind increases to more than 15 knots, the entire ocean may turn white.

Winds blowing offshore have a different effect. They push water away from land, exposing structure not seen on normal low tides. These winds also push the warm surface water offshore and can drop surf temperatures by 10° to 15°F. This sudden temperature drop is seldom beneficial to surf fishing.

If you crest the top of the dune line at low tide, you can survey a considerable stretch of beach. Look for waves breaking on an offshore bar that is

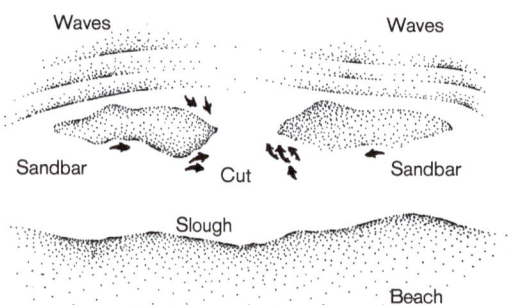

Although waves will break on sandbars, there will be no waves in the cut between the bars, and fish will be located as shown here.

close enough to be in casting range. A break in the bar or a place where the bar comes to the beach will funnel fish to you.

Set up a station close to the break or the point, and you will be in position for some action on the rising tide. Walk-on anglers will stay in one area, but those with four-wheel-drive vehicles can move about looking for the best action. Drive slowly and stop often to watch wave action and water color. Birds feeding close to shore are a positive sign, especially if big fish are observed breaking under the birds.

Watch not only the water, birds, and fish, but other anglers. When everyone is sitting in chairs or leaning on their vehicles talking, the action is pretty slow. A tight group of anglers standing at the water's edge, holding rods without a sand spike in sight, indicates that someone recently caught something. If most of the rods are bent, you've found a good place to fish, and you better get started.

Every beach is a separate entity. Some are similar but none are exactly the same. A rocky coast in Maine or California fishes completely different from a sandy beach in North Carolina. The only way to learn how to read the beach where you fish is experience. The more time you put in on the beach, the more knowledge you'll gain. For example, you should learn when stripers stage on the end of a certain bar, or when pompano move over an outer bar, or at what stage of the tide you can expect to find flounder in a particular slough. No matter how much you read or how many old salts you talk to, the only way to learn how to read the beach is to get out there and fish.

Night Fishing

Many fish species move into the surf at night to feed when they feel safer in the shallow water. Striped bass, weakfish, and red drum are among the fish that are taken regularly after dark.

Fishing the surf at night is similar to fishing in daylight but does require a few modifications. Avoid bright lights at all cost. Fish have very sensitive eyes, and the beam from a flashlight, headlights, or searchlight will send them to deeper, darker water. Never approach a fishing site with the headlights on or scan the water with a flashlight or searchlight. Should you violate this rule, those anglers who were catching fish before your arrival will do things to hasten your departure.

It's a good idea to arrive at the beach before dark to scout the waters and allow your eyes to adjust. Scouting out the situation in daylight will make the return trip easier and safer because you will have seen the territory earlier in the light. You should always be careful when wading in the surf but especially so after dark. An angler who is knocked down by a wave or who steps into a deep hole may go unnoticed until it is too late. A miner's light worn around the neck or on a hat helps surf anglers keep track of one another without shedding enough light on the water to spook the fish. The same light is also handy for close work when tying knots or unhooking fish.

Dress appropriately for night fishing because even the warmest summer day can turn into a chilly night on the beach. This is amplified when water temperatures are cold and the wind is blowing in.

Casting into a totally dark ocean using the sound of breaking waves as a guide takes a bit of getting used to. Any available moonlight helps, as do permanent shore lights. Fortunately, the tops of breaking waves are white and reflect even the smallest amount of available light.

Surf casters who work the night tides are a pretty dedicated bunch. Usually standoffish at first, they will come around when a newcomer demonstrates that he or she is capable and as dedicated as they are. Of course, it may take 15 to 20 years, but they will come around.

Playing/Landing Fish
Surf anglers face several obstacles when playing and landing fish. The quarry is quite a distance from the angler, which allows wind, tide, current and seaweed to play havoc with the fishing line. The long line gives a big fish plenty of room to swim up or down the beach, picking up the lines of neighboring anglers and creating quite a mess.

In almost every surf fishing situation, the angler will use heavy tackle and put as much pressure as possible on the fish. Heavy is relative, since 10-pound test may be fine for small fish in calm water but 50-pound may not be heavy enough for a big fish in heavy seas with crowded anglers.

It is seldom necessary to set the hook when fishing with bait. The fish hooks itself when it moves away with the bait and tries to pull the sinker out of the sand. Live or dead baits on fishfinder rigs are an exception, since the fish is allowed to run with the bait before the angler takes up all the slack and sets the hook.

Lures, of course, require some hooksetting, but they are generally fished on a shorter line than bait, and the angler will be aware of the strike. A quick upward sweep of the rod tip is enough to set the hook. Continued hooksetting is unnecessary and may pull the hook out of the fish.

Once hooked, the fish should be brought to the beach as quickly as possible. Keep the rod tip high, and crank in the line at a steady pace. If you crank too fast, the fish may come to the top, tumbling head over tail until the hook is free. A slow retrieve allows the fish too much time to figure out how to get away. Fish with a soft mouth do require a bit of finesse; a slow but steady retrieve will keep pressure on the hook and hold the fish on the line.

The real problem with landing a fish from the beach occurs at the surf line. Breaking waves tumble fish, which allows the line to go slack and gives the hook an opportunity to come out. Watch the waves and time your retrieve so that the fish rides the back of the wave without going over the top. The bigger the waves and the bigger the fish, the harder the job.

Once through the waves, the fish will be pulled back to sea by the undertow. Be careful not to exert much pressure on the fish, holding it in place until the undertow subsides. At this point, the prize should be lying on wet sand, waiting for you to pick it up.

Fish weighing up to 20 pounds can be landed with relative ease. Those over 20 are more difficult. Big fish are going to take line, but drag tension must be high. Fish usually run toward deeper water, but some will go up and down the beach instead of heading offshore. In either case, try to get as close to the water's edge as possible to shorten the distance between you and the fish.

Snook are sought in the frothy Caribbean surf of Costa Rica, where warm water makes wet wading practical.

Keep the rod tip as high as possible when the fish is taking line; then drop down and crank before lifting up again to gain line. Always apply maximum pressure to tire the fish as quickly as possible. The longer the fight, the better the odds the fish will win.

Using quality tackle and tying good knots is the most important aspect of landing a big fish in the surf. Cheap rods, reels with jerky drags, rusty hooks, and weak knots will work on small fish; but when that trophy of a lifetime is finally hooked, everything had better be first-rate.

For more information on this topic, *see: Playing Fish*.

Access and Responsibility
For the most part, coastal beaches are controlled by federal, state, and municipal governments, as well as by private individuals, organizations, and corporations. In most cases, you must have permission to access a particular portion of beach. Many government agencies have established access points for a good deal of oceanfront. Most charge a fee to use a four-wheel-drive vehicle, if that is allowed at all (a special permit is usually issued, and it may require the holder to have a pail, tow rope or chain, shovel, fishing rod, and other items in the vehicle while on the beach). A few beaches are free for walk-on anglers, but very few have free and unrestricted access to the ocean for beach buggies.

As coastal areas become more populated and increasingly utilized, fishing space becomes a rarer commodity. The fate of all beaches is susceptible to many influences, and anglers may find it increasingly difficult to gain access to beaches or to convince policymakers that they are entitled to recreate there as well. Some angling organizations and surf fishing clubs have been able to hold their ground, but pressure to ban access has grown and is likely to continue.

Surf anglers must be aware of this problem and do what they can to establish and maintain a good image and a good rapport with others. Exercising common sense is important. Always leaving the beach as clean as, or cleaner than, you found it, even if this involves cleaning up someone else's mess, is a good way to start. Dispose of unused or discarded bait properly. Take off cleats or creepers when walking on wooden boardwalks or access lanes. Do not cross a strip of private property without permission simply because it is the easy way to get to a desirable fishing spot. If someone is swimming or surfing right in the middle of your favorite fishing spot, leave it and come back later. Beach buggy owners must be particularly careful. Stay in designated areas, do not drive on or even near the dunes, and avoid nesting bird habitat, especially that of piping plovers. Don't take an unnecessary risk. If the sand looks a little soft, get out of the vehicle and walk across; if you sink, your beach buggy will go down to the axles, and it may put one more nail in the coffin of other vehicular users.

Fishing when less people are present will help avoid user conflicts. The best surf fishing is often at dawn, at dusk, at night, in poor weather, and in the fall, all of which are times when there are few others on the beach. Nevertheless, you shouldn't crowd in on another angler's spot, or put out more than two rods.

Surf anglers seldom make a significant dent in fish populations, but they must be mindful of the need to conserve. As is also true for other fishing, surf anglers must obey all regulations, keep only the fish they plan to eat, and never kill unwanted fish or leave them to die on the beach.

SURFACE LURE

An artificial lure that is strictly, or primarily, retrieved on the water's surface.

Surface lures, which are also known as topwater lures, are almost exclusively fished by casting and retrieving, and many require proper manipulation to be effective. As a category, surface lures are the most presumptuous of all lure types because they must draw fish to a place where they spend the least amount of their time—the surface. Thus, surface lures appeal to highly aggressive fish and to species that attack from hiding places or gang up on prey and "corner" them at the surface, but not to bottom-dwelling species, true deep-water denizens, and fish that don't hunt near the surface in packs.

Salmon, for example, though aggressive fish in open water, do not find any of their prey on the surface; likewise, walleyes prowl deep water, often near the bottom. However, largemouth bass, smallmouth bass, northern pike, and striped bass are freshwater species that sometimes feed on or close to the surface. In saltwater, species that maraud baitfish schools (like bluefish) and pin them near the surface, and those that use and feed near cover (like snook), are also candidates for surface fishing, while those that feed deep (like groupers) or mainly pick shrimp off the bottom (like bonefish), are not.

Without question, surface fishing is highly appealing to anglers. Ask trout anglers if they prefer to catch a fish on a dry fly or on a subsurface fly, and they will certainly vote for the former, even though the vast majority of trout feed and are caught beneath the surface. The extra visual stimulus to every kind of surface fishing is of exceptional entertainment value, and can be exciting no matter when or where it is experienced.

Because surface fishing requires aggressive fish behavior, it is more of a warmwater phenomenon than a coldwater one, which also restricts its suitability in many places (summertime for most species, especially in temperate climates). For some species—freshwater bass, for example—surface lures are more effective in shallow water and places with cover than in open deep-water environs. But that depends on the nature of the fish. Some saltwater species may be taken on the surface miles from the nearest shore, when they happen to be feeding on baitfish that have been pushed to the surface.

For the most part, however, because more surface fishing is done in freshwater (for bass) and near some form of cover, being an accurate caster and having full mastery over the workings of these lures is important in surface fishing. The keys to successful surface fishing include knowing when, and when not, to use them; knowing what type to use and how; knowing where to use them; knowing when to stop fishing on the surface (a common mistake for many anglers is staying with surface fishing long after the surface activity has petered out); and being able to put those lures in the position where they will be most productive.

Basically, any lure that is worked on the surface or is fished both on the surface or within the first 1 to 3 feet of the surface, is part of this category. There are basically four types of surface lures: popping and wobbling plugs, floating/diving plugs and darters, propellered lures, and stickbaits. There is also, in the broadest sense, the dry fly, which is detailed separately because it is vastly different in principle and application from other lures, as is the fly rod popper or bug *(see: fly)*.

Poppers and Wobblers

There are two distinct lures in this category: plugs that pop or chug and those that wobble. Some poppers are also called chuggers and they are also known as popping plugs; they come in small sizes for light-tackle casting in freshwater to long heavy versions used in surf casting. Many are short and squat, some are long and slender, and the rear treble hook on many is dressed with bucktail or synthetic material for extra pizzazz. Wobblers are strictly a freshwater lure for bass fishing, and less numerous than poppers. All these plugs are strictly fished on top of the water.

A popper doesn't actually resemble the actions

of any prevalent form of fish food, since nothing deliberately calls attention to itself or makes popping or chugging sounds. It is possible, however, that the noise generated by these lures is construed by fish as the surface feeding activity of other fish. More likely, this sound simply attracts feeding fish or calls some out of hiding for curiosity's sake. Poppers are most effective on largemouth and smallmouth bass in freshwater, particularly the former, and on striped bass and bluefish in saltwater.

Nearly all poppers have a concave, scooped out mouth. They function mainly as a noisemaker and attractor. They may be worked in a continuous retrieve manner in locations where fish feed on schools of bait, but otherwise they should be fished with pauses of varying duration during the retrieve. The actual popping or forward chugging motion is made by jerking the rod up or back, not by reeling line in, to achieve the proper movement.

In freshwater, in generally close quarters fishing, it's best to keep the rod low and pointed toward the lure; this helps avoid slack to work the lure well and puts the rod in the best possible position to react to a strike. In saltwater, where casting long distances may be common, it is often necessary to keep the rod tip up to help work the lure properly, especially when there is much wave action; when a strike occurs, drop the rod tip while reeling up slack, and quickly set the hook.

Popping plugs should be worked with varying degrees of emphasis. Seldom is it worthwhile to jerk the rod hard to create a loud commotion. This can occasionally be effective for schooling striped bass, but seldom is it warranted for other fish, especially largemouth bass, and even then when they're schooling and chasing baitfish pods near the surface. Usually when the surface is calm, you need only to effect a mild popping noise; a loud noise under this condition is alarming. When the surface is disturbed by a mild chop, make a slightly noisier retrieve.

If it appears that fish are feeding fairly actively, you can shorten the time between retrieval strokes, but in nonfrenzied situations it's usually best to maintain pauses of several seconds' duration. When worked slowly and enticingly in places with good concentrations of fish, especially largemouth bass, they can be dynamically effective. A good tactic is to let a popper lie motionless awhile after splashdown, then reel up all slack line and gently jiggle the rod just enough to impart the slightest sign of life to the lure. This tactic works well for just about all surface lures and sometimes makes a striker out of a fish, usually bass, that has been attracted to the landing of the plug in the water but might be spooked by the first quick motion. In situations where there is plenty of bait or where there is surface-feeding commotion, however, work the popper with a quicker motion.

Poppers are obviously time-consuming lures to use, and do not cover a lot of area very well. They

A frog-patterned popper is eyed by a largemouth bass.

work best near cover and in water that is not too deep, roughly to 12 feet in freshwater. Early and late in the day (particularly in the summer), night, and cloudy days are the best fishing times for this lure. Don't use a popper continuously unless you're having exceptionally good success. Poppers are good for spot fishing, that is, making a few casts in selected areas and then switching to another, different type of lure.

Wobbling plugs are used much in the manner of poppers. They are more effective for largemouths, but can produce some dandy smallmouths at night, and are probably more effective in the dark than at dusk, daylight, or dawn.

Wobblers are characterized by their to and fro undulating action, resulting in large part from a wide, spoonlike metal lip or metal side "wings" that rock the lure from side to side. The common retrieval method is a straight, continuous motion. At times, though, a worthwhile technique is to make the lure stop and go, or to give it a pull-pause motion, particularly as it swims next to an object like a stump or dock support. As long as there is some cover present or the water is not excessively deep under the boat, it's wise to work these lures all the way back to you; they may be struck at any point along the retrieve, especially at night.

Keep your rod tip low and resist the urge to reel too fast. Wobblers don't have as good an action when retrieved quickly as they do when worked slowly. Moreover, a fast retrieve is more conducive to missed strikes. Many bass strike and miss wobbling surface lures. This may be because they have difficulty pinpointing the lure's location or more often because they're intending to stun this surface swimming creature. Try a more frequent stop-and-go retrieval cadence if the fish keep missing it.

For some reason, many fish that strike and miss fail to hit the lure when you toss it out a second time. Resist the urge to set the hook the instant a fish slashes at the lure, and momentarily wait to feel the fish take your plug before setting the hook sharply. This hard to master delay is very effective in fishing weedless spoons in the grass, and works well with wobbling surface plugs too. If the fish misses altogether, try stopping the lure in its tracks and twitching it a little, then moving it a few inches and stopping it. Repeat this before resuming the retrieve.

Very light or very dark colors are preferred in poppers and wobblers by many anglers. Black is especially favored in freshwater, but chrome, clear, and frog-patterned models are also effective; in saltwater, silver and blue-and-white are popular.

Floating/Diving Lures

Probably the most universally applied method of surface or near surface fishing involves the use of floating/diving plugs. These lures are made either of plastic or wood and are generally minnow-shaped, which cause them to be generically called minnow plugs by some anglers. They have a small lip that serves to bring the lure beneath the surface at a maximum of about 3 feet on a conventional cast and retrieve. (These same minnow plugs, incidentally, will get down to a depth of 6 or 7 feet when trolled slowly and when using at least 150 feet of light line.) This type of lure is manufactured in sizes from 2 inches up to 8 inches; the most practical size for bass fishing is the 4- to 6-inch model, and larger versions are used for pike, muskie, and striped bass.

These lures are most effectively worked in a deliberately erratic fashion to imitate a crippled baitfish. A small dying fish lies on its side, wiggles its tail fin occasionally, goes around in circles, and sometimes gets up enough energy to swim a few inches underwater before bobbing to the surface. This is essentially the activity to mimic in the retrieval of a floating/diving lure. Opportunistic gamefish are likely to charge such a defenseless morsel with gusto, creating an electrifying strike.

To get the most out of this lure, it has to be fished convincingly. Results are directly proportional to the action put into it. Start a retrieve by reeling in all slack line, and keep the rod pointed low in case a fish strikes a well-cast surface lure shortly after it hits the water or has been retrieved a few feet. If a fish hits that lure while it's first sitting still in the water and you have either slack line or a sky busting rod, it's very hard to set the hook.

The objective with a floater/diver is to make it gyrate as enticingly as possible in a stationary position. Keep the rod tip pointed low toward the water and use your wrist to move the rod. Jiggle the rod tip in a controlled, not frantic, fashion. Then jerk the lure back toward you a few inches. Then gyrate it some more, all the time reeling in an appropriate amount of line to keep the slack to a minimum. This is not very difficult to accomplish, particularly if you have a rod with a fairly limber tip; stiff-tipped rods don't allow for soft lure movement.

Another way to use this lure type is on a straight retrieve, allowing it to run a foot or two beneath the surface. This is more like using it as a crankbait, and sometimes fish strike it this way. But a better technique, especially when fish won't hit this plug on top of the water, is to make it run just below the surface in a series of short jerk-pause movements, running it forward half a foot with each motion. This retrieve is more in the style of darters, those plugs that float but have no significant surface action and are used solely just below the surface. Some lures that are fished this way, incidentally, are called "jerkbaits" by bass anglers, and some manufacturers use the words jerking or ripping in labeling such lures that they make for stop-and-go retrieves.

There are good floating/diving plugs made from wood (usually balsa) or plastic. The balsa lures do not seem to rise as quickly to the surface after being pulled under as do many of the plastic products; however, some of these lures have neutral buoyancy and suspend when they're pulled under the surface, or can be made to do so with adhesive weight add-ons. A host of colors have merit in both freshwater and saltwater, although the silver (gray) version with black back probably out catches all the others combined.

In freshwater, perhaps the best location for the use of a floating/diving plug is over submerged grass that comes to within a few feet of the surface. This lure is not only good for catching bass in such a locale, but also for locating possible concentrations of fish, which may then be tapped by the use of a plastic worm. Any type of relatively shallow cover can be a target for this lure. In less covered locations, it can be quite effective as well, including spots such as long, shallow points; the backs of bays; and rocky shorelines. Smallmouth bass are particularly receptive to this lure in late spring and early summer when they're in shallow water. Look for every sizable rock or boulder and toss a floating/diving minnow plug to it.

Propellered Lures

Plugs. Propellered surface plugs catch pickerel, pike, inland stripers, and some saltwater fish, but are mostly associated with largemouth and smallmouth bass. These lures, in 2- to 6-inch sizes, are basically shaped like small cigars or torpedoes; they may feature propeller-like blades both fore and aft, or have one or two blades at the rear. Smaller sizes are better for smallmouths, but all sizes are productive for largemouth bass, and it is likely that the larger plugs account for the larger fish, too.

The basic retrieval technique is similar to the surface retrieve of floating/diving minnow plugs, which was outlined previously. The retrieve constitutes an erratic jiggling-jerking-pausing motion that represents a struggling or crippled baitfish. As in fishing with floating/diving lures, you need to keep the rod down, utilize the rod tip to effectively

---

The largest group of living fish, Actinopterygii (ray-finned fish), contains some 23,000 species; the oldest specimens have been dated to 410 million years ago.

impart action, and make your wrist do the rod-manipulating work.

You can retrieve a propellered plug either quickly or slowly. The slow retrieve is good when prospecting for unseen fish, using a deliberate, convincing action. The propellers will make a loud churning noise with some bubbly effect, and this may aid in attracting the attention of bass in the vicinity. A rapid, ripping retrieve is warranted for schooling largemouths, and the noise thereby created seems to imitate the slashing surface breaking feeding activity common to this situation. At this time, if you can keep with the school and if they stay near the surface, it is possible to have a lot of action on a propellered plug. This generally occurs (with varying degrees of frequency) in southern impoundments with abundant concentrations of threadfin shad, where bass have gathered to chase and feed on these baitfish. Summer and fall are productive fishing times for this lure, usually early and late in the day. Areas with heavy cover are prime; in northern waters especially, shore hugging weedlines before a gradual dropoff are quite productive. These lures do not work well in deeper water, other than for school-feeding situations.

Buzzbaits. Another type of propellered lure is a buzzbait, which is not a plug but a sinking spinnerbait-like lure that is fished strictly on the surface. It is solely used in freshwater and almost entirely for largemouth bass, although it does catch pike and occasionally muskie, and has been known to catch the occasional peacock bass. In warm water, it especially appeals to the aggressive nature of largemouths.

Buzzbaits have either in-line or overhead configuration. The overhead version resembles a spinnerbait *(see)* in its construction—an overhead arm with a blade and a lower arm with a lead head and single skirted hook—while the in-line version features a weedless spoon or a bucktail or rubber skirt behind the blade. The revolving "buzz" blade itself is of unique design, vaguely resembling an airplane propeller, and having cupped ends that give the lure a clicking, chop-chop-chop sound that accounts for the name of the lure.

The noise of a buzzbait is not only attractive to feeding bass, but also to shallow nonfeeding bass. Its effectiveness is not limited to one time of the day, to one season, or to a specific geographic locale. Moreover, this lure is an excellent producer of big fish, and certainly of larger than average bass. It works well in spring, summer, and fall, under most weather conditions, and during the day as well as at night. It is generally not very productive in bright sunlight, but good for warm water and hot weather conditions.

A buzzbait is at its very best in areas with thick cover. It is deadly in emergent vegetation that is not too thick to prevent free lure passage and over submerged vegetation that comes fairly close to the surface. It is also highly effective around brush, in timber, and around any fallen wood that might conceal a bass. The closer you can work a buzzbait to such cover, the better.

A well designed buzzbait is reasonably weed-free and can be fished effectively in all but dense concentrations of matted vegetation. Even in fairly thick areas, with accurate casting and a little side-to-side rod manipulation, you can pick your spots and work a buzzer. Mid- to late spring, when lily pads and grass have not fully grown up, is an excellent buzzbait season, provided the water is warm enough.

Bass don't seem to mind how warm the water is in order to hit a buzzer, but they won't come up for it if the water is too cold. The upper 60s is the lower water temperature range for buzzbait action. The summer and early fall are consistently productive buzzbait times, usually in the first few hours of the morning, in late evening, and at night.

Like all surface lures, buzzbaits are basically shallow water products. They seldom produce fish in water over 12 feet deep, even if the vegetation comes to the surface. Furthermore, they allow anglers to cover a lot of water in search of feeding fish.

When bass strike a buzzer, they usually crush it. There are times, however, when they either miss (this happens a lot at night) or strike short. A lot of short strikers can be caught by placing a trailer hook on the bend of the lure's main hook. This is rigged the same as a spinnerbait trailer.

There are many buzzbaits available. In selecting, look for a lure that can be worked effectively at a slow retrieval speed, a bullet-shaped lead head that can cut through the water and ride over vegetation neatly, heavy duty gauge shaft arms, an overall slim profile for lightweight lures to permit easy casting with baitcasting tackle, and large hooks, generally in the 4/0 or 5/0 sizes. Triple-cupped plastic blades are favored by some people for their subtlety rather than a clanking metal blade, but various blade styles and combinations exist. Black, white, and chartreuse are good skirt or body colors, as are combinations, but selection depends on the color and clarity of the water and the relative lightness of the day. Sometimes, color makes no difference.

Stickbaits

Resembling a cigar or tapered broom handle in basic shape, the unimaginatively named stickbait is the antithesis of the natural shape and imitation design of many lures. An artsy paint job may dress up this lure, but essentially it's still a torpedo in costume. Most of the lures that fit into this category of surface plug are similar in size and conformation to propellered plugs, except that they don't have propellers or a lip. They are retrieved much like, and are fished in the same areas as, propellered plugs and to a lesser extent floating/diving lures. However, they have a more pronounced walking or wide swimming action than other surface plugs, and this can be very seductive

Surface Lure

A stickbait is "walked" around a flooded bush; the low rod position is necessary to effect the right lure action.

when done in a slow and deliberate manner or in a fast and frantic manner.

Stickbaits do not have a lip or concave mouth, but a rounded head. They're weighted in the tail so the head sits off the water and the tail rests slightly under the surface. Stickbaits are also known as "splash" baits, "jumpers," and "walkers" because of their darting activity on the surface and the way they splash and seem to be lurching in and out of the water.

Although appearance has little to do with a stickbait's fish catching appeal, its activity when retrieved has everything to do with it. A stickbait can't be tossed out with abandon and then cranked back in. The secret of its effectiveness lies in a masterful retrieval technique. All of the action must be supplied by the angler, making the stickbait foremost among lures for which retrieval skill is of paramount importance.

Many anglers find stickbait retrieval difficult to master. Perhaps this difficulty has been a factor in the relatively lower popularity of these lures compared to other surface plugs. Stickbaits are effective for largemouth, smallmouth, and spotted bass, and also productive at times in angling for stripers, muskies, pike, pickerel, peacock bass, snook, tarpon, and an assortment of other saltwater fish.

Stickbaits come and go among manufacturers, but the one standard of this field is Heddon's Zara Spook, which is widely known and even revered in some circles. The largest and most productive of the Spooks are the $3/4$- and $7/8$-ounce versions, which are $4^1/_2$ inches long.

Learning to retrieve stickbaits comes easily to anglers who are familiar with techniques for fishing floating/diving minnow plugs. The principal stickbait retrieve causes the lure to step from side to side. This side-stepping technique for stickbaits is called "walking the dog," a term that originated with the Zara Spook; this, and an advanced technique known as "half stepping," is described and illus-trated under that entry (see: walking the dog).

A propensity to attract big fish, incidentally, is one of the prime virtues of stickbaits. On the average, these lures produce bigger fish than most other types, and it seems that the larger the plug, the larger the fish.

One difficulty with these lures is that they are hard to fish from a sitting position, especially from a low seat. Sitting on a pedestal seat or, preferably standing, improves retrieval ability. Also, a relatively limber tipped rod is preferable to a stiff tipped one.

Using a snap or a loop knot with a stickbait is especially important; it allows the line to go back and forth quickly and unimpeded. Tying a conventional knot snug to the eye of the lure definitely hinders the action. Also, using thinner diameter line enhances the movement of these lures (less drag).

Stickbaits can be productive in all cover situations where you'd expect to find fish that ambush their prey. You can work specific objects or fish blindly. These lures are especially effective, however, around wood, particularly stumps, logs, and fallen trees, and for calling up bass from submerged timber. They should be worked along the full length of logs and as close to stumps and bushes as possible. When casting to a specific object, land the lure well past your target. Slow walk the lure up to the object, then fast walk it past. Vary retrieval speeds. A moderate retrieve is often best, though there are times when the best approach is to work the lure slowly and seductively, or with a very quick, constant retrieval speed (this is when there is very active fish feeding).

Wind and wave action is a prohibiting factor in working stickbaits because they affect the line and impede retrieval. A light wind that ripples the surface is sometimes desirable, and cloudy, overcast, drizzly conditions are good. Bright sun can be inhibiting. When the angle of the sun is low, retrieve the lure toward the sun, rather than away from it.

A lot of fish strike or boil after a stickbait and miss it. Many of these fish can be enticed to strike again if you can control your reflexes. When fish strike a stickbait, the over anxious angler often rears back to set the hook and jerks the lure away from the fish. Try to hold back your reaction until the fish has clearly taken the lure. If the fish misses the plug and you don't jerk it away but keep it walking along, there's a good chance it will strike again. If you jerk the lure clear away from the fish, you probably won't get a second hit. Then it pays to toss out a different lure to the same spot immediately if another one is handy.

It's important to cast a stickbait very accurately. In thick cover, you'll need to lay the line in such a way that you help direct a clear path of travel for the lure. If you've been fishing another type of lure for some time and then switch to a stickbait, you'll find it hard to cast precisely in close quarters until you get accustomed to the larger, heavier lure.

Pay close attention to the working action of every stickbait you fish. These are critically balanced lures, and though they may come from the same manufacturer, they are not identical. Some lures may need smaller treble hooks to perform well; with others you may have to fiddle with the line-tie screw to lower the angle. It's not uncommon to find one stickbait that works better than an identical one from the same manufacturer. Out of a dozen, it's a fair bet that one or two will have superior action.

As with other lures, colors run the full gamut, and there are many opinions on what to use. The species and clarity of the water will have a lot to do with selection. Try clear (transparent) models if you can find them, as well as Walkers and frog-, perch-, and shad-colored models for bass. Silver, chrome, blue and white, and red and white are among the good saltwater choices. Try dark models on dark days and light colors in clear water.

Specialty Surface Lures
There are a few surface lures that do not quite fit into the standard categories previously mentioned. The soft plastic frog or mouse is such a lure, as are other styles of soft and hard plastic lures that are meant to swim through and over heavy cover in fishing for freshwater bass. These lures are generally preferred in natural colors, with white or yellow bellies, and in all green and all black versions.

These lures are strictly for fishing the vegetation—the thicker the better. Some can be retrieved steadily along while others, like frogs, must be fished extremely slowly and deliberately and with a delay in setting the hook. The latter requires a lot of patience on the angler's part, and with soft plastic lures, it's best to work two on separate rods at the same time, in different locations, alternating between retrieving them.

When a fish hits, delay your hook setting momentarily until you actually feel the fish with the lure. This is less of a problem with soft lures than others because of their consistency, which makes it feel more natural to the fish and results in the bass holding it a bit longer than it might otherwise. When you do set the hook, it must be done hard.

See: Lure; Plug.

SURFPERCH
Also called seaperch and surffish, this group of 21 members of the Embiotocidae family is abundant along the eastern Pacific and is rare among

Barred Surfperch

marine fish for being viviparous, or producing live offspring. This characteristic was first noticed at Sausalito, California, in 1853, when an angler named A. C. Jackson discovered a number of small fish swimming in a pail into which he had just placed some recently caught adult black surfperch. This led to the discovery and naming of the surfperch family by Louis Agassiz.

Unlike most other fish, female surfperch do not scatter eggs outside their body but nourish young fish internally and then spawn them live into the surf. Just as remarkably, these young fish are sexually mature at or before their birth, and infant males can inseminate infant females soon after birth.

Two members of this family occur off Japan and Korea, and the remainder occur along the Pacific coast of North America from Alaska to Baja California, Mexico. All are marine with the exception of the small tule perch (*Hysterocarpus traski*), which is found in California's Sacramento and Russian Rivers.

None of the species in the family is large; their maximum size ranges from 4 to 18 inches. They have compressed bodies, more or less oval in shape and generally silvery, and large fleshy lips. The spiny and soft-rayed dorsal fins are joined. Most species inhabit the surf along both sandy and rocky coasts, but several species live mainly in bays or in similar shallow inshore waters. One species occurs in relatively deep water (to more than 700 feet), and two smaller species inhabit only tidal pools. They primarily consume small crustaceans, but some also feed on worms, small crabs, shrimp, and mussels. The larger species are popular with anglers and are caught year-round from docks, piers, kelp, the surf line, tidepools, and a variety of other sites. They contribute to the commercial catch but not to a significant extent.

The shiner surfperch (*Cymatogaster aggregata*) is probably the number one fish caught by youngsters along the California coast. They range from Baja California, Mexico, to Wrangell, Alaska, and are most abundant around bays and eelgrass beds and the pilings of wharves and piers. They grow to a maximum of only 8 inches and are generally greenish or silvery but may be reddish.

The barred surfperch (*Amphistichus argenteus*) is one of the larger members of the group, growing to

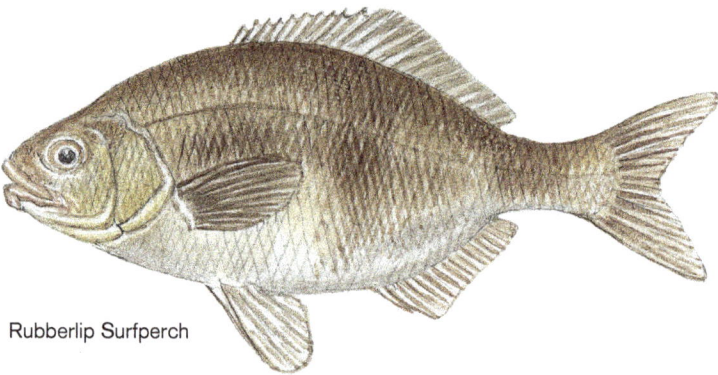

Rubberlip Surfperch

a maximum of 17 inches and $4^1/_2$ pounds, although it is usually much smaller. It occurs along sandy coasts from central California to Baja California. Its sides are marked with a series of dusky, brassy vertical bars with spots between them. The back and sides are gray to olive, and the belly is white. This is among the most popular surfperch with anglers.

The redtail surfperch (*A. rhodoterus*) is more northern in range than the barred species; it ranges from Vancouver Island, British Columbia, to central California. Its vertical bars and the pelvic and caudal fins are usually reddish; it may grow to 16 inches.

The calico surfperch (*A. koeizi*) occurs from Cape Flattery, Washington, to Northern California and grows to 12 inches. It is similar to the redtail, but has a deeper body. It is also similar to the barred, but its lower jaw projects slightly beyond the upper; in the barred surfperch, the lower jaw is shorter than the upper jaw.

The walleye surfperch (*Hyperprosopon argenteum*), occurring from British Columbia to Baja California, is another surfperch that is highly popular with anglers, and the most frequent catch from piers. It grows to about 11 inches and is distinguished by its large eyes and by the black tips on its pelvic, anal, and caudal fins. The back and sides are bluish, the belly is white or silvery. The last spiny rays of the dorsal fin are higher than any of the rays of the soft dorsal.

Relatives of the walleye surfperch include the spotfin surfperch (*H. anale*), found from central California to Baja California; it has no black tips on its fins but does have a distinctive black spot on its spiny dorsal fin and sometimes a black blotch on the anal fin. The silver surfperch (*H. ellipticum*) ranges from Vancouver, British Columbia, to Baja California and is one of the most frequently caught surfperch. It has no black markings on its body and grows to a maximum of $10^1/_2$ inches. All three of these species are found mostly along sandy shores.

The rainbow surfperch (*Hypsurus caryi*) grows to 12 inches and lives principally along rocky shores from northern California to northern Baja California. Somewhat less oval in shape than other surfperch, its silvery body is striped horizontally with blue, orange, and red. The fins are generally orange, and a large black blotch appears on both the soft dorsal and the anal fins.

The white surfperch (*Phanerodon furcatus*) is distinguished by its deeply forked tail and has a rather slim body compared to other surfperch. Growing to 12 inches long, it ranges from Vancouver Island, British Columbia, to northern Baja California, occurring mainly off sandy coasts. There is usually a black spot on the anal fin. This is the species most commonly caught by commercial fishermen due to its schooling tendencies.

Largest in the surfperch family is the rubberlip seaperch (*Rhacocilus toxotes*), which reaches 18 inches in length. Occurring from central to Southern California, it is distinguished by thick white to pinkish lips, so large in some individuals that they droop. The whitish background color is usually tinged with a smoky or blackish color, and the pectoral fins are yellow.

Closely related to the rubberlip is the pile surfperch (*R. vacca*), which ranges from Alaska to Baja California. It is only slightly smaller and is distinguished by a deeply forked tail and very high first rays in the second dorsal fin. The color is silvery, with a blackish or brownish cast on the back, and it has dark fins.

The black surfperch (*Embiotoca jacksoni*) reaches a length of 15 inches. Found from Northern California to central Baja California, it is dark brownish black and often tinged with blue or yellow. It has thick reddish lips. A group of scales between the pectoral and pelvic fins are exceptionally large, and the spiny rays of the dorsal fin are all shorter than the soft rays. The tail is slightly forked.

The striped surfperch (*E. lateralis*) ranges from Baja California to Alaska and is most abundant in the cooler waters north of Point Conception. It has a less forked tail than the black surfperch, and its coppery body is striped horizontally with orange and blue. The scales are spotted with black above the lateral line.

SURGEON'S KNOT
A fishing knot for line-to-line connections.
See: Knots, Fishing.

SURGEON'S LOOP
A fishing knot for line-to-line connections, primarily used in fly fishing for loop-to-loop leaders.
See: Knots, Fishing.

SURGICAL TUBE LURE
A long, slender, hollow trolling lure fashioned from rubber tubing; many are now made from plastic.
See: Trolling Lures, Saltwater; Umbrella Rig.

SURVEY
A tool used by fisheries managers to determine the needs and desires of anglers, the extent of the fish

harvest, methods of angling, and the condition of fish populations. Multiple surveys are used in fisheries management and can include angler surveys, biological surveys, and tagging surveys.
See: **Fisheries Management.**

SURVIVAL

Most anglers find it hard to imagine themselves in a survival situation. This is something that most people associate with extremely remote areas and extraordinary weather conditions. Given the state of sophisticated communications and population density, some people cannot imagine being in a situation where survival is really an issue. Yet, every angler is exposed to the elements, and one can easily imagine scenarios in which people can be suddenly and unexpectedly placed into a situation that is, or can become, life threatening.

A capsized boat, a flash flood, a breakaway ice floe are just some of the things that can happen to anglers. What if you're deep in the Everglades, lose all electric power, and can't get your motor started? What if you're on a big lake in the Far North, 20 miles from camp, and you damage the lower unit of the motor on a reef and have to spend the night ashore with the black flies and without any wood? What if one evening you're on a trout stream just a half mile from the nearest house and you fall and break your leg? What if a storm rises, the waves pitch into your boat, the bilge pump fails, and you find yourself capsized miles from shore?

These are not far-fetched what-ifs. These and a lot more unexpected circumstances affect anglers every year whether they fish big water in a boat, hike into mountain lakes, or take a snowmobile for miles across a frozen lake. Some circumstances obviously have the potential for danger, but many do not. Storms and heavy winds often are the cause of unexpected events, and anglers should realize that even in routine activities they may sometime face a short- or long-term survival predicament. Even though the odds are against your being in a life or death situation, it is foolish to think that you're immune from it, and practical to be aware of and prepared for it.

In essence, survival is the art of making efficient use of any available resource for sustenance. If individuals are able to think clearly and objectively about an emergency situation—usually because they have prepared for it—they are far more likely to survive than those who panic and are unable to take full advantage of resources that may be at hand.

In a survival situation, there are five basic needs: sustenance, medical, fire, shelter, and rescue. Few survival situations are identical, and some needs are more urgent than others. However, when thinking about and planning for survival, you must prepare for emergencies in a way that will meet all of these needs. Equally important is thinking about these

Strong wind, as experienced on this remote Ontario lake, can be especially dangerous for small boats.

needs in the context of the environment that you'll be in. The following basic information pertains to these needs within the context of the angling world, although it is apropos of other outdoor enthusiasts as well. There is also a review of water safety issues, since anglers are more likely to encounter such issues than others.

Planning Ahead

Survival situations often strike unexpectedly, and they strike the ill-prepared. The angler with only light clothing invariably is the one caught in the "unexpected" late spring snowstorm. Boats never seem to sink when there are enough life jackets to go around.

Planning and preparing for emergencies is more than proper clothing or PFDs, and it is more than carrying a Swiss army knife with you. Preparation requires investing time so that you are physically and mentally fit; it requires thoughtful planning and intelligent selection of resources so that they will be available when you need them. Since you are unlikely to remember all this information (and this is just a primer on survival), it would be a good idea to copy it, laminate it, or otherwise make it waterproof, so you can keep it with you should you ever be in an emergency situation.

Angler's survival kit. It's a smart idea to assemble into a kit all the items necessary for a survival situation; then you can tote the kit wherever you go. Far more is involved than simply buying a prepackaged "survival kit," and it is unlikely that any single kit will meet your specific needs.

Select the items for your survival kit based on their versatility, multifunctionality, and practicality. Although the ability to improvise is not one of the five basic needs of survival, it is an important process in bringing all these needs together. The surgical tubing that you selected as a tourniquet for the first aid kit, for example, can be used to collect water from an improvised solar still; the tubing also makes a straw for drinking out of your water container, or even a slingshot.

The following items are recommended for day or weekend anglers and are versatile for all survival-related emergencies. However, no kit can be entirely right for every situation. These items form a foundation to build upon depending on your activity and the environment. Although the list may seem long, many items are small and light, and some are tools you may want along anyway for everyday use. The GPS navigational unit is optional, but handheld versions are becoming more of a staple for backcountry travelers.

- ❏ One-gallon water bag or container (collapsible or folded)
- ❏ Water purification tablets
- ❏ Nonperishable food ration, 3,600 calories
- ❏ Hard candy
- ❏ Container for boiling water
- ❏ Large fixed-blade knife
- ❏ Pocket knife, with locking blade
- ❏ Flint-and-steel fire starter
- ❏ Tinder for lighting a fire
- ❏ Windproof and waterproof matches (strike-anywhere versions are best)
- ❏ Waterproof match case
- ❏ Lighter
- ❏ Flashlight with spare batteries
- ❏ Three 12-hour high-intensity cyalume light sticks (activated by snapping and shaking)
- ❏ Signal mirror
- ❏ Whistle
- ❏ Compass
- ❏ Compact strobe light
- ❏ First aid kit (should be adequate for environment and include prescription medicines and large compresses)
- ❏ Saw
- ❏ Multiperson emergency tube shelter
- ❏ Survival bag
- ❏ Mylar space blanket sleeping bag
- ❏ Space blanket
- ❏ Wool gloves
- ❏ Wool hat
- ❏ Dry socks
- ❏ Emergency poncho or rain jacket
- ❏ Cord or rope
- ❏ Sewing kit
- ❏ Fishing line and hooks (and also perhaps a few sinkers, small jigs, and streamers)
- ❏ Multifunction tool
- ❏ Sharpening stone
- ❏ Carry/storage bag (sealed for pilfer resistance)
- ❏ Handheld GPS *(see)* navigational unit

Vehicle survival kit. Like the survival kit for anglers, a survival kit for a vehicle is something that few people assemble, whether they are anglers or not. If you travel off the beaten path, in places where help may be hard to get, and in places subject to extreme weather, then a vehicle survival kit is especially important. Savvy north-country drivers have some or all of these items in their vehicle in case they get stuck on the road in a snowstorm; this kind of situation can happen to people who are simply driving home from work.

The following products are recommended for a complete vehicle survival kit. They include some of the items in the angler's traveling survival kit; you might be wise to have both, since a situation may occur when you have access to one kit but not the other. Items like jumper cables, tire chains, and road flares are normally considered safety items rather than part of a vehicle survival kit, but many survival situations have started along the side of the road because these items were not present. Be ready to improvise. For example, if your vehicle overheats because of a ruptured hose, wait for the car to cool and fix the rupture with duct tape. This may not be the perfect fix but it will probably get you to the next town or nearest phone.

- ❏ Cellular phone
- ❏ Spare tire
- ❏ Flashlight
- ❏ Vehicle jack
- ❏ Gas can
- ❏ Spool of 20-gauge wire
- ❏ Tire chains
- ❏ Flat tire repair items
- ❏ Ground tarp
- ❏ Jumper cables
- ❏ Tool kit
- ❏ Tow rope
- ❏ Road flares (or red light sticks)
- ❏ Shovel
- ❏ Duct tape
- ❏ One gallon of water
- ❏ Blanket
- ❏ Saw
- ❏ Emergency poncho or rain jacket
- ❏ Wool gloves
- ❏ Wool hat
- ❏ Multifunction tool
- ❏ Strapping cord or rope
- ❏ Large emergency tube shelter/tarp
- ❏ Water storage container
- ❏ Water purification tablets
- ❏ Six red, 12-hour Cyalume light sticks
- ❏ Six 12-hour high-intensity yellow cyalume light sticks
- ❏ Nonperishable food ration, 3,600 calories
- ❏ Signal mirror
- ❏ Whistle
- ❏ Compact strobe light
- ❏ First aid kit (should include prescription medicines, trauma dressings, and other large bandages)
- ❏ Surgical tubing
- ❏ Large fixed-blade survival knife
- ❏ Pocket knife with locking blade

- ❑ Flint-and-steel fire starter
- ❑ Tinder for lighting a fire
- ❑ Windproof and waterproof matches (strike-anywhere version)
- ❑ Waterproof match case
- ❑ Lighter
- ❑ Compact sewing kit
- ❑ Handheld GPS navigational unit

Sustenance

Sustenance is providing food and water to supply energy, increase metabolism, regulate temperature, and allow the mind to work rationally. Most healthy adults can miss a few meals without significant distress. However, even the healthiest adults can go no longer than a few days without water before they become delirious and lose vital body functions. Although ready-to-eat low-water rations make an excellent addition to many survival kits, far too much emphasis is placed on food and not nearly enough on water, water storage, and water purification. The following information assumes that you are in a pure survival situation without food or water/beverage and without a means of catching fish or hunting game.

Making potable water. Rainwater collected in clean containers or from plants is generally safe for drinking. However, you must purify water from lakes, ponds, swamps, springs, or streams, especially those near human habitation. When at all possible, disinfect all water obtained from vegetation or from the ground by using iodine or chlorine or by boiling it.

You can purify water by using one of the following methods:

- Use water purification tablets.
- Pour 5 drops of 2 percent tincture of iodine in a canteen full of clear water, and 10 drops in a canteen full of cloudy or cold water. Let the canteen of water stand for 30 minutes before drinking.
- Boil water for 1 minute at sea level, adding 1 minute for each additional 1,000 feet above sea level, or boil for 10 minutes no matter where you are.
- Use a commercial water purification device.

Potable drinking-water system devices. Having to purify water is a bother. The only reason to carry any drinking water purifier at all is to protect your health against microbiological and chemical contaminants. Water-related health threats can occur anytime you're in contact with water: drinking it directly, using it as a food or beverage ingredient, using it for bathing or for brushing teeth, and using it to clean cookware.

Primary exposure to drinking-water contaminants occurs at various times. It can happen when you are collecting raw water for purification: Use a separate container, whenever possible, for raw water supply; be selective and choose a source least likely to be badly polluted. Other situations inviting exposure to contamination can occur: during purification (don't let dirty water drip or flow into purified water); during storage of the purifier (at meal and campsites); and during handling of the unit while placing it in a pack or performing maintenance tasks.

The micro-organisms of concern in most wilderness recreation areas are tough, hardy cystic parasites that resist heat, freezing cold, drought, chlorine, iodine, and just about everything else. Although bacteria are relatively fragile and have very short life cycles, often less than a day, cysts can exist for months. All micro-organisms of chief concern are invisibly small, and they cannot be seen, smelled, or detected in any quick and easy manner. Accordingly, you must rely on knowledge of the area and on common sense.

It is widely known today that Giardia and/or Cryptosporidia have been found in water supplies in almost every country in the world. Therefore, you should always protect against parasitic cysts, and you should insist on 100 percent reduction. Since one cyst is enough to infect, 99.9 percent reduction may not be good enough, especially when there is no known treatment for some cysts.

Pesticides, herbicides, and other chemicals can be present anywhere downwind or downstream from major agricultural and industrial areas, and perhaps hundreds of miles away. These contaminants concentrate in streams, rivers, and lakes. Asbestos fibers can be found in very high numbers of more than a million fibers per liter in most western and some eastern wilderness waters. Even though trace amounts of these chemicals won't make you ill, no one wants to drink such fibers if they can easily be avoided.

Micron ratings from potable drinking-water treatment systems must be absolute to be meaningful, and precise measurements are essentially impossible to make. Micron ratings pertain only to physical removal or straining of particles, so absolute micron ratings are only one means of evaluating effectiveness. Removal of pesticides, herbicides, tastes, odors, and most colors and solvents requires other purification (separation) mechanisms. Many units, even those with very low micron ratings, have little or no ability to remove anything other than particles.

According to United States federal regulations, all water purification devices are defined as being either pesticide or device products. Pesticide products rely on chemically poisoning organisms (pests), and devices rely on physically removing them. It's easy to tell whether a product is categorized as a pesticide or a device. All products must carry an EPA Establishment Regulation Number; pesticide products must carry two EPA registration numbers, one for the manufacturing establishment

---

Some common expressions with fish-related origins include: loan shark; fluke; red herring; fish or cut bait; swallow hook, line, and sinker; and stewed to the gills.

and one for the pesticide being used. So, decide on a device or a pesticide product for water purification needs, and check the label to choose the right type. In certain applications, it may be desirable to use a pesticide to pretest water. Complete removal of the pesticide is very desirable after enough kill time is allowed. Iodine resins are not effective against cysts.

Solar still for safe water. No matter how fresh and clean water may appear to be, even in a wild stream or creek, you can never be sure that it isn't contaminated with chemicals and bacteria that make it unsafe for drinking. It is good common sense to always carry a safe container of water with your gear, especially in warm climates where dehydration is a danger.

In a survival situation, you can get safe drinking water by building a solar still, which will usually provide at least a pint of water every 24 hours. Here's how to use the sun to get safe drinking water:

1. Dig a hole in the ground about 2 feet deep and 3 feet across.
2. Place a clean bucket or pan at the bottom of the hole.
3. Set a plastic sheet over the hole, and hold it in place by piling stones or dirt around the edges.
4. Place a small stone in the center of the plastic sheet, so that the water formed by condensation on the sheet's sides is funneled into the catch container.

The sun causes condensation to form on the sides of the plastic sheet. As the water collects at the bottom of the sheet, it drips into the bucket. As an extra precaution, boil the water for 10 minutes or add a commercial water treatment tablet.

Wild plants for food. After water, food is your most urgent need. In a survival situation, you should always be on the lookout for wild foods and live off the land whenever possible. Plants are a valuable food source. Although they may not offer a balanced diet, they will sustain you. Many plant foods, such as nuts and seeds, will provide enough protein for normal efficiency. Roots, green vegetables, and plant food containing natural sugar will provide calories and carbohydrates that will give your body energy.

Being able to recognize wild edible plants is important in a survival situation. There are certain factors you should keep in mind when collecting edible plants:

- Cultivated plants and wild plants growing in or near cultivated plants may have been sprayed with pesticides. Thoroughly wash whatever plants you collect.
- The surface of any plant food that grows on, or is washed in, contaminated water is also contaminated. To eat the plant raw, wash it in water suitable for drinking.
- Some plants may have fungal toxins that are extremely poisonous. To lessen the chances that these toxins are present, collect fresh seeds, fruit, or leaves, but not those that have fallen to the ground.
- Plants of the same species may differ in the amount of toxic or subtoxic compounds they contain because of different environmental and genetic factors. One example is the foliage of the common chokeberry. Some chokeberry plants have high concentrations of cyanide compounds, other plants low concentrations.
- Some people are more susceptible than others to gastric upset from plants. Those who are sensitive this way should avoid unknown wild plants. If you are extremely sensitive to poison ivy, avoid products from this family, including drinks made from sumacs, mangos, and cashews.
- There are some edible wild plants, such as acorns and water lily rhizomes, that are bitter. These bitter substances (usually tannin compounds) make them unpalatable. Boiling in several changes of water will help remove these substances.
- Many valuable wild plants have high concentrations of oxalate compounds. Oxalates usually produce a sharp burning sensation in your mouth. And they are bad for the kidneys. Boiling usually destroys these oxalates.
- The only way to tell if a mushroom is edible is by proper examination. Even then, some species are questionable, so do not eat mushrooms.

There are many, many plants throughout the world. Tasting or swallowing even a small portion of some can cause severe discomfort, extreme internal disorders, or even death. Therefore, if you have the slightest doubt about the edibility of a plant, apply the Universal Edibility Test (which follows) before eating any part of it.

Before testing a plant for edibility, make sure that there are a sufficient number of the plants to make testing worth your time and effort. You need more than 24 hours to apply the edibility test. Keep in mind that eating large amounts of plant food on an empty stomach may cause diarrhea or cramps. Familiar foods that cause this problem are green apples and too many fresh berries. Even if you've tested plant food and found it safe, eat it in moderation with other foods. You can see from the steps and time involved in testing edibility just how important it is to be able to identify edible plants.

Universal Edibility Test

1. Test only one part of a potential food plant at a time.

2. Break the plant into its basic components: leaves, stems, roots, buds, and flowers.
3. Smell the food for strong or acidic odors. Smell alone is not an indication of edibility.
4. Do not eat for eight hours before starting the test.
5. During the eight hours you are abstaining from eating, test for contact poisoning by placing on the inside of your elbow or wrist a piece of the plant part being tested. Usually 15 minutes is enough time to allow for a reaction.
6. During the test period, take nothing by mouth except purified water and the plant part being tested.
7. Select a small portion of a single component and prepare it the way you plan to eat it.
8. Before putting the prepared plant part in your mouth, touch a small portion (a pinch) to the outer surface of the lip to test for burning or itching.
9. If after 3 minutes there is no reaction on your lip, place the plant part on your tongue, holding it there for 15 minutes.
10. If there is no reaction, thoroughly chew a pinch and hold it in your mouth for 15 minutes. *Do not swallow.*
11. If no burning, itching, numbing, stinging, or other irritation occurs during the 15 minutes, swallow the food.
12. Wait eight hours. If any ill effects occur during this period, induce vomiting and drink a lot of water.
13. If no ill effects occur, eat one-half cup of the same plant part prepared the same way. Wait another eight hours. If no ill effects occur, the plant part as prepared is safe for eating.

Caution: Test all parts of the plant for edibility, since some plants have both edible and inedible parts. Also, do not assume that a part that proved edible when cooked is also edible when raw. Test the part raw to ensure edibility before eating raw.

Do not eat unknown plants that:

- Have a milky sap or a sap that turns black when exposed to air.
- Are mushroomlike.
- Resemble onion or garlic.
- Resemble parsley, parsnip, or dill.
- Have carrotlike leaves, roots, or tubers.

Preparation of plant food. Although some plants or plant parts are edible raw, others must be cooked to be edible or palatable. Some methods of improving the taste of plant food are soaking, parboiling, cooking, or leaching. (Leaching is done by crushing food, placing it in some sort of strainer, and pouring boiling water through it.)

Leaves, stems, and buds should be boiled until tender; several changes of water help to eliminate bitterness.

Roots and tubers can be boiled, baked, or roasted. Boiling removes harmful substances such as oxalic acid crystals.

Nuts can be leached or soaked in water to remove the bitterness. Although chestnuts are edible raw, they are tastier roasted or steamed.

Grains and seeds may be parched to improve the taste, or ground into meal to use as a thickener with soups or stews or to use as flour to make bread.

To get sugar, sap is dehydrated by boiling until the water is gone.

Fruit is baked or roasted if it is tough with heavy skin. Boil juicy fruit.

Medical

You need not be a member of the medical profession to be prepared to meet basic medical and health needs. Good outdoor first aid kits are available, but be sure to take your specific circumstances into account and supplement any kit with items you will need. This means taking sufficient quantities of any prescribed medicines, bringing extra contact lenses or pairs of glasses, and taking additional supplies (bug spray, antivenin, seasickness medication) that are appropriate for the environment. A separate entry on first aid has more information on medical and health issues.

See: First Aid.

Fire

It is often said that the presence of a fire means that a person is going to survive. Although this is not an absolute truth, it is true that in a survival situation nothing can warm the soul, calm fear, and bring hope more than a warm fire. Fire is a versatile and often essential survival resource. Cold weather, wind, and moisture are three impediments to survival. A good fire can help fight and prevail against them all. Fire also helps meet other needs, like purifying water, sterilizing bandages, signaling, etc.

Unfortunately, most survival kits offer only mediocre fire-making implements, and fire is seldom given the attention it deserves in survival guides. It takes skill to build a warming fire in the pouring rain. For a small investment of time, learning this skill can help save your life.

Use good judgment when selecting fire-making implements for your own survival kit, and think about how the tools you're selecting might fail under various conditions. For example, most lighters work poorly in extreme cold temperatures, can blow out in the wind, and last only as long as the butane fuel source. Most waterproof matches are waterproof only at the striking head and will stay lit for only four to five seconds.

In the hands of someone who has practiced with it, there is no better all-purpose fire-starting device than a large piece of flint and something to scrape it. Flints work effectively in the wind or rain and

The Queensland lungfish, genera Neoceratodus from Australia, is one of the world's most primitive fish and has changed little in 100 million years.

last a long time. Commercially made flint-based fire-starter tools are excellent choices for a survival kit.

Commercial fire starters or fuels should be chosen with care to ensure that they will work in wet weather. For those wanting to save a few pennies, a good homemade tinder is a 100 percent cotton ball saturated with Vaseline. Ten to 20 of these can be crammed into a waterproof match case or empty film canister.

Of course, good cutting tools can help immeasurably when you're preparing to make a fire. First, it makes sense to carry both a fixed-blade and a folding knife. A large fixed-blade knife is great for cutting into the heart of dry wood. A smaller folding locking-blade knife is good for preparing shavings and fire-starting materials.

Rescue

The chances of being rescued can be dramatically improved if you know and can use basic signaling skills. Being seen or heard is the key. No one should ever venture far afield or go anywhere in a car, boat, or plane, without a signal mirror and a whistle.

You can't outscream a good whistle, and you can't sustain the effort of screaming or hollering. But you can blow a good whistle long and often. A signal mirror is second only to electronic communication devices (radios, phone, e-mail–capable GPS, etc.) for conveying the need for help. When those other devices are unavailable, it may be your only means. Except for military personnel, who have a signal mirror in their survival kit and who use this device religiously, the general public has only limited knowledge of the value of the signal mirror. The key is having a targetable signal mirror, such as the official Air Force Star Flash, so that the signal flash can be aimed.

Other widely available signaling devices include flashlights, strobe lights, and chemical lights. High-intensity 12-hour chemical lights are a better choice in most instances than a flashlight because they're lighter in weight and don't require batteries. A small string tied to the end of a chem light and spun in a circle overhead makes an excellent night signal that can be seen from a great distance. Anglers who venture offshore in large boats should have a flare gun for signaling.

With signaling and rescue devices, the key is to be seen. Bigger, louder, and more is better. A recognized international distress call is a series of three signals: three blasts of your whistle, three long honks of your car horn, three shots of a flare, or three small fires (smoke or flame), etc.

Shelter and Personal Protection

The need for shelter encompasses all aspects of covering or protecting the human body according to the circumstances and with regard to facing wind, sun, heat, cold, rain, snow, insects, snakebite, and more.

Clothing is the most obvious element of protection and one that sometimes gets little attention. People tend to dress for the conditions that exist at the moment they leave their home, RV, camp, etc., and not for what might be encountered. While appropriate clothing should be worn according to the weather, workload, and activity, you must take into account possible extremes and worst-case scenarios. When venturing on the water, always ask yourself if your clothes would be sufficient to spend the night in them if you had to.

Personal survival protection items like space blankets, emergency tube shelters, and others lead many people to a false sense of security. Most space blankets claim to reflect up to 90 percent of your body heat back to you. This might be true when used in perfect conditions, but these blankets can tear in the wind and are open at the end. The best lightweight shelters are Mylar (or equivalent-film) sleeping bags. This is because you can get inside them and trap the heat while minimizing the loss of heat through convection. Bodily heat transfer in cold weather is done by evaporation, radiation, convection, conduction, and respiration. Fifty percent of all body heat can be lost through the head alone.

The better reflective-type blankets are reinforced by polyethylene or polypropylene materials. These resist tearing and damage. Survival bags (oversize and double strength garbage bags that go from head to toe) are widely available. This item should be part of a survival kit and makes an excellent emergency shelter to climb into, especially when used in conjunction with a Mylar space blanket sleeping bag. It is important to recognize, however, that these emergency shelters are not self-regulating and that they can become exceptionally hot and wet inside when moisture is not allowed to escape.

Sheltering not only affects the body directly but is important in meeting other survival needs. It is

If these Nunavut Territory anglers all suddenly lean to the same side when landing their fish, one or more could wind up in the frigid water and suddenly be in a survival situation.

very difficult to build a fire in the pouring rain if you cannot keep the material you're preparing dry or, for that matter, your hands.

Combating cold. You can't beat the cold, but you can learn how to survive in it. Modern clothing is insulated, waterproof, and windproof, but you can still get into trouble. Hypothermia is the cold-weather killer, and it is caused by exposure to wind, rain, snow, or wet clothing. If the body's core temperature drops below 98.6°, you'll start to shiver and stamp your feet to keep warm. If these early signs are ignored, the next symptoms will be slurred speech, memory lapses, fumbling hands, and drowsiness. If not treated quickly, hypothermia can kill its victim when body temperature drops below 78°, and this can happen within 90 minutes after shivering begins.

If you detect these symptoms in yourself or a friend, start treatment immediately. Get to shelter and warmth as soon as possible. If no shelter is available, build a fire. Get out of wet clothing and apply heat to head, neck, chest, and groin. Use body heat from another person. Give the victim warm liquids, chocolate, or any food with a high sugar content. Never give a victim alcohol; this will impair judgment, dilate blood vessels, and prevent shivering, which is the body's way of producing needed heat.

You'll be better prepared to survive the cold if you've stayed in shape and have had a good night's sleep before going outdoors. Carrying candy, mixed nuts, raisins, and other high-energy food helps. To avoid hypothermia in a survival situation, stay as dry as possible and avoid overheating your body, which produces perspiration and damp clothes. Most importantly, dress properly. This means several layers of clothing and rain gear. Wear a wool hat with ear protection. An uncovered head can lose up to 50 percent of the body's heat. If you are thrust into a situation without proper clothing protection, you must seek shelter and find a way to stay warm. It is very dangerous to risk cold elements when you don't have the right clothing. Anglers should keep in mind that going out on a large body of cold water can be greatly different than being onshore at the same time. A moderate breeze coming across a cold body of water mandates heavy clothing, even though people on land may be dressed much lighter.

Combating heat. To survive in extreme heat, you must understand how heat affects the human body, and you must be prepared for it. You have to determine what you need, how you can combat the heat, and what impact the environment will have on you.

The body's normal temperature is 98.6°, and the body gets rid of excess heat by sweating. The warmer the body becomes, the more it sweats and thus the more moisture it loses. Sweating is the principal cause of water loss. A person who stops sweating during periods of high air temperature and heavy work or exercise could have a heat stroke, which is an emergency that requires immediate medical attention.

Understanding how the air temperature and your physical activity affect your water requirements allows you to take measures to get the most from your water supply. These measures include:

- Find shade. Get out of the sun. Place something between you and the hot ground. Limit your movements.
- Conserve your sweat. Wear all your clothes, including tee shirt; roll the sleeves down, cover your head, and protect your neck with a scarf or similar item. This will protect your body from hot blowing winds and the direct rays of the sun. Your clothing will absorb your sweat, keeping it against your skin so you gain its full cooling effect. By staying in the shade quietly, fully clothed, not talking, keeping your mouth closed and breathing through your nose, your water requirement for survival drops dramatically.
- If water is scarce, do not eat. Food requires water for digestion. Eating food will use water that you need for cooling.

Thirst is not a reliable guide for your need for water. A person who uses thirst as a guide will drink only two-thirds of the daily requirement. To prevent this "voluntary" dehydration, use this guide: at temperatures below 100°, drink 1 pint of water every hour; at temperatures above 100°, drink 1 quart of water every hour.

Drinking water at regular intervals helps the body to remain cool, thus decreasing sweating. Even when your water supply is low, sipping water constantly will keep your body cooler and will reduce water loss through sweating. Conserve water by reducing activity during the heat of the day; this minimizes perspiration. Do not ration your water, or you stand a good chance of becoming a heat casualty.

Intense sunlight/heat. Intense sunlight and heat are present in all arid areas. Air temperature can rise as high as 140°F during the day. Heat gain results from direct sunlight, hot blowing winds, reflective heat (the sun's rays bouncing off the sand), and conductive heat from direct contact with sand and rock. The temperature of sand and rock averages 30 to 40° more than that of the air. For instance, when the air temperature is 110°F, the sand temperature may be 140°. Intense sunlight and heat increase the body's need for water. To conserve your body sweat and energy, you need a shelter that will reduce your exposure to the heat of the day.

Temperatures may get as high as 130°F during the day and as low as 50° at night in arid areas. The drop in temperature at night occurs rapidly and will chill a person who lacks warm clothing and is unable to move about. At night you'll find a wool sweater, long underwear, and a wool stocking cap very helpful.

Sunburn results from overexposing skin to ultraviolet rays, so in extreme situations try to keep your body completely clothed, including gloves on your hands and a scarf around your neck. Use sunscreen *(see)* liberally on all exposed areas. Sun poisoning equals nausea and dehydration. In addition, burns may become infected, causing more problems. So you must protect yourself from overexposure. There is as much danger of sunburn on cloudy days as on sunny days, especially at high altitudes. Most sunscreens do not give complete protection against excessive exposure.

The glare on sand causes eyestrain, and wind-blown, fine sand particles can irritate the eyes and cause inflammation. Wear goggles and use eye ointments to protect your eyes. The combination of wind and sand or dust can cause your lips and other exposed skin to chap. Use lip and skin balms or ointments to prevent or overcome this problem. Rest is essential in this environment. You need 20 minutes of rest for each hour in the heat, and a minimum of six hours of sleep each day.

See: Safety.

Water Safety

For anglers, some survival circumstances occur as the result of mishaps on the water, such as a boat capsizing. Dealing with such an event is covered in greater detail in other entries *(see: boat; safety)*. Finding yourself in the water, especially if that water is cold (and essentially anything under normal body temperature is cold) presents an immediate survival concern due to the potential for hypothermia, and the colder the water the greater the concern. Anglers who find themselves having to fend for survival on the land, as wilderness travelers might, will also have to deal with water, probably in terms of crossing or traveling along it, so it's worth reviewing both of these matters.

Surviving in cold water. If you are suddenly the victim of a capsizing, you can survive if you follow a few important rules.

First, don't panic. Clothing will trap body heat, so don't remove your clothes. If you're wearing a life jacket (PFD), restrict your body movements and draw your knees up to your body, which is a position that will reduce heat loss.

Don't try to swim or tread water. That will just pump out warm water between your body and clothing. Get into a protective posture and wait for a rescue. There are body positions that will minimize heat loss and increase your chances for survival. For solo survival, H.E.L.P. (Heat Escape Lessening Posture) is the body position that will best minimize heat loss. If you're wearing waders, keep them on, and assume a sitting position. The trapped air in the waders will help keep you afloat.

To survive in cold water when alone and wearing a PFD, draw your knees up to your chest and hold them there with locked arms; this is the Heat Escape Lessening Posture. Two or three people should huddle together to conserve body heat.

Cover head and neck if possible. Two or more persons in cold water should huddle together to conserve body heat. A small group in this position can extend survival time 50 percent longer than by swimming.

Crossing rivers and streams. In a wilderness survival situation, you'll likely encounter some type of water that needs crossing when you are finding your way through the country. Rivers and streams are the most tempting, since the distance across is less than it is in a pond or lake. A river or stream may be narrow or wide, shallow or deep, slow or fast, and fed by ice or snow, making it colder than would be comfortable or wise to cross.

The first thing to do is find a place where the river is basically safe for crossing. Look for a high vantage point to scout the water and find a place for crossing. Check the river carefully for the following:

1. A level stretch where it breaks into a number of channels. Two or three narrow channels are usually easier to cross than a single wide section.
2. Obstacles on the opposite side of the river that might hinder travel. Try to select the spot from which your exit will be safest and easiest.
3. A ledge of rocks that crosses the river. This often indicates dangerous rapids or canyons.
4. A deep or rapid waterfall or a deep channel. Never attempt to ford a stream directly above or even close to such spots.
5. Rocky places. Avoid these; you can be seriously injured from falling on rocks. An occasional rock that breaks the current, however, may assist you.
6. A shallow bank or sandbar. If possible, select a point upstream from a shallow bank or sandbar so that the current will carry you to it if you lose your footing.
7. A course across the river that leads downstream so that you will cross the current at about a 45-degree angle.

Crossing rapids. Crossing a deep, swift river or rapids is not as dangerous as it looks. If you must swim across, swim with the current. Never fight it. Try to keep your body horizontal to the water to reduce the danger of being pulled under.

In fast, shallow rapids, float on your back, feet first; fin your hands alongside your hips to add buoyancy and to fend away from submerged rocks. Keep your feet up to avoid getting them bruised or pinned by rocks, and also to fend off any objects.

In deep rapids, float on your belly, head first; angle toward shore whenever you can. Breathe between wave troughs. Be careful of backwater eddies and converging currents as they often contain dangerous swirls. Avoid bubbly water under falls; it has little buoyancy.

When fording a swift, treacherous stream, remove your pants and underpants so that the water will have less grip on your legs. Keep your shoes on to protect your feet and ankles from rocks and to provide firmer footing. Tie your pants and important articles securely to the top of your pack. If you have to release the pack, all of your articles will be together. It is easier to find one large pack than to find several small items.

Carry your pack well up on your shoulders so you can release it quickly if you are swept off your feet. Not being able to get a pack off quickly enough can drag even the strongest of swimmers under.

Find a strong pole about 5 inches in diameter and 7 to 8 feet long to help you ford the stream. Grasp the pole and plant it firmly on your upstream side to break the current. Plant your feet firmly with each step, and move the pole forward a little downstream from its previous position, but still upstream from you. With your next step, place your foot below the pole. Keep the pole well slanted so that the force of the current keeps the pole against your shoulder.

If there are other people with you, cross the stream together. Make sure that everyone has prepared a pack and clothing as above. The heaviest person should be downstream of the pole and the lightest person at the end of the group. This way, the upstream person breaks the current, and the persons below can move with comparative ease in the eddy formed by the upstream person. If the upstream person is temporarily swept off his or her feet, the others can hold steady while that wader regains footing.

As in all fording, move so that you will cross the downstream current at a 45-degree angle. Currents too strong for one person to stand against can usually be crossed safely in this manner. Do not be concerned about the weight of your pack because the weight will help rather than hinder you in fording the stream. Just make sure you can release the pack quickly if necessary.
See: Boat; Compass; First Aid; Navigation; Safety.

SURVIVAL SUIT
A name for a full-body garment with maximum flotation capability, usually classified as a Type V flotation device. It is designed to provide upright flotation, with face and head out of the water, and to provide longer protection in life-threatening cold water than other devices or garments. It is worn by some anglers who boat in cold weather for both personal comfort as well as for lifesaving values in case they get wet or wind up in cold water and have a chance of developing hypothermia (see).

Many survival suits have hoods and inflatable collars or head rests. They are often brightly colored or have patches of reflective material to aid in spotting for rescue purposes, although some that are used for hunting may be in camouflage patterns. Anglers who venture onto cold water should consider wearing a U.S. Coast Guard–approved and rated survival suit in lieu of a PFD because of the increased chances of quickly developing hypothermia in cold water.
See: Personal Flotation Device; Safety.

SUSPENDING
The habit of some fish, mainly freshwater species, to hold steady in midwater; this is distinguished from species that normally live in midwater levels, cruising in pursuit of baitfish. A fish that is located 10 feet off the bottom in 40 feet of water is often said to be suspended. Certain lures that float on the surface but dive on retrieve have the ability to suspend by virtue of neutral buoyancy; when the retrieval action is stopped, the lure stays where it is in the water column, neither rising nor sinking. This most accurately mimics the behavior of fish and may be useful in some angling situations.
See: Plug.

SUSTAINABLE FISHERIES ACT
See: Fishery Conservation Act.

SWAYBACK
The distance that a trolled line and weight, especially downrigger weight, inclines back from a perpendicular position beneath a boat, caused by current or speed.
See: Downrigger Fishing.

SWEDEN
Spanning more than 2,000 kilometers from north to south, Sweden is blessed with tens of thousands of lakes and roughly the same number of rivers and streams, as well as a lengthy coastline along the Gulf of Bothnia, the Baltic Sea, and the North Sea. Small wonder that it is a nation with plenty of angling opportunity and a diversity of fish species.

Sweden's western saltwaters have such typical

northern species as cod, lire (pollack), and mackerel, and its eastern and more brackish waters contain mostly pike (big ones), zander (pike-perch), and perch. The rivers and small streams host Atlantic salmon, brown trout, pike, perch, carp, and various coarse species. With the exception of salmon, these species are present in an almost uncountable number of big and small lakes (about 100,000).

Diversity is also found in the country's climate, thanks to the distance between north and south. In January, the temperature can be above 0°C with no snow or ice in southernmost Sweden, but it may be 20° to 30° below zero with several meters of ice and snow on the lakes in the northern region of Lapland. Spring normally begins in March or April in the south, but it may not arrive until June in the north, when the snow and ice begin to melt.

As a result, the waters in the north are ice-free for only three or four months per year, whereas some are ice-free year-round in most places in the south, especially on the coasts. Seasonal activity, therefore, varies according to latitude; for instance, April is normally a very good month for pike and brown trout in the south, but in the north April is a prime period for ice fishing.

Methods and Tackle

Casting with spinning and fly tackle is most common in Sweden's lakes, although coarse fishing and trolling can also produce good results for certain species, and ice fishing is popular.

Fishing with spinning tackle is the most common, and often the most effective, method of pursuing predator species. Sinking and floating plugs are common lures for pike, zander, salmon, and brown trout, but standard spinners and different kinds of spoons can produce good catches. Long, slender spoons, often combined with a dropper fly, can be rewarding for sea trout along the coast. Heavy diamond jigs (100 to 300 grams) are used for heavy-tackle coastal fishing, including deep jigging for cod and coalfish (pollock).

Fly fishing is very common in Sweden, mainly for trout and grayling, but good opportunities also exist to catch arctic charr, salmon, and sea trout on fly tackle. Perch and pike can be pursued with fly tackle, and, along the coast—especially in the south—fly fishing for sea trout has grown in popularity.

Coarse fishing techniques are favored for perch, pike, and zander, especially by those who prefer live or dead baits. Opportunities to catch big roach, tench, bream, ide, and coarse species are extremely good, perhaps because relatively few Swedes practice this kind of fishing. Many waters contain especially good stocks of coarse species.

A particularly popular method for catching salmon and trout is trolling, especially in southern Sweden and in Lakes Vänern and Vättern. The boats for this type of fishing are normally well equipped with downriggers, sonar, GPS navigational units, and the like. It is also common to troll the old and original way—by towing a couple of wobblers (plugs) behind a small boat.

Ice fishing, of course, is a very common activity in northern Sweden, where the ice is thick for six to eight months per year. A popular and exciting local ice fishing tactic has anglers lie belly down on a reindeer skin placed on the ice, then shade their eyes with their hands while looking through a hole and watching their bait until a fish takes it. The equipment for northern ice fishing in Sweden includes an ice drill, an ice fishing rod about 30 centimeters long, a line that doesn't freeze, and special jigging spoons that are often baited with maggots.

Lakes and Tarns

In southern Sweden there are mostly lowland lakes, which especially hold pike, zander, perch, and coarse species. As one heads northward, the landscape changes and becomes more hilly and covered with large, forested areas that have many fish-rich lakes. Pike, perch, and carp species are dominant, but many lakes have brown trout.

Massive forests cover the middle part of Sweden, and these contain a good number of lakes, primarily containing pike, perch, and carp species, as well as brown trout, grayling, and zander. Zander become increasingly scarce in this region, whereas trout, grayling, and arctic charr become more prevalent. In the lightly populated northern region, the landscape opens up and becomes more rugged, and huge spruce forests dominate up to the tree line. There are many lakes here, and brown trout (known as "lake" trout when inhabiting Swedish lakes), grayling, pike, and perch are the predominant species.

In the lakes and tarns (small mountain lakes or ponds) of southern Sweden, fishing for brown trout and pike is normally best in spring and autumn. In summer, zander and coarse species are extremely active. In the middle region of Sweden the fishing season on open water is a little shorter. Generally, pike and brown trout fishing begins later and finishes earlier than in the southern part of the country. On the other hand, lower water temperature makes summer fishing better in the middle region. In northern Sweden, all fishing in open water occurs from May through October. The best time here is from June through August.

The Great Lakes

With a surface area of 5,600 square kilometers, Lake Vänern is one of Europe's largest lakes. It includes more than 20,000 islands, and 35 species of fish live in this gigantic lake. This combination naturally creates fantastic angling possibilities. A large population of landlocked Atlantic salmon provides excellent trolling, which is also a good method for pike and zander. Pike fishing is usually best after spawning in the spring, and salmon fish-

---

Bass is derived from the Middle English word basse, which is either a corruption of the Old English word baers, meaning bristly or spiny, or of the Dutch word for perch, barse.

ing can be good from spring through autumn.

Lake Vättern is also large at 130 kilometers long and 30 kilometers wide. This deep-water lake has big pike, as well as brown trout, salmon, and grayling, but the main attraction is large arctic charr that reach weights over 10 kilograms. These charr lie in deep water, and trolling with downriggers is the best method of catching them.

Mälaren is yet a another big lake with many islands and bays. The common game here are perch, pike, and zander, and the population of coarse species is good. Casting from shore is common, but trolling also produces big pike and zander. The best times for pike are spring and autumn. Zander, perch, and coarse anglers are most successful during the summer.

The West Coast
Warm northerly flowing current from the Atlantic Ocean brings a good supply of saltwater to the west coast of Sweden, providing good fishing. On the northern part of this coast, many areas offer relatively deep water close to shore, making it possible for anglers to cast lures and baits from the cliffs. Cod, mackerel, pollack, garfish, and sea trout are all caught this way. Even anglers in small boats can have rewarding fishing without venturing into the open sea. Deep-sea fishing farther offshore, however, is possible, and mackerel, cod, ling, pollock, and pollack are the targets of a great number of charter boats with experienced skippers.

In some places along the coast, the water is shallow and there are almost no skerries (a group of small rocky islands or reefs) at all. Here it is possible to wade and catch sea trout, flatfish, cod, and—during late spring—garfish. Anglers also fish from piers and breakwaters for mackerel and eels. In the south, the Öresund Strait is well known for its excellent cod fishing during winter, especially in January and February.

Cod fishing along the west coast is best during spring and autumn. Sea trout fishing peaks in April. Garfish arrive along the coast at the end of May, closely followed by mackerel; these species are caught throughout the summer. Autumn is also a productive time, offering good catches both from the coast and farther offshore.

The South Coast
Since the salt content of the Baltic water along the South Coast is lower than that on the west coast, fewer species thrive here, although cod and garfish are present. The brackish water of the Baltic Sea, however, provides good conditions for pike fishing. Angling from shore or small boats can produce big pike and sea trout. One of the best areas for these species is Hanöbukten, where it is also possible to troll for heavy salmon on their way to entering the Mörrumsån. Salmon over 25 kilograms have been caught on rod and reel here, and many anglers believe that Hanöbukten offers one of the world's best salmon fisheries.

Fishing for sea trout along the South Coast starts as early as January but reaches its peak during April, when pike fishing also begins to be good. In May, big salmon arrive, and trolling continues throughout the summer and into autumn, although the size of salmon drops as the season progresses. The autumn months offer good sea trout fishing all season long. Pike fishing run through late autumn as well, with good chances then of catching fish over 10 kilograms.

The East Coast
This coast stretches all the way from southern Sweden to the border with Finland and has a wide variety of environments, climate, and fish species. Large areas of the East Coast are scattered with skerries and, unlike the West Coast, are rich in vegetation and protected.

Fishing for sea trout and pike is the favorite activity along the southern part of this coast up to the Swedish capital of Stockholm. Fishing from the shore or small boats provides an excellent chance of catching big specimens. Every year, pike of 10 to 15 kilograms are caught here. The large Öland and Gotland Islands also have coasts that offer good fishing for pike and sea trout.

As one moves north, the salinity weakens, and only freshwater species—such as perch, zander, and coarse fish—continue to thrive. Pike and sea trout fishing are still interesting, and along the northern region there are good populations of coarse species and grayling. The main angling methods along the entire East Coast are spinning, fly fishing, and coarse fishing, from shore or small boats.

In the southern section of this coast, fishing for pike and sea trout is usually best during spring and autumn (April through May, and September through October). The season begins later farther north, because melting ice in the Baltic keeps the water cooler. In the very north in Bottenviken, it is usually possible to fish in open water only from the end of May through September.

Coastal Rivers
A large number of rivers along the East Coast host Atlantic salmon and sea trout. The best-known river here is the Mörrumsån, which is about 500 kilometers south of Stockholm. Due to increasing numbers of salmon and sea trout, it attracts thousands of anglers every year.

Even along the western side of Sweden there are 10 rivers with salmon. A few of them also offer sea trout. These rivers are slow-flowing and are situated in rich countryside. A few hundred salmon are typically taken from each western river, but some yield more than 1,000 salmon per river in a season. Fishing for Atlantic salmon usually starts in May or June, but the best chance to catch them is in autumn, although this is dependent on rainfall and water temperature.

An angler casts in a remote, wild site in Lapland.

The angler who wishes to fish for wild salmon on the eastern side of Sweden should go north of Stockholm. One of the best rivers there is Nedre Dalälven, where the fishing begins in January and continues into the autumn. Heavy fly and spinning tackle are recommended, since this is a big, deep river, and the fish often lie on the bottom.

North of this river are several other salmon rivers, but the catches in these large waters are varied, and the angler often needs local knowledge in the form of a guide to ensure success. In recent years these rivers have become increasingly more productive. Summer and autumn are the best fishing periods.

Inland Rivers

The rivers in southern and middle Sweden have pike, perch, and coarse species, and sometimes brown trout, whereas rivers and brooks in the northern area contain brown trout, grayling, and arctic charr. Many of the rivers in southern and middle Sweden can sometimes have good fishing for eels and zander.

Casting with spinning tackle, and coarse fishing, are the most common fishing methods in southern Sweden. In the middle and northern regions, fly and spinning tackle are both popular. Even in flowing water, the season stretches from spring through autumn. Farther north, the fishing season concentrates around the summer months.

For the versatile angler, there are good opportunities for diverse and exciting river fishing throughout the season. During spring and autumn, for example, pike fishing can be excellent in southern Sweden; in May, when the mayflies are hatching, the fly angler goes into action for brown trout; spinning, coarse, and fly anglers have all summer in different parts of the country to experience good fishing for pike, perch, bream, ide, tench, trout, grayling, and eels.

Large Northern Rivers

With a few exceptions, the really big river systems are in the northern part of Sweden. These are up to 200 kilometers long and extremely powerful as they rush through the wild landscape. Fishing possibilities in these huge waters are normally especially good, and they provide an unforgettable experience. All of the big northern rivers flow out into the upper parts of the Baltic Sea and run through big valleys from east to west.

These big river systems have many slow pools, rapids, and waterfalls, and a local guide is advisable to improve your chances. Furthermore, in the thinly populated areas of this region, where there are large areas of true wilderness, you might have to walk long distances to reach the fishing spots, although in some places there are roads to and along the rivers.

Brown trout, grayling, and arctic charr are the main species, although you might find good pike fishing on the slower stretches. Very large trout sometimes linger in the deep pools, but you must fish for them selectively with relatively heavy tackle.

Both spinning and fly fishing are effective. The season stretches from May through October depending on northern latitude. Generally, June through August are good months; during this period, daylight lasts nearly 24 hours a day, although the mosquitoes can be bad.

Lapland's Mountain Fishing

Mountain fishing in Lapland is probably the most exotic angling sport Sweden can offer. Midnight sun, northern lights, vast open spaces, unpopulated mountain plateaus, snow-covered peaks, and top-class fishing are a few benefits you can expect. Unexplored and road-free mountain and forest areas here offer many lakes, brooks, and rivers.

Lapland is often described as Europe's last wilderness and is only sparsely populated. In this vast area there are countless rivers and lakes, most of which contain brown trout, arctic charr, and grayling, and many of which have pike and perch. The large river systems are generally best, as spawning areas are large and fishing pressure is low.

Although the wild natural habitat of northern Sweden is alluring, it can be dangerous. Roads are few, the weather can change very fast, and a long walk to comfort and rest may await you. The angler who isn't familiar with mountain travel but who wishes to experience fishing north of the Arctic Circle has the option of staying at a fishing camp. Small aircraft and helicopters transport anglers to many such camps, which have comfortable cabins and often have a service shop and boats for hire, in some cases even a restaurant. With a fishing camp as a base, it is possible to safely experience the north and to enjoy fine fishing for trout, grayling, and charr.

The two main fishing seasons in Lapland are the short summer and long winter. July and August are the peak months for fly and spinning tackle in open water. March, April, and sometimes even the first half of May are the best times for ice fishing for trout and charr.

Licenses and Regulations

All waters in Sweden are private and may be administered by the owner or a fishing club. Every angler needs a license to fish in all lakes and rivers, except for the four biggest lakes (Vänern, Vättern, Hjälmaren, and Storsjön), where it is free to fish with a rod and reel. Private water may be accessed for a fee, which is nominal in most cases. Salmon rivers are the exception. Fishing from or along the coast is also free. Some areas and/or species may be protected, however. In some places, restrictions pertaining to a minimum size for certain species, angling methods, or seasons may apply. Anglers should check the regulations, which are printed (in Swedish) on the back of licenses. Licenses are obtainable at tourist centers, tackle shops, and guest houses.

SWEETFISH
See: Ayu.

SWELL
A long, huge free ocean wave that moves away from its origin, releasing its energy along the continental margins; a long-crested wave that moves steadily without breaking.
See: Waves.

SWIM
A term predominantly used by British coarse anglers to refer to a particular spot that is fished from the bank; anglers fishing a swim do not rove but remain stationary, working one location and usually baiting and/or prebaiting that spot.

SWIMFEEDER
A perforated cylinder containing chum (see), used for coarse species (see: coarse fish). Swimfeeders are weighted to facilitate casting, and they remain on the bottom where their contents are dispersed.

SWITZERLAND
If any European country is predetermined to become a country of anglers, Switzerland certainly qualifies. The most mountainous country in Europe, with 70 percent of its landmass covered by the Alps in the central and southern sections, and the Jura in the northwest, Switzerland is the source of many of Europe's greatest rivers. The Rhône and Rhine Rivers emerge from the very heart of this country in the mountain massif of Saint Gotthard. The origin of the Ticino River is also nearby. The Ticino becomes a main tributary of the big Italian river, the Po. From the Alpine Engadine Valley in the south of the canton (state or province) of Graubünden, the River Inn flows down to Austria and gives its name to the famous town of Innsbruck before reaching Germany and finally flowing into the Danube.

Water from the Swiss Alps therefore feeds the Atlantic Ocean as well as the Mediterranean, Adriatic, and Black Seas. One can easily understand the pride with which the Swiss call their country the "Aquatic Heart of Europe." This bounty also attracts some nonresident visitors.

Within Switzerland's 41,293 square kilometers are many large and small rivers with a total length of roughly 50,000 kilometers, as well as roughly 2,000 lakes and reservoirs. Switzerland is well known for its lakes, especially those in the Alpine region, which are oft-visited for their scenic beauty. Covering roughly 4 percent of the highly structured Alpine topography, these inland waters—surpassed in quantity, in Europe, only by some Nordic and eastern countries—represent a great variety of aquatic habitats.

One measure of the fisheries resources of Switzerland can be gleaned from its commercial fishery: The 14 largest lakes provide approximately 300 professional (commercial) fishermen with a full-time living from netting fish, and another 200 with a part-time living. The total number of annual or seasonal angling permits issued by the cantonal fishery offices is about 200,000, not including the countless people who acquire private angling permits or profit from the right to fish free of charge from the banks and shores of some of the bigger rivers and lakes.

The Swiss lakes and rivers are populated by 58 species of fish, of which 45 are indigenous and 13 have been introduced. The latter originated mainly from North America and include rainbow trout, arctic charr, and lake trout (which are called namaycush), and from Asia, from which originated fish of the carp family.

Brown trout are the foremost game species for Swiss anglers. A native fish, they are primarily pursued in rivers (where they are called *bachforelle*) but are also found in lakes (where they are called *seeforelle*, which literally means "lake trout" but refers to lake-resident brown trout). Rainbow trout *(regenbogenforelle)* have become a favorite of many anglers, and exist in numerous rivers and lakes. Grayling *(äsche)*, lake trout *(kanadische seeforelle)*, and arctic charr *(saibling)* have more limited distribution and following among the coldwater species, whereas pike *(hecht)*, perch *(barsch)*, zander (called pike-perch), carp, and various coarse species are among the warmwater interests.

Large catches of some of these are possible, including pike over 20 pounds, zander over 10 pounds, and brown trout over 3 pounds, all in the midlands, plus namaycush over 10 pounds in the mountain lakes. Trolling in the big lakes is very popular for trout as well as for pike, and the latter are also caught on dead or live bait. Fly fishing in rivers has an enthusiastic following, but the majority of anglers use spinning tackle and assorted lures.

Eight other species—among them Atlantic salmon and sea trout—died out between 50 and 150 years ago. Numerous hydroelectric dams and pollution on the Rhine River stopped these fish from swimming upstream to their traditional spawning grounds in the pre-Alpine freshwater rivers. Since the late 1980s, however, the water quality has improved significantly, and it is hoped that a new salmon restoration program will be a complete success in the early twenty-first century.

The program, initiated by a group of Swiss anglers from the Basle area with the support of fishing authorities and angler associations, has been rearing salmon smolts in local tributaries of the Rhine and then releasing them to swim downstream to the Atlantic Ocean, anticipating that they will come back to their native waters to spawn. Atlantic salmon have been seen as far upstream as the lowest of the barrier dams near the German city of Freiburg. Because hydroelectric power companies have committed themselves to construct fish passages on the dams after the year 2000, there is real hope that the Swiss will see Atlantic salmon return to their river systems in the very near future.

Lake Fishing

In 1995 the total catch of fish on the 14 largest Swiss lakes (Lakes Geneva, Neuchâtel, Konstanz, Lucerne, Zurich, Thun, Locarno, Biel, Zug, Lugano, Brienz, Walenstadt, Murten, and Sempach) was approximately 1.8 million kilograms, of which 1.5 million, or 85 percent, was netted by professional fishermen and the remainder caught by recreational anglers. Although these numbers might seem alarming, they beg comparison by the percentage of different species of fish.

Professional fishermen mainly fish for different species of whitefish and perch. In these big lakes (they no longer fish in the smaller lakes), they account for 97 percent of all whitefish caught and 73 percent of all perch, which together represent more than 90 percent of their income. Natural reproduction of perch is fully guaranteed in all the bigger lakes, although this is not the case with whitefish. In the big cantons (Bern, Zurich, St. Gall, among others) and in the smaller cantons (such as Lucerne), the professional fishermen operate special fish nurseries for the breeding of whitefish fry.

Professional fishermen also have a bycatch of many other species in large quantities, especially roach (97 percent of the total catch), zander (96 percent), eels (89 percent), and burbot (76 percent). Although recreational anglers may be as keen as professionals to catch lake whitefish, their chances are greatly diminished because the professionals are more efficient at netting. This is also true in the big lakes for recreational perch anglers; in addition, perch are subject to restricted bag limits, as these are particularly valuable to professionals and are highly desired as table fare. The professional fishermen, in protecting their income, have arranged for legal restriction on the numbers of perch taken by anglers.

In addition to perch and whitefish, the lake angler pursues other species, and records indicate that recreational anglers in the 14 largest lakes catch 57 percent of all arctic charr, 51 percent of northern pike, and 48 percent of lake-resident brown trout. In the 1990s, in some lakes in the west of Switzerland, zander stocks have increased phenomenally for unknown reasons, becoming a favorite catch of local anglers.

Bream, dace, carp, perch, pike, roach, rudd, and tench exist in great numbers in the big lakes, as well as in ponds and smaller lakes, and most of these species are favorite catches of many coarse anglers. Burbot live in the deep waters of numerous pre-Alpine lakes but are pursued only by keen specialists. European catfish live in the restricted area of only two western lakes (Lake Murten and Lake Neuchâtel), and in the Broye and Zihl Canals that link them.

In small Alpine lakes, anglers often find good stocks of arctic charr, brown trout, and namaycush. A species of shad that lives in the Adriatic Sea and once came up the Po and Ticino Rivers for spawning in Lakes Lugano and Maggiore (which is located at Locarno and is Switzerland's lowest point at 636 feet above sea level) before returning to the sea, became resident in these lakes about 100 years ago and has lived there ever since in great quantities; these fish are caught by local anglers who preserve them in salt, as is usual with fish of the herring family. In the same southern lakes, as well as in some lakes in the Swiss midland, anglers also land pumpkinseed panfish, and there is some angling for these.

River Fishing

Brown trout is the predominant species in many of the bigger and all of the smaller Swiss rivers, as well as in mountain lakes and reservoirs, which are subject to the same fishing regulations as are applied to the rivers. This species is the favorite catch of Swiss anglers because of its table value and the sport it provides. Due to the popularity of brown trout and the ensuing pressure on population levels, an annual stocking program is applied to waterways. The application of this program is controlled by the cantonal fishery offices. Depending on the area, the raising and stocking of brown trout is either carried out by cantonal or commercial nurseries or by individual groups of anglers with their own facilities.

Also found in the Alpine lakes are arctic charr and/or namaycush. Namaycush were introduced in the 1880s by the Federal Fishery Inspectorate because of their suitability as a stocked fish for lakes in the cold mountainous regions.

At the same time the inspectorate initiated a similar program of stocking rainbow trout in closed water systems and especially in commercial fish farms. Over the years, rainbow trout have become more widespread and are nowadays found in many rivers and lakes. Despite the fact that this fish adapted exceptionally well to its Swiss habitat and was recognized as a native fish by the average person, recent federal legislation has reclassified it as a foreign species. Hence, stocking of rainbow trout is again restricted to closed water systems. Numerous anglers and their clubs disagree wholeheartedly with this federal finding because in some areas where pollution and modern technology and construction work has tipped the natural balance of the waterways, brown trout have declined while rainbow trout have survived such adverse conditions.

The elusive grayling exists for the dedicated angler in such diverse locations as the River Inn in the Engadine Valley, located at 1,700 meters above sea level; the Doubs River in the Jura Mountains on the Swiss-French border; the Aare River between Thun and Berne; the Reuss River not far from the outflow of Lake of Lucerne; the Linth Canal, which links the lakes of Walenstadt and Zurich; and the Rhine River between Lake Konstanz (Bodensee) and the famous Rhein Falls.

Below the Alpine areas the variety of fish species increases in the larger rivers, which course through to the flatland. Depending on such factors as river size and depth, height above sea level, and the regions through which they flow, there will be species like barbel, nose, carp, chub, dace, bream, carp, roach, rudd, tench, perch, and pike, and in the last few years an increasing number of zander. Some small species of fish, such as European minnows and bleak, are caught by anglers for use as baitfish.

A Regulation Jungle

Fishing and angling practices in Switzerland are mainly regulated by the laws and decrees of the 26 cantons. The regulations can therefore be very diverse. The cantons decide such practical matters as the permitted equipment, tackle and methods of angling, and the compulsory restocking of rivers with brown trout.

The Federal Fishery Act of 1994 declares the main objectives of fishery policies and lists all native and introduced species of fish and crayfish that exist in Swiss waters. In the interest of preserving certain species, the act also regulates some basic fishing practices, such as the closed season for catching trout, charr, whitefish, grayling, pike, and native crayfish, and the minimum catch size for the same species and for perch. The cantons can apply stricter size limits and closed seasons, however, to guarantee the perpetuation of certain fish species.

The professional fishermen and most of the lake anglers who fish the 14 largest lakes of Switzerland are legally obliged to register their catches and report the annual results to their cantonal fishery office. Therefore, the total weight of fish caught in general and per species every year in these lakes is known.

For the rivers, smaller lakes, and Alpine reservoirs there are no catch figures available because in a number of the Swiss cantons—among them three of the biggest, Graubünden, Tessin, and Wallis, which cover two-fifths of the country—such registering and reporting is not compulsory. This situation may change, and catch results may become compulsory in the future.

The issue of fishing permits is a complex matter because each of the 26 cantons has its own rules and regulations. There are mainly three different systems operated by the cantons, however. Some cantons (like Appenzell Innerrhoden, Freiburg, Geneva, Graubünden, Ticino, Waadt, and Wallis) use a general cantonal permit, which is known as a patent, for all the public waters within their territory. Other cantons (Aargau, Appenzel, Ausserrhoden, and Solothurn, among others) close the general access to their public waterways and apply a method of leasing, whereby fishing is restricted to

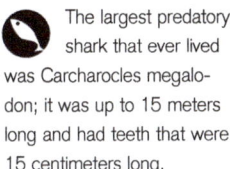

The largest predatory shark that ever lived was Carcharocles megalodon; it was up to 15 meters long and had teeth that were 15 centimeters long.

certain stretches of water for a limited number of anglers. A third group of cantons (including Berne, Lucerne, St. Gall, and Zurich) combine the patent and leasing systems, opening the bigger lakes and rivers with a general permit to everyone, and closing general access to the smaller ones by leasing them to restricted groups of anglers.

For the visiting angler it is worth bearing in mind that there are several inland lakes and waterways surrounded by more that one canton; therefore, special fishing regulations have been reached by mutual agreement between the cantons. A similar situation applies to some lakes and rivers that border Switzerland and surrounding countries, whereby fishing regulations are mutually agreed.

Outside the cantonal jurisdiction there still exist a few very old, private-family or corporate fishery rights. A permit to angle these private waters is usually obtainable locally through tackle shops, tourist offices, and the like.

The visiting angler faced with such a convoluted cocktail of different laws, rules, and systems may feel the need for guidance out of this labyrinth. One channel leading to all the necessary information (in the German language only) is the office of the Swiss angling magazine *Petri-Heil,* Readers Services, P.O. Box CH-8645, Jona (phone: 055225-5030; fax: 055225-5039). Also available from the same address is the annually issued Swiss Fishing Calendar, which provides a concise source of all the current rules and regulations.

SWIVEL

A freely turning metal connector that is meant to prevent twist in fishing line that would otherwise be caused by the action of a lure, bait, or sinker *(see)*. Swivels are used by themselves in connecting two lines or a line and one or more leaders, or used in conjunction with a snap *(see),* in which case the combined entity is known as a snap-swivel. They are not attached directly to a hook.

Like some other types of terminal tackle, swivels can lead to problems by breaking or by failing to actually swivel, and should only be used if really necessary. Poor quality swivels, or light swivels used with too heavy tackle, are the main causes of problems. They can be the weakest link in the angler-to-fish scenario due to their strength. If the rated breaking strength of a swivel is less than the fishing line, it's possible that you could break the swivel and lose the lure and/or fish when maximum pressure is applied. Most swivels are relatively strong, so this is less likely to be a problem with them than with snaps or split rings *(see)*.

Swivels used without a snap technically belong in one of two categories: slide bearing and ball bearing. Most slide-bearing swivels are of the two-way barrel, the chain, or the three-way dropper variety. The bearing surface of these types of swivels—the strand and curved barrel or ring body—slide

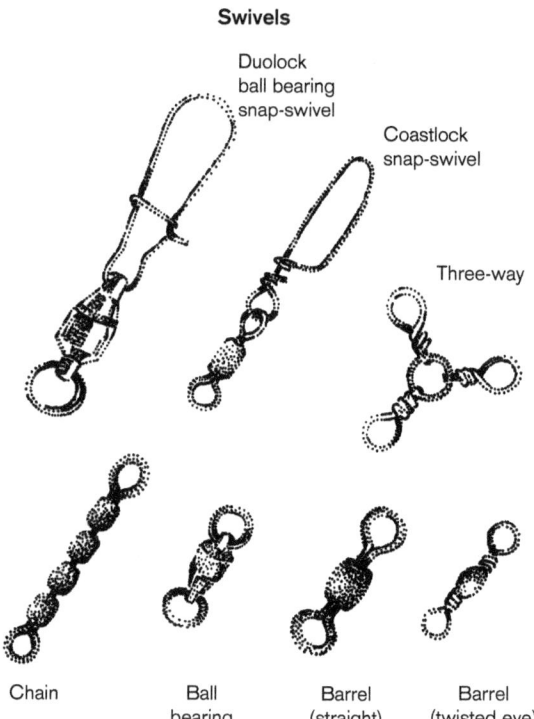

Swivels
Duolock ball bearing snap-swivel
Coastlock snap-swivel
Three-way
Chain
Ball bearing
Barrel (straight)
Barrel (twisted eye)

against each other and, when subjected to linear tension and torque, become deformed and bind, thereby negating their effectiveness.

Barrel swivels that have a twisted and single-strand head are the cheapest and poorest style available, and often unreliable. A little better in performance, because they're less prone to binding, are barrel swivels that have a straight and double-strand head; these are sometimes called crane swivels. Both of these styles are made of brass, and are used singly or as part of a snap-swivel. Three-way swivels are made of brass and feature three twisted and single-strand rings equally spaced on a ring. These are used to separate bait or lure from sinker via separate leaders. They are even more subject to binding than similar quality barrel swivels and rarely swivel well.

A chain swivel is a series of barrel-like swivels with an eye at each end; the better ones are made of stainless steel, are less prone to binding than barrel swivels, and are mainly used in conjunction with trolling sinkers. A dropper-line arrangement exists with some models that have a second chain attached to the middle of them, forming a T-shaped setup.

Although brass barrel swivels are by far the most commonly used swivels, especially among freshwater anglers, they are not nearly as functional as ball bearing swivels, which are much more expensive but greatly superior in operation and reliability. The rings of the best quality ball bearing swivels rotate freely due to highly polished stainless steel ball bearings and tapered design. These may be solid rings or split rings.

Swivels are often used when they don't have to be. For example, some anglers use barrel swivels as stops on a line to halt the movement of a slip sinker, even though a simpler device like a small split shot pinched on the line would do better and pose less trouble. As with other terminal tackle, it is best to use the smallest size that is compatible with the size of lure, strength of line, and type of fishing to be done.

Snap-swivels. A snap-swivel is strictly intended for attaching an artificial lure directly to a line, or leader to an artificial lure. It is only used with some spoons, and with spinners (especially when trolling or when retrieving these lures in current), and is unnecessary with other lures. Snap-swivels are distinct from snaps *(see)* in function, even though they may be used together. Swivels used with a snap are always barrel-shaped, with closed-eye rings at both ends; snaps may be of various design.

The same issues that apply to swivels and to snaps apply to the combined product. Preventing twist is their primary purpose, and providing a convenient means of quick attachment and detachment is their secondary purpose. Lures that do not need both of these (which is the majority of them) should not be fished with a snap-swivel. It is one more piece of equipment that can cause a problem, and may be the weakest part of the terminal tackle. Moreover, it can inhibit the action of some lures.

It's best to tie your line directly to a lure whenever you can, and to change knots when putting new lures on. However, some situations demand the use of snap-swivels, and these should be of the highest quality in terms of strength and durability in both the snap and the swivel.

SWORDFISH *Xiphias gladius.*

Other names—broadbill, broadbill swordfish; Arabic: *kheil al bahar;* French: *espadon;* Hawaiian, *a'u ku;* Italian, *pesce sapda;* Japanese: *dakuda, medara, meka, mekaiiki;* Norwegian: *sverdfisk;* Portuguese: *agulha, espadarte;* Spanish: *aja para, aibacora, espada.*

The only member of the Xiphidae family, the swordfish is one of the most highly regarded big-game species in the ocean, yet one that has been caught by relatively few anglers in modern times. Thus, any rod-and-reel catch today is a notable distinction regardless of size. Big-game fishing for swordfish was pioneered by author Zane Grey a century ago, and in the 1940s and 1950s it was popularly sought by other pioneering anglers who had the means and equipment to best these giants in their offshore haunts. Then the average catch well exceeded 200 pounds, and much larger monsters were often lost. Today, fish under 100 pounds—which have likely never had the opportunity to spawn once—are primarily encountered, and in some places only rarely, and too few are released alive (this is hard to do with larger specimens).

Unfortunately, swordfish have been especially coveted in world seafood markets—the meat of the swordfish is excellent—making this fish the object of large commercial fisheries and resulting in overexploitation virtually worldwide, as well as contributing to a demise in large specimens. Commercial fishermen take them in gillnets, with harpoons, and, most successfully, on longlines. Approximately 95 percent of swordfish harvested by U.S. commercial fishermen in the Atlantic are caught on longline gear.

Once almost unsalable, swordfish meat gained popularity following World War II and continuing through the early 1970s, when the U.S. and Canadian swordfish fishery was essentially terminated following restrictions imposed on the sale of swordfish found to contain certain levels of mercury. The acceptable level of mercury was raised in 1979, and then changed again in 1984, when it was determined that methyl mercury was the toxic component of the total mercury concentration and a test specific for methyl mercury became available. Since then, both the commercial catch and fishing effort have been exceedingly high in the Atlantic Ocean, with swordfish meat commanding top prices in the marketplace. An increasing amount of swordfish is now harvested from the South Atlantic and the Pacific, much of it destined for North American consumption.

Because these fish cross international boundaries, multination cooperation is critical to achieve effective swordfish management, but this has been painfully slow in occurring, and many countries have not complied with international catch reduction efforts. The body responsible for the multilateral coordination of Atlantic swordfish management is the International Commission for the Conservation of Atlantic Tunas (ICCAT), and most anglers have been dissatisfied with their management efforts for this species.

The countries that have the highest swordfish catches in the North Atlantic are Spain, the United States, Canada, Portugal, and Japan. In the South Atlantic, Brazil, Japan, Spain, Taiwan, and Uruguay dominate the swordfish fisheries. In the mid-1990s, approximately 50 percent of the world's total swordfish catch came from the Atlantic Ocean, with the Indian Ocean producing 15 percent and the Pacific Ocean 35 percent of the total. Recreational catches have been insignificant in the total harvest, in part because recreational catch numbers are low, the fish are found far offshore and are not often encountered, and they are not caught by the same water-covering methods used for other billfish.

Adult swordfish have few natural enemies, with the exceptions of large sharks and sperm and killer whales. They are easily frightened by small boats, yet, paradoxically, large craft are often able to draw very near without scaring them. This makes swordfish easy to harpoon, although that once-prominent commercial-capture method is rarely used today.

Identification. The swordfish has a stout, fairly rounded body and large eyes. The first dorsal fin

Swordfish

is tall, nonretractable, and crescent-shaped. The second dorsal fin is widely separated from the first and very small. Both are soft rayed, having thin, bony rods that extend from the base of the fin and support the fin membrane. The anal fins approximate the shape of the dorsal fins but are noticeably smaller. Ventral fins, on the underside of the fish, are absent. There is a strong longitudinal keel, or ridge, on either side of the caudal peduncle, which leads to a broad, crescent-shaped tail. Adult swordfish have neither teeth nor scales.

The back may be dark brown, bronze, dark metallic purple, grayish blue, or black. The sides may be dark like the back or dusky. The belly and lower sides of the head are dirty white or light brown.

The swordfish snout elongates into a true sword shape. Measuring at least one-third the length of the body, it is long, flat, pointed, and very sharp (especially on smaller fish), and significantly longer and wider than the bill of any other billfish. The lower jaw is much smaller, although just as pointed, ending in a very wide mouth.

The bodies of swordfish fry are quite different from those of adults. Their upper and lower jaws are equally prolonged; the bodies are long, thin, and snakelike; and they are covered with rough, spiny scales and plates, are rounded, and have just one long dorsal and anal fin.

Although they are distinctive fish, they do bear some resemblance to the spearfish (see), which is distinguished from the swordfish by its rounded sword, small teeth, a long continuous dorsal fin, and ventral fins.

Size/Age. Swordfish are capable of growing well over a thousand pounds, although fish of this size are unheard of in modern times. In the North Atlantic, a fish weighing more than 400 pounds is extremely unusual, and the average fish caught in the commercial fishery there weighs less than half of that amount; reports vary from under 90 pounds to under 200 pounds. The National Marine Fisheries Service reports that the largest swordfish ever caught in the North Atlantic weighed 1,210 pounds—more than double the size of the largest known in that region on rod and reel. The all-tackle world record for the species was caught in 1953 in Chile and weighed 1,182 pounds. The larger fish measure approximately 15 feet in length and have a 10-foot-long body and a 5-foot-long sword. Female swordfish grow faster, live longer, and are proportionally heavier than their male counterparts. Very large swordfish are always females; males seldom exceed 200 pounds.

The maximum longevity of swordfish is unknown, but they do live for at least nine years. The majority of swordfish caught in the North Atlantic sportfishery are thought to be immature fish only up to two years old.

Distribution. Swordfish occur in tropical, temperate, and occasionally cold waters of the Atlantic, Pacific, and Indian Oceans. They generally migrate between cooler waters in the summer to warmer waters in the winter for spawning. In the Atlantic Ocean, swordfish range from Canada to Argentina in the west, and from Ireland to South Africa in the east, including the Mediterranean and Black Seas. Swordfish are also found in the Indian and Pacific Oceans.

Habitat. These are pelagic fish living within the water column rather than on the bottom or in coastal areas. They typically inhabit waters from 600 to 2,000 feet deep and are believed to prefer waters where the surface temperature is above 58°F, although they can tolerate temperatures as low as 50°F. There seems to be some correlation between larger size and the ability to tolerate cooler temperatures. Few fish under 200 pounds are found in waters with temperatures less than 64°F.

In the western Atlantic, swordfish are summer and fall visitors to New England waters, entering the warming Atlantic coastal waters from far offshore in the Gulf Stream around June and departing in late October. Evidence suggests that such onshore-offshore seasonal migrations are more prevalent than are migrations between the northern feeding areas off Cape Hatteras and the southern spawning grounds off Florida and the Caribbean.

Life history/Behavior. Swordfish are not schooling fish. They swim alone or in loose aggregations, separated by as much as 10 meters from a neighboring swordfish. They are frequently found basking at the surface, airing their first dorsal fin. Boaters report this to be a beautiful sight, as is the powerful free jumping for which the species is known. This free jumping, also called breaching, is thought by some researchers to be an effort to dislodge pests, such as remoras or lampreys. It could also be a way of surface feeding by stunning small fish. They reach sexual maturity at about two to three years of age.

Food and feeding habits. Swordfish feed daily, most often at night. They may rise to surface and near-surface waters in search of smaller fish, or prey upon abundant forage at depths to 1,200 feet. They have been observed moving through schools of fish, thrashing their swords to kill or stun their prey and then quickly turning to consume their catch. Squid is the most popular food item, but many species of midwater and deep-sea pelagic fish, such as menhaden, mackerel, bluefish, silver hake, butterfish, herring, dolphin, and others are part of their diet.

This fish also uses its sword for defense. Occasional attacks on boats have been authenticated by the recovery of swords found broken off in wooden hulls. One swordfish attacked *Alvin,* the Woods Hole Oceanographic Institute submarine, at a depth of 330 fathoms, and wedged its sword so tightly into a seam that it could not be withdrawn.

Angling. Swordfish are vigorous, powerful fighters and impressive jumpers. When hooked or harpooned, they have been known to dive so quickly that they have impaled their swords up to their eyes in the ocean bottom. Anglers normally fish for them by trolling and drift fishing, and have had a slightly increased catch rate since the mid-1970s, when night drifting with squid for bait was adopted.

As mentioned, swordfish often bask on the surface with their dorsal and tail fins protruding from the water, so anglers intent on fishing during daylight will actually scan the water looking for a fish to present a trolled bait to. Swordfish are finicky, however, and are easily frightened by an approaching boat. They rarely strike blindly; typically, the bait must be presented carefully and repeatedly before the swordfish will take it. Once a swordfish has been spotted, the speed of the boat should not be changed appreciably and the bait should be eased quietly and gently in front of the fish. Squid is the most popular bait, although Spanish mackerel, eel, mullet, herring, tuna, and live or dead bonito are also used.

The soft mouth makes hookup uncertain, and the slashing bill can make short work of an angler's line or leader. Sighted swordfish are most often attracted by a trolled, rigged squid or baitfish on a long line. This must be done in such a manner as to keep the boat from spooking the finning fish but still bring the offering in front of it. This often results in avoidance by the swordfish. When it does attract the sword's attention, a strike can result, but the slashing fish often does not inhale the bait and is frequently not hooked. Casting live bait to surface-finning swords is also practiced.

A 200-pound-class swordfish is about to be released (note the tag below its dorsal fin) at La Guaira, Venezuela.

One reason why swordfish are not actively pursued in daytime is that they rarely feed actively during daylight, and thus are not often interested in anglers' offerings. Because this sport usually takes many sightings and presentations—which is not common in some places but is more common in others—the odds are not especially good.

The odds of catching swordfish are generally better for nighttime anglers, although the option of fishing at night far offshore does not appeal to many anglers and probably restricts greater angling activity. Depths run a wide gamut, from 60 to 80 feet below the surface to 1,200 feet and much more, depending on geographical location, water temperature, and moon phase. Often, baits are staggered at various levels, and light sticks are employed at least 6 feet above the baits to call attention to them, with balloons attached to the line with rubber bands to help indicate pickups.

Tackle for swordfish can be as light as 30- to 50-pound outfits with lever-drag reels, primarily in shallow water, but ranges up to 130-pound tackle for deeper water and larger fish. Line capacity is of great concern, as swordfish may be hooked exceptionally deep and run a long way. In their fight they may also rush the surface at any time and leap out of the water, then continue with blistering runs. Some of the most epic angling battles have occurred with swordfish, which fortifies their reputation as the "Gladiator of the Sea," which is the translation of their Latin name. Although the average swordfish caught today is small, landing one is considered by many to be the highest achievement in angling.

See: Big-Game Tackle; Billfish; Offshore Fishing.

Conversion Charts

THE SYSTEM OF WEIGHTS AND MEASURES USED IN MOST COUNTRIES AND IN ALL SCIENTIFIC work is the International System of Units (SI), which is commonly referred to as the metric system. A notable and influential exception to this is the United States, where the general public, and non-scientific publications, use the U.S., or U.S. customary, system of weights and measures. Throughout the *Ken Schultz's Fishing Encyclopedia & Worldwide Angling Guide*, there is a liberal use of both metric and U.S. customary weights and measures without parenthetical conversions to equivalent weights or measures. Some anglers, especially those who travel widely and those who pay close attention to world-record fish weights and fishing line classifications, are accustomed to both systems, which are often found mixed at boat docks, fish camps, and tackle shops throughout the world. The following information is provided to help the reader make the conversion from one system to another.

U.S. To Metric Conversion Formulas

When You Know...	Multiply By...	To Determine...
Inches (in)	25.4	Millimeters (mm)
Inches (in)	2.54	Centimeters (cm)
Inches (in)	0.0254	Meters (m)
Square Inches (sq in)	645.0	Square Millimeters (sq mm)
Square Inches (sq in)	6.45	Square Centimeters (sq cm)
Square Inches (sq in)	0.00064	Square Meters (sq m)
Feet (ft)	30.5	Centimeters (cm)
Feet (ft)	0.305	Meters (m)
Feet (ft)	0.0003	Kilometers (km)
Square Feet (sq ft)	0.093	Square Meters (sq m)
Fathoms (fath)	1.827	Meters (m)
Fathoms (fath)	0.0018	Kilometers (km)
Yards (yd)	0.914	Meters (m)
Square Yards (sq yd)	0.836	Square Meters (sq m)
Statute Miles (mi) (5,280 ft)	1.61	Kilometers (km)
Nautical Miles (n mi) (6,020 ft)	1.852	Kilometers (km)
Square Miles (sq mi)	2.56	Square Kilometers (sq km)
Miles per hour (mph)	1.61	Kilometers per hour (kph)
Knots per hour	1.84	Kilometers per hour (kph)
Acres	0.405	Hectares
Ounces of Weight (oz)	28.3	Grams (g)
Ounces of Weight (oz)	0.0283	Kilograms (kg)
Ounces of Fluid (fl oz)	29.6	Milliliters (mL)
Pounds (lb)	454.0	Grams (g)
Pounds (lb)	0.454	Kilograms (kg)
Pints (pt)—U.S.	0.473	Liters (L)
Pints (pt)—Imperial	0.568	Liters (L)
Quarts (qt)—U.S.	0.946	Liters (L)
Quarts (qt)—Imperial	1.14	Liters (L)
Gallons (gal)—U.S.	3.79	Liters (L)
Gallons (gal)—Imperial	4.55	Liters (L)
degrees Fahrenheit (°F)	0.555 (after subtracting 32)	degrees Celsius (°C)

Metric To U.S. Conversion Formulas

When You Know...	Multiply By...	To Determine...
Millimeters (mm)	0.039	Inches (in)
Centimeters (cm)	0.394	Inches (in)
Centimeters (cm)	0.0328	Feet (ft)
Square Centimeters (sq cm)	0.155	Square Inches (sq in)
Meters (m)	39.37	Inches (in)
Meters (m)	3.281	Feet (ft)
Meters (m)	1.09	Yards (yd)
Meters (m)	0.547	Fathoms (fath)
Square Meters (sq m)	1.2	Square Yards (sq yd)
Kilometers (km)	3,279.0	Feet (ft)
Kilometers (km)	1,093.0	Yards (yd)
Kilometers (km)	546.0	Fathoms (fath)
Kilometers (km)	0.621	Statute Miles (mi)
Kilometers (km)	0.545	Nautical Miles (n mi)
Square Kilometers (sq km)	0.386	Square Miles (sq mi)
Kilometers per hour (kph)	0.621	Miles per hour (mph)
Kilometers per hour (kph)	0.545	Knots per hour
Hectares	2.47	Acres
Grams (g)	0.035	Ounces of Weight (oz)
Grams (g)	0.002	Pounds (lb)
Kilograms (kg)	35.2736	Ounces (oz)
Kilograms (kg)	2.2	Pounds (lb)
Milliliter (mL)	0.034	Fluid Ounces (oz)
Liters (L)	2.11	Pints (pt)—U.S.
Liters (L)	1.76	Pints (pt)—Imperial
Liters (L)	1.06	Quarts (qt)—U.S.
Liters (L)	0.880	Quarts (qt)—Imperial
Liters (L)	0.264	Gallons (gal)—U.S.
Liters (L)	0.22	Gallons (gal)—Imperial
degrees Celsius (°C)	1.8 (and add 32)	degrees Fahrenheit (°F)

Table Of Metric and U.S. Equivalent Line Strengths

Metric	U.S. Customary	Metric	U.S. Customary
1 kg	2.2 lb	10 kg	22.0 lb
2 kg	4.4 lb	15 kg	33.0 lb
3 kg	6.6 lb	24 kg	52.8 lb
4 kg	8.8 lb	37 kg	81.4 lb
6 kg	13.2 lb	60 kg	132.0 lb
8 kg	17.6 lb		

Table of Fish Weights

Metric	U.S. Customary	Metric	U.S. Customary
1 kg	2.2 lb	60 kg	132.0 lb
2 kg	4.4 lb	70 kg	154.0 lb
3 kg	6.6 lb	80 kg	176.0 lb
4 kg	8.8 lb	90 kg	198.0 lb
5 kg	11.0 lb	100 kg	220.0 lb
6 kg	13.2 lb	200 kg	440.0 lb
7 kg	15.4 lb	300 kg	660.0 lb
8 kg	17.6 lb	400 kg	880.0 lb
9 kg	19.8 lb	500 kg	1,100.0 lb
10 kg	22.0 lb	600 kg	1,320.0 lb
20 kg	44.0 lb	700 kg	1,540.0 lb
30 kg	66.0 lb	800 kg	1,760.0 lb
40 kg	88.0 lb	900 kg	1,980.0 lb
50 kg	110.0 lb	1,000 kg	2,200.0 lb

www.ingramcontent.com/pod-product-compliance
Lightning Source LLC
Chambersburg PA
CBHW040933240426
43673CB00054B/1965